# Lecture Notes in Computer Science

Vol. 1: GI-Gesellschaft für Informatik e.V. 3. Jahrestagung, Hamburg, 8.–10. Oktober 1973. Herausgegeben im Auftrag der Gesellschaft für Informatik von W. Brauer. XI, 508 Seiten. 1973.

Vol. 2: GI-Gesellschaft für Informatik e.V. 1. Fachtagung über Automatentheorie und Formale Sprachen, Bonn, 9.–12. Juli 1973. Herausgegeben im Auftrag der Gesellschaft für Informatik von K.-H. Böhling und K. Indermark. VII, 322 Seiten. 1973.

Vol. 3: 5th Conference on Optimization Techniques, Part I. (Series: I.F.I.P. TC7 Optimization Conferences.) Edited by R. Conti and A. Ruberti. XIII, 565 pages. 1973.

Vol. 4: 5th Conference on Optimization Techniques, Part II. (Series: I.F.I.P. TC7 Optimization Conferences.) Edited by R. Conti and A. Ruberti. XIII, 389 pages. 1973.

Vol. 5: International Symposium on Theoretical Programming. Edited by A. Ershov and V. A. Nepomniaschy. VI, 407 pages. 1974.

Vol. 6: B. T. Smith, J. M. Boyle, J. J. Dongarra, B. S. Garbow, Y. Ikebe, V. C. Klema, and C. B. Moler, Matrix Eigensystem Routines – EISPACK Guide. XI, 551 pages. 2nd Edition 1974. 1976.

Vol. 7: 3. Fachtagung über Programmiersprachen, Kiel, 5.–7. März 1974. Herausgegeben von B. Schlender und W. Frielinghaus. VI, 225 Seiten. 1974.

Vol. 8: GI-NTG Fachtagung über Struktur und Betrieb von Rechensystemen, Braunschweig, 20.–22. März 1974. Herausgegeben im Auftrag der GI und der NTG von H.-O. Leilich. VI, 340 Seiten. 1974.

Vol. 9: GI-BIFOA Internationale Fachtagung: Informationszentren in Wirtschaft und Verwaltung. Köln, 17./18. Sept. 1973. Herausgegeben im Auftrag der GI und dem BIFOA von P. Schmitz. VI, 259 Seiten. 1974.

Vol. 10: Computing Methods in Applied Sciences and Engineering, Part 1. International Symposium, Versailles, December 17–21, 1973. Edited by R. Glowinski and J. L. Lions. X, 497 pages. 1974.

Vol. 11: Computing Methods in Applied Sciences and Engineering, Part 2. International Symposium, Versailles, December 17–21, 1973. Edited by R. Glowinski and J. L. Lions. X, 434 pages. 1974.

Vol. 12: GFK-GI-GMR Fachtagung Prozessrechner 1974. Karlsruhe, 10.–11. Juni 1974. Herausgegeben von G. Krüger und R. Friehmelt. XI, 620 Seiten. 1974.

Vol. 13: Rechnerstrukturen und Betriebsprogrammierung, Erlangen, 1970. (GI-Gesellschaft für Informatik e.V.) Herausgegeben von W. Händler und P. P. Spies. VII, 333 Seiten. 1974.

Vol. 14: Automata, Languages and Programming – 2nd Colloquium, University of Saarbrücken, July 29–August 2, 1974. Edited by J. Loeckx. VIII, 611 pages. 1974.

Vol. 15: L Systems. Edited by A. Salomaa and G. Rozenberg. VI, 338 pages. 1974.

Vol. 16: Operating Systems, International Symposium, Rocquencourt 1974. Edited by E. Gelenbe and C. Kaiser. VIII, 310 pages. 1974.

Vol. 17: Rechner-Gestützter Unterricht RGU '74, Fachtagung, Hamburg, 12.–14. August 1974, ACU-Arbeitskreis Computer-Unterstützter Unterricht. Herausgegeben im Auftrag der GI von K. Brunnstein, K. Haefner und W. Händler. X, 417 Seiten. 1974.

Vol. 18: K. Jensen and N. E. Wirth, PASCAL – User Manual and Report. VII, 170 pages. Corrected Reprint of the 2nd Edition 1976.

Vol. 19: Programming Symposium. Proceedings 1974. V, 425 pages. 1974.

Vol. 20: J. Engelfriet, Simple Program Schemes and Formal Languages. VII, 254 pages. 1974.

Vol. 21: Compiler Construction, An Advanced Course. Edited by F. L. Bauer and J. Eickel. XIV. 621 pages. 1974.

Vol. 22: Formal Aspects of Cognitive Processes. Proceedings 1972. Edited by T. Storer and D. Winter. V, 214 pages. 1975.

Vol. 23: Pr... ium, IBM Germa... ⊃. E. Hackl. VI, 5(...

Vol. 24: Parallel Processing. Proceedings 1974. Edited by T. Feng. VI, 433 pages. 1975.

Vol. 25: Category Theory Applied to Computation and Control. Proceedings 1974. Edited by E. G. Manes. X, 245 pages. 1975.

Vol. 26: GI- 4. Jahrestagung, Berlin, 9.–12. Oktober 1974. Herausgegeben im Auftrag der GI von D. Siefkes. IX, 748 Seiten. 1975.

Vol. 27: Optimization Techniques. IFIP Technical Conference. Novosibirsk, July 1–7, 1974. (Series: I.F.I.P. TC7 Optimization Conferences.) Edited by G. I. Marchuk. VIII, 507 pages. 1975.

Vol. 28: Mathematical Foundations of Computer Science. 3rd Symposium at Jadwisin near Warsaw, June 17–22, 1974. Edited by A. Blikle. VII, 484 pages. 1975.

Vol. 29: Interval Mathematics. Procedings 1975. Edited by K. Nickel. VI, 331 pages. 1975.

Vol. 30: Software Engineering. An Advanced Course. Edited by F. L. Bauer. (Formerly published 1973 as Lecture Notes in Economics and Mathematical Systems, Vol. 81) XII, 545 pages. 1975.

Vol. 31: S. H. Fuller, Analysis of Drum and Disk Storage Units. IX, 283 pages. 1975.

Vol. 32: Mathematical Foundations of Computer Science 1975. Proceedings 1975. Edited by J. Bečvář. X, 476 pages. 1975.

Vol. 33: Automata Theory and Formal Languages, Kaiserslautern, May 20–23, 1975. Edited by H. Brakhage on behalf of GI. VIII, 292 Seiten. 1975.

Vol. 34: GI – 5. Jahrestagung, Dortmund 8.–10. Oktober 1975. Herausgegeben im Auftrag der GI von J. Mühlbacher. X, 755 Seiten. 1975.

Vol. 35: W. Everling, Exercises in Computer Systems Analysis. (Formerly published 1972 as Lecture Notes in Economics and Mathematical Systems, Vol. 65) VIII, 184 pages. 1975.

Vol. 36: S. A. Greibach, Theory of Program Structures: Schemes, Semantics, Verification. XV, 364 pages. 1975.

Vol. 37: C. Böhm, λ-Calculus and Computer Science Theory. Proceedings 1975. XII, 370 pages. 1975.

Vol. 38: P. Branquart, J.-P. Cardinael, J. Lewi, J.-P. Delescaille, M. Vanbegin. An Optimized Translation Process and Its Application to ALGOL 68. IX, 334 pages. 1976.

Vol. 39: Data Base Systems. Proceedings 1975. Edited by H. Hasselmeier and W. Spruth. VI, 386 pages. 1976.

Vol. 40: Optimization Techniques. Modeling and Optimization in the Service of Man. Part 1. Proceedings 1975. Edited by J. Cea. XIV, 854 pages. 1976.

Vol. 41: Optimization Techniques. Modeling and Optimization in the Service of Man. Part 2. Proceedings 1975. Edited by J. Cea. XIII, 852 pages. 1976.

Vol. 42: James E. Donahue, Complementary Definitions of Programming Language Semantics. VII, 172 pages. 1976.

Vol. 43: E. Specker und V. Strassen, Komplexität von Entscheidungsproblemen. Ein Seminar. V, 217 Seiten. 1976.

Vol. 44: ECI Conference 1976. Proceedings 1976. Edited by K. Samelson. VIII, 322 pages. 1976.

Vol. 45: Mathematical Foundations of Computer Science 1976. Proceedings 1976. Edited by A. Mazurkiewicz. XI, 601 pages. 1976.

Vol. 46: Language Hierarchies and Interfaces. Edited by F. L. Bauer and K. Samelson. X, 428 pages. 1976.

Vol. 47: Methods of Algorithmic Language Implementation. Edited by A. Ershov and C. H. A. Koster. VIII, 351 pages. 1977.

Vol. 48: Theoretical Computer Science, Darmstadt, March 1977. Edited by H. Tzschach, H. Waldschmidt and H. K.-G. Walter on behalf of GI. VIII, 418 pages. 1977.

# Lecture Notes in Computer Science

Edited by G. Goos and J. Hartmanis

## 98

## Towards a Formal Description of Ada

Edited by D. Bjørner and O. N. Oest

Springer-Verlag
Berlin Heidelberg New York 1980

**Editors**

D. Bjørner
Department of Computer Science
Technical University of Denmark
Building 343
DK-2800 Lyngby/Denmark

O. N. Oest
Danish Datamatics Centre
Electrovigbuilding 341
DK-2800 Lyngby/Denmark

AMS Subject Classifications (1980): 68-02, 68 A 05, 68 A 30


ISBN 3-540-10283-3 Springer-Verlag Berlin Heidelberg New York
ISBN 0-387-10283-3 Springer-Verlag New York Heidelberg Berlin

Printing and binding: Beltz Offsetdruck, Hemsbach/Bergstr.
2145/3140-5432

CONTENTS

------------------------------------------------------------------------
*  Each asterisked paper lists its Contents at its very beginning.

## PRELUDE

### Aims & Purposes of this Volume

The aim of this volume is to present the arguments, some of the experiments, and the thoughts that were part of the project whose result is also presented: namely (the construction of) a formal, basically denotational semantics definition of Ada.

Rather than (just) presenting you with the finished product: a suitably annotated formal definition - part II of this volume - instead, oftentimes extensively, this volume argues choices and discusses variants of modelling Ada constructs formally. As such we believe that this volume serves two purposes: it contributes to the analytical study of Ada semantics, and it contributes to the body of knowledge about the abstract modelling of advanced software constructs -- including such embodying parallelism.

The volume, in part III, also contributes to the field of Computer Architectures, by illustrating how one can systematically "derive" a formal definition of a multi-processor computer architecture "optimally" suited for the concurrent execution of Ada tasks.

### On: "The Formal Definition of Ada"

This volume does not (purport to) present THE formal definition of Ada. The United States Government, through its Department of Defence (US DoD) has commissioned such a formal definition. This volume, we repeat, is NOT it. The so-commissioned, officially (to be) approved formal definition of Ada is due soon. The work on that definition has been carried out by a group at the French Governments' "information- & automation science institute", INRIA. Intermediate versions of that definition have graciously been put at our disposal. These versions have, however, not influenced our construction effort noticeably.

This volume is otherwise not the place to compare the two definition efforts.

### The Basis for Our Definition Work

Two sources of information have played the major role as input to the process of constructing our formal definition. Both are referred to here:

(A)  Preliminary Ada Reference Manual
     ACM SIGPLAN Notices
     Vol.14, No.6, part A, June 1979

(B)  Rationale for the Design of the Ada Programming Language
     ACM SIGPLAN Notices
     Vol.14, No.6, part B, June 1979

The definition presented here, as 'Consolidated Formulae' appendices to the papers of part II of this volume, have however lately been updated to reflect:

(C)  Reference Manual for the Ada Programming Language
     Proposed Standard Document
     Cii Honeywell Bull, July 1980


## Completeness & Validity of the Present Definition

The Ada being modelled here is believed to be rather close to, if not directly modelling, the proposed standard Ada, i.e. ref.(C). But the present
definition is not complete. Roughly speaking two, minor, aspects have been
left out. Due to lack of time most of the rather straightforward definitions of expression semantics is omitted. And due to some, by us, perceived
ambiguities & incompletenesses of the reference manual specification of
'Generic Program Units' (ref.(C) chapter 12), we have also left out variant
models of Generics.

The main effort behind the Ada definition work presented here went into deciding upon the "most fitting" forms of abstraction. Robustness of the chosen model, with respect to expected language changes -- introduced between
the times of issue of refs.(A,B) and (C) -- was of prime concern. We believe, however, that not only are the model (semantic) Domains reasonable,
but also that most, if not all, uses thereof, validly reflects ref.(C). --
But see end of next section: 'Disclaimer'.


## The Danish Ada Definition Project

### -- Student Masters Theses

The papers of parts II & III of this volume are the result of four
M.Sc.Thesis projects. These were carried out within the faculty of Electri-
cal Engineering. Each lasted 6 months. Altogether 5 students were involved
-- during the spring and summer of 1980.


### -- Educational Prerequisites

Before embarking on these projects the students had received education in
'Denotational Semantics' and 'Software Abstraction Principles' -- corres-
pondng to, in fact based on, the books:

(D)  The Vienna Development Method:The Meta-Language
     eds.:D.Bjorner & C.B.Jones
     Springer-Verlag, Lecture Notes in Computer Science
     Vol.61, May 1978 (2nd printing July 1980)

(E)  Abstract Software Specifications
     ed.:D.Bjorner
     Springer-Verlag, Lecture Notes in Computer Science
     Vol.86, June 1980

-- in the latter volume, ref.(E), only the material on 'Constructive', i.e.
Denotational definitions is relevant. We urge the reader of the present volume to consult either ref.(D) or ref.(E) for a comprehensive introduction
to the techniques of language modelling, to the particular (VDM META-IV) semantics definition language used, and -- in ref.(E) -- to J. Stoy's
enlightened expose of the mathematics underlying such definitions.

-- Project Prerequisites

The same students had also participated in smaller student projects concerned with the likewise formal definition of CHILL.


-- CHILL

CHILL is an acronym. It stands for "Communications HIgh Level Language".
CHILL is a language for programming Stored Program Controlled (SPC) Telephone Exchanges. CHILL has been commissioned by the C.C.I.T.T.   C.C.I.T.T.
stands for the International Consultative Committee on Telephony & Telegra-
phy. C.C.I.T.T. is part of ITU:  the International Telecommunications
Union. ITU is part of the United Nations. CHILL represents a workable com-
promise between the interests of National and Public Utility Telephone Ad-
ministrations (PTTs etc.) and Telephone Equipment Manufacturers of the whole
world! The actual design of CHILL was carried out in the  period  1974-1979
by representatives from almost 30 such organizations from more than 2 dozen
countries spread over five continents!


-- The Formal Definition of CHILL

"C.C.I.T.T. Recommendation Z200" presents an informal, but very rigorous,
and precise, specification of CHILL. A planned "Supplement" to Z200, presently in the form of a C.C.I.T. "Manual", attached to Z200, presents THE
formal definition of CHILL. This C.C.I.T.T. officially (to be) approved,
formal definition was produced at the Computer  Science  Department of the
Technical University of Denmark in a joint project with the Danish Telecommunications Research Laboratory.

   (F)   The Formal Definition of CHILL
        eds.:P.L.Haff & D.Bjorner
        C.C.I.T.T. Recommendation Z200 Supplement
        ITU Geneva, Switzerland, March 1981

provides a reference -- advance copies may be obtained, at reproduction
cost, from the address of the editors of this volume.


-- CHILL & Ada

This is otherwise not the place for a discussion of these two languages.
Such a comparison would be quite worthwhile -- provided it was carried out
with reference to precise formal definitions. The two languages are roughly
of the "same order of complexity". Both languages 'compete' in very similar
areas of application. For the purposes of a proper understanding of the
background for the work behind the present volume it suffices with the following more detailed characteristics: CHILL appears to have a more  complex
type (mode) system than Ada. CHILL (also) seems more complex in the area of
visibility & referability than is Ada. Finally CHILL has three sets of  independent constructs for handling processes, where Ada has one, "smaller",
set of task handling constructs.

The experience gained, with around 18 students, in producing the formal definition of CHILL gave us confidence in our ability to produce, reasonable
swiftly, also an Ada definition.

-- State-of-the-Art of Formal Definition Work

We believe that the present volume justifies the confidence expressed in the previous paragraph.

We conclude, therefore, that one can now, 10 years after the pioneering works of Dana Scott and the late Christopher Strachey, expect of todays software engineers & computer scientists, that they -- as an everyday matter of concern -- can produce formal software specifications of even very complex software systems, should anyone still want such bastards!


-- A Disclaimer

But it should be emphasized that the present Ada definition is the result of only 2 (relatively inexperienced) man-years of (student) work, limited to within the period March-September 1980.

No rigorous, exhaustive, "refereed" attempt has yet been made to compare our formal definition with the proposed standard for Ada (ref.(C)). Although all formulae here have been extensively scrutinized, and "somewhat" buddy-checked, they have yet to be subjected to the same careful procedure of "validation" that our CHILL formal definition has been, and still is, subjected to. It is calculated that more than one man-year of highly technical work has gone into this CHILL "validation". No ultimate security is anyway (formally) possible. But a rather high degree of informal confidence, on an international level, that the informal and the formal CHILL specifications "agree", has already been attained.


## Overview of Papers

There are three parts to this volume -- and an appendix.

The center part, part II, contains three papers on respective aspects of an Ada definition.

The problem of tackling the modelling of the so-called static semantics of (languages like Euclid, CHILL and) Ada is a difficult, non-trivial one. We have come to believe that this problem exceeds, by a manpower estimate alone, 3-4 times that of modelling e.g. the dynamic semantics of the sequential parts of (those languages and) Ada.

(Some rough statistics can be given. It relates the sizes of expressing the static- & the dynamic semantics, and the relative complexity, of a number of languages:

Size of Semantics

| | | | | |
|---|---|---|---|---|
| Static Semantics: | 22% | 26% | 45% | 55% |
| Dynamic Semantics: | 78% | 74% | 55% | 45% |

| | ALGOL 60 | PL/1 | CHILL | Ada |
|---|---|---|---|---|
| Relative "Complexity": | 1 | 5 | 8 | 8 |

The table indicates the extent to which the CHILL and Ada languages embodies notions of statically decidable properties. In the vernacular: "more and more is being checked at compile-time, in particular aspects that have to do with the disciplining of the co-operation among programmers". We refer here to the module/package concepts.)

(By the static semantics we mean those semantic aspects of a language which a compiler for that language must, or at least can, check. That is: the statically decidable context-conditions. By a dynamic semantics we mean those semantics aspects of a language which corresponds to the code generated by a compiler for that language, exclusive of that which only has to do with static semantics checks -- should a compiler design choose so. That is: dynamic semantics reflect the run-time properties of the language. It is justified to call both aspects for semantics. In both cases we can speak of a "computation" based on, i.e. over, a/the program text.)


You may therefore find the paper:

1. A Denotational (Static) Semantics Method                21-212
   for Defining Ada Context Conditions
   by Jorgen Bundgaard & Lennart Schultz

somewhat studious to follow. It deals with a hard problem.

The modelling of the static environment- (surrounding-), or as they are called here: dictionary-, Domains for languages of the (Euclid, CHILL and) Ada kind, have, up till now, not received the attention required. In the pioneering paper by Bekic & Walk [BeWa 71] the problem of modelling Storage of PL/1 and ALGOL68 recieved a lucid, almost final, treatment. The foundation was laid, it turned out, for all subsequent models of the Storage concept of PL/1, ALGOL60, Pascal, CHILL and Ada. What we hope is that somebody will elucidate, one day, in a similarly foundational paper, the proper techniques for modelling the static dictionary problem of modular languages. Languages which permit such "weird" things as exporting & importing names, thereby "freeing" their visibility & referability properties from being syntactically tied to the phrase structure of any program.


The paper:

2. A Formal Semantics Definition of Sequential Ada        213-308
   by Jan Storbank Pedersen

carefully treats all the difficult aspects of (modelling) the dynamic semantics of those parts of Ada which are not related to tasking. In its content it is more in line with the, by now, classical treatments of dynamic semantics. The paper contains a model of Ada Storage. That is: of the Ada con-

cept of variables, composite values, including variant records with discriminants, and their locations. The present Storage model stems from models
first worked out by J.Bundgaard, in June 1979, and later extensively
(update-) revised by H.H.Lovengreen, in January 1980 [Lo 80a].

Many formal definers of languages fail to give such formal definitions of
the, basically axiomatically formulated, properties of locations & values;
allocation-, initialization-, assignment- & update to, contents taking- and
freeing of storage.

### Advice

We have this advice to give: before embarking on the systematic,
laborious and somewhat straightforward, i.e. "easy", writing of
static wellformedness- and dynamic elaboration function definitions, make sure to get the underlying Domains straightened out
first. Work out, in detail, not only all these Domains, but also
all the auxiliary function needed to construct, modify & use objects of these Domains.

### End-of-Advice

Failure to do so, i.e. to complete these parts, early in a definition project, usually proves disastrous -- ultimately requiring the complete rewrite
of masses of formulae. Luckily in this project we were spared such
blunders. (We hope, and "pray", with some trepidation, that the present Do-
main- and function definition structures are robust enough to meaningfully
cope with the unfinished modelling of Generics!)


The paper:

3. Parallelism in Ada                                      309-433
   by Hans Henrik Lovengreen

tackles, and solves, the (new) problem of modelling all of the Ada tasking
semantics as abstractly, i.e. as implementation-unbiased as possible; and
of embedding its parallel meta-process model in an otherwise Denotational
model of sequential Ada. (The official, formal definition of Ada, mentioned
above, does not give a model of Ada tasking.) The modelling principles of
the present Ada tasking definition are basically the same as those used in
ref.(F). CHILL, as mentioned previously, possesses many more process primitives than Ada. The semantics of the latters "fewer" constructs appears,
however, to be more involved. Measured in definition (page) size alone:

Size of Dynamic Semantics

| | | |
|---|---|---|
| Sequential | 75% | 67% |
| Parallel | 25% | 33% |

CHILL     Ada

We attribute this seeming anomaly to the involved, very high level rules for
Ada task exception handling and task termination, due primarily to the "hierarchy"-notions involved herein. (Both of the above comparisons (i.e.
table contents) are normalized, in the sense of all definitions being expressed in the same meta-language, using basically the same modelling prin-

ciples.)

The center part, part II, is bracketed by two papers.

The opening, part I, paper:

outlines the use of a formal definition of a programming language (like Ada
and CHILL) in projects aimed at systematically & rigorously developing compilers & run-time systems for such languages. By extensively referring to
the, by now established journal-, but not yet text-book, literature, the
paper shows how one can arrive at such compilers, and such run-time systems,
in whose correctness one can obtain a far greater degree of confidence than
heretofore attainable.

The simple message is this:

> Following classical, e.g. text-book techniques is not , we be-
> lieve, the way to construct compilers etc. for Ada and CHILL.
> The complexity of these languages is simply such, that many steps
> of careful development, each carefully documented and related back
> to its antecedent, are a sheer necessity. In all other engineer-
> ing branches such well-documented, objectively stated and related
> designs are commonplace. Their hierarchilization of work permits
> engineers of different educational background and skills to work
> at different levels of the project. No one in these engineering
> professions would dream of not first producing architecture spec-
> ifications, formally expressed; from these derive engineering de-
> signs, again formally expressed, and backward related; from these
> construction blue-prints, suitably marked-up, but still formal,
> etc., etc.. Time has come to raise programming to a professional,
> engineering, emotionally detached level.

The DDC stands for the Danish Datamatics Centre. DDC is a not-for-profit
Computer Science Research-, an Advanced Software Engineering (Development)-,
an edp-Consultancy-, and Continued Education Institute affiliated with the
Danish Academy for the Technical Sciences. The DDC presently is embarked
upon several software development projects (CHILL, Ada, Office Automation,
etc.), which are pursued according to the formal techniques espoused above.

The closing, part III, paper:

reports on the process of deriving from an in-depth semantic analysis of Ada
-- while also formally defining -- a (Virtual) Machine for Ada. That is:
the state Domain, and an instruction repertoire: their syntaxes & semantics. The defined computer is deemed "optimally" suited for executing compiled Ada programs. It should be noted here that the defined computer is
one containing an indefinite number of processors sharing storage.

We are presently implementing this A-Code Machine in two out of three ways:

(i) in software, written in standard, hence portable, Pascal, but currently available only in an IBM System/370 VS version; and (ii) in hardware, bit-slized from conventional, AMD2900 series LSI circuits, and otherwise micro-programmed. We are also planning, once the details of project (ii) have been analyzed, (iii) to commission the custom-design of a VLSI circuit for this Ada/A-Code micro multi-processor computer. Its dataflow reflects rather directly the objects of the semantic Domains of the definition. And its control logic otherwise corresponds to the elaboration functions of the formal definition.

(The present design of the A-Code Machine is protected property.)

An appendix, pilfered basically from ref.(F), i.e. the CHILL formal definition, provides a comprehensive:

A:

for all of the papers (0.-4.) closes the current volume. A closer study of just this literature reference & bibliography list reveals much of the technical background for work in the subject area of this volume.

## ACKNOWLEDGEMENTS

The editors take pleasure in extending thanks to the students, now engineers, whose theses form the main part of this volume. For their courage in embarking upon all of Ada, for their dilligent and hard work, and for their willingness -- lately -- to spend hours re-editing their thesis reports for purposes of this publication. We trust they will be rewarded.

All of us, editors & authors, extend thanks to Veronique Donzeau-Gouge, of INRIA, for her gracious help in pointing out, in January 1980, our misunderstanding of aspects of the Ada Storage concept; to Gilles Kahn, also of INRIA, for a general presentation, and discussion, in June 1980, confirming vaguely held suspicions, and for otherwise keeping us informed about the substance of the INRIA formal definition work on Ada; and to Hans Bruun, the Department of Computer Science at the Technical University of Denmark, for invaluable advice on how to break down the static semantics aspects of Ada into manageable pieces.

Special thanks are due to a referees' most relevant and helpful comments on paper 1.

Finally we acknowledge the contribution of the Danish Datamatics Centre in providing comfortable office facilities during the thesis project, and this and much more, in the last month, during preparation of this volume. Similar thanks goes to the Department of Computer Science at the Technical University of Denmark. In particular to Lasse H.Ostergaard without whose assistance in preparation publication of this volume would have been further delayed.

# AUTHOR AFFILIATIONS

Dines Bjorner &
Hans Henrik Lovengreen:

Department of Computer Science
Building 343
Technical University of Denmark
DK-2800 Lyngby, Denmark
Phones: ++45-2-881566 & ++45-2-872622
Telex: 37529 dthdia dk


Jorgen Bundgaard,
Ole Henrik Dommergaard,
Ole Nybye Oest, &
Jan Storbank Pedersen:

Danish Datamatics Centre
Elektrovej, Bldg.341
DK-2800 Lyngby, Denmark
Phone: ++45-2-872622
Telex: 37704 ddc dk


Lennart Schultz:

Crone & Koch EDP K/S
Ordrupvej 101
DK-2920 Charlottenlund, Denmark
Phone: ++45-1-631122
Telex: 16014 crone dk

# THE DDC ADA COMPILER DEVELOPMENT METHOD

*Dines Bjørner & Ole Nybye Oest*

*April 1980*

Abstract:

This paper outlines the specific development methods used in a large scale, full Ada compiler & run-time system development project. The most significant feature of this project is its insistence on using formal, mathematics based definition-, specification- and implementation techniques. The basis for the compiler is twofold: First a formal, denotational & abstract semantics specification of Ada, including tasking; then an abstract compiling algorithm derived from the dynamic semantics (denotational) specification from Ada into (so-called) A-code.

Table of contents                                                       Page

Summary

Project work reported upon in this volume will, after an initial effort by the Dept. of Computer Science (ID) of the Technical University of Denmark (DTH), mostly take place within the Danish Datamatics Centre (DDC), with remaining work being done in participating industries.

The project (as outlined in this document) will result in

- a formal definition of full Ada,

- an Ada Compiler, AC, derived systematically from the formal definition and generating code for a virtual 'A-code' machine,

- an Ada Compiler Environment Support, ACES, administering separately compiled modules - ACES can be seen as that part of a full STONEMAN [Stoneman] environment which is necessary for the compiler,

- an Ada Run Time Environment System, ARTES, including an A-code interpreter, a kernel for tasking and 'rudimentary' Input/Output as specified by the standard Ada prelude.

The compiler and the A-code interpreter will be coded so as to be easily portable to the systems of the participating industry companies. The compiler environment support and the remaining parts of the run time environment system will be coded and documented so as to require a minimal re-coding effort by these companies in order to interface with their operating systems. The coding language of the Ada compiler (AC) and of as large parts of the Ada Compiler Environment Support (ACES) and Run Time System (ARTES) will be a subset of Standard PASCAL. This subset is the maximum such which permits a mechanical transformation into Ada, thus boot-strapping the compiler itself. Through manual intervention further Ada constructions should be applied to the boot-strapped Ada compiler (etc.) in Ada so as to obtain maximally portable systems.

Specific phases of the project will establish precise specifications (abstract models) for those external software interfaces for which the companies themselves have to produce final design and/or coding.


In summary: The DDC Ada project itself will operate on a computer system chosen-by/available to DDC; minor parts of the Ada system must necessarily be re-coded/re-fitted by/or for participating companies.

## 1. What is Ada

Ada is a high order programming language suited for a wide application domain, e.g. numerical applications, system programming applications and embedded computer system applications including real-time applications [Ada 79a & b].

The language belongs to the Algol/Pascal family by being block structured, but extends the program structuring by providing modules, called 'packages', which are collections of data types, constants, variables, subprograms and modules. Modules and subprograms can be compiled separately without loss of security and made available to more users through a common library. For handling parallellism, 'tasks' are provided. This mechanism allows a program to be divided into more processes running in parallel on multi-processors or in quasi-parallel on single-processors.

Combined with the facilities in Ada for handling hardware and software exceptions (interrupts) as well as for reading the clock the tasking facilities make the language well suited for embedded (and/or) real-time systems.

The language provides simple data types (integer, character, enumeration, real, access (reference)) as well as composite (arrays and records with elements of simple and composite types). Furthermore the programmer can define his own enumeration types as well as subtypes of any of the types. As Ada is strongly typed a large amount of checking can be done at compile time.

Representation specifications can be used for specification of the mapping between data types and the concrete representation, e.g. how the components of a record are to be placed in storage.

Ada supports hierarchical (top-down) as well as configurative (bottom-up) program development through its module concept and the facilities for separate compilation. For example, within a subprogram or module where a subunit (subprogram or module) is declared, the corresponding body can be represented by a body stub. The body itself can then be developed later and compiled separately.

## Development History

Ada was developed on behalf of US Department of Defense at CII-Honeywell-Bull in Paris by a design team led by Jean Ichbiah, and including Bernd Krieg-Brueckner, Brian A. Wichman, Henry F. Ledgard, Jean-Claude Heliard, Jean-Raymond Abrial, John G. P. Barnes, and Olivier Roubine. The language was named to honour the world's first programmer Ada Augusta, Lady Lovelace, colleague of Charles Babbage, and the daughter of Lord Byron.

## 2. The DDC Ada Compiler and Run Time System Development Method

This chapter expresses a "Credo", something to which all project personnel will subscribe: the tightly related set of theory-based and theory-derived methods according to which the various components of the compiler and run time system are to be developed.

It should be noted, that the methods are in or beyond the front of the "state-of-the-art". Hence there are two aspects of the compiler development project:

* The production of a portable Ada compiler with run time system using formal and systematic software engineering methods

* Propagation of these software engineering methods using the Ada compiler development project as a case study.

Note also, that the sections below deal primarily with the 'internal' DDC Ada project – that is an A-code generating and interpreting system implemented on, but not for, a computer chosen by DDC. The implications of and interactions with participating companies' systems will be elaborated upon in the subsequent parts 1 and 2 of the development plan – which are to be agreed between DDC and these companies.

### Note

When, in the following, we speak of models, we mean Abstract Software Specifications expressed, basically, in the Denotational Semantics Style. References [BjJo 78, Bj 80] outline the methods used in constructing such models.

### End-of-Note

### 2.0 The Ada Compiler & Run-Time System Components

There are three major components in the Ada Compiler & Run-Time System:

* The Ada Compiler, AC, which works in conjunction with ACES (see below) and which separately compiles ADA modules and subprograms into into A-Code (see ARTES, below).

* The Ada Compiler Environment Support System, ACES, which permits the separate compilation of Ada modules. ACES works in conjunction with the Host Computer Operating & File system, and further manages a library of already compiled modules.

* The Ada Run-Time Environment Support, ARTES, which supports the execution of a compiled Ada program potentially leading to a dynamically varying number of tasks. The ARTES works in conjunction with the Target Computer Operating- & File System.

Both the Host- and the Target Systems may consist of just a single, or may be composed of multiple CPUs.

These three major components are detailed in sections 2.3 to 2.5 below, whereas sections 2.1 and 2.2 deal with the formal definition of Ada and the compiling algorithm, which form the basis of the development of the Compiler System.


## 2.1 Denotational Semantics Definition of Ada

The basis for the DDC Ada project is a formal definition of the complete Ada language including an abstract model of the ADA parallelism (tasking) components.

The initial development of this formal definition takes place as an internal university project carried out at the Department of Computer Science at the Technical University of Denmark by M. Sc. Computer Science thesis students during spring/summer 1980. Only the extensive update revision/completion of the formal definition will take place as a part of the DDC Ada project.

We insist on a formal definition as the project basis for several reasons:

(1) The development of the formal definition will give a thorough understanding of the Ada language necessary for the successful compiler development.

(2) The formal definition will constitute a reference document:

    (a) from which the compiler can be derived systematically enhancing the correctness,

    (b) against which the DDC Ada compiler (or any ADA compiler) can be verified,

    (c) to serve as basis for proving properties of ADA programs,

    (d) to serve as a basis for informal descriptions/manuals of Ada - or interesting parts of Ada.

(3) A formal definition is the only means we have to state precisely the semantics of a programming language.

The formal definition is thus considered mandatory for the compiler development and will be an integral part of the final documentation of the DDC Ada compiler.

The style of the formal definition will be that of denotational semantics [BeWa 71, ScSt 71, Sc 72, Wa 72, Be 74, Te 76, Bj 77a, MiSt 77, St 77, BjJo 78, Jo 79, St 79], as this style offers a compact, comprehensive, now well-established form of programming language definition, and as a complete compiler development methodology centered around denotational semantics has emerged during the last years [McCaPa 67, LaBu 69, JoLu 71, Re 72, WeMi 72, Mo 73, Jo 74, WeHe 75, Jo 76, Bj 77b, Bj 78, Jo 78, Jo 80, and the Aarhus Conference Wo 80], permitting a systematic, stepwise derivation of a compiler from the formal definition of the language.

In the formal definition three components can be identified:

(1) The abstract Ada syntax and static semantics.

(2) The dynamic semantics.

(3) The abstract model of Ada parallelism.

The specific method of definition will be according to the principles outlined in the references given above and likewise applied in [HaBj 80].

## 2.1.1 Abstract Syntax and Static Semantics

This part of the definition gives an abstract syntax for the Ada language; that is a syntax description dealing entirely with the semantic contents of the various constructs of the language; the abstract syntax is thus completely free of concrete representational details such as language keywords, delimiters, linearizations, group ordering, etc.

The static semantics deals with those aspects of a given ADA program, which can be validated statically, that is at 'compile time'. This includes checking the visibility & referability rules, declarations, type checking all occurrences of variables, checking that parameters are used according to their modes, resolving overloading etc. The formal definition of the static semantics could take the form of a function which maps any abstract Ada program conforming to the static semantics rules (that is being 'well-formed') into true, and any other abstract program into false. The structure of this function will correspond to the abstract syntax, so that for each language component (conditional statement, say) a corresponding function dealing with the 'well-formedness' of this component can be identified.

The 'context condition checker' component of the compiler (cf. section 2.4.3) will be derived from this static semantics part of the formal definition - and the abstract syntax will be used when designing the parser of the compiler (section 2.4.2).

Examples of Abstract Syntax & Static Semantics expressed according to the method & style planned for Ada is given in [Be 74, HeJo 78, HaBj 80].

The paper by Bundgaard and Schultz of this volume gives a model of the Static Semantics.

## 2.1.2 Dynamic Semantics

This second part of the formal definition gives the semantics - the meaning - of the (abstract) Ada language constructs.

This is done by functional composition of meanings ascribed to the constituent parts of such constructs. In this way the dynamic semantics defining formulae will inherit the structure of the abstract syntax as did the static semantics formulae: To a given language construct 'e.g. IfStmt' (i.e. the if-statement) the static semantics will define a well-formedness predicate 'is-wf-IfStmt', whereas the dynamic semantics will define the meaning through an evaluation or interpretation function 'elaborate-IfStmt' denoting the corresponding state-to-state [etc.] transformation on an underlying abstract machine.

The semantics of a complete Ada program is thus defined as a state-to-state transformation, where the state contains the input/output to/from the program and where the transformation is composed of the transformations of the constituents of the program.

Alternatively the dynamic semantics formulae can be considered as an interpreter of abstract Ada programs on an abstract machine, whose state component contains a model of a storage and of the input/output system.

The dynamic semantics formulae provide the basis of the derivation of the compiling algorithm, cf. section 2.2.

Examples of Dynamic Semantics expressed according to the method & style planned for Ada is given in [Be 74, HeJo 78, HaBj 80].

The paper by Storbank Pedersen of this volume gives a model of the Dynamic Semantics.

### 2.1.3 An abstract Model of Parallelism in Ada

Whereas the elaboration functions of the Ada tasking components are included in the dynamic semantics part described above, the part of the abstract interpreter handling tasking (task initiation, termination, intertask communication, sharing of variables) is treated separately by defining an abstract model handling these aspects.

The reason for this is rather pragmatic: Where the dynamic semantics leads to the compiling algorithm and thereby to the code generation part of the compiler, the parallelism model will be refined into a component of the run-time environment, namely the kernel for Ada tasking, cf. section 2.5.2. Furthermore a distinct kernel has to be derived for each implementation of the Ada compiler system, naturally to separate out the tasking model already in the language definition.

### On the Mechanical Semantics of Ada Tasking

To cope with the parallelism a mechanical semantics will be provided. By a mechanical semantics is here meant one which explains tasks (processes) of Ada in terms of definitional (meta-) language processes, and which therefore deals with the explicit scheduling of Ada tasks. The meta-language (of the denotational semantics part) is therefore extended to cope with meta-processes, their synchronization and inter-communication. This extension basically derives from the very elegant notions of "CSP" [Ho 78, FoBj 79]. As a research project in ID experiments are carried out with the aim of expressing Ada tasking via Milners Behavior Algebras [Mi 80].

An extensive example of Tasking Semantics expressed in the CSP like style planned for Ada is given in [HaBj 80]. That definition is more complex than is expected for Ada Tasking. This is due to CHILL's richness of Tasking (Process) Primitives.

The paper by Lovengreen of this volume gives such a model of tasking.

## 2.2  Compiling Algorithm

The compiling algorithm is a formal specification of the code to be
generated for any given abstract Ada program.

The algorithm takes as 'input' an abstract Ada program (i.e. an object
belonging to the class of objects denoted by the abstract Ada syntax and
being well-formed) and produces likewise abstract target machine code. The
target machine code in question is the so-called A-code. Therefore the
definition of the A-code must be carried out before - or in parallel with -
the specification of the compiling algorithm. The A-code definition will
also involve specification of I/O and tasking primitives, in the A-code, and
hence to some extent the interface to the run time environment components:
Kernel and I/O system.

The compiling algorithm is to be derived from the dynamic semantics formulae
in a systematic way [McCaPa 67, WeMi 72, WeHe 75, Bj 77b, Ne 77, Bj 78, Jo
78] and will inherit the structure of these formulae and hence of the
abstract syntax (i.e. of the Ada language) structure, making it possible to
identify which code any individual construct generates.

Whereas the compiling algorithm formulae will make use of semantic 'compile
time' objects (e.g. an identifier dictionary) the generated target code will
be 'pure' A-code not referencing any such 'compile time' objects.

In addition to the dynamic semantics of section 2.1.2 the parallelism model
of section 2.1.3 will (indirectly) influence the compiling algorithm as this
model will be used when defining the A-code tasking primitives.

The paper by Dommergaard of this volume contains an appendix which gives,
for a large fully interesting section of Ada, such a compiling algorithm.

## 2.3 The Ada Compiler Environment Support System, ACES

The Ada Language Definition [Ada 79a & b] specifies that Ada programs may have their (immediate) constituent modules separately compiled. Hence a sub-system, acronymously called ACES, is required which works in conjunction with the ADA compiler, AC. The distinct functions of these two components, which together form the Ada Compiler System, ACS, are:

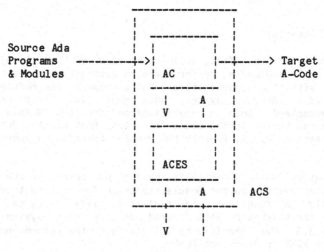

File System

Ada source programs, or separately compilable Ada modules are input to the AC which is directed to perform compilation, possibly in conjunction with already compiled modules. The result, if a complete program has now been compiled, is target A-code, which is handed over to the Operating System for further disposition. Or the result is yet another separately compiled module, which is handed over to the ACES. Or the result is both. The ACES thus can be seen to provide various filing, book keeping and cross-module checking functions. We somewhat prematurely distinguish three parts of the ACES — described in the subsections 2.3.1 to 2.3.3.

### 2.3.0 The ACES Model-Design-Code

The main purpose of ACES is to support the separate compilation of Ada modules and subprograms. In order to understand the notion of separate compilation we first establish an overall, abstract model of ACES, by providing models for its two major components, see 2.3.1-2. In order to be able to perform the next step towards the coding of ACES we must provide an abstract model of the host machine system, cf. section 2.3.3. Having established this model, we are able to refine the models of the ACES components into specifications of these two components.

The last prerequisites for the final design and coding of ACES from the specifications above, are a (probably informal) specification of the ACES features required, i.e. the facilities & capabilities provided to the user (the ADA programmer), cf. section 2.3.4 - and a specification of the interface between AC and ACES, this latter specification will be established from and while working on the design of the compiler structure.

### 2.3.1  Separate Compilation Component

We construct, on paper, an abstract model of Separate Compilation as outlined above. As for any abstract model it disregards notions of efficiency and the actual host machine system. Using the Host Machine System Interface Model of section 2.3.3 we therefore object refine & operation decompose this abstraction into a specification of the structure and components of the separate compilation sub-system of ACES. Then the Separate Compilation part of ACES is coded from this specification.

### 2.3.2  Module Librarian

Given idealized, or simplified, rudimentary views of the file system, i.e. e.g. such generally available, we formulate an abstract model of the Module Librarian -- with the module library being those of the Module Librarian designated files of the file system. This model is object refined and operation decomposed into a specification for the Module Librarian implementation now taking into account the actual Host machine Interface via the model of section 2.3.3. Finally the Module Librarian is coded from this specification.

The implementation will potentially have to be redone for the respective industry computer systems as the Module Librarian for efficient realizations depends heavily on functions and facilities offered by the respective systems. But a first version will depend on the host system interface defined in 2.3.3 thus sacrificing efficiency to the convenience of being able to use the ACES on different hosts.

### 2.3.3  Host Machine/Computer Interface

For each Host Machine in question, an abstract model of the File System and Operating System must be provided. From these models we derive a common ACES/Host interface, which can be implemented on all Hosts in question. This common interface is defined through an abstract model, and the contracting industries should implement this interface so as to allow the ACES as developed by DDC to run on their machines.

### 2.3.4  ACES Features: Facilities & Capabilities

In cooperation with the contracting industries DDC will establish which features shall be available in ACES with regards to the maintenance of the Module Library, merging of libraries etc. Furthermore the interface to the user operating the Module Library should be specified. Time and space resources available should also be specified as should any additional requirements imposed on ACES by the contracting industries.

### 2.4  The Ada Compiler, AC

In this section the components of the compiler will be identified, and the bases for the development of the individual components given. All in all these bases sum up to the denotational semantics of section 2.1, the compiling algorithm of section 2.2 and the Ada compiler environment system of section 2.3.

## 2.4.0 Multi-pass and ACES Interface Administrator

As the compiler has to run on small as well as medium size (micro, mini) computers the compiler will be designed as a multi-pass compiler [Na 63]. The multi-pass administrator shall, besides initiating the passes and control the data flow between the passes, take care of the interface to the environment, the ACES of section 2.3.

The partitioning into passes will be established from the nature and size of the computers to be used (that is from models of these computers having to be established beforehand, see e.g. 2.3.3), from the static semantics and from the compiling algorithm. From these separable components can be identified.

The remaining four components of the compiler (besides the multi-pass administrator) are described in the subsequent sections with no regards to the actual partitioning into passes - which (cf. above) cannot be decided upon in this report.

## 2.4.1 Lexical Scanner

The lexical scanner takes as input an Ada compilation unit [Ada 79a] (e.g. a package, package body or complete program) in the form of a string of characters. The scanner identifies the lexical elements of the compilation unit (identifiers, keywords etc.) as defined in the language definition and outputs the compilation unit to the parser as a sequence of these lexical units with associated attributes carrying the semantic contents like values of numbers, actual names of identifiers.

## 2.4.2 Error Correcting Parser

The parser takes as input the sequence of lexical elements and checks that they correspond to a syntactically correct compilation unit while constructing and outputting the compilation unit in the form of the corresponding syntax tree with semantic attributes associated with the nodes and leaves of the tree. Some of these attributes will take the form of (references to) name tables etc. for use by the subsequent compiler components. The syntax tree can be considered a realization of the abstract syntax tree of the denotational semantics definition.

Thus the bases of the parser are the scanner output definition, the abstract syntax defining Ada compilation units plus the static semantic domains of the Static Semantics and the Compiling Algorithm, which help to identify the semantic attributes of the grammar.

The parser will be theory-based full syntax error correcting, so that syntactical errors will not inhibit the checking of the rest of the compilation unit.

Note that the parser as well as the scanner can be constructed by more or less automatic tools - and at an early stage of the project.

## 2.4.3 Context Condition Checker

This component is a realization of the static semantics formulae of section 2.1.1, and performs all compile time checking of the semantics of the compilation unit. The Context Condition Checker will work on the tree representation generated by the parser, and will build dictionaries and environment description tables to aid in the analysis of the compilation units. These semantic objects are also to be used by the code generator below.

Ada is deliberately designed to allow a comprehensive amount of the semantic checking to be carried out at compile time -- thus the Context Condition Checker will constitute a rather large portion of the compiler.

### 2.4.4 Non-Optimizing Code Generator

The code generator is a realization of the compiling algorithm of section 2.2. The code generator will take as input the tree structure form of the compilation unit generated by the parser and will utilize the semantic tables of the context condition checker. An example of a concretization of an abstract compiling algorithm can be found in [Bj 78]. The code is generated for the virtual machine of section 2.5.1.

It will be possible to introduce various optimizing techniques into the code generator - this is, however, not considered a part of the DDC Ada project but is left to the individual implementors of Ada. Such optimizations will have to be defined formally and integrated into the abstract compiling algorithm before being introduced in the code generator. Correctness arguments showing the equivalence between the optimized code and the dynamic semantics should be carried out.

### 2.4.5 AC Features: Facilities & Capabilities

Before the design of the compiler structure can be carried out, a specification of the 'external' requirements to the compiler must be provided. Such requirements are, for example: The kind & quality of diagnostics, the speed of the compiler, the size of the compiler, provision of interfaces from Ada programs to programs/modules written in other languages.

### 2.5 The Ada Run-time Environment Support System, ARTES

We have decided to compile Ada programs into code for a virtual machine. We call the code for A-code. At run-time an A-code interpreter, which is a part of ARTES, interprets A-code. ADA specifies that programs, when executed (i.e. interpreted) may lead to an indefinite number of 'concurrently' executing tasks. These may communicate according to the Ada 'rendez-vous' principle, and otherwise must obey a number of 'hierarchy' properties: sharing storage, exception handling task termination etc. And Ada specifies a (traditional, conventional, but quite satisfactory) Input/Output stream and record oriented architecture.

In toto we therefore find that ARTES has three major sub-components:

- The A-code interpreter,

- The tasking kernel,

- The I/O system.

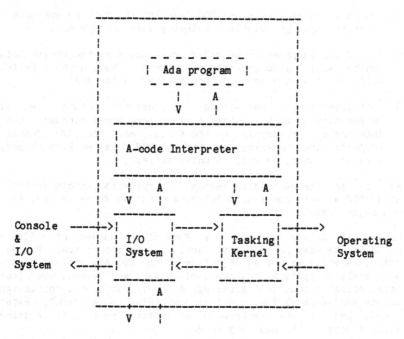

File System

### 2.5.0  The ARTES Model-Design-code

The following prerequisites must be available before ARTES can be designed and coded:

- An abstract model of the A-Code, the A-Code Interpreter specification derived therefrom (see section 2.5.1),

- An abstract model of tasking and the derived specification of the tasking kernel/nucleus (see section 2.5.2),

- An abstract model of the predefined, recommended Ada I/O packages, (see section 2.5.3),

- An abstract model of the Target Machine System (see section 2.5.4),

- The specification of the required ARTES Features (see section 2.5.5).

From these the overall design of ARTES can be carried out and the individual components coded as described in the following sections.

### 2.5.1  The A-Code Interpreter

A number of reasons motivate the decision to compile into code, called A-code, for a virtual machine, i.e. code which must be interpreted, to begin with, by a software implemented A-code Interpreter:

(1)   The  Ada  compiler, as the DDC develops it, must be portable to, and
       generate code for, distinct industry computer systems.

(2)   The  CHILL Compiler, also under development by the Danish Datamatics
       Centre  will,  also generate code for a virtual machine (effectively
       believed to be the same, A-code machine as for ADA).

(3)   Next-generation   main-frame   processors   could   be   directly
       implementing,  in bit-sliced & micro-programmed hardware, the A-code
       interpreter, in addition to the Kernel  and  Ada  I/O  System  (such
       projects  are  underway  at  the  ID/DTH,  as  well as at many other
       places: industry as well as universities).

(1)  is,  by  far,  the overriding reason. (2) reflects certain desires on the
part of ID/DTH as well the Danish Telecommunication Research Lab. (3)  could
become a major reason.

The  notion  of  A-code  is  not  new. Part of the success of PASCAL must be
attributed to its easy portability, partly due to its virtual, P-code,  code
generation.  Now  it is not an objective of the DDC Ada project to propagate
ADA; but merely to apply sound, state-of-the-art and beyond, techniques. And
with  theoretical & practical knowledge & clarification of, and insight into
appropriate P-/A-code virtual machines now  being  more  firmly  established
[DoBo  80],  and  on  the  background  of  motivation (1), it is deemed that
generating A-code is the best way to go.

The  paper  by  Dommergaard  of  this  volume presents the A-Code design and
model.


## Target Code Generation

This  does  not  preclude  that  the  DDC Ada compiler cannot be modified to
generate  code  for  an  actual,  real (physical) target machine. On  the
contrary.  The  DDC Ada compiler will indeed be easily modifiable to do just
that. In this proposal no plans are established in the direction of defining
Compiling  Algorithms, and specifying, and implementing such code generators
directly from Ada into target machine code.

## A-Code Interpreter Development

Developing  the  A-code  interpreter  has  four  aspects: (1) deciding on an
appropriate A-code instruction  set;  (2)  formally  defining  the  evolving
virtual   machine;   (3)   specifying  a  design  structure  for  an  A-code
interpreter; and (4) finally coding this interpreter. The  designs  must  be
properly integrated into the ARTES.

## 2.5.2  A Kernel for Ada Tasking

The  Ada Run-Time Environment System as developed by DDC is oriented towards
supporting the execution of a single ADA program on a  single,  or  multiple
mini/midi mono-processors. The sub-system kernel which short-term schedules,
the dynamically varying, indefinite number of 'concurrently'  running  tasks
is called KAT.

The  requirements  to  be  fulfilled  by  KAT are precisely defined by the
abstract model of Ada parallelism -- see section 2.1.3 - - which  is  really
the  abstract model of KAT. Hence we derive from this model the design, i.e.
structure, of KAT as partly determined by interfaces to  possibly  available

operating system facilities (thus we assume at this stage a model of these facilities to be present, see 2.5.4). From this design we finally code a realization.

## 2.5.3 An Ada Input/Output System

Ada specifies a set of predefined modules describing recommended stream- and record-oriented Input/Output. The proposed functions are all rather conventional -- & should hence all be easily realizable on any computer system in terms of their (assumed) already existing I/O (incl. backing store facilities). The Ada definition I/O modules rely on a small set of very primitive functions. The I/O modules use these to build up a rather more powerful set of I/O functions and I/O data types. The 'standard/prelude' oriented inclusion of those I/O modules in any Ada program therefore has led us to include these directly in a formal definition of Ada. That is: It is as if the compiler specification recognizes the I/O module functions & data-types, and instead of compiling the I/O modules, generates appropriate (SVC-like) calls to an optimized I/O component of ARTES. From the formal definition of Ada incl. I/O, we therefore develop an abstract model of the I/O component of ARTES, and from it we code the I/O component.

## 2.5.4 Target Machine/Computer System Interface

A prerequisite of the design of ARTES is an abstract model of the interface between ARTES and the Target machine System. One such model must be developed for each Target machine System in question - and from these preferably one 'standard' model derived. This 'standard interface' must then be implemented by the contracting industries on their target machines.

## 2.5.5 ARTES Features: Facilities and Capabilities

The facilities and capabilities which ARTES shall possess must be specified before the designing of ARTES can take place. Some of the facilities which could be convenient in ARTES could influence the design of the compiler, too, e.g. how much information should be made available to the programmer when an Ada program fails during execution. A simple ARTES could provide no more than a dump of the current activation records, whereas a more elaborate ARTES might indicate the point of error by referring to the source text, and might allow for inspection in symbolic form (i.e. using the programmer defined names of variables and types etc.) all variables visible - or reachable - at the point of program failure; it might allow for checkpoint setting with print-out of the contents of indicated variables at specified checkpoints, etc. A proper balance between features and cost must be established and specified.

## 3. Quality Assurance

The primary means of Quality Assurance is the development methodology itself starting from (a formal definition of) the Ada language and from abstract models of the environment of the compiler and run-time system - and from these systematically in a stepwise manner arive at the actual, concrete compiler and run-time system. At each step correctness arguments are carried out to increase confidence in the correctness of the derivation step. We do not claim, however, that the Ada Compiler System will be error free - but we believe that the development method outlined above will keep errors to a minimum compared to any other method currently in use - and that errors will not be too difficult to trace and to correct. Each derivation will be properly documented to ease such error tracing - and to ease the implementation of later language changes and/or introduction of compiler optimizing techniques.

It is recognized, that in addition to the development methodology outlined above certain traditional means of project management and structuring, programming practices and testing will have to be employed.

The project planning will partition the project into smaller, manageable parts or phases and include reviews between the parts as well as at selected points during the individual phases to allow for updating the plan, assessing whether the project direction is feasible, allowing for iterations in the work of the phase. Included will be a documentation production plan dealing with what documentation to provide as well as with when these documents shall be available. Other traditional means to be employed are outlined in the following sub-sections.

### 3.1 The 'Buddy' Checking System

The 'buddy' checking system will be used throughout the project. That is each project member will have a fellow project member allocated as his/her buddy. This buddy regularly (e.g. more frequent than once a week), reviews and comments the work done since the last review. In this way further errors can be detected and corrected in an early stage and, equally important, the detailed knowledge of the various project activities will be spread among more project members.

One further advantage is obtained where project members working in parallel on interdependent project activities are assigned as buddies of each other: The required exchange and sharing of information between the activities are then obtained at no extra cost.

### 3.2 The Chief Programmer Teams

The functional organization of the project especially when in the program design and code phases will be that of the Chief Programmer Teams, cf. [Ba 72]. The permanent members of the team are: The chief programmer, the backup programmer and the programming librarian.

### 3.2.1 Chief Programmer

The responsibility of each project activity is assigned to a chief programmer, who produces the critical nucleus and specifies and integrates all other components of the activity. This is valid for detailed development of programs as well as for development of abstract models/specifications which in this case can be considered a programming activity on an abstract level.

In case of smaller components the chief programmer may produce them entirely – and the team has no members but the above mentioned permanent ones. In the normal case, however, more programmers will be assigned to the team.

### 3.2.2 Backup Programmer

The backup programmer – who potentially could be a chief programmer of another activity – shall follow the work in the activity and be available as a discussion partner. The primary role is to be able to take over the work as chief programmer of the activity – temporarily or permanently – without causing any delay in the progress of the activity. It will probably be advantageous to have a chief programmer's 'buddy' and backup programmer to be one and the same person.

### 3.2.3 EDP Assistant/Programming Librarian

The programming librarian carries out the keying in of actual code, the removal of trivial coding errors and performs the test runs, before presenting the output (diagnostics) to the rest of the team. Furthermore the programming librarian maintains the documentation of the activity releasing the updated documents and source texts to the document librarian as soon as these texts have reached a well-defined – or closed – state.

### 3.3 Programming Implementation Manual

The programming implementation manual will specify how the concrete programming has to be performed, including which language to use, which program structuring principles, module interfacing, error handling etc to use, that is the now traditional ways of writing readable, reliable, robust and modifiable code. An existing programming guide can most likely be used.

### 3.4 Test Library

A library of Ada test programs will be developed and maintained for use in the verification/testing of the compiler system.

Ada programs each exercising separate parts of the Ada language should be provided on an 'orthogonal' basis; furthermore full Ada programs using more features in combination should be provided in this library.

These Ada programs are considered a part of the final documentation of the Ada compiler system and should be re-exercised whenever changes are introduced into the system. The library must include input data to the Ada programs as well as the expected and the actual output produced.

To the greatest extent possible the test program library will draw upon the library of the Ada-Europe Validation Centre being set up now. When selecting the actual testing methodology the DDC will consult the expertise of the validation centre(s).

## 4. Software Engineering Support

This chapter describes tools and techniques concerning the software engineering support which - together with the techniques of chapter 3 - are considered necessary for the DDC Ada project.

### 4.1 Document Processing System

In order to keep all documentation up to date and to keep track of changes made to documentation and program modules, a computer based document processing system must be available along the following lines:

#### 4.1.1 Text/Program Editing and Formatting

Basically the DDC will use a TEX/META-FONT system for technical text, also adopted by the American Math. Society [Kn 79].

An interactive editor must be available allowing input and editing of pure texts (reports) as well as source program texts. Furthermore various text/program formatting functions must be provided either embedded in the editor or as separate system programs.

The text formatting must include: paragraph justification, page splitting, page numbering, extraction of chapter and section headers into tables of contents, index preparation.

The program 'formatting' must include: Indentation corresponding to the structure of the program, highlighting keywords, splitting long lines into multiple lines to fit given document formats. The text 'output' device must allow for a full mathematical text character set.

#### 4.1.2 Document Librarian

A document librarian must be allocated to the DDC Ada project. The responsibilities of the librarian are:

- Taking care of all source programs, data files, documentation texts and their history and current status (level of completion).

- Filing all output from test runs together with the corresponding input data.

- Providing for backup of all files and facilitating the retrieval of any version of the files.

- Producing surveys of the existing source texts and documentation including their status thus giving the basis of the complete project status survey.

- Producing intermediate reports documenting project progress by collecting existing documents whether complete or in draft form. Such intermediate reports are to be submitted to interested parties at certain predefined checkpoints/milestones in the project.

# A DENOTATIONAL (STATIC) SEMANTICS METHOD FOR DEFINING ADA CONTEXT CONDITIONS

*Jørgen Bundgaard & Lennart Schultz*

Abstract:

This paper outlines a denotational semantics like method for defining the statically decideable context conditions that Ada programs must satisfy. The resulting definition illustrates representational & operational abstraction by - in contrast to conventional attribute/affix grammar methods - not referring to any compiler realization.

Contents                                                      page
--------                                                      ----

## 1.0 Introduction

### 1.1 Background

This paper constitutes the thesis presented to obtain the degree of Master of Science in engineering, at the Technical University of Denmark, Department of Computer Science. The preceding work was carried out in collaboration with Ole Dommergaard, Hans Henrik Løvengreen and Jan Storbank Pedersen. Regular discussions with these people gave us a thorough understanding of the ideas behind Ada, as well as they revealed the deepest implications of the language changes that came up during the project period.

Dealing with the context sensitive properties of Ada, this paper is one of four, constituting the initial development of a formal definition of Ada. The three others are [StPe 80], concerning the dynamic semantics, including storage handeling [Lø 80a] and parallelismn (Ada Tasking) [Lø 80b].

The style of definition is that of Denotational Semantics, using the Meta-Language (META-IV) of The VIENNA DEVELOPMENT METHOD (VDM) [BjJo 78]. This method has succesfully been applied to the formal definitions of the PL/1, Algol 60 and CCITT-CHILL programming languages. [Be 74], [HeJo 78] and [HaBj 80].

We hereby wish to express our gratefulness to those people, who took part in our work during the project period, and from whom we received much inspiration and encouragement.
We especially wish to thank Jan Storbank Pedersen, Ole Dommergaard, Hans Henrik Løvengreen, Ole N. Oest and Hans Bruun.
We do owe a debt of gratitude to Professor Dines Bjørner, who has supported our educational efforts so much during the past two years.

### 1.2 This Paper

This paper will concentrate on the analysis of the static semantics of Ada, in order to define the well-formedness predicates that abstract Ada programs must satisfy.
Appendix A holds a set of formulae, defining context conditions for an abstract, experimental language, called A6, which is the 7th language in a series of languages which approach Ada more and more, A9 being the full abstract Ada.
Experimental languages A0 through A6 were designed in order to study static aspects with increasing complexity systematically, and to keep the current model up to date, according to language changes that came up during the project period. A0 was based on preliminary Ada, while A6 is based on the current version of the language as defined by [Ada 80].
By means of small, orthogonal examples, various Ada aspects are identified and discussed. The correspondence to the formal model is illustrated by means of annotated abstract domain equations and recursively defined applicative formulae.

Section 2 holds the conclusion. The completeness of the formal definition of Ada context conditions presented in this paper is discussed. The main modelling problems are identified together with some particular interesting aspects of Ada static semantics.

Section 3 concentrates on the analysis of the package properties of Ada. This serves to group related data types, variables and subprograms, and to limit the scope and visibility of corresponding identifiers to certain ranges of text. Experience with similar projects with other languages shows that the formal model of the static semantics is heavily influenced by the scope and visibility rules of the language. A static semantics model includes and maintaines symboltable-like compile-time (also called static) objects usually called dictionaries. The thus needed static domains are designed in Section 3.

Section 4, referring to relevant syntactic domains of compilation units, packages, blocks, declarative parts and declarations will show how to check that these constructs are well-formed. These constructs are the syntactic constructs from which most dictionary information is extracted. Consequently the details of the corresponding static domains are analysed in this section.
A suggestion for modelling the concept of libraries is given. It has however not been finished since the notion of separate compilations is not yet covered by our model.

Section 5 covers the notion of subprograms. We discuss overloading, forward declaration, derived subprograms, predefined subprograms and user defined subprograms. It is shown that a unified description of procedures, functions and operators can be given.

Section 6 covers the modelling of the notion of types. It is shown how to associate a description with a user defined type or subtype. The description is to be derived from the declaration at the type and to be used when expressions are type-checked.

Section 7 elaborates further on the subject of the previous section. The details of the various datatypes of Ada is discussed and proper dictionary descriptions af these are designed.

Section 8, referring to the syntactic domains of expressions will show how to use the information in the dictionary. We discuss overloading resolving and type check of expressions. Various expressions are included.

Section 9 elaborates on the notion of names. As names are also expressions, this section is closely related to the previous. This section shows how to lookup names in the dictionary. In fact the dictionary was designed to make this as easy as possible.

Section 10 addresses statements and blocks. We will show that it is a relatively simple task to check the well-formedness of these constructs.

Section 11 discusses two aspects: (1) how to extend the model of the "A6" context conditions to cover full Ada; and (2) the work to be done if this definition should be transformed into another definition, from which the non-code-generating passes of an Ada compiler can be systematically derived.

Section 12 holds an index to all formulas given in sections 3 to 11. Otherwise consult the index of appendix A.

Before any modelling aproach is presented we give an introduction to what modelling static semantics is all about.

## 1.3 Abstract Syntax and Static Semantics

The context sensitive properties (colloquially called the static semantics) of Ada are those syntactic properties which cannot be expressed even by an abstract (context free) grammar defining the syntactic objects of Ada (i.e. Ada compilation units, etc), but which can be checked for correctness statically, that is by inspection of the program text itself, without reference to any execution of that text.

In The VIENNA DEVELOPMENT METHOD the syntax of Ada constructs is representationally abstracted using domain equations; and the context sensitive properties are operationally abstracted by a set of recursively defined applicative functions. The latter basically applies to objects of the syntactic domains and yields truth values. The thus defined well-formedness or invariant predicate functions are normally expressed in terms of an auxiliary object, here called the "Surroundings". The Surroundings *) abstractly summarise what is statically known about a program text at given program points.

The task of designing the static semantics defining formulae of Ada includes that of defining suitable abstract syntaxes for the syntactic domains, and of defining functions which gather appropriate information from program text for inclusion in the surroundings.

The thesis of this paper is that the static semantics of Ada can be formulated denotationally and as a homomorphism. That is: to each identifier of a program (whether a package name, subprogram name, object name, type name, etc.) is associated its static semantics denotation; and the well-formedness of a compound Ada construct can be expressed as a function of the well-formedness of the constituent constructs.

Modelling the context sensitive properties of a language construct such as a statement or an expression requires knowledge of the set of visible identifiers, and what they identify at a given point of text.

This information is obtained from the declarations of the identifiers, and is in the model kept in an auxiliary object, called the "Dictionary". The Dictionary is a map from identifiers into their static semantic denotation (object identifiers are mapped into object-descriptors, etc.).

The previous mentioned surroundings will as its most important component, contain such a dictionary.

The well-formedness predicates are complemented by so-called "Rebuild-functions". These are functions which maps abstract Ada programs conforming to an abstract syntax "AS1" into an equivalent abstract program now conforming to an abstract syntax "AS2" better suited for the dynamic semantics definition.

This includes substituting all composite name-occurences with unique "internal" identifiers, associating to such identifiers a description (package, type, etc.). That is: distributing the dictionary information, evaluating static expressions, performing the (macro-like) expansion of generic instantiations, etc., over the abstract program text.

---

*) Not to be confused with the notion of "Environment" of Ada-programming systems. (eg. text editors, library management, runtime-system etc. )

## 2.0  Conclusion

At the present stage the model of A6 is considered as being a "well-off-the-ground" definition of the static semantics of full Ada. The language aspects not covered by A6 (Tasks, exception-handlers and associated statements: accept, select, raise etc.) are variations over the themes: Packages and statements, and can, without changing the fundamental static domains, be "appended" to the existing model. Whether this also applies to the concept of "generics" and "separate compilation" is yet to be considered.

The main problem in defining the static semantics turned out to be the handeling of derived subprograms and the arranging of a proper model of the scope of "predefined operators".

The present model handels this rather mechanical in the literal sense: Derived subprograms and predefined operators are modeled as being "explicitly declared" with a well defined "scope". This in return makes it possible to handle user defined- as well as predefined subprograms, in particular operators, universally.

From the analysis of overloading it appears that the existence of a proper resolving can always be detected by means of a single bottom up pass. The identification of overloaded expressions can be done in a subseqent top down pass. (The two passes can be local to the functions dealing with the expression tree.)

It is observed that the evaluation of static (compile time) expressions requires a "rebuilding" of the expression (the transformation from "AS1" into "AS2"), involving resolving overloading.

Ada introduces a new class of expressions, which is neither static expressions nor dynamic (run time) expressions. This is the class of "constant expressions", whose evaluation can be guaranteed to have no side effects. These expressions which refer only to values, constants (which could have dynamically computed values) and to predefined operators and functions can only be identified when overloading within the expression is resolved. If default values of subprogram parameters given in a (forward) subprogram declaration were not to be repeated with the corresponding subprogram body (and guaranteed to yield the same value as before) the identification of this class of expressions could be avoided.

The modelling style applied here represents the "pure" understanding of the context conditions that Ada programs must satisfy, while a more refined/elaborated "rebuild" specification would serve as a better basis for systematic derivation of a "Context-Condition-Checker"

## 3.0 The Fundamental Static Domains

### 3.1 Introduction

This section analyses the visibility-control facilities provided in Ada. We
do so in order to design the overall structure of the static domains. These
must reflect the intended purpose of those tools. The prime aspect is that
of nested packages. Packages group declarations which define names referr-
able from outside the package. Outside as well as inside a package specification, an item declared there can be referenced as a selected component of
the package. This also applies to blocks when named with the usual restriction that one can never use identifiers local to the block when not inside
it. (Cf.: storage local to a block is freed when the block is left.)
Though the same entity can be referenced through several (syntactically
different) names, we dislike keeping multiple copies of information. Such
would make dictionary updates cumbersome. We outline a dictionary
(symbol-table like) structure with the required properties but without redundancy.
It is also important to keep track af the level of program text nesting such
that eg. types with the same name but at different level can be uniquely
marked as beeing different. This makes type checking of expressions possible.
Visibility of identifiers locally declared in package specifications can be
"opened" as a result of a use clause mentioning that package name.
Therefore there must be a way to represent this "opening". To do so we maintain a second symbol-table like object where information about these identifiers is held. It should not be merged into the dictionary since it represents only temporary opening of visibility unlike that of explicitly declared identifiers.
There must be a way to model the existence of predefined operators of the
language. Since the user can define his own operators overloading or rede-
claring the predefined, it is convinient to represent also the predefined
operators as two-parameter functions. The description of the predefined operators are keept in a separate symbol-table like object since the rules
determining their visibility is not quite similar to those of user defined
operators.
This was a sketch of the static domains, which models the "Surroundings".
The next section elaborates details and motivations.

### 3.2 The Dictionary and The Surroundings

First we analyse the concept of nested declarative constructs. Since nested
subprograms and nested blocks (when named) exhibit properties equivalent to
those of nested package specifications, we shall in an introductory, small
example, consider the latter only. We believe that the example is sufficient to argue the need for a hierarchical dictionary structure.

Consider the declarative part of an unnamed Ada block. It contains declarations of types, objects (of these types) and packages. Comments (--) mark
some type names, usable in object declarations.

```
declare

package P1 is
   type T1 is....;
   -- T1 and P1.T1 are here different names for the same type

   package P2 is
      type T2 is ...;
      -- T2, P2.T2 and P1.P2.T2 are here different names for
      -- the same type
      ...
   end P2;
   ....
end P1;

package P3 is

   package P4 is
      type T4 is...;
      ....
   end P4;

   package P5 is

      package P6 is
         type T6 is ...;
         type T7 is ...;
         -- T6, P6.T6, P5.P6.T6, P3.P5.P6.T6 are here
         -- different names for the same type
         ...
      end P6;
      -- P6.T6, P5.P6.T6, P3.P5.P6.T6 are legal names
      -- for the type above
   end P5;
   -- P5.P6.T6, P3.P5.P6.T6 are legal names for the type above
end P3;
-- P3.P5.P6.T6 is the only legal name for the type above

begin
....
end;
```

fig. 1

Omitting Ada-keywords, the example can with unchanged meaning be written as:

```
P1:┌
   │T1:...
   │P2:┌
   │   │T2:...
   └   └

            — this is point 1 (see below )

P3:┌
   │P4:┌
   │   │T4:...
   │   └
   │
   │P5:┌
   │   │P6:┌
   │   │   │T6:...
   │   │   │      — point 2
   │   │   │T7:...
   │   │   │      — point 3
   │   │   └            fig. 2
   │   └
   └
```

At any point of the text where a name appears on the right hand side  of  an
object declaration, that name must represent (stand for) a type.
It can be a selected component of some visible package,  or  it  can  be  an
identifier from a preceding type declaration in the same declaration list.
Ada thus permits referring to a certain type via  different  names,  because
one  can  always prefix a name with the identifier of the directly enclosing
package.  Names obtained in this manner can again be prefixed with the identifier of the directly enclosing package etc.  - and still be a name for the
same type.

The modeling experience shows, that the dictionary structure should  reflect
this prefix naming concept.
An abstract syntax is given for the simple language used in this example:


```
1.0   Program       = Declaration*
 .1   Declaration   = Package-decl | Type-decl | Object-decl
 .2   Package-decl  :: Id Declaration*
 .3   Type-decl     :: Id Type-expr
 .4   Object-decl   :: Id ( Type-expr | Type-name )
 .5   Type-expr     = INT | BOOL | ...
 .6   Type-name     = Id+
```

Dict(ionary) is a map from id(entifiers) into their static semantic  denotation.   The domain of the dictionary will be the set of identifiers that are
directly visible.
Type-descriptors contain a unique mark which is the "path of names" from the
outermost  level,  or  in other words, the longest possible name of the type
they describe.  We also refer to this as the "Unitname" or just "Name".
Objects  inherit  these  marks  from  their type, thus prepared for the
"strong type match"-rules  in  Ada.  A hierarchical/recursively defined dic-
tionary-object can reflect the visibility and referabillity rules of  this
Ada-subset:

```
2.0   Dict         =  Id  m-> Descriptor
 .1   Descriptor   =  Package-descr | Type-descr | Object-descr
 .3   Package-descr :: Dict
 .4   Type-descr   :: Datastructure Unitname
 .5   Object-descr :: Type-descr
 .6   Datastructure =  INT | BOOL |  ...
 .7   Unitname     =  Id+
```

Since no name or identifier can be referred to before it is introduced and
since it can be referred to in its own declaration list as soon as it is introduced (textual order plays an important role!) the dictionary "changes"
with each and every declaration in a list of declarations. We speak of a
dictionary that is "valid" at a certain point of text. We show how the dictionary reflects the visibility rules of Ada – at points 1,2 and 3 (in
fig.2):

point 1:
  dict:

$$
\left[ P1 \rightarrow \text{mk-pack-descr}\left( \left[ \begin{array}{l} T1 \rightarrow \text{mk-type-descr}(\ldots), \\ P2 \rightarrow \text{mk-pack-descr}([~T2 \rightarrow \text{mk-type-descr}(\ldots)]) \end{array} \right] \right) \right]
$$

fig. 3

Using a shorthand:

point 1:

$$
\left[ P1 \rightarrow \left[ \begin{array}{l} T1 \rightarrow \ldots \\ P2 \rightarrow [~T2 \rightarrow \ldots~] \end{array} \right] \right]
$$

fig. 4

point 2:

$$
\left[ \begin{array}{l}
P1 \rightarrow \left[ \begin{array}{l} T1 \rightarrow \ldots \\ P2 \rightarrow [\overline{T2} \rightarrow \ldots] \end{array} \right] \\[2ex]
P3 \rightarrow \left[ \begin{array}{l} P4 \rightarrow [\overline{T4} \rightarrow \ldots] \\ P5 \rightarrow \left[ P6 \rightarrow \left[ \begin{array}{l} T6 \rightarrow \ldots \\ *) \end{array} \right] \right] \end{array} \right] \\[3ex]
P4 \rightarrow [T4 \rightarrow \ldots] \\[1ex]
P5 \rightarrow \left[ P6 \rightarrow \left[ \begin{array}{l} T6 \rightarrow \ldots \\ *) \end{array} \right] \right] \\[2ex]
P6 \rightarrow \left[ \begin{array}{l} T6 \rightarrow \ldots \\ *) \end{array} \right] \\[2ex]
T6 \rightarrow \ldots \\
*)
\end{array} \right]
$$

fig. 5

Point 3: All the *) becomes T7 -> ...

Consider the dictionary which is valid at point 2:

1.  T4 is not in the domain of the dictionary, hence it is not visible,
    but it can be referred to as a selected component in two ways,
    namely as P4.T4 and as P3.P4.T4. Thus the dictionary exhibits re-
    dundancy.

2.  Updating the dictionary (when introducing T7) involves the diction-
    ary to be updated at several points, hence it is hard to guarantee
    the well-formedness of the dictionary (what we mean by this is  yet

to be formally stated).


The hierarchical dictionary exhibits visibility and referabillity properties
rather directly while it the same time is easy to use.
We give the lookup-function:


```
3.0  lookup(name)(dict)=
 .1  ( let id = hd name in
 .2    if id ~E dom dict then exit
 .3      else(let descriptor = dict(id) in
 .4            if tl name = <> then descriptor else
 .5              cases descriptor
 .6              ( mk-Package-descr(localdict) -> lookup(tl name)
                                                    (localdict),
 .7                    T                       -> exit)))

 .8  type: Id+ -> ( Dict -> Descriptor )
```


This function goes recursively down the hierarchy of the dictionary, returning a description of the given name.  It might instead exit reporting static
errors (it is for example illegal to select components in a type).


We have now seen that due to the prefix-naming concept (dot selection),  the
dictionary  must  exhibit  some  "depth",  that is:  it must be hierarchical
structured.
At the same time it must be "flat", that is:  global identifiers (when  not
redeclared)  can  be  referred  to,  simply by using their identifier.  This
latter case  is  similar  to  that  of  simple,  block-oriented  programming
languages like Algol 60 and PL/1.
Since identifiers can be referenced through their full name as soon as  they
are  introduced, a "flat-deep" dictionary structured model would be troubled
by cumbersome, multiple updatings (see the example fig.  5, where  the  type
T7 is to be introduced).  Besides, it would contain undesired redundancy.
The proposed "high" dictionary combined with the "level"-information provide
a fairly simple model:
All updatings are performed on the "high" dictionary which  when  used  (eg.
by lookup-functions) is always flattened with respect to the level.

In the following we present the fundamental concepts of the  dictionary  and
surroundings model, which is used throughout this paper.

```
4.0  Surroundings    ::  Dict    Dict-level  ...
 .1  Dict            =   ( Id | BLK )  m->  Descriptor
 .2  Dict-level      =   Unitname
 .3  Descriptor      =   Pack-descr | Block-descr | ...
 .4  Pack-descr      ::  Dict  Unitname ...
 .5  Block-descr     ::  Dict  Unitname
 .6  ...
 .7  Unitname        =   ( Id | BLK )*
```

### annotations:

The Surroundings of a given point of program text is defined as:
.1 The hierarchical dictionary (hdict) with only the identifiers that  are
   visible at the outermost level in its domain.
.2 The level of nesting, ie. the unitname of the package (or named block)
   that is directly enclosing the given point of program text.
   The term will be "dictionary-level" (level). The  dictionary-level  is
   equivalent  to unitnames, which are tuples of identifiers and BLK's.
   (BLK is used in absence of an explicitly given block name)
   A package-descriptor is the local dictionary of the visible part of the
   package plus the unitname of the package.

### Example:

The surroundings of point 2 (fig. 2) are:

$$
\begin{aligned}
\text{mk-Surr(} &\left[ P1 \to \left( \left[ \begin{array}{l} T1 \to \dots \\ P2 \to ( [\ T2 \to \dots\ ],\ \langle P1,P2 \rangle ) \end{array} \right],\ \langle P1 \rangle \right), \right.\\
&\quad P3 \to \left( \left[ \begin{array}{l} P4 \to ( [\ T4 \to \dots\ ],\ \langle P3,P4 \rangle ),\\ P5 \to \left( \left[ P6 \to \left( \left[ \begin{array}{l} T6 \to \dots \\ *) \end{array} \right], \langle P3,P5,P6 \rangle \right) \right], \langle P3,P5 \rangle \right) \end{array} \right], \langle P3 \rangle \right), \\
&\qquad \langle P3,P5,P6 \rangle,\ \dots\ )
\end{aligned}
$$

The surroundings at point 3 (fig. 2) is obtained by replacing
*) by  T7 -> ...    in the object above.

The dictionary with all the visible identifiers in its domain can be  obtained  by means of a "flattening" of the dictionary component with respect to
the dictionary-level. We give the "flattening" function.

```
5.0 flatten (dict)(level) =
 .1 if ~(E id E dom dict)(is-enclosing(dict |{id})(level))
 .2     then dict
 .3     else (let id E dom dict be s.t. is-enclosing(dict | {id})
                                                        (level) in
 .4           let nextdict = cases dict(id):
 .5              ( mk-Pack-descr(localdict, ) -> localdict ,
 .6                .                                        ,
 .7                .                                        ,
 .8                .                                ) in
 .9           dict + flatten(nextdict)(level)  )

 .10 type: Dict -> ( Id* -> Dict )
```

## Annotations:

The non-redundant hierarchical dictionary is "unraveled" (like a chinese box) as long as the "level" indicates a certain "path" pointing further into the structure.
.5 If the level points into a package, the local dictionary of this package is flattened and "put on the top of" the enclosing dictionary (overwrite-plus is used in .9 because inner re-declarations of identifiers "hide" the outer declaration).

A dictionary is said to enclose a certain level, if in the range of the dictionary there exists a package (...named block, subprogram, ...) whose unit-name is equal to the given level or if its local (here visible) dictionary is enclosing the level.

```
6.0 is-enclosing(dict)(searchlevel) =
 .1 (E id E dom dict)(cases dict(id):
 .2                    ( mk-Pack-descr(localdict,packname) ->
 .3                       (packname=searchlevel  or
 .4                        is-enclosing(localdict)(searchlevel)),
 .5                        .
 .6                        .
 .7                        .
 .8                       T -> false ))

 .9 type: Dict -> ( Id* -> BOOL )
```

Obviously the surroundings of point 3 (fig. 2) must be different from the surroundings of point 2, since the type T7 has been introduced. We shall in section 5 deal with the specific problems of extracting a type-descriptor from a type definition, but here, assuming an "extension" or a "partial dictionary"

$$[ \; T7 \; -> \; \underline{mk}\text{-Type-descr}( \; ... \; ) \; ]$$

we show how to extend the dictionary component of the surroundings.

```
7.0 extend(dict)(level)(extension) =
.1 if level = <> then dict + extension
.2     else (let id = hd level                          in
.3           dict + [id -> cases dict(id):
.4               ( mk-Pack-descr(localdict,packname) ->
.5                   mk-Pack-descr( extend(localdict)
.6                                  (tl level)(extension),
.7                                  packname ),
.8                 .
.9                 .
.10                .
.11                ) ]   )

.12 type: Dict -> ( Id* -> ( Dict -> Dict ))
```

Annotations:

.1  "Overwrite-plus" is used, because the dictionary is (sometimes) updated, rather than extended.
.4  When the local dictionary of a package is extended, only the dictionary component is changed.


## 3.3 Overloaded Identifiers

Enumeration-literals, subprogram-identifiers and operators can be overloaded, that is, the same identifier/operator may have different meanings depending on the context in which it is used.
Subprogram identifiers may be overloaded for two or more subprograms if the parameters and the (possible) result type are not equivalent.

The reader should notice that in the dictionary model so far described identifiers declared at an inner level always hides an identifier with the same name declared global to the inner level.
This is due to the usage of "overwrite-plus" at line 5.9 in "flatten".
In Ada this overwriting/hiding should only occur when the identifiers cannot be overloaded.


The static domains associated with overloading are:

```
8.0  Dict            ::  (Id | Char-lit | Operator | BLK) m-> Descr
 .1  Descr           =   Pack-descr | Block-descr | Overload-descr
 .2                      | ...
 .3  Overload-descr  ::  (Literal-descr | Sub-prog-descr) - set
 .4  Literal-descr   ::  Type
 .5  Type            ::  ...
 .6  Operator        =   + | - | * | / | and | or | ...
 .7  Char-lit        ::  TOKEN
 .8  Sub-prog-descr  ::  Dict  Unitname  s-entr:Entrance
 .9  Entrance        ::  Parm-descr*  s-return:[ Type ][OPERATOR]
 .10 Parm-descr      ::  Id+  Mode  Type  [ Expr ]
 .11 Mode            =   in | in out | out
 .12 Unitname        =   (Id | Char-lit | Operator | BLK | N1)*
```

## Annotations:

.0 The domain of dictionary contains character-literals and operator-symbols, since characters are enumeration-literals and operator-symbols may denote subprograms.

.3 The static semantic denotation of an overloaded identifier/character-literal/operator is a set of Literal-descriptors and subprogram descriptors.

.4 A Literal-descriptor contains the "Type" of the enumeration type of which it is a literal.

.8 A Subprogram-descriptor contain a dictionary of locally declared items. This is necessary, since such items can, from inside the subprogram body, be refered as a selected component of the subprogram.

.12 A subprogram-descriptor also contains a Unitname, which is equivalent to that of packages and blocks except for an extra element (a natural number) which is concatenated to the otherwise not unique Unitname in order to make the Unitnames of overloaded subprograms different.

.9 It also contains an "Entrance" which is used whenever it must be decided whether a certain subprogram is overloading or is hiding a former declared with the same identifier or designator.

The "overwrite-plus" in 5.9, 7.1 and 7.3 must be substituted with "overload-plus". Only when the identifiers, operators or character-literals in dictionary as well as in the extension denote overloadable entities, the map returned from this function will be different from the map returned from "overwrite-plus", (ie.+) when applied to the same arguments.

```
9.0 overload(dict)(extension) =
.1 [id -> cases:
.2   (id E dom dict and id E dom extension ->
.3       cases( dict(id),extension(id)):
.4       ((mk-Overload-descr(set1),mk-Overload-descr(set2)) ->
.5           mk-Overload-descr({ spd E Sub-prog-descr |
.6               spd E set2 or
.7               (spd E set1 s.t.
.8               (Ɐ spd' E set2)
.9               (is-overloadable(s-entr(spd))(s-entr(spd'))))}
.11
.10               U { ltd E Literal-descr |
.11                       ltd E set1 or ltd E set2 } ),
.12       T   ->
.13               extension(id)  ),
.14   id E dom dict        -> dict(id) ,
.15   id E dom extension -> extension(id)  )
.16 | id E dom dict U dom extension ]

.17 type: Dict -> ( Dict -> Dict )



10.0  is-overloadable(entrance1)(entrance2) = ( ... )
  .1 type: Entrance -> ( Entrance -> BOOL )
```

This concludes the representational abstraction of overloading in Ada.  In section 6 we show how to use these domains in the resolving of overloading within expressions and names.


### 3.4  Strong- and Weak Visible Identifiers

The Ada programmer has the abillity to extend the set of strong visible identifiers (that is: the identifiers, that can be referenced using simply the identifier itself) with identifiers declared in the visible part of package specifications by means of Use clauses mentioning these package names.  Use clauses are declarative items and can appear among the declarations in any declarative part.
We resume the rules concerning this visibility control tool in terms of our own definitions:

1. The range of text in which a use clause has an effect is called the scope of the use clause.

2. The effect of use clauses given in the declarative part of a block, package- or subprogram body extends from its introduction throughout the block or body.

3. The effect of use clauses given in a package specification extends from its introduction to the end of the specification.  It also extends over the corresponding package body.

4. Strong visible identifiers constitute the domain of the "strong

dictionary". The strong dictionary is exactly what we get if we flatten the high dictionary component of the surroundings with respect to the level.

5.  Identifiers declared in the visible part of packages, mentioned in use clauses given at any level, up to the level of the compilation unit itself are said to be candidates for weak-visibility.

6.  Identifiers that are declared in one and only one of the packages mentioned in the use clauses so far, are said to be weak-visible in the scope of the use clauses. They constitute the domain of the "weak dictionary".

7.  Identifiers that are either in the domain of the strong dictionary or in the domain of the weak dictionary are said to be 'visible'. They constitute the domain of the 'visible dictionary'.

8.  The visible dictionary is the weak dictionary overloaded by the strong dictionary. That is: whenever an identifier is in the intersection of the domains of the strong- and weak dictionary, its static semantic denotation in the visible dictionary will be that of the strong dictionary, unless the identifier can be overloaded. Therefore, some of the weak visible identifiers may not be visible at all. The visible dictionary is formally defined by the equation:

11.0  <u>let</u> visible-dict = overload(weakdict)(strongdict) <u>in</u> ...

## 3.5 Modelling Weak Visibility

Use clauses are language constructs for gathering the candidates for weak visibility, from which the weak dictionary is formed.
It is important to notice, that a use clause not always extends the weak dictionary, it might also restrict it.: Therefore the weak dictionary cannot be expanded directly into the dictionary-component of the surroundings, as we would do if the semantics of use clauses was a simulated repeated declaration of the identifiers from the visible part of the "used" packages.

40

```
declare
        package P is
           W, Z : INT;
        end P;

        package Q is
           X, Y, Z : FLOAT;
        end Q;

        package R is
           X, Y, W : BOOL;
        end R;

              -- weak visible identifiers here: none.
        use Q;
              -- -      -        -          - : X, Y, Z
        use R;
              -- -      -        -          - : Z, W
        use P;
              -- -      -        -          - : none.
begin ... end;
```

The candidates for weak visibility are gathered in a component of the surroundings called the Weak-map. A weak-map is a mapping from unique package
names into the visible (local) dictionary of the same packages. The domain
of the weak-map will consist of the unitnames of packages, which have been
mentioned in use clauses being in effect at the point of program text, for
which the current "Surroundings" is valid.


12.0  Surroundings :: Dict  Dict-level  s-wm: Weak-map    ...
  .1  ...
  .2  Weak-map     =   Unitname  m-> Dict


The weak dictionary is then at any point of text defined as the "merging" of
the dictionaries in the range of the weak-map component of the surroundings,
following the rules above.
We give the function, that preforms this merging:

```
13.0 weak-merge(weakmap) =
 .1 (let double-non-overloadable-ids =
 .2    {id|(E n1,n2 E dom weakmap)
 .3    (n1≠n2 and
 .4      let d1 = weakmap(n1), d2 = weakmap(n2)   in
 .5      (id E dom d1 and id E dom d2      and
 .6 ~(is-Overload-descr(d1(id)) and is-Overload-descr(d2(id))))))
 .7                                                      } in
 .8  let new-wm = [ n -> weakmap(n)\double-non-overloadable-ids
 .9                ! n E dom weakmap ]                    in
 .10 let map-of-ovl-dsc =
 .11    [id -> mk-Overload-descr(set1) |
 .12     (¥ ds1,ds2 E set1)
 .13     ((is-Literal-descr(ds1) or
 .14      ((ds1 ≠ ds2 and is-Sub-prog-descr(ds1) and
 .15                      is-Sub-prog-descr(ds2)    ) =>
 .16       is-overloadable(s-entr(ds1))(s-entr(ds2))            )
 .17      and
 .18      (E n E new-wm)( id E new-wm(n) and
 .19                      cases (new-wm(n))(id):
 .20                      (mk-Overload-descr(set2) -> ds1 E set2,
 .21                       T                       -> false) in
 .22 merge( ldict \ dom map-of-ovl-dsc | ldict E rng new-wm )
 .23 U map-of-ovl-dsc

 .24 type: Weak-map  ->  Dict
```

Annotations:

.8  First remove all identifiers that are not possibly overloadable and
    happen to be in more than one of the local dictionaries, from those
    dictionaries, thereby obtaining a new weakmap.
.10 Then create a dictionary of identifiers of Overload-descriptors of
.13 all literals (which can always be overloaded) and of
.14-.16 all subprograms, which are overloadable.
.22 Finally merge the dictionaries of those identifiers that are not "dou-
    ble" and not overloadable.  These dictionaries have disjoint domains.
    Add to the merged dictionaries the dictionary of overloadable identif-
    iers - and we have the weak dictionary !!


We show how to use the surroundings with the weak-map included:

14.0 lookup-name(name)(sur) =
 .1   lookup(name)(extract-dict(sur))

 .2 type: Name  ->  (  Surroundings  ->  Descriptor  )


15.0 extract-dict(mk-Surroundings(dict,level,weakmap,... )) =
 .1   overload(weak-merge(weakmap))(flatten(dict)(level))

 .2 type:  Surroundings  ->  Dict


The strong dictionary can be extracted by simulating "no use clauses given",
ie.:  by extracting the visible dictionary from surroundings, where the
weak-map component is empty:


16.0 extract-strong-dict(sur) =
 .1   extract-dict(sur+(s-wm:->[]))

 .2 type: Surroundings  ->  Dict


3.6  A Model of Predefined Operators

Some of the predefined operators in Ada have parameters  of  the  predefined
types, and returns values of predefined types.
In Ada, the predefined operators "+","*",....,"&" can be overloaded or hidden
(redeclared)  by  user  defined  operators.  The manual very, very carefully
describes the scope and visibility rules for user defined subprograms, which
of  course,  includes user defined operators. These may be either strong visible, visible but only weak visible, or they may be hidden.  Visible operators can be overloaded.
However, the visibility of the predefined operators in relation to the  user
defined operators is unfortunatly not precisely stated in the manual.
There are several aspects; one might be, to consider eg. to  the  operator
"+"  as  defined  on  the predefined type INTEGER and as "universal-integer"
(and therefore defined at the same place as the predefined  INTEGER  is  declared);   Since  all user defined integer types are derived from the predefined INTEGER, the predefined "+" is also derived for the user  defined  integer types.  In Ada it is such that:


    Certain subprograms having a parameter or result of the parent type (or
    one  of  its  subtypes) are derived by derived type. These subprograms
    are implicitly declared at the place of the  derived  type  definition,
    but may be redefined in the same declaration-list.

consider the following Ada block:


B: declare
    package P is
      type MY_INTG is range 1..100;-- new integer type
      -- function "+"(X,Y:MY_INT) return MY_INT is
      -- derived, hence implicitly declared here!
    end P;
    I,J,K:P.MY_INTG:=10;
  begin
    I:=J+K; -- note: which plus?
  end B;

It is very unreasonable to consider the "+" in the statement above as being
the implicitly declared "+" of the declarative part of package P; One reson
is that this implicitly declared "+" is not visible (which neither a explicitly declared "+" would be, nor a derived user defined "+" would be) within
the begin end of block B.


For the same reson, predefined operators for user defined types (eg.  "&")
should not be considered as implicitly declared at the place of the type definition.
consider the following Ada block:

C:declare
  package P is
    type AR is array(INTG range <>) of ELEM;
    -- implicit declared "&"(AR,AR) -> AR
    -- implicit declared "&"(AR,ELM) -> AR
  end P;
  V1,V2,V3 : P.AR(1..10);
begin
  V1:=V2(1..5) & V3(6..10); -- which "&" ?
end C;

These examples has shown, that predefined operators cannot be treated as
user defined operators, ie. be subject ordinary scope rules.

Another aspect is to consider all predefined operators as (implicitly) declared at the outermost level. Implicitly generated operators (as "&" in
the above example) should be kept at this level, in the dictionary of the
model. This will not work since the predefined operators may only be be directly visible (when not hidden) within and only within the scope of the
type, that coursed the (implicit) declaration of the predefined operator.
This is due to the fact, that operators are applicable to values
(eg.overloaded aggregates) of the type. Such values should be meaningless
outside the scope of the type of which they are values.
Implicitly declared at outermost level, the visibility of an operator would
exceed the scope of the type.

example:

```
B:declare
    package P is
        package Q is
            package R is
                type T is range 1..100;    -- Scope of type T
            end R;                          -- is also scope
        end Q;                             -- the scope for
    end P;                                 -- "+"(T,T) -> T and
    V1,V2,V3:P.Q.R.T:=7;                   -- "*"(T,T) -> T
    V4:P.Q.R.T:=V1+V2;                     -- etc.
begin                                      --
    V2:=6*V1;                              --
end B;                                     --
```

We assume that predefined operators should have the status to be "more weak visible" than weak visible user defined operators (ie. operators introduced in a use-clause). That is, if a weak visible user defined operator cannot overload a predefined operator, it must be the user defined operator that is visible! Just as strong visible user defined operators hide predefined operators that cannot overload.

However, it may often be the case, that the predefined operator "wins the game"

consider the example:

```
declare
    package P is
        type INT is range 1..100;
        -- implicit declaration of "+"(INT,INT) -> INT
        ...
        function "+"(X,Y:INT) return INT;
    end P;
use P;
A,B:INT:=5;
begin
A:=A+B;  --overloading can be resolved without knowledge of
end;     --weak visible operators(ie. P."+").
```

It must be possible to determine, whether a user defined operator is a redeclaration or an overloading of a predefined operator.
This is rather important, since there may be cases, where within expressions, a user defined as well as a predefined operator is matching the parameters and the context.
As shown (in section 4.6) it is quite easy to determine whether two user defined operators are overloadable or not. This can be done whenever the "entrance"-components of the "Subprogram descriptors" are known. Consequently, the modeling principle applied here requires predefined operators to be described (and to contain such "entrance" components) in the static domains.

The static semantic description of user defined operators are subprogram
descriptors. These are generated, based on the exact knowledge of the parameter and result types, which are provided by the subprogram specifications, in the declaration of an operator (see section 4.6).
Our conclusion is, that predefined operators should be explicitly collected
at the level of the declarative part of the innermost block, subprogrambody,
package private part, or package body enclosing the type definition, of the
type, for which the predefined operators are defined.
The collection of predefined operators is inherited by inner nested blocks,
subprograms, etc. .

For this purpose, the surroundings contains a dictionary of the predefined
operators, that have parameter and result types of user defined types.
This dictionary is updated whenever a type definition is elaborated (see
section 5.5).

```
17.0  Surroundings  ::  ... Operator-dict ...
   .1  Operator-dict = Operator  m-> Overload-descr
   .2  Overload-descr :: (Sub-prog-descr | ... )-set
```

Since predefined operators are even "weaker" visible than weak-visible user
defined operators, the dictionary of visible identifiers and operators, etc.
must be extracted as follows:

```
18.0  extract-dict(mk-Surroundings(dict,level,wkmap,opdict,.. )) =
   .1  overload( overload(opdict)(weak-merge(wkmap)) )
   .2          ( flatten(dict)(level)                 )

   .3  type: Surroundings  ->  Dict
```

## 3.7  Program Text Nesting.

The status component of the Surroundings is a track of the program text
nesting. Each of these stack-elements will contain information, all to be
discussed in the relevant context. An obvious motivation for the inclusion
of the status, is that the Exit-statement (see section 10.5) may only appear
within loops and it may not transfer control out of a package body (or a
task body) or a subprogram body. The status stack contains information
enough to check the legality of exit-transfers.

```
19.0 Surroundings  :: s-dict  : Dict
  .1                  s-level : Unitname
  .2                  s-wm    : Weak-map
  .3                  s-opmap : Operator-dict
  .4                  s-status: Status#
  .5 ...
  .6 Status        = In-Pack-spec  |
  .7                 In-Pack-body |  In-Sub-prog    |
  .8                 In-Block     |  In-Loop        | ...
  .9 In-Pack-spec :: ...
  .10 ...
```

## 3.8  Summary

We summarize the contents of this section by giving the static domain  equations  which,  together with the syntactic domain equations, form the foundation of the model.

```
20.0 Surroundings  :: s-dict   : Dict
  .1                  s-level  : Unitname
  .2                  s-wm     : Weak-map
  .3                  s-opmap  : Operator-dict
  .4                  s-status : Status#

  .5 Dict          = Dict-entry m-> Descr
  .6 Weakmap       :: Unitname m-> Dict
  .7 Operator-dict = Operator m-> Overload-descr
  .8 Status        = In-Pack-spec | In-Pack-body |
  .9                 In-Sub-prgr | In-Block | In-Loop

  .10 Dict-entry   = Id | Char-lit | Operator | BLK | LOOP

  .11 Descr        = Obj-descr | Numb-descr | Type-descr |
                     Pack-descr | Loop-descr |
  .12                Overload-descr | Block-descr
  .13                INTRODUCED | COMPONENT | nil

  .14 Obj-descr    :: s-tp: Type   s-con: [CONSTANT]
  .15 Numb-descr   :: ( INTG | NUM )

  .16 Type-descr   :: s-tp: Type   s-attr: Attributes
  .17 Pack-descr   :: s-vis    : Dict
  .18                 s-priv   : Dict
  .19                 s-name   : Unitname
  .20                 s-wm     : Weak-map
  .21                 s-sub-prgr : Sub-prgr-set
  .22                 s-opmap  : Operator-dict

  .23 Overload-descr :: ( Sub-prgr-descr | Literal-descr )-set
```

```
.24 Block-descr    :: Dict Unitname
.25 Loop-descr     ::      Unitname
.26 Literal-descr  :: Type
.27 Sub-prgr-descr :: Dict    Unitname   s-entr:Entrance
.28 Entrance       :: Parm-descr* s-return:[Type] [OP ¦ PREDEF-OP]
.29 Parm-descr     :: Id+ Mode Type [Expr]
.30 Attributes     =  Designator  m-> Unitname-set
.31 Unitname       =  ( Designator ¦ Char-lit ¦ N1 ¦ BLK ¦ LOOP )*
```

## Annotations:

.14 Objects can be constants.  Objects belong to specific types.

.15 Numbers are either universal-integer or universal-real numbers.

.17 The first dictionary component of a package descriptor is the diction-
    ary of the visible part.

.18 The next dictionary component is the dictionary of the visible- and
    private part together.  This,

.20 and the weakmap (representing the weak dictionary as it was inside the
    specification) and

.22 the map of operators, that are predefined on types defined in the pri-
    vate part of the package specification, must be available when the cor-
    responding package body is checked for well-formedness.

.25 Loops must be represented in the dictionary, since  loop-names  can  be
    used in exit statements.

.28 Subprogram-entrances are (also) used to determine whether two  subpro-
    grams can be overloaded or not.

.29 Whenever the subprogram body is separated from the  specification,  op-
    tional  default parameter values (given by expressions) in the two sep-
    arated formal parameter list, must (for the corresponding formal param-
    eter) evaluate to the same value.
    The manual  states  that  this  should  be  checked  at  compile  time.
    Therefore the expressions given with the forwarded specification should
    be  available  when  the  corresponding  body  is  checked  for
    well-formedness.

## 4.0 Declarative Parts, Declarative Items and Compilation


### 4.1 Introduction

This section will deal with the declarative elements of Ada.  These are used
to declare program compilation units and to associate (declare) identifiers
with the meaning they will have throughout their scope.  The point is now to
extract the meaning from the declaration, include it in the dictionary and
keep it there throughout the scope of the identifier.
Declarations are in Ada elaborated in the order in which they appear in  the
list of declarations.  Therefore a declared identifier is included in the
dictionary as soon as its declaration is elaborated, such that the next  declaration can be elaborated in a context where the effect of the previous is
known.
The scope of an identifier always ends, where the block  or  subprogram-body
or package-body, in which it is declared, ends. Consequently a dictionary,
which is valid inside the these constructs only, is build based on the local
declarations  plus  a dictionary inherited from outer scope. When the block
or body is left, knowledge of this local dictionary is no  longer  required.
Section  4.2  will  show  how the linear elaboration rules and scope binding
rules are modelled.

An identifier can be entered into the dictionary only if  the  corresponding
declaration is well formed.  For this reason checks are merged into the dic-
tionary-building functions.  Sections 4.3 and 4.6 will show how  to  extract
the  meaning  from package specifications and how to check the corresponding
bodies.  In sections 4.4 and 4.5 it is shown how to extract the meaning from
object-  and  constant  declarations,  and  how to model the effect of use
clauses.

There are several conditions that declarative parts must  satisfy  when  the
local  dictionaries  (eg.  for blocks) are to be extracted . Some of these
conditions can only be checked for satisfaction with full knowledge of  the
dictionary information of the preceding declarations.  For example, the name
given in the subtype indication in an object declaration should refer  to  a
type, not to a record component, etc.
Some conditions can be checked with reference only to the text  of  the  declarative  part  itself.  Example:  the same identifier may not be declared
more than once in the same declarative part - except if it could possibly be
overloaded.  Type identifiers can never be overloaded - subprograms can.
The latter conditions can be checked while at the same time handling and updating the dictionary, but modeling experience shows that it would hopeless-
ly  damage  the  transparency  of  the  dictionary building functions.  The
pre-conditions are therefore checked before anything else.

Finally a rudimentary model of the Compiling and Library concept  is  given.
This  part of the model is subject to change, since seperate compilation has
not yet been considered.

## 4.2  Declarative Parts

Functions checking declarations and declarative parts, deliver a new surrounding, hence the well-formedness functions for declarations have the types:

'Syntactic Domain' -> Surroundings ~-> Surroundings

If 'decl-part' is a given declarative part and 'sur' is the surroundings just before the declarative part, the surroundings after the declarative part is:

let mk-Decl-part(decll,bodyl) = decl-part in
    get-decl-part-sur(decll^bodyl)(sur)

Textual order plays an important role in Ada, the next function reflects this:  A declaration is checked for well-formedness in surroundings where information extracted from the preceding declarations is included.

1.0 get-Decl-part-sur(iteml)(sur) =
.1 if iteml=<> then sur else
.2 (let prefix^<item> = iteml in
.3   let prefixsur=get-Decl-part-sur(prefix)(sur) in
.4     get-sur-if-wf-decl-item(item)(prefixsur)  )

.5 type: (Decl-Item ¦ Body)* -> Surroundings -> Surroundings

A declarative item list constitutes together with the body list the declarative parts of blocks, packages and subprograms. Furthermore, item lists constitute the visible and the private part of package specifications.

| Decl-part | :: | Decl-item* Body* |
|---|---|---|
| Decl-item | = | Use-clause ¦ Declaration |
| Use-clause | :: | Name-set |
| Declaration | = | Obj-decl ¦ Const-decl ¦ Numb-decl ¦ Type-decl ¦ |
|  |  | Sub-type-decl ¦ Sub-prgr-spec ¦ Pack-spec |
| Body | = | Pack-spec ¦ Pack-body ¦ Sub-prgr-spec ¦ |
|  |  | Sub-prgr-body |

This section will concentrate on how to check well-formedness of declarative items and bodies, and to associate to them a static semantics denotation. This denotation is, in fact, always a function from surroundings to surroundings, ie.  each element in the list denotes an "updating" of the surroundings.  This is operationally abstracted by:

```
2.0  get-sur-if-wf-decl-item(item)(sur) =
 .1  cases item:
 .2  (mk-Use-clause()      -> get-use-sur(item)(sur) ,
 .3   mk-Obj-decl()        -> get-obj-decl-sur(item)(sur),
 .4   mk-Pack-spec()       -> get-pack-spec-sur(item)(sur),
 .5   mk-Pack-body         -> if is-wf-Pack-body(item)(sur)
                                 then sur
                                 else exit ,
 .6   mk-Sub-prgr-spec() -> get-sub-prgr-spec-sur(item)(sur),
 .7   mk-Sub-prgr-body() -> get-sub-prgr-body-sur(item)(sur),
 .8   mk-Type-decl()       -> get-type-decl-sur(item)(sur) ,
      ....

 .9  type: (Decl-item | Body) -> Surrounding -> Surrounding
```

The updating of the surroundings, as a result of the static elaboration of a declaration, is shortly and informally described here.

Use-clause:
   Update the weakmap component of the dictionary

Object-declaration:
   Updating the dictionary with object-descriptors, also updating the op-erator-dictionary if an anonymous array-type is introduced.

Package-specification:
   Update the dictionary with a package descriptor, and update the opera-tor dictionary with predefined operators of any type defined in the vi-sible part (also for nested packages) within this package specifica-tion.

Package-body:
   No updating.

Sub-program-specifications:
   Update the dictionary with a subprogram descriptor and - if the specif-ication is a forward declaration in a package specification - update the attributes of the types which are defined in the same package spec-ification and are either parameter- or result type of the subprogram (this is a record of which subprograms to derive from these types).

Sub-program-body:
   The status contains a set of the subprograms defined in each declara-tive part. When the body is encountered the status is updated, such that it is recorded that the body belonging to a certain specification is found. There must be a body to each specification (the latter check is one which could not be performed by the pre-check function, because overloading resolving requires dictionary information).

Type-declaration:
   Updating dictionary with a type-descriptor. Updating the operator dic-tionary with the predefined operators defined for the type and for any anonymous types (this is the case when record types contain anonymous array types). Derived type definitions cause derived subprograms to be updated too.

Subtype-declaration:
    The dictionary is updated with a type descriptor.

To conclude this section, we show a simplified version of the function which
performs the pre-checks of declartive parts. The complete version is found
in appendix A.  It requires the following auxiliary static domains :


```
Pre-decl    =  Body | Decl-item | Pre-item
Pre-item    =  Pre-literal | Pre-block | Pre-loop
Pre-literal ::  (Designator | Char-lit)
Pre-block   ::  Id
Pre-loop    ::  Id
```

Pre-literal is a description of a declared literal after having been  transformed by the function "split-decll", Pre-block and Pre-loop are descriptors
of the identifiers of blocks and loops.  It is necessary to have these  descriptors, because the manual states that literals are implicitly declared in
the same declarative part as the type they are literals of – and identifiers
of  blocks  and loops are implicitly declared in the declarative part of the
innermost enclosing unit.

```
3.0  Pre-check-decl-part(visdecll,privdecll,bodydecll) =
 .1  (let visl = split-decll(visdecll)    in
 .2   let privl = split-decll(privdecll)   in
 .3   let bodyl = split-decll(bodydecll)   in
 .4   let decll = visl^privl^bodyl         in
 .5   (A i E ind decll)
 .6    (let posind = {j|j E ind decll\{i}  and
                       get-id(decll[i]) = get-id(decll[j])} in
 .7     cases decll[i]:
 .8     (mk-Pack-spec(id,vl,pl) ->
 .9      cases posind:
 .10      ( { } -> (~(E j E ind(vl^pl))(is-Sub-prgr-spec(
                                            (vl^pl)[j]))
 .11                   and Pre-check-decl-part(vl,pl,<>)),
 .12       {j} -> (j>i and is-Package-body(decll[j]))   ,
 .13       T   -> false) ,
 .14     mk-Pack-body(id,mk-Decl-part(dl,bl),stmtl) ->
 .15        cases posind :
 .16        ({j} -> (j<i and decll[j]=mk-Pack-spec( ,vl,pl)and
 .17                 Pre-check-decl-part(vl,pl,dl^bl^
                        get-loop-and-block-ids(stmtl)) and
                       (A stmt E stmtl)(Pre-check-Stmt(stmt)),
 .19           T    -> false ),
 .20     mk-Pre-literal()      ->
 .21        (A j E posind)(is-sub-prgr-or-literal(decll[j])),
 .22     mk-Type( ,mk-Private-td() )   ->
 .23        (1<=i<=ln visl and
 .24         cases posind:
 .25         ({j} -> (is-Type-decl(decll[j]) and
 .26                  ln visl<j<ln(visl^privl) ),
 .27          {j,k}-> ....
 .28          T    ->  false ),
        ....
 .29     T                      -> posind={} )))

 .30  type: Pre-decl* Pre-decl* Pre-decl* -> BOOL
```

---

**Annotations:**

.0  pre-check of a visible declaration list, a  private  declaration  list,
    and a body list is

.1-.4 for each declaration-list split the compound declarations  in  simple
    declarations and make one long list.

.5-.7 for each declaration the pre-conditions - depending on  the  declara-
    tion that must be satisfied are:

.6  To check the pre-conditions, select all the declarations declared  with
    the same identifier as the declaration which is going to be checked.

.8  The pre-conditions for a package specification are:

.10 If there is no corresponding package body there must  be  specified  no
    subprograms in the specification, and of course the pre-conditions must
    be satisfied for the local declarations.

.11 If there is another declaration with the same identifier, the other de-
    claration  must be a corresponding package body (the further pre-checks
    will be performed when reaching the corresponding body).

.14 The pre-conditions for a package body are:  there must exist a  corres-
    ponding package specification, and - remembering that the local declar-

ation list in a package specification and the local declaration list in the corresponding package body should be regarded as one declaration list - the pre-conditions must be satisfied for the local declarations (including the identifiers of blocks and loops), and for all statements in the statement list of the body, the pre-conditions must be satisfied too.

.20 The pre-conditions for a enumeration literal are: all other declarations with the same identifier, must be subprogram declarations or other enumeration literals.

.22 The pre-conditions for a private type declaration are: the declaration must appear in the visible part of a package specification. There must at least exist one other declaration with the same identifier, and that other declaration must be a type declaration appearing in the private part of the same package specification (there could be two other declarations: in case where the corresponding type declaration is an incomplete access type declaration, where there must exist a complete access declaration too, but this problem the manual has not even mentioned).

.29 In the cases with no special conditions, eg. object declarations and type declarations (except private type declarations and incomplete access type definitions) the pre-conditions are: there must exist no other declaration in the same declarative part with the same identifier.

```
4.0  split-decll(decll) =
 .1    conc < decl | 1<=i<= ln decll and
 .2    decl= cases decll[i]:
 .3        (mk-Obj-decl(idl,otype,ex) ->
 .4           <mk-Obj-decl(id,otype,ex)|1<=j<=ln idl and id=idl[j]>,
 .5         mk-Type-decl( ,mk-Enum-td(elml)) ->
 .6           <decll[i]> ^
 .7           <mk-Pre-literal(elm)|1<=j<=ln elml and elm=elml[j]> ,
 .8         mk-Use-clause() -> <>,
 .9           T                -> <decll[i]> >

 .10  type: Pre-decl* -> Pre-decl*
```

Annotations:

.0  Split-decll given a declaration list splits the multiple declarations of the list in a list of single item declarations:

.3-.4 Object declarations with a list of identifiers to be declared are divided in a list of object declarations each only containing a single identifier to be declared.

.5-.7 Enumeration type declarations are divided in the type declaration itself and a list of declarations, one for each literal of the type.

.8  Use clauses are eliminated as there are no pre-conditions to be checked for use clauses.

.9  In all other cases it is the declaration itself.

## 4.3  Package Specifications and Bodies

A package is divided into its specification and its body, and between  these
other  declarations  can appear.  Besides, the specification is divided in a
visible and a private part where the items declared in the visible part  are
referable  from  outside  the package.  Inside the package the visible part,
the private part, and the declarative part of the body is considered as  one
declarative part.
In the model the "elaboration" of a package specification results in a  description  of the package.  This description is entered in the dictionary and
serves several purposes:  It contains dictionary information of the  locally
declared  items,  which are referable from outside the package.  It contains
all the information extracted from the specification, such that it is available,  when  the  body is encountered and checked for well-formedness.  This
includes dictionary information of items declared in the private part of the
specification.   This includes knowledge of the identifiers that were candidates for weak visibility in the specification since they must also be so in
the  body.   It  includes the unitname of the package.  Knowlegde of subprograms defined in the specification, since their bodies must be found in  the
package body.  Because of overloading this cannot be pre-checked.  Knowledge
of predefined operators which are generated as results of types  defined  by
the  user  in the private part of the package specification.  Such operators
are not known outside the scope of the type declared in private part of  the
package  specification.  The scope of such a type extends over the (rest of)
the private part of the specification and over the body.

The surroundings object which is used when a package specification is elaborated  has a status stack as one of its components.  On top of this "pushed"
an object which contains information gathered and used through the  elaboration  of the package specification.  The object is "pop'ed" when the package
specification is elaborated.  It contains the names of the types and a  description  of  the  subprograms  defined in the package.  This information is
used when derived types are elaborated.

Syntactic domains associated with packages are:

```
Pack-spec       :: Id Decl-item* s-private:Decl-item*
Pack-body       :: Id Decl-part Stmt*
```

The static domains associated with packages are:

```
Pack-descr        :: s-vis      : Dict
                     s-priv     : Dict
                     s-name     : Unitname
                     s-wm       : Weak-map
                     s-sub-prgr : Sub-prog-set
                     s-opmap    : Operator-dict

Status            = In-Pack-Spec | In-Pack-Body | ...

In-Pack-spec      :: s-defined-types:    Unitname-set
                     s-defined-sub-prgr: Sub-prgr-set
In-Pack-body      :: s-defined-sub-prgr: Sub-prgr-set

Sub-prgr          :: Unitname Entrance [BODY]
Entrance          :: -- something by which overloaded subprograms
                     -- can be distinguished.
```

We show how to update the surroundings with the information extracted from a package specification:

```
5.0  get-Pack-spec-sur(mk-Pack-spec(id,vil,privl))(sur) =
 .1  let mk-Surroundings(dict,level,wm,opd,status) = sur      in
 .2  let packname = level^<id>                                in
 .3  let packdescr = mk-Pack-descr([],[],packname,[],{})      in
 .4  let presur    = update-sur([id->packdescr],<id>,[],[],
                                 mk-In-Pack-spec({}{}))(sur)  in
 .5  let vissur    = get-Decl-part-sur(vil)(presur)           in
 .6  let visdict   = lookup-local-dict(packname)(vissur)      ,
 .7      export-op = s-opdict(vissur)                         in
 .8  let privsur   = get-Decl-part-sur(privl)(vissur)         in
 .9  let pack-wm   = s-weakmap(privsur)                       ,
 .10     priv-dict = lookup-local-dict(packname)(privsur)     ,
 .11     pack-op   = s-opdict(privsur)                        ,
 .12     mk-In-Pack-spec( ,ps) = hd s-status(privsur)         in
 .13 update-sur([id->mk-Pack-descr(visdict,priv-dict,packname,
                                   pack-wm,ps,pack-op)],
             <>,[],export-op,nil)(sur)

 .14 type: Pack-spec -> Surroundings -> Surroundings
```

Annotations:

.2-.4 Introduce the package by making an empty package descriptor and insert it in the surroundings.

.5-.7 Update the surroundings with the declarations of the visible part, and get the visible items, and the predefined operators of the visible part.

.8-.12 Update the surroundings with the declarations of the private part, and extract all the information, which is needed to check the package body.

.13 Update the outside surroundings with full information about the package and export the predefined operators defined in the visible part of the package.

```
6.0  is-wf-Pack-body(mk-Pack-body(id,declpart,stmtl))(sur) =
.1   trap exit with false in
.2   (let mk-Surroundings( ,un,wm,,statusl) = sur            in
.3   let mk-Decl-part(iteml,bodyl)          = declpart       in
.4   let mk-Pack-descr( ,pdict,pun,pwm,psd,opm)=
                    lookup-Unitname(un^<id>)(sur)            in
.5   let pack-status = mk-In-Pack-body(psd)                  in
.6   let pack-descr  = mk-Pack-descr(pdict,[],pun,[],{},[])  in
.7   let presur      = update-sur([id->pack-descr],<id>,pwm,opm,
                             packstatus)(sur)                in
.8   let bodysur     = get-Decl-part-sur(iteml^bodyl)(presur)in
.9   let mk-In-Pack-body(subprgrs) = hd s-status(bodysur)    in
.10  (~(E subprgr E subprgrs) (subprgr=mk-Sub-prgr( ,nil) ) and
.11  (¥ stmt E elems stmtl)(is-wf-Stmt(stmt)(bodysur)) )

.12  type: Package-body -> Surroundings -> BOOL
```

Annotations:

.4-.7 "Connect" the package body with its specification, and restore the informations for the package specification in the surroundings
.7 get the surroundings of checking the declarations and
.8 be sure of that there are missing no subprogram bodies

4.4 Use Clauses.

The rules determining which identifiers to be introduced as weak visible in the scope of a use clause are discussed in section 3.4.
We now show how to gather informations from use clauses for inclusion in the weakmap component of the surroundings:

Use-clause :: Name-set

A use-clause should only mention visible package names. The effect of the use-clause, ie. the updating of weakmap, takes place immediatly after the use-clause itself (this semantics implies that we can use a "set" of names instead of a "list", in the domain equation for use-clauses):

```
7.0 get-Use-sur(use-clause)(sur) =
.1 let newwm = get-weakmap(use-clause)(sur) in
.2     sur+(s-wm:wm -> wm+newwm)

.3 type: Use-clause -> Surroundings ~-> Surroundings
```

Annotations:

.2 the new weakmap overrides the old weakmap:
   If the programmer should (accidentally) "use" the same package twice or
   more, it would have no effect. We have chosen this semantics, since
   the manual doesn't cover the matter.

Consider the example:
declare
```
        package P is
            A,B,C:INT;
        end P;
        package Q is
            A,B,C:BOOL;
        end Q;

        use P; — A,B,C weak visible

        use P; — A,B,C still weak visible

        use Q; — A,B,C are not visible any longer
                  they appear in P as well as in Q
begin ... end;
```

The weakmap is extracted as shown in the formula:

```
8.0 get-weak-map(mk-Use-clause(nset))(sur) =
.1 if (∀ n E nset)(is-Pack-descr(lookup-name(n)(extr-dict(sur))))
.2    then [ packname -> visdict |
.3          (E n E nset)
.4             (mk-Pack-descr(visdict,,packname, ) =
                                    lookup(n)(extr-dict(sur)) in
.5             and packname ≠ <s-level(sur)[i]|1<=i<=ln packname>)]
.6    else exit

.7 type: Use-clause -> Surroundings ~-> Weak-map
```

Annotations:

.5 If a use clause should mention an enclosing package it will have no effect, since everything locally declared in this package would already
   be strongly visible.

## 4.5  Object- and Constant Declarations

Object and constant declarations are the simplest declarations.  First  the
identifiers of a declaration are introduced, pre-checks guarantee that there
are no two identical identifiers in the list, hereafter the  type  is  established.  If  there  is  an  expression, the expression is checked for
well-formedness in a context, where the objects and their type are known.
Constant declarations are quite similar to object declarations  except  that
constants must have an initialization expression. The initialization can be
deferred if the constant is declared in the visible part of  a  package  and
the type is a private type declared in the same package specification.
A component descriptor (in records and arrays) inherits the constant indication  of  its  enclosing  object descriptor at the time when it is selected.
(see "lookup-selected-component")

Syntactic and semantic domains associated with objects and constants:

```
Obj-decl        :: Id+ Type-expr  s-init: [Expr]
Const-decl      :: Id+ Type-expr  s-init: [Expr]
Obj-descr       :: s-tp: Type     s-con: [CONSTANT]
```

The function, which updates the surroundings as the result of elaborating an
object declaration:

```
9.0   get-obj-decl-sur(mk-Obj-decl(idl,tex,expr))(sur) =
 .1   (let presur   = update-sur-dict([id->INTRODUCED|
                                      id E elems idl])(sur) in
 .2    let otype    = make-type(tex)(sur)                   in
       let predef-op-dict = ....
 .3    let objdescr= mk-Obj-descr(otype,nil)                in
 .4    let objsur = update-sur-dict([id->objdescr| id E
                                    elems idl])             in
 .5    if type-expr-compatibility(otype)(expr)(objsur)
         ...
 .6       then objsur ...
 .7       else exit )

 .8    type: Obj-decl -> Surroundings ~-> Surroundings
```

Constants are handled by changing line .3 in the above formula to:

```
 .3a  if ~(expr=nil => is-local-and-private(otype)(sur)) then exit
 .3b  else let objdescr=mk-Obj-descr(otype,CONSTANT) in
```

## 4.6 Predefined Surroundings and Compilation

Ada has a vararity of predefined identifiers, denoting constants, types, packages, enumeration literals, operators etc. (eg.: PI, INTEGER, TEXTIO, 'A', "&" etc.). These are assumed to be declared in a package named STANDARD. Also the packages and subprograms in the users library that are referenced during a compilation are assumed to be declared in STANDARD. Even the units of a given compilation are assumed to be declared in package STANDARD, so everything can be referenced as a selected component of this package.
To model this, we - so to speak - "start out" with a "surroundings" object, which indicates that package STANDARD is being compiled. Hence the predefined "environment" is declared in this package, followed by the users compilation units.
We can now define an abstract syntax for the input to a context condition checker. We call this input a "Program".


Program          ::  s-predef:   Decl-part
                     s-library:  Library
                     s-comp:     Compilation

Library          =   Id m-> Libinfo
Libinfo          =   Pack-info | Subprog-info
Pack-info        ::  Pack-descr  Operator-dict
Subprog-info     ::  Overload-descr

Compilation      =   Comp-unit*
Comp-unit        ::  Context* Body

Context          ::  s-with:Id-set   s-use: [Use-clause]

Body             =   Pack-spec | Pack-body | Sub-prgr-spec |
                     Sub-prgr-body

Decl-part        ::  Decl-item* Body*
Decl-item        =   Use-clause | Declaration

Use-clause       ::  Name-set
Declaration      =   Obj-decl | Const-decl | Type-decl | Pack-spec | ...


The important point is, that in the "predefined" declarative part, the bodies corresponding to predefined subprograms are empty (ie. begin null; end;) since their implementation is not relevant to the static semantics modelling. In modelling the dynamic semantics, the bodies is the interesting aspect.
The "surrounding" object, used when the outermost (very odd) package STANDARD is compiled is not completely empty. In order to model the concept of "universal-integer" and "universal-fixed" some operators having such pseudo parameter types, are present. The dictionary component has pseudo identifiers (which cannot be redeclared by identifiers of the program) in its domain. We now elaborate on the details of the predefined surroundings:

```
10.0 generate-predefined-sur() =
   .1 mk-Surroundings(pre-dict,pre-level,pre-wm,pre-opdict,pre-status)

   .2 type: () -> Surroundings
```

pre-dict=
[STANDARD->mk-Pack-Descr(standarddict,[],<STANDARD>,[],(,,),[])]

where standarddict =

```
[  $_INTEGER           ->    -- description of predefined INTEGER,
   $_FLOAT             ->    -- description of predefined FLOAT,
   $_any-integer       ->    -- description of a type with
                                   such a datastructure
   $_universal-fixed   ->    -- description af a type with
                                   such a datastructure            ]
```

A name prefixed with "$" cannot be redefined by names in a program.   Hence,
in the model we can always get hold of predefined INTEGER and FLOAT from the
usual dictionary. We use this trick because integer and float type definitions should be treated as explicitly derived from the predefined INTEGER
and FLOAT: eg.

type MY_INT is range L..R; -- is modelled as if it was:
type MY_INT is new $_INTEGER range L..R;


pre-level = <STANDARD>

pre-wm    = []

pre-opmap = []

pre-status = <mk-In-Pack-spec({<STANDARD,$_INTEGER>,
                               <STANDARD,$_FLOAT>  } )>


Some of the operators declared as predefined reference the types
"$_any-integer" and "$_universal-fixed" instead of regular type names, as
parameters. These are:

```
mod , rem        (FLOAT ,$_any-integer) -> FLOAT


*  , /           ($_univ-fixed , $_univ-fixed ) -> $_univ-fixed
                 (FIXED         ,$_any-integer ) -> FIXED
                 ($_any-integer, FIXED         ) -> FIXED
```

The result of compiling an extended "Program" is an extended "Library".   The
library can be used in subsequent compilations, the user can delete entries
and so on.  Since we do not consider separate compilation, this part of the
model is subject to change.  However, it covers the main "events" during a

compilation: (1) When eg. a package specification is compiled, the library
is extended with a package-information-descriptor, which contains the well
known Pack-descr and a map of operators generated from type declarations in
the package specification. (2) When a compilation unit has some "context"
specified, the information about library units mentioned in this context is
retrived from the library and restored in the surroundings prior to the compilation. The unit can now reference the library units, select components,
call subprograms etc. (3) To generalize the concept of context, the context
given with eg. a package specification is explicitly forced onto the corresponding body in a first "pass". If the body itself has some context
specifyed, it should match that of the specification. Otherwise it is an
error. As a consequence of this semantics, a body can never reference more
than the corresponding specification can reference.

we show the functions that perform the compilation and library extention:

```
11.0 compile(mk-Program(declpart,lib,complist))=
 .1 trap exit with PROGRAM-IN-ERROR                                in
 .2 (~pre-check-Decl-part(<>,<>,<s-body(complist[i])|
 .3                               1<=i<= len complist>)  -> exit,
 .4  T                                                   ->
 .5  (let sur1=get-Decl-part-sur(declpart)(generate-predefined-sur()) in
 .6   extend-library(lib,insert-context(<>,[],complist))(sur1)

 .7 type: Program ~-> Library



12.0 insert-context(head,cmap,tail)=
 .1 if tail=<> then head else
 .2 (let mk-Comp-unit(con,body)=hd tail                            in
 .3 cases body:
 .4 (mk-Pack-spec(id,, ),
 .5  mk-Subprog-spec(id,, )                    ->
 .6    (insert-context(head^<hd tail>,cmap U[id->con],tl tail)),
 .7  mk-Pack-body(id,, )                        ->
 .8    (let con'=cmap(id) in
 .9     if con≠nil => con=con'
 .10      then insert-context(head^<mk-Comp-unit(con',body)>,
 .11                     cmap, tl tail )
 .12     else exit ),
 .13 mk-Subprog-body(mk-Subprog-spec(id,, )->
 .14    (let con'=cmap(id) in
 .15     if con≠nil => con=con'
 .16      then insert-context(head^<mk-Comp-unit(con',body)>,
 .17                     cmap, tl tail )
 .18     else exit )))

 .19 type:(Comp-unit* Id m->Context Comp-unit*) ~-> Comp-unit*
```

```
13.0 extend-lib(lib,complist)(presur)=
 .1 if complist=<> then lib else
 .2 let mk-Comp-unit(context,body)=hd complist              in
 .3 let sur1=get-context-sur(con,lib,presur)               in
 .4 let sur2=get-Sur-if-wf-declpart-item(body)(sur1)        in
 .5 let lib-extention =
 .6 cases body:
 .7 (mk-Pack-spec(id,, )    -> get-pack-info(id,sur2),
 .8  mk-Subprog-spec(id,, )-> get-subprog-info(id,sur2),
 .9  mk-Subprog-body(mk-Subprog-spec(id,},, )
 .10                         -> get-subprog-info(id,sur2),
 .11 T                      -> [])                          in
 .12 extend-lib(lib+libextention,tl complist)(presur)

 .13 type: (Library Comp-unit*) -> Surr. ~-> Library


14.0 get-context-sur(con,lib,sur)=
 .1 if con=<> then sur else
 .2 let mk-Context(withset,use)=hd con                      in
 .3 if(E idEwithset)(id~Edom lib)
 .4    then exit
 .5    else(let (con-dict,con-opmap)=
 .6              insert-lib-info(s-dict(sur),s-opmap(sur),
 .7                                    withset,lib ) in
 .8         let con-sur= sur+(s-dict:<-con-dict,
 .9                           s-opmap:<-con-opmap)          in
 .10        let nextsur=if use=nil then consur else
 .11                   get-Use-sur(use)(consur)            in
 .12        get-context-sur(tl con,lib,nextsur) )

 .13 type: (Context* Library Surr] ~-> Surroundings


15.0 get-pack-info(id,sur)=
 .1 let packdescr=extract-dict(sur)(id)                     in
 .2 let opmap    =s-opmap(sur)                              in
 .3 let name     =s-name(packdescr)                         in
 .4 let opmap'   =
 .5    [id'->mk-Overload-descr(spset)  |
 .6     id'E dom opmap  and
 .7     (let mk-Overload-descr(spset')=opmap(id')  in
 .8      (¥ spdEspset)(spdEspset'  and
 .9              spd=mk-Sub-prog-descr( ,sname, ) and
 .10             (sname[i]=((name^<id'>)[i] |
 .11              1<=i<=len sname-1            )))] in
 .12   [id->mk-Pack-info(packdescr,opmap') ]

 .13 type:(Id Surroundings) -> Library
```

```
16.0 get-subprog-info(id,sur)=
  .1 let mk-Overload-descr(spset)=extract-dict(sur)(id)   in
  .2 [id->mk-Subprog-info(mk-Overload-descr(spset')) |
  .3  ∀ sp ∈ spset')(sp∈ spset and is-Subprog-descr(sp))]

  .4 type: (Id Surroundings) -> Library


17.0 insert-lib-info(dict,opmap,withset,lib)=
  .1 if withset={} then (dict,opmap) else
  .2 let id ∈ withset in
  .3 cases lib(id):
  .4 (mk-Pack-info(pd,opd) ->
  .5    insert-lib-info(extend-dict(dict)(<mk-Id(STANDARD)>)
  .6                  ([id->pd]), withset\{id}, lib      ),
  .7 mk-Subprog-info(ovld)->
  .8    insert-lib-info(extend-dict(dict)(<mk-Id(STANDARD)>)
  .9                  ([id->ovld]), withset\{id}, lib     ))

  .10 type:(Dict Operator-dict Id-set Library) -> (Dict Operator-dict)
```

## 5.0 Subprograms

### 5.1 Introduction

This section will discuss the concept of Subprograms. It will be shown that a unified description of procedures, functions and operators can be designed for inclusion in the dictionary. Such descriptors are designed such that overloaded subprograms can be distinguished. The concept of forward declaration of subprograms is covered. Derived subprograms are explicitly entered into the dictionary of the current surroundings. Likewise are predefined operators generated and entered in the operator dictionary of the current surroundings. Finally the subprogram calls are discussed by addressing the actual parameter checking function.

Subprograms (functions, procedures and operators) consist of a specification and a body. Subprograms are overloadable with other subprograms and with enumeration literals. The subprogram specification can be given in the visible part of a package, so that it can be used from outside the defining package, and be given as a forward declaration for mutually dependent recursive subprograms.
The subprogram body includes also a specification, and if a forward specification as well as a body is given the specification-part of the body must be equal to the "forward declared" specification:
The parameter identifiers, the subtype indications and any default values must be the same and be given in the same order. The only variation allowed is that names can be written differently, provided that they have the same meaning.
Subprogram descriptors are derived directly from subprogram specifications; they contain 3 components:
(1) The dictionary component of a subprogram descriptor contains the description of the locally declared items. This dictionary is only non empty, when 'inside' a subprogram body. Inside a subprogram body the subprogram name can be used as prefix to local identifiers as within packages. In the model the lookup functions use the dictionary component of the subprogram descriptor, ie. being inside a subprogram body is like being inside a package as far as this matter is concerned. From outside the subprogram body it is not possible to select items declared locally to the subprogram.
(2) The unitname of the subprogram. Subprograms have an extra element (a unique number) in their unique name. Thereby overloaded subprograms declared at the same level will always have different names.

$$\text{get-unique-number}() = ( \ldots )$$

is a 'magic' function which when called returns a (n integer) number which is distinct from those returned in any preceding calls. This requires an internal 'state' which we do not define. Alternatively we could keep a set of "used numbers" in the dictionary and always select one not in the set for the subprogram and then include it as used. Thereby the homomorphism thesis would not be violated.
(3) An Entrance. Subprogram entrances are descriptors of parameter names, modes and types plus the (optional) function result type plus an indication of whether the function is a (predefined) operator or not. Entrances are used when checking legality of subprogram calls. Entrances are also used to distinguish overloaded subprograms, since these must differ in their parameter names, -order or -types. Or optional result type (functions only).

To check that these default values are equal it is necessary to rebuild the expressions and the subtype indications such that they only contain unique names and values (the rebuild functions transform from AS1 to AS2). The manual also requires that initializing expressions of parameters must have no side effect (this is not (?) claimed for the subtype indications !). This rule can (also) only be checked when the expressions are rebuilt. Hence a description of a parameter will contain an optional rebuilt expression.

Syntactic domains associated with subprograms:

```
Sub-prgr-spec   :: Designator Parm-decl* s-return:[Subtype-indic]
Sub-prgr-body   :: Sub-prgr-spec Decl-part Stmt*
Parm-decl       :: Id+ [Mode] Subtype-indic [Expr]
```

Semantic domains associated with subprograms:

```
Overload-descr  :: ( Sub-prog-descr ¦ Literal-descr )-set

Sub-prgr-descr  :: Dict    Unitname   s-entr:Entrance
Entrance        :: Parm-descr* s-return:[Type] [OP ¦ PREDEF-OP]
Parm-descr      :: idl: Id+ Mode Type [Reb-sub-type] [Reb-expr]
Mode            = in ¦ inout ¦ out
```

## 5.2 Overloading

This section describes the aspects of a list of declarations including forward subprogram specifications and subprogram bodies, where the following rules must be obeyed:
(1) When two subprograms have the same designator, they can be overloaded if their specifications are "different enough".
(2) To a forward declared subprogram specification there must be a corresponding body. The corresponding body is identified by having the same designator and a specification equivalent to that of the forward specification.
(3) The "same" subprogram must only be declared once in the same declarative part. In our model we define that two specifications are equal if their corresponding entrances derived from the specifications are equal. But even if the entrances are different the corresponding subprograms are not necessary overloadable, consider following example:

```
procedure P(X,Y:INT);
procedure P(X:INT,Y:INT);
```

These two subprograms cannot be overloaded, although they have different entrances:

mk-Entrance(<mk-Parm-descr(<X,Y>,in,<..INT>,nil)>,nil,nil)

mk-Entrance(<mk-Parm-descr(<X>,in,<..INT>,nil),
        mk-Parm-descr(<Y>,in,<..INT>,nil)>,nil,nil)

The order of the parameters are different, though the names and types are
identical.

As seen in the example above, entrances are not sufficient to check whether
two subprograms can be overloaded or not. To check this we have a function
"convert-entrance" which converts an entrance to an object of the auxiliary
domain:

> Overloadable :: (Id Type [INITIALIZED])* s-return: [Type]

Two subprograms are overloadable if their "overloadable" are different:
That is: Two subprograms can be overloadable if just one parameter is initialized in one of the subprogram specifications, and the subprograms are
otherwise equal. Consider the following example:

```
procedure P(X:INT);
procedure P(X:INT:=0);
```

A call such as P(5); is ambiguous, and likewise is P(X=>5); The only legal
call is P(); And if one new procedure is introduced:

```
procedure P();
```

any call would be ambiguous. If two subprograms are declared in the same
declarative part they must differ at more than just the parameter identifiers. In this case we test for overloadablilty by checking in-equality relations among elements of the domain:

> XXX :: (Type [INITIALIZED])* s-return:[Type]

For operators it is only the parameter types and the result type that have
influence on overloading, so here we use the auxiliary domain:

> YYY :: Type+

## 5.3 Forward Declarations

In the status component of the surroundings, we keep track of the subprograms declared in a declarative part. Using this track, we can always detect whether a given subprogram declaration
(1) is declaring a subprogram which is overloading an already declared subprogram of the same declaration list, or
(2) is an illegal redeclaration. A subprogram may not be redeclared in the same declaration list.
We can also detect that the body corresponding to a forward declared subprogram is found. There should be a body for each declared subprogram. The "s-body" component of a "Sub-prog" (see above) indicates, whether the body is found (=BODY) or not (=nil). If separate compilation was considered one would add "SEPARATE" as a possible value of the "s-body" component.
We can now show the functions, which extracts subprogram descriptors for inclusion in the dictionary while at the same time checking the subprogram specification and the body.

```
Status          =  In-Pack-spec | In-Pack-body | In-Sub-prog |
                   In-Block     | In-Loop

In-Pack-spec    :: s-defined-types:    Unitname-set
                   s-defined-sub-prgr: Sub-prgr-set
In-Pack-body    :: s-defined-sub-prgr: Sub-prgr-set
In-Sub-prgr     :: s-defined-sub-prgr: Sub-prgr-set
In-Block        :: s-defined-sub-prgr: Sub-prgr-set
In-Loop         :: s-loopname:         Unitname

Sub-prgr        :: Unitname  s-entr: Entrance  s-body: [BODY]
```

```
1.0  get-Sub-prgr-spec-sur(mk-Sub-prgr-spec(id,parml,rtn))(sur) =
 .1  let entrance = get-Entrance(id,parml,rtn)(sur)                    in
 .2  if sub-prgr-exists(id,entrance)(hd s-status(sur))
 .3     then exit else
 .4  (let unitname = s-level(sur)^<id>^<get-unique-number()> in
 .5   let sub-descr= mk-Sub-prgr-descr([],unitname,entrance) in
 .6   let sub-prgr = mk-Sub-prgr(unitname,entrance,nil)       in
 .7   let statussur= insert-in-status(sub-prgr)(sur)          in
 .8   let ovldescr = mk-Overload-descr([sub-descr])           in
 .9   let subsur   = update-sur-dict([id->ovldescr])(statussur) in
 .10      make-Sub-prgr-to-attribute(id,unitname,entrance)(subsur) )

 .11  type: Sub-prgr-descr -> Surroundings ~-> Surroundings
```

```
2.0  get-Sub-prgr-body-sur(mk-Sub-prgr-body(sp,declp,stmtl))(sur) =
.1   let mk-Sub-prgr-spec(id,parml,rtn) = sp                      in
.2   let mk-Decl-part(iteml,bodyl)       = declp                  in
.3   let sub-descr= connect-body-with-spec(spec) (sur)            in
.4   let mk-Sub-prgr-descr( ,unitname,entrance)=sub-descr         in
.5   let sub-prgr = mk-Sub-prgr(unitname,entrance,body)           in
.6   let statussur = insert-in-Status(sub-prgr)(sur)              in
.7   let parmdict  = get-parm-dict(entrance)                      in
.8   let ovldescr  = mk-Overload-descr([sub-descr])               in
.9   let newlevel  = <unitname[i]|(ln unitname -1) <= i<=
                                  ln unitname >                   in
.10  let sub-sur   = update-sur-dict([id->ovldescr])(sub-sur) in
.11  let presur    = update-sur([],newlevel,[],[],
                                  mk-In-Sub-prgr({}))(statussur) in
.12  let parmsur   = update-sur-dict(parmdict)(presur)            in
.13  let bodysur   = det-Decl-part-sur(iteml^bodyl)(parmsur)      in
.14  let mk-In-Sub-prgr(sprgrs) = hd s-status(bodysur)            in
.15  if (~(E sp E sprgrs)(s-body(sp)=nil ) and
         (¥ stmt E elems stmtl)(is-wf-Stmt(stmt)(bodysur)))
.16      then sub-sur
.17      else exit

.18  type: Sub-prgr-body -> Surroundings ~-> Surroundings
```

## Annotations:

.3   Get a subprogram descriptor by connecting the subprogram body with a forward declared subprogram specification.

.5-.6 update the status component with the information that a body is found.

.7   Convert the parameters to normally declared objects and constants.

.10  Introduce the subprogram

.11  and prepare the surroundings for the locally declared items of the subprogram

.12  insert the parameters in the local dictionary of the subprogram (the pre-check functions have checked that no parameter have the same name as any of the items locally declared in the subprogram)

.13  check the declarative part of the subprogram

.14-.15 be sure, that all locally declared subprogram specifications have a corresponding body.

## 5.4 Derived Subprograms

Subprograms declared in a package specification having parameter- or result types of any types declared in the same package specification, are said to be subprogram attributes of the types. A derived type will derive the subprogram attributes of the parent type. These derived subprograms are implicitly declared at the same place as the derived type. Now, the declaration of a subprogram may imply that several types represented in the local dictionary of the package shall have their descriptor updated. Such that their new subprogram attribute is included. Therefore "get-Sub-prgr-spec-sur" must call the function "make-Sub-prgr-to-Attributes":

```
3.0 make-Sub-prgr-to-attribute(id,unitname,entrance)(sur)=
.1  cases hd s-status(sur):
.2  (mk-In-Pack-spec(typenames, ) ->
.3    (let parmtypn = extract-types-of-entrance(entrance) in
.4     let aff-types = typenames  parmtypn             in
.5     let local-dict = get-local-dict(sur)            in
.6     let up-loc-dict=
.7        [tid -> typedescr | atype Є aff-types   and
.8         tid = atype[ln atype]                  and
.9         let attributes = s-attr(local-dict(tid))    in
.10        let new-attr =
.11           (if id Є dom attributes
.12            then attributes+[id->attributes(id)U{unitname}]
.13            else attributesU[id->{unitname}])    in
.14        typedescr=local-dict(tid)+(s-attr:->newattr)] in
.15     update-sur-dict(up-loc-dict)(sur)) ,
.16  T          -> sur)

.17  type: Id Unitname Entrance -> Surroundings -> Surroundings
```

## 5.5 Generating Predefined Operators

We show how to generate descriptors for predefined operators. These are identical to those of user defined operators, thus enabling a reasonable overloading resolving algorithm (see sections 8.2 and 8.3).
We give the relevant static domains:

```
Dict            = ( ...| Operator | .. ) m-> Descr
Descr           = Overload-descr | ...
Overload-descr  :: ( Sub-prgr-descr | Literal-descr )-set
Sub-prgr-descr  :: ... Unitname s-entr:Entrance
Entrance        :: Parm-descr* s-return:[Type] [OP | PREDEF-OP]
Parm-descr      :: Id+ Mode Type [Expr]
Mode            = in | inout | out
```

```
4.0  create-usertype-dep-op-dict(typ)(sur) =
.1  (is-not-private(typ)(sur)  ->
.2              create-type-predef-opdict(typ)(s-level(sur)),
.3   is-not-limited-private(typ)(sur) ->
.4              create-eq-neq-opdict(typ)(s-level(sur)),
.5   T   ->         []                                    )

.6 type: Type -> Unitname -> Operator-dict
```

## Annotations:

.1 For types which are not private all (relevant) predefined operators are generated.
.3 For types which are private but not limited only the equality and in-equality operators are generated.
.5 For types which are limited private or contains components of such types, the equality and in-equality operators are not predefined. The user may, however, define the equality (not the in-equality) operator explicitly.

We show how to create the in-equality operator ("/=") for a type which is not limited private:

```
5.0  create-neq-opdict(typ)(level) =
 .1  let left-arg-descr  = mk-Parm-descr( ,in,typ)        ,
 .2      right-arg-descr = left-arg-descr                in
 .3  let entrance = mk-Entrance(<left-arg-descr,right-arg-descr>,
 .4                 predef-bool-type(),PREDEF-OP)         in
 .5  [mk-Operator(/=) -> mk-Overload-descr( {
 .6       mk-Sub-prog-descr([],level^<mk-Operator(/=)^
 .7       <get-unique-number()>,entrance)})]

 .8  type: Type  ->  Unitname -> Operator-dict
```

## Annotations:

.1 Parameter names are insignificant for operators.
.2 Same left and right-hand type.
.4 In-equality returns predefined boolean type.
.6 The predefined operator is implicitly "declared" at the same "level" as the type.

## 5.6  Subprogram Calls

To check whether an actual parameter list matches names and types of the formal parameters of a given subprogram, we use the function "parameter-checker". "parameter-checker" is a boolean function, which when given an entrance, an actual parameter list and the surroundings, yields true if the actual parameter list matches the entrance, that is if the actual parameters match the formal parameters.

```
6.0   parameter-checker(entrance)(actual-parm-list)(sur) =
 .1   trap exit with false in
 .2   (let formall = convert-entrance-to-parm-check(entrance) in
 .3    let mk-Act-parm-list(posl,namel) = actual-parm-list      in
 .4    let given-ids = {s-Id(namep)|namep E elems namel}        in
 .5    if (ln formall < ln actual-parm-list              or
 .6        (E i E ind posl)(s-Id(formall[i]) E given-ids) or
 .7        (E i E ind formall)( i>ln posl and
 .8         s-Id(formall[i]) ~E given-ids=>s-Expr(formall[i])≠nil))
 .9    then exit else
.10    (V i E ind posl)
.11       (check-parm(s-Expr(posl[i]),formall[i])(sur)) and
.12    (V parm E elems namel) (E fparm E elems formall)
.13       (s-Id(parm)=s-Id(fparm) and
.14        check-parm(s-Expr(parm),fparm)(sur)))

.15    type: Entrance -> Actuel-parm-list -> Surroundings -> BOOL
```

## 6.0 The Notion of Types in Ada

### 6.1 Introduction

The ability to define named distinct types is one of the main features of Ada. The philosophy of strong typing is applied: Definitions of compatibility are based on type names not on data structures. The dictionary must then contain descriptions of the types which are defined so that type-compatibility and type-convertability within expressions can be statically checked.

This introduction will discuss the design of proper type descriptors based on the rules for defining types, subtypes and derived types. The following sub-sections will consider the static elaboration of type- and subtype declarations. This elaboration will result in the inclusion of type descriptors in the dictionary of the current surroundings. It may also result in inclusion of predefined operators defined on the types in the operator dictionary of the current surroundings. Next sub-section will discuss the notion of subprogram attributes of types and their inclusion in the dictionary of the current surroundings. The last section will cover the elaboration of derived types.

We will now discuss the design of a type descriptor. It must contain a component which describes the characteristics of the type: Type name, datastructure, statically determinable constraints etc. Futhermore it must contain the unitnames of the subprogram attributes associated with the type. This latter is discussed in a subsection.

The characteristics of a type is assembled in an object which is called a "Type". The design of a "Type" is influenced by the concept of strong typing, the concept of subtypes, private types and derived types.

Strong typing implies that each type definition in the program introduces a distinct type. This type can be marked by the unitname of the type. The typemark of anonymous types, eg.

A : array(1..10) of ELEM;

is the unitname of the object A. It will never clash with other type names. A subtype can always be referenced through its defined name but it denotes no new distinct type. Futhermore it inherits the typemark and the datastructure characteristics of the type of which it is a subtype. The datastructure characteristics are inherited even if they are not known at the time when the subtype is declared. This is the case when subtypes of private types are declared. The datastructure of the subtype should, of course, be referable where the datastructure of the base type is referable. As a consequence all reference to datastructure components of "Types" must address the base type. This is done via a "pointer" into the dictionary. This pointer value is simply the typemark of the base type. The constraints on a (sub) type is, however, always associated with the named subtype. Constraints are represented by semantic objects called "Substructures" and must be associated with the descriptor of the subtype itself. A type is by definition a subtype of itself.

Private types are concidered as types with a special datastructure namely "EMPTY". Possibly a record-like structure if it has discriminants. Each type and subtype is marked if it is "PRIVATE" or possibly "LIMITED". Thereby we can determine whether the user may define his own "="-operator for the type or not (he may define "=" only for his own limited types and

the "=" and "/=" operators are predefined for all his private types).
Derived types are new distinct types. Hence they are marked uniquely with
the unitname of type itself. Derived types derive their datatype characteristics (and sometimes the constraints) from the parent type. However, as
with subtypes, their datastructure may be unknown at the point of definition. Therefore reference to the datastructure component must address the
datastructure component of the parent type. There must also be a reference
to the parent type. This must likewise be performed via a pointer into the
dictionary. There must also be a reference to the parent type since derived
types can be converted to their parent type and vice versa. A non-derived
type is by definition its own parent.
We will summarize the design criteria for "Types": There must be a typemark
(= a unique name). There must be a reference to the description of the datastructure. The typemark of the parent type must be known. There must be
a description of the datastructure and the substructure. The private types
must be marked.

We have discussed datastructures. Section 7 will elaborate on the details
of the construction of "Datastructure" objects based on type definitions.
Also the construction of "Substructure" objects based on constraints given
in subtype indications etc. is elaborated in detail.

We now return to the second component of a type descriptor, namely the subprogram attribute names. Subprogram attributes are associated with types
and not with subtypes. When the attributes of a type are required, one
should find them with the base type. We summarise this discussion by giving
the syntactic and semantic domains associated with types. But first a small
example:

```
package P is
    type PT is private;
    PV : PT;
    package Q is
        QV : PV; -- in the specification of Q, the structure of PV
                 -- is not referable, neither is the structure of QV
    end Q;
private
    type PT is array( ... ) of ... ;
                 -- in the rest of P, incl body, the structure of
                 -- objects of type PT is referable
end P;
 .
 .              -- the structure of P.Q.QV is private
 .
package body P is
        .        -- structure of objects of type PT is referable
        .
    package body Q is
        .
        .        -- structure of QV referable here!
        .
    end Q;
 .
end P;
```

Syntactic domains:

```
Type-decl       :: Id Type-def

Sub-type-decl   :: Id Subtype-indic

Type-def        = Enum-td | Intg-td | Float-td | Fixed-td | Array-td
                  | Record-td | Access-td | Derived-td | Private-td

Subtype-indic   :: Name [Constraint]

Derived-td      :: Subtype-indic

Constraint      = ...
...
```

Types are the in the dictionary associated with identical structured type-descriptors, whether the types are declared in type-declarations, sub-type-declarations, or as derived- or private types.

We give the static domains of type-descriptors:

```
Type-descr      :: Type Attributes

Type            :: s-name      : Unitname
                   s-parent    : Unitname
                   s-structure : Unitname
                   s-ds        : [Datastructure]
                   s-sub       : Substructure
                   s-lim       : [PRIVATE | LIMITED]

Unitname        = ( Id | N1 | BLK | ... )*
Datastructure   = ...

Substructure    = ...

Attributes      = Unitname m-> Unitname-set
```

## 6.2  Type Declarations

In the following we show how to update the surroundings with the informations obtained from a type declaration. It is assumed that if the type was prede-clared as a private type or as an access type, its information will now be overwritten in the dictionary with a new description. If the type was prede-clared as private with discriminants then the full declaration must repeat the discriminants correctly. This is checked by "is-wf-full-decl-of-private-type". Futhermore if it is an integer- or float type declaration, it is transformed into an equivalent derived type definition as required by the Ada manual. It is observed that a type definition is elaborated in a context where the type iden-tifier have been introduced.

```
1.0  get-Type-decl-sur(typedecl)(sur) =
 .1  let mk-Type-decl(id,typedef) = typedecl,
 .2      localdict = lookup-local-dict(sur)                    in
 .3  let early = (id E dom localdict -> localdict(id),
 .4               T                  -> nil          )         in
 .5      pre-sur = update-sur-dict([id->INTRODUCED])(sur),
 .6      eqvl-tdcl = transform(typedecl)(sur)                  in
 .7  cases eqvl-tdcl:
 .8  ( mk-Derived-td() ->
 .9          get-derived-type-sur(eqvl-tdcl)(early)(presur),
 .10   T                ->
 .11         get-defined-type-sur(eqvl-tdcl)(early)(presur) )

 .12 type: Type-decl  -> ( Surroundings ->  Surroundings )
```

Annotations:

.3 If the type was incompletely predeclared this is the full declaration.
   Get hold of the previous descriptor.
.5 The rule is that the type definition must be elaborated in a context
   where the type-identifier have been introduced (as unusable).
.6 Integer and float types are modeled as if they were derived from the
   predefined INTEGER and FLOAT type.

```
2.0  get-defined-type-sur(typedecl)(early)(sur) =
 .1  let mk-Typedecl(id,typedef) = typedecl,
 .2      newname = s-level(sur)^<id>                           in
 .3  let (typ,opdict1) =
 .4      make-type(typedef)(newname)[](nil)(TYPE)(sur)  in
 .5  let opdict2 = create-usertype-dep-op-dict(typ)(sur) in
 .6  let predefopdict = overload(opdict1)(opdict2),
 .7      newstatus = cases hd s-status(sur):
 .8          (mk-In-Pack-spec(def-tps,def-spgs) ->
 .9             (<mk-In-Pack-spec(def-tps U {newname},def-spgs)>
 .10              ^ tl s-status(sur)  ),
 .11          T -> s-status(sur)                       ),
 .12 let literaldict = get-enum-literal-dict(typ)             in
 .13 let attributes = cases:
 .14     (early = nil  -> [],
 .15      is-Access(s-ds(s-tp(early)))-> s-attr(early),
 .16      ~is-wf-full-decl-of-private-type(typ)(s-tp(early))
 .17                      -> exit,
 .18      T              -> s-attr(early))                     in
 .19 let extension = [id->mk-Type-descr(typ,attributes)]
 .20               U literaldict                              in
 .21 update-sur(extension,<>,{},predefopdict,<>)
 .22         ( sur+(s-status:->newstatus)    )

 .23 type: Type-decl -> [Type-decl] -> Surroundings
                                    -> Surroundings
```

## Annotations:

.2 The unique name of a new type is the unitname of the type.

.3 Types are generated from type definitions. If the type definition was a record type definition containing anonymous array type definitions the predefined operators (eg. >, >=, & etc.) defined for these array types are generated too.

.5 For this type some operators are predefined. These are overloadable with those of the anonymous types.

.9 Record that this type is defined in this package specification.

.12 The declaration of an enumeration type implies that its literals are declared too.

.13 The attributes of a the type are those defined on the type when (if) it was already introduced as an incompletely predeclared access-type or as a private type.

.16 If this is the full declaration of a private type, some special conditions must be satisfied.

.21 The static elaboration of a type-declaration results in an updating of the dictionary, the set of predefined operators and the status of the surroundings.


## 6.3 Subtype Declarations

Subtypenames are abbreviations for the name of the (base) type, plus a constraint. Constraints restrict the set of possible values for objects of the subtype. When a subprogram is an attribute of a type, it is also an attribute of the subtype. Even when the subprogram is declared before the subtype:

```
declare
    type T is range 1..1000;
    function MIX(X,Y:T) return T;     -- an attribute of T
    subtype ST is T range 10..100;
    V1,V2,V3 : ST := 66;
    function MIX(X,Y:T) return T is .... end MIX;
begin
  V1 := MIX(V1,V2);
  declare
    type NT is new ST;
    VN : NT := MIX( NT(V1), NT(V2) ); -- also attribute of NT
  begin null; end;
end;
```

The Type-descriptor of a subtype should contain a 'Type' which is a copy of that of the base type, except that the Datastructure component should be NIL and the Substructure component should be derived from the constraint given with the Subtype-indication (substructures are related to subtypes, not types).

If the base type is private or limited private, the subtype is that too. A subtype introduces no new types, thus no new predeclared operators are introduced. The attribute component of the Type-descriptor of the subtype should likewise contain no attributes, since these must be obtained from those of the parent type (Attributes are related to type names, not to structures).


We give the syntactic domains:

```
Sub-type-decl   :: Id Subtype-indic
Subtype-indic   :: Base [Constraint]
Base            =  Name
Constraint      =  Range-constr | Index-constr | Discrim-constr |
                   Float-constr | Fixed-constr
```


We show the surrounding updating effect of a subtype declaration.

```
3.0  get-subtype-decl-sur(st-decl)(sur) =
 .1  let mk-Subtype-decl(id,mk-Subtype-indic(name,constr))=st-decl in
 .2  let pre-sur = update-dict-sur([id->INTRODUCED])(sur)            in
 .3  let mk-Type-descr(basetype, )=lookup-type(name)(presur)        in
 .4  let subtype =
 .5      constrain-type(basetype)(constr)({})(nil)(TYPE)(presur)    in
 .6  update-sur-dict([id->mk-Type-descr(subtype,[])])(sur)

 .7  type: Subtype-decl -> Surroundings -> Surroundings
```


Annotations:

.2 The subtype declaration must be elaborated in a context where the identifier of the subtype have been introduced.
.4 The substructure is derived from the base type and a constraint (the parameters to "constrain-type" is discussed later).


## 6.4  The Subprogram Attributes of Types

Subprograms are said to be attributes of a type T if they have a parameter and/or result of type T. These attributes must be associated with the type T (in fact with the base type of T because T might be a subtype identifier) to record those subprogram attributes, which must be derived together with the types derived from T.
For a type declared in a package specification, the subprograms that are derived are those declared in the same package specification; however such subprograms are not inherited by a derived type definition itself given in the same package specification.
The subprograms inherited by a derived type can be further inherited if this type is used as parent type in another derived type definition.

Example:

```
declare
   package P is
      type T is range 1..10;
      function "+"(X,Y:T) return T;  -- an attribute of T
      type NT1 is new T;             -- inherits no attributes
   end P;

   package Q is
      type NT3 is new P.T;           -- inherits "+"(NT3,NT3)->NT3
      function "-"(X,Y:NT3) return NT3;
                                     -- "-" is also attribute of NT3
   end Q;

begin ... end;
```

Note: the types T, NT1 and NT3 have, of course, the predefined operators defined. However, "+" is redefined for type T and NT3 and "-" is redefined for NT3. The predefined operators are not treated as user defined operators, since they obey different scope rules (see section 3.6).

The attribute component of a type descriptor is a map from the designators of those subprograms that are attributes of the (base) type into the set of unique names of those which have the same (overloaded) designator.
In the status component, when inside a package specification, there is a recording of the set of types and the set of subprograms defined so far in the package specification.
Only types defined in package specifications have subprogram attributes (which can be derived) and these subprograms must be declared in the same package specification. We dislike these rules, because they imply that derived types a l s o derive subprograms that are defined in the private part of the package specification (see next example).
The rules should be changed such that only if the subprograms were declared in the same v i s i b l e part of the package specification as the type they were derivable subprogram attributes.

```
declare
   package P is
      type T is private;          -- private declaration
      function VISIBLE(X:T) return T;
   private
      function NOTVISIBLE(Y:T) return T;
      type T is range 1..1000;  -- full declaration
   end P;

   package Q is
      type T is new P.T;
      -- Q.VISIBLE:    Q.T -> Q.T  implicitly declared here
      -- Q.NONVISIBLE: Q.T -> Q.T  -           -          -
   end Q;

   V1 : P.T;   V2 : Q.T;   use Q, P; -- functions visible

   package body P is
      function VISIBLE   (X:T) return T is ... end VISIBLE;
      function NONVISIBLE(Y:T) return T is ... end NONVISIBLE;
   begin
      V1 := 10;  V2 := 100;  -- or whatever you like
   end P;

begin  V1 := VISIBLE   (V1); -- ok
       V1 := NOTVISIBLE(V1); -- illegal
       V2 := VISIBLE   (V2); -- ok, a derived function
       V2 := NOTVISIBLE(V2); -- ok, but we dislike it !
end;
```

## 6.5  Derived Types

Derived types are types which are structural equivalent to the type from
which they are derived (reference to same structure type). They share the
same collection of values.
When the full declaration of a private type is given as a derived  type  definition,  the  type  may derive subprograms, but these may be redeclared by
subprograms defined for the type when it was known as private.

```
package R is
   type T is array(1..10) of SOMETHING;
   function "&"(X,Y:T) return T;          -- R."&"
end R;

package Q is
   type P is private;
   function "&"(X,Y:P) return P;
private
   type P is new R.T;     -- Q.P derives R."&" but it is
                          -- already hidden by Q."&"
end Q;
```

We conclude the discussion of derived types by giving the functions which handle derived type declarations: The annotations will pinpoint the v e r y complicated rules. Complicated rules, of course, implies complicated formal specifications. These are shown in full extent:


```
4.0  get-derived-type-sur(typedecl)(early)(sur) =
 .1  let mk-Type-decl(id,mk-Derived-td(sub-t-indic))=typedecl in
 .2  let mk-Subtype-indic(name,constr) = sub-t-indic          in
 .3  let newname = s-level(sur) ^ <id>                           in
 .4  let mk-Type-descr(parenttype, ) = lookup-type(name)(sur) in
 .5  let base-of-parent = lookup-base-type(parenttype)(sur)   in
 .6  let dtype = base-of-parent + (s-name    :-> newname,
 .7                                s-parent:-> s-name(parent),
 .8                                s-ds    :-> nil          )in
 .9  let subtype = cases constr:
 .10  ( nil -> dtype + (s-sub: -> s-sub(parenttype))          ,
 .11    T  -> constrain-type(dtype)([])(nil)(TYPE)(sur) )  in
 .12(~is-wf-full-decl-of-private-type(subtype,s-tp(early))(sur)
 .13                                                    -> exit,
 .14 T -> get-sur-of-derived-type(id,subtype)(early)(sur)    )

 .15 type:Type-decl->[Type-descr]->Surroundings->Surroundings
```


## Annotations:

.6 This type is assembled from the base type of the parent type (the base type is by definition unconstrained).
.8 The datastructure is referenced through the structure type of the base type.
.9 If no explicit constraint is given,
.10 the constraint is inherited from the parent type.
.11 Otherwise the explicitly given constraint is imposed.


Derived subprograms are entered to the dictionary. But there must be a "filter", such that those already declared are not entered again.

```
5.0 get-sur-of-derived-type(id,typ)(early)(sur) =
.1 let parent-attr = s-attr(lookup-unitname(s-parent(typ))(sur))in
.2 let (deriv-attr,new-state) =
.3   cases hd s-status(sur):
.4   (mk-In-Pack-spec(def-tp,def-sp) ->
.5     ((if s-parent(typ) E def-tp
.6        then (let def-attr={ un | mk-Sub-prgr(un,, ) E
.7                            def-sp}                    in
.8              parent-attr \ def-sp)
.9        else   parent-attr        ),
.10      mk-In-Pack-spec(def-tp U {s-name(typ)},def-sp) ^
.11                        tl s-status(sur)),
.12   T -> ( {parent-attr}, s-status(sur) )              ) in
.13let attributes = filter-attr(deriv-attr)(s-attr(early))( .. )in
.14let new-attr = excl-old-attr(attributes)(s-attr(early)( .. ) in
.15let deriv-sp-dict = get-sp-attr-dict(new-attr,typ)(sur)      in
.16let literaldict = get-enum-literal-dict(typ)                 ,
.17    predef-opdict = create-usertype-dep-op-dict(typ)(sur)    ,
.18    type-dict = [id -> mk-Type-descr(typ,attributes) ]      in
.19let dict-ext = overload(deriv-sp-dict)(literaldict)
.20               + type-dict                                  in
.21update-sur(dict-ext,<>,[],predef-opdict,<>)
.22                        (sur+(s-status:->newstatus))

.23 type:(Id Type)->[Type-descr]->Surroundings->Surroundings
```

## Annotations:

.5-.8 Derived types declared in the same package specification as their parent type do not derive the subprograms declared in the same specification list (only the attributes which the parent type itself has derived (if any) are derived).

.13 The attributes are those derived, plus those defined when (if) the type was only known as a private type. The latter may override the former.

.14 Derived subprograms are implicitly declared with the type,

.15 but only the new ones!

.16 The declaration of an enumeration type implies the declaration of its literals.

.17 A type definition causes the introduction of a set of predefined operators.

.21 The denotation of a derived type declaration is an extension of the dictionary, predefined operator set and status of surroundings.

7.0  The Data Types in Ada

7.1  Introduction

This section will cover the details of the different datatypes in Ada.
These are the record-, private-, access-, array-, enumeration-, integer-,
fixed- and float data types.  Task types are not covered.  A subsection is
devoted to private types since these may be concidered as a special datatype.  Namely a data type where the structural details cannot be referred
to.  We show in detail how the "Datastructure", which is a semantic object,
is constructed for the particular data types as a result of the static elaboration af a type definition.  We also show in detail how the "Substructure" which is also a semantic object is constructed as the result of the
static elaboration of a subtype indication or a constraint.

We give the syntactic domains for type definitions:

```
Type-def     = Enum-td | Integer-td | Float-td | Fixed-td |
               Array-td | Record-td | Access-td | Derived-td |
               Private-td
```

The corresponding static domains are Datastructure's:

```
Datastructure = Scalar | Record | Array | Access | EMPTY
Scalar       = Discrete | FIXED | FLOAT | univ-fixed
Discrete     = ENUM | BOOL | INTG | any-integer
Numeric      = INTG | FIXED | FLOAT
```

The datastructure component of "Types" is constructed:

```
1.0  make-type(typeexpr)(newname)(dmap)(rlevel)(tdusg)(sur) =
 .1  cases typeexpr:
 .2  (mk-Subtype-indic() ->
 .3       (make-subtype(typeexpr)(dmap)(rlevel)(tdusg)(sur),[]),
 .4   mk-Record-td()      ->
 .5         make-record-type(typeexpr)(newname)(sur),
 .6   mk-Array-td()       ->
 .7       ...
 .8   ...
 .9   mk-Private-td()     -> ...         )

 .10 type: (Type-def|Subtype-indic) -> Unitname -> Discrim-map
 .11        -> Record-level -> Type-def-usage -> Surroundings
 .12        -> ( Type  Operator-dict )
```

Annotations:

.4 No extra predefined operators from subtypes but
.6 possibly from a record type definition if it contains  anonymous  array
type definitions.


3 of the parameters of the above function have not  been  described  before.
These are:

2.0  Discrim-map   =  Id m-> Obj-descr
 .1  Record-level  =  [IN-RECORD]
 .2  Typ-def-usage =  ( TYPE | COMPONENT )


## Annotations:

.0 A Discriminant map is a map from record-type  discriminant  identifiers
   into  their  object-descriptors.   Record components may depend on discriminants.  Precise knowledge of these discriminants when  generating
   the types (or subtypes) for a record component is therefore necessary.
.1 So it must be known when to use the discriminant.
.2 Whenever a type definition or subtype indication is a part of an object
   or  record component declaration it must not designate an unconstrained
   array type or an unconstrained record type with un-initialized discriminants.


Substructures are derived from Subtype-indications, that is:   from  a  base
type  and  a  constraint.   The function "constrain-type" does the work.  We
give the syntactic domains:

Subtype-indic :: Name [Constraint]
Constraint     =  Range-constr | Index-constr | Discrim-constr |
                  Float-constr | Fixed-constr
Range-constr  :: ...
Index-constr  :: ...
...


The corresponding static domains are "Substructures":

Substructure =  Enum | Intg | Fixed | Float | Array-sub |
                Record-sub | ACCESS-SUB | PRIVATE-SUB
Enum          :: ...
Intg          :: ...
...


We show the function that creates the substructure component of  types  (ie.

constrains a Type) provided that the given constraint is legal:

```
 3.0  constrain-type(typ)(constr)(dmap)(rlevel)(tdusg)(sur) =
  .1  cases s-sub(typ):
  .2  (mk-Record-sub()  ->
  .3     constrain-record-type(typ)(constr)(dmap)(rlevel)
                                              (tdusg)(sur),
  .4  mk-Array-sub()  ->
  .5     constrain-array-type(typ)(constr)(dmap)(rlevel)
                                              (tdusg)(sur),
  .6  mk-Intg()        ->
  .7     constrain-intg-type(typ)(constr)(sur),
  .8  ...
  .9  PRIVATE-SUB  -> exit  )

 .10  type: Type -> [Constraint] -> Discrim-map -> Record-level
 .11       -> Typ-def-usage -> Surroundings ~-> Type
```

Annotations:

.9 Private types with discriminants are treated as records (with empty
   component list). Private types without discriminants cannot be constrained.

## 7.2  Record Types

Record types are recursively defined, ie. variant parts contain
component-lists, which again may contain variant parts etc. Therefore, the
formulae, which generate the corresponding (recursively defined) description
are recursively defined.
Records may have decriminants. A variant part of a record type depends on a
discriminant of the type. An index constraint or a discriminant constraint
can depend on the value of the discriminant of the record type. Finally, if
an array type definition is given in a record component declaration, the
component type (subtype red.) of the array may depend on a discriminant.
This dependency must be direct. In case of an index constraint, a bound can
be a discriminant, but it cannot be another expression involving the discriminant. The same rule applies to a discriminant value specified in a
discriminant constraint. A record component can be a dynamic array if the
bounds that are not static are discriminants. This implies that whenever a
component declaration is elaborated (checked for well-formedness and the
static denotation entered in the dictionary) full knowledge of the discriminants of the record type must be available. The map of discriminants

$$\text{Discrim-map} = \text{Id m-> Obj-descr}$$

is therefore given as parameter to several of the functions in the model.

Record components may not depend on each other, but a component may use it's
own attributes in an (optional) initializing expression.

```
declare
  A : INTEGER;
  N : INTEGER := ... ;
  B : BOOLEAN;
  type R (D1 : INTEGER range 1..N := 10) is record
          C : array(1..D1) of X := (C'FIRST .. C'LAST => X0);
          B : BOOLEAN := A = 100; --outer A used, outer B hidden
          E,D : BOOLEAN := B or TOO_BAD; --illegal
  end record;
begin null; end;
```

For this reason, the dictionary (in which the record type is checked) is extended several times during the elaboration of a component declaration:

| Stepwise elaboration: | dictionary extended with: | contents of d-map: |
|---|---|---|
| type R | [R   -> INTRODUCED] | |
| (D1 | [D1 -> INTRODUCED] | |
| :INT) is record | [D1 -> COMPONENT] | [D1 -> Objdescr] |
| C: | [C   -> INTRODUCED] | [D1 -> Objdescr] |
| array(1..D) of X | [C   -> Objdescr(array)] | [D1 -> Objdescr] |
| := (C'FIRST..); | [C   -> COMPONENT] | [D1 -> Objdescr] |
| . | . | . |
| . | . | . |
| . | . | . |
| end record; | [R   -> Typedescr(record([D -> .. | |
| | C -> .. | |
| | ..-> ..]))] | |

When a record type contains components of anonymous array types, the predefined operators defined on these array types are implicitly generated at the place of the component declarations.  Consider the example:

```
  type ERRORDATA is record
      HEAD: array(1...100) of CHAR:= MESSAGE1 & SP &
                                    MESSAGE2 & '.' & CRLF;
          --- "&" must be available
      ... --- other components
  end record;
```

The result of "make - record type" must therefore be:

$$... -> ( \text{Type} \quad \text{Operator-dict} )$$

It is easy to check the well-formedness of discriminant constraints.  The effect of a "correct" discriminant constraint is that the generated record subtype has a substructure which is:

$$\text{substructure} = \underline{\text{mk-Recordsub}}(\underline{\text{DISCRIM-LOCK}})$$

Such a subtype must not be further constrained.  Discriminant constraints may be omitted in record object-declarations if the decriminants all have default values.

Private types may have discriminants and these discriminants (names, order, subtype and default value) must be repeated with the full declaration of the private type. The rule is that names within the implied expressions may be written differently (provided they have the same meaning). To check this the implied expressions must be rebuild and should not contain calls to non-predefined functions since no sideeffects are allowed.


Associated syntactic domains:

```
Type-def         =  Record-td | ...
Record-td        :: Discrim-decl* Comp-list
Discrim-decl     =  Obj-decl
Comp-list        :: Obj-decl* [Variant-part]
Variant-part     :: Id ( s-chl:Choice+  s-compl:Comp-list )*
                    s-oth:[Comp-list]
Choice           =  Expr | Range | Named-discr-rng
Range            :: Expr Expr
Named-discr-rng  :: Name [Range]

Constraint       =  Discrim-constr | ...
Discrim-constr   :: s-pos:Expr* s-named:(Id Expr)*
```


Associated static domains:


```
Datastructure    =  | Record | ...
Record           :: s-discrim:[Discrim-descr] s-compl:Compl-descr
Discrim-descr    :: s-obj-map: Id m-> Obj-descr
                    s-order   : Id <-m-> N1
                    s-init    : [INIT] [Rebuild-item+]

Compl-descr      :: s-obj-map : Id m-> Obj-descr
                    s-order    : Id <-m-> N1
                    s-var-part:[Var-part-descr]
Var-part-descr   :: Id ( OTH | VAL-set ) m-> Compl-descr
VAL              =  ...

Substructure     =  Record-sub | ...
Record-sub       :: s-lock: [DISCRIM-LOCK]
```


Relevant functions:

```
make-record-type  ( ... )( ... )( ... ) = ( ... )
type: Record-td -> Unitname -> Surr. -> (Type Operator-dict)

constrain-record-type  ( ... )( ... )( ... )( ... ) = ( ... )
type: Type -> [Constraint] -> Discrim-map -> Type-def-usage ->
                                    Surrroundings -> Type


flatten-record ( ... ) = ( ... )
type: Type -> Dict
```

This function flattens   the nested component lists, thereby   all variants are
 revealed.

```
pre-check-record ( ... ) = ( ... )
type: Record-td -> BOOL
```

The (rather interesting) topic of checking the compatibility  of  aggregates
with record types has yet to be elaborated.  However the Record - datastructure has been designed with that in mind.


## 7.3  Private Types

Privte type-definitions can appear only in the visible  part  of  a  package
specification  and  they must be declared in full in the private part of the
package specfication.  These conditions are pre-checkable.
The private type is, when the package-descriptor is entered in the  dictionary,  represented in the visible dictionary component as well as in the private dictionary component of the package-descriptor. In  the  visible  dictionary component, in which entries can be referenced from outside the package, the "Datastructure" and the "Substructure" component of the "Type" have
the  values  "EMPTY" (usually) and "PRIVATE-SUB".  Thereby we can always detect illegal references to these. There is  an  exception:   Private  types
with  discriminants  have the Datastructure of "Record"s instead of "EMPTY".
In the private dictionary component the type will have the same  description
as  in the visible, until the full declaration is elaborated.  When the full
declaration is elaborated the Type-component is generated  in  the  function
"make-type"  used  in "get-defined-type-sur".  The interesting point is that
the full declaration must satisfy some rules with respect to the early (private)  declaration.   These  rules  are  checked  for  satisfaction by the
function: "is-wf-full-decl-of-private-type".
In the visible as well as in the private dictionary component  the  type  is
marked  as  "PRIVATE" (or as "LIMITED").  This indicates whether or not the
"=" and "/=" operators should be generated for the type.

Associated syntactic domains:

```
Type-def          = Private-td | ....
Private-td        :: [Discrim-decl+] [limited]
```

Associated static domains:

```
Datastructure     = Record | EMPTY | ...
Substructure      = PRIVATE-SUB | ...
```

We show how to extract the Type-component of the Type-descr of a type defined as private:

```
4.0  make-private-type(texpr)(nawname)(sur) =
 .1 let mk-Private-td(discrim,limited) = texpr        in
 .2 (discrim = nil ->
 .3     mk-Type(newname,newname,newname,EMPTY,PRIVATE-SUB,
 .4              cases limited: ( nil -> PRIVATE,
 .5                               T   -> LIMITED)       ),
 .6  T              ->
 .7     let (tp, ) =
 .8     make-record-type(mk-Record-td(discrim,
 .9                  mk-Compl(<>,nil)))(newname)(sur) in
 .10    (tp+(s-lim:-> cases limited:(nil->PRIVATE,
 .11                             T  ->LIMITED))))

 .12 type: Private-td -> Unitname -> Surroundings ~-> Type
```

Annotations:

```
 .6 If the private type has discriminants it is treated as a record with an
    empty component list and no variant part.
```

```
5.0  is-wf-full-decl-of-private-type(full)(early)(parlim)(sur)=
 .1 parlim ≠ LIMITED   and
 .2 cases sel-ds(full)(sur):
 .3 (mk-Record(discrim-descr,compl-descr) ->
 .4   (discrim-descr ≠ nil =>
 .5   (∀ id ∈ dom s-obj-map(discrim-descr))
 .6   (is-not-limited-private(s-tp(s-obj-map(discrim-descr)
                                              (id)))(sur)
 .7     and no-limited-components(compl-descr)))
 .8   and (compatible-datastructure-and-discriminants(full)
                                        (early)(sur))),
 .9  mk-Array( ,obj-descr)            ->
 .10    (s-lock(s-sub(full)) = INDEX-LOCK  AND
 .11     is-not-limited-private(s-tp(obj-descr))(sur) ),
 .12 T                                -> true)
 .13 and (no-circularity(full)(s-name(full))(FIRST)(sur))

 .14 type: Type -> Type -> Surroundings -> BOOL
```

## Annotations:

.1 The type must not be directly derived from a limited private type.
.2 The datastructure is obtained through the structure type, since the full declaration might be in terms of a derived type definition. If this structure type was known to be a
.3 record or an array (.9), it should contain no components for which assignment and equality is not defined.
.8 The discriminants must be repeated correctly.
.9 If the type is an array type it must be constrained.
.12 If the full declaration is unstructured the private declaration should contain no discriminants.

Consider the examples:

```
declare
  package P is            -- begin first example
    type T is private;    -- private declaration
    package Q is
      type R is record
              F1 : T;  -- possible circularity
                       -- cannot be detected here
            end record;
    end Q;
  private
    type T is record      -- full declaration
            F1 : Q.R  -- circularity via nested
                      -- structures
          end record;
  end P;                  -- end first example

  package S is            -- begin second example
    type T is private;    -- private declaration
  private
    package Q is
      type N is private;
    private
      type N is new T;    -- ok, T not limited
    end Q;
    type T is new Q.N;    -- full declaration
                          -- and circularity!
  end S;                  -- end second example
begin ... end;
```

However, these circularities, direct or via structures, can easily be detected. Consider the recursive "predicate":

```
6.0   no-circularity(typ)(searchname)(which)(sur) =
 .1   cases which:
 .2   (FIRST -> (s-structure(typ)=searchname) =>
 .3                           (s-parent(typ)=searchname ) ,
 .4     NEXT -> (s-structure(typ) ≠ searchname )          )
 .5   and cases sel-ds(typ)(sur):
 .6        (mk-Record(discrim-descr,compl-descr) ->
 .7           let rec-dict =
                    flatten-record(discrim-descr,compl-descr) in
 .8           (A id E dom rec-dict)
 .9           (no-circularity(s-tp(rec-dict(id)))(searchname)(sur) ),
 .10       mk-Array( ,obj-descr)  ->
 .11          no-circularity(s-tp(obj-descr))(searchname)(sur),
 .12       T                          -> true)

 .13 type: Type->Unitname->(FIRST|NEXT)->Surroundings->BOOL
```

## Annotations:

.2 in the very first of the recursive steps the structure type may only be
   the type itself if it also is its "own" parent. Otherwise it is a variant of the second example above.
.4 in all following recursive steps the name of the type concerned  should
   not occur.
.5 In the first as well as in the following steps the same predicate  must
   hold for the components.
.7 Reveal all variants.
.12 The recursion stops when the  datastructure  is  EMPTY  thus  reaching
    another  incompletely predeclared private type (there is no circularity
    detectable yet), when the datastructure is an access (allowed  mutually
    dependency) and when the datastructure is not composite.

```
compatible-datastructure-and-discriminants( ... )( ... )( ... ) = ( ... )
type: Type -> Type -> BOOL
```

This function is yet to be written. The only interesting point is that  it
uses a function which checks that the "rebuilded" item-lists of two discrim-
inant-descriptors are equal.

The programmer may declare subtypes of private types, and  iff  the  private
type  has discriminants a (discriminant) constraint may be given. The function "constrain-type" will report static error if an attempt is made to constrain a type with substructure PRIVATE-SUB.

## 7.4 Access Types

The interesting point of access types (pointer types) in Ada is the fact that they can be incompletely forwardly declared with the full declaration at a textually later point. This is for the purpose of recursively and mutually dependent access types.

```
type LINK is access;                 -- incomplete declaration
type LIST_ELEM is record
               KEY:KEYTYPE;
               ....
               NEXT:LINK;
           end record;
type LINK is access LIST_ELEM;        -- complete declaration
```

In the dictionary the description of an access type is represented as a functional object and an indication of whether the accesstype is incompletely declared or not. When an incomplete predeclaration of an access type is encountered the access type is entered into the dictionary as being INCOMPLETE. At the textually later point when the complete declaration is encountered the descriptor is overwritten to denote a COMPLETE access type.
This allows for several usages of the access type: components, objects, subtypes and derived types can be declared of incomplete access types, as long as no constraints are imposed, and as long as no structure of the accessed type (which is unknown) is referenced.

The Ada manual is only dealing with record component declarations of incomplete access types, but we assume that above mentioned cases are all legal.

The functional object yields when applied to the high dictionary the accessed type. The accessed type is always regarded as a subtype. If the access type was directly represented in the dictionary, eg. as Access::...Type..., the dictionary representation of LIST_ELEM would be infinite.
Besides, these funtional objects may be generated when incomplete access types are declared. In this case they will detect errors if the structure of the accessed type is referenced before the type is completely declared.
When the access type is completely declared the functions will yield the accessed type. We show this trick in the function "make-accesstype".
The force of this method is that if objects or subtypes (with no constraints) are declared of an incomplete access type their description will always be "updated" when the access type is completly declared since they always, when their functional object is applied to a dictionary, will obtain their structure via this access type, ie. via their "structure type".

Constraints may be imposed on an access type:

Assume:

1)   type SOMETHING(D:INT) is record ... end record;
2)   type ACCESSTYPE is access SOMETHING [constraint];

If the constraint in 2) is given, further constraints in the following declarations are illegal. If the constraint is not given, the constraints in the following are optional.

```
3)  MY_ACCESS :                          ACCESSTYPE [constraint];
4)  type ACCESS_TO_ACCESS is access  ACCESSTYPE [constraint];
5)  subtype SUB_ACCESSTYPE is access ACCESSTYPE [constraint];
6)  type NEW_ACCESSTYPE    is new    ACCESSTYPE [constraint];
7)  MY_ACCESS := new SOMETHING constraint; -- constraint mandatory
```

("constraint" denotes (D=>expr) in the above example)


The rules for constraints are that only index constraints and discriminant
constraints may be given for access types, and only when the accessed type
is an unconstrained array or record type respectively. So far the manual is
quite clear. It is easy to check wether the constraints are legal. The effect however of the possible constraints 3),4) and 5) in relation to the
static semantics of the language is unclear.
The manual considers allocators where it is stated that the typemark given
in an allocator denotes the type of the object created; the type of the access value returned by the allocator is defined by the context. If the typemark given in an allocator denotes an unconstrained array type or an unconstrained record type with discriminants, the allocator must contain either an explicit initial value or an index or discriminant constraint.
We conclude that constraints imposed on an access type are only relevant to
the dynamic semantics of the language [StPe 80]. That is: the constraints
(if any) imposed on the access object must correspond to those imposed on
the accessed object. This is to be checked during execution.



Associated syntactic domains:

```
Type-def       = Access-td | ...
Access-td      :: [Subtype-indic]
```



Associated static domains:

```
Datastructure  = Access | ...
Substructure   = ACCESS-SUB | ...
Access         :: Dict ~-> Type  s-com:(COMPLETE | INCOMPLETE)
```

(L denotes the Greek letter lambda)

```
7.0   make-accesstype(access-td)(newtypename)(sur) =
 .1   let mk-Access-td(subtypeindic) = access-td in
 .2   let ds = cases subtypeindic:
 .3   (nil -> (let func = L hdict.
 .4            (let mk-Type( ,,structure,, )=
 .5                  lookup-Unitname(newtypename)(hdict) in
 .6            cases structure:
 .7            (mk-Access(f,COMPLETE) -> f( ),
 .8             T                    -> exit) ) in
 .9            mk-Access(func,INCOMPLETE)),
 .10  T   -> (let accessedtp =
 .11          make-subtype(subtypeindic)([])(nil)(TYPE)(sur) in
 .12          mk-Access( L().accessedtp,COMPLETE))) in
 .13  mk-Type(newtypename,newtypename,newtypename,ds,ACCESS,nil)

 .14  type: Access-td -> Unitname -> Surroundings ~-> Type
```

We show how to constrain an accesstype:

```
8.0   constrain-access-type(subtype)(constr)(sur) =
 .1   let mk-Access(fct, ) = sel-ds(subtype)(sur)             in
 .2   if ((is-Index-constr(constr) or is-Discrim-constr(constr)
 .3        or constr=nil) and
 .4       constr≠nil =>
 .5       (trap exit with false in
 .6       (let accstype = fct(s-dict(sur))                    in
 .7        let newstype =
 .8        constrain-type(accstype)(constr)([])(nil)(sur) in
 .9        true)))
 .10  then subtype+(s-ds:->nil)
 .11  else exit

 .12  type: Type -> Constraint ->Surroundings ~-> Type
```

Annotations:

.1  the structure type of the (sub)type to be constrained is
.2  known to be an access type. The imposed constraint (if any) must be an
    index or discriminant constraint,
.8  which must be applicable to the accessed subtype:
    that is: the accessed subtype must have array or record structure
    type, and it must not already have been constrained
.6  if the accessed subtype is not yet known, or the
.8  constraint is illegal, the static error is
.5  locally trapped and
.11 propagated. If everything fits,
.10 the access subtype (ds=nil indicates subtype) is returned

## 7.5 Array Types

The most interesting aspects of array types are: (1) The index types may be
given implicitely, ie.  as  a range - loop parameters may also have their
type implicitly given by a range - so it is not  an  isolated  problem  (see
membership  expressions  section  8.7  and loop statement section 10.4.  (2)
Bounds may depend on discriminants of record types when the thus constrained
array  type  is used as the type of a component of that record type (see re-
cordtypes section 7.2).  (3) An array subtype (which in the  model  has  its
indices  "LOCKED")  may  not  be  further constrained.  The only alowed array
types for objects are constrained array types.  All array types  are  alowed
array  types for constants, but if the array type is not constrained the indices must be extraced from the initial value.

Associated syntactic domains:

```
Type-def        =  Array-td | ...
Array-td        :: ( Discrete-range+ | Index+ ) Subtype-indic
Discrete-range  =  Named-discr-rng | Range
Named-discr-rng :: Name [Range]
Range           :: Expr Expr
Index           :: s-name: Name
Subtype-indic   :: Name [Constraint]
Constraint      =  Index-constr | ...
Index-constr    :: Discrete-range+
```

Associated static domains:

```
Datastructure   =  Array | ...
Substructure    =  Array-sub | ....
Array           :: Type+ Obj-descr
Array-sub       :: s-lock: [INDEX-LOCK]
```

We show how to get index types from ranges:

```
9.0  generate-index-type(dis-rng)(discr-map)(reclevel)(sur) =
 .1  let xsur = update-sur-dict(discr-map)(sur)               in
 .2  let indextype =
     s-type(generate-obj-descr-from-discr-range(dis-rng)(xsur) in
 .3  if  reclevel=IN-RECORD =>
 .4      is-valid-index-constraint(indextype)(dis-rng)
                                  (discr-map)(INRECORD)(sur))
 .5      then indextype
 .6      else exit

 .7  type: Discrete-range ->Discrim-map -> Record-level ->
             Surroundings ~-> Type
```

Annotations:

.1 the range-constraint may use a discriminant
.2 see loop statement section 10.4 (it is only the type of the object that
   is used here).
.3 if the array was defined inside a record the discriminants may be used.


7.6 Enumeration Types

Associated syntactic domains:

Type-def          = Enum-td | ......
Enum-td           :: (Id | Char-lit)+


Associated static domains:

Datastructure     = ENUM | ...
Substructure      = Enum | ...
Enum              :: (Id | Charlit)* [STATIC]
Descr             = Overload-descr | ...
Overload-descr    :: (Literal-descr | Sub-prgr-descr)-set
Literal-descr     :: Type


Annotations:

4  The only interesting aspect is the component in the substructure  indicating  whether the range in the other component is staticaly determinable or not.  If it is, the subtype name may be  used  to  determine  a
   static  range (index constraints on arrays defined inside records, choices in a case statement, etc.).
6  Since character literals can be enumeration literals the domain of  the
   dictionary  must  include  charater literals. Enumeration literals may
   overload subprogram identifiers.


See formulas:

make-enum-type( ... )( ... )( ... ) = ( ... )
type: Enum-td -> Unitname -> Surroundings ~-> Type

constrain-enum-type( ... )( ... )( ... ) = ( ... )
type: Type -> [Constraint] -> Surroundings ~-> Type


in Appendix A.

## 7.7  Integer Types

It should be possible to record that an integer subtype has a static range (see enumeration types section 7.6). Therefore the descriptor of an Int(e)g(er) sub-structure contains the optional quotation "STATIC". When the range constraint is elaborated and the data structure component is generated, the indicator of static range is set to either nil or "STATIC". If the range is static the two integer components denote the lower and upper bounds. The range constraint given with in an integer type definition must be statically determinable. The range constraint given with an integer subtype indication may be dynamic. In Ada integer literals (INTG) are assumed to belong to the predefined type INTEGER whenever used in array index constraints:

        A : array (1..10) of ...;

or in for-clauses:

        for I in 1..100 loop ... end loop;

Since object- and constant descriptors must contain a type descriptor and array type descriptors must contain the index types, it is very useful to have a function which can return the predefined INTEGER type. The predefined integer type has the same name, parent, and structure type (The integer defined in package STANDARD), it has implementation dependent, but statically range, and is not a private type. As required by the Ada manual, all integer types are simulated derived types of the predefined STANDARD.INTEGER .

Associated syntactic domains:

```
Constraint       = Range-constr | ...
Intg-td          :: Range-constr
Range-constr     :: Range
Range            :: Expr Expr
Subtype-indic    :: Name [Constraint]
```

Associated static domains:

```
Datastructure    = INTG | any-integer | ...
Substructure     = Intg | ...
Intg             :: INTG INTG [STATIC]
```

```
pre-def-intg-type() =
mk-Type( <mk-Simp-name(STANDARD),mk-Simp-name(INTEGER)>,
         <mk-Simp-name(STANDARD),mk-Simp-name(INTEGER)>,
         <mk-Simp-name(STANDARD),mk-Simp-name(INTEGER)>,
         INTG,
         mk-Intg(implementation-defined-lover-bound,
                 implementation-defined-upper-bound,
                 STATIC                             ),
         nil)

type:  () -> Type
```

See also the formulas:

```
transform-type-decl( ... )( ... ) = ( ... )
type: Type-decl -> Surroundings ~-> Type-decl

constrain-intg-type( ... )( ... )( ... ) = ( ... )
type: Type -> [Constraint] -> Surroundings ~-> Type
```

in Appendix A .

## 7.8  Fixed and Floating Point Types

The interesting point is that floating point type declarations are equivalent  to the declaration of a type derived from one of the predefined floating point types, while the same thing is not true for fixed point  type declarations.   This  implies  that floating point types derive the predefined
subprograms READ, WRITE, etc. as attributes from the predefined type  FLOAT
in package STANDARD. Fixed point types derive no subprograms. But the dictionary may contain equivalent (overloaded) subprograms with  parameter  or
result type of "universal-fixed" which matches any fixed type (see the modeling of this aspect in the function "type-expr-compatibility" ).
The usage of "universal-fixed" instead of ordinary "Type"-objects in subprogram parameter descriptors is a 'trick' which makes it possible to have certain operators for fixed point types in the operator dictionary.

The types of these operators are:

```
*,/ : (universal-fixed,universal-fixed) -> universal-fixed
*,/ : ( Fixed-type , any-integer)       -> (same) Fixed-type
*,/ : (any-integer , Fixed-type)        -> (same) Fixed-type
```

When the declaration of a fixed point type is elaborated, the predefined  *,
/-operators having any integer type as one parameter type are generated (see
the function "create-usertype-dep-op-dict").

Associated syntactic domains:

```
Type-def          :: Fixed-td | Float-td | ...
Fixed-td          :: Fixed-constr
Float-td          :: Float-constr
Fixed-constr      :: Expr [Range-constr]
Float-constr      :: Expr [Range-constr]
Range-constr      :: Range
Range             :: Expr Expr
```

Associated static domains:

```
Datastructure     = FIXED | FLOAT | univ-fixed | ...
Substructure      = Fixed | Float | ...
Fixed             :: s-delta: NUM
Float             :: s-digits: INTG
```

Relevant formulas:

```
make-fixed-type( ... )( ... )( ... ) = ( ... )
type: Fixed-td -> Unitname -> Surroundings ~-> Type

transform-typedecl( ... )( ... ) = ( ... )
type: Type-decl -> Surroundings -> Type-decl

constrain-fixed-type( ... )( ... )( ... ) = ( ... )
type: Type -> [Constraint] -> Surroundings ~-> Type

constrain-float-type( ... )( ... )( ... ) = ( ... )
type: Type -> [Constraint] -> Surroundings ~-> Type
```

## 8.0 Expressions


## 8.1 Introduction

This section describes the static aspects of Ada expressions. Although expressions include names these are treated separately in section 9. So what here is said about expressions in general is also related to names. In particular, operators are described in this section together with the infix expressions, while function calls are described in the section on names.

However,the discussion of overloading resolving is in this section also for functions. It would thus be ideal if this section could be read in parallel with the next.

This introduction discusses first the reasons for the complexity of expressions in Ada, compared to eg. Pascal. Finally the abstract syntax for expressions is given. In the following subsections overloading is discussed. It is shown that only one pass is needed to detect whether overloading can be resolved or not. And that the resolving can be done (if possible) in a second pass. In the next subsection we show how to check whether a given expression and a given type is compatible or not. With those tools ready we show how to check infix expressions, qualified expressions, type conversions and membership expressions. The model also includes the check of prefix expressions, see appendix A. The function which checks aggregates is not written yet but it will be easy to do. Now to the point: Why is expression checking so complex in Ada ?

In a language with the ability to declare types but not with overloading (except for certain predefined operators: $*$, $/$, $+$, $-$, $=$, $/=$ eg. Pascal [JeWi78]) expressions can usually be checked for well-formedness without reference to the context in which they appear. Furthermore when well-formed the type of an expression is well-defined and extractable:

    extr-type-if-wf-Expr(expr)(sur) = ( ... )
    type : Expression -> Surroundings -> Type

unless the expression is denoting a dynamically allocated object (which may match several pointer types). In case of dynamically allocated objects (or the value NIL) the pointer, (and the pointer type) is always known. The function needed is thus:

    type-expr-compatibility(pointer-type)(allocator)(sur) = ( ... )
    type : Type -> Expr -> Sur -> BOOL

The pointer type defines the context. In Pascal the only overloaded literal is the pointer value NIL. In Algol 60 all types are predefined thereby simplifying the type·checking [HeJo 79 ]. Compared to Pascal, type checking in Ada is much more complicated. This is due to the following : (1) More overloaded primaries: Integer- and real- numbers (literals), the access (pointer) value NULL, allocators and aggregates can be overloaded. No unique type can be extracted from these expressions.

(2) User defined operators and functions and enumeration literals (zero-adic functions) can be overloaded: The context in which an expression appears must/may be used to determine which of several overloaded functions or operators to use. In particular, the right hand side types of an assignment may influence the resolving of overloaded functions called (yielding eg. index values) at the left hand side.

We conclude this introduction by giving the abstract syntax for expressions. The abstract syntax for expressions is derived from the concrete grammar by means of a - further unspecified - transforming function, which generates the parse tree, thereby resolving operator hierarchy, thus yielding expressions where all parentheses are explicit (this transforming function is usually just the parser of the compiler). Note the distinction between operators which can be defined by the programmer, and those which can not.

```
Expr            = Infix | Prefix | Primary | Membership

Primary         = Name | Qualif-expr | Type-conv | Aggregate |
                  Allocator | Literal

Composite-expr  = Aggregate | Allocator | String

Literal         = INTG | NUM | null | Char-lit | String

Type-conv       :: Name Expr

Qualif-expr     :: Name Expr

Infix           :: Expr Dop Expr

Prefix          :: Mop Expr

Aggregate       :: ( Positional-list | Named-list ) s-others:[Expr]

Positional-list = Expr+

Named-list      = ( Choice+ Expr )+

Allocator       :: Name [ Expr | Discrim-constr | Index-constr ]

String          = Char-lit*

Membership      :: Expr ( Range | Subtype-indic ) [not]

Operator        = Mop | Dop

Mop             = + | - | not

Dop             = Declarable-Dop | andthen | orelse | /=

Declarable-Dop  = = | < | <= | > | >= | and | or | xor |
                  + | - | & | * | / | mod | rem | **
```

## 8.2  Overloading Resolving

Expressions and in particular names can have several possible meanings as a result of overloading.
The purpose of this section is to show how to detect whether overloading can be resolved, rather than actually resolving the overloading.
The subject is treated in [PeWi 79], but this paper is based on the assumption that the possible types can always be extracted from an expression,

which implies that the possible types of an aggregate is the total set of referable record and array types. Our approach is based on the following:

For each expression and its context we define:

1. available types:
a list of the types of the possible meanings of the expression. No references to the context.

2. required types:
a list of the types of acceptable meanings of the expression. The context defines the acceptability.

Well-formedness of an entire expression (eg. the righthand-side of an assignment statement or an actual parameter in a subprogram call) with respect to its context is:

1. If available types can be extracted from the expression there must exist exactly one type in the list of available types such that there exists exactly one of the required types such that the names of these two types are the same (strong typing).

2. If available types cannot be extracted from the expression (which in this case is an overloaded primary) there must exist exactly one type among the required types, such that the type is compatible with the expression.

The required types can always be extracted. These are either the types of the possible meanings of the left hand side of assignment statements (names), the parameter types of a set of (overloaded) subprograms, a qualifying type, the type in type conversion, or predefined boolean type in conditions.
If available types can be extracted the first check above is performed; otherwise the second check is. If these checks fail the expression is not well-formed.
To find the set of overloaded subprograms for which the parameters given in the call is valid we use the function "parameter-checker". "parameter-checker" uses the function "compatibility". Thus the method is based on successive usage of "extract-available-types" which works bottom up, and "compatibility", which works top down.
The theorem is:

1. The detection of whether or not overloading can be resolved within entire expressions, knowing the context (and of course whether only referable names are used) - can be done in one passage bottom up.

2. If this resolving is possible, the overloaded items (subprograms, operators, literals) can be identified in a second pass, top down.

Proof (the validity of the second part of the theorem is also proved in [PeWi 79]).
The function "get-available-object-list" extracts the maximum set of available overloaded subprograms, and forms a list whose elements represent values of the result types of these subprograms. If "true ambiguity" occurs (that is if two or more subprograms of the maximum set return values of the same type), this value is represented twice (or more) in the list of extracted types.

Example:
Let (1,2) -> 3 represent a function (or operator) with operands of types 1
and 2 and returning a value of type 3.
Let mk-expr(<1,2>,<2>) represent an infix expression where the available values of the left hand side are either of type 1 or type 2, and the available
value(s) of the right hand side is type 2.
Assume some overloaded operators(subprograms):

```
(1,1) -> 1      (3,3) -> 3
(1,2) -> 2      (3,4) -> 4
(1,1) -> 2      (1,3) -> 5
(2,2) -> 2      (2,3) -> 6
```

Consider the following "expression"

mk-expr( <mk-expr(<1>  ,<1,2>) >  ,  <mk-expr(<3> ,<3,4>) > )

For left- and right hand-side extract the maximum set of available operators
for which the parameter requirements are satisfied (no true ambiguity)

```
        (1,1) -> 1              (3,3) -> 3
        (1,2) -> 2              (3,4) -> 4
        (1,1) -> 2
```

Form a list of returned value types:

mk-expr( <1,2,2>          ,        <3,4> )
         (true ambiguity)   (no true ambiguity)

Extract the maximum set of overloadable subprograms:

```
            (1,3) -> 5
```

but neither    (2,3) -> 6
nor            (2,4) -> 2

because the required left hand-side parameter type <2> cannot match exactly
one of the available value types <1,2,2>. The only available value type of
the initial expression is <5>.


Iff the set of overloadable subprograms is not empty at any level of the
parse tree we know that at the root we have a non empty list of available
value types. If this list exhibits true ambiguity we know that this is the
only possible true ambiguity in the tree since the effect of lower level ambiguities are eliminated. If the true ambiguity of the root expression is
eliminated by the context (could be if the required type only exists once in
the list) we know that a top down walk in the tree (identifying which of the
set of available subprograms to use) will always contain at least one, returning the required type (otherwise the "value-type-list" of the root expression would be empty), on the other hand at most one, since true ambiguity is eliminated. Thus overloading can be resolved.
Otherwise, iff the list of overloadable value types of the root expression

is empty, or if true ambiguity cannot be eliminated by the context, overloading cannot be resolved. This completes the proof.

## 8.3  Type- Expression Compatibility

If overloaded subprograms or enumeration literals used in expressions can be
unambiguous identified - using only the knowledge of identifiers that are
strong visible, they are unambiguously identified. Otherwise they must be
unambiguously identifyable using all visible identifiers.
This modelling principle is applied in the functions
"type-expr-compatibility" and "is-wf-Assign" :

```
1.0   type-expr-compatibility(required-type) (expr) (sur) =
.1    let strongsur=sur+(s-wm->[ ])                     in
.2    (     compatibility(required-type) (expr) (strongsur)
.3       or compatibility(required-type) (expr) (sur) )

.4    type : Type -> Expr -> Surroundings -> BOOL
```

## Annotations:

When the required type of the expression is given beforehand (eg. in
object-initializing expressions) the type and expression must be compatible
using only the strong visible identifiers, or using all visible identifiers.


We give the compatibility checking function and (some of) its implications:

```
2.0   compatibility(reqtp)(expr)(sur)=
.1    cases expr :
.2    ( mk-Aggregate() -> Aggregate-compatibility(reqtp)(expr)(sur),
.3      mk-Allocator() -> ...
.4      null            -> ...
.5      INTG            -> ...
.6      NUM             -> ...
.7      T               ->
.8           (let typel = extr-available-types(expr)(sur)        in
.9            (E! i E ind typel) (cases typel[i]:
.10              ( mk-Pseudo-type(val)->
                          compatibility(reqtp)(val)(sur),
.11               mk-Type(univ-fixed,,,, ) -> false,
.12               mk-Type()-> s-name(typel[i])=s-name(reqtp)))

.13 type : (Pseudotype | Type) -> Expr -> Surroundings -> BOOL
```

## Annotations:

   .2 -.6 available types cannot be extracted from aggregates, allocators,
      the null-value, and universal real- and integer numbers, but compati-
      bility can be checked.
   .7-.9 The "type" is one of the required types, of these there must exist

exactly one for which the compatibility function yields true.
.11 In particular no type is compatible with expressions of the type "universal-fixed" (except in type conversions, see 4.8).


```
3.0  extr-available-types(expr)(sur)=
.1   cases expr:
.2   ( mk-Name()          -> extr-name-types( expr ) (sur),
.3     mk-Infix()         -> ...
.4     mk-Prefix()        -> ....
.5     mk-Qualif-expr()   -> ...
.6     mk-Type-conv()     -> ...
.7     mk-Membership()    -> get-pre-def-bool-type-if-wf-membership
                                  ( expr) (sur)           ,
.8     mk-String()         -> get-pre-def-string-type()    ,
.9     Char-lit           -> ...
.10    T                  -> /* extracting types impossible
                               see the pre-condition of
                               this function              */ )

.11  type : Expr -> Surroundings -> Type*
.12  pre  : expr ~E { Allocator,Aggregate,null,INTG,NUM }
```

Annotations:

Membership expressions return the predefined boolean type.


```
4.0  extract-name-types(name)(sur) =
.1   let descrl = lookup-name(name) (sur)                    in
.2   conc < cases descrl[i]:
.3     ( mk-Obj-descr(otype, )  -> <otype> ,
.4       mk-Overload-descr(ds)  ->
.5       ( let list E Type* be.s.t
.6             card elems list = ln list and
.7             elems list = {ltype |
                            mk-Literal-descr(ltype)E ds }) in
.8         list)
.9       mk-Number(val)         -> <mk-Pseudotype(val)> ,
.10      T                      -> <> )
.11    | i E ind descrl>

.12  type : Name -> Surroundings -> ( Type | Pseudotype )*
```

Annotations:

.4 - .8 In case of an enumeration literal, make a list of all the types
which have it defined as a literal.

## 8.4  The Infix Expression

Due to the unified description of procedures, functions and operators this function exhibits the full generality of the concept of overloaded operators:

```
5.0  extr-infix-types(infix)(sur) =
 .1  let mk-Infix( ,op, )      = infix                   in
 .2  let mk-Overload-descr(ds) = (extr-dict(sur))(op)    in
 .3    extr-infix-ret-types(infix)(ds)(sur)

 .4  type : Infix -> Surroundings -> Type*
```

### Annotations:

.2 any operator has a static semantics denotation which is an overload-descr, which again contains only subprogram descriptors (eg.: "and" cannot be an enumeration literal). This static semantics denotation is the set of overloading user- and predefined operators. User defined operators may have redeclared (and thereby hidden) the predefined operator.

```
6.0  extr-infix-ret-types(infix)(dset)(sur) =
 .1  if dset = { } then <> else
 .2    ( let d E dset , mk-Infix(e1,,e2)   = infix           in
 .3       let mk-Sub-prgr-descr( ,,entrance)= d               in
 .4       let mk-Entrance( ,rtn, )         = entrance        in
 .5      extr-infix-ret-types(infix)(dset\{d})(sur) ^
 .6      ( rtn=nil -> <>,
 .7        paramchecker(entrance)
                        (mk-Act-param-list(<e1,e2>,<>))(sur)
 .8              -> <rtn>,
 .9        T         -> <>))

 .10 type : Infix -> Sub-prgr-descr-set -> Surroundings -> Type*
```

### Annotations:

The available types of an infix expression are the elements in a list of the returned types of those of the available subprograms in the "set" which are functions (the return type /= nil), and where the types of the left- and right hand side expressions are compatible with the types of the formal parameters of the operator.

```
7.0 extr-dict(mk-Surroundings(hdict,dlevel,wm,opdict, )) =
 .1 overload( overload(opdict) (weakmerge(wm)) )
            ( flatten(hdict) (dlevel) )

 .2 type: Surroundings -> Dict
```

## Annotations:

Operators that are only weak visible are "stronger" than predefined operators.

## 8.5  Qualified Expression.

Qualified expressions are used to explicitly state the type of expressions.
Therefore as one may expect, it must be unambiguously determinable which
type the name denotes:

$$Qualif\text{-}expr :: Name\ Expr$$

The returned type of a qualified expression is the type denoted by the
"Name", and the expression must be compatible with the base type of this
type.

```
8.0 extract-Qualif-type(mk-Qualif-type(name,expr))(sur) =
 .1 let mk-Type-descr(qtype, )=lookup-type(name)(sur) in
 .2 let basetype = lookup-base-type(qtype)(sur)          in
 .3 if compatibility(basetype)(expr)(sur)
 .4    then <qtype>
 .5    else <>

 .6 type : Qualif-expr -> Surroundings -> Type*
```

## 8.6  Type Conversion

Type conversions are a little more complicated than qualified expressions.
This is due to the fact that the "compatibility" function is substituted by
"explicit-conv-compatibility" which is rather complicated due to the conversion rules of Ada.

Type-conv :: Name Expr

Note that expressions of type "universal-fixed" can be converted to any fixed type!


```
9.0 extract-Type-conv-type(mk-Type-conv(name,expr))(sur) =
 .1 let mk-Type-descr(convtype, ) = lookup-type(name)(sur) in
 .2 if explicit-conv-compatibility(convtype)(expr)(sur)
 .3    then <convtype>
 .4    else <>

 .5 type: Type-conv -> Surroundings -> Type*
```


```
10.0 explicit-conv-compatibility(type1)(expr)(sur) =
 .1 cases expr:
 .2 (mk-Aggregate() -> aggregate-compatibility(type1)(expr)(sur),
 .3  null            -> allocate-compatibility(type1)(expr)(sur),
 .4  INTG            -> is-Numeric(sel-ds(type1)(sur))            ,
 .5  NUM             -> is-Numeric(sel-ds(type1)(sur))            ,
 .6  T               ->
 .7  (let typel=extract-available-types(expr)(sur)                 in
 .8   (E! i E ind typel)
 .9    ((is-derived-or-compatible-types(type1)(typel[i])(sur) or
 .10    (is-Array(sel-ds(type1)(sur))        and
 .11    is-Array(sel-ds(typel[i])(sur)) and
 .12    (let basetp1 = lookup-base-type(type1)(sur)            in
 .13    let mk-Array(tl1,objd1, ) = sel-ds(basetp1)(sur)  in
 .14    let mk-Array(tl2,objd2, ) = sel-ds(typel[i])(sur)) in
 .15    (ln tl1 = ln tl2 and
 .16    (¥ i E ind tl1)
 .17    (is-derived-or-compatible-types(tl1[i])(tl2[i])(sur))
 .18    and is-derived-or-compatible-types(s-type(objd1))
 .19                       (s-type(objd2))(sur)))))))))

 .20 type : Type -> Expr -> Surrounding -> BOOL
```

```
11.0 is-derived-or-compatible-types(type1)(type2)(sur) =
.1 cases type2:
.2 (mk-Pseudotype()              -> is-Numeric(sel-ds(type1)(sur)),
.3  mk-Type( ,,,univ-fixed,, ) -> is-Numeric(sel-ds(type1)(sur)),
.4  mk-Type(name2,parent2,,,, )->
.5     (let mk-Type( name1,parent1,,,, ) = type1 in
.6          name1  E {name2,parent2} or
.7          name2  E {name1,parent1}     ))

.8 type: Type -> ( Type | Pseudotype ) -> BOOL
```

## 8.7  Membership Expression

The extraction of a type from a range is rather cumbersome.  This is due  to
overloading.

          Membership  ::  Expr ( Range | Subtype-indic ) [not]

We show how to do this extraction which, besides in membership  expressions,
is  relevant  when loop statement parameter types are defined by the type of
some (discrete) range.

```
12.0 get-predef-bool-type-if-wf-membership(mbs)(sur) =
.1 (let mk-Membership(expr,rangeden) = mbs in
.2  if cases rangeden:
.3   (mk-Range(ex1,ex2)   ->
.4     (let rtype =extr-type-from-range(rangeden)     in
.5        (is-Pseudotype(rtype) or is-Scalar(s-ds(rtype))) and
.6         type-expr-compatibility(rtype)(expr)(sur) )   ,
.7    mk-Subtype-indic(name,constr)  ->
.8    (let rtype=make-subtype(rangeden)([])(nil)(TYPE)(sur)in
.9         (is-Pseudotype(rtype) or is-Scalar(s-ds(rtype))) and
.10        type-expr-compatibility(rtype)(expr)(sur) )   ,
.11   then predef-bool-type() else exit)

.12  type: Membership -> Surroundings -> Type
```

```
13.0   extract-type-from-range(mk-range(ex1,ex2))(sur)=
  .1   if is-Composite(ex1) or ex1=null or
          is-Composite(ex2) or ex2=null
  .2   then exit else
  .3   (is-INTG(ex1) and is-INTG(ex2) -> predef-Intg-type() ,
  .4    is-NUM (ex1) and is-NUM (ex2) -> mk-Pseudotype(ex1) ,
  .5    T                             ->
  .6      (let tl1 = extract-overloadable-types(ex1)(sur)    in
  .7      (let tl2 = extract-overloadable-types(ex2)(sur)    in
  .8      let test= get-test-fct(tl1)(tl2)(sur)              in
  .9      if (E! i E ind tl1) (E! j E ind tl2)(test(i)(j))
  .10        then (let i E ind tl1,j E ind tl2 be s.t. test(i)(j) in
  .11            cases tl1[i],tl2[j]:
  .12              (mk-Type(),T -> tl1[i],
  .13               T,mk-Type() -> tl2[j],
  .14               T           -> tl1[i]))
  .15        else exit) ) )

  .16  type: Range -> Surroundings -> Type
```

Annotations:

We state how, in general, to find the type of a range.
.3 Either both expressions must be integer literals in which case the type
   is the predefined integer type, or both
.4 expressions must be universal reals in which case the type is a pseudo-
   type (this is only relevant in membership expressions;  loop parameters
   must be of discrete types),
.12 or the available types must be extracted from one of the expressions in
    which  case  this  is the type of the range (if the other expression is
    compatible with that type).


L denotes  the Greek letter lambda:

```
14.0  get-check-fct(11)(12)(sur)= Li. Lj.cases (11[i],12[j]):
  .1  (mk-Type(name,,dsname, ),mk-Type(name2, ) ->
          is-Scalar(s-ds(lookup-unitname(dsname)(sur))) and
          name1=name2 ,
  .2   mk-Type(),mk-Pseudotype(val)               ->
          type-expr-compatibility(11[i])(val)(sur) ,
  .3   mk-Pseudotype(val),mk-Type()               ->
          type-expr-compatibility(12[j])(val)(sur) ,
  .4   mk-Pseudotype(v1),mk-Pseudotype(v2)        ->
          (is-INTG(v1) and is-INTG(v2)) or
          (is-NUM(v1) and is-NUM(v2))
  .5   T                                          -> false)

  .6   type: Type* -> Type* -> Surroundings ->
              ( INTG -> INTG -> BOOL)
```

Annotations:

"get-check-fct" is used in "extr-type-from-range" and  delivers  a  function
which checks if it is possible to extract a type of a range.

## 9.0  Names


### 9.1  Introduction

A name is perhaps the most interesting expression in Ada.  It is so  because
names  include  indexed  components,  selected  components,  slices, function
calls and de-referenced objects.  Futhermore functions can be overloaded and
can  return  values  in  which  components  can  be  indexed,  selected etc.
Therefore one must find all possible meanings of a  name,  corresponding  to
all possible overloaded function return values where slicing, selecting etc.
is possible.  Only if there is exactly one usable  meaning  in  the  context
where the name appears, the name is well-formed.
In this section we give the abstract syntax for Ada names and we show how to
lookup names in the dictionary.  We show the Meta-IV functions which handles
calls to overloaded Ada functions and the Meta-IV functions  which  "lookup"
selected  components.   The latter is particular interesting since it proves
easy to model, once having the hierarchical dictionary structure.
Finally we argue that the set of possible meanings of a name  is  a  synthesized attribute of parse trees generated for names.

We give the abstract syntax for names.  It is derived directly from the concrete (context-free) grammar.

```
Name             =  Simp-name | Index-component | Select-component |
                    Attr-name | Slice-name | All-name | Func-call

Simp-name        :: ( Designator | Char-lit )

Index-component  :: Name Expr+

Select-component:: Name Simp-name

Attr-name        :: Name Attr

Slice-name       :: Name Discrete-range

All-name         :: Name

Func-call        :: Name Act-param-list

Attr             =  Attr-id | Attr-fct

Attr-id          =  base | digits | first | last | .....

Attr-fct         =  Pos | Succ | Pred | Val | First | Last | ....

Pos              :: ( Id | Char-lit )
Succ             :: ( Id | Char-lit )
Pred             :: Id
Val              :: INTG
First            :: INTG
Last             :: INTG

Id               :: Token
Char-lit         :: Token
Designator       =  Id | Mop | Declarable-Dop
```

## 9.2  Looking up Names in The Dictionary

```
1.0 lookup-name(name)(sur) =
 .1 let dict = extract-dict(sur)                          in
 .2 cases name:
 .3 ( mk-Simp-name(id) ->
         if id E dom dict then <dict(id)> else <>        ,
     mk-Select-component() ->
         lookup-selected-component(name) (sur)           ,
 .7   .....
 .8  mk-Func-call()          ->
         lookup-available-function-result-descrs(name)(sur) )

.10 type : Name -> Surroundings -> Descr*
```

The function returns a list of possible descriptions of a name.
Types (and subtypes), objects (maybe constants), numbers, packages,  blocks,

and loops are described with their usual descriptors: Type-descr, ...
,Loop-descr.
For names denoting subprograms and/or enumeration literals an Overload-descr
is returned.
This is the way the model reflects that the name might have several possible
meanings.


## 9.3 Function Calls

For a name denoting a function-call the "meaning" is a value. This is modeled as an object-descriptor denoting a CONSTANT of the result type of the
function.
If the function is overloaded a list of possible returned object descriptors
is returned.
This list will contain more than one element if the given parameters match
the parameter requirements of more than one of the overloaded subprograms.
The possible meanings of function calls are extracted as follows:


```
2.0  lookup-available-funct-result-descrs(name) (sur) =
 .1  ( let mk-Func-call(name',act-parm-list) = name        in
 .2    let descrl = lookup-name(name')(sur)                 in
 .3    conc < cases descrl[i]:
 .4         ( mk-Overload-descr(ds)   ->
 .5              get-available-obj-list(act-parm-list)
 .6              ({d | d E ds and is-Subprgr-descr(d)})(sur),
 .7              T                         -> <> )
 .8           | i E ind descrl > )

 .9 type : Func-call -> Surroundings -> Obj-descr*
```


```
3.0  get-available-obj-list(parms)(pset)(sur)=
 .1  if pset = { } then <> else
 .2  let d E pset in
 .3  let mk-Subprgr-descr( ,,entrance) = d    in
 .4  ((if s-return(entrance) ≠ nil and
            parameter-checker(parms)(entrance)(sur)
 .5    then <mk-Obj-descr(s-return(entrance),CONSTANT)>
 .6    else <> )) ^
 .7    get-available-obj-list(parms)(pset\d)(sur) ) )

 .8 type : Act-parm* -> ( Subprgr-descr)-set ->Sur -> Obj-descr*
```


## Annotations:

If the name component of the function call denoted an overload-descr an explicitly constructed list of object descriptors is returned. An object des-

criptor (or value descriptor) is inserted in the list as many times as there are a function where the actual parameters match the formal parameters in the overloaded subprograms returning such objects (values of such types). (Note this list is a realization of a "bag").


## 9.4 Nested Subprogram Bodies

Where nested subprograms are overloaded there is the problem of identifying selected components in these subprograms if the components have the same identifiers.
In the following example F.X can mean Q.F.F.X as well as Q.F.X:


```
Q:declare
    function F(A:INT) return INT is
      X:INT;                          -- Q.F.X
      function F(B:BOOL) return BOOL is
        X,T:INT;                      -- Q.F.F.X
      begin
        T:= F.X                       -- which X?
        return true;
      end F;
    begin
      return 10;
    end F;
  begin
    null;
  end Q;
```


Which X - or in other words - which F (which of the overloaded functions) is meant ?
Whenever two or more meanings of a name - which is a selected component - are possible the name is ambiguous, hence illegal. This programming problem is due to overloading of nested subprograms and can always be solved by pre-fixing the name with the (unambiguous) name of the enclosing unit. It is easy to model that a selected component must always be uniquely identified, see "lookup-selected-component", line .8 .


## 9.5 Selected Components

We show how the list of possible meanings of a selected component is looked up:

```
4.0  lookup-selected-component(name)(sur) =
 .1  let mk-Select-component(prefix,mk-Simp-name(id))= name in
 .2  let descrl = lookup-name(prefix) (sur)                       in
 .3  conc < cases descrl[i] :
 .4         ( mk-Pack-descr(visdict,,,,, ) ->
 .5            if id E dom visdict then <visdict(id)> else <>,
 .6           mk-Overload-descr(ds)        ->
 .7             ( let sp = {mk-Sub-prgr-descr(ldict,, ) E ds|
                                          id E dom ldict} in
 .8               cases sp:
                  ({es} ->(let mk-Sub-prgr-descr(l,, )=
                                          es in<l(id)>),
                   T ->-<> )
 .9           mk-Obj-descr(typ,con) ->
 .10           (cases sel-ds(typ)(sur):
 .11           mk-Record(dis,compl) ->
 .12             (let rdict=flatten-record(dis,compl) in
 .13              if id E dom rdict then <rdict(id)+
                                     (s-const:->con)>
 .14                               else <> ) ,
 .15          mk-Access(fct, )     ->
 .16             (cases sel-ds(fct(s-dict(sur))):
 .17              (mk-Record(dis,compl) ->
 .18                 (let rdict=flatten-record(dis,compl)  in
 .19                  if id E dom rdict then <rdict(id)>
 .20                                   else <>            ),
 .21                    T                 ->-<> )),
 .22                 T                 -> <> ),
                  ...
 .23              T                        -> <>
 .24  | i E ind descrl >

 .25  type : Select-component -> Surroundings -> Descr*
```

## Annotations:

.6-8 See the example above. There may only be one such subprogram descrip-
     tor containing the named component in its dictionary of local identif-
     iers. Note, that only the descriptors of subprograms, whichs bodies
     surround the text point here, have a dectionary component, which is not
     empty.
.13 If a record object is a constant, its components must inherit this pro-
     perty.
.19 The accessed object is never a constant.
.23 You cannot select components in eg. types
.24 The order of the list is unspecified.


9.6  Possible Meanings of a Name

As names are checked for validity from left to right, bottom up, the list of
possible descriptors is a synthesized attribute of the parse tree eg.:

example: PACK1.F(B=>12).C

```
                                   name.descrlist :

                  name          <mk-Obj-descr(int,CONST),
                   |             mk-Obj-descr(real,CONST)>
            selected-component
           /      |       \
          name    .      id (=C)<mk-Obj-descr(rec1,CONST),
           |                     mk-Obj-descr(rec2,CONST)>
        function-call
       /      |      \    \
     name   ( parm-ass*  )       <mk-Overload-descr( .. )>
      /               \
  selected-component  (B => 12)
   /      \
name     id    (=F)             <mk-Pack-descr( .PACK1. )>
  /
simple-name
  |
 id  (= PACK1)
```

---

<u>Annotations:</u>

When the name (the root of the tree) is looked up its attribute "Descr-list"
may  contain two elements for example, the package PACK1 contained two overloaded functions named F, parameter A of the same integer type, both returning a record type, that contains elements with the name C.  The context must
then be used to determine which C-descriptors to "use".  If  the  list  contains more than one "usable" descriptor the name is illegal (ambiguous).  If
the descriptor-list is empty or contains no "usable" descriptors the name is
also illegal.

The abstraction of the "possible meaning" of a name must be a list (but  the
order of the elements is insignificant), not a set.  Consider two overloaded
subprograms returning values of exactly the same type:


type MY_RECORD is record MY_FIELD:MY_REAL;... end record;
function F(A:INT:=10,B:BOOL) return MY_RECORD;
function F(C:INT,D:BOOL) return MY_RECORD;
 ....

 ...   F(6,true).MY_FIELD ...  -- a name


In this case it is impossible to identify the  overloaded  subprogram.   The
possible meaning of the name is a list containing two identical

                  mk-Obj-descr('my-real-type',CONSTANT)

thus signifying that the name is ambiguous (this is called true ambiguity).

9.7  Predefined Attributes

Names can denote predefined attributes.  Attributes can be identifiers (eg.
MY_REALTYPE'DIGITS)           or           "functional           attributes"
(eg. MY_ARRAY_TYPE'FIRST(10) ).
The latter kind is not treated as function calls in the model since they are
much simpler (only one parameter which must be a value).
The meaning of an attribute is either a type-descr (eg.  MY_SUB_TYPE'BASE ),
or a value (an object-descriptor denoting a constant).

## 10.0  Statements


## 10.1  Introduction

The statements included in our model show usage of all parts of the surroundings, in particular the Status (which is a stack) component is used in
the checks of Loop-, Exit- and Return-statements. The dictionary of predefined operators is updated according to the types defined within the declarative part of the block. The check of procedure calls are similar to that
of function calls, but simpler. The If statement is at the present stage of
the model not really interesting but if labels and goto statement were considered it would be: eg. checking for jumps between its branches which is
not allowed.
The well-formedness of a compound statement or a statement list is expressed
as a function of the well-formedness of its constituent statements. The
order in which the constituent statements appear is insignificant.
Note, this was not the case in preliminary Ada, where labels were visible
from the point of their appearance and to the end of the statement list in
which they appeared. Note also, that we do not (so far) consider labels and
goto statements in this model.
As one will see in the following it is relativly easy to check
well-formedness of statements once the required dictionary and surroundings
information is available.


First we give the syntactic domains:


```
Stmt            =  Assign | Proc-call | Return | Block | Exit
                   Loop-stmt | If-stmt | null | ...
Assign          :: Name Expr
Proc-call       :: Name Act-param*
Return          :: [Expr]
Block           :: [Id] Declpart Stmt*
Loop-stmt       :: [Id] [Iteration-clause] Stmt*
Exit            :: [Name] [Expr]
If-stmt         :: Cond-stl+ [Stmt+]
   ...
```


1.0 is-wf-Stmt-list(stmtl)(sur) =
.1 (∀ stmt E elems stmtl) (is-wf-Stmt(stmt)(sur))

.2 type: Stmt* -> Surroundings -> BOOL
.3 pre : stmtl≠<> (syntactically there is at least one)

```
2.0  is-wf-Stmt(stmt)(sur) =
 .1  cases stmt:
 .2  (mk-Assign()        -> is-wf-Assign(stmt)(sur),
 .3   mk-Block()         -> ...
 .4   mk-Loop-stmt()     -> ...
 .5   mk-Exit()          -> ...
 .6   mk-Return()        -> ...
 .7   mk-Proc-call()     -> ...
 .8   mk-If-Stmt()       -> ...
 .9   ...
 .10  null               -> true)

 .11 type: Stmt -> Surroundings -> BOOL
```

## 10.2 Assignment Statement

The assignment statement is said to be well-formed, iff in the list of  possible meanings of the name component there is exactly one "meaning" denoting an object or component of a given type such that the expression is  compatible with that type.
Furthermore this single object (or component) may  not  denote  a  constant. The type of the object (or component) may not be limited private (or contain such components). The assignment statement is first checked  in  a  context where  only  the  strong visible identifiers are known. If this check fails another is made in a context where also the weakly visible  identifiers  are known.  If  one  of these checks is succesful the statement is well-formed. Otherwise it is not (see also 8.3).

```
3.0  is-wf-Assign(assign) (sur) =
 .1  (    half-check-Assign(assign)(STRONG)(sur)
 .2   or half-check-Assign(assign)(VISIBLE)(sur))

 .3 type: Assign -> Surroundings -> BOOL
```

## Annotations:

STRONG and VISIBLE indicates which set of identifiers that have to  be  used when  "checking  validity  /  extracting  possible  meanings"  of  the Name-components of the assignment statement.

```
4.0 half-check-Assign(mk-Assign(name,expr))(test)(sur) =
 .1 let testsur = cases test : ( STRONG -> sur+(s-wm:->[ ])
 .2                              T      -> sur)                    in
 .3 let descrl = look-up-name(name) (testsur)                     in
 .4 ( E! i E ind descrl )
 .5    (mk-Obj-descr(otype, )=descrl[i] and
 .6     type-expr-compatibility(otype)(expr)(sur) and
 .7     (let mk-Obj-descr(otype,const) E elems descrl be s.t.
 .8                  type-expr-compatibility(otype)(expr)(sur) in
 .9         const ≠ CONSTANT and is-not-limited(otype)))

 .10 type: Assign -> (STRONG|VISIBLE) -> Surroundings -> BOOL
```

## 10.3 Blocks

A block is as in Algol 60 a compound statement with the possibility to declare local items.

Block :: [Id] Decl-part Stmt+

Unlike packages it is not possible to select items declared inside the block
from outside the block, but if the block is named it is possible from inside
the block (as inside subprogram bodies) to use the identifier of the block
as a prefix in a selected component name. This means that inside a named
block the block acts as a package.
Because of the possibility to use the identifier of a block as a part of a
name it is necessary to have a description of blocks in the dictionary, and
according to the possibility to declare items inside a block the block descriptor must contain a (local) dictionary and the unitname of the block;
besides there must be a status for blocks containing a description of locally declared subprograms (as for packages).

We have the following static domains:

```
        Block-descr :: Dict Unitname
        In-block    :: s-defined-sub-prgr: Sub-prgr-set
```

But since there is the possibility to omit the block identifier, and since
the model requires a description of the block, we accept the quotation "BLK"
in the domain of the dictionary, hence the block :

```
    declare
        A:INTEGER;
    begin
        null;
    end;
```

would, when inside the block, appear in the dictionary as:

```
        [ BLK -> mk-Block-descr([A -> ...],< ...,BLK>) ]
```

```
5.0  is-wf-Block(mk-Block(id,mk-Decl-part(decll,bodyl),stmtl)(sur) =
 .1   trap exit with false in
 .2   (let id' = if id=nil then BLK else id        in
 .3    let presur=update-Sur([id'->
                        mk-Block-descr([],s-level(sur)^ <id'>)],
                        <id'>>,[],[],<mk-In-block({})>)(sur) in
 .4    let blocksur = get-Decl-part-Sur(decll^bodyl)(presur) in
 .5    let mk-In-block(subprgrs) = hd s-statusl(blocksur)    in
 .6   ( ~(E subprgr E subprgrs)(subprgr=mk-Sub-prgr( ,,nil)) and
 .7     is-wf-Stmt-list(stmtl)(blocksur) ))

 .8   type:Block -> Surroundings -> BOOL
```

## 10.4  Loop Statement

```
Loop-stmt       :: [Id] [Iteration-clause] stmt*
Iteration-clause = For-clause | While-clause
For-clause      :: Id Discr-range [reverse]
While-clause    :: Expr
```

If the loop statement contains an iteration clause which is a For-clause,
the loop parameter is implicitly declared as a constant object of a type extractable from the given range.

If the discrete range is in form of:

```
Range :: Expr Expr
```

the type extraction is a rather complicated affair. This is, of course, due
to the overloading resolving within the expression pair that constitutes the
range. In the model range types are extracted by the function
"extr-type-from-range" (see "membership-expression"). If the type is extractable from the range (which it must be), this type must be a discrete
type.
There are two interesting aspects of the loop statement: (1) Within the
loop the loop-parameter must be a visible identifier denoting a constant of
the range type. (2) The legality of exit statements within the loop must
be checkable. To fulfil (1) the dictionary is updated with a map from the
identifier of the loop parameter into a constant object descriptor of the
type of the range. To accomplish (2) the dictionary is updated with a map

from the loop identifier (or the quotation "LOOP" if the latter is not given) into a Loop descriptor:

$$Loop-descr :: Unitname$$

containing the unique name of the loop.  Exit statements

$$Exit :: [Name] \quad [Condition]$$

may name a loop if they occur within it.  To indicate that the statements of a loop is within a loop, the Status stack has the component:

$$In-loop :: Unitname$$

pushed onto the top.  The purpose of this is shown in the formulas that check exit statements.
These updatings of the surroundings are local to the loop;  thus outside the loop the loop parameter and the loop name are not referable.
We show how to check the well-formedness of the loop statement:
One should notice, that the iteration clause is elaborated in a context where the loop parameter is INTRODUCED as unusable.

```
6.0   is-wf-Loop(mk-Loop-stmt(lid,iteration,stmtl))(sur) =
 .1     let id = (lid=nil -> LOOP,T -> lid)                    in
 .2     let ldict = [id -> mk-Loop-descr(s-level(sur)^<id>] in
 .3     cases iteration:
 .4     (mk-For-clause(pid,discrrange) ->
 .5        (let presur = update-Sur-Dict([pid -> INTRODUCED)) in
 .6         let pdict  = [pid->generate-obj-descr-from-discr-rng
                                 (discrrange)(presur)]          in
 .7        check-loop(ldict+pdict)(stmtl)(id)(sur)) ,
 .8     mk-While-clause(condition)      ->
 .9        type-expr-compatibility(pre-def-bool-type())(condition)
                                    (update-Sur-dict(ldict)(sur) )
 .10       and check-loop(ldict)(stmtl)(id)(sur)             ,
 .11    nil                       ->
              check-loop(ldict)(stmtl)(id)(sur) )

 .12   type: Loop-stmt -> Surroundings -> BOOL
```

Before the statements of the loop can be checked, the status of the local surroundings of the loop must have a Loop descriptor pushed onto the top.
The static elaboration, or static check of a loop does not update the surroundings.

```
7.0 check-loop(loopdict)(stmtl)(id)(sur) =
 .1 let newsur=
        Update-sur(loopdict,,,mk-In-Loop(s-level(sur)^<id>)) in
 .2 (¥ stmt E elems stmtl)(is-wf-Stmt(stmt)(newsur))

 .3 type: Dict -> Stmt* -> Id -> Surroundings -> BOOL
```

We show how to generate the object decriptor for the loop parameter. If the
discrete  range is named by the type of the expression - the type in the object descriptor will simply be this type. Otherwise the type  is  extracted
from the expression.
The type component of the object descriptor of the loop parameter denotes  a
subtype.  Hence the datastructure component is nil.

```
8.0  generate-obj-descr-from-discr-rng(discr-range)(sur) =
 .1   cases discr-range:
 .2   ( mk-Named-discr-rng(name,range) ->
 .3      (let typ = lookup-structure-type(name)(sur) in
 .4       if is-Discrete(s-ds(typ)) and
 .5       range ≠ nil =>  type-range-compatible(typ)(range)(sur)
 .6       then mk-Obj-descr(typ+(s-ds:->nil),CONSTANT)
 .7       else exit) ,
 .8    mk-Range(ex1,ex2) ->
 .9      (let typ =extr-type-from-range(discr-range)(sur) in
 .10      if is-Discrete(s-ds(typ))
 .11        then mk-Obj-descr(typ+(s-ds:->nil),CONSTANT))
 .12        else exit)))

 .13 type: Discrete-range -> Surroundings ~-> Obj-descr
```

## 10.5  Exit Statement

Exit statements can be checked rather straightforward:

$$\text{Exit :: [Name] [Condition]}$$

```
9.0   is-wf-Exit(mk-Exit(loopname,condition))(sur) =
 .1   condition ≠ nil =>
               type-expr-compatibility(pre-def-bool-type())
                                       (condition) (sur)        and
 .2   (name ≠ nil  ->
               cases lookup-name(name)(sur):
               (mk-Loop-descr(unitname) ->
                       check-transfer(unitname)(s-status(sur)),
                 T              -> false),
         T              -> check-transfer(nil)(s-status(sur)))

      type:Exit -> Surroundings -> BOOL
```

## Annotations:

An exit statement is well-formed if the condition is either nil or it is  an
expression of the predefined boolean type.  Furthermore if the name is given
it must uniquely name a loop.   Whether  the  name  is  given  or  not,  the
transfer out of loops must satisfy some conditions.

```
10.0   check-transfer(loopname)(statuslist) =
  .1         if statuslist = <> then false else
  .2           cases hd statuslist:
  .3           (mk-In-Pack-body() -> false,
  .4            mk-In-Task-body() -> false,
  .5            mk-In-Subprgr()   -> false,
  .6            mk-In-Loop(name)  ->
  .7                  (loopname=name or loopname=nil or
  .8                     check-transfer(loopname)(tl statuslist) ),
  .9            T -> check-transfer(loopname)(tl statuslist))

  .10   type: Unitname -> Status* -> BOOL
```

## Annotations:

.1 an exit is illegal if there is no enclosing loop construct
.3 if it transfers control out of a package body,
.4 task body or
.5 subprogram body.
.6 an exit is legal when it mentions a loop name and that loop is  enclosing, or it mentions no loop name , and a loop is enclosing
.7 .8 exits may transfer control out of blocks and nested loops

10.6  Return Statement

A return statement must not transfer control out of a package body or a task
body.
A return statement transfers control out of a subprogram body, and  must  in
case  of  a function subprogram contain an expression of the function result
type.
In case of a procedure subprogram, the return statement must not contain any
expression.

Return :: [Expr]

We show how to check these rules, using the status stack  component  of  the
surroundings.

11.0  is-wf-Return(mk-Return(expr))(sur) =
.1   trap exit with false in
.2   (let mk-In-Subprgr(rtype)=
              get-subprgr-status(s-status(sur)) in
.3   (rtype=nil -> expr=nil,
.4   T            -> type-expr-compatibility(rtype)(expr)(sur)))

.5 type : Return -> Surroundings -> BOOL

12.0  get-sub-prgr-status(statuslist)=
.1   if statuslist=<> then exit else
.2   cases hd statuslist:
.3   (mk-In-Pack-body() -> exit,
.4    mk-In-Task-body() -> exit,
.5    mk-In-Subprgr()   -> hd statuslist,
.6    T                 -> get-sub-prgr-status(tl statuslist))

.7 type : Status* ~-> In-Subprgr

.6 this case corresponds to exit a loop or a block with a return statement.

## 10.7  The Procedure Call Statement

The manual states that overloading of function subprograms within expressions must be unambiguously resolvable either (1) when neglecting use-clauses (in the model: exclude the weak visible identifiers from the domain of the visible dictionary), (2) when obeying the effect of use-clauses.
Nothing like this is said about procedure subprogram overloading resolving within procedure calls so we assume no special rules here. The procedure call must be well-formed within a context, where strong as well as weak visible identifiers are referable.


```
13.0  is-wf-Proc-call(mk-Proc-call(name,act-parml))(sur) =
  .1  cases lookup-name(name)(sur):
  .2  ( <mk-Overload-descr(dset)>  ->
  .3      ( E! mk-Subprgr-descr( ,,entrance) E dset)
  .4        (s-return(entrance) = nil and
  .5           Parameterchecker(act-parml)(entrance)(sur) ) ,
  .6    T                            -> false)

  .7  type: Proc-call -> Surroundings -> BOOL
```


## Annotations:

  .0 A procedure call is well-formed in its context
  .1 if the given name
  .2 uniquely denotes a set of overloaded subprograms
  .3 in which there is exactly one
  .4 procedure
  .5 where the actual parameters match the formal parameters


## 10.8  If Statement

```
      If-stmt      ::  Cond-stl+ [Stmt+]
      Cond-stl     ::  Expr  Stmt+
```

The if statement is checked in the following way:
All the conditions must be wellformed boolean expressions - besides all the statements must be wellformed.

```
14.0  is-wf-If-stmt(mk-If-stmt(list,last))(sur) =
  .1  (∀ mk-Cond-stl(condition,stl) ∈ elems list)
  .2    (type-expr-compatibility(predef-bool-type())
                              (condition)(sur)
  .3    and is-wf-Stmt-list(stl)(sur)) and
  .4  (last≠nil => is-wf-Stmt-list(last)(sur))

  .5  type: If-stmt -> Surroundings -> BOOL
```

## 11.0  Remaining Work


### 11.1  Introduction

In this section we outline how to complete the formal definition af Ada context conditions.  We discuss the design of a tree-building parser and the
specification af a context condition checker. We give  the  characteristics
of intermediate languages which will be the output of these functions.
Finally we summarise the aspects of Ada which  is  not  covered  by  the  A6
language  and  the aspects of A6 which is not fully elaborated in the formulae.


### 11.2  The Parser Specification

We give a specification of a function which can transform concrete Ada  programs  into an abstract tree otherwise described by the abstract syntax AS1.
This function may be implemented using, as the first part, a  table  driven,
error  correcting  parser which produces a (parse) tree. Having an abstract
syntax AS0 for such parse trees, we can specify the second  part  (ie.  the
AS0  -> AS1 transforming function) in Meta-IV also.  We show the ideas using
the loop statement and the infix expressions as examples. We note that  all
kinds  of  "syntactic sugar" has disappeared from programs conforming to AS1
syntax.  Likewise operator hierarchy has been resolved.


"BNF" :

```
Loop-stmt    ::= [loop-id :] [iteration-clause] [basic-loop] [loop-id];
basic-loop   ::= loop sequence-of-statements end loop
iteration-clause ::=
                 for loop-parm in [reverse] discrete-range
               | while condition
    ...
```

"AS0" :

```
Loop-stmt         :: [Id] [Iteration-clause] Stmt+ [Id]
Iteration-clause  :: For-clause  |  While-clause
For-clause        :: Id [REVERSE] Discrete-rng
While-clause      :: Expression
Expression        :: Relation ( (and|or|.. ) Relation )*
Relation          :: Simp-expr [(=|>|.. ) Simp-expr ]
Simp-expr         :: [(+|-)] Term ((+|-|&|.. ) Term )*
Term              :: ...
```


The parser specification is a function, which transforms AS0-programs  into
equivalent  programs,  conforming  to  a new syntax "AS1", better suited for
Context Condition Checking.  The operator hierarchy is resolved:

"AS1" :

```
Loop-stmt          :: [Id] [Iteration-clause] Stmt+ [Id]
Iteration-clause   :: For-clause  |  While-clause
For-clause         :: Id Discreteirng [REVERSE]
While-clause       :: Expr
Discrete-rng       :: Named-discr-rng | Range
Named-discr-rng    :: Name [ Range ]
Range              :: Expr Expr
Expr               = Infix | Prefix | ...
Infix              :: Expr  Dop  Expr
Prefix             ::       Mop  Expr
Mop                = + | - | ...
Dop                = + | - | & | ...
```

We outline the transformation function:

```
1.0 transform(as0-expr) =
 .1 cases as0-expr:
 .2 (mk-Expression(relation, rel-list) ->
 .3    (rel-list = <> -> transform(relation),
 .4     T             ->
 .5       (let (op,next) = hd rel-list                        in
 .6         mk-Infix(transform(relation, op,
 .7                  transform(mk-Expression(next,
 .8                                          tl rel-list))))),
 .9  mk-Relation(simp-left,right)      ->
 .10    (right = nil   -> transform(simple-left),
 .11     T             ->
 .12       (let (op,simp-right) = right                        in
 .13         mk-Infix(transform(simple-left),op,
 .14                  transform(simp-right)))),
 .15 mk-Simple(mop,term,term-list)     ->
 .16    (let t1 = transform(term)                              in
 .17     let e1 = cases mop: (nil->t1,T->mk-Prefix(mop,t1)     in
 .18     cases term-list:
 .19     (<> -> e1,
 .20      T  -> (let (op,next-term) = hd termlist              in
 .21             mk-Infix(e1,op,
 .22                transform(mk-Simple(nil,next-term,
 .23                                    tl term-list)))))),
 .24 mk-Term( ... )                    -> ... ,
 .25 ...                                                       )

 .26 type: (Expression | Relation | Simple | Term |... ) -> Expr
```

## 11.3  The Context Condition Checker Specification

This specification is derived from the well-formedness predicate  functions, and specifies equivalent well-formedness predicates as well as the "rebuild-ing" of AS1 programs into equivalent programs conforming to an abstract syn-tax  AS2,  better suited for dynamic semantics (ie.  intrepertation and com-piling algorithm specification).  A complete definition of Ada AS2 is  given in  [StPe 80]  and  [Do 80].   AS2-programs are different from corresponding AS1's.  All static checks are performed, overloading is resolved, predefined and  user  defined  operators are identified, the type of each expression is determined and unique identifiers are substituted  for  all  occourences  of names.   Futhermore each block and body contain relevant dictionary informa-tion which is used when the local environment is established.  The  diction-ary  information  is  much  simpler  than the informations needed to perform static checks.  Again we use the loop statement as example:

"AS2" :

```
Loop'               :: [Id] (Uncond-loop ¦ While-loop ¦ For-loop)
Uncond-loop         :: Stmt'+
While-loop          :: Expr' Stmt'+
For-loop            :: Id [REVERSE] Discr-rng' Stmt'+
Discr-rng'          :: Type-id [ Range' ]
Type-id             = Id
```

We show how the AS1 Loop-stmt is rebuilded to an AS2 Loop:

```
 2.0 rebuild-loop-stmt(mk-Loop-stmt(lid,itcl,stlist,elid))(sur) =
  .1 (lid ≠ elid -> exit, T -> let id = (lid=nil->LOOP,T->lid)) in
  .2 let loop-dict = [id->mk-Loop-descr(s-level(sur)^<id>)]      in
  .3 mk-Loop'((lid=nil->nil,T->mk-Id(s-level(sur)^<lid>)),
        cases itcl:
  .4    (nil  ->
  .5       mk-Uncond-loop(rebuild-loop(loop-dict)(stlist)(id)(sur),
  .6
  .7    mk-For-clause(pid,discr-rng,reverse) ->
  .8       (let presur = update-sur-dict([pid->INTRODUCED](sur) in
  .9        let discr-rng'= rebuild-discr-rng(discr-rng)(presur)in
  .10       let pdict =
  .11         [pid->mk-Obj-descr(get-tp(discr-rng'),CONSTANT)] in
  .12       mk-For-loop(pid,reverse,discr-rng',
  .13          rebuild-loop(loop-dict+pdict)(stlist)(id)(sur)  )),
  .14
  .15   mk-While-clause(expr)    ->
  .16      (let xsur = update-sur-dict(loop-dict)(sur)              in
  .17       let expr'= rebuild-expr(expr)(BOOL)(xsur)          in
  .18       mk-While-loop(expr',
  .19          rebuild-loop(loop-dict)(stlist)(id)(sur) ))     ))

  .20 type: Loop-stmt -> Surroundings -> ~-> Loop'
```

```
3.0  rebuild-loop(ldict)(stlist)(lid)(sur) =
 .1  let local-sur =
 .2      update-sur(ldict,,,mk-In-Loop(s-level(sur)^<lid>)) in
 .3      rebuild-stmt-list(stmtlist)(local-sur)

 .4  type: Dict -> Stmt+ -> (Id|LOOP) -> Surroundings~-> Stmt'+


4.0  rebuild-stmt-list(stlist)(sur) =
 .1  if stlist = <> then <> else
 .2      rebuild-statement(hd stlist)(sur) ^
 .3      rebuild-stmt-list(tl stlist)(sur)

 .4  type: Stmt* -> Surroundings ~-> Stmt'*
```


## 11.4  From A6 to Ada

The aspects of Ada not covered by A6 are:

Separate compilation, generics, exception handlers, task types, task specifications, task bodies. Renaming declaration, exception declaration and labels. Representation specification and pragma. Case statement, entry call
statement, accept-, select-, delay-, and abort statement, goto statement and
code statement. Static expression evaluation.
Except for generics, the above mentioned declarations and statements are  to
be considered as variations over well-elaborated themes.


The formulas of A6, which has not been completed, are:

Checking compatibility of aggregates and  strings with  record- and  array
types.  Checking  that discriminant declarations are repeated properly with
the full declaration of a private type with discriminants.  Checking  that
parameter  default  values  are repeated properly with the body of a forward
declared subprogram.

132

## 12.0 Index to Formulas

APPENDIX A

CONTENTS
--------

## 1.0  Syntactic domains for A6

### 1.1  Compilations

```
Program        :: s-predef:   Decl-part
                  s-library:  Library
                  s-comp:     Compilation

Compilation    =  Comp-unit*
Comp-unit      :: Context* Body
Context        :: s-with:Id-set   s-use: [Use-clause]
Body           =  Pack-spec | Pack-body | Sub-prgr-spec |
                  Sub-prgr-body

Pack-spec      :: Id Decl-item* s-private:Decl-item*

Pack-body      :: Id Decl-part Stmt*

Sub-prgr-spec  :: Designator Parm-decl* s-ret:[Subtype-indic]

Sub-prgr-body  :: Sub-prgr-spec Decl-part Stmt*
```

### 1.2  Simple names

```
Id             :: Token

Char-lit       :: Token

Designator     =  Id | Mop | Declarable-Dop
```

### 1.3  Declarations

```
Decl-part      :: Decl-item* Body*

Decl-item      =  Use-clause | Declaration

Use-clause     :: Name-set

Declaration    =  Obj-decl | Const-decl | Numb-decl | Type-decl
                  | Sub-type-decl | Sub-prgr-spec | Pack-spec
```

```
Obj-decl          :: s-idl: Id+ Type-expr  s-init: [Expr]

Const-decl        :: s-idl: Id+ Type-expr  s-init: [Expr]

Type-expr         =  Subtype-indic | Array-td

Numb-decl         :: s-idl: Id+ Expr

Type-decl         :: Id Type-def

Sub-type-decl     :: Id Subtype-indic

Parm-decl         :: Id+ [Mode] Subtype-indic [Expr]

Mode              =  in | inout | out

Type-def          =  Enum-td | Intg-td | Float-td | Fixed-td |
                     Array-td | Record-td | Access-td
                     | Derived-td | Private-td

Subtype-indic     :: Name [Constraint]
```

## 1.4  Constraints & Ranges

```
Constraint        =  Range-constr | Index-constr | Discrim-constr
                     | Float-constr | Fixed-constr

Range-constr      :: Range

Index-constr      :: Discrete-range+

Discrim-constr    :: s-pos:Expr* s-named:( Id Expr )*

Float-constr      :: Expr [Range-constr]

Fixed-constr      :: Expr [Range-constr]

Range             :: Expr Expr

Discrete-range    =  Named-discr-rng | Range

Named-discr-rng   :: Name [Range]
```

## 1.5  Type definitions

```
Enum-td           :: ( Id | Char-lit )+

Integer-td        :: Range-constr

Float-td          :: Float-constr
```

```
Fixed-td          :: Fixed-constr

Array-td          :: ( Discrete-range+ | Index+ ) Subtype-indic

Record-td         :: Discrim-decl* Comp-list

Discrim-decl      =  Obj-decl

Comp-list         :: Obj-decl* [Variant-part]

Variant-part      :: Id ( s-chl:Choice+  s-compl:Comp-list )*
                                         s-oth: [Comp-list]

Choice            =  Expr | Discrete-range

Index             :: s-name: Name

Access-td         :: [Subtype-indic]

Derived-td        :: Subtype-indic

Private-td        :: [Discrim-decl+] [limited]
```

## 1.6  Statements

```
Stmt              =  Assign | Proc-call | Return | Block | Exit
                     Loop-stmt | If-stmt | null

Assign            :: Name Expr

Proc-call         :: Name Act-param-list

Act-param-list    :: s-pos:Expr* s-named:( Id Expr )*

Return            :: [Expr]

Block             :: [Id] Declpart Stmt+

Loop-stmt         :: [Id] [Iteration-clause] Stmt+

Iteration-clause  =  For-clause | While-clause

For-clause        :: Id Discrete-range [reverse]

While-clause      :: Expr

Exit              :: [Name] [Expr]

If-stmt           :: Cond-stl+ [Stmt+]

Cond-stl          :: Expr Stmt+
```

## 1.7  Names

```
Name              =  Simp-name | Index-component | Select-component
                     | Attr-name | Slice-name | All-name | Func-call

Simp-name         :: ( Designator | Char-lit )

Index-component   :: Name Expr+

Select-component  :: Name Simp-name

Attr-name         :: Name Attr

Slice-name        :: Name Discrete-range

All-name          :: Name

Func-call         :: Name Act-param-list

Attr              =  Attr-id | Attr-fct

Attr-id           =  base | digits | first | last | .....

Attr-fct          =  Pos | Succ | Pred | Val | First | Last | ....

Pos               :: ( Id | Char-lit )

Succ              :: ( Id | Char-lit )

Pred              :: Id

Val               :: INTG

First             :: INTG

Last              :: INTG
```

## 1.8  Expressions

```
Expr              =  Infix | Prefix | Primary | Membership

Primary           =  Name | Qualif-expr | Type-conv | Aggregate |
                     Allocator | Literal

Composite-expr    =  Aggregate | Allocator | String

Literal           =  INTG | NUM | null | Char-lit | String

Type-conv         :: Name Expr

Qualif-expr       :: Name Expr

Infix             :: Expr Dop Expr
```

```
Prefix          :: Mop Expr

Aggregate       :: (Positional-list | Named-list) s-others:[Expr]

Positional-list =  Expr+

Named-list      =  ( Choice+ Expr )+

Allocator       :: Name [ Expr | Discrim-constr | Index-constr ]

String          =  Char-lit*

Membership      :: Expr ( Range | Subtype-indic ) [not]
```

## 1.9  Operators

```
Operator        =  Mop | Dop

Mop             =  + | - | not

Dop             =  Declarable-Dop | andthen | orelse | /=

Declarable-Dop  =  = | < | <= | > | >= | and | or
                   | xor | + | - | & | * | / | mod
                   | rem | **
```

## 2.0  Static domains for A6

### 2.1  Surroundings

```
Surroundings    :: s-dict    : Dict
                   s-level   : Unitname
                   s-wm      : Weak-map
                   s-opmap   : Operator-dict
                   s-status  : Status*

Dict            = Dict-entry m-> Descr

Weakmap         :: Unitname m-> Dict

Operator-dict   = Operator m-> Overload-descr

Status          = In-Vis-Pack | In-Priv-Pack | In-Pack-body |
                  In-Sub-prgr | In-Block | In-Loop

Dict-entry      = Id | Char-lit | Operator | BLK | LOOP
```

### 2.2  Descriptors

```
Descr           = Obj-descr | Numb-descr | Type-descr | Pack-descr |
                  Overload-descr | Block-descr | Loop-descr |
                  INTRODUCED | COMPONENT | nil

Obj-descr       :: s-tp: Type    s-con: [CONSTANT]

Numb-descr      :: ( INTG | NUM )

Type-descr      :: s-tp: Type    s-attr: Attributes

Pack-descr      :: s-vis      : Dict
                   s-priv     : Dict
                   s-name     : Unitname
                   s-wm       : Weak-map
                   s-sub-prgr : Sub-prgr-set
                   s-opmap    : Operator-dict

Overload-descr  :: ( Sub-prgr-descr | Literal-descr )-set

Block-descr     :: Dict Unitname
```

```
Loop-descr       ::        Unitname

Literal-descr    :: Type

Sub-prgr-descr   :: Dict    Unitname    s-entr:Entrance

Entrance         :: Parm-descr* s-return:[Type] [OP|PREDEF-OP]

Parm-descr       :: s-idl:Id+ Mode Type [Reb-sub-type] [Reb-expr]

Attributes       =  Designator  m-> Unitname-set

Unitname         =  ( Designator | Char-lit | N1 | BLK | LOOP )*
```

## 2.3  Types

```
Pseudotype       :: ( NUM | INTG )

Type             :: s-name      : Unitname
                    s-parent    : Unitname
                    s-structure : Unitname
                    s-ds        : [Datastructure]
                    s-sub       : Substructure
                    s-lim       : [PRIVATE | LIMITED]

Datastructure    = Scalar | Record | Array | Access | EMPTY

Scalar           = Discrete | FIXED | FLOAT | univ-fixed

Discrete         = ENUM | BOOL | INTG | any-integer

Numeric          = INTG | FIXED | FLOAT

Record           :: s-discrim:[Discrim-descr] s-compl:Compl-descr

Discrim-descr    :: s-obj-map: Id m-> Obj-descr
                    s-order   : Id <-m-> N1
                    s-init    : [INIT] [Rebuild-item+]

Compl-descr      :: s-obj-map : Id m-> Obj-descr
                    s-order    : Id <-m-> N1
                    s-var-part:[Var-part-descr]

Var-part-descr   :: Id ( OTH | VAL-set ) m-> Compl-descr

VAL              = ...

Array            :: Type+ Obj-descr

Access           :: Dict ~-> Type  s-com:(COMPLETE | INCOMPLETE)

Substructure     = Enum | Intg | Fixed | Float | Array-sub |
                   Record-sub | ACCESS-SUB | PRIVATE-SUB
```

```
Enum            :: ( Id | Char-lit )*  s-static: [STATIC]

Intg            :: INTG INTG    s-static: [STATIC]

Fixed           :: s-delta: NUM

Float           :: s-digits: INTG

Record-sub      :: s-lock: [DISCRIM-LOCK]

Array-sub       :: s-lock: [INDEX-LOCK]
```

## 2.4  Status

```
In-Pack-spec    :: s-defined-types:    Unitname-set
                   s-defined-sub-prgr: Sub-prgr-set

In-Pack-body    :: s-defined-sub-prgr: Sub-prgr-set

In-Sub-prgr     :: s-defined-sub-prgr: Sub-prgr-set

In-Block        :: s-defined-sub-prgr: Sub-prgr-set

In-Loop         :: s-loopname:         Unitname

Sub-prgr        :: Unitname  s-entr:Entrance  s-body:[BODY]
```

## 2.5  Pre-check domains

```
Pre-decl        =  Body | Decl-item | Pre-item

Pre-item        =  Pre-literal | Pre-block | Pre-loop

Pre-literal     :: (Designator | Char-lit)

Pre-block       :: Id

Pre-loop        :: Id
```

## 2.6  Other domains

```
Type-def-usage  =  ( TYPE ◁ COMPONENT )

Record-level    =  [IN-RECORD]

Discrim-map     =  Id m-> Obj-descr

Rebuild-item    :: Reb-sub-type | Reb-Expr | Reb-Range
```

```
Reb-sub-type    =  Reb-Range

Reb-Expr        :: ...

Reb-Range       :: s-tp: Unitname Reb-Expr Reb-Expr


Library         =  Id m-> Libinfo

Libinfo         =  Pack-info | Sub-prgr-info

Pack-info       :: Pack-descr Operator-dict

Sub-prge-info   :: Overload-descr
```

## 3.0  Formulae


### 3.1  Surroundings & Dictionary

```
.0 update-sur-dict(extention)(sur) =
.1 sur + (s-dict:d -> extend(d)(s-level(sur))(extention))

.2 type: Dict -> Surroundings -> Surroundings
```


```
.0 update-sur(dext,lext,wext,oext,stext)(sur)=
.1 sur + (s-dict:   d  -> extend(d)(s-level(sur))(dict),
.2        s-level:  l  -> l ^ lext,
.3        s-wm:     w  -> w + wext,
.4        s-opmap:  o  -> overload(o)(oext),
.5        s-status: sa -> stext ^ sa)

.6 type: (Dict Unitname Weak-map Operator-dict Status*) ->
         (Surroundings -> Surroundings)
```


```
.0 extract-strong-dict(sur) =
.1    extract-dict(sur+(s-wm:->[]))

.2 type: Surroundings  -> Dict
```


```
.0 extract-dict(mk-Surroundings(dict,level,wkmap,opdict,sta)) =
.1  overload( overload(opdict)(weak-merge(wkmap)) )
.2          ( flatten(dict)(level)                 )

.3 type: Surroundings  -> Dict
```

```
.0 extend(dict)(level)(extention) =
.1 if level=<> then overload(dict)(extention)
.2 else (let id=hd level in
.3        if id ~E dom dict then /*error in this model */ else
.4           dict + [id -> cases dict(id):
.5        (mk-Pack-descr(visdict,d,u,w,sp,o) ->
.6            mk-Pack-descr(extend(visdict)(tl level)(extention),
                               d,u,w,sp,o)                        ,
.7         mk-Block-descr(localdict,u)           ->
.8            mk-Block-descr(extend(localdict)(tl level)(extention),u),
.9         mk-Overload-descr(descr-set)    ->
.10           (let descr E descr-set be s.t.
.11            (descr=mk-Sub-prgr-descr(localdict,name,e) and
.12             name[ln name] = hd (tl level))                in
.13            mk-Overload-descr(descr-set\descr +
.14              mk-Sub-prgr-descr(extend(localdict)(tl tl level)
.15                                         (extention),name,e),
.16       T -> /* error in this model */ ] )

.17 type: Dict -> Unitname -> Dict -> Dict
```

```
.0 flatten(dict)(level) =
.1 if ~ (E id E dom dict) (is-enclosing(dict|{id})(level))
.2   then dict
.3   else (let id E dom dict be s.t. is-enclosing(dict|{id})(level) in
.4         let next-dict = cases dict(id):
.5            (mk-Pack-descr(visdict,,,,, )  -> visdict,
.6             mk-Block-descr(localdict, )   -> localdict,
.7             mk-Overload-descr(descr-set)  ->
.8                (let mk-Sub-prgr-descr(ld,un, ) E descr-set
.9                    be s.t. level=un or
.10                            is-enclosing(ld)(level) in
.11                ld ) ,
.12            T -> /* this function called illegal in this model */) in
.13       overload(dict)(flatten(next-dict)(level)))

.14 type: Dict -> Unitname -> Dict
```

```
.0 is-enclosing(dict)(searchname) =
.1 (E id E dom dict)
.2   (cases dict(id):
.3     (mk-Pack-descr(visdict,,packname,,, )         ->
.4        packname=searchname or is-enclosing(visdict)(searchname) ,
.5      mk-Block-descr(localdict,blockname)         ->
.6        blockname=searchname or is-enclocing(localdict)(searchname),
.7      mk-Overload-descr(descr-set)              ->
.8        (E mk-Sub-prgr-descr(ldict,subname, ) E descr-set)
.9         (subname=searchname or is-enclosing(ldict)(searchname))
.10     T -> false))

.11 type: Dict -> Unitname -> BOOL
```

```
.0 overload(dict)(extension) =
.1 [id ->
.2   (id E dom dict and id E dom extension ->
.3      cases( dict(id),extension(id)):
.4      ((mk-Overload-descr(set1),mk-Overload-descr(set2)) ->
.5            mk-Overload-descr({ spd E Sub-prgr-descr |
.6                  spd E set2 or
.7                  (spd E set1 s.t.
.8                  (¥ spd' E set2)
.9                  (is-overloadable(s-entr(spd))(s-entr(spd'))))}
.10                U { ltd E Literal-descr |
.11                          ltd E set1 or ltd E set2 } ),
.12      T    -> extension(id) ),
.13   id E dom dict       -> dict(id) ,
.14   id E dom extension -> extension(id) )
.15 | id E dom dict U dom extension ]

.16 type: Dict -> ( Dict -> Dict )
```

```
.0 weak-merge(weakmap) =
.1 (let double-non-overloadable-ids =
.2   {id|(E n1,n2 E dom weakmap)
.3   (n1≠n2 and
.4    let d1 = weakmap(n1), d2 = weakmap(n2)   in
.5    (id E dom d1 and id E dom d2    and
.6    ~(is-Overload-descr(d1(id)) and is-Overload-descr(d2(id)))))
.7                                                } in
.8 let new-wm = [ n -> weakmap(n)\double-non-overloadable-ids
.9              | n E dom weakmap ]                        in
.10 let map-of-ovl-dsc =
.11    [id -> mk-Overload-descr(set1) |
.12    (¥ ds1,ds2 E set1)
.13    ((is-Literal-descr(ds1) or
.14    ((ds1 ≠ ds2 and is-Sub-prgr-descr(ds1) and
.15                     is-Sub-prgr-descr(ds2)   ) =>
.16     is-overloadable(s-entr(ds1))(s-entr(ds2))         )
.17    and
.18    (E n E new-wm)( id E new-wm(n) and
.19                     cases (new-wm(n))(id):
.20                     (mk-Overload-descr(set2) -> ds1 E set2,
.21                      T                        -> false   ) in
.22 merge( ldict \ dom map-of-ovl-dsc | ldict E rng new-wm )
.23 U map-of-ovl-dsc)

.24 type: Weak-map -> Dict
```

```
.0 is-overloadble(entr1)(entr2) =
.1 let mk-Entrance(pdl1,ret1,op1 ) = convert(entr1),
.2     mk-Entrance(pdl2,ret2, ) = convert(entr2)     in
.3   ~ ( ln pdl1 = ln pdl2  and
.4        (∀ i ∈ ind pdl1)
.5        (let mk-Parm-descr(<id1>,,type1, ) = pdl1[i] ,
.6             mk-Parm-descr(<id2>,,type2, ) = pdl2[i] in
.7        (s-name(type1) = s-name(type2) and
.8         ~(ret1=nil xor ret2=nil)          and
.9         ret1 ≠ nil => (s-name(ret1)=s-name(ret2)) and
.10        op1=nil     => (id1=id2) )))

.11 type: Entrance -> Entrance -> BOOL
```

```
.0 convert(mk-Entrance(pdl,rtntype,operetor)) =
.1 mk-Entrance(conc <<mk-Parm-descr(<idl[i]>,nil,ptype,nil,nil) |
.2                    1<= i <= ln idl > |
.3                    1<= j <= ln pdl and
.4                    pdl[j]=mk-Parm-descr(idl,,ptype, ) > ,
.5            rtntype,operator)

.6 type: Entrance -> Entrance
```

```
.0 lookup-unitname(unitname)(hdict) =
.1 let descr = hdict(hd unitname) in
.2 if tl unitname=<> then descr else
.3 cases descr:
.4 (mk-Pack-descr(visdict,,,,, )    ->
.5    lookup-unitname(tl unitname)(visdict),
.6 mk-Block-descr(localdict, )      ->
.7    lookup-unitname(tl unitname)(localdict),
.8 mk-Sub-prgr-descr(localdict,, ) ->
.9    lookup-unitname(tl unitname)(localdict),
.10 mk-Overload-descr(dset)          ->
.11   (let mk-Sub-prgr-descr(localdict,name, ) ∈ dset be s.t.
.12     (<name[i] | ln name - 1 <= i <= ln name> =
.13       <unitname[i] | 1 <= i <= 2> )                in
.14    lookup-unitname(tl unitname)([name[ln name] -> d])))

.15 type: Unitname -> Dict -> Dict
```

let <u>L</u> denote the greek letter lambda <u>in</u>

```
.0 lookup-base-type(btype)(sur) =
.1 let ds = sel-ds(btype)(sur) in
.2 btype + (s-ds:-> cases ds:
.3         (mk-Access(fct,compl)->
.4            mk-Access(Ld.lookup-base-type(fct(d))
.5                         (sur+(s-dict:->d))),compl) ,
.6         T -> ds) ,
.7       s-sub:-> cases ds:
.8       (mk-Array()  -> nil,
.9        mk-Record() -> nil,
.10       T            -> s-sub(btype))  )
```

.11 <u>type</u>: Type -> Surroundings -> Type

```
.0 lookup-local-dict(sur) =
.2 cases lookup-unitname(s-level(sur))(s-dict(sur)):
.2 (mk-Pack-descr(visdict,,,,, )      -> visdict,
.3  mk-Block-descr(localdict, )       -> localdict,
.4  mk-Sub-prgr-descr(localdict,, )  -> localdict)
```

.5 <u>type</u>: Surroundings -> Dict

```
.0 sel-ds(stype)(sur)=
.1 s-ds(s-tp(lookup-unitname(s-structure(stype))(s-dict(sur))))
```

.2 <u>type</u>: Type -> Surroundings -> Datastructure

## 3.2 Compilation Units

```
.0 compile(mk-Program(declpart,lib,complist))=
.1 trap exit with PROGRAM-IN-ERROR                              in
.2 (~pre-check-Decl-part(<>,<>,<s-body(complist[i])|
.3                                 1<=i<= len complist>) -> exit,
.4  T                                                    ->
.5   (let sur1=get-Decl-part-sur(declpart)(generate-predefined-sur()) in
.6     extend-library(lib,insert-context(<>,[],complist))(sur1)

.7 type: Program ~-> Library
```

```
.0 insert-context(head,cmap,tail)=
.1 if tail=<> then head else
.2 (let mk-Comp-unit(con,body)=hd tail in
.3 cases body:
.4 (mk-Pack-spec(id,, ),
.5  mk-Sub-prgr-spec(id,, )                  ->
.6    (insert-context(head^<hd tail>,cmap U[id->con],tl tail)),
.7  mk-Pack-body(id,, )                       ->
.8    (let con'=cmap(id) in
.9      if con≠nil => con=con'
.10       then insert-context(head^<mk-Comp-unit(con',body)>,
.11                     cmap, tl tail )
.12      else exit ),
.13 mk-Sub-prgr-body(mk-Sub-prgr-spec(id,, ) ->
.14    (let con'=cmap(id) in
.15      if con≠nil => con=con'
.16       then insert-context(head^<mk-Comp-unit(con',body)>,
.17                     cmap, tl tail )
.18      else exit )))

.19 type:(Comp-unit* Id m->Context Comp-unit*) ~-> Comp-unit*
```

```
.0 extend-lib(lib,complist)(presur)=
.1 if complist=<> then lib else
.2 let mk-Comp-unit(context,body)=hd complist               in
.3 let sur1=get-context-sur(con,lib,presur)                 in
.4 let sur2=get-Sur-if-wf-declpart-item(body)(sur1)         in
.5 let lib-extention =
.6 cases body:
.7 (mk-Pack-spec(id,, )       -> get-pack-info(id,sur2),
.8  mk-Sub-prgr-spec(id,, ) -> get-sub-prgr-info(id,sur2),
.9  mk-Sub-prgr-body(mk-Sub-prgr-spec(id,},, )
.10                     -> get-sub-prgr-info(id,sur2),
.11 T                    -> [])                             in
.12 extend-lib(lib+libextention,tl complist)(presur)

.13 type: (Library Comp-unit*) -> Surr. ~-> Library
```

```
.0 get-context-sur(con,lib,sur)=
.1 if con=<> then sur else
.2 let mk-Context(withset,use)=hd con in
.3 if(E id E withset)(id ~E dom lib)
.4    then exit
.5    else(let (con-dict,con-opmap)=
.6              insert-lib-info(s-dict(sur),s-opmap(sur),
.7                                       withset,lib ) in
.8         let con-sur= sur+(s-dict:<-con-dict,
.9                           s-opmap:<-con-opmap)        in
.10        let nextsur=if use=nil then consur else
.11                    get-Use-sur(use)(consur)          in
.12        get-context-sur(tl con,lib,nextsur) )

.13 type: (Context* Library Surr] ~-> Surroundings
```

```
.0 get-pack-info(id,sur)=
.1 let packdescr=extract-dict(sur)(id)                in
.2 let opmap     =s-opmap(sur)                        in
.3 let name      =s-name(packdescr)                   in
.4 let opmap' =
.5     [id'->mk-Overload-descr(spset)  |
.6      id'E dom opmap  and
.7      (let mk-Overload-descr(spset')=opmap(id')   in
.8      (V spd E spset)(spd E spset'  and
.9                      spd=mk-Sub-prog-descr( ,sname, )
.10                     and (sname[i]=((name^<id'>)[i] |
.11                          1<=i<=len sname-1      )))] in
.12 [id->mk-Pack-info(packdescr,opmap') ]

.13 type:(Id Surroundings) -> Library
```

```
.0 get-sub-prgr-info(id,sur)=
.1 let mk-Overload-descr(spset)=extract-dict(sur)(id)   in
.2 [id->mk-Sub-prgr-info(mk-Overload-descr(spset')) |
.3 (V sp E spset')(spE spset and is-Sub-prgr-descr(sp))]

.4 type: (Id Surroundings) -> Library
```

```
.0 insert-lib-info(dict,opmap,withset,lib)=
.1 if withset={} then (dict,opmap) else
.2 let id E withset in
.3 cases lib(id):
.4 (mk-Pack-info(pd,opd)     ->
.5   insert-lib-info(extend-dict(dict)(<mk-Id(STANDARD)>)
.6               ([id->pd]), withset\{id}, lib       ),
.7  mk-Sub-prgr-info(ovld) ->
.8   insert-lib-info(extend-dict(dict)(<mk-Id(STANDARD)>)
.9               ([id->ovld]), withset\{id}, lib     ))

.10 type:(Dict Operator-dict Id-set Library) -> (Dict Operator-dict)
```

## 3.3  Declarative Parts

```
.0 get-Decl-part-sur(iteml)(sur) =
.1 if iteml=<> then sur else
.2 (let prefix^<item> = iteml in
.3    let prefixsur=get-Decl-part-sur(prefix)(sur) in
.4        get-sur-if-wf-decl-item(item)(prefixsur)  )

.5 type: (Decl-Item | Body)* -> Surroundings -> Surroundings



.0 get-sur-if-wf-decl-item(item)(sur) =
.1 cases item:
.2 (mk-Use-clause()      -> get-Use-sur(item)(sur) ,
.3  mk-Obj-decl()        -> get-obj-decl-sur(item)(sur),
.4  mk-Pack-spec()       -> get-Pack-spec-sur(item)(sur),
.5  mk-Pack-body         -> if is-wf-Pack-body(item)(sur)
                               then sur
                               else exit ,
.6  mk-Sub-prgr-spec() -> get-Sub-prgr-spec-sur(item)(sur),
.7  mk-Sub-prgr-body() -> get-Sub-prgr-body-sur(item)(sur),
.8  mk-Type-decl()       -> get-type-decl-sur(item)(sur) ,
.9  mk-Sub-type-decl() -> get-sub-type-decl-sur(item)(sur),
.10 mk-Const-decl()      -> get-const-decl-sur(item)(sur),
.11 mk-Number-decl()     -> .......
.12 ..... )

.13 type: (Decl-item | Body) -> Surrounding -> Surrounding
```

```
.0 pre-check-Decl-part(vl,pl,bl) =
.1 (let visl  = split-decll(vl),
.2      privl = split-decll(pl),
.3      bodyl = split-decll(bl)        in
.4  let decll = visl ^ privl ^ bodyl in
.5  (∀ i Ε ind decll)
.6   (let posinds={ id ¦ j Ε ind decll \ {i} and
.7                    get-id(decll[i])=get-id(decll[j]) } in
.8    cases decll[i]:

.9    (mk-Pack-spec(id,vl,pl)                        ->
.10      (cases posinds:
.11       ({}  -> (~Ε j Ε ind (vl^pl))(is-Sub-prgr-spec((vl^pl)
                                                         [j]))
.12                and pre-check-Decl-part(vl,pl,<>) ,
.13       {j} -> (j>i and is-Pack-body(decll[j])),
.14       T  -> false )),

.15    mk-Pack-body(id,mk-Decl-part(dl,bl),stmtl)) ->
.16      (cases posinds:
.17       ({j} -> (j<i and decll[j]=mk-Pack-spec( ,vl,pl)  and
.18                (let lbls=get-block-a-loop-ids(stmtl) in
.19                 pre-check-Decl-part(vl,pl,dl^bl^lbls) ) and
.20                (∀ stmt Ε elems stmtl)(pre-check-stmt(stmt))),
.21       T  -> false)),

.22    mk-Type-decl( ,mk-Access-td(ti))              ->
.23      (cases posinds:
.24       ({}  -> ti ≠ nil,
.25       {j} -> (decll[j]=mk-Type-decl( ,mk-Access-td(tj)) and
.26                cases ti:
.27                (nil -> (tj≠nil and i < j and
.28                          i <= ln visl => j <= ln visl),
.29                 T   -> (tj=nil and j < i and
.30                          j <= ln visl => i <= ln visl) )),
.31       {j,k} -> (let mini = min{i,j,k} ,
.32                     maxi = max{i,j,k} ,
.33                     midi = {i,j,k} \ {mini,maxi} in
.34                 mk-Type-decl( ,mk-Private-td())=decll[mini] and
.35                 mk-Type-decl( ,mk-Access-td(nil))=
                                          decll[midi] and
.36                 cases decll[maxi]:
.37                 (mk-Type-decl( ,mk-Access-td(t)) -> t ≠ nil,
.38                  T -> false)),
.39       T -> false)),

.40    mk-Type-decl( ,mk-Private-td())                 ->
.41       ( 1<= i <= ln visl and
.42        cases posinds:
.43       ([j] -> (is-Type-decl(decll[j]) and
.44               ln visl < j <= ln (visl^privl)),
.45       [j,k] ->(mk-Type-decl( ,mk-Access(nil))=decll[min{j,k}]
.46            and mk-Type-decl( ,mk-Access(t))=decll[max{j,k}]
.47            and t ≠ nil
.48            and ln visl < min{j,k}<=ln(visl^privl)),
.49       T -> false),
```

```
.50    mk-Sub-prgr-spec(id,parml, )                     ->
.51       (trap exit with false in
.52        let pre-parml=get-pre-parml(id,parml) in
.53        (∀ j E posinds)(sub-prgr-or-literal(decll[j]))),

.54    mk-Sub-prgr-body(sub-spec,mk-Decl-part(dl,bl),stmtl) ->
.55       (trap exit with false in
.56        let mk-Sub-prgr-spec(id,parml, )        in
.57        let pre-parml=get-pre-parml(id,parml)   in
.58        ((∀ j E posinds)(sub-prgr-or-literal(decll[j])) and
.59         (let lbls=get-block-a-loop-ids(stmtl) in
.60          pre-check-Decl-part(<>,<>,dl^bl^labels)) and
.61         (∀ stmt E elems stmtl)(pre-check-stmt(stmt)))),

.62    mk-Pre-literal()                               ->
.63       (∀ j E posinds)(sub-prgr-or-literal(decll[j])),

.64    mk-Const-decl(id,,nil)                          ->
.65       (cases posinds:
.66        ({j} -> ( 1 <= i <= ln visl and
.67                  ln visl < j <= ln(visl^privl)  and
.68                  mk-Const-decl( ,,expr)=decll[j] and
.69                  expr ≠ nil),
.70           T   -> false)) ,

.71    T -> posinds={}))))

.72 type: Pre-decl* Pre-decl* Pre-decl* -> BOOL
```

```
.0 split-decll(decl)=
.1 conc <decl | 1 <= i <= ln decll and
.2        decl = cases decll[i]:
.3             (mk-Obj-decl(idl,tp,ex)   ->
.4                  <mk-Obj-decl(<id>,tp,ex) |
.5             mk-Const-decl(idl,tp,ex)  ->
.6                  <mk-Const-decl(<id>,tp,ex) |
.7             mk-Numb-decl(idl,ex)      ->
.8                  <mk-Numb-decl(<id>,ex) |
.9             mk-Type-decl(id,mk-Enum-td(eleml)) ->
.10                 <decll[i]>^
.11                 <mk-Pre-literal(elm) |
.12            mk-Use-clause() -> <>,
.13            T -> <decll[i]>        >
```
```
                 1 <= j <= ln idl and id=idl[j]>,
                 1 <= j <= ln idl and id=idl[j]>,
                 1 <= j <= ln idl and id=idl[j]>,
                 1 <= j <= ln eleml and elm=eleml[j]>,
```

.14 type: Decl* -> Pre-decl*


```
.0 get-id(decl) =
.1 (cases decl:
.2 (mk-Sub-prgr-body(mk-Sub-prgr-spec(id,, ),, ) -> id,
.3  mk-Sub-prgr-spec(id,, )                       -> id,
.4  mk-Pack-body(id, )                            -> id,
.5  mk-Pack-spec(id, )                            -> id,
.6  mk-Obj-decl(<id>,, )                          -> id,
.7  mk-Const-decl(<id>,, )                        -> id,
.8  mk-Numb-decl(<id>, )                          -> id,
.9  mk-Type-decl(id, )                            -> id,
.10 mk-Sub-type-decl(id, )                        -> id,
.11 mk-Pre-literal(id)                            -> id,
.12 mk-Pre-block(id)                              -> id,
.13 mk-Pre-loop(id)                               -> id))
```

.14 type: Pre-decl -> Designator

```
.0 get-pre-parml(id,parml) =
.1 (let pre-parml = < pre-parm | 1 <= i <= ln parml          and
.2                    mk-Parm-decl(idl,mo,tp,ex)=parml[i] and
.3                    test-mode(mo,ex) and
.4                    pre-parm=mk-Obj-decl(idl,tp,nil) >        in
.5 (is-Operator(id) ->
.6    (let checkl=split-decll(pre-parml) in
.7     cases id:
.8      (+,-,NOT -> (if 0 <= ln checkl <= 2
.9                      then pre-parml
.10                     else exit),
.11       T       -> (if ln checkl=2
.12                     then pre-parml
.13                     else exit))),
.14   T -> pre-parml))

.15 type: Designator Parm-decl* -> Obj-decl*
```

```
.0 test-mode(mode,expr)=
.1 cases (mode,expr):
.2 ((T,nil) -> true,
.3 (IN,T) -> true,
.4 (nil,T) -> true,
.5 T      -> exit)

.6 type: [Mode] [Expr] -> BOOL
```

```
.0 sub-prgr-or-literal(decl)=
.1 ( is-Sub-prgr-spec(decl) or is-Sub-prgr-body(decl) or
.2   is-Pre-literal(decl))

.3 type: Pre-decl -> BOOL
```

```
.0 get-block-and-loop-ids(stmtl)=
.1 < balid | 1 <= i <= ln stmtl and
.2   balid = cases stmtl[i]:
.3            (mk-Block(id,, )     -> if id=nil then nil
                                      else mk-Pre-Block(id),
.4             mk-Loop-stmt(id,, ) -> if id=nil then nil
                                      else mk-Pre-Loop(id),
.5.            T                   -> nil)
.6   and balid ≠ nil>

.7 type: Stmt* -> Pre-decl*
```

```
.0 pre-check-Stmt(stmt) =
.1 (cases stmt:
.2  (mk-Block( ,mk-Decl-part(dl,bl),stmtl) ->
.3     (let lbls = get-block-a-loop-ids(stmtl) in
.4      pre-check-Decl-part(<>,<>,dl^bl^lbls)) and
.5     (∀ stmt ∈ elems stmtl)(pre-check-Stmt(stmt))),
.6   mk-Loop-stmt( ,,stmtl)        ->
.7     (let lbls = get-block-a-loop-ids(stmtl) in
.8      pre-check-Decl-part(<>,<>,lbls)) and
.9     (∀ stmt ∈ elems stmtl)(pre-check-Stmt(stmt))),
.10  mk-If-stmt(con-sl,els)            ->
.11     (∀ stmtl ∈ {s-stmtl(elems con-sl} U {els}))
.12       ((let lbls = get-block-a-loop-ids(stmtl) in
.13         pre-check-Decl-part(<>,<>,lbls)) and
.14         (∀ stmt ∈ stmtl)(pre-check-Stmt(stmt))),
.15  T -> true))

.16 type: Stmt -> BOOL
```

## 3.4  Use Clauses

```
.0  get-Use-sur(use-clause)(sur) =
.1  let newwm = get-weakmap(use-clause)(sur)  in
.2    sur+(s-wm:wm -> wm+newwm)

.3  type: Use-clause -> Surroundings ~-> Surroundings



.0  get-weak-map(mk-Use-clause(nset))(sur) =
.1  if (∀ n E nset)(cases lookup-name(n)(sur):
.2                  (<mk-Pack-descr()> -> true, T -> false ))
.3    then [ packname -> visdict |
.4          (E n E nset)
.5            (<mk-Pack-descr(visdict,,packname,,, )> = lookup-name(n)
.6                                                                (sur)
.7              and packname ≠ <s-level(sur)[i] | 1<=i<=ln packname>)]
.8    else exit

.9  type: Use-clause -> surroundings ~-> Weak-map
```

## 3.5 Object- & Constant Declarations

```
.0 get-obj-decl-sur(obj-decl)(sur) =
.1 let pre-sur = update-sur-dict([id->INTRODUCED |
                                  id E elems s-idl(objdecl)])(sur) in
.2 let (obj-id-dict,op-dict) =
       get-obj-id-dicts(objdecl)([])(nil)(s-level(sur))
                       (COMPONENT)(presur)              in
.3 update-sur(obj-id-dict,<>,[],op-dict,<>)(sur)

.4 type: Obj-decl -> Surroundings -> Surroundings
```

```
.0 get-object-id-dicts(decl)(dmap)(reclevel)(psname)(tdu)(sur) =
.1 let mk-Obj-decl(idl,tex,initex) = decl                        in
.2 let xname  = psname ^ <hd idl>                                in
.3 let typ    = make-type(tex)(xname)(dmap)(reclevel)
                                          (tdu)(sur)             in
.4 let opdict = cases tex:
.5                (mk-Array-td() ->
                            create-user-dep-operator-dict(typ)(sur),
.6                 T -> [])                                      in
.7 let obdict = [id -> mk-Obj-descr(typ,nil)|id E elems idl]     in
.8 let t-sur  = update-sur(obdict,<>,[],opdict,<>)(sur)          in
.9 if ~ (initex=nil =>
        type-expr-compatibility(typ)(initex)(t-sur))
.10   then exit
.11   else (obdict,opdict)

.12 type: Obj-decl -> Discrim-map -> Record-level ->
          Unitname -> Type-def-usage -> Surroundings ->
          (Dict Operator-dict)
```

```
.0 get-const-decl-sur(cdecl)(sur) =
.1 (let pre-sur = update-sur([id->INTRODUCED |
                 id E elems s-idl(cdecl)])(sur)     in
.2  let mk-Const-decl(idl,tpex,initex) = cdecl       in
.3  let xobject = mk-Obj-decl(idl,tpex,initex)       in
.4  let (obdict,opdict) =
        get-obj-id-dicts(xobject)([])(nil)(s-level(sur))
                        (COMPONENT)(pre-sur)        in
.5  let typ = (let descr E rng(obdict) in s-Type(descr)) in
.6  if (is-Aggragate(initex) =>
        contains-no-others-choice(initex))
.7     then (let const-dict=
.8            [id -> mk-Obj-descr(typ,CONSTANT) |
.9             id E dom obdict and
.10            typ = s-Type(obdict(id))]) in
.11           update-sur(const-dict,<>,[],opdict,<>)(sur))
.12    else exit)

.13 type: Const-decl -> Surroundings -> Surroundings
```

```
.0 is-local-and-private-type(typ)(sur) =
.1 cases hd s-status(sur):
.2 (mk-In-pack-spec(def-types) -> (s-name(typ) E def-types and
                                   s-sub(typ)  = PRIVATE-SUB),
.3  T                          -> false)

.4 type: Type -> Surroundings -> BOOL



.0 contains-no-others-choice(aggragate) =
.1 (let mk-Agggregate(list,others)=aggregate  in
.2  others=nil and
.3  (¥ el E elems list)
.4    (let xex = cases el:(( ,expr)->expr,T->el) in
.5     is-Aggregate(xex) =>
.6     contains-no-others-choice(xex)))

.7 type: Aggragate -> BOOL
```

## 3.6 Packages

```
.0  get-Pack-spec-sur(mk-Pack-spec(id,vil,privl))(sur) =
.1  let mk-Surroundings(dict,level,wm,opd,status) = sur        in
.2  let packname = level^<id>                                  in
.3  let packdescr = mk-Pack-descr([],[],packname,[],{})        in
.4  let presur    = update-sur([id->packdescr],<id>,[],[],
                               mk-In-Pack-spec({}{}))(sur) in
.5  let vissur    = get-Decl-part-sur(vil)(presur)             in
.6  let visdict   = lookup-local-dict(packname)(vissur)      ,
.7      export-op = s-opdict(vissur)                            in
.8  let privsur   = get-Decl-part-sur(privl)(vissur)           in
.9  let pack-wm   = s-weakmap(privsur)                          in
.10     priv-dict = lookup-local-dict(packname)(privsur)      ,
.11     pack-op   = s-opdict(privsur)                         ,
.12     mk-In-Pack-spec( ,ps) = hd s-status(privsur)          in
.13 update-sur([id->mk-Pack-descr(visdict,priv-dict,packname,
                               pack-wm,ps,pack-op)],
             <>,[],export-op,nil)(sur)

.14 type: Pack-spec -> Surroundings -> Surroundings




.0  is-wf-Pack-body(mk-Pack-body(id,declpart,stmtl))(sur) =
.1  trap exit with false in
.2  (let mk-Surroundings( ,un,wm,,statusl) = sur                in
.3   let mk-Decl-part(iteml,bodyl)         = declpart           in
.4   let mk-Pack-descr( ,pdict,pun,pwm,,psd)=
                       lookup-Unitname(un^<id>)(sur)            in
.5   let pack-status = mk-In-Pack-body(psd)                     in
.6   let pack-descr = mk-Pack-descr(pdict,[],pun,[],[],{}       in
.7   let presur     = update-sur([id->pack-descr],<id>,pwm,[],
                               packstatus)(sur)                 in
.8   let bodysur     = get-Decl-part-sur(iteml^bodyl)(presur)in
.9   let mk-In-Pack-body(subprgrs) = hd s-status(bodysur)       in
.10  (~(E subprgr E subprgrs) (subprgr=mk-Sub-prgr( ,nil) ) and
.11   (V stmt E elems stmtl)(is-wf-Stmt(stmt)(bodysur)) )

.12 type: Package-body -> Surroundings -> BOOL
```

## 3.7  Subprograms

```
.0  get-Sub-prgr-spec-sur(mk-Sub-prgr-spec(id,parml,rtn))(sur) =
.1  let entrance = get-Entrance(id,parml,rtn)(sur)                in
.2  if sub-prgr-exists(id,entrance)(hd s-status(sur))
.3     then exit else
.4  (let unitname = s-level(sur)^<id>^<get-unique-number()> in
.5   let sub-descr= mk-Sub-prgr-descr([],unitname,entrance) in
.6   let sub-prgr = mk-Sub-prgr(unitname,entrance,nil)         in
.7   let statussur= insert-in-status(sub-prgr)(sur)            in
.8   let ovldescr = mk-Overload-descr([sub-descr])             in
.9   let subsur   = update-sur-dict([id->overldescr])(statussur) in
.10      make-Sub-prgr-to-attribute(id,unitname,entrance)(subsur) )

.11  type: Sub-prgr-descr -> Surroundings ~-> Surroundings
```

```
.0  get-Sub-prgr-body-sur(mk-Sub-prgr-body(spec,declpart,stmtl))(sur) =
.1  let mk-Sub-prgr-spec(id,parml,rtn) = spec                 in
.2  let mk-Decl-part(iteml,bodyl)      = declpart             in
.3  let sub-descr = connect-body-with-spec(spec)(sur)         in
.4  let mk-Sub-prgr-descr( ,unitname,entrance)=sub-descr      in
.5  let sub-prgr  = mk-Sub-prgr(unitname,entrance,body)       in
.6  let statussur = insert-in-Status(sub-prgr)(sur)           in
.7  let parmdict  = get-parm-dict(entrance)                   in
.8  let ovldescr  = mk-Overload-descr([sub-descr])            in
.9  let newlevel  = <unitname[i]|(ln unitname -1) <= i<=
                                    ln unitname >             in
.10 let sub-sur   = update-sur-dict([id->ovldescr])(sub-sur)  in
.11 let presur    = update-sur([],newlevel,[],[],
                              mk-In-Sub-prgr({}))(statussur)  in
.12 let parmsur   = update-sur-dict(parmdict)(presur)         in
.13 let bodysur   = det-Decl-part-sur(iteml^bodyl)(parmsur)   in
.14 let mk-In-Sub-prgr(sprgrs) = hd s-status(bodysur)         in
.15 if (~(E sp E sprgrs)(s-body(sp)=nil.) and
       (¥ stmt E elems stmtl)(is-wf-Stmt(stmt)(bodysur)))
.16    then sub-sur
.17    else exit

.18  type: Sub-prgr-body -> Surroundings ~-> Surroundings
```

```
.0 make-Sub-prgr-to-attribute(id,unitname,entrance)(sur)=
.1 cases hd s-status(sur):
.2 (mk-In-Pack-spec(typenames, ) ->
.3    (let parmtypn = extract-types-of-entrance(entrance) in
.4    let aff-types = typenames  parmtypn               in
.5    let local-dict = get-local-dict(sur)               in
.6    let up-loc-dict=
.7        [tid -> type-descr | atype E aff-types  and
.8         tid = atype[ln atype]                  and
.9         let attributes = s-attr(local-dict(tid))      in
.10        let new-attr  =
.11            (if id E dom attributes
.12            then attributes+[id->attributes(id)U{unitname}]
.13            else attributesU[id->{unitname}])          in
.14       typedescr=local-dict(tid)+(s-attr:->newattr)]  in
.15      update-sur-dict(up-loc-dict)(sur)) ,
.16    T          -> sur)

.17    type: Id Unitname Entrance -> Surroundings -> Surroundings
```

```
.0  parameter-checker(entrance)(actual-parm-list)(sur) =
.1  trap exit with false in
.2  (let formall = convert-entrance-to-parm-check(entrance) in
.3   let mk-Act-parm-list(posl,namel) = actual-parm-list   in
.4   let given-ids = {s-Id(namep)|namep E elems namel}      in
.5   if (ln formall < ln actual-parm-list              or
.6      (E i E ind posl)(s-Id(formall[i]) E given-ids) or
.7      (E i E ind formall)( i>ln posl and
.8       s-Id(formall[i]) ~E given-ids=>s-Expr(formall[i])≠nil))
.9      then exit else
.10     (∀ i E ind posl)
.11        (check-parm(s-Expr(posl[i]),formall[i])(sur)) and
.12     (∀ parm E elems namel)  (E fparm E elems formall)
.13       (s-Id(parm)=s-Id(fparm) and
.14       check-parm(s-Expr(parm),fparm)(sur)))

.15    type: Entrance -> Actuel-parm-list -> Surroundings -> BOOL
```

```
.0 get-parm-dict(entrance) =
.1 let parml = convert-entrance(entrance) in
.2 [id -> mk-Obj-descr(typ,const) |
.3   mk-(<id>,mo,typ) E elems parml and
.4   const = cases mo:(in->CONSTANT,T->nil)]

.5 type: Entrance -> Dict
```

```
.0 insert-in-status(sub-prgr)(sur) =
.1 (let <status>^tail = s-status(sur)              in
.2  let dsps = s-defined-sub-prgrs(status)         in
.3  let mk-Sub-prgr(un,entrance,body)=sub-prgr in
.4  let new-dsps =
.5     (if (E sp E dsps)
.6          (sp=mk-Sub-prgr(un,entrance, ))
.7        then dsps ¦ {sp} U {sub-prgr})
.8        else dsps U {sub-prgr})               in
.9  let new-status = status+(s-defined-sub-prgrs:->new-dsps) in
.10 sur+sur(s-status:-><new-status>^tail)

.11 type: Sub-prgr -> Surroundings -> Surroundings
```

```
.0 connect-body-with-spec(sub-spec)(sur) =
.1 (let mk-Sub-prgr-spec(id,parml,rtn) = sub-spec        in
.2  let entrance = get-entrance(id,parml,rtn)(sur)       in
.3  let dsps     = s-defined-sub-prgrs(hd s-status(sur)) in
.4  if (E sp E dsps)
.5     (sp=mk-Sub-prgr(prefix^<id,n>,entrance,body))
.6     then (if body ≠ nil then exit
.7              else mk-Sub-prgr-descr([],prefix^<id,n>,
                                               entrance))
.8     else if (E sp' E dsps)
.9          (sp'=mk-Sub-prgr(prefix^<id,n'>,entrance',body')
.10          and
            convert-entrance-in-same-decl-part(entrance)=
            convert-entrance-in-same-decl-part(entrance'))
.11         then exit
.12         else (let un=prefix^<id,get-unique-number()> in
.13              mk-Sub-prgr-descr([],un,entrance)))

.14 type: Sub-prgr-spec -> Surroundings -> Sub-prgr-descr
```

```
.0 convert-entrance-in-same-decl-part(entrance) =
.1 let mk-Entrance(parml,rtn,op) = entrance in
.2 cases op:
.3  (nil -> (let list =
.4           conc < xl ¦ 1 <= i <= ln parml and
.5           let mk-Parm-descr(idl,,typ,expr,, )=parml[i]    in
.6           let init=(if expr=nil then nil else INITIALIZED) in
.7           xl=< mk-(typ,init) ¦ 1 <= j <= ln idl> >        in
.8           mk-(list,rtn)),
.9   T   -> (let list=
.10          conc <xl ¦ 1 <= i <= ln parml and
.11          let mk-Parm-descr(idl,,typ,,, )=parml[i] in
.12          xl= <typ ¦ 1 <= j <= ln idl> >          in
.13          list^<rtn>))

.14 type: Entrance -> ( (((Type [INITIALIZED])* [Type]) ¦ Type+)
```

```
.0 sub-prgr-exsists(id,entrance)(status) =
.1 let dsps = s-defined-sub-prgr(status) in
.2 (E sp E dsps)
.3   (sp = mk-Sub-prgr(prefix^<id,n>,entrance', ) and
.4     convert-entrance-in-same-decl-part(entrance) =
.5     convert-entrance-in-same-decl-part(entrance')  )

.6 type: Id Entrance -> Status -> BOOL



.0 get-ids-of-parms(parml) =
.1 union {ids | mk-Parm-descr(idl,,, ) E elems parml and
.2          ids=elems idl}

.3 type: Parm* -> Id-set



.0 get-parm-descrl(parml)(sur) =
.1 <mk-Parm-descr(idl,mode',typ,rebexpr) |
.2   1 <= i <= ln parml and
.3   mk-Parm-decl(idl,mode,subtypind,expr)=parml[i] and
.4   typ=make-Sub-type(subtypind)(nil)(TYPE)(sur)   and
.5   rebexpr=(if expr=nil then nil else rebuild-item(expr)(sur)) and
.6   mode'=(if mode=nil then nil else mode) >

.7 type: Parm* -> Surroundings -> Parm-descr*



.0 get-Entrance(id,parml,rtn)(sur) =
.1 (let pre-dict = [id->INTRODUCED|id E get-ids-of-parms(parml)] in
.2  let pre-sur  = update-sur-dict(pre-dict)(sur)            in
.3  let parm-descrl = get-parm-descrl(parml)(pre-sur)        in
.4  let rtntype  = if rtn=nil then nil
                   else make-Sub-type(rtn)(nil)(TYPE)(pre-sur)   in
.5  if is-Operator(id)
.6    then get-operator-entrance(id,parm-descrl,rtntype)
.7    else mk-Entrance(parm-descrl,rtntype,nil))

.8 type: Id Parm* Sub-type-indic -> Surroundings -> Entrance
```

```
.0 get-operator-entrance(operator,parml,rtn) =
.1 (if rtn ≠ nil and
.2     cases parml:
.3     (<mk-Parm-descr(<id>,in,t,nil)>          ->
.4                     operator E {+,-,NOT},
.5     <mk-Parm-descr(<id1,id2>,in,t,nil)> ->
.6                     cases operator:
.7                     (= -> (is-limited(t) and
                                   rtn=get-pre-def-bool-type()),
.8                      T -> true),
.9     <mk-Parm-descr(<id1>,in,t1,nil),
       mk-Parm-descr(<id2>,in,t2,nil)>          ->
.10                    cases operator:
.11                    (= ->(t1=t2 and is-limited(t1) and
                                   rtn=get-pre-def-bool-type()),
.12                     T -> true),
.13    T -> false)
.14    then mk-Entrance(parml,rtn,OP)
.15    else exit)

.16 type: Operator Parm-descr* Type -> Entrance
```

```
.0 check-parm(expr,mk-Parm-descr(id,mo,typ,, ))(sur) =
.1 (type-expr-compatibility(typ,expr) and
.2  cases mo:
.3  (in  -> true,
.4   T   -> (is-Name(expr)                    ->
.5             (let list=lookup-name(expr)(sur) in
.6              cases list:
.7              (<mk-Obj-descr( ,nil)> -> true,
.8               T                     -> false)),
.9           expr=mk-Type-conv( ,expr') ->
.10            (is-Name(expr') ->
.11              (let list=lookup-name(expr')(sur) in
.12               cases list:
.13               (<mk-Obj-descr( ,nil)>  -> true,
.14                T                      -> false)),
.15            T   -> false),
.16         T -> false)))

.17 type:Expr Parm-descr -> Surroundings -> BOOL
```

```
.0 extr-types-of-entrance(mk-Entrance(parml,rtn, ))(sur) =
.1 let types = {typ | mk-Parm-descr( ,, typ) E elems parml} U
.2            (if rtn=nil then {} else {rtn})                in
.3 {unitname | mk-Type(unitname,,,, ) E types}

.4 type: Entrance -> Surroundings -> Unitname-set
```

```
.0 convert-entrance-to-parm-check(entrance) =
.1 let mk-Entrance(parml,rtn,op) = entrance in
.2 conc < xl | 1 <= i <= ln parml and
.3              let mk-parm-descr(idl,mo,typ,init)=parml[i] in
.4              xl=<mk-(id,md,typ,init) |
.5                   i <= j <= ln idl and id=idl[j] > >

.6 type: Entrance -> Parm-descr*
```

## 3.8 Type- & Subtype Declarations

```
.0  get-Type-decl-sur(typedecl)(sur) =
.1  let mk-Type-decl(id,typedef) = typedecl              ,
.2      localdict = lookup-local-dict(sur)               in
.3  let early = (id E dom localdict -> localdict(id)     ,
.4              T                   -> nil          )    in
.5      pre-sur = update-sur-dict([id->INTRODUCED])(sur) ,
.6      eqvl-tdcl = transform(typedecl)(sur)             in
.7  cases eqvl-tdcl:
.8  ( mk-Derived-td() ->
.9          get-derived-type-sur(eqvl-tdcl)(early)(presur),
.10   T               ->
.11         get-defined-type-sur(eqvl-tdcl)(early)(presur) )

.12 type: Type-decl -> ( Surroundings -> Surroundings )
```

```
.0  get-subtype-decl-sur(st-decl)(sur) =
.1  let mk-Subtype-decl(id,mk-Subtype-indic(name,constr))=st-decl in
.2  let pre-sur = update-dict-sur([id->INTRODUCED])(sur)          in
.3  let mk-Type-descr(basetype, )=lookup-type(name)(presur)       in
.4  let subtype =
.5          constraint-type(basetype)(constr)({}(nil)(TYPE)(presur) in
.6  update-sur-dict([id->mk-Type-descr(subtype,[])])(sur)

.7  type: Subtype-decl -> Surroundings -> Surroundings
```

```
.0  get-defined-type-sur(typedecl)(early)(sur) =
.1  let mk-Typedecl(id,typedef) = typedecl                      in
.2  let newname = s-level(sur)^<id>                             in
.3  let (typ,opdict1) =
.4      make-type(typedef)(newname)[](nil)(TYPE)(sur)           in
.5  let opdict2 = create-usertype-dep-op-dict(typ)(sur)         in
.6  let predefopdict = overload(opdict1)(opdict2)               in
.7  let newstatus = cases hd s-status(sur):
.8      (mk-In-Pack-spec(def-tps,def-spgs) ->
.9        (<mk-In-Pack-spec(def-tps U {newname},def-spgs)>
.10        ^ tl s-status(sur) ),
.11       T -> s-status(sur) )                                  in
.12 let literaldict = get-enum-literal-dict(typ)                in
.13 let attributes = cases:
.14     (early = nil                  -> [],
.15      is-Access(s-ds(s-tp(early)))-> s-attr(early),
.16      ~is-wf-full-decl-of-private-type(typ)(s-tp(early))
.17                                    -> exit,
.18      T                            -> s-attr(early)) in
.19 let extension = [id->mk-Type-descr(typ,attributes)]
.20              U literaldict                          in
.21 update-sur(extension,<>,{},predefopdict,<>)
.22          ( sur+(s-status:->newstatus)      )

.23 type: Type-decl -> [Type-decl] -> Surroundings -> Surroundings



.0  get-derived-type-sur(typedecl)(early)(sur) =
.1  let mk-Type-decl(id,mk-Derived-td(sub-t-indic))=typedecl    in
.2  let mk-Subtype-indic(name,constr) = sub-t-indic             in
.3  let newname = slevel(sur) ^ <id>                            in
.4  let mk-Type-descr(parenttype, ) = lookup-type(name)(sur)    in
.5  let base-of-parent = lookup-base-type(parenttype)(sur)      in
.6  let dtype = base-of-parent + (s-name   :-> newname,
.7                                s-parent:-> s-name(parent),
.8                                s-ds     :-> nil         ) in
.9  let subtype = cases constr:
.10   ( nil -> dtype + (s-sub: -> s-sub(parenttype))         ,
.11     T   -> constraint-type(dtype)([])(nil)(TYPE)(sur) )  in
.12 (~is-wf-full-decl-of-private-type(subtype,s-tp(early))(sur)
.13                                              -> exit,
.14  T -> get-sur-of-derived-type(id,subtype)(early)(sur)    )

.15 type: Type-decl-> [Type-descr] -> Surroundings -> Surroundings
```

```
.0   get-sur-of-derived-type(id,typ)(early)(sur) =
.1   let parent-attr = s-attr(lookup-unitname(s-parent(typ))(sur)) in
.2   let (deriv-attr,new-state) =
.3     cases hd s-status(sur):
.4     (mk-In-Pack-spec(def-tp,def-sp) ->
.5        ((if s-parent(typ) E def-tp
.6             then (let def-attr={ un | mk-Sub-prgr(un,, ) E
.7                                         def-sp}              in
.8                       parent-attr \ def-sp)
.9             else    parent-attr            ),
.10      mk-In-Pack-spec(def-tp U {s-name(typ)},def-sp) ^
.11                                   tl s-status(sur)),
.12     T -> ( {parent-attr}, s-status(sur) )                 ) in
.13  let attributes = Filter-attr(deriv-attr)(s-attr(early))( .. ) in
.14  let new-attr = excl-old-attr(attributes)(s-attr(early)( .. ) in
.15  let deriv-sp-dict = get-sp-attr-dict(new-attr,typ)(sur)      in
.16  let literaldict = get-enum-literal-dict(typ)                 in
.17  let predef-opdict = create-usertype-dep-op-dict(typ)(sur)    in
.18  let type-dict = [id -> mk-Type-descr(typ,attributes) ]       in
.19  let dict-ext = overload(deriv-sp-dict)(literaldict)
.20                    + type-dict                              in
.21  update-sur(dict-ext,<>,[],predef-opdict,<>)
.22                         (sur+(s-status:->newstatus))

.23  type: (Id Type) -> [Type-descr] -> Surroundings -> Surroundings



.0   get-enum-literal-dict(typ) =
.1   cases s-sub(typ):
.2   ( mk-Enum( lit-list ) ->
.3       [ lid -> mk-Overload-descr({mk-Literal-descr(typ)})
.4       | lid E elems lit-list ],
.5     T -> [] )

.6   type: Type -> Dict



.0   create-usertype-dep-op-dict(typ)(sur) =
.1   let level = s-level(sur) in
.2   (is-not-private(typ)(sur)          ->
.3                create-type-predef-opdict(typ)(level),
.4    is-not-limited-private(typ)(sur) ->
.5                create-eq-neq-opdict(typ)(level),
.6     T  -> [] )

.7   type: Type -> Unitname -> Operator-dict
```

```
.0 create-type-eq-neq-op-dict(typ)(level) =
.1 generate-op-dict(mk-Operator(=))(typ,typ,predef-bool-type())
                                                        (level) U
.2 generate-op-dict(mk-Operator(/=))(typ,typ,predef-bool-type())
                                                        (level)

.3 type: Type -> Unitname -> Dict



.0 generate-op-dict(op)(lt,rt,rtnt)(level) =
.1 let pdl=mk-parm-descr( ,in,lt,nil) in
.2 let pdr=mk-parm-descr( ,in,rt,nil) in
.3 let entr = mk-Entrance(<pdl,pdr>,rtnt,PREDEFOP) in
.4 [ op -> mk-Overload-descr(
.5          {mk-Sub-prgr-descr([],level^<op,get-unique-number()>,
                 entrance) } ) ]

.6 type: Operator -> (Type Type Type) -> Unitname -> Dict



.0 generate-operator-list-dict(list)(typ)(level) =
.1 merge (generate-op-dict(list[i])(typ,typ,typ)(level) |
          i E ind list )

.2 type: Operator* -> Type -> Dictlevel -> Dict



.0 is-one-dim-array(mk-Array( ,typel,, )) =
.1 ln typel = 1

.2 type: Array -> BOOL



.0 is-not-private(typ) =
.1 s-lim(typ)=nil and is-notlimited(typ)

.2 type: Type -> BOOL



.0 generate-monadic-op-dict(op,typ)(level) =
.1 let pd   = mk-Parm-descr( ,IN,typ,nil)      in
.2 let entr = mk-Entrance(<pd>,typ,PREDEF-OP) in
.3 [op -> mk-Overload-descr({
.4        mk-Sub-prgr-descr([],level^<op,get-unique-number()>,
               entr)})]

.5 type: (Operator Type) -> Unitname -> Dict
```

```
.0 generate-sign-op-dict(typ)(level) =
.1 generate-monadic-op-dict(mk-Operator(+),typ)(level) U
.2 generate-monadic-op-dict(mk-Operator(-),typ)(level)

.3 type: Type -> Unitname -> Dict



.0 generate-fixed-multipling-op-dict() =
.1 let list = <*,/> in
.2 generate-operator-list-dict(list)(universal-fixed)
                                    (universal-fixed)(<>)

.3 type: () -> Dict



.0 is-not-limited-private(typ)(sur) =
.1 let mk-Type( ,,,ds,sub,lim) = typ in
.2 lim ≠ LIMITED and
.3 cases sel-ds(typ)(sur):
.4 (mk-Record(discrim,comp)          ->
.5    ((discrim≠nil =>
.6      (∀ id E dom s-map(discrim)
.7       (is-not-limited(s-type((discrim)(id)))) and
.8    no-limited-components(comp)(sur)),
.9 mk-Array( ,mk-Obj-descr(typ', ), ) ->
.10    is-not-limited(typ'),
.11 T -> true)

.12 type: Type -> BOOL



.0 no-limited-components(mk-Compl-descr(map,,varpart))(sur) =
.1 (∀ id E dom map)(is-not-limited(s-type(map(id)))(sur)) and
.2 (varpart ≠ nil =>
.3    (let mk-Varpart-descr( ,map')=varpart in
.4     (∀ d E dom map')(no-limited-components(map'(d))(sur))))

.5 type: Compl-descr -> BOOL
```

```
.0 create-type-predef-op-dict(typ)(level) =
.1 let ds = sel-ds(typ) in
.2 create-usertype-eq-neq-op-dict(typ)(level)  U
.3 cases ds:
.4 (INTG  -> create-intg-op-dict(typ)(level),
.5  FLOAT -> create-float-op-dict(typ)(level),
.6  FIXED -> create-fixed-op-dict(typ)(level),
.7  BOOL  -> create-bool-op-dict(typ)(level),
.8  ENUM  -> create-enum-op-dict(typ)(level),
.9  mk-Array() ->
.10      (is-one-dim-array(ds) ->
                    create-1-dim-array-op-dict(typ)(level),
.11      T -> []),
.12 T -> [])

.13 type: Type -> Unitname -> Operator-dict
```

```
.0 create-intg-op-dict(typ)(level) =
.1 let dict1 =
.2 (let list = <+,-,*,/,mod,rem,**> in
.3  generate-operator-list-dict(list)(typ)(level) U
.4  create-rel-op-dict(typ)(level))                        in
.5 let dict2 = generate-sign-op-dict(typ)(level)           in
.6 overload(dict1)(dict2)

.7 type: Type -> Unitname -> Operator-dict
```

```
.0 create-float-op-dict(typ)(level) =
.1 let dict1 =
.2 (let list = <+,-,*,/>  in
.3  generate-operator-list-dict(list)(typ)(level) U
.4  create-rel-op-dict(typ)(level)                  U
.5  generate-op-dict(mk-Operator(**))(typ,any-integer(),typ)
                                        (level) ) in
.6 let dict2 = generate-sign-op-dict(typ)(level) in
.7 overload(dict1)(dict2

.8 type: Type -> Unitname -> Operator-dict
```

```
.0 create-fixed-op-dict(typ)(level) =
.1 let dict1=
.2 (let list = <+,-> in
.3  generate-operator-list-dict(list)(typ)(level)    U
.4  create-rel-op-dict(typ)(level)                   U
.5  generate-op-dict(mk-Operator(*))
                    (typ,any-integer(),typ)(level)  U
.6  generate-op-dict(mk-Operator(*))
                    (any-integer(),typ,typ)(level)  U
.7  generate-op-dict(mk-Operator(/))
                    (typ,any-integer(),typ)(level)  U
.8  generate-op-dict(mk-Operator(/))
                    (any-integer(),typ,typ)(level)  U
.9 let dict2 = generate-sign-op-dict(typ)(level)    in
.10 overload(dict1)(dict2)

.11 type: Type -> Unitname -> Operator-dict



.0 any-integer() =
.1 mk-Type(T,T,T,any-integer,T,T)

.2 type: () -> Type



.0 create-bool-op-dict(typ)(level) =
.1 (let list = < and,or,xor,andthen,orelse,
                 >,>=,<,<= >                        in
.2  generate-operatop-op-dict(list)(typ)(level) U
.3  generate-monadic-op-dict(mk-Operator(not))
                            (typ)(level) )

.4 type: Type -> Unitname -> Operator-dict
```

```
.0 create-1-dim-array-op-dict(typ)(level) =
.1 (let mk-Type(mk-Array( ,objdescr, ),,, ) = typ                    in
.2  let d1=generate-op-dict(mk-Operator(&))(typ,typ,typ)
                                            (level)                  in
.3  let d2=generate-op-dict(mk-Operator(&))
                             (typ,s-type(objdescr),typ)(level) in
.4  overload(d1)(d2))   U
.5  (if is-Discrete(s-ds(s-type(objdescr)))
.6     then create-rel-op-dict(typ)(level)
.7     else [])            U
.8  (if is-Bool(s-ds(s-type(objdescr)))
.9     then (let list = <and,or,xor> in
.10          generate-operator-list-dict(list)(typ)(level) U
.11          generate-monadic-op-dict(mk-Operator(not))
                                      (typ) (level) )
.12     else [])

.13 type: Type -> Unitname -> Dict



.0 create-rel-op-dict(typ)(level) =
.1 (let list = < >,>=,<,<= > in
.2  merge [generate-op-dict(mk-Operator(list[i])
                            (typ,typ,pre-def-bool-type())(level)
.3          | i E ind list] )

.4 type: Type -> Unitname -> Dict
```

176

## Missing Functions
----------------

.0 filter-attr()()( ... ) = ( ... )
.0 excl-old-attr()()( ... ) = ( ... )

.1 type: Attributes -> Attributes -> ... -> Attributes

### 3.9  Datastructures

```
.0 make-type(typeexpr)(newname)(dmap)(rlevel)(tdu)(sur) =
.1 cases typeexpr:
.2 (mk-Subtype-indic()    ->
.3        (make-subtype(typeexpr)(dmap)(rlrvel)(tdu)(sur),[]),
.4  mk-Private-td()       ->
.5        (make-private-type(typeexpr)(newname)(sur),[]),
.6  mk-Record-td()        ->
.7        make-record-type(typeexpr)(newname)(sur),
.8  mk-Array-td()         ->
.9        (make-array-type(typeexpr)(newname)(dmap)(rlevel)
                                        (tdu)(sur),[]),
.10 mk-Access-td()        ->
.11        (make-access-type(typeexpr)(newname)(sur),[]),
.12 mk-Fixed-td()         ->
.13        (make-fixed-type(typeexpr)(newname)(sur),[]),
.14 mk-Enum-td()          ->
.15·       (make-enum-type(typeexpr)(newname)(sur),[])

.16 type: (Typedef | Subtype-indic) -> Unitname ->
            Descrim-map -> Record-level -> Type-def-usage ->
            Surroundings -> (Type Operator-dict)
```

```
.0 make-subtype(subtype-indic)(dmap)(rlevel)(tdu)(sur) =
.1 let mk-Subtype-indic(neme,constr)=subtype-indic  in
.2 let mk-Type-descr(typ, )=lookup-type(name)(sur)  in
.3  constraint-type(typ)(constr)(dmap)(rlevel)(tdu)(sur)

.4 type: Subtype-indic -> Discrim-map -> Record-level ->
           Type-def-usage -> Surroundings -> Type
```

```
.0 make-record-type(rtd)(typename)(sur) =
.1 (if ~ pre-check-record(rtd) then exit else
.2 let (datastructure,opmap) =
.3   (let mk-Record-td(discrim,compl)=rtd                              in
.4    let discrim-descr=extract-discrim-descr(discrim)(sur)            in
.5    let dmap = cases discrim-descr:
.6              (nil->[],T->s-obj-map(discrim-descr))                  in
.7    let presur =
.8              update-sur-dict([id->COMPONENT |
                                id E dom dmap] )(sur)                  in
.9    let (compl-descr,op-dict) =
.10             extr-compl-descr(compl)(dmap,typename)(presur) in
.11   (mk-Record(discrim-descr,compl-descr),op-dict))                 in
.12  let substructure =
.13      mk-Recordsub(cases discrim-descr:
                      (nil -> DISCRIM-LOCK,T -> nil)) in
.14  (mk-Type(typename,typename,typename,datastructure,
              substructure,nil), opmap)))

.15 type: Record-td -> Unitname -> Surroundings ->
         (Type Oprator-dict)




.0 pre-check-record(mk-Record-td(discrim,compl)) =
.1 let pseudo-obj-decl =
.2     discrim ^ extract-copl-decll(compl)                            in
.3 let idtuple        =
.4     conc<s-idl(pseudo-obj-decl[j]| i E ind pseudo-obj-decl> in
.5 (ln idtuple=card elems idtuple and
    s-varpart(compl) ≠ nil => discrim ≠ nil)

.6 type: Record-td -> BOOL




.0 extract-compl-decll(mk-Comp-list(fields,varpart)) =
.1 fields ^ cases varpart:
.2         (mk-Variant-part( ,chl,oth) ->
.3             (conc<extract-compl-decll(s-compl(chl[i])) |
                    i E ind chl >   ^
.4                cases oth:
.5                (mk-Comp-list() ->
.6                    extract-compl-decll(oth),
.7                 nil -> <>) ),
.8         nil -> <>)

.9 type: Comp-list -> Obj-decl*
```

```
.0 extr-discrim-descr(discrim)(sur) =
.1 if discrim=<> then nil else
.2 if ( ~(∀ mk-Obj-decl( ,,typeexpr, ) E elems discrim)
.3        ( cases typeexpr:
.4            (mk-Subtype-indic(name, ) ->
.5                      is-Discrete(sel-ds(s-tp(lookup-type(name)(sur))
                                                              (sur)),
.6            T -> false) ) or
.7      (E i,j E ind discrim)
.8          (i ≠ j => s-expr(discrim[i] = nil  xor
                                    s-expr(discrim[j] = nil))
.9      then exit
.10     else let objmap = extract-field-dict(discrim)([])(<>)(sur) in
.11          let ordmap = [id <-m-> oneway(id) | id i$ dom oneWay and
                             oneway = extr-ordermap(discrim) ]      in
.12          let unit  = (s-expr(hd discrim)≠nil->INIT,T->nil)      in
.13          let initl = <mk-Obj-decl( ,stp,expr)=discrim[i] in
.14                 <rebuild(stp)(sur)>^<rebuild(expr)(sur)> |
                           1 <= i <= ln discrim >                   in
.15          mk-Discrim-descr(obj-map,ordmap,unit,initl)

.16 type:Obj-decl+ -> Surroundings -> Discrim-descr
```

```
.0 extr-order-map(obj-decl-l) =
.1 let fids = conc<s-idl(obj-decl-l[i] | 1<=i<=ln obj-decl-l> in
.2 [fids[i] <-> i | i E ind fids]

.3 type: Obj-decl* -> (Id <-m-> N1)
```

```
.0 extr-compl-descr(compl)(dmap,recunit)(sur) =
.1 let mk-Comp-list((fields,varpart) = compl                    in
.2 let (field-dict,opmap1) =
.3        extr-field-dict(fields)(dmap)(recunit)([])(sur)        in
.4 let ordermap = extr-order-map(fields)                         in
.5 let presur   =
.6        update-sur([id->COMPONENT],<>,[],opmap1,<>)(sur)       in
.7 let (varpart-descr,opmap2) =
.8        extr-variant-descr(varpart)(dmap,recunit)(presur) in
.9 (mk-Compl-descr(field-dict,ordermap,varpart-descr,
.10               overload(opmap1)(opmap2))

.11 type: Comp-list -> (discrim-map Unitname) -> Surroundings
          (Compl-descr Operator-dict)
```

```
.0 extr-variant-descr(varpart)(dmap,recunit)(sur) =
.1 (varpart = nil -> (nil,[]),
.2  ~ precheck-variant(varpart)(dmap)(sur) -> exit,
.3  T ->
.4  (let mk-Variant-part(id,casel,othl) = varpart                    in
.5   let casemap'=
.6       [extr-static-choice(s-ch(casel[i])(s-tp(dmap(id)))(sur) ->
.7        extr-Compl-descr(s-compl(casel[i]))(dmap,recunit)(sur) |
.8        i E ind casel ]  U
.9     cases othl:
.10      (nil -> [],
.11       T   -> [OTH->extr-compl-descr(othl)(dmap,recunit)(sur)] in
.12  let casemap =
.13      [alternative -> compldescr | alternative E dom casemap' and
.14                     (compldescr, ) = casemap'(alternative) ] in
.15  let operator-dict =
.16      multioverload({opdict | ( ,opdict) E rng casemap'})          in
.17 (mk-Varpart-descr(id,casemap),operator-dict)

.18 type: [Variant-part] -> (Discrim-map Unitname) -> Surroundings ->
          ([Var-part-descr] Operator-dict)



.0 multioverload(oset) =
.1 if oset = {} then [] else let o E oset in
.2 overload(o)(multioverload(oset|{o}))

.3 type: Operator-dict-set -> Operator-dict



.0 pre-check-varpart(varpart)(dmap)(sur) =
.1 let mk-Variant-part(id,chl,oth) = varpart in
.2 (id E dom dmap and
.3  (let choicel = conc<s-ch(chl[i]) | i E ind chl> in
.4   let ev-chl  = conc<eval-static-choice(chl[i])(s-tp(dmap(id)))
                                                           (sur) |
.5                     i E ind choicel >             in
.6  (card elems ev-chl = ln ev-chl and
.7   oth=nil =>
.8   cases s-sub(s-tp(lookup-unitname(s-structure(s-tp(dmap(id))))
                                            (s-dict(sur)))):
.9   (mk-Enum(idl, )        -> elems idl  = elems ev-chl,
.10   mk-Intg((low,high), ) -> {low:high} = elems ev-chl)))

.11 type: Variant-part -> Discrim-map -> Surroundings -> BOOL
```

```
.0 extract-field-dicts(fieldlist)(dmap,recunit)(sur) =
.1 if fieldlist=<> then ([],[]) else
.2 let prefix ^ <last> = fieldlist in
.3 let (compdict,opdict) =
.4    extract-field-dicts(prefix)(dmap,recunit)(sur)  in
.5 let exsur =
.6    extend-sur([id->COMPONENT|id E compdict],<>,[],
                                  opdict,<>)(sur) in
.7 let (objdict,objopdict) =
.8    get-obj-id-dicts(last)(dmap)(IN-RECORD)(recunit)
                                  (COMPONENT)(exsur) in
.9 (compdict U objdict , overload(objopdict)(opdict))

.10 type: Obj-decl* -> (Discrim-map Unitname) -> Surroundings ->
         (Dict Operator-dict)



.0  make-private-type(texpr)(nawname)(sur) =
.1 let mk-Private-td(discrim,limited) = texpr in
.2 (discrim = nil ->
.3    (mk-Type(newname,newname,newname,EMPTY,PRIVATE-SUB,
.4              cases limited: ( nil -> PRIVATE,
.5                               T  -> LIMITED)   )),
.6 T              ->
.7    (let (tp, ) =
.8    make-record-type(mk-Record-td(discrim,
.9              mk-Compl(<>,nil)))(newname)(sur) in
.10   (tp+(s-lim:-> cases limited:(nil->PRIVATE,
.11                               T  ->LIMITED)))))

.12 type: Private-td -> Unitname -> Surroundings ~-> Type



.0  is-wf-full-decl-of-private-type(full)(early)(parlim)(sur)=
.1 parlim ≠ LIMITED  and
.2 cases sel-ds(full)(sur):
.3 (mk-Record(discrim-descr,compl-descr) ->
.4   (discrim-descr ≠ nil =>
.5   (∀ id E dom s-obj-map(discrim-descr))
.6 (is-not-limited-private(s-tp(s-obj-map(discrim-descr)(id)))(sur)
.7   and no-limited-components(compl-descr)))
.8   and (compatible-datastructure-and-discriminants(full)(early)(sur))),
.9   mk-Array( ,obj-descr)            ->
.10   (s-lock(s-sub(full)) = INDEX-LOCK  and
.11    is-not-limited-private(s-tp(obj-descr))(sur) ),
.12 T -> true )
.13 and (no-circularity(full)(s-name(full))(FIRST)(sur))

.14 type: Type -> Type -> Surroundings -> BOOL
```

```
.0   no-circularity(typ)(searchname)(which)(sur) =
.1   cases which:
.2   (FIRST -> (s-structure(typ)=searchname) =>
.3                        (s-parent(typ)=searchname )) ,
.4     NEXT -> (s-structure(typ) ≠ searchname ) )
.5   and cases sel-ds(typ)(sur):
.6       (mk-Record(discrim-descr,compl-descr) ->
.7        let rec-dict = flatten-record(discrim-descr,compl-descr) in
.8        (∀ id ∈ dom rec-dict)
.9        (no-circularity(s-tp(rec-dict(id)))(searchname)(sur) ) ,
.10      mk-Array( ,obj-descr)  ->
.11          no-circularity(s-tp(obj-descr))(searchname)(sur) ,
.12      T  -> true  )

.13 type: Type -> Unitname -> (FIRST¦NEXT) -> Surroundings -> BOOL
```

```
.0  make-array-type(atd)(newname)(dmap)(rlevel)(tdu)(sur) =
.1  let mk-Array-td(list)(subtype-indic) = atd in
.2  (is-Index(hd list) and tdu=COMPONENT -> exit ,
.3  T ->
.4   (let objdescr = mk-Obj-descr(make-subtype(subtype-indic)(dmap)
.                                  (rlevel)(tdu)(sur),nil)    in
.5   let indextypes = cases hd list:
.6      (mk-Index()            ->
.7          let typelist =
.8          <lookup-type(s-name(list[i])(sur)¦ 1<= i <= ln list> in
.9          ((∀ typ ∈ elems list)(is-Discrete(sel-ds(typ)(sur))) ->
.                                                       typelist,
.10         T -> exit),
.11      mk-Discrete-range() ->
.12         <generate-index-type(list[i])(dmap)(rlevel)(sur) ¦
.13          1 <= i <= ln list> )                            in
.14  let arraysub =cases hd list:
.15             (mk-Index() -> mk-Arraysub(nil),
.16              T          -> mk-Arraysub(INDEX-LOCK)) in
.17 mk-Type(newname,newname,newname,
.          mk-Array(indextypes,objdescr),arraysub,nil)

.18 type: Array-td -> Unitname -> Discrim-map -> Recordlevel ->
.          Type-def-usage -> Surroundings -> Type
```

```
.0 generate-index-type(discrrng)(dmap)(rlevel)(sur) =
.1 let xsur = update-sur-dict(dmap)(sur)                              in
.2 let indextype = s-type(generate-objdescr-from-discrrng(discrrng)
                                                         (xsur) in
.3 if (rlevel = IN-RECORD =>
.4     is-valid-index-constr(indextype)(discrrng)(dmap)(IN-RECORD)
                                                         (xsur)
.5     then indextype
.6     else exit

.7 type: Discrete-range -> Discrem-map -> Record-level ->
        Surroundings -> Type


let L denote the greek letter lambda in

.0  make-accesstype(access-td)(newtypename)(sur) =
.1  let mk-Access-td(subtypeindic) = access-td                       in
.2  let ds = cases subtypeindic:
.3  (nil -> (let func = Lhdict.
.4          (let mk-Type( ,,,structure,, )=
.5             lookup-Unitname(newtypename)(hdict) in
.6          cases structure:
.7          (mk-Access(f,COMPLETE) -> f(),
.8           T  -> exit) )                                  in
.9       mk-Access(func,INCOMPLETE)),
.10 T  -> (let accessedtp =
.11          make-subtype(subtypeindic)([])(nil)(TYPE)(sur) in
.12      mk-Access(L().accessedtp,COMPLETE))) in
.13 mk-Type(newtypename,newtypename,newtypename,ds,ACCESS,nil)

.14 type: Access-td -> Unitname -> Surroundings ~-> Type


.0 make-enum-type(etd)(newname)(sur) =
.1 let mk-Enum-td(tokenlist) =etd in
.2 (ln tokenlist ≠ card elems token -> exit,
.3  T -> mk-Type(newname,newname,newname,ENUM,
.4              mk-Enum(tokenlist,STATIC),nil))

.5 type: Enum-td -> Unitname -> Surroundings -> Type
```

```
.0 transform-type-decl(tdc)(sur) =
.1 let mk-Type-decl(id,typedef) = tdec in
.2 cases typedef:
.3  (mk-Intg-td(mk-Range-constr(mk-Range(e1,e2))) ->
.4      (let int = get-predef-inttype()                    in
.5       let v1 = eval-static-expr(e1)(int)(sur) in
.6       let v2 = eval-staric-expr(e2)(int)(sur) in
.7      mk-Typedecl(id,mk-Derived-td(
.8        mk-Subtype-indic(mk-Id(ENTEGER),
.9                         mk-Range-constr(mk-range(v1,v2))))),
.10  mk-Float-td(mk-Float-constr(ex,constr))       ->
.11      (let flt = get-predef-flt-type()          in
.12       let static-constr = cases constr:
.13          (nil -> nil,
.14           mk-Range-constr(mk-Range(e1,e2)) ->
.15           (let v1=eval-static-expr(e1)(flt)(sur) in
.16            let v2=eval-static-expr(e2)(flt)(sur) in
.17           mk-Range-constr(mk-Range(v1,v2)))) in
.18          mk-Typedecl(id,mk-Derived-td(
.19          mk-Subtype-indic(mk-Id($FLOAT),
.20                           mk-Float-constr'ex,static-constr)))))

.21 type: Type-decl -> Surroundings -> Type-decl
```

```
.0 make-fixed-type(fld)(newname)(sur) =
.1 let mk-Fixed-td(mk-Fixed-constr(ex,constr)) = ftd in
.2 let fix = get-predef-fix-type()                    in
.3 let static-constr = cases constr:
.4 (nil -> nil,
.5  mk-Range-constr(mk-Range(el,eh)) ->
.6     (let vl = eval-static-expr(el)(fix)(sur) in
.7      let vh = eval-static-expr(eh)(fix)(sur) in
.8     mk-Range-constr(mk-Range(vl,vh))))        in
.9 let newfix=
.10    mk-Type(newname,newname,newname,FIXED,s-sub(fix),nil) in
.11 constraint-fixed-type(newfix)(mk-Fixed-constr(ex,static-constr))(sur)

.12 type: Fixed-td -> Unitname -> Surroundings -> Type
```

## Missing Functions
------------------

.0  compatible-datastructure-and-discriminants
.1  <u>type</u>: Type -> Type -> Surr -> BOOL

## 3.10 Substructures

```
.0 constraint-type(typ)(constr)(dmap)(rlevel)(tdu)(sur) =
.1 cases s-sub(typ):
.2 (mk-Record-sub() ->
.3     constraint-record-type(typ)(constr)(dmap)(tdu)(sur),
.4 mk-Array-sub()  ->
.5     constraint-arraytype(typ)(constr)(dmap)(rlevel)(tdu)(sur),
.6 mk-Enum()    -> constraint-enum-type(typ)(constr)(sur),
.7 ACCESS-SUB   -> constraint-access-type(typ)(constr)(sur),
.8 mk-Intg()    -> constraint-intg-type(typ)(constr)(sur),
.9 mk-Fixed()   -> constraint-fixed-type(typ)(constr)(sur),
.10 mk-Float()  -> constraint-float-type(typ)(constr)(sur),
.11 PRIVATE-SUB -> exit)

.12 type: Type -> [Constraint] -> Discrim-map ->
          Record-level -> Type-def-usage -> Surroundings ->
          Type
```

```
.0 constraint-record-type(typ)(constr)(dmap)(tdu)(sur) =
.1 let mk-Record(discrim-descr, ) = sel-ds(sur) in
.2 (constr ≠ nil and
.3 (discrim-descr=nil or ~ is-Discrim-constr(constraint) or
.4  s-lock(s-sub(typ))                            -> exit,
.5 tdu=COMPONENT and constr=nil and discrim-descr≠nil and
.6 s-init(descrimdescr)=INIT and
.7 s-lock(s-sub(typ))≠ DISCRIM-LOCK               -> exit,
.8 constr = nil  -> typ+(s-ds:->nil),
.9 T ->
.10 (let mk-Discrim-descr(objmap,order,, ) = discrimdescr in
.11 let mk-Discrim-constr(pos,nam)     = constr       in
.12 (ln pos+ln nam ≠ card dom objmap              -> exit ,
.13 ~(∀ i,j E ind nam)
.14     (i≠j => s-id(nam[i])≠s-id(nam[j]) and
.15      s-id(nam[i])E{id|idE dom order   and
.16      order(id) > ln pos} )                    -> exit,
.17 ~(∀ i E ind pos)
.18    (is-valid-discrim(dmap)(s-tp(objmap(ordermap-1(id))))
.19                        (pos[i])(sur)           -> exit,
.20 ~(∀ (id,ex) E elems nam)
.21   (is-valid-discrim(dmap)(s-tp(objmap(id)))
.22                              (ex) (sur)    -> exit,
.23 T -> typ+(s-ds:->nil,s-sub:->mk-Recordsub(DISCRIM-LOCK)))))

.24 type: Type -> [Constraint] -> Discrim-map ->
          Type-def-usage -> Surroundings -> Type
```

```
.0 is-valid-discrim(dmap)(discrim-tp)(dexpr)(sur) =
.1 (is-Simp-name(dexpr) and dexpr E dom dmap ->
.2     s-name(discrim-tp)=s-name(s-tp(dmap(dexpr))),
.3 T -> type-expr-compatibility(discrim-tp)(dexpr)(sur))

.4 type: Discrim-map -> Type -> Expr -> Surroundings -> BOOL
```

```
.0 constraint-array-type(typ)(constr)(dmap)(tdu)(rlevel)(sur) =
.1 let mk-Array(typelist, ) = sel-ds(typ)(sur) in
.2 (constr ≠ nil and (~ is-Index-constr(constr) or
.3                     s-lock(s-sub(typ))=INDEX-LOCK) -> exit,
.4 tdu = COMPONET and constr ≠ nil and
.5                     s-lock(s-sub(typ))=INDEX-LOCK  -> exit,
.6 constr=nil -> typ+(s-ds:->nil),
.7 T ->
.8 (let mk-Index-constr(discr-rngl) = constr in
.9  (ln typelist ≠ ln discr-rngl                      -> exit,
.10  ~(∀ i E ind typelist)
.11     (is-valid-index-constr(typelist[i])(discr-rngl[i])
.12                     (dmap)(rlevel)(sur))  -> exit,
.13  T -> typ+(s-ds: -> nil,
.14             s-sub:->mk-Arraysub(INDEX-LOCK))))

.15 type: Type -> [Constraint] -> Discrim-map ->
           Type-def-usage -> Record-level ->
           Surroundings -> Type
.16 assert rlevel ≠ IN-RECORD => dmap=[]
```

```
.0 is-valid-index-constr(itype)(discr-rng)(dmap)(rlevel)(sur) =
.1 cases rlevel:
.2 (nil -> type-range-compatibility(itype)(discr-rng)(sur),
.3  IN-RECORD ->
.4     (type-range-compatibility(itype)(discr-rng)
.5        (update-sur-dict(dmap)(sur))        and
.6     cases discr-rng:
.7     (mk-Named-discr-rng(name,nrng) ->
.8       (nrng=nil ->
.9          s-static(s-sub(s-tp(lookup-type(name)(sur))))=STATIC,
.10      T        ->
.11        is-valid-range(discr-rng)(dmap)(itype)(sur)),
.12     mk-Range()                 ->
            is-valid-range(discr-rng)(dmap)(itype)(sur)))

.13 type: Type -> Discr-range -> Discrim-map -> Record-level ->
           Surroundings -> BOOL
```

```
.0 is-valid-range(rnge)(dmap)(itype)(sur) =
.1 let mk-Range(e1,e2)=rnge in
.2 (is-static-expr(e1)(itype)(sur) or
.3  (is-Simple-name(e1) and e1 E dom dmap)) and
.4 (is-static-expr(e2)(itype)(sur) or
.5  (is-Simple-name(e2) and e2 E dom dmap)) )

.6 type: Range -> Discrim-map -> Type -> Surroundings -> BOOL



.0 constraint-enum-type(typ)(constr)(sur) =
.1 let mk-Enum(idl,static) = s-sub(typ) in
.2 (constr = nil -> typ+(s-ds:->nil),
.3 ~is-Range-constr(constr)                       -> exit,
.4 T ->
.5 (let mk-Range-constr(rnge)=constr in
.6  (~ type-range-compatibility(typ)(rnge)(sur) -> exit,
.7   s-static(s-sub(typ)) ≠ STATIC              -> exit,
.8   T ->
.9   (let mk-Range(v1,v2)=eval-if-static-expr(rnge)(typ)(sur) in
.10   v1=nil or v2=nil ->
.11     typ+(s-ds:->nil,s-static o s-sub:->nil),
.12   T -> (let i,j E ind idl
.13           be s.t. idl[i]=v1 and idl[j]=v2  in
.14         typ+(s-ds:-> nil,s-sub:->
.15             mk-Enum(<idl[k]|k E {i:j}>,STATIC)))))

.16 type: Type -> [Constraint] -> Surroundings -> Type



.0 constraint-access-type(subtype)(constr)(sur) =
.1 let mk-Access(fct, ) = sel-ds(subtype)(sur) in
.2 if ((is-Index-constr(constr) or is-Discrim-constr(constr) or
.3      constr=nil) and
.4     (constr≠nil =>
.5      (trap exit with false in
.6      (let accstype = fct(s-dict(sur))                        in
.7       let newstype =
.8          constraint-type(accstype)(constr)([])(nil)(sur)) in
.9       true)))
.10    then subtype+(s-ds:->nil)
.11    else exit

.12 type: Type -> Constraint ->Surroundings ~-> Type
```

```
.0 constraint-fixed-type(typ)(constr)(sur) =
.1 (constr=nil -> typ+(s-ds:->nil),
.2 T -> (let mk-Fixed(delta) = s-sub(typ) in
.3 cases constr:
.4 (mk-Fixed-constr(ex,rng-constr) ->
.5       let new-delta = eval-static-expr(ex)(typ)(sur) in
.6       (new-delta < delta                         -> exit,
.7        T -> constraint-fixed-type(typ+(s-delta o s-sub:->new-delta))
.8                                   (rng-constr)(sur) ),
.9  mk-Range-constr(range)          ->
.10      (~type-range-compatibility(typ)(range)(sur) -> exit,
.11       T -> typ+(s-ds:->nil)),
.12 T -> exit))

.13 type: Type -> [Constraint] -> Surroundings -> Type



.0 constraint-intg-type(typ)(constr)(sur) =
.1 (constr=nil -> typ+(s-ds:->nil),
.2 ~is-Range-constr(constr) -> exit,
.3 T ->
.4 (let mk-Range-constr(mk-Range(e1,e2)) = constr in
.5 (~type-range-compatibility(typ)(mk-Range(e1,e2))(sur) -> exit,
.6  s-static o s-sub(typ) ≠ STATIC -> typ+(s-ds:->nil),
.7  T->
.8  (let v1=eval-if-static-expr(e1)(typ)(sur) in
.9   let v2=eval-if-static-expr(e2)(typ)(sur) in
.10  (v1=nil or v2=nil ->
.11      typ+(s-ds:->nil,s-static o s-sub:->nil),
.12   T -> typ+(s-ds:->nil,s-sub:->mk-Intg(v1,v2,STATIC))))))

.13 type: Type -> [Constraint] -> Surroundings -> Type



.0 constraint-float-type(typ)(constr)(sur)=
.1 (constr=nil -> typ+(s-ds:->nil),
.2 T -> let mk-Float(digits) = s-sub(typ) in
.3 cases constr:
.4 (mk-Float-constr(expr,rng-constr) ->
.5      let newdigits = eval-static-expr(expr)(predef-intg-type())
                                                    (sur) in
.6      (newdigits > digits -> exit,
.7       T                  ->
.8               constraint-float-type(typ+s-digits o s-sub:->newdigits))
                                   (rng-constr)(sur)) ,
.9  mk-Range-constr(range)          ->
.10      (~type-range-compatibility(typ)(range)(sur) -> exit,
.11       T -> typ+(s-ds:->nil)),
.12 T -> exit))

.13 type: Type -> [Constraint] -> Surroundings -> Type
```

Missing functions
------------------

The following functions are variations over a theme:

```
.0  eval-static-choice()()() = ( ... )
.1  type: (Expr|Discrete-range)->Type->Surr~-> VAL-set
```

```
.0  eval-static-expr()()() = ( ... )
.1  type: Expr -> Type -> Surr ~-> VAL
```

```
.0  eval-if-static-expr()()() = ( ... )
.1  type: Expr -> Type -> Surr -> [VAL]
```

```
.0  is-static-expr()()() = ( ... )
.1  type: Expr -> Type -> Surr -> BOOL
```

They use these functions:

```
.0  rebuild-expr()() = ( ... )

.1  type: Expr -> Surr ~-> Reb-expr

.0  rebuild-range()() = ( ... )
.1  type: (Discrete-range|Sub-type-indic) -> Surr ~-> Reb-range
```

## 3.11  Names

```
.0 lookup-type(name)(sur) =
.1 let descrlist=lookup-name(name)(sur) =
.2 cases descrlist:
.3 (<mk-Type-descr()> -> hd descrlist,
.4  T -> exit)

.5 type: Name -> Surroundings -> Type-descr
```

```
.0 lookup-name(name)(sur) =
.1 let dict = extract-dict(sur) in
.2 cases name:
.3 (mk-Simple-name(id)    -> if id E dom dict then <dict(id)> else <>,
.4  mk-Index-component()  -> lookup-index-component(name)(sur),
.5  mk-Select-component()-> lookup-select-component(name)(sur),
.6  mk-Attr-name()        -> lookup-attr-name(name)(sur),
.7  mk-Slice-name()       -> lookup-slice-name(name)(sur),
.8  mk-All-name()         -> lookup-all-name(name)(sur),
.9  mk-Function-call      ->
.10    lookup-avaiable-func-result-descrs(name)(sur))

.11 type: Name -> Surroundings -> Descr*
```

```
.0 lookup-index-component(name)(sur) =
.1 let mk-Index-component(name',expr-list) = name in
.2 let descr-list = lookup-name(name')(sur)          in
.3 conc < cases descr-list[i]:
.4       (mk-Obj-descr(typ,const) ->
.5          cases sel-ds(typ)(sur):
.6          (mk-Array(typelist,objdescr) ->
.7           (if ln expr-list = ln typelist and
.8              (compatibility(typelist[j])(expr-list[j])(sur))
.9               (j E ind typelist)
.10              then <objdescr+(s-con:->CONSTANT)> else <>),
.11       mk-Access(fct, )         ->
.12         (cases sel-ds(fct(s-dict(sur))):
.13          (mk-Array(typelist,objdescr) ->
.14            if ln expr-list = ln typelist and
.15               (compatibility(typelist[j])(expr-list[j])(sur))
.16                (j E ind typelist)
.17               then <objdescr> else <> ,
.18          T -> <>),
.19         T -> <>),
.20       mk-Overload-descr()            ->
.21         lookup-avaiable-func-result-descrs(name)(sur),
.22       T -> <>)
.23 | i E ind descr-list>

.24 type: Name -> Surroundings -> Descr*
```

```
.0   lookup-selected-component(name)(sur) =
.1   let mk-Select-component(prefixname,mk-Simp-name(id))= name in
.2   let descrl = lookup-name(prefixname) (sur)                    in
.3   conc < cases descrl[i] :
.4        ( mk-Pack-descr(visdict,,,,, )   ->
.5            if id E dom visdict then <visdict(id)> else <> ,
.6          mk-Overload-descr(ds)           ->
.7            ( let sp = {mk-Sub-prgr-descr(ldict,, ) E ds |
.                         id E dom ldict}                    in
.8              cases sp:
.                ({es} ->(let mk-Sub-prgr-descr(l,, )=es in<l(id)>),
.                 T ->(> )
.9          mk-Obj-descr(typ,con)            ->
.10           (cases sel-ds(typ)(sur):
.11           mk-Record(dis,compl) ->
.12             (let rdict=flatten-record(dis,compl)          in
.13             if id E dom rdict then <rdict(id)+(s-const:->con)>
.14                               else <> ) ,
.15           mk-Access(fct, )      ->
.16             (cases sel-ds(fct(s-dict(sur))):
.17              (mk-Record(dis,compl) ->
.18                 (let rdict=flatten-record(dis,compl)  in
.19                  if id E dom rdict then <rdict(id)>
.20                                    else <> ),
.21               T -> <> )),
.22            T -> <> ),
.24         mk-Block-descr(localdict, )       ->
.24            if id E dom lovaldict then localdict(id) else <> ,
.25         T -> <>
.26  |   i E ind descrl >

.27  type: Select-component -> Surroundings -> Descr*
```

```
.0 flatten-record(discrim,comp) =
.1 if discrim= nil then [] else
.2 ((let mk-Discrim-descr(dmap,,, ) = discrim in
.3   dmap) U flatten-comp-descr(comp))

.4 type: [Discrim-descr] Compl-descr -> Dict


.0 flatten-compl-descr(mk-Compl-descr(objmap,,varpartdescr)) =
.1 objmap U
.2 (if varpartdescr = nil then [] else
.3  (let mk-Varpart-descr( ,choicemap) = varpartdescr in
.4   merge [flatten-comp-descr(choicemap(ch) ¦ ch E dom choicemap]))

.5 type: Compl-descr -> Dict


.0 look-up-attr-name(name)(sur) =
.1 let mk-Attr-name(name',attribute) = name in
.2 let descrl = lookup-name(name')(sur)      in
.3 conc < cases descrl[i]:
.4  ( mk-Typedescr() ->
.5      type-descr-attributes(descr)(attribute)(sur),
.6    mk-Obj-descr() ->
            ....
          .
          .
          .
.7    T -> <> ¦ i E ind descrl>

.8 type: Name -> Surroundings -> Descr*


.0 type-descr-attributes(descr)(attribute)(sur) =
.1 let mk-Type-descr(typ, ) = descr in
.2 cases attribute:
.3 (BASE   -> (let basetp = lookup-base-type(typ)(s-dict(sur)) in
.4             <mk-Type-descr(basetp,[])>),
.5  FIRST  -> get-first-descriptor(typ)(sur),
.6  DIGITS -> get-digits-descriptor(typ)(sur),
.7  LAST   -> ....
          .
          .
          .
.8    )

.9 type: Type-descr -> Attr -> Surroundings ->
         (Type-descr ¦ Obj-descr)
```

```
.0 lookup-slice-name(name)(sur) =
.1 let mk-Slicename(name',descr-rng) = name in
.2 let descr-list = lookup-name(name')(sur) in
.3 conc < cases descr-list[i]:
.4  (mk-Obj-descr(typ, ) ->
.5     cases sel-ds(typ)(sur):
.6     (mk-Array(typelist, ) ->
.7      (if ln typelist=1 and
.8         type-range-compatibility(typelist[1])(descr-rng)(sur)
.9         then <descr-list[i]> else <>),
.10    mk-Access(fct, )       ->
.11      (let accessedtp = fct(s-dict(sur)) in
.12      cases sel-ds(accessedtp)(sur):
.13      (mk-Array(typelist, ) ->
.14       (if ln typelist=1 and
.15          type-range-compatibility(typelist[1])(descr-rng)(sur)
.16          then <mk-Obj-descr(accessedtp,nil)> else <>),
.17        T -> <>),
.18     T -> <>),
.19 T -> <>)
.20 | i E ind descr-list>

.21 type: Slice-name -> Surroundings -> Descr*


.0 lookup-all-name(name)(sur) =
.1 let mk-All-name(name') = name            in
.2 let descr-list = lookup-name(name')(sur) in
.3 conc <cases descr-list[i]:
.4  (mk-Obj-descr(typ, ) ->
.5     cases sel-ds(typ)(sur) :
.6     ( mk-Access(fct) -> <mk-Obj-descr(fct(s-dict(sur)),nil)>,
.7       T -> <>),
.8  T -> <>) | i E ind descrl>

.9 type: All-name -> Surroundings -> Descr*


.0  lookup-available-funct-result-descrs(name) (sur) =
.1 ( let mk-Func-call(name',act-parm-list) = name          in
.2    let descrl = lookup-name(name')(sur)                 in
.3    conc < cases descrl[i]:
.4          ( mk-Overload-descr(ds)    ->
.5              get-available-obj-list(act-parm-list)
.6                ({d | d E ds and is-Subprgr-descr(d)}) (sur),
.7             T                           -> <> )
.8          | i E ind descrl > )

.9 type: Func-call -> Surroundings -> Obj-descr*
```

```
.0 get-available-obj-list(parms)(pset)(sur)=
.1 if pset = { } then <> else
.2 let d E pset in
.3 let mk-Subprgr-descr( ,,entrance) = d   in
.4 ((if s-return(entrance) ≠ nil and
          parameter-checker(parms)(entrance)(sur)
.5       then <mk-Obj-descr(s-return(entrance),CONSTANT)>
.6       else <> )) ^
.7 get-available-obj-list(parms)(pset\d)(sur) ) )

.8 type: Act-parm* -> ( Subprgr-descr)-set ->Sur -> Obj-descr*
```

3.12  Type Check of Expressions

```
.0 type-range-compatibility(type1)(range)(sur) =
.1 cases range:
.2 (mk-Range(e1,e2)                         ->
.3     (type-expr-compatibility(type1)(e1)(sur) and
.4      type-expr-compatibility(type1)(e2)(sur) ),
.5  mk-Named-descr-range(name,rnge) ->
.6     (let mk-Type-descr(type2, ) = lookup-type(name)(sur) in
.7      (s-name(type1)=s-name(type2) and
.8       type-range-compatibility(type2)(rnge)(sur))),
.9  nil -> true)

.10 type: Type -> Discrete-range -> Surroundings -> BOOL
```

```
.0  type-expr-compatibility(required-type)(expr)(sur) =
.1  let strongsur=sur+(s-wm->[ ])                      in
.2  (    compatibility(required-type) (expr) (strongsur)
.3    or compatibility(required-type) (expr) (sur) )

.4  type: Type -> Expr -> Surroundings -> BOOL
```

```
.0  compatibility(reqtype)(expr)(sur) =
.1  cases expr :
.2  ( mk-Aggregate() -> Aggregate-compatibility( reqtype)(expr)(sur),
.3    mk-Allocator() -> Allocate-compatibility(reqtype)(expr)(sur),
.4    null           -> Allocate-compatibility(reqtype)(null)(sur),
.5    INTG           -> Integer-compatibility(reqtype),
.6    NUM            -> Real-compatibility(reqtype),
.7    T              ->
.8        (let typel = extr-available-types(expr)(sur)            in
.9         (E! i E ind typel) (cases typel[i]:
.10           ( mk-Pseudo-type(val)         ->
                          compatibility(reqtype)(val)(sur),
.11          mk-Type(univ-fixed,,,, ) -> false,
.12          mk-Type()                ->
                          s-name(typel[i])=s-name(reqtype)))

.13 type: (Pseudotype | Type) -> Expr -> Surroundings -> BOOL
```

```
.0  integer-compatibility(reqtype) =
.1  s-ds(reqtype) = any-integer or is-Intg(s-sub(reqtype))

.2  type: Type -> BOOL




.0  real-compatibility(reqtype) =
.1  s-ds(reqtype) = universal-fixed   or
.2  is-Float(s-sub(reqtype))          or
.3  is-Fixed(s-sub(reqtype))

.4  type: Type ->  BOOL




.0  extr-available-types( expr ) (sur)
.1  cases expr:
.2  ( mk-Name()           -> extr-name-types( expr ) (sur),
.3    mk-Infix()          -> extr-infix-types(expr)(sur),
.4    mk-Prefix()         -> extr-prefix-types(expr)(sur),
.5    mk-Qualif-expr()    -> extr-qualif-type(expr)(sur),
.6    mk-Type-conv()      -> extr-conv-type(expr)(sur),
.7    mk-Membership()     ->
              get-pre-def-bool-type-if-wf-membership(expr)(sur),
.8    mk-String()         -> get-pre-def-string-type()    ,
.9    Char-lit            -> extr-char-lit-types(expr)(sur),
.10   T                   -> /* extracting types impossible
                               see the pre-condition of
                               this function            */ )

.11 type: Expr -> Surroundings -> Type*
.12 pre  : expr ~E { Allocator,Aggregate,null,INTG,NUM }




.0  extract-name-types( name ) (sur) =
.1  let descrl = lookup-name(name) (sur) in
.2  conc < cases descrl[i]:
.3          ( mk-Obj-descr(otype, )  -> <otype> ,
.4            mk-Overload-descr(ds)  ->
.5              ( let list E Type* be.s.t
.6                  card elems list = ln list and
.7                  elems list = {ltype |
                              mk-Literal-descr(ltype)E ds }) in
.8              list)                   ,
.9            mk-Number(val)          -> <mk-Pseudotype(val)> ,
.10           T                       -> <> )
.11     | i E ind descrl>

.12 type: Name -> Surroundings -> ( Type | Pseudotype )*
```

```
.0 extr-char-types(charlit)(sur) =
.1 let dict = extract-dict(sur)                     in
.2 let mk-Overload-descr(cset)=dict(charlit)        in
.3 let s = {tp | (E mk-Literal-descr(tp) E cset)} in
.4     list E Type* s.t. (card elems list = ln list and
.5                             elems list = s)

.6 type: Char-lit -> Surroundings -> Type*
```

```
.0  extr-infix-types(infix)(sur) =
.1  let mk-Infix( ,op, )       = infix                in
.2  let mk-Overload-descr(ds) = (extr-dict(sur))(op) in
.3    extr-infix-ret-types(infix)(ds)(sur)

.4  type: Infix -> Surroundings -> Type*
```

```
.0  extr-infix-ret-types(infix)(dset)(sur) =
.1  if dset = { } then <> else
.2    ( let d E dset , mk-Infix(e1,,e2) = infix      in
.3       let mk-Sub-prgr-descr( ,,entrance)= d        in
.4       let mk-Entrance( ,rtn, )        = entrance   in
.5       extr-infix-ret-types(infix)(dset\{d})(sur) ^
.6        ( rtn=nil -> <>,
.7          paramchecker(entrance)
                         (mk-Act-param-list(<e1,e2>,<>))(sur)
.8                  -> <rtn>,
.9          T        -> <>))

.10 type: Infix -> Sub-prgr-descr-set -> Surroundings -> Type*
```

```
.0 extr-prefix-types(prefix)(sur) =
.1 let mk-Prefix(op,ex) = prefix in
.2 let mk-Overload-descr(dset) =(extr-dict(sur))(op)  in
.3   extr-prefix-return-types(ex)(dset)(sur)

.4 type: Prefix -> Surroundings -> Type*
```

```
.0 extr-prefix-return-types(expr)(dset)(sur)=
.1 if dset={} then <> else
.2 (let d E dset                                               in
.3  let mk-Subprgr-descr( ,,entrance) = d                      in
.4  let mk-Entrance( ,rtn, )            = entrance in
.5  extr-prefix-return-types(expr)(dset \ {d})(sur)^
.6  (ret = nil -> <>,
.7   paramchecker(entrance)(mk-Act-Param-list(<expr>,<>))(sur) -> <rtn>,
.8   T -> <>))

.9 type: Expr -> Subprgr-descr-set -> Surroundings -> Type*
```

```
.0 extract-qualif-type(mk-Qualif-type(name,expr))(sur) =
.1 let mk-Type-descr(qtype, )=lookup-type(name)(sur) in
.2 let basetype = lookup-base-type(qtype)(sur)              in
.3 if compatibility(basetype)(expr)(sur)
.4    then <qtype>
.5    else <>

.6  type: Qualif-expr -> Surroundings -> Type*
```

```
.0 extract-type-conv-type(mk-Type-conv(name,expr))(sur) =
.1 let mk-Type-descr(convtype, ) = lookup-type(name)(sur) in
.2 if explicit-conv-compatibility(convtype)(expr)(sur)
.3    then <convtype>
.4    else <>

.5  type: Type-conv -> Surroundings -> Type*
```

```
.0  explicit-conv-compatibility(type1)(expr)(sur) =
.1  cases expr:
.2  (mk-Aggregate() -> aggregate-compatibility(type1)(expr)(sur),
.3  null             -> allocate-compatibility(type1)(expr)(sur) ,
.4  INTG             -> is-numeric(sel-ds(type1)(sur))             ,
.5  NUM              -> is-numeric(sel-ds(type1)(sur))             ,
.6  T                ->
.7   (let type1=extract-available-types(expr)(sur)               in
.8    (E! i E ind type1)
.9      ((is-derived-or-compatible-types(type1)(type1[i])(sur) or
.10      (is-Array(sel-ds(type1)(sur))           and
.11      is-Array(sel-ds(type1[i])(sur))         and
.12      (let basetp1 = lookup-base-type(type1)(sur)             in
.13       let mk-Array(tl1,objd1, ) = sel-ds(basetp1)(sur)       in
.14       let mk-Array(tl2,objd2, ) = sel-ds(type1[i])(sur)      in
.15       (ln t1 = ln tl2 and
.16       (V i E ind tl1)
.17       (is-derived-or-compatible-types(tl1[i])(tl2[i])(sur))
.18       and is-derived-or-compatible-types(s-type(objd1))
.19                              (s-type(objd2))(sur)))))))))

.20 type: Type -> Expr -> Surrounding -> BOOL



.0  is-derived-or-compatible-types(type1)(type2)(sur) =
.1  cases type2:
.2  (mk-Pseudotype()                -> is-Numeric(sel-ds(type1)(sur)),
.3  mk-Type( ,,,univ-fixed,, ) -> is-Numeric(sel-ds(type1)(sur)),
.4  mk-Type(name2,parent2,,,, )->
.5    (let mk-Type( name1,parent1,,,, ) = type1 in
.6       name1  E {name2,parent2} or
.7       name2  E {name1,parent1}       ))

.8  type: Type -> ( Type | Pseudotype ) -> BOOL



.0  get-predef-bool-type-if-wf-membership(mbs)(sur) =
.1  (let mk-Membership(expr,rangeden) = mbs in
.2   if cases rangeden:
.3    (mk-Range(ex1,ex2)                     ->
.4     (let rtype =extr-type-from-range(rangeden) in
.5      ( is-Pseudotype(rtype) or is-Scalar(s-ds(rtype)) ) and
.6       type-expr-compatibility(rtype)(expr)(sur) )   ,
.7     mk-Subtype-indic(name,constr)  ->
.8      (let rtype=make-subtype(rangeden)([])(nil)(TYPE)(sur)in
.9       ( is-Pseudotype(rtype) or is-Scalar(s-ds(rtype)) ) and
.10       type-expr-compatibility(rtype)(expr)(sur) ))
.11   then predef-bool-type() else exit)

.12   type: Membership -> Surroundings -> Type
```

```
.0  extract-type-from-range(mk-range(ex1,ex2))(sur)=
.1  if is-Composite(ex1) or ex1=null or
       is-Composite(ex2) or ex2=null
.2  then exit else
.3  (is-INTG(ex1) and is-INTG(ex2) -> predef-Intg-type() ,
.4   is-NUM (ex1) and is-NUM (ex2) -> mk-Pseudotype(ex1) ,
.5   T                             ->
.6     (let tl1 = extract-overloadable-types(ex1)(sur)     in
.7      (let tl2 = extract-overloadable-types(ex2)(sur)     in
.8      let test= get-test-fct(tl1)(tl2)(sur)              in
.9      if (E! i E ind tl1) (E! j E ind tl2)(test(i)(j))
.10        then (let i E ind tl1,j E ind tl2 be s.t. test(i)(j) in
.11             cases tl1[i],tl2[j]:
.12              (mk-Type(),T -> tl1[i],
.13               T,mk-Type() -> tl2[j],
.14               T           -> tl1[i]))
.15         else exit) ) )

.16 type: Range -> Surroundings -> Type
```

let L denote the greek letter lambda in

```
.0 get-check-fct(l1)(l2)(sur)= Li. Lj.cases (l1[i],l2[j]):
.1 (mk-Type(name,,dsname, ),mk-Type(name2, ) ->
      is-Scalar(s-ds(lookup-unitname(dsname)(sur))) and
      name1=name2 ,
.2 mk-Type(),mk-Pseudotype(val)              ->
      type-expr-compatibility(l1[i](val)(sur) ,
.3 mk-Pseudotype(val),mk-Type()              ->
      type-expr-compatibility(l2[j](val)(sur) ,
.4 mk-Pseudotype(v1),mk-Pseudotype(v2)       ->
      (is-INTG(v1) and is-INTG(v2)) or (is-NUM(v1) and is-NUM(v2))
.5 T                                         -> false)

.6 type: Type* -> Type* -> Surroundings -> ( INTG -> INTG -> BOOL)
```

```
.0 pre-def-intg-type() =
.1 mk-Type( <mk-Simp-name(STANDARD),mk-Simp-name(INTEGER)>,
.2          <mk-Simp-name(STANDARD),mk-Simp-name(INTEGER)>,
.3          <mk-Simp-name(STANDARD),mk-Simp-name(INTEGER)>,
.4          INTG,
.5          mk-Intg(implementation-defined-lover-bound,
.6                  implementation-defined-upper-bound,
.7                  STATIC                    ),
.8          nil)

.9 type: () -> Type
```

Missing Functions
------------------


```
.0  allocate-compatibility()()() = ( ... )
.1  type: Type -> Allocator -> Surr -> BOOL


.0  aggregate-compatibility()()() = ( ... )
.1  type: Type -> Aggregate -> Surr -> BOOL


.0  get-predef-bool-type() = ( ... ) type: () -> Type
.1              fixed
.2              float
.3              string
.4              character
```

## 3.13 Statements

```
.0 is-wf-Stmt-list(stmtl)(sur) =
.1 (∀ stmt E elems stmtl) (is-wf-Stmt(stmt)(sur))

.2 type: Stmt* -> Surroundings -> BOOL
.3 pre : stmtl≠<> (syntactically there is at least one)
```

```
.0  is-wf-Stmt(stmt)(sur) =
.1  cases stmt:
.2  (mk-Assign()          -> is-wf-Assign(stmt)(sur),
.3   mk-Block()           -> is-wf-Block(stmt)(sur),
.4   mk-Loop-stmt()       -> is-wf-Loop(stmt)(sur),
.5   mk-Exit()            -> is-wf-Exit(stmt)(sur),
.6   mk-Return()          -> is-wf-Return(stmt)(sur),
.7   mk-Proc-call()       -> is-wf-Proc-call(stmt)(sur),
.8   mk-If-Stmt()         -> is-wf-if-stmt(stmt)(sur),
.9   ....
.10  null                 -> true)

.11 type: Stmt -> Surroundings -> BOOL
```

```
.0  is-wf-Assign(assign) (sur) =
.1  (     half-check-Assign(assign)(STRONG)(sur)
.2     or half-check-Assign(assign)(VISIBLE)(sur) )

.3 type: Assign -> Surroundings -> BOOL
```

```
.0 half-check-Assign(mk-Assign(name,expr))(test)(sur) =
.1 let testsur = cases test : ( STRONG -> sur+(s-wm->[ ])
.2                              T      -> sur)  in
.3 let descrl  = look-up-name(name) (testsur)   in
.4 ( E! i E ind descrl )
.5   (mk-Obj-descr(otype, )=descrl[i]              and
.6    type-expr-compatibility(otype)(expr)(sur) and
.7    (let mk-Obj-descr(otype,const) E elems descrl be s.t.
.8                 type-expr-compatibility(otype)(expr)(sur) in
.9       const ≠ CONSTANT and is-not-limited(otype)))

.10 type: Assign -> (STRONG|VISIBLE) -> Surroundings -> BOOL
```

```
.0  is-wf-Block(mk-Block(id,mk-Decl-part(decl1,body1),stmt1))(sur) =
.1  trap exit with false in
.2  (let id' = if id=nil then BLK else id                              in
.3   let presur=update-Sur([id'->mk-Block-descr([],s-level(sur)^<id'>)],
                           <id'>,[],[],<mk-In-block({})>)(sur) in
.4   let blocksur = get-Decl-part-Sur(decl1^body1)(presur)            in
.5   let mk-In-block(subprgrs) = hd s-status1(blocksur)               in
.6   ( ~(E subprgr E subprgrs)(subprgr=mk-Sub-prgr( ,,nil)) and
.7     is-wf-Stmt-list(stmt1)(blocksur) ))

.8  type:Block -> Surroundings -> BOOL
```

```
.0  is-wf-Loop(mk-Loop-stmt(lid,iteration,stmt1))(sur) =
.1  let id = (lid=nil -> LOOP,T -> lid)                         in
.2  let ldict = [id -> mk-Loop-descr(s-level(sur)^<id>] in
.3  cases iteration:
.4  (mk-For-clause(pid,discrrange) ->
.5      (let presur = update-Sur-Dict([pid -> INTRODUCED)) in
.6       let pdict  = [pid -> generate-obj-descr-from-discr-rng
                            (discrrange)(presur)        ] in
.7       check-loop(ldict+pdict)(stmt1)(id)(sur)) ,
.8   mk-While-clause(condition)      ->
.9      type-expr-compatibility(pre-def-bool-type())(condition)
                              (update-Sur-dict(ldict)(sur) )   and
.10     check-loop(ldict)(stmt1)(id)(sur)             ,
.11  nil                       ->
        check-loop(ldict)(stmt1)(id)(sur) )

.12  type: Loop-stmt -> Surroundings -> BOOL
```

```
.0  check-loop(loopdict)(stmt1)(id)(sur) =
.1  let newsur=Update-sur(loopdict,,,mk-In-Loop(s-level(sur)^<id>)) in
.2  (V stmt E elems stmt1)(is-wf-Stmt(stmt)(newsur))

.3  type: Dict -> Stmt* -> Id -> Surroundings -> BOOL
```

```
.0  generate-obj-descr-from-discr-rng(discr-range)(sur) =
.1  cases discr-range:
.2  ( mk-Named-discr-rng(name,range) ->
.3     (let typ = lookup-structure-type(name)(sur) in
.4      if is-Discrete(s-ds(typ)) and
.5         range ≠ nil => type-range-compatible(typ)(range)(sur)
.6         then mk-Obj-descr(typ+(s-ds:->nil),CONSTANT)
.7         else exit) ,
.8     mk-Range(ex1,ex2)             ->
.9      (let typ =extr-type-from-range(discr-range)(sur) in
.10      if is-Discrete(s-ds(typ))
.11         then mk-Obj-descr(typ+(s-ds:->nil),CONSTANT))
.12         else exit)))

.13 type: Discrete-range -> Surroundings ~-> Obj-descr



.0  is-wf-Exit(mk-Exit(loopname,condition))(sur) =
.1  (condition ≠ nil => type-expr-compatibility(pre-def-bool-type())
.2                    (condition) (sur)) and
.3  (name ≠ nil   ->
.4       cases lookup-name(name)(sur):
.5        (mk-Loop-descr(unitname) ->
.6              check-transfer(unitname)(s-status(sur)),
.7           T                      -> false),
.8     T            -> check-transfer(nil)(s-status(sur)))

.9 type:Exit -> Surroundings -> BOOL



.0  check-transfer(loopname)(statuslist) =
.1   if statuslist = <> then false else
.2     cases hd statuslist:
.3      (mk-In-Pack-body() -> false,
.4       mk-In-Task-body() -> false,
.5       mk-In-Subprgr()   -> false,
.6       mk-In-Loop(name)  ->
.7          (loopname=name or loopname=nil or
.8             check-transfer(loopname)(tl statuslist) ),
.9        T               -> check-transfer(loopname)(tl statuslist))

.10 type: Unitname -> Status* -> BOOL



.0  is-wf-Return(mk-Return(expr))(sur) =
.1  trap exit with false in
.2  (let mk-In-Subprgr(rtype)=get-subprgr-status(s-status(sur)) in
.3  (rtype=nil -> expr=nil,
.4   T          -> type-expr-compatibility(rtype)(expr)(sur)))

.5 type: Return -> Surroundings -> BOOL
```

```
.0  get-sub-prgr-status(statuslist)=
.1  if statuslist=<> then exit else
.2  cases hd statuslist:
.3  (mk-In-Pack-body() -> exit,
.4   mk-In-Task-body() -> exit,
.5   mk-In-Subprgr()   -> hd statuslist,
.6   T                 -> get-sub-prgr-status(tl statuslist))

.7  type: Status* ~-> In-Subprgr
```

```
.0  is-wf-Proc-call(mk-Proc-call(name,act-parml))(sur) =
.1  cases lookup-name(name)(sur):
.2  ( <mk-Overload-descr(dset)>  ->
.3      ( E! mk-Subprgr-descr( ,,entrance) E dset)
.4          (s-return(entrance) = nil and
.5             Parameterchecker(act-parml)(entrance)(sur) ) ,
.6   T                              -> false)

.7  type: Proc-call -> Surroundings -> BOOL
```

```
.0  is-wf-If-stmt(mk-If-stmt(list,last))(sur) =
.1  (¥ mk-Cond-stl(condition,stl) E elems list)
.2    (type-expr-compatibility(predef-bool-type())(condition)(sur)
.3     and is-wf-Stmt-list(stl)(sur))
.4     and (last≠nil  => is-wf-Stmt-list(last)(sur))

.5  type: If-stmt -> Surroundings -> BOOL
```

3.14  Transform & Rebuild Functions

```
.0 transform(as0-expr) =

.1 cases as0-expr:
.2 (mk-Expression(relation, rel-list) ->
.3    (rel-list = <> -> transform(relation),
.4     T               ->
.5       (let (op,next) = hd rel-list                      in
.6        mk-Infix(transform(relation, op,
.7                 transform(mk-Expression(next,tl rel-list))))),
.8
.9 mk-Relation(simp-left,right)      ->
.10   (right = nil   -> transform(simple-left),
.11    T             ->
.12    (let (op,simp-right) = right                        in
.13    mk-Infix(transform(simple-left),op,transform(simp-right)))),
.14
.15 mk-Simple(mop,term,term-list)      ->
.16   (let t1 = transform(term)                            in
.17    let e1 = cases mop: (nil->t1,T->mk-Prefix(mop,t1)   in
.18    cases term-list:
.19    (<> -> e1,
.20     T -> (let (op,next-term) = hd termlist             in
.21          mk-Infix(e1,op,
.22            transform(mk-Simple(
.23                      nil,next-term,tl term-list)))))),
.24 mk-Term( ... )                        -> ...  ,
.25 ...                                        )

.26 type: (Expression | Relation | Simple | Term |... ) -> Expr


.0 rebuild-loop-stmt(mk-Loop-stmt(lid,itcl,stlist,elid))(sur) =
.1 (lid ≠ elid -> exit, T -> let id = (lid=nil->LOOP,T->lid)) in
.2 let loop-dict = [id->mk-Loop-descr(s-level(sur)^<id>)]   in
.3 mk-Loop'((lid=nil->nil,T->mk-Id(s-level(sur)^<lid>)),cases itcl:
.4    (nil                                -> 
.5        mk-Uncond-loop(rebuild-loop(loop-dict)(stlist)(id)(sur),
.6
.7     mk-For-clause(pid,discr-rng,reverse) ->
.8        (let presur = update-sur-dict([pid->INTRODUCED](sur)   in
.9         let discr-rng'= rebuild-discr-rng(discr-rng)(presur)  in
.10        let pdict =
.11          [pid->mk-Obj-descr(get-tp(discr-rng'),CONSTANT)]     in
.12        mk-For-loop(pid,reverse,discr-rng',
.13          rebuild-loop(loop-dict+pdict)(stlist)(id)(sur) )),
.14
.15    mk-While-clause(expr)                  ->
.16        (let xsur = update-sur-dict(loop-dict)(sur)          in
.17         let expr'= rebuild-expr(expr)(BOOL)(xsur)           in
.18        mk-While-loop(expr',
.19          rebuild-loop(loop-dict)(stlist)(id)(sur) ))     ))

.20 type: Loop-stmt -> Surroundings -> ~-> Loop'
```

208

```
.0  rebuild-loop(ldict)(stlist)(lid)(sur) =
.1  let local-sur =
.2      update-sur(ldict,,,mk-In-Loop(s-level(sur)^<lid>)) in
.3      rebuild-stmt-list(stmtlist)(local-sur)

.4  type: Dict -> Stmt+ -> (Id|LOOP) -> Surroundings~-> Stmt'+




.0  rebuild-stmt-list(stlist)(sur) =
.1  if stlist = <> then <> else
.2      rebuild-statement(hd stlist)(sur) ^
.3      rebuild-stmt-list(tl stlist)(sur)

.4  type:  Stmt* -> Surroundings ~-> Stmt'*
```

# 4.0 Index

# A FORMAL SEMANTICS DEFINITION OF SEQUENTIAL ADA

*Jan Storbank Pedersen*

Abstract:

This paper gives a formal denotational dynamic semantics definition of the sequential parts of Ada. It describes the 'meaning' of (abstract) Ada constructs by state-to-state transformations on an abstract machine.

Contents
========

# 1 Introduction

This paper is the result of a student project that took place during the spring and summer of 1980 at the Department of Computer Science, Technical University of Denmark, to attain the degree of master of science in engineering. The initial work was carried out in collaboration with Jørgen Bundgaard, Ole Dommergaard, Hans Henrik Løvengreen and Lennart Schultz. Since we were covering different parts of the language Ada: Jørgen Bundgaard and Lennart Schultz the static semantics, Hans Henrik Løvengreen the tasking model, Ole Dommergaard the definition of a virtual target machine (A-code machine) and I the dynamic semantics, the discussions on Ada revealed all the different aspects represented by the different points of view. Especially the close relation between the dynamic semantics, the tasking model and the A-code machine lead to fruitful discussions with Hans Henrik Løvengreen and Ole Dommergaard.

This report contains a formal definition of the sequential parts of the programming language Ada. The definition is presented in the style of "The Vienna Development Method" (called VDM) of Dines Bjørner and Cliff B. Jones: in "The Vienna Development Method: The Meta-Language" [BjJo 78].

When constructing a compiler for a programming language it is of course important to know 'all' about the programming language. First of all the concrete syntax of the language must be known. Means for defining such syntaxes have long been known and used in e.g. reference manuals. The most widely used method is to define a BNF-grammar for the language. Such grammars are then used as a basis of making scanners and syntax analysers. But as to checking context sensitive conditions (e.g. type checking), generating code and constructing a runtime system there is no method, generally agreed on, for describing these aspects formally or constructing the corresponding compiler components.

This paper is one of three parts constituting a formal definition of these three aspects:
A definition of the context sensitive conditions to be satisfied by a program, and called the static semantics [BuSch 80].
A definition of the dynamic semantics of (sequential) Ada (this report) and a model of parallelism in Ada [Lø 80b].

The compiler development method of which defining these three models is an essential part is described in the paper by Dines Bjorner and Ole Oest in this book.

The rest of this paper is divided into the following parts:

- The textual part of the model, with some examples.

- The domains and formulas of the model as appendices A and B.

I wish to express my gratitude for the valuable comments made on this model by Hans Henrik, Jørgen, Lennart and Ole. Furthermore Dr. Ole N. Oest pointed out aspects concerning the relations between an earlier version of this model and a compiling algorithm; this relation is described in the joint paper [DDC 80/14]. Finally thanks to my teacher professor Dines Bjørner for introducing abstract software specification to me, and the influence that this had on the course of the later part of my study.

## 2 Dynamic Semantics of Sequential Ada

This chapter is a formal definition of the dynamic semantics of essential parts of sequential Ada. One essential part is however not dealt with in this model. That is the concept of generics. However, it seems to be a feature of the language that does not call for major extensions of the modelling of the dynamic semantics.

The definition consists of two major parts: the abstract domains and the formulas. The domains are divided into two categories, the semantic domains and the syntactic domains. The objects belonging to the semantic domains are the objects on which the formulas operate when elaborating, interpreting or evaluating objects of the syntactic domains. In a model in this style, as in any formal model of a programming language, the semantic domains are the storage and the environment, and the syntactic domains are essentially those belonging to the abstract syntax of the language (here called "AS2").

The model defines the semantics of complete programs as a state-to-state transformation, most of the formulas are thus imperative. A 'complete' program is in this model is seen as a block even though it in concrete Ada is a list of compilation units. This way of looking at a program has been chosen as the aspects concerning compilation units, separate compilation and library packages are not the subject of this report. However no generality is lost by this way of modelling a program: The block just has to contain all the packages used by the actual program. The semantics of running an Ada program is then defined as the interpretation of this block in a predefined environment and given an initial (empty) storage.

In this chapter we discuss the construction of the syntactic and semantic domains constituting the basis of the remaining parts of the model. Furthermore we give illustrative examples of modelling characteristic concepts of Ada like types and subtypes. The domains and formulas presented here are a subset of the model given in appendices A and B, and this chapter is therefore also an introduction to the model presented in these appendices.

The chapter consists of four parts:

First a brief description of the influence of the tasking model on this sequential model.

The second part discusses the definition of the abstract syntax, AS2, which describes the syntactic properties of programs that have passed the static analysis and have undergone a transformation. This transformation is informally described. A formal definition of this transformation will constitute a part of the static semantics definition when this is complete.

The third part deals with the definition of a model for the storage, and with the environment component of our dynamic semantics definition.

The fourth part is four examples of the modelling of certain concepts of Ada showing how the former defined domains are used as a basis for elaboration, interpretation and evaluation, and pointing out some of the Ada that makes parts of modelling somewhat difficult (e.g. discriminant relations inside records). Other aspects however are easily modelled. This may in some sense express that the concept modelled is 'simple' (for example does the modelling of the exception mechanism in section 2.4.1 not require an extensive set of formulas).

## 2.1 The Influence from Parallel Ada

As mentioned in chapter 1 the definition of the dynamic aspects of Ada programs is divided into two parts: a denotational part defining the semantics of the sequential parts of the language, and a more mechanical model defining the tasking parts. The interpretation of statements which involves heavy meta-process communication (the statements of chapter 9 of [Ada 80]) is for practical reasons included as a part of [Lø 80b] even though it logically belongs to the dynamic semantics in the sense that interpretation of statements corresponds to code generation in a compiler and not directly to the tasking primitives/kernel of the run time system.

The existence of tasks affects the sequential model in several ways. First of all the formulas defined (excluding those belonging to the storage handler, see later) belong to or are used by task processes of the meta-language. This means that when the meta-state is present (indicated by the capital greek letter sigma $\Sigma$ ) in the type of a meta-function this means the state of all meta-processes: task processes, monitor, storage handler and the other processes defined in the tasking model. A detailed discussion on the meta-state when processes are involved is given in the tasking-model [Lø 80b]. The symbol => is used for $\Sigma \to \Sigma$ in the types of the formulas.

All communication between meta-processes is 'hidden' in the sequential model (as we call functions to handle this communication). These functions which are defined in the tasking-model can then be changed to e.g. reflect various choices as to which extend tasks share storage without affecting the sequential model.

The fact that the formulas of this model are used by meta-processes make them lose some of their denotational style. The reason is that an Ada task can be affected by other tasks e.g. the failure exception may be raised or the task may be aborted. To model this one has two choices (using meta-processes): either (almost) all the formulas of this report should at various points of text call functions inquiring whether an abnormal situation has occurred due to external factors like abortion. Such a solution would make the formulas cumbersome to read. The other solution is to say that these calls are implicitly present at various generally defined points, and then use a special symbol to mark those points where such calls for some reason are not present. Thus the symbol $\odot$ denotes the usual functional composition of the ';' with no possibility of interruption between the application of the two functions. A more detailed discussion on the 'uninterruptable semicolon' is found in the tasking-model [Lø 80b]. When reading the formulas of this report all one has to notice as to this aspect is that a meta-exit may be performed (almost) everywhere because of some external factor.

Another consequence is that the modelling of the storage is separated in two

parts:   One part belongs to the task processes and the other belongs to the
storage handler.  The various aspects regarding the storage model are  found
in section 2.3 on storage and environment modelling.

The functions used in this report and defined in the tasking model [Lø  80b]
are listed in Appendix B.5.


## 2.2 Definition of an Abstract Syntax for Ada

This section will deal with the definition of the abstract  syntax  for  Ada
called  AS2.   It has been defined in collaboration with Ole Dommergaard due
to our the mutual interest (his from an A-code point of view).   The  syntax
has been chosen so as to provide the information necessary for the definini-
tion of the dynamic semantics of Ada.  This information  is  represented  as
convenient  as possible for the dynamic semantics formulas.  This means that
some   static   transformations   are   performed   during   the   AS1->AS2
transformation:   e.g.   overloading  is  solved by unique naming of subprograms, and some static information concerning types and subprograms  is  inserted  in  the declarative parts.  The effect of the AS1->AS2 transformation
will in special cases be described when the syntactic  construct  is  explained, but a few general transformations are described below.

The first important transformation is the transformation  of  names.   Since
the  static  analysis is checking scope and visibility rules, and since programs in AS2 are statically correct, a unique identifier  can  replace  that
part of a name which is used to select a component of a package, subprogram,
block, task body or loop.  Also overloaded subprograms are uniquely named to
avoid resolving overloading dynamically since it is by nature a static problem.  This name transformation makes use clauses unnecessary for the dynamic
semantics (they are static by nature), so they are excluded from the syntax.

The second transformation concerns types and will be explained in detail  in
section 2.4.2.

A general philosophy in the design of the syntax is that when the  order  of
the components of a concrete syntactic domain is of no importance dynamically they are represented as sets or maps in the abstract syntax.   Two  examples:   The  variable identifiers of an object declaration are seen as a set
and  not  a  list.   A  record aggregate is in  AS2  a  mapping  from
field-identifier-sets  to expressions because the order of evaluation of the
expressions is not defined by the language [Ada 80 section 4.3] (more  about
aggregates later).

The complete abstract syntax (excluding generics) is given in Appendix A and
follows  the  structure  and section numbers of the revised reference manual
[Ada 80].

The rest of this section will comment on those parts of  the  syntax  which
differ  from  what  could be expected from the concrete syntax and which are
not described elsewhere in this report.  The syntax for  statements  closely
related  to  tasks (accept, abort etc.) is described in the tasking-model of
[Lø 80b].

Declarations:

Declarative parts in general are described in section 2.4.1 on blocks, declarations ad exceptions.

Object declarations are described in section 2.3 on the storage and environment modelling.

All declarations related to types are described in section 2.4.2.

Procedure- and function- declarations and bodies are described in section
2.4.3.

Package- and task-type- declarations and bodies are described in section
2.4.4.

The remaining declarations in Ada are number declarations, exception declarations and renaming declarations. A number declaration is simply not present in AS2 because the expression defining the number is a literal expression and hence statically evaluable. So it is evaluated during the AS1->AS2
transformation, and the value is inserted for each of the number identifiers
in the remaining parts of the program. Exception declarations are also ignored as the exception mechanism is modelled through the exit-mechanism of
the meta-language (see section 2.4.1) instead of a continuations model.
Thus the exception declarations serves but statical purposes (checking visibility).

Renaming declarations however are present in AS2 because of their dynamical
nature. The various kinds of renaming declarations are described below:

```
Renaming-dcl   =   Object-rename  |  Failure-rename  |
                   Proc-rename    |  Entry-rename    |
                   Fct-rename

Object-rename  ::  Var-id   Type-id   Name

Failure-rename ::  Excp-id   Name

Proc-rename    ::  Proc-id   Formal-part   Proc-id

Entry-rename   ::  Proc-id   Formal-part
                   Name   Entry-name

Fct-rename     ::  Fct-id   Formal-part
                   Subtype-def   Fct-id
```

This syntax differs in several ways from the corresponding concrete syntax.
The object renaming in this model also covers task renaming since all task
objects belong to a type having a name (see section 2.4.4). The renaming of
exceptions is reduced to the renaming of the failure exception since all
other exception renamings are of a static nature and hence ignored in the
sense that the renamed exception identifier is statically inserted for the
newly introduced identifier. The name present in this
failure-renaming-declaration is the name of the task in which the failure
exception is to be raised when raising the newly introduced identifier (see
section 2.4.1 on blocks, declarations and exceptions). Since all packages
are uniquely identified in AS2, the package renaming declaration of concrete
Ada is eliminated in AS2 leading to substitutions in the remaining parts of

the program.

The renaming of procedures, entries and functions are on the other hand present and syntactically separated to make modelling easier. Due to the unique naming of procedures the renaming of a procedure contains as identification of the renamed procedure only a procedure identifier (not a general name as in concrete Ada). The formal part is described in section 2.4.3 on procedures and functions. An entry renaming is like a procedure renaming except that the renamed procedure identifier is replaced by a name (denoting a task object) and an entry name (consisting of an entry identifier and an optional expression selecting a member in the case of a family). Function renaming is similar to procedure renaming with an additional result type definition. Renaming a user defined operator is like renaming a function, whereas renaming a predefined operator in Ada is in AS2 not viewed as a renaming declaration because the predefined operators are not associated with function denotations in the environment (see later in this section on expressions). So the renaming of, say the predefined * operator for integers as MULT, is by the AS1->AS2 transformation changed to the AS2 object corresponding to the following piece of Ada program:

```
function MULT (a,b: integer) return integer is
  begin
    return (a * b);
  end MULT;
```

This means that it is seen as a new function definition, which returns the value yielded by applying the renamed operator to the parameters of the function.


Names:

Due to the name transformation mentioned earlier, the major difference between concrete Ada and AS2 with respect to names is that a selected component is either the selection of a field of a record or the all-select used for getting the object designated by an access value. It is not selection of entities from packages or from outer blocks, subprograms, task bodies or loops. Furthermore the implicit '.all' in case of e.g. the selection of a component of an object designated by an access value is explicitly inserted in AS2 during the AS1->AS2 transformation. This means that whenever selecting a component, indexing etc. it is known that no '.all'-selection is performed unless it is explicitly present. It makes the formulas of the model simpler by not having to check whether an implicit '.all' is to be performed and it reflects what I think is the reason behind permitting the omision of it in concrete Ada: it is nothing but a syntactical shorthand.

The remaining names are straightforward abstractions of the corresponding concrete names, except for function calls explained in section 2.4.3.


Expressions:

    Expr    ::  Type-id Expr'

The expressions of AS2 have two parts: a type identifier and what could be called an 'ordinary' expression. The type identifier is that of the (statically known) type result of the expression. This type identifier is used

when manipulating fixed and float values (see section 2.4.2 on types) and
when evaluating positional array aggregates (described later). The prefix-
ing of expressions is possible because all types in this model, including
the in Ada possibly anonymous array types, have been named during the AS1 ->
AS2 transformation (see section 2.4.2 on types).

```
Expr'        =   VAL                  |
                 Aggregate            |
                 Name                 |
                 Allocator            |
                 Qualified-expr       |
                 Type-conversion      |
                 Prefix               |
                 Infix                |
                 Range-test           |
                 Subtype-test
```

An expression (without prefix) can be:

1. A value. Values correspond to literals and the results of evaluating
static expressions, and they are described in section 2.3 on storage and environment modelling.

2. An aggregate. The aggregates used in AS2 are syntactically divided in
four disjoint classes:

```
Aggregate       =   Record-Aggregate            |
                    Named-Array-Aggregate       |
                    Positional-Array-Aggregate  |
                    One-Comp-Aggregate

Record-Aggregate             ::  Field-id-set m-> Expr

Named-Array-Aggregate        ::  (DiscreteVal-set m-> Expr)
                                 [Expr]

Positional-Array-Aggregate   ::  (N1 m-> Expr) [Expr]

One-Comp-Aggregate           ::  [Choice-set] Expr

Choice          =   Expr                |
                    Discrete-range
```

Record aggregates in AS2 have always named components. The transformation
of a positional aggregate into a named aggregate is possible because the
following two conditions are satisfied: Overloading of aggregates is statically solved so that the type of the aggregate is known, and the expression
specifying the value of a discriminant used in a variant part must be static, implying that it is statically known which fields are present [Ada 80
section 4.3.1]. So the record is seen as a mapping from sets of field identifiers to expressions, where all the field identifiers of one set is to be
associated with the same value in the resulting record value.

A named array aggregate is the model of an array aggregate that has more
them one component association. Since there is more than one component as-

sociation each 'choice' (except others) of the concrete aggregate must be
static expressions [Ada 80 section 4.3.2]. The set of choices associated
with the same expression is therefore evaluated statically and the (discrete) values are (as a set) mapped to the corresponding expression. The
last optional component is the expression used for the choice others if present.

Positional array aggregates have expressions for some index positions (the
position given as a natural number N1) and possibly an 'others' alternative
for the rest. Again here a map have been chosen to model the first part to
show that even though the positions of the expressions do matter the evaluation of these expressions is performed in an order not defined by the
language [Ada 80 section 4.3].

The last sort of aggregate is a socalled one component aggregate having only
one component association. In this case the choices don't have to be static. In this model 'no choices' corresponds to 'others' and the choices present are dynamically evaluated to yield the index values of the array (the
socalled one component aggregates are array aggregates).

3. A name, described earlier.

4. An allocator. Allocators consist of a type identifier of the allocated
object and an optional part describing the value to be assigned initially to
the allocated object.

```
Allocator   :: Type-id [(Expr           |
                         Discrim-constr  |
                         Index-constr   )]
```

This domain corresponds to the concrete Ada-allocator except that aggregates
are not explicitly mentioned in AS2 as an optional part of an allocator
since they fall into the class of Expr, (which they by the way also do in
Ada, so why they are explicitly mentioned is not clear).

5. and 6. Type convertions and qualified expressions are just as in concrete Ada.

7. and 8. Prefix and infix expressions are used to model expressions involving the predefined operators. All expressions including one or more
predefined operators are by the AS1->AS2 transformation changed to fit into
one of these two classes, e.g. a+b+c (+ is the predefined operator) will be
transformed into the AS2 object corresponding to (a+b)+c [Ada 80 section
4.5]. The reason for letting the predefined operators appear as purely syntactic objects in the syntax rather than as calls to predefined function denotations is, that a model where e.g. the evaluation of x+y (predefined +)
may cause allocation of parameter locations, checking parameters, freeing
locations etc., seems to complex. One would have to describe all the denotations in a description of the predefined environment. The solution chosen
implies that formulas must be defined for evaluation of infix and prefix expressions using the types of the operand(s) to determine the operation to be
performed.

9. and 10. Range- and subtype-tests are as in concrete Ada.

Statements:

Any statement of an AS2 program may have at most one label. In Ada it may have more than one but a static transformation will be able to make at most one and transform the gotos involved accordingly.

The statements are all modelled in a straightforward manner, but the traditional separation in simple and compound statements is avoided because there is really no difference in semantics. Just the one being changed mostly by the AS1->AS2 transformation is described here (a second transformed statement, the procedure call is described in section 2.4.3). The statement described here is the case statement.

        Case    ::  Expr  (DiscreteVal m-> Stmt-list)
                          [Stmt-list]

The case statement is abstracted as consisting of an expression, which is the one dynamically determining the statement list to be interpreted and a mapping from discrete values to statement lists and an optional statement list for the choice others, if present. The discrete values of the map are the statically evaluated choices [Ada 80 section 5.4] and the choices are 'expanded' in the sense that each value represented in an evaluated choice is in this map associated with the corresponding statement list. This means that the statement lists of a concrete case statement may be present several times in this mapping once for each value associated with the list. This transformation is performed to make the interpretation of the case statement easier (see Appendix B.2).

The statements related to tasking (those described in chapter 9 of [Ada 80].) are discussed in the tasking-model [Lø 80b].

The exception handler and raise statement are described in section 2.4.1 on blocks, declarations and exceptions.

The dictionary part (of declaration lists) is a mapping from identifiers to descriptors. The descriptors are either descriptors of types or subprograms (and entries) and the information is discussed in sections 2.4.2 and 2.4.3 respectively. The dictionary is generated during the AS1->AS2 transformation.

Even though the AS1->AS2 transformation is not yet defined (AS1 is not at this moment fully defined but is at a state called A6 in the definition of the static semantics [BuSch 80]) the transformation of a program into the abstract syntax AS2 is not 'impossible' in the sense of requiring information not present in AS1 or in the dictionary used during the static analysis. The unique naming of entities is already in a way performed during the static analysis for the subset A6 of AS1 because the socalled 'unitname' used in [BuSch 80] is a unique identification of any referable entity at a given point of the program.

The AS2 will have to be extended when the subject of generics is included, and when the I/O-parts of the language is defined. The idea concerning the I/O-definition is to let the calls to I/O-functions and procedures appear as expressions/statements in AS2 and then evaluate/interpret these in the way expressions involving predefined operators are evaluated without assuming the existence of function/procedure denotations in the environment. Thus this I/O-definition requires just an extension of AS2 (not a general revision) and some formulas defining the semantics of these new constructs.

This concludes the description of the abstract syntax.


2.3 Storage and Environment Modelling

As mentioned earlier two fundamental elements of this formal model are the
environment and the storage. The modelling of these concepts will be described and discussed in detail in this section.


The Storage:

The storage is modelled as a mapping from non-structured locations to possibly structured values (records and arrays). This part of the storage model
is based on the model proposed by Hans Henrik Løvengreen et al in [Lø 80a].
It would not always convenient to use non structured locations for structured values when updating variant records. But the rules in Ada for assignment to discriminants (discriminant assignment is only permitted by complete record assignment) makes the use of non structured locations convenient. The concept of sublocations is nevertheless necessary because of two
independent reasons: an identifier may, if it is introduced by a renaming
declaration, denote a subcomponent of an object,and likewise for a formal
parameter of a subprogram, in the case of parameter transfer by reference.
Such a sublocation consists of a non structured location containing the possibly structured value and a list describing the path to a specific subva-
lue. An alternative would have been to use structured locations as in the
formal definitions of the languages PL/I [Be 74] and CHILL [HaBj 80]. But
since the storage concept of Ada is simpler than that of these two
languages, that fact should be taken advantages of in the model I think.

The storage is due to the parallelism of Ada administered by a meta process
called a storage handler, with which the task processes communicate when accessing the storage. This means that the functions belonging to the
storage-model are divided into two groups: one belonging to the task
processes (e.g. check-and-assign) and one belonging to the storage handler
(e.g. stg-allocate). The functions belonging to the task processes use
functions which involve meta process communication. Functions involving
such communications are defined in the tasking-model [Lø 80b]. In the modelling of the storage the functions involving meta-process communication
correspond to functions belonging to the storage handler. An example:
calling the function allocate involving meta-process communication results
in calling stg-allocate in the storage handler. This means that if a totally sequential model is wanted (Ada without tasking) the functions prefixed
by stg- can be viewed as definitions of the corresponding unprefixed functions.

The domains involved in the storage model are:

    STG    =    LOC m-> VAL

    ACTV   =    ActId m-> LOC-set

    ActId  ::   TOKEN

```
Values:

VAL      _   =   DiscreteVal | URealVal   |
                 FixedVal    | FloatVal   |
                 ArrayVal    | RecordVal  |
                 TV          | AccessVal  |
                 UNDEF

DiscreteVal  =   IntegerVal | EnumVal

IntegerVal   ::  INTG

EnumVal      ::  Id | QUOT

URealVal     ::  NUM

FixedVal     ::  INTG

FloatVal     ::  NUM

ArrayVal     ::  (N1+ m-> VAL)
                 order: (DiscreteVal+ <-m-> N1+)

RecordVal    ::  Field-id m-> VAL

TV           ::  TOKEN

AccessVal    ::  LOC | NULL

Locations:

LOC          ::  TOKEN

VarLoc       =   SubLoc | SliceLoc

SubLoc       ::  LOC (N1+ | Field-id)*  Alloc

Alloc        =   STATIC | DYN

SliceLoc     ::  SubLoc  N1  N1
```

The storage administered by the storage handler is as explained earlier in this section modelled as a mapping from nonstructured locations to possibly structured values. The second component used by the storage handler is a mapping from activation identifiers to sets of locations and divides the locations of the storage into (disjoint) subsets. Each of these subsets contains locations that are to be removed when leaving the activation (e.g. block) to which they are associated. For dynamically allocated objects (by evaluating an allocator) the manual mentions nothing about freeing the locations. In this model they are freed when the activation containing the access type definition is left, because they cannot be accessed outside that activation (see eval-Allocator in Appendix B.3). Another alternative had been not to free them at all by associating these locations to a special activation-identifier. This component of the storage handler is especially convenient when stopping the elaboration of a declaration list because of an exception, and the locations so far allocated have to be given free.

The relation between two actual values of the domains STG and ACTV present in the storage handler can be expressed by the following well-formedness-criteria:

```
is-wf-ACTV(actv)(stg) =
 (( ∀ loc E dom stg)
   ( E! actid E dom actv)(loc E actv(actid))
     and union rng actv = dom stg)
 type: ACTV -> (STG -> BOOL)
```

The formula expresses that each location of the storage is represented in exactly one of the location-sets of the activation-map, and that locations present in the activation-map are exactly those of the storage.


Values:

The values of Ada are represented by elements of the syntactic domain VAL.

Integers are represented by elements of the meta-domain of integers called INTG.

Enumeration values are either trees of identifiers or quotations. The boolean values are represented as the enumeration values mk-EnumVal(TRUE) and mk-EnumVal(FALSE).

The Ada concept of universal real values is modelled by a domain capable of representing any number.

Fixed values are represented by integers. This integer is the one by which the actual delta of the type is to be multiplied to give the value represented. The delta can always be obtained from the context. If the value is associated with a variable, the denotation of that variable contains the type information necessary to find the actual delta. If the value is the result of the evaluation of a part of an expression, that part is statically prefixed by the typename of the result. The modelling of fixed values as integers implies that some operations on fixed values of the same type can be performed on the integer values alone (e.g. addition). This model corresponds to the Ada concept of model numbers.

Float values are modelled using a domain capable of representing any number. The fact that the actual representation is not exact, is modelled by having the values small and having binary digits associated with the type in the environment (see the section on types 2.4.2).

Array values are modelled as two mappings, one from tuples of position numbers to values (components of the arrays) and a one-to-one ordering map from tuples of discrete values being the actual index lists to tuples of position numbers. This splitting of an array value may look strange in the sense that one mapping: DiscreteVal+ m-> VAL intuitively should be sufficient. But if an array value of the latter kind is stored in a location and that location is accessed using a formal parameter accessing by reference and this formal parameter has a constraint different from that of the actual parameter, some sort of index transformation has to be performed when indexing that formal parameter. I have chosen to put this transformation into the denotation of an index constraint (see section 2.4.2) and let the value consist of a mapping from socalled unified position tuples to values. These position tuples contain for each index position a positional number relative to the index constraint, so that the lower bound has positional number 1 and the upper bound a positional number equal to the number of index values for that index position. The result of this is that indexing (and slicing) is performed in a standard way so that e.g. inside a subprogram a parameter acts like an ordinary variable.

A record value is modelled as a mapping from field identifiers of that record type to component values. This mapping includes the discriminants if any. The reason for choosing a map rather than some sort of list is that the positions of the fields are of no importance for the dynamic semantics since the only operation on record values involving the positions is assignment of positional aggregates, but such aggregates are statically transformed into named aggregates. This is possible because the value of any discriminant determining variant parts must be static, and the rules concerning evaluation of aggregates states that the order of evaluation of the components is not defined by the language [Ada 80 section 4.3]. An important thing to notice about a record value is that only the fields currently present in the value are in the mapping. This means that fields not being present due to the value of some discriminant are simply not in the record value. It is only possible to do this because of the fact that the values of discriminants can only be changed by a complete record assignment (this is checked statically) so that all the (new) fields are present in the record value after the current fields of the record has changed.

A task value is simply a token by which the monitor process and storage handler identify a task when communicating with it. Such a value is created and stored in a location whenever a task object is created.

An access value is either a location designating a dynamically allocated object or a null value designating no value at all.

The last sort of value is an undefined value used when a value is totally undefined.


Locations:

The locations used in the storage map are as mentioned nonstructured, but variable locations are structured. Such locations can be either sublocations or slice locations.

A sublocation denotes a subcomponent of a nonstructured location. This subcomponent is identified by the nonstructured location in which it resides and an access path selecting the component. The access path is empty if the sublocation is the total nonstructured location. Otherwise it describes the path to the subcomponent using a list of either tuples of natural numbers (in the case that the sublocation denoted by the access path up to this point is associated with an array), or a field identifier selecting its path into a record. The third component of a sublocation describes whether this sublocation is allocated statically or dynamically (by means of an allocator), and this component is used for determining whether the special rules applying to dynamically allocated objects are to be satisfied by this sublocation (non-changing discriminant values).

A slice location contains a sublocation denoting an array and two natural numbers determining the lower and upper bound of the slice. The numbers are the relative positions of the corresponding actual indices determining the slicelocation (see section 2.4.2 on types).

Before examples can be given of functions operating on the storage the environment has to be described.

The Environment:

As usual when modelling block oriented languages with recursive procedures, an environment associating identifiers with their 'denotations' is used. The 'denotation of e.g. a variable identifier is some information about its subtype and a variable location 'containing' its value.

The environment contains information of various kinds used when interpreting statements, elaborating declarations and evaluating expressions.

An important thing to notice is that the environment is in a sense 'flat'. By 'flat' is meant that the elaboration of a package declaration/body does not result in a sub environment placed as a nested component of the surrounding environment, but the elaboration causes the current environment to be extended by the identifiers introduced in the package declaration/body. This type of environment requires that names using 'dot'-notation to get into packages or to outer block structures are transformed into unique identifiers during the AS1->AS2 transformation.

One could have chosen a sort of hierarchical environment where the denotation of a package contains a sub environment and thus let the environment reflect the visibility of identifiers. But then all the static name resolving, including calculating the effect of use-clauses, would have to be performed dynamically when searching for the denotation of a name. Even then one still had to generate unique identifiers for entities declared immediately inside a block because of the possibility of referring to outer entities using block identifiers, unless a solution is chosen where entering a block causes the creation of a sub-environment similar to the usage of the static concept of a dictionary used by Jørgen Bundgaard and Lennart Schultz in [BuSch 80]. But it seems to me that using such a model for the environment implies doing the same things twice: once during the static analysis and once in the dynamic semantics.

The information placed in the environment can be roughly divided in two classes: denotations of identifiers and other information. The abstract syntax for the environment is:

```
ENV  =  ((Id | QUOT) m-> DEN)     U (EXCP m-> Excp-id) U
        (RESTP m-> Subtype-den)   U (ACTID m-> ActId) U
        (CRID m-> CrId)           U (Excp-id m-> TaskFailure)

DEN  =  Type-den | Elem-den | Var-den | Proc-den |
        Fct-den | Entry-den | Package-den
```

The denotation of an identifier can be some sort of type or subtype information. Such type related denotations are described in detail in section 2.4.2.

If an identifier denotes a variable (or constant) a variable denotation is present in the environment. This denotation is described later in this section.

Procedure- and function-denotations are described in section 2.4.3. It should just be noted here that user defined operators are viewed as functions and that they are associated with function denotations in the environment.

The description of entry denotations and package denotations is found in section 2.4.4 on packages and tasks.


The other components of the environment are:

One holding the exception being handled at the moment. This is used to be able to re-raise that exception inside the handler and it is only present in the environment inside a handler. The usage of this component can be seen in section 2.4.1 on blocks, declarations and exceptions.

Another component holding the result subtype of a function is only present when interpreting the statement list of a function and it is used to be able to interpret a return statement (more on its use in section 2.4.3).

A third component always present contains the current activation identifier. It is used to manage the freeing of locations and to assure that a block having dependent tasks is not left before all such tasks are terminated. A new activation identifier is created and placed in the environment when entering block like structures and when calling subprograms because allocation of parameter locations is performed at the place of the call and such locations have to be freed after the subprogram call (discussed in section 2.4.3). Its usage is described in section 2.4.1 on blocks and in the tasking-model [Lø 80b].

A fourth component even more tightly connected to the tasking-model than the activation identifier is the creation identifier. It is used by the monitor process to group together tasks that have been created and which have to be activated at the 'same' time like e.g. before interpreting the first statement of a block or package body.

The last component is a mapping from exception identifiers to something called a task failure, the latter consisting of a task value. This mapping is used to contain information concerning exception identifiers but only those introduced by a renaming declaration and renaming the failure exception of some task. For all the other exception identifiers no denotation is needed in the environment due to the use of the exit mechanism of the meta-language for modelling transfer of control (see section 2.4.1 on blocks, declarations and exceptions).

The predefined environment in which a program is interpreted contains at least the result of elaboration of the package STANDARD of Ada. But in this model the definition of the (overloaded) predefined operators is not considered as function definitions to be elaborated in the usual sense since the predefined operators in contrary to user defined are present as syntactic elements of the program (using ordinary prefix and infix expressions in AS2), see section 2.2. What is present in the predefined environment is e.g. denotations of the predefined types as integer type(s) and some enumeration types like BOOLEAN and CHARACTER (see section 2.4.2).


The operations involving the storage and the environment are now to be illustrated by interpreting an assignment statement, but first a variable denotation will be described.

    Var—den    ::   Subtype-den   VarLoc

A variable denotation consists of a subtype denotation  holding  information
about  the  type  of the variable and any constraints to be satisfied by the
value associated with the variable location of the denotation.  Subtype  denotations are defined in section 2.4.2 on types and subtypes.

An assignment statement in AS2 is similar to that of  concrete  Ada  in  the
sense that it contains two parts:  a name and an expression, where the value
of the expression is to be assigned to the variable location  designated  by
the evaluated name.

    Assign  ::  Name  Expr

The interpretation of such an assignment statement is defined by the following formulas.


int-Assign(mk-Assign(name,expr))env=
   (def mk-(loc,subtpden,env') : eval-Name(name)env,
        val : eval-Expr(expr)env;
   check-and-assign(mk-Var-den(subtpden,loc),val)env')

type : Assign -> (ENV => )

The interpretation consists of - in undefined order - to evaluate  the  name
of the left-hand-side and the expression of the right-hand-side, followed by
the checking assignment of the value to the location of the  left-hand-side.
The  evaluation of the left-hand-side results in a triplet consisting of the
variable location of the evaluated name, the subtype denotation of that  location and a new environment.  The latter is needed due to the fact that the
evaluation of the name may involve insertion of discriminant values  in  the
constraints of the array elements of an array inside a record and hence in a
sense expands the element denotation of such component into subtype  denotations  (see section 2.4.2 on types).  The complete definition of the evaluation of a name is found in Appendix B.3.  In general  the  evaluation  of  a
name  may  yield either a location or a value as its first component, but in
this case it is statically checked that the left-hand-side will evaluate  to
a  location if an exception is not raised by e.g.  trying to dereference the
access-value NULL.

The checking assignment is defined in the following way:

```
check-and-assign(mk-Var-den(subtpden,varloc),val)env=
   (let mk-Subtype-den(base,constr) = subtpden in
    cases env(base) :
      (mk-Access-den(tid, )  ->
          (cases val :
             (mk-AccessVal(NULL)  ->  I,
              mk-AccessVal(loc)   ->
                  (let subloc = mk-SubLoc(loc,<>,DYN) in
                   def val' : value-of(subloc);
                   subtype-check(val',subtpden)env))),
       T                         ->
          (cases varloc :
             (mk-SubLoc( , ,statordyn)                    ->
                 (if statordyn = DYN
                     then (def val' : value-of(varloc);
                              check-dyn-values(val,val',subtpden)env)
                     else subtype-check(val,subtpden)env),
              mk-SliceLoc(mk-SubLoc( , ,statordyn), , )  ->
                  (if statordyn = DYN
                      then (def val' : value-of(varloc);
                               check-dyn-values(val,val',subtpden)env))));
   assign(varloc,val))

type : Var-den VAL -> (ENV => )
```

Before assigning a value to a location it must be checked that this value
satisfies any constraint imposed on it by the subtype of the location. This
checking depends on the base type of the location. If the type is an access
type and the access value to be assigned is not NULL (in which case no check
is performed) the value contained in the location forming the access value
is checked against any constraint imposed by the subtype denotation (see Appendix B.1). If the type is not an access type and the location is dynamically allocated (by an allocator) it is checked that no discriminant value
if present is changed by the assignment. If the location is not dynamically
allocated an ordinary subtype checking is performed. If the checks did not
raise the exception CONSTRAINT-ERROR the assignment is performed using the
function assign which involves meta-process communication - this function is
hence defined in the tasking-model [Lø 80b]. It transfers the information
contained (variable location and value) to the storage handler, which then
uses the function stg-assign defined below.

```
stg-assign(varloc,val)=
   cases varloc :
      (mk-SubLoc(loc,path, )                         ->
          (def oldval : (c Stg)(loc);
           def newval : update-value(oldval,path,nil,val);
           Stg := c Stg + [loc -> newval]),
       mk-SliceLoc(mk-SubLoc(loc,path, ),lb,ub)  ->
          (def oldval : (c Stg)(log);
           def newval : update-value(oldval,path,mk-(lb,ub),val);
           Stg := c Stg + [loc -> newval]))

type : VarLoc VAL =>
```

The assign function applied by the storage handler updates the storage by updating values of nonstructured locations. If the variable location is a sublocation the old total value is found in the storage. This value is then updated using the new value, that is to be a subcomponent of the new updated value, and a path describing the way to the corresponding subcomponent of the old value. This updated value is then stored back in the original location. If the variable location is a slicelocation a similar updating is performed, this time with the additional information of the lower and upper bounds of the slice. In any case the attempt to follow the given path into the old value may fail. That is, a field selection may try to select a non-existing component of a record value (raising a CONSTRAINT-ERROR exception). This may happen if the left-hand-side of the assign statement is evaluated first giving as result among other things this path, and then the evaluation of the right-hand-side expression has the side effect of changing a discriminant of the left hand side. The same remarks apply to indexing an array being a component of a record and depending on a discriminant. Such situations are detected by the function update value and CONSTRAINT-ERROR is raised here and transferred to the meta-process issuing the call of assign. The updating function is found in Appendix B.4 on storage functions together with the other storage functions like stg-allocate.

This concludes the section on storage and environment modelling.

## 2.4 Modelling Special Aspects

This section contains four parts, each describing various aspects of Ada from a dynamical point of view. The first will deal with blocks, declarations and exceptions, the second with types and subtypes, the third with procedures and functions and the last with packages and tasks. These parts are examples of the usage of the semantical domains (storage and environment) and the syntactic domains (AS2) and are extracted from the model given in appendices A and B, and some of the formulas defined in the following may depend on formulas only defined in Appendix B.

## 2.4.1 Blocks, Declarations and Exceptions

This section will deal with the various aspects concerning blocks. A block is a statement but it includes from a dynamic point of view all the essential parts of Ada. The block contains a declarative part capable of holding e.g. object-, type-, subprogram- and package-declarations, a statement list and possibly one or more exception handlers. What is left out from blocks are the problems concerning compilation units, but they are not dealt with in this model at all.

First an abstract syntax (part of AS2) for a block and related constructs is given followed by the functions interpreting a block.

    Block        :: Dcl-part  Stmt-list  [Excphdl]

```
Dcl-part     ::  Dict  Dcl*

Stmt-list    =   Stmt*

Excphdl      ::  (Excp-id m-> Stmt-list)  oth: [Stmt-list]

Dcl          =   Object-dcl | ...

Object-dcl   ::  Var-id-set  [CONST]
                 Subtype-def [Expr]

Stmt         ::  [Label-id]  Unlab-stmt

Unlab-stmt   =   Goto | Raise

Goto         ::  Label-id

Raise        ::  [Excp-id | Name]
```

A block consists of three parts: a declarative part, a statement list and
an exception handler (containing one or more Ada exception handlers). The
optional block identifier of a concrete Ada block is removed in AS2 because
the unique naming of identifiers makes it useless (one cannot exit to it
anyway).

The declarative part contains a dictionary and a list of declarations. The
dictionary contains basically static information concerning two aspects:
types and subprograms, and these aspects will be discussed in the respective
sections: types in section 2.4.2 and subprograms in section 2.4.4. The declarations are either object declarations or some other declarations not
described here (types and subtypes in section 2.4.2, packages and tasks in
2.4.3 and subprograms in 2.4.4).

An object declaration consists of a set of variable identifiers, a component
designating whether the object is a constant or not, a subtype definition
and possibly an initialization expression.

The exception handler part of a block contains if present two parts: one
for the explicitly mentioned exceptions and one optional for the anonymous
'others'. The part handling explicitly named exceptions is a mapping from
every singly mentioned exception identifiers of the concrete Ada handler(s),
to the corresponding statement lists. This means that the handler is statically expanded during the AS1->AS2 transformation. The part handling
'others' contains if present the corresponding statement list.

Statements may contain a label. In AS2 there is at most one label per
statement. This is obtained by statically choosing just one label if the
concrete statement has several and then transforming any goto statement accordingly. The only statements considered in this section are the goto and
raise statements.

```
int-Block(mk-Block(mk-Dcl-part(dict,dcllist),stmtl,excpthdlr))env=
  (def actid : get-new-ActId()ⓖ
   let env' = env + [ACTID -> actid] + get-type-dens(dict)(actid) in
   always block-epilogue(actid) in
      (def crid : create-CrId(actid);
       let env'' = env' + [CRID -> crid] in
       def env''' = extend-env(dict,dcllist)(env'')env''';
       trap exit (mk-Excp(eid)) with
                   handle(mk-Excp(eid),excpthdlr)env''' in
        (activate-tasks(crid);
         int-Stmtlist(stmtl)env''')))

type : Block -> (ENV=> )


extend-env(dict,dcllist)(env)env'=
  (if dcllist=<>
    then return(env)
    else (def env'' : elab-Dcl(hd dcllist)(dict)(env)env';
          extend-env(tl dcllist)(env'')env'))

type : Dict Dcl* -> (ENV -> (ENV => ENV))


block-epilogue(actid)=
  (await-termination(actid)ⓕ
   free-locations(actid))

type : ActId =>
```

Interpretation of a block starts with the creation of a new activation identifier and then informing the monitor that a block with this activation
identifier is being entered. This activation identifier serves two purposes, the first is to keep track of locations to be freed when leaving the
block, the second is for the monitor to keep track of tasks dependent of
this block. The latter use is described in detail in the report on tasking
[Lø 80b]. This new activation identifier is entered into the environment
together with the type denotations obtained from the dictionary (see section
2.4.2). Then a trap is set up defining the action to be taken when leaving
the following compound meta-statement whether it is left by means of a
meta-exit or 'normally' by reaching the end. The block epilogue to be performed consists of: Awaiting the termination of any task dependent of the
block followed (uninterruptably) by the freeing of locations belonging to
this activation. The creation of the activation identifier, the extension
of the environment and the setting up of the trap is performed uninterruptably, so that the activation identifier is always removed when leaving a
block.

Inside the trap the following is performed: First a socalled creation identifier is made (by the storage handler). This identifier is used by the
monitor to group together tasks that are to be activated together. The
identifier is put in the environment. Then the environment is extended to
reflect the elaboration of the declarations of the block. This extension is
defined by a recursive equation in the sense that the resulting environment
is used as one of the parameters to the extension function. This resulting
environment must of course be used with 'extreme care' by the extension
function to assure a solution to this equation. The only declarations whose

elaboration uses this environment are subprogram bodies because of (mutually) recursive subprogram calls (explained in detail in section 2.4.4), and
renaming declarations, provided it is legal to rename a subprogram before
its body has been elaborated (the reference manual is not specific on this
point [Ada 80 section 8.5]).

Following this extension of the environment yet another trap is set up.
This trap is only used for catching exits caused by exceptions raised during
the rest of the function and such exits are treated by attempting to handle
the exception in question using the exception handler (if any) of the block
and using the newly extended environment. The function handling exceptions
is described later in this section. Having set up this trap the tasks, if
any, created during the elaboration of the declaration list of the block,
are activated. These tasks are identified by the creation-identifier of the
block. Following this activation the statement list of the block is interpreted.

The extension of the environment mentioned above is performed stepwise one
declaration at the time using the dictionary of the declaration list and two
environments: the one existing just prior to the elaboration of the declaration in question and the one containing the result of the elaboration of
the total declaration list! The same extension function is used for the declaration list of packages described in section 2.4.3. The elaboration of
each declaration gives as its result a new environment used for the elaboration of the rest of the declarations and so on until the end of the list.

The only declaration whose elaboration is described in this section is the
object declaration. The elaboration of an object declaration will use functions not described in this part of the report but these can be found in the
model (Appendix B.1).

```
elab-Object-dcl(mk-Object-dcl(vids,oconst,subtpdef,opexpr))env=
   (def subden : elab-Subtype-def(subtpdef)env;
    def env' : env + get-vardens(vids,subden)env;
    if opexpr = nil
      then (for all vid E vids do
               (def val : get-init-VAL(subden)(CREATE)env';
                assign(s-VarLoc(env'(vid)),val));
             return(env'))
      else (def val : eval-Expr(opexpr)env';
            for all vid E vids do
            check-and-assign(env'(vid),val)env';
            if const = CONST
               then return(update-subtypes(vids,val,subden)env')
               else return(env')))
```

type : Object-dcl -> (ENV => ENV)


The elaboration of an object declaration consists of first elaborating the
subtype definition and then creating variable denotations for the variable
identifiers and putting these denotations into the environment. This creation of variable denotations includes allocation of locations for the variables. If there is no initialization expression an initial value is generated for each variable using the subtype denotation found above. The generation of such an initial value includes the creation of a task value for
each component of the subtype denotation being of a task type. The value is

then assigned to the location, of course without any subtype checks. If on
the other hand an initialization expression is present this expression is
evaluated and that value is assigned to all variables checking any constraint imposed by the subtype denotation. After this an updating of the subtype denotations is performed in the case that the objects are constants.
This updating only has an effect if the subtype is an unconstrained array
type. Then the bounds obtained from the value is used to constrain the original type.

The next subject considered is the interpretation of a statement list and
especially the gotos of the list.

```
int-Stmtlist(stmtlist)env=
  tixe [mk-Go(lab) -> int-Stmtlist-without-trap(gotomap(lab))env |
                      (gotomap = create-gotomap(stmtlist) and
                       lab E dom gotomap)] in
     int-Stmtlist-without-trap(stmtlist)env

type : Stmt-list -> (ENV => )


create-gotomap(stmtlist)=
  [lab -> stmtl | (E j E ind stmtlist)(mk-Stmt(lab, ) = stmtlist[j] and
                  lab ≠ nil and
                  stmtl = <stmtlist[i] | j =< i =< ln stmtlist>)]

type : Stmt-list -> (Label-id m-> Stmt-list)


int-Stmtlist-without-trap(stmtlist)env=
  for i = 1 to ln stmtlist do
    int-Stmt(stmtlist[i])env

type : Stmt-list -> (ENV => )
```

The interpretation of a statement list consists of first setting up a trap
for meta-exits performed because of gotos. The trap associates labels of
this statement list with the interpretation of a statement list starting
from the statement with the label in question and continuing to the end of
the statement list for which the trap is being set up, in a
continuation-like way. The trap is of a special kind in the sense that an
exit from 'within' the interpretation of the statement lists of the trap may
be caught by the same trap (if the label identifier matches one in the domain of the trap). After setting up this trap the statements of the list are
interpreted one by one without at that level trapping the meta-exits to labels of this statement list. The auxiliary function create-gotomap makes a
mapping from the labels of a statement list to statement lists characterized
by the fact that they start with the statement having one such label and
contain all the statements following this statement in the original statement list. In an earlier version of this model where gotos were permitted
to transfer control between the internal statement lists of if and case
statements this function was used when interpreting these statements. The
goto statement mk-Goto(labid) is interpreted as simply exit(mk-Go(labid)).

The exit-mechanism has been chosen for modelling transfer of control whether this transfer is caused by a goto statement, an exit statement, a return statement or a raise statement. One could have chosen a continuation model, but especially in the the case of the raise statement, when raising failure in another task the exit-mechanism fits better into the tasking model (being of a somewhat mechanical nature) the form of which affects this sequential model strongly. So the exit-mechanism is used to handle all cases of transfer of control. The special use in the case of exceptions and exception handlers is described below:

```
handle(mk-Excpt(eid),excpthdlr)env=
  cases excpthdlr :
    (mk-Excphdl(excpmap,others)  ->
      (let env' = env + [EXCP -> eid] in
       (eid E dom excpmap  ->  int-Stmtlist(excpmap(eid))env',
        others ≠ nil       ->  int-Stmtlist(others)env',
        T                  ->  raise(eid))),
    nil                        ->  raise(eid))

type : Excpt [Excphdlr] -> (ENV => )


int-Raise(mk-Raise(opexname))env=
  (opexname = nil
   is-Excp-id(opexname)  ->  (if opexname E dom env
                              then (let tf = env(opexname) in
                                    raise-failure(s-TV(tf)))
                              else raise(opexname)),
   T                     ->  (def mk-(varloc, , ) : eval-Name(opexname)env;
                              raise-failure(value-of(varloc))))

type : Raise -> (ENV => )


raise(eid)=
  exit(mk-Excpt(eid))

type : Excp-id =>
```

The attempt to handle an exception proceeds as follows: If there is no handler the exception is raised again, that is, a new exit is performed. Otherwise the identifier of the exception to be handled is put into the environment. This is done to be able to perform a reraise statement inside the handler. If the exception identifier is among the explicitly mentioned exceptions of the handler the corresponding statement list is interpreted, otherwise if an others exists in the handler, the statement list belonging to this alternative is interpreted. Finally if there was no others alternative the exception is raised again since the attempt to handle the exception failed.

Raising an exception is interpreted in the following manner: If there is no exception name it is a reraise statement, and it is statically known that the statement appears inside a handler so the environment contains the identifier of the current exception and this exception is raised. If the raise statement contains an exception identifier and this identifier is in the environment, it is known that it due to a renaming denotes a failure exception for the task designated by the task value associated with this identifier in

the environment, and a failure exception is raised in that task by the monitor. If on the other hand the identifier does not belong to the domain of
the environment it is an internal exception and a normal raise is performed.
The last case being that of a name denoting a task is used for raising failure in the task corresponding to the evaluated name. This failure exception is again raised by the monitor in the task in question.

This relatively small set of formulas used to explain the exception mechanism of Ada shows that the exception concept is simple from a sequential dynamic semantics point of view. The trouble stems from tasks and especially
the failure exception that appears to have a special status. As explained
in section 2.1 this exception is one of the reasons for using the uninterruptable semicolon in these formulas at crucial points.
This concludes the description of blocks, declarations and exceptions.


## 2.4.2 Types and Subtypes


The type concept known from other languages like Pascal and CHILL being used
for e.g. type- checking, is in Ada supplied with the more dynamic concept
of subtypes. Types will in this section be viewed as being of a static nature with the exception of record types, because of the possibility of initializing components of a record type. This static view causes some devia-
tions in AS2 from what could be expected from the reference manual alone.

An important rule in this model is that a type always has a name. This implies that the only anonymous sort of type in Ada, the array type, has to be
named when declaring objects of such a type. The main reason for this naming is that the evaluation of an expression in general requires knowledge of
the type of the result. This is in particular important for array types
when determining indices for a positional aggregate. This naming is performed during the AS1->AS2 transformation. Due to the existence of a name
(a type identifier) for every type, subtypes can be modelled as a type identifier and an optional constraint.

Another important thing to notice is that the concept of derived types is of
no significance for the dynamic semantics. All that is left from a derived
type declaration in AS2 is the declaration of the type name as a subtype
having the constraints (if any) imposed by the original derived type declaration (see section 3.4 of [Ada 80]).

The static nature of most types (except records) makes it desirable to avoid
elaborating the declaration of such types dynamically. The declaration of
e.g. an enumeration type is purely static. Now the idea is that all this
static information should be passed from the static analysis to AS2 in a
convenient form. The solution chosen is for each declaration list (appearing in blocks, subprograms, packages or tasks) to add this information in a
sort of dictionary generated during the AS1->AS2 transformation. This dictionary will for some type.identifiers declared in the following declaration
list associate them with some static information. The types for which information is present in the dictionary are: Enumeration types, fixed types,
float types, array types, access types and private types. This information
is entered into the environment before elaborating the declaration list in
question. The only really dynamical action involved in this transformation
of information concerns access types. This is due to the existence of tasks

and is explained in section 2.4.1 on blocks.

The information in the dictionary about types takes the following form:

Enum-descr :: EnumVal <-m-> NO

That is an enumeration-type is described by a one-to-one mapping between the enumeration values of the type and their position number, the first value having the number zero.

Fixed-descr :: adelta: URealVal  udelta: URealVal
               lb: FixedVal  ub: FixedVal

Float-descr :: small: URealVal  bdigits: N1
               [lb: URealVal  ub: URealVal]

These descriptors are identical to the denotations and their components are described later. The descriptor of an array type is as follows:

Array-descr :: index: Type-id+  elem: Type-id

An array type declaration in Ada such as:

type AT is array (1..10,2..10) of integer range 3..8;

is transformed into the AS2-construct corresponding to:

subtype element is integer range 3..8;
subtype AT is arraytype (1..10,2..10);

and the dictionary for the declaration list in which this type declaration appears will contain the identifier arraytype associated with the following type descriptor: mk-Array-descr(<INTEGER,INTEGER>,element). That is a type identifier is made for the subtype of the array element during the AS1->AS2 transformation and this type identifier is used in the array-type descriptor. This causes some trouble when an anonymous array type is introduced inside a record, but this aspect will be discussed when describing the modelling of record types. In the case of an unconstrained array-type definition in Ada the same transformations as above will be performed except that no subtype- declaration is made for the result.

Access-descr :: Type-id

The type identifier is that of the base type of the object accessed by objects of the access type. That is the concrete Ada access type declaration is transformed into an Access-descr in the dictionary and a subtype declaration constraining the access type (by constraining the accessed object) e.g.:

type ACC is access R(D=>7);

where R is assumed to be a record type with the discriminant D (of type integer) is transformed into:

subtype ACC is AC(D=>7);

where in the dictionary AC is associated with mk-Access-descr(R). Since the dictionary information is transferred to the environment at the start of the declaration list, it is available during the elaboration of the declarations of the list. Hence the concept of incomplete access-type definitions is of no importance and the forward declarations are removed.

For private types all that one needs to know is that the identifier denotes a private type.

Before describing the representation of types and subtypes in the environment the influence of private types and limited private types is discussed. The mere existence of (limited) private types in Ada is a matter of hiding details concerning types from the external user of a package. This hiding is a static property and it is my opinion that from a dynamic point of view the denotation of a (limited) private type is the denotation of the complete type (obtained from the private part of the package), hence the border between the visible and private part of a package specification is removed during the AS1->AS2 transformation. This means that the (limited) private type declaration in general should not appear in AS2, but a temporary private type denotation containing no other information than that it is a private type is obtained from the dictionary.

One serious problem arises when one declares objects of (limited) private types in the visible part of the package containing the private type declaration. First of all it is not stated anywhere in the reference manual whether or not it is legal to declare non-constant objects of a (limited) private type in the visible part of the package containing the private type declaration. In the case of a deferred constant the (first) incomplete declaration is simply removed from the declaration list during the AS1->AS2 transformation. If we assume that variable declarations of that kind are not allowed there is no problem, but on the other hand if they are allowed a problem occurs: The complete type declaration has not been elaborated. In the first place this is against the sequential 'spirit' of Ada (I think) and secondly it may cause allocation problems in a realization in the case of dynamic arrays. The choice made in this model is hence to say that the declaration of variables (not constants) of (limited) private types cannot occur textually before the complete type definition. In any case a clarification of section 7.4 of the reference manual is needed on this subject.

Below the abstract syntax for type and subtype declarations is presented together with the corresponding denotations in the environment which are the result of elaborating the declarations. Furthermore some of the elaboration formulas will be given.

As mentioned at the start of this section enumeration types, fixed types, float types, array types, access types and private types are not declared in the declaration list but their denotations are found using the dictionary.

For the predefined integer type(s) a denotation exists in the predefined environment and it has the form:

    Integer-den :: lb: IntegerVal    ub: IntegerVal

where the two integer values are the lower and upper bounds respectively, and should the result of an operation on objects of this type fall outside these values the exception NUMERIC-ERROR is raised. All integer-type definitions occurring in an Ada program are transformed into subtype definitions using (one of) the predefined integer type(s) following the note from section 3.5.4 in [Ada 80].

Enumeration-, fixed-, float- and array-denotations are simple copies of the corresponding descriptors found in the dictionary.

    Enum-den   ::   EnumVal <-m-> N0

As this denotation is a one-to-one mapping between enumeration values and position numbers it is quite easy to use the attributes of such a type (POS, SUCC, PRED, VAL).

    Fixed-den   ::   adelta: URealVal   udelta: URealVal
                      lb: FixedVal     ub: FixedVal

A fixed type is characterized by two deltas, one is the actual delta, a universal real value, the other is the user defined delta, also a universal real value. The actual delta is used when e.g. multiplying values of fixed types, and the user delta is used to determine when the result of comparing two fixed values is undefined (a difference less than the user delta). The two fixed values constrain the values of the type to this range.

    Float-den   ::   small: URealVal    bdigits: N1
                      [lb: URealVal    ub:URealVal]

Float types are characterized by the smallest positive number of the type. This number is used to determine whether a comparison between two floats is defined independent of the implementation. The number of binary digits is used to simulate that the values of the type are not represented exactly, and it forms a basis on which type conversions between floats can be explained. The last component is the optional static range given in a floating point definition.

    Array-den   ::   index: Type-id+   elem: Type-id

An unconstrained array type is defined by a list of type identifiers one for each index position and a type identifier for the subtype of the elements.

    Access-den  ::  Type-id  ActId

The type identifier of an access denotation is that of the base type of the objects accessed by objects of this access type. The activation identifier, which is inserted when transferring the type identifier from the dictionary, is needed in this model because of tasking, as tasks accessed by an object of an access type is dependent on the block where the access type is declared (see section 2.1 on the influence from parallel Ada).

The remaining types are defined by declarations in AS2. These declarations are presented together with the denotations resulting from the elaboration of the declarations.

    Record-type-dcl    ::   Type-id  Record-type-def

    Record-type-def     ::   discrim: Field-id-<u>set</u>
                            Fieldortype-descr*
                            fixed: Field-id-<u>set</u>
                            [Varpart-descr]

    Fieldortype-descr  =   Field-descr | Type-in-Rec-dcl

    Field-descr        ::   Field-id-<u>set</u>  Elem-descr  [Expr]

```
Type-in-Rec-dcl    ::   Type-id  Elem-descr

Elem-descr         =    Subtype-def          |
                        Bound-Record-def     |
                        Bound-Array-def

Bound-Record-def   ::   Type-id (Discrim-spec |
                                  (Field-id Field-id))-set

Bound-Array-def    ::   Type-id
                        (lb: (DiscreteVal | Field-id)
                         ub: (DiscreteVal | Field-id))+

Varpart-descr      ::   Field-id (DiscreteVal m->
                        (Field-id-set [Varpart-descr]))
                        oth: [Field-id-set
                              [Varpart-descr]]


Record-den         ::   discrim: Field-id-set  Field-dens
                        fixed: Field-id-set
                        [Varpart-descr]

Field-dens         =    Field-id m-> (Elem-den  VAL)

Elem-den           =    Subtype-den |
                        Bound-Record-den | Bound-Array-den

Bound-Record-den   ::   Type-id
                        (Field-id m-> (DiscreteVal |
                                       Field-id      ))

Bound-Array-den    ::   Type-id
                        (lb: (DiscreteVal | Field-id)
                         ub: (DiscreteVal | Field-id))+
```

A record-type definition consists of four parts. The first is the set of field identifiers corresponding to the discriminants if any. The second part is a list of either field descriptors or type declarations in a record, the latter not corresponding to concrete Ada syntax but used to declare type identifiers for array component subtypes. The third component is the set of field identifiers that are fixed that is: always present. The last part is optional and describes the dependence relations between discriminants and the existence of fields in the varying part.

The corresponding record denotation is obtained by elaborating the descriptor list getting field denotations and simply transferring the remaining three components.

The descriptor list contains a field descriptor for each field in the record including any discriminant and any field of the variant part if such one exists. The descriptor list is constructed during the AS1->AS2 transformation. The field descriptors of the descriptor list are elaborated yielding field denotations by elaborating the element descriptor and evaluating the initialization expression if any. A type declaration in the list is elaborated by elaborating the element descriptor and putting the resulting denotation into the environment (see formulas below).

The element descriptors can be divided into two categories: Subtype definitions that do not refer to any record discriminant in their constraint, and
two 'bound' definitions where the constraint contains one or more references
to discriminants. A bound definition can be a bound record definition, in
which case it contains a type identifier of the record type and a set of either ordinary discriminant specifications or a pair of field identifiers
where the first field identifier is the discriminant being constrained (the
inner), and the second is the discriminant constraining (the outer). In the
denotation of such a bound record the constraint takes the form of a mapping
from the discriminant fields being constrained to either discrete values or
field identifiers of some outer discriminants. Arrays in records are not
allowed to be dynamic in any other way than through dependence on discriminants [Ada 80 section 3.7.1]. Hence a bound array definition consists of
the type identifier of the unbound array type and a list of bounds each of
which consists of a pair of either discrete values (statically evaluated) or
the field identifier of a discriminant.

The variant part descriptor will in the case of a variant part in the record
contain three parts. The first is the field identifier of the discriminant
determining which of the alternatives of the variant part is present. The
second part is a mapping from discrete values to descriptions of which
fields are present when the discriminant has the corresponding value. That
is the explicit choices given in the concrete Ada program are statically
evaluated (they are static expressions [Ada 80 section 3.7.3]) and for each
value the field identifiers of the corresponding list are collected in a set
and associated with this discriminant value together with an optional descriptor (of the same sort) for nested variant parts. The third part is optional and describes the same kind of field existence information for the
choice others if present.

The formulas performing the elaboration of record-type declarations and record component descriptors are given below.

```
elab-Record-type-dcl(mk-Record-type-dcl(tid,rtpdef))env=
   (let mk-Record-type-def(discrim,descrs,fixed,ovarpart) = rtpdef in
    def mk-(fielddens,env') : elab-Descrs(descrs)env;
    let rden = mk-Record-den(discrim,fielddens,fixed,ovarpart) in
    return(env' + [tid -> rden]))

type : Record-type-dcl -> (ENV => ENV)


elab-Descrs(descrs)env=
   (if descrs = <>
      then return(mk-([],env))
      else (def mk-(fden,env') : elab-Descr(hd descrs)env;
            def mk-(fdens,env'') : elab-Descrs(tl descrs)env';
            return(mk-(fdenUfdens,env''))))

type : Fieldortype-descr* -> (ENV => (Field-dens ENV))
```

```
elab-Descr(descr)env=
  cases descr :
    (mk-Field-descr(fids,elemdescr,opexpr)  ->
      (def elemden : elab-Elem-descr(elemdescr)env;
       def val : (if opexpr = nil
                    then get-init-fieldval(elemden)env,
                    else (let env' = [fid -> elemden | fid E fids],
                              env'' = env + env' in
                          def v : eval-Expr(opexpr)env'';
                          subtype-check(v,elemden);
                          return(v)));
      return(mk-([fid -> mk-(elemden,val) | fid E fids],env))),
    mk-Type-in-Rec-dcl(tid,elemdescr)    ->
      (def elemden : elab-Elem-descr(elemdescr)env;
       return(mk-([],env + [tid -> elemden]))))

type : Fieldortype-descr -> (ENV => (Field-dens ENV))


elab-Elem-descr(elemdescr)env=
  cases elemdescr :
    (mk-Subtype-def( , )         -> elab-Subtype-def(elemdescr)env,
     mk-Bound-Record-def( , ) -> elab-Bound-Record-def(elemdescr)env,
     mk-Bound-Array-def( , )  -> elab-Bound-Array-def(elemdescr))

type : Elem-descr -> (ENV => Elem-den)


elab-Bound-Record-def(mk-Bound-Record-def(tif,constrs))env=
  (let base = (cases env(tid) :
                  (mk-Subtype-den(oldbase, )  -> oldbase,
                   T                          -> tid)) in
   def constraints : eval-Rec-constr-in-Rec(base,constrs)env;
   return(mk-Bound-Record-den(base,constraints)))

type : Bound-Record-def -> (ENV => Bound-Record-den)


eval-Rec-constr-in-Rec(tid,sonstrs)env=
  (if constrs = {}
     then return([])
     else (let constr E constrs in
            (cases constr :
                (mk-Discrim-spec(fid,expr)  ->
                   (let fden = s-Elem-den((s-Field-dens(env(tid)))(fid)) in
                    def val : eval-Expr(expr)env;
                    subtype-check(val,fden)env;
                    return([fid -> val])),
                mk-(fidinner,fidouther)   ->
                   return([fidinner -> fidouther])) U
             eval-Rec-constr-in-Rec(tid,constrs{constr})env))

type : Type-id (Discrim-spec | (Field-id Field-id))-set -> (ENV =>
          (Field-id m-> (DiscreteVal | Field-id)))
```

```
elab-Bound-Array-def(mk-Bound-Array-def(tid,indexconstr))=
  return(mk-Bound-Array-den(tid,indexconstr))

type : Bound-Array-def => Bound-Array-den


get-init-fieldval(elemden)env=
  (is-Subtype-den(elemden)  ->  get-init-VAL(elemden)(nil)env,
   T                        ->  return(UNDEF))

type : Elem-den -> (ENV => VAL)
```

Private types with discriminants are a special case of private types.
Such private type declarations take the form:

```
    Private-Rec-with-discrim-dcl  ::
              Type-id (Field-id-set Subtype-def [Expr])+
```

This introduces the type identifier and gives a definition of the discriminants.  The elaboration yields an incomplete record denotation in the sense
that all other fields are not described. The corresponding complete record
declaration has been chosen to be syntactically different from that of a
usual record-type declaration. This transformation is performed during the
AS1->AS2 transformation, since it is statically known when a record-type declaration is a full definition of a private type and when it is not.

```
    Complete-private-Rec-dcl  ::  Type-id Record-type-def
```

This declaration is elaborated without re-elaborating the discriminant part
and the complete denotation (an ordinary record denotation) is the result.

The following will deal with subtypes. That is, the declaration of such
subtypes and the denotation of subtypes.

```
    Subtype-decl         ::  Type-id  Subtype-def

    Subtype-def          ::  Type-id  [Constr]

    Constr               =   Range-constr  |
                             Index-constr  |
                             Discrim-constr

    Range-constr         ::  Type-id  Range

    Range                ::  lb: Expr  ub: Expr

    Index-constr         ::  Discrete-range+

    Discrete-range       =   Range-constr | Type-id

    Discrim-constr       ::  Discrim-spec-set

    Discrim-spec         ::  Field-id  Expr


    Subtype-den          ::  Type-id  [Constraint]
```

```
Constraint              =   Range-Constraint |
                            Index-Constraint |
                            Discrim-Constraint

Range-Constraint        ::  lb: VAL   ub:VAL

Index-Constraint        ::  (lb: DiscreteVal
                             ub: DiscreteVal)+
                            order: (DiscreteVal+ <-m-> N1+)

Discrim-Constraint      ::  Field-id m-> DiscreteVal
```

The subtype declaration and definition follow the concrete syntax of Ada in a straigthforward way. The denotation obtained by elaborating a subtype declaration contains a type identifier, being the identifier of the base type, and an optional evaluated constraint. The syntactic constraints are either range-, index- or discriminant- constraints. The first thing one might notice is the lack of an accuracy constraint specifying delta or digits for reals, but the delta and digits are statically determinable and since this report does not include the modelling of representation details values of a subtype are assumed to be represented as values of their base type, and furthermore the delta (small) used in comparision is the delta (small) of the type and not the subtype [Ada 80 section 4.5.2]. An accuracy constraint containing a range constraint is transformed into an ordinary range constraint during the AS1->AS2 transformation.

The syntactic range constraint consists of the base type of the expressions of the range, the latter being two expressions. The evaluated range constraint contains the two evaluated bounds.

A syntactic index constraint is a list of discrete ranges, the latter being range constraints or type identifiers as in concrete Ada. The semantic index constraint consists of two components, the first being a list of pairs of discrete values describing the bounds of this subtype, the second component being an ordering relation between index lists and lists of relative positions of the index values of each index. This is used when indexing a variable of this subtype. The need of this component arises due to the fact that when accessing an actual parameter of a subprogram by reference, if we have a subtype of the actual parameter which is different from that of the formal parameter an index transformation has to be performed either in the subprogram or somewhere else. The first implies that one inside the subprogram should know whether an identifier denotes a parameter accessing by reference. This is against the general idea (see section 2.4.3) of subprogram parameters: That they from the inside of the subprogram 'look like' ordinary variables and are accessed similarily. This leads to the conclusion that if a subtype denotation contains this transformation information (and variable denotations contain subtype denotations) the accessing is performed in a unified way (see section 2.3 on storage- and environment modelling). This has been chosen.

A syntactic discriminant constraint consists of a set of discriminant specifications, the latter being pairs containing the field identifier of the discriminant and the expression whose value is used to constrain the discriminant. The evaluated discriminant constraint is a mapping from discriminants to their (discrete) values.

This concludes the description of the modelling of the Ada type concept. The model constitutes a basis on which e.g. the consequences of the more or

less complicated relations between a record and its component is explainable
in a reasonable way when used as in the evaluation of names (Appendix B.3)
and the creation of initial values for a variable (Appendix B.3 and section
2.4.1).

2.4.3 Procedures and Functions

The topic of this section is procedures and functions as seen from a dynamical semantics point of view. First a few general remarks on procedures and
functions (operators) are given , next their declarations and bodies are
presented, and last their denotations and some elaboration- and interpreta-
tion- formulas are presented.

Subprograms are declared in a declaration list, and in concrete Ada (and in
AS1 as well) the declaration may be separated in two so that the socalled
subprogram specification occurs twice: the first time to introduce the subprogram identifier and its parameters (and result-type in the case of a
function). The second time it appears together with the rest of the subprogram body. This division is required if two subprograms are mutually recursive, because of the strictly sequential way identifiers are introduced in
an Ada program.

If a separate subprogram specification occurs in Ada the rules of the
chapter on subprograms [Ada 80 section 6.3] states that the specification is
elaborated when first met and is not to be re-elaborated when reaching the
subprogram body. In order to treat the elaboration of a subprogram body in
a uniform way regardless of the existence of an earlier specification the
declaration of a subprogram is always split during the AS1->AS2 transformation into what is called a subprogram declaration and a subprogram body.
The subprogram body used here is somewhat 'degenerated' in the sense that
all that is left from the specification part of the original body is the
subprogram identifier. This is possible due to a name-transformation secur-
ing that all subprograms (including those being overloaded) get unique identifiers so that the correspondence between declaration and body is given by
their names being identical. For user-defined operators the following rule
applies in AS2: They are as functions. This means that they are defined as
functions given a new unique function identifier and they are called like
functions not as the predefined operators. This is possible because overloading is statically solved.

Furthermore the declaration is statically transformed so that the mode information is extracted and placed in the dictionary associated with the declaration list in which the subprogram declaration occurs. This mode information is only present for procedures, since the mode of any parameter of a
function is known to be IN. But for procedures as well as for functions an
ordering relation for parameters is found in its descriptor in the dictionary. This ordering is only used when elaborating the renaming of a subprogram (entry), where the positions of the parameters are used and not their
names, and all subprogram calls are transformed so that named parameters are
used.

The descriptors have the following form:

```
Proc-descr    ::   (Parm-id m-> Parmmode)
                   order: (Parm-id <-m-> N1)

Fct-descr     ::   order: (Parm-id <-m-> N1)

Parmmode      =    IN | OUT | INOUT
```

The abstract syntax of subprogram declarations and bodies is as follows:

```
Proc-dcl      ::   Proc-id   Formal-part

Fct-dcl       ::   Fct-id    Formal-part   Subtype-def

Formal-part   =    Parm-id-set m-> (Subtype-def [Expr])

Subprog-body  ::   (Proc-id | Fct-id)  Block
```

A procedure declaration consists of a procedure identifier and a formal part. The latter associates sets of parameter identifiers with pairs consisting of a subtype definition and an optional initialization expression. This formal part is like the formal part of concrete Ada except that the mode information has been removed and placed in the dictionary instead.

A function declaration contains the same two parts as the procedure declaration plus an additional component: a subtype definition defining the result subtype of the function.

Subprogram bodies are modelled as consisting of an identifier (procedure- or function-identifier) and a part being a block. The identifier corresponds to the specification part of a concrete Ada subprogram and the block to the rest. A block is used to model the main part of a subprogram body because they contain the same elements: A declarative part, a sequence of statements and possibly an exception handler. The only difference is that a concrete Ada block may contain a block identifier but it is removed in AS2 as the unique naming of identifiers makes it useless.

The denotations that are the results of elaborating subprogram declarations and bodies are now presented:

```
Proc-den      ::   (Parm-id m-> (Subtype-den
                                 Parmmode
                                 (REF | COPY)))
                   init: (Parm-id m-> VAL)
                   order: (Parm-id <-m-> N1)
                   [Proc]

Fct-den       ::   (Parm-id m-> (Subtype-den
                                 (REF | COPY)))
                   init: (Parm-id m-> VAL)
                   order: (Parm-id <-m-> N1)
                   restp: Subtype-den
                   [Fct]

Proc          =    (Parm-id m-> Var-den) -> (∑ -> ∑ )

Fct           =    (Parm-id m-> Var-den) -> (∑ -> (∑ VAL))
```

A procedure denotation consists of three parts that are always present and an optional fourth functional component.

The first component is a description of the parameters of the procedure. This description associates with each parameter identifier three parts of information: The subtype denotation of the parameter, the mode and a part designating whether the actual parameter of a call corresponding to this formal parameter is accessed by reference or it is transferred by copying. The presence of this last part implies that the parameter transfer method is determined in some way (see later) when elaborating the procedure declaration and hence is the same (for a given parameter) in every call.

The second component is a mapping from those parameters having an initialization value into their values. Such parameters are known to be of mode IN.

The third component is an ordering of the parameters. This ordering is obtained directly from the dictionary mentioned earlier in this section.

The last optional component is a functional object. All the three previously described components are placed in the denotation as the result of elaborating the procedure declaration. But this last component is not inserted before the procedure body has been elaborated. The function is (when present) a function from a mapping between parameter identifiers and variable denotations, the mapping having the form of an environment, into a state transformation. This means that when this functional object is applied to a mapping being as described above it results in a state transformation.

The denotation of a function is similar to that of a procedure except for the following: No mode information is present (all parameters are of mode IN ), a result-subtype denotation is present as being the result of elaborating the corresponding component of the function declaration, and the functional component is one that - when applied - besides causing a state transformation (it may be the identity transformation corresponding to no side effects) returns a value.

The elaboration of a procedure declaration, function declaration and subprogram body is illustrated in the following with the use of auxiliary functions which are defined in appendix B.1 on declarations.

```
elab-Proc-dcl(mk-Proc-dcl(procid,formalpart))(dict)env=
  (let mk-Proc-descr(modes,order) = dict(procid) in
   def parmdens : eval-Formal-part(formalpart)env;
   let parminit = [pid -> val | pids E dom parmdens and
                                pid E pids and val ≠ nil and
                                ( ,val) = parmdens(pids)],
       extpdens = extend-p-parmdens(parmdens,modes))env,
       procden = mk-Proc-den(extpdens,parminit,order,nil) in
   return(env + [procid -> procden]))

type : Proc-dcl -> (Dict -> (ENV => ENV))
```

The elaboration of a procedure declaration uses the dictionary of the declaration list containing the declaration. The first thing done is to extract the procedure descriptor from the dictionary. Secondly the formal part is evaluated yielding a mapping from sets of parameter identifiers to pairs consisting of a subtype denotation and an optional initialization

value. From this mapping the default-value-map to be used in the initialization is extracted, and an extended version of the mapping is created to be
used for the parameter descriptor part of the procedure denotation. This
extension includes determining the parameter transfer mechanism (reference
or copying). At last a procedure denotation containing the three permanent
parts and no functional part (nil) is made and placed in the environment.


```
elab-Fct-dcl(mk-Fct-dcl(fctid,formalpart,result))(dict)env=
   (let mk-Fct-descr(order) = dict(fctid) in
    def parmdens : eval-Formal-part(formalpart)env;
    def subtpden : eval-Subtype-def(result)env;
    let parminit = [pid -> val ¦ pids E dom parmdens and
                                pid E pids and val ≠ nil and
                                ( ,val) = parmdens(pids)],
        extpdens =extend-f-parmdens(parmdens)env,
        fctden = mk-Fct-den(extpdens,parminit,order,subtpden,nil) in
   return(env + [fctid -> fctden]))

type : Fct-dcl -> (Dict -> (ENV => ENV))
```


Elaborating a function declaration is similar to the elaboration of a procedure declaration. The main differences are that a subtype definition is
evaluated for the result type of the function, and that no mode information
is placed in the denotations of the parameters.


```
elab-Subprog-body(mk-Subprog-body(sid,block))(env)env'=
   cases env(sid) :
     (mk-Proc-den(extparmdescr,parminit,order,nil)     ->
         (let proc(parmassoc) =
               (let env'' = env' + parmassoc in
                trap exit(mk-Ret(nil)) with I in
                     int-Block(block)env'') in
        let pden = mk-Proc-den(extparmdescr,parminit,order,proc) in
        return(env + [sid -> pden])),
      mk-Fct-den(extpdescr,parminit,order,restp,nil)   ->
         (let func(parmassoc) =
               (let env'' = env' + parmassoc + [RESTP -> restp] in
                trap exit(mk-Ret(val) with return(val) in
                     (int-Block(block)env'';
                      exit(mk-Ret(UNDEF))))) in
        let fden = mk-Fct-den(extpdescr,parminit,order,restp,func) in
        return(env + [sid -> fden])))

type : Subprog-body -> (ENV -> (ENV => ENV))
```


Elaborating a subprogram body requires two environments: The one existing
just prior to the elaboration and the one being the result of elaborating
the declaration list of the enclosing block, subprogram- or task-body. This
last environment is used to handle such subprogram calls inside the subprogram body, that refer to this same subprogram or a subprogram whose body is
not yet elaborated (but, its specification is). This is the case of (mutually) recursive subprograms. The need for this second environment occurs
due to the fact that in denotational semantics the denotation of a subprogram must be fully known before interpreting a call to this subprogram even

if the call occurs inside another subprogram body and thus is not to be performed before calling this latter subprogram.

The elaboration depends on whether the body is that of a procedure or that
of a function. If the subprogram identifier is associated with an (incomplete) procedure denotation in the environment a functional object is created. This function takes an argument having the form of an environment being
a parameter association - and the following is performed: The total environment is extended by this parameter association and a trap is set up for
catching meta-exits caused by interpreting a return statement inside the
subprogram body. Such return exits are known to contain no value since this
is a procedure and not a function, and when trapped they cause no state
change (the identity transformation). Inside this trap the block of the
subprogram body is interpreted. This constitutes the definition of the
functional object which is placed in the environment that existed just prior
to this elaboration.

In the case where the body belongs to a function, another kind of functional
object is created. It also takes as its argument a parameter association
and does the following: The total environment is extended by the parameter
association and the subtype denotation of the result in order to be able to
interpret return statements of the body. Next a trap is set up for
meta-exits caused by interpreting a return statement. This return exit will
always contain a value since the exit is performed inside a function.
Catching such an exit causes a meta return containing the value of the exit.
Having set up this trap the block of the body is interpreted followed by a
return exit with the value UNDEF. This last return-exit is only reached if
no exits have been performed when interpreting the block, and it corresponds
to leaving the body by reaching the end which causes the value of the result
to be undefined [Ada 80 section 6.5]. This defines the functional object.
It is placed in the denotation and the latter is put in the environment that
existed prior to this elaboration.

As could be seen from the elaboration of a subprogram body the functional
component of a procedure/function denotation does not manage the parameter
passing: Allocation of locations for actual parameters passed by copying,
restoring of actual parameters (copying) etc.. In this model this is performed at the place of the call. This implies that the functional component
has no information concerning parameter passing and all parameters are treated alike from the point of view of this function. The opposite solution:
To let the functional component take care of the parameter passing could
have been chosen instead. Choosing between these two alternatives is in my
opinion a matter of taste since both solutions have their advantages. If we
look at the amount and complexity of the formulas involved, the two solutions are almost identical, it is just a question about whether the formulas
to handle the passing of parameters are used when creating the functional
component of the subprogram denotation or at the point of call. But if one
looks at it from a code generation point of view the two models are representatives of two different strategies. The solution not chosen corresponds
to generating transfer-handling code just once, whereas the other corresponds to code generation at each point of call. The latter however will in
a reasonable compiler generate simpler (less) code for this at each point of
call than the other will generate in the subprogram code block because static information concerning actual parameters can be utilized. All in all it
would have been better in a formal model to be able to describe parameter
passing without making any decision as to where this parameter passing is
handled. This is, however, to the best of my knowledge not possible, so one
of the two possibilities have been chosen (the point of call), and if one

wants a compiler to use the other form one should write the corresponding formal definition and argue (or perhaps even prove) the equivalence of the two models.

In the following a procedure call is described and interpreted. The corresponding evaluation of a function call, and the auxiliary functions used, are defined in appendices B.3 and B.2.

    Procedure-call  ::  Proc-id  (Parm-id m-> Expr)

A procedure call consists of an identifier of the procedure to be called and parameter associations. The identification is a procedure identifier and not a general name (as in concrete Ada) since the name transformation performed during the AS1 >AS2 transformation has generated a unique identifier for each subprogram and this is the one used. The parameter associations are in AS2 always named associations and they are viewed as a mapping from the formal parameter identifiers to the actual expressions. This mapping contains no ordering of the parameters corresponding to the rule for evaluation of parameter associations [Ada 80 section 6.4.1]: the order is not defined by the language. All parameter associations are named, as can be seen. This is chosen because it is more general than positional parameters due to the possibility of omitting an actual parameter if a default value exists. The consequence of this possibility is that any positional parameter can be statically transformed to a named parameter, whereas the opposite is not always the case (default values cannot be statically inserted in a positional list).

The interpretation formula for a procedure call is now given.

```
int-Procedure-call(mk-Procedure-call(pid,parmexprs))env=
   (let mk-Proc-den(extpdescr,pinit, ,proc) = env(pid) in
    def actid : create-ActId();
    let env' = env + [ACTID -> actid] in
    always free-locations(actid) in
      (def pla : eval-p-parmassoc(extpdescr,pinit,parmexprs)env';
       let copyenv = extract-copyenv(pla),
           parmassoc = extract-parmassoc(pla) in
       always p-call-epilogue(extpdescr,pla)env' in
         (proc(parmassoc);
          restore-params(parmassoc,copyenv))env')))

type : Procedure-call -> (ENV => )
```

A procedure call is interpreted by first finding the procedure denotation to be used. An activation identifier is created and placed in the environment. It is used to handle the freeing of any location allocated for parameters transferred by copying. Then (uninterruptable) a trap is set up describing what is to happen when the rest of the formula is left whether by an exit or by reaching the end. The action to be performed when leaving the interpretation of a procedure call is to free any location allocated during the evaluation of the parameter associations. Inside the trap the parameter associations are evaluated yielding a mapping from formal parameter identifiers to pairs consisting of the variable denotation to be used by the functional component of the procedure denotation and an optional variable denotation corresponding to the evaluated actual parameter name. The latter is only present in the case of an <u>OUT</u> or <u>INOUT</u> parameter and is used to restore the actual parameters upon returning from the procedure. This mapping is now split into two: one containing the information to be used when restoring the parameters transferred by copying and one to be used as argument to the functional component of the procedure denotation. Then another trap is set up to ensure that the value of a parameter transferred by reference satisfies any constraint imposed by the actual parameter, otherwise the exception CONSTRAINT-ERROR is raised. Inside this trap the functional component is applied to the parameter association extracted above yielding a state transformation. After this the parameters transferred by copying are restored.

This concludes the section on procedures and functions. The remaining formulas concerning calls are found in Appendix B.2.

## 2.4.4 Packages and Tasks

The subject of this section is packages and tasks from a dynamic semantics point of view. Packages are described first:

```
Package-dcl    ::  Package-id  Dcl-part

Package-body   ::  Package-id  Dcl-part
                   Stmt-list  [Excphdl]
```

A package declaration consists of a package identifier and a declarative part. This declarative part is like that in a block, that is it is not separated in a visible and a private part from a dynamic semantics point of view (for a discussion on private type declarations see section 2.4.2).

The package body has the following parts: a package identifier, a declarative part, a statement list and perhaps an exception handler. The first thing to notice is that an 'empty' package body is statically inserted in a declaration list in which package declaration with object declarations of a task type but no original package body occurs (see [Ada 80 section 9.3]). This 'empty' body contains a declarative part with an empty dictionary and an empty declaration list, a null statement and no exception handler. Since the environment is in a sense flat the elaboration of a package declaration/body does not give rise to a sub environment as part of a package denotation. The items declared in a package are so to speak made accessible in the block, subprogram or task in whose declaration list the package declaration/body resides.

```
Package-den    ::  CrId
```

A package denotation contains only one single component: a creation identifier used to govern the activation of task objects declared in the package. The formulas for interpreting package declarations/bodies are now given.

```
elab-Package-dcl(mk-Package-dcl(pid,dclpart))env=
  (def crid : create-CrId(env(ACTID));
   let mk-Dcl-part(dict,dcllist) = dclpart,
       env' = env + get-type-dens(dict)(env(ACTID) in
   def env'' = extend-env(dict,dcllist)(env' + [CRID -> crid])env'';
   let env''' = env'' + [pid -> mk-Package-den(crid)] in
   return(env''' + [CRID -> env(CRID)])))

type : Package-dcl -> (ENV => ENV)


elab-Package-body(packbody)(env)env'=
  (let mk-Package-body(pid,dclpart,stmtl,excphdlr) = packbody,
       crid = s-CrId(env(pid)),
       mk-Dcl-part(dict,dcllist) = dcllist,
       env'' = env + get-type-dens(dict)(env(ACTID)) in
   def env''' : extend-env(dict,dcllist)(env'' + [CRID -> crid])env';
   trap exit (mk-Excpt(eid)) with
             handle(mk-Excpt(eid),excphdlr)env''' in
     (activate-tasks(crid);
      int-Stmtlist(stmtl)env''';
      return(env''' + [CRID -> crid])))

type : Package-body -> (ENV -> (ENV => ENV))
```

The elaboration of a package declaration consists of first creating a creation identifier used to control the activation of task objects created in
the declaration list of the package declaration. The type descriptors of
the dictionary are made into denotations and placed in the environment. The
environment is next extended by the effect of elaborating the declaration
list of the declarative part using as initial environment, one containing
the newly generated creation identifier. The result of elaborating the
package declaration is a new environment being like the result of the elaboration of the declaration list of the declarative part with the package denotation inserted and the creation identifier component restored.

When elaborating a package body one needs two environments: the one existing just prior to the elaboration and the one obtained by elaborating the
declaration list of the enclosing block, subprogram or task body in which
the package body resides. The latter environment is needed because of the
possibility of declaring (mutually) recursive subprograms involving calls to
subprograms whose bodies are not yet elaborated (see section 2.4.3 on subprograms). The first thing done is getting the creation identifier corresponding to the package identifier (created when elaborating the package declaration). Then the type denotations obtainable from the dictionary are
placed in the environment. The next step is to extend the environment by
elaborating the declaration list using the newly found creation identifier.
After this a trap is set up for catching exception exits from the following
part of the elaboration just as when interpreting the statements of a block
(see section 2.4.1). Having set up this trap the tasks, if any, created
using the creation identifier of the package are activated followed by the
interpretation of the statement list. The result is the environment found
by the extension above but with the creation identifier component restored.


For tasks the following is important to notice: The declaration of a single
task by a task specification in Ada is in AS2 statically transformed into

the declaration of a task type having a unique identifier and the declaration of the object of that introduced type according to the equivalence stated in [Ada 80 section 9]. The abstract syntax for task-type declarations and task bodies is:

    Task-type-dcl    ::   Type-id  Dict  Entry-dcl*

    Entry-dcl        ::   Entry-id  [Discrete-range]
                          Formal-part

    Task-type-body   ::   Type-id  Dcl-part
                          Stmt-list  [Excphdl]

The denotations:

    Task-type-den    ::   Entries [TaskFct]

    Entries          =    Entry-id m-> Entry-den

    Entry-den        ::   (Parm-id m-> (Subtype-den
                                        Parmmode
                                        (REF | COPY)))
                          init: (Parm-id m-> VAL)
                          order: (Parm-id <-m-> N1)
                          fam: [Subtype-den]

    TaskFct          =    $\Sigma \rightarrow \Sigma$

A task type declaration consists of the type identifier introduced, a dictionary containing information concerning the entries declared in the following declaration list. Such an entry declaration is similar to that of a procedure except for an optional discrete range present in the case of a family of entries. A formal part is described in the section on procedures and functions 2.4.3. A task type body is like a block but its elaboration results in the completion of the task type denotation by adding the functional component. The task type denotation has a component describing its entries and this component is created when elaborating the task type declaration. The second component is the functional part describing the effect of running that task, and it is inserted after elaborating the corresponding task type body. The description of the entries is viewed as associating an entry denotation to each entry identifier declared. Such an entry denotation contains three components that are of the same kind as those present in a procedure denotation (see section 2.4.3) and an optional fourth component present in the case of a family of entries, and it will the describe the subtype with the constraint to be satisfied by any index value used to get a member of the family.

elab-Task-type-dcl(mk-Task-type-dcl(tid,dict,entrydcls))env=
  (def entries : elab-entrylist(entrydcls)(dict)env;
   return(env + [tid -> mk-Task-type-den(entries,nil)]))

type : Tak-type-dcl -> (ENV => ENV)

```
elab-entrylist(entrydcls)(dict)env=
  (if entrydcls = <>
    then return([])
    else (let mk-Entry-dcl(eid,oprange,formalpart) = hd entrydcls,
              mk-Proc-descr(parmmodes,order) = dict(eid) in
          def parmdens : eval-Formal-part(formalpart)env;
          let parminit = [pid -> val | pids E dom parmdens and
                                       pid E pids and val ≠ nil and
                                       ( ,val) = parmdens(pids)],
              extpdens = extend-p-parmdens(parmdens,parmmodes)env in
          def fam : (if oprange = nil
                       then return(nil)
                       else (def mk-(tid,constr) :
                                    eval-Discrete-range(oprange)env;
                             return(mk-Subtype-den(tid,constr))));
          let entryden = mk-Entry-den(extpdens,parminit,order,fam) in
          (return([eid -> entryden]) U
           elab-entrylist(tl entrydcls)(dict)env)))

type : Entry-dcl* -> (Dict -> (ENV => Entries))


elab-Task-type-body(tasktbody)env=
  (let mk-Task-type-body(tid,dclpart,stmtl,excphdlr) = tasktbody,
       mk-Task-type-den(entries,nil) = env(tid),
       env' = env + entries,
       taskfct = create-TaskFct(dclpart,stmtl,excphdlr)env' in
   return(env + [tid -> mk-Task-type-den(entries,taskfct)]))

type : Task-type-body -> (ENV => ENV)
```

The elaboration of a task type declaration consists of elaborating the entry list  and placing this entry information in the environment as part of a new task type denotation.  Elaborating a list of entry declarations is performed sequentially  entry by entry.  For each entry its descriptor (being a proce- dure descriptor) is extracted from the dictionary.  The formal part is eva- luated as for a procedure (see section 2.4.3), initial values are extracted, and mode information and parameter transfer information is inserted.   If a discrete  range  is  given corresponding to a family, it is evaluated giving the family information (a subtype denotation).  From all this an entry deno- tation is made and placed in the descriptor of entries.

When elaborating a task type body entry descriptors are found  corresponding to this task type in the environment.  These entry descriptors are placed in the environment before creating the task function.  The creation function is defined  in  the  tasking model [Lo 80b].  The task function thus created is used to make the task type denotation complete and this complete  denotation is placed in the environment.

This concludes the description of packages and tasks from a  sequential  dy- namic semantics point of view.

258

# 3. Conclusion

When defining a formal model of a language, in this case the dynamic semantics of Ada, one starts by reading the relevant manuals describing the
language more or less informally. Having read the reference manual [Ada
79a] and the rationale [Ada 79b] for Ada I fealt that Ada was quite well designed and described. But when definition of the first formal model of that
version of Ada had begun, it became evident that some very specific questions, that had to be answered when defining a model were not answered by
the manual.

In general, making a formal model of a subject being more or less informally
described forces one to analyse the subject in detail, and thereby one gets
a thorough understanding of the intrinsic properties of the subject.

In this specific case of the definition of the dynamic semantics of Ada, the
model will, when completed, serve two purposes. One is to be a sort of formal 'reference manual' defining concisely the semantics of any language construct and thus applicable for answering very specific questions about the
language. The second is to be the basis for a systematic derivation of a
compiling algorithm mapping abstract Ada programs into A-code as defined by
Ole Dommergaard [Do 80], where this compiling algorithm formally defines the
effect of the code generating parts of a compiler. So the long-term goal of
the compiler development method is that of constructing better (i.e. more
correct) compilers.

259


Appendices:   The Model.

A.  Semantic and Syntactic Domains


Semantic Domains.

```
Env        = ((Id ¦ QUOT) m-> DEN)            U
             (EXCP       m-> Excp-id)          U
             (RESTP      m-> Subtype-den)      U
             (ACTID      m-> Actid)            U
             (CRID       m->  CrId)            U
             (Excp-id    m-> TaskFailure)

DEN        = Type-den          ¦ Elem-den          ¦
             Var-den           ¦ Proc-den          ¦
             Fct-den           ¦ Entry-den         ¦
             Package-den

Type-den   = Integer-den       ¦ Enum-den          ¦
             Real-den          ¦ Array-den         ¦
             Record-den        ¦ Access-den        ¦
             Task-type-den     ¦ Private-den

Elem-den   = Subtype-den          ¦ Bound-Array-den    ¦
             Bound-record-den

Var-den    :: Subtype-den  VarLoc

Proc-den   :: (Parm-id m-> (Subtype-den (REF ¦ COPY)))
              init:(Parm-id m-> VAL)  order:(Parmid <-m-> N1)
              [Proc]

Fct-den    :: (Parm-id m-> (Subtype-den (REF ¦ COPY)))
              init:(Parm-id m-> VAL)  order:(Parmid <-m-> N1)
              restp: Subtype-den   [Fct]

Entry-den  :: (Parm-id m-> (Subtype-den Parmmode
                                         (REF ¦ COPY)))
              init:(Parm-id m-> VAL)  order:(Parm-id <-m-> N1)
              fam:[Subtype-den]

Package-den :: Crid

Integer-den :: lb:IntegerVal  ub:IntegerVal

Enum-den    :: EnumVal <-m-> NO

Real-den    = Fixed-den ¦ Float-den

Fixed-den   :: adelta:URealVal  udelta:URealVal
               lb:FixedVal  ub:FixedVal

Float-den   :: small:URealVal  ldigits:N1
               [lb:URealVal  ub:URealVal]

Array-den   :: index:Type-id+  elem:Type-id
```

```
Record-den    :: discrim:Field-id-set  Field-dens
                 fixed:Field-id-set  [Varpart-descr]

Field-dens    =  Field-id m-> (Elem-den  VAL)

Access-den    :: Type-id  Actid

Task-type-den :: Entries  [TaskFct]

Entries       =  Entry-id m-> Entry-den

Task-Fct      :: ∑ -> ∑

Private-den   :: ()

Subtype-den   :: base:Type-id  [Constraint]

Constraint    =  Range-Constraint    | Index-constraint    |
                 Discrim-Constraint

Range-constraint :: lb:VAL  ub:VAL

Index-Constraint :: (lb:DiscreteVal  ub:DiscreteVal)+
                    order:(DiscreteVal+ <-m-> N1)

Discrim-Constraint :: Field-id m-> DiscreteVal

Parmmode      =  IN | OUT | INOUT

Proc          =  (Parm-id m-> Var-den)  -> ( ∑ ->∑ )

Fct           =  (Parm-id m-> Var-den)  -> ( ∑ -> ( ∑ VAL))

Actid         :: TOKEN

Cr Id         :: TOKEN

TaskFailure   :: TV
```

Locations:

```
VarLoc      =  Subloc | SliceLoc

SubLoc      :: LOC  (N1+ | Field-id)*  Alloc

SliceLoc    :: Subloc  N1  N1

Alloc       =  STATIC | DYN

LOC         :: TOKEN
```

Values:

```
VAL           =  DiscreteVal          |  URealVal              |
                 FixedVal             |  FloatVal              |
                 ArrayVal             |  RecordVal             |
                 TV                   |  AccessVal             |
                 UNDEF

DiscreteVal   =  IntegerVal  |  EnumVal

IntegerVal    :: INTG

EnumVal       :: Id  |  QUOT

URealVal      :: NUM

FixedVal      :: INTG

FloatVal      :: NUM

ArrayVal      :: (N1+ m-> VAL)  order:(DiscreteVal+ <-m-> N1+)

RecordVal     :: Field-id m-> VAL

TV            :: TOKEN

AccessVal     :: LOC  |  NULL
```

Domains of The Storage Handler.

```
STG           =  LOC m-> VAL

ACTV          =  ActId m-> LOC-set
```

Auxiliary semantic Domains used by the Exit Mechanism:

```
Go            :: Label-id

Ret           :: [VAL]

Ex            :: [Loop-id]

Excpt         :: Excp-id
```

Syntactic Domains.

The Abstract Syntax AS2.


2.3

| | | |
|---|---|---|
| Var-id | = | Id |
| Type-id | = | Id |
| Field-id | = | Id |
| Attribute-id | = | Id |
| Label-id | = | Id |
| Loop-id | = | Id |
| Proc-id | = | Id |
| Fct-id | = | Id |
| Parm-id | = | Id |
| Package-id | = | Id |
| Entry-id | = | Id |
| Excp-id | = | Id      ¦ |
| | | Predef-excp-id |

Predef-excp-id  =  <u>FAILURE</u>         ¦
                   <u>CONSTRAINT-ERROR</u> ¦
                   <u>NUMERIC-ERROR</u>    ¦
                   <u>SELECT-ERROR</u>     ¦
                   <u>STORAGE-ERROR</u>


Id            :: TOKEN

3
        Dcl-part          :: Dict  Dcl*

3.1
        Dcl             = Object-dcl                  |
                                      Subtype-dcl               |
                                      Private-Rec-with-discrim-dcl |
                                      Complete-private-Rec-dcl   |
                                      Record-type-dcl           |
                                      Proc-dcl                  |
                                      Fct-dcl                   |
                                      Subprog-body             |
                                      Package-dcl               |
                                      Package-body             |
                                      Task-type-dcl            |
                                      Task-type-body          |
                                      Renaming-dcl

3.2
        Object-dcl       :: Var-id-set [CONST] Subtype-def [Expr]

3.3
        Subtype-dcl      :: Type-id  Subtype-def

        Subtype-def      :: Type-id  [Constr]

        Constr           = Range-constr          |
                                      Index-constr          |
                                      Discrim-constr

3.5
        Range-constr     :: Type-id  Range

        Range            :: lb: Expr  ub: Expr

        Index-constr     :: Discrete-range+

        Discrete-range   = Range-constr            |
                                      Type-id

3.7

```
Private-Rec-with-discrim-dcl
              :: Type-id (Field-id-set Subtype-def [Expr])+

Complete-private-Rec-dcl
              :: Type-id  Record-type-def

Record-type-dcl :: Type-id  Record-type-def

Record-type-def :: discrim: Field-id-set  Fieldortype-descr*
                   fixed: Field-id-set [Varpart-descr]

Fieldortype-descr = Field-descr  |  Type-in-Rec-dcl

Field-descr     :: Field-id-set  Elem-descr [Expr]

Type-in-Rec-dcl :: Type-id  Elem-descr

Elem-descr      = Subtype-def            |
                  Bound-Record-def       |
                  Bound-Array-def

Bound-Record-def:: Type-id
                   (Discrim-spec | (Field-id Field-id))-set

Bound-Array-def :: Type-id  (lb: (DiscreteVal | Field-id)
                            ub: (DiscreteVal | Field-id))+

Varpart-descr   :: Field-id (DiscreteVal m->
                            (Field-id-set [Varpart-descr]))
                   oth: [Field-id-set [Varpart-descr]]
```

3.7.1

```
Discrim-constr  :: Discrim-spec-set

Discrim-spec    :: Field-id  Expr
```

4.1

```
    Name              =  Simple-name         |
                         Indexed-component   |
                         Slice               |
                         Selected-component  |
                         Attribute           |
                         Fct-call

    Simple-name      :: Var-id
```

4.1.1

```
    Indexed-component
                     :: Name  Expr+
```

4.1.2

```
    Slice            :: Name  Discrete-range
```

4.1.3

```
    Selected-component
                     =  Field-select |
                        All-select

    Field-select     :: Name  Field-id

    All-select       :: Name
```

4.1.4

```
    Attribute        :: Name  Attribute-id
```

4.3

```
    Aggregate         =  Record-Aggregate            |
                         Named-Array-Aggregate       |
                         Positional-Array-Aggregate  |
                         One-Comp-Aggregate

    Record-Aggregate           :: Field-id-set m-> Expr

    Named-Array-Aggregate      :: (DiscreteVal-set m-> Expr) [Expr]

    Positional-Array-Aggregate :: (N1 m-> Expr)  [Expr]

    One-Comp-Aggregate         :: [Choice-set]  Expr

    Choice                     =  Expr             |
                                  Discrete-range
```

4.4

| Expr | :: Type-id  Expr' |
|---|---|

| Expr' | = VAL | &#124; |
|---|---|---|
| | Aggregate | &#124; |
| | Name | &#124; |
| | Allocator | &#124; |
| | Type-conversion | &#124; |
| | Qualified-expr | &#124; |
| | Prefix | &#124; |
| | Infix | &#124; |
| | Range-test | &#124; |
| | Subtype-test | |

4.5

| Prefix | :: Mop  Expr |
|---|---|

Mop          = $\pm$ &#124; $-$ &#124; not

Infix        :: Expr  Dop  Expr

Dop          = $+$ &#124; $-$  &#124; $*$ &#124; $/$  &#124; mod &#124; rem  &#124;
               $=$ &#124; $/=$ &#124; $<$ &#124; $<=$ &#124; $>$  &#124; $>=$ &#124;
               $\&$ &#124; $**$ &#124;
               and &#124; or &#124; xor &#124; and then &#124; or else

Range-test   :: Expr  [NOT]  Range

Subtype-test :: Expr  [NOT]  Subtype-def

4.6

Type-conversion :: Type-id  Expr

4.7

Qualified-expr  :: Type-id  Expr'

4.8

Allocator    :: Type-id
                [(Expr &#124; Discrim-constr &#124; Index-constr)]

5.1
```
Stmt-list       =  Stmt*

Stmt            :: [Label-id]  Unlab-stmt

Unlab-stmt      =  Null               |
                   Assign             |
                   Exit               |
                   Return             |
                   Goto               |
                   Procedure-call     |
                   Entry-call         |
                   Delay              |
                   Abort •            |
                   Raise              |
                   Code               |
                   If                 |
                   Case               |
                   Loop               |
                   Block              |
                   Accept             |
                   Select

Null            :: ()
```

5.2
```
Assign          :: Name  Expr
```

5.3
```
If              :: (Expr  Stmt-list)+ [Stmt-list]
```

5.4
```
Case            :: Expr  (DiscreteVal m-> Stmt-list)
                             [Stmt-list]
```

5.5
```
Loop            :: [Loop-id] ( Uncond-loop  |
                               While-loop   |
                               For-loop     )

Uncond-loop     ::                               Stmt-list

While-loop      :: Expr                          Stmt-list

For-loop        :: Var-id [REV] Discrete-range Stmt-list
```

5.6
```
Block           :: Dcl-part  Stmt-list  [Excphdl]
```

5.7
```
Exit            :: [Loop-id]  [Expr]
```

5.8
```
Return          :: [Expr]
```

5.9
```
Goto            :: Label-id
```

6.1

```
Proc-dcl        :: Proc-id   Formal-part

Fct-dcl         :: Fct-id    Formal-part   Subtype-def

Formal-part     =  Parm-id-set m-> ( Subtype-def [Expr])
```

6.3

```
Subprog-body    :: (Proc-id | Fct-id)  Block
```

6.4

```
Procedure-call  :: Proc-id  (Parm-id m-> Expr)

Fct-call        :: Fct-id   (Parm-id m-> Expr)
```

7.1

```
Package-dcl     :: Package-id  Dcl-part

Package-body    :: Package-id  Dcl-part  Stmt-list  [Excphdl]
```

8.5

```
Renaming-dcl    =  Object-rename       |
                   Failure-rename      |
                   Proc-rename         |
                   Entry-rename        |
                   Fct-rename

Object-rename   :: Var-id  Type-id                        Name

Failure-rename  :: Excp-id                                Name

Proc-rename     :: Proc-id  Formal-part                   Proc-id

Entry-rename    :: Proc-id  Formal-part  task:Name        Entry-name

Fct-rename      :: Fct-id   Formal-part  Subtype-def      Fct-id
```

9.1

```
Task-type-dcl   :: Type-id  Dict  Entry-dcl*

Task-type-body  :: Type-id  Dcl-part
                   Stmt-list [Excphdl]
```

9.5

```
Entry-dcl       :: Entry-id [Discrete-range] Formal-part

Entry-call      :: Name  Entry-name  (Parm-id m-> Expr)

Entry-name      :: Entry-id [Expr]

Accept          :: Entry-id [Expr] Stmt-list
```

9.6

```
Delay           :: Expr
```

9.7

```
Select          = Selective-wait            ¦
                  Conditional-entry-call     ¦
                  Timed-entry-call
```

9.7.1

```
Selective-wait :: ([Expr] Select-alt)* [Stmt-list]

Select-alt      = Accept-alt                 ¦
                  Delay-alt                  ¦
                  Terminate-alt

Accept-alt      :: Accept  Stmt-list

Delay-alt       :: Delay   Stmt-list

Terminate-alt   :: ()
```

9.7.2

```
Conditional-entry-call
                :: Entry-call  Stmt-list  Stmt-list
```

9.7.3

```
Timed-entry-call
                :: Entry-call  Stmt-list  Delay-alt
```

9.10

```
Abort           :: Name+
```

11.2
  Excphdl    :: (Excp-id m-> Stmt-list)  oth: [Stmt-list]

11.3
  Raise     :: [Excp-id | Name]

13
  Repr-spec   = Length-spec
         ...

13.2
  Length-spec  :: INTG

13.8
  Code     :: Aggregate

```
Dict           =  Id m-> Descr

Descr          =  Type-descr  | Proc-descr  | Fct-descr

Type-descr     =  Enum-descr  | Real-descr   | Array-descr |
                  Access-descr | PRIVATE

Enum-descr     :: EnumVal <-m-> NO

Real-descr     =  Fixed-descr  | Float-descr

Fixed-descr    :: adelta: URealVal   udelta: URealVal
                  lb: FixedVal   ub: FixedVal

Float-descr    :: small: URealVal   bdigits: N1
                  [lb: URealVal   ub: URealVal]

Array-descr    :: index: Type-id+  elem: Type-id

Access-descr   :: Type-id

Proc-descr     :: (Parm-id m-> Parmmode)
                  order: (Parm-id <-m-> N1)

Fct-descr      :: order: (Parm-id <-m-> N1)

Parmmode       =  IN  |  OUT  |  INOUT
```

B.  Formulas


B.1 Blocks, declarations and exceptions

```
int-Block(mk-Block(mk-Dcl-part(dict,dcllist),stmtl,excpthdlr))env=
  (def actid : get-new-ActId()ⓒ
   let env' = env + [ACTID -> actid] + get-type-dens(dict)(actid) in
   always block-epilogue(actid) in
     (def crid : create-CrId(actid);
      let env'' = env' + [CRID -> crid] in
      def env''' = extend-env(dict,dcllist)(env'')env''';
      trap exit (mk-Excp(eid)) with
                   handle(mk-Excp(eid),excpthdlr)env''' in
        (activate-tasks(crid);
         int-Stmtlist(stmtl)env''')))

type : Block -> (ENV=> )



extend-env(dict,dcllist)(env)env'=
  (if dcllist=<>
     then return(env)
     else (def env'' : elab-Dcl(hd dcllist)(dict)(env)env';
              extend-env(tl dcllist)(env'')env'))

type : Dict Dcl* -> (ENV -> (ENV => ENV))



block-epilogue(actid)=
  (await-termination(actid)ⓒ
   free-locations(actid))

type : ActId =>



get-type-dens(dict)(actid)=
  [id -> create-typedens(dict(id))(actid) | id ∈ dict and
                                      is-Type-descr(dict(id))]

type : Dict -> (ActId -> ENV)
```

```
create-typeden(tpdescr)(actid)=
index create-typeden
  cases tpdescr :
    (mk-Enum-descr(vmap)                    ->
        mk-Enum-den(vmap),
     mk-Fixed-descr(mdelta,udelta,lb,ub)    ->
        mk-Fixed-den(mdelta,udelta,lb,ub),
     mk-Float-descr(small,bdigits,oprange)  ->
        mk-Float-den(small,bdigits,oprange),
     mk-Array-descr(index,elem)             ->
        mk-Array-den(index,elem),
     mk-Access-descr(typeid)                ->
        mk-Access-den(typeid,actid),
     T                                      ->
        mk-Private-den( ))

type : Type-descr -> (ActId -> Type-den)



handle(mk-Excpt(eid),excpthdlr)env=
  cases excpthdlr :
    (mk-Excphdl(excpmap,others)  ->
        (let env' = env + [EXCP -> eid] in
        (eid E dom excpmap  ->  int-Stmtlist(excpmap(eid))env',
         others ≠ nil        ->  int-Stmtlist(others)env',
         T                   ->  raise(eid))),
     nil                            ->  raise(eid))

type : Excpt [Excphdlr] -> (ENV => )
```

```
elab-Dcl(decl)(dict)(env)env'=
  cases decl :
    (mk-Object-dcl( , , , )                    ->
        elab-Object-dcl(decl)env,
    mk-Subtype-dcl( , )                        ->
        elab-Subtype-dcl(decl)env,
    mk-Private-Rec-with-discrim-dcl( , )  ->
        elab-Private-Rec-with-discrim-dcl(decl)env,
    mk-Complete-private-Rec-dcl( , )         ->
        elab-Complete-private-Rec-dcl(decl)env,
    mk-Record-type-dcl( , )                    ->
        elab-Record-type-dcl(decl)env,
    mk-Proc-dcl( , )                           ->
        elab-Proc-dcl(decl)(dict)env,
    mk-Fct-dcl( , , )                          ->
        elab-Fct-dcl(decl)(dict)env,
    mk-Subprog-body( , )                       ->
        elab-Subprog-body(decl)(env)env',
    mk-Package-dcl( , )                        ->
        elab-Package-dcl(decl)env,
    mk-Package-body( , , , )                   ->
        elab-Package-body(decl)(env)env',
    mk-Task-type-dcl( , , )                    ->
        elab-Task-type-dcl(decl)env,
    mk-Task-type-body( , , , )                 ->
        elab-Task-type-body(decl)env,
    T                                          ->
        elab-Renaming-dcl(decl)(dict)(env)env')

type : Dcl -> (Dict -> (ENV -> (ENV => ENV)))



elab-Object-dcl(mk-Object-dcl(vids,oconst,subtpdef,opexpr))env=
  (def subden : elab-Subtype-def(subtpdef)env;
   def env' : env + get-vardens(vids,subden)env;
   if opexpr = nil
     then (for all vid E vids do
              (def val : get-init-VAL(subden)(CREATE)env';
               assign(s-VarLoc(env'(vid)),val));
           return(env'))
     else (def val : eval-Expr(opexpr)env';
           for all vid E vids do
             check-and-assign(env'(vid),val)env';
           if const = CONST
             then return(update-subtypes(vids,val,subden)env')
             else return(env')))

type : Object-dcl -> (ENV => ENV)
```

```
get-vardens(vids,subden)env=
   (if vids = {}
      then return([])
      else (let vid E vids in
              def varloc : mk-SubLoc(allocate(env(ACTID)),<>,STATIC);
              (return([vid -> mk-Var-den(subden,varloc)]) U
              get-vardens(vids\{vid},subden)env)))

type : Var-id-set Subtype-den -> (ENV => ENV)


get-init-VAL(subtpden)(creation)env=
   (let mk-Subtype-den(base,constr) = subtpden in
    cases env(base) :
      (mk-Array-den( ,elem)                                     ->
          (let mk-Index-Constraint( ,order) = constr in
           def vmap : get-A-valuemap(elem,order)(creation)env;
           return(mk-ArrayVal(vmap,order)))),
      mk-Record-den(discrim,fielddens,static,vpartdescr)  ->
          (let discrvals =
                 (if constr = nil
                     then [fid -> val | fid E discrim and
                                        val = s-VAL(fielddens(fid))]
                     else (let mk-Discrim-Constraint(discrvals') = constr in
                              discrvals')),
               curfields = static U
                           get-currentfields(vpartdescr,discrvals) in
           def vmap : get-R-valuemap(fielddens|curfields,discrvals)
                                         (creation)env;
           return(mk-RecordVal(vmap))),
      mk-Access-den( , )                                        ->
          return(mk-AccessVal(NULL)),
      mk-Task-type-den( , )                                     ->
          (if creation = CREATE
              then return(mk-TV(create-task(base)env))
              else return(UNDEF)),
      T                                                         ->
          return(UNDEF)))

type : Subtype-den -> ([CREATE] -> (ENV => VAL))


get-A-valuemap(elem,order)(creation)env=
   (if order = []
      then (let dvt E dom order in
              def val : get-init-VAL(env(elem))(creation)env;
              (return([order(dvt) -> val]) U
              get-A-valuemap(elem,order\{dvt})(creation)env)))

type : Type-id (DiscreteVal+ <-m-> N1+) -> ([CREATE] ->
          (ENV => (N1+ <-m-> VAL)))
```

```
get-R-valuemap(fielddens,discrvals)(creation)env=
  (if fielddens = []
   then return([])
   else (let fid E dom fielddens
             mk-(elemden,val) = fielddens(fid) in
          def mk-(subtpden,env') :
                insert-discrimvalues(elemden,discrvals)env';
          def val : get-init-VAL(subtpden)(creation)env;
          (return([fid -> val]) U
           get-R-valuemap(fielddens\{fid},discrvals)(creation)env')))

type : Field-dens (Field-id m-> DiscreteVal) -> ([CREATE] ->
         (ENV => (Field-id m-> VAL)))


insert-discrimvalues(elemden,discrvals)env=
  cases elemden :
    (mk-Subtype-den( , )                    ->
       return(mk-(elemden,env)),
    mk-Bound-Array-den(tid,constr)    ->
       (let newconstr = <mk-(lv,uv) | 1 =< i =< ln constr and
                                      mk-(lb,ub) = constr[i] and
                                      lv = get-value(lb,discrvals) and
                                      uv = get value(ub,discrvals)>,
            mk-Array-den(index,elem)=env(tid) in
        def mk-(newden,env') :
              insert-discrimvalues(env(elem),discrvals)env;
        let order = find-order(newconstr,index)env,
            indexconstr = mk-Index-Constraint(newconstr,order),
            subtpden = mk-Subtype-den(tid,indexconstr) in
        check-Index-Constraint(newconstr,index)env;
        return(mk-(subtpden,env' + [elem -> newden]))),
    mk-Bound-Record-den(tid,constr)   ->
       (let newconstr = [fid -> val | fid E dom constr and
                            val = get-value(constr(fid),discrvals)],
            fdens = s-Field-dens(env(tid)),
            discrimconstr = mk-Discrim-Constraint(newconstr) in
        check-Discrim-Constraint(newconstr,fdens)env;
        return(mk-(mk-Subtype-den(tid,discrimconstr),env)))))

type : Elem-den (Field-id m-> VAL) -> (ENV => (Subtype-den ENV))


get-value(fidorval,discrvals)=
  (is-DiscreteVal(fidorval)  ->  fidorval,
   T                         ->  discrvals(fidorval))

type : (Field-id | DiscreteVal) (Field-id m-> DiscreteVal) -> DiscreteVal
```

```
update-subtypes(vids,val,subden)env=
    (let mk-Subtype-den(base,constr) = subden in
     if constr = nil
       then (cases val :
                 (mk-ArrayVal(vmap,order)  ->
                     (let indexconstr = find-Index-Constraint(order),
                         newsubden = mk-Subtype-den(base,indexconstr) in
                      env + [vid -> mk-Var-den(newsubden,vloc) |
                                       vid E vids and
                                       vloc = s-VarLoc(env(vid))]),
                 T
                                       ->  env))
       else env)

type : Var-id-set VAL Subtype-den -> (ENV -> ENV)



find-Index-Constraint(order)=
    (let lower E dom order be s.t.
          (¥ dvt E dom order)((¥ i E ind order(dvt))
                                     (order(dvt)[i] >= order(lower)[i])) in

     let upper E dom order be s.t.
          (¥ dvt E dom order)((¥ i E ind order(dvt))
                                     (order(dvt)[i] =< order(upper)[i])) in
     let constr = <mk-(lower[i],upper[i]) | i =< i =< ln lower> in
     mk-Index-Constraint(constr,order))

type : (DiscrVal+ <-m-> N1+) -> Index-Constraint



elab-Subtype-dcl(mk-Subtype-dcl(tid,subtpdef))env=
    (def subtpden : elab-Subtype-def(subtpdef)env;
     return(env + [tid -> subtpden]))

type : Subtype-dcl -> (ENV => ENV)



elab-Subtype-def(mk-Subtype-def(tid,constr))env=
    cases env(tid) :
      (mk-Subtype-den(base,oldconstr)  ->
          (def newconstr : eval-Constr(constr,base)env;
           if newconstr = nil
             then return(env(tid))
             else (check-Constraints(newconstr,oldconstr,base)env;
                   return(mk-Subtype-den(base,newconstr)))),
      T                                  ->
          (def newconstr : eval-Constr(constr,tid);
           if newconstr = nil
             then return(mk-Subtype-den(tid,nil))
             else (check-Constraints(newconstr,nil,tid)env;
                   return(mk-Subtype-den(tid,newconstr)))))

type : Subtype-def -> (ENV => Subtype-den)
```

```
eval-Constr(constr,base)env=
  cases constr :
    (mk-Range-constr( ,mk-Range(lb,ub))           ->
        (def lv : eval-Expr(lb)env,
             uv : eval-Expr(ub)env;
         return(mk-Range-Constraint(lv,uv))),
     mk-Index-constr(discreterngl)               ->
        (def constrl : <eval-Discrete-range(discreterngl[i]env |
                              1 =< i =< ln discreterngl>;
         let typeidl = <s-Type-id(constrl[i] | 1 =< i =< ln constrl>,
             bounds = <mk-(lb,ub) | 1 =< i =< ln constrl and
                          mk-( ,mk-Range-Constraint(lb,ub)) = constrl[i]> in
         let order = find-order(bounds,typeidl)env in
         return(mk-Index-Constraint(bounds,order))),
     mk-Discrim-constr(discrimspecs)             ->
        (def constrm : [fid -> eval-Expr(expr)env |
                          mk-Discrim-spec(fid,expr) E discrimspecs];
         return(mk-Discrim-Constraint(constrm))),
     T                                           -> return(nil))

type : [Constr] Type-id -> (ENV => Constraint)



eval-Discrete-range(discrrng)env=
  cases discrrng :
    (mk-Range-constr(tid,mk-Range(lb,ub))  ->
        (def lv : eval-Expr(lb)env,
             uv : eval-Expr(ub)env;
         return(mk-(tid,mk-Range-Constraint(lv,uv)))),
     T                                           ->
        (let mk-Subtype-den(tid,constr) = env(discrrng) in
         return(mk-(tid,constr))))

type : Discrete-range -> (ENV => (Type-id Range-Constraint))



find-order(constrl,typeidl)env=
  (let valposllist = <get-valposl(get-base(typeidl[i]env,constrl[i])env|
                          1 =< i =< ln typeidl> in
   [vt -> ot | ln vt = ln ot = ln valposllist and
              (¥ i E ind vt)(E j E ind valposllist[i])
                   ((valposllist[i])[j] = mk-(vt[i],ot[i]))])

type : (DiscreteVal DiscreteVal)+ Type-id+ -> (ENV ->
        (DiscreteVal+ <-m-> N1+))
```

```
get-valposl(tid,mk-(lb,ub)))env=
  cases env(tid) :
    (mk-Integer-den( , )    ->
        <mk-(mk-IntegerVal(i),i-mn+1) | mn =< i =< mx and
                                       mk-IntegerVal(mn) = lb and
                                       mk-IntegerVal(mx) = ub>,
    mk-Enum-den(enummap)    ->
        <mk-(enummap-1(i),i-mn+1) | mn =< i =< mx and
                                    enummap(lb) = mn and
                                    enummap(ub) = mx>)

type : Type-id (DiscreteVal DiscreteVal) -> (ENV -> (DiscreteVal N1)+)



check-Constraints(new,old,base)env=
  cases old :
    (mk-Range-Constraint(olb,oub)     ->
        (let mk-Range-Constraint(nlb,nub) = new in
         if (less-than(nlb,olb,base)env or less-than(oub,nlb,base)env or
             less-than(nub,olb,base)env or less-than(oub,nub,base)env)
           then raise(CONSTRAINT-ERROR)
           else I),
    nil                               ->
        (cases new :
          (mk-Index-Constraint(iclist, )     ->
              (let arrayden = (cases env(base) :
                                (mk-Access-den(tid, )  ->  env(tid),
                                 T                      ->  env(base))) in
               check-Index-Constraint(iclist,s-index(arrayden))env),
          mk-Discrim-Constraint(dmap)        ->
              (let recden = (cases env(base) :
                              (mk-Access-den(tid, )  ->  env(tid),
                               T                      ->  env(base))) in
               check-Discrim-Constraint(dmap,s-Field-dens(recden))env),
          mk-Range-Constraint( , )           ->  I)))

type : Constraint Constraint Type-id -> (ENV => )



check-Index-Constraint(iclist,index)env=
  (for all i E ind iclist do
    (let mk-(lb,ub) = iclist[i],
         mk-Subtype-den(base,constr) = env(index[i] in
     cases constr :
       (mk-Range-Constraint(lv,uv)  ->
           check-range(lb,ub,lv,uv,base)env,
        T                           ->  I)))

type : (DiscreteVal DiscreteVal)+ Type-id+ -> (ENV => )
```

```
check-Discrim-Constraint(dmap,fielddens)env=
   (for all fid E dom dmap do
      (let mk-(sybtpden, ) = fielddens(fid) in
       subtype-check(dmap(fid),subtpden)env))

type : (Field-id m-> DiscreteVal) Field-dens -> (ENV => )



check-range(lb,ub,lv,uv,base)env=
   (if less-than(lb,lv,base)env or less-than(uv,lb,base)env
      then raise(CONSTRAINT-ERROR)
      else (if less-than(ub,lb,base)env
               then I
               else (if less-than(uv,ub,base)env
                        then raise(CONSTRAINT-ERROR)
                        else I)))

type : DiscreteVal DiscreteVal DiscreteVal DiscreteVal Type-id -> (ENV => )



subtype-check(val,mk-Subtype-den(base,constr))env=
   cases constr :
      (nil                                    ->  I,
       mk-Range-Constraint(lb,ub)            ->
          (if less-than(val,lb,base)env or less-than(ub,val,base)env
             then raise(CONSTRAINT-ERROR)
             else I),
       mk-Index-Constraint(bounds,order)  ->
          (let mk-ArrayVal(vmap, ) = val in
           if rng order = dom vmap
             then I
             else raise(CONSTRAINT-ERROR)),
       mk-Discrim-Constraint(dmap)            ->
          (let mk-RecordVal(vmap) = val in
           if dmap ⊆ vmap
             then I
             else raise(CONSTRAINT-ERROR)))

type : VAL Subtype-den -> (ENV => )



elab-Private-Rec-with-discrim-dcl(decl)env=
   (let mk-Private-Rec-with-discrim-dcl(tid,dl) = decl in
    def mk-(fielddens, ) : elab-Descrs(dl)env;
    let rden = mk-Record-den(dom fielddens,fielddens,{},nil) in
    return(env + [tid -> rden]))

type : Private-Rec-with-discrim-dcl -> (ENV => ENV)
```

```
elab-Complete-private-Rec-dcl(decl)env=
  (let mk-Complete-private-Rec-dcl(tid,defin) = decl,
       mk-Record-type-def(discrims,fdescrs,fixed,vpdescr) = defin,
       mk-Record-den(discrs,fdens,{},nil) = env(tid),
       newfdesrs = remove-discrim(fdescrs,discrims)env in
   def mk-(fielddens,env') : elab-Descrs(newfdesrs)env;
   let rden = mk-Record-den(discrims,fielddensUfdens,fixed,vpdescr) in
   return(env' + [tid -> rden]))

type : Complete-private-Rec-dcl -> (ENV => ENV)


remove-discrim(fdescrs,discrims)=
  <fdescrs[i] | 1 =< i =< ln fdescrs and
                cases fdescrs[i] :
                  (mk-Field-descr(fids, , )  -> fids ∩ discrims = {},
                   T                          -> true)>

type : Fieldortype-descr* Field-id-set -> Fieldortype-descr*


elab-Record-type-dcl(mk-Record-type-dcl(tid,rtpdef))env=
  (let mk-Record-type-def(discrim,descrs,fixed,ovarpart) = rtpdef in
   def mk-(fielddens,env') : elab-Descrs(descrs)env;
   let rden = mk-Record-den(discrim,fielddens,fixed,ovarpart) in
   return(env' + [tid -> rden]))

type : Record-type-dcl -> (ENV => ENV)


elab-Descrs(descrs)env=
  (if descrs = <>
      then return(mk-([],env))
      else (def mk-(fden,env') : elab-Descr(hd descrs)env;
            def mk-(fdens,env'') : elab-Descrs(tl descrs)env';
            return(mk-(fdenUfdens,env''))))

type : Fieldortype-descr* -> (ENV => (Field-dens ENV))
```

```
elab-Descr(descr)env=
  cases descr :
    (mk-Field-descr(fids,elemdescr,opexpr)  ->
      (def elemden : elab-Elem-descr(elemdescr)env;
       def val : (if opexpr = nil
                    then get-init-fieldval(elemden)env,
                    else (let env' = [fid -> elemden | fid E fids],
                               env'' = env + env' in
                          def v : eval-Expr(opexpr)env'';
                          subtype-check(v,elemden);
                          return(v)));
       return(mk-([fid -> mk-(elemden,val) | fid E fids],env))),
    mk-Type-in-Rec-dcl(tid,elemdescr)       ->
      (def elemden : elab-Elem-descr(elemdescr)env;
       return(mk-([],env + [tid -> elemden])))))

type : Fieldortype-descr -> (ENV => (Field-dens ENV))



elab-Elem-descr(elemdescr)env=
  cases elemdescr :
    (mk-Subtype-def( , )          ->  elab-Subtype-def(elemdescr)env,
     mk-Bound-Record-def( , )  ->  elab-Bound-Record-def(elemdescr)env,
     mk-Bound-Array-def( , )   ->  elab-Bound-Array-def(elemdescr))

type : Elem-descr -> (ENV => Elem-den)



elab-Bound-Record-def(mk-Bound-Record-def(tif,constrs))env=
  (let base = (cases env(tid) :
                  (mk-Subtype-den(oldbase, )  ->  oldbase,
                   T                          ->  tid)) in
   def constraints : eval-Rec-constr-in-Rec(base,constrs)env;
   return(mk-Bound-Record-den(base,constraints)))

type : Bound-Record-def -> (ENV => Bound-Record-den)



eval-Rec-constr-in-Rec(tid,sonstrs)env=
  (if constrs = {}
     then return([])
     else (let constr E constrs in
             (cases constr :
                 (mk-Discrim-spec(fid,expr)  ->
                    (let fden = s-Elem-den((s-Field-dens(env(tid)))(fid)) in
                     def val : eval-Expr(expr)env;
                     subtype-check(val,fden)env;
                     return([fid -> val])),
                  mk-(fidinner,fidouther)    ->
                     return([fidinner -> fidouther])) U
          eval-Rec-constr-in-Rec(tid,constrs{constr})env))

type : Type-id (Discrim-spec | (Field-id Field-id))-set -> (ENV =>
          (Field-id m-> (DiscreteVal | Field-id)))
```

```
elab-Bound-Array-def(mk-Bound-Array-def(tid,indexconstr))=
  return(mk-Bound-Array-den(tid,indexconstr))

type : Bound-Array-def => Bound-Array-den


get-init-fieldval(elemden)env=
  (is-Subtype-den(elemden)  ->  get-init-VAL(elemden)(nil)env,
   T                        ->  return(UNDEF))

type : Elem-den -> (ENV => VAL)


elab-Proc-dcl(mk-Proc-dcl(procid,formalpart))(dict)env=
  (let mk-Proc-descr(modes,order) = dict(procid) in
   def parmdens : eval-Formal-part(formalpart)env;
   let parminit = [pid -> val | pids E dom parmdens and
                                pid E pids and val ≠ nil and
                                ( ,val) = parmdens(pids)],
       extpdens = extend-p-parmdens(parmdens,modes))env,
       procden = mk-Proc-den(extpdens,parminit,order,nil) in
   return(env + [procid -> procden]))

type : Proc-dcl -> (Dict -> (ENV => ENV))


elab-Fct-dcl(mk-Fct-dcl(fctid,formalpart,result))(dict)env=
  (let mk-Fct-descr(order) = dict(fctid) in
   def parmdens : eval-Formal-part(formalpart)env;
   def subtpden : eval-Subtype-def(result)env;
   let parminit = [pid -> val | pids E dom parmdens and
                                pid E pids and val ≠ nil and
                                ( ,val) = parmdens(pids)],
       extpdens =extend-f-parmdens(parmdens)env,
       fctden = mk-Fct-den(extpdens,parminit,order,subtpden,nil) in
   return(env + [fctid -> fctden]))

type : Fct-dcl -> (Dict -> (ENV => ENV))
```

```
eval-Formal-part(formalpart)env=
  (if formalpart = []
    then return([])
    else (let pids E dom formalpart in
            let mk-(subtpdef,expr) = formalpart(pids) in
            def stden : elab-Subtype-def(subtpdef)env;
            def val : (if expr = nil
                          then return(nil)
                          else (def v : eval-Expr(expr)env;
                                subtype-check(v,stden)env;
                                return(v)));
            (return([pids -> mk-(stden,val)]) U
             eval-Formal-part(formalpart{pids})env)))

type : Formal-part -> (ENV => (Parm-id-set m-> (Subtype-den [VAL])))


extend-p-parmdens(parmdens,modes)env=
  (let flatpdens = [pid -> subtpden | pids E dom parmdens and
                                      pid E pids and
                                      (subtpden, ) = parmdens(pids)] in
  [pid -> mk-(stden,mode,refcopy) | pid E dom flatpdens and
                                    stden = flatpdens(pid) and
                                    mode = modes(pid) and
                                    refcopy =
                                      param-transfer(pid,stden)env])

type : (Parm-id-set m-> (Subtype-den [VAL])) (Parm-id m-> Parmmode) ->
          (ENV -> (Parm-id m-> (Subtype-den Parmmode (REF | COPY))))


extend-f-parmdens(parmdens)env=
  (let flatdens = [pid -> subtpden | pids E dom parmdens and
                                     pid E pids and
                                     (subtpden, ) = parmdens(pids)] in
  [pid -> mk-(stden,refcopy) | pid E dom parmdens and
                               stden = flatdens(pid) and
                               refcopy = param-transfer(pid,stden)env])

type : (Parm-id-set m-> (Subtype-den [VAL])) -> (ENV ->
          (Parm-id m-> (Subtype-den (REF | COPY))))


param-transfer(parmid,mk-Subtype-den(base, ))env=
  cases env(base) :
    (mk-Integer-den( , )   -> COPY,
     mk-Fixed-den( , , , ) -> COPY,
     mk-Float-den( , , )   -> COPY,
     mk-Access-den( , )    -> COPY,
     T                     -> (by-ref(parmid,base)env -> REF,
                               T                      -> COPY))

type : Parm-id Subtype-den -> (ENV -> (REF | COPY))
```

by-ref is an implementation defined function, determining whether an actual
parameter corresponding to 'parmid' is transferred by copying or is accessed
by reference.  The function yields true if reference is chosen by the implementation.

```
elab-Subprog-body(mk-Subprog-body(sid,block))(env)env'=
  cases env(sid) :
    (mk-Proc-den(extparmdescr,parminit,order,nil)      ->
        (let proc(parmassoc) =
                (let env'' = env' + parmassoc in
                 trap exit(mk-Ret(nil)) with I in
                     int-Block(block)env'') in
         let pden = mk-Proc-den(extparmdescr,parminit,order,proc) in
         return(env + [sid -> pden])),
     mk-Fct-den(extpdescr,parminit,order,restp,nil)  ->
        (let func(parmassoc) =
                (let env'' = env' + parmassoc + [RESTP -> restp] in
                 trap exit(mk-Ret(val) with return(val) in
                 (int-Block(block)env'';
                     exit(mk-Ret(UNDEF)))) in
         let fden = mk-Fct-den(extpdescr,parminit,order,restp,func) in
         return(env + [sid -> fden])))

type : Subprog-body -> (ENV -> (ENV => ENV))
```

```
elab-Package-dcl(mk-Package-dcl(pid,dclpart))env=
  (def crid : create-CrId(env(ACTID));
   let mk-Dcl-part(dict,dcllist) = dclpart,
       env' = env + get-type-dens(dict)(env(ACTID) in
   def env'' = extend-env(dict,dcllist)(env' + [CRID -> crid])env'';
   let env''' = env'' + [pid -> mk-Package-den(crid)] in
   return(env''' + [CRID -> env(CRID)]))

type : Package-dcl -> (ENV => ENV)
```

```
elab-Package-body(packbody)(env)env'=
  (let mk-Package-body(pid,dclpart,stmtl,excphdlr) = packbody,
       crid = s-CrId(env(pid)),
       mk-Dcl-part(dict,dcllist) = dcllist,
       env'' = env + get-type-dens(dict)(env(ACTID)) in
   def env''' : extend-env(dict,dcllist)(env'' + [CRID -> crid])env';
   trap exit (mk-Excpt(eid)) with
           handle(mk-Excpt(eid),excphdlr)env''' in
     (activate-tasks(crid);
      int-Stmtlist(stmtl)env''';
      return(env''' + [CRID -> crid])))

type : Package-body -> (ENV -> (ENV => ENV))
```

```
elab-Task-type-dcl(mk-Task-type-dcl(tid,dict,entrydcls))env=
  (def entries : elab-entrylist(entrydcls)(dict)env;
   return(env + [tid -> mk-Task-type-den(entries,nil)]))

type : Tak-type-dcl -> (ENV => ENV)



elab-entrylist(entrydcls)(dict)env=
  (if entrydcls = <>
     then return([])
     else (let mk-Entry-dcl(eid,oprange,formalpart) = hd entrydcls,
               mk-Proc-descr(parmmodes,order) = dict(eid) in
           def parmdens : eval-Formal-part(formalpart)env;
           let parminit = [pid -> val | pids E dom parmdens and
                                       pid E pids and val ≠ nil and
                                       ( ,val) = parmdens(pids)],
               extpdens = extend-p-parmdens(parmdens,parmmodes)env in
           def fam : (if oprange = nil
                        then return(nil)
                        else (def mk-(tid,constr) :
                                      eval-Discrete-range(oprange)env;
                              return(mk-Subtype-den(tid,constr))));
           let entryden = mk-Entry-den(extpdens,parminit,order,fam) in
           (return([eid -> entryden]) U
            elab-entrylist(tl entrydcls)(dict)env)))

type : Entry-dcl* -> (Dict -> (ENV => Entries))



elab-Task-type-body(tasktbody)env=
  (let mk-Task-type-body(tid,dclpart,stmtl,excphdlr) = tasktbody,
       mk-Task-type-den(entries,nil) = env(tid),
       env' = env + entries,
       taskfct = create-TaskFct(dclpart,stmtl,excphdlr)env' in
   return(env + [tid -> mk-Task-type-den(entries,taskfct)]))

type : Task-type-body -> (ENV => ENV)
```

B.2 Statements


```
int-Stmtlist(stmtlist)env=
  tixe [mk-Go(lab) -> int-Stmtlist-without-trap(gotomap(lab))env |
                       (gotomap = create-gotomap(stmtlist) and
                        lab E dom gotomap)] in
     int-Stmtlist-without-trap(stmtlist)env

type : Stmt-list -> (ENV => )




create-gotomap(stmtlist)=
  [lab -> stmtl | (E j E ind stmtlist)(mk-Stmt(lab, ) = stmtlist[j] and
                   lab ≠ nil and
                   stmtl = <stmtlist[i] | j =< i =< ln stmtlist>)]

type : Stmt-list -> (Label-id m-> Stmt-list)




int-Stmtlist-without-trap(stmtlist)env=
  for i = 1 to ln stmtlist do
     int-Stmt(stmtlist[i])env

type : Stmt-list -> (ENV => )




int-Stmt(mk-Stmt( ,unlabstmt))env=
  cases unlabstmt :
    (mk-Null( )               ->  I,
     mk-Assign( , )           ->  int-Assign(unlabstmt)env,
     mk-Exit( , )             ->  int-Exit(unlabstmt)env,
     mk-Return( )             ->  int-Return(unlabstmt)env,
     mk-Goto(labid)           ->  exit(mk-Go(labid)),
     mk-Procedure-call( , )   ->  int-Procedure-call(unlabstmt)env,
     mk-Entry-call( , , )     ->  int-Entry-call(unlabstmt)env
     mk-Delay( )              ->  int-Delay(unlabstmt)env,
     mk-Abort( )              ->  int-Abort(unlabstmt)env,
     mk-Raise( )              ->  int-Raise(unlabstmt)env,
     mk-Code( )               ->  int-Code(unlabstmt)env,
     mk-If( , )               ->  int-If(unlabstmt)env,
     mk-Case( , , )           ->  int-Case(unlabstmt)env,
     mk-Loop( , )             ->  int-Loop(unlabstmt)env,
     mk-Block( , , )          ->  int-Block(unlabstmt)env,
     mk-Accept( , , )         ->  int-Accept(unlabstmt)env,
     T                        ->  int-Select(unlabstmt)env)

type : Stmt -> (ENV => )
```

```
int-Assign(mk-Assign(name,expr))env=
  (def mk-(loc,subtpden,env') : eval-Name(name)env,
       val : eval-Expr(expr)env;
   check-and-assign(mk-Var-den(subtpden,loc),val)env')

type : Assign -> (ENV => )



check-and-assign(mk-Var-den(subtpden,varloc),val)env=
  (let mk-Subtype-den(base,constr) = subtpden in
   cases env(base) :
     (mk-Access-den(tid, )  ->
         (cases val :
            (mk-AccessVal(NULL)  -> I,
             mk-AccessVal(loc)   ->
               (let subloc = mk-SubLoc(loc,<>,DYN) in
                def val' : value-of(subloc);
                subtype-check(val',subtpden)env))),
      T                       ->
         (cases varloc :
            (mk-SubLoc( , ,statordyn)                  ->
                (if statordyn = DYN
                   then (def val' : value-of(varloc);
                           check-dyn-values(val,val',subtpden)env)
                   else subtype-check(val,subtpden)env),
             mk-SliceLoc(mk-SubLoc( , ,statordyn), , )  ->
                (if statordyn = DYN
                   then (def val' : value-of(varloc);
                           check-dyn-values(val,val',subtpden)env)))));
   assign(varloc,val))

type : Var-den VAL -> (ENV => )
```

```
check-dyn-values(newval,oldval,subtpden)env=
  (let mk-Subtype-den(base, ) = subtpden in
  cases env(base) :
    (mk-Record-den(discrim,fdens, , ) ->
        (let mk-RecordVal(oldmap) = oldval,
             mk-RecordVal(newmap) = newval in
         if (E fid E discrim)(oldmap(fid) ≠ newmap(fid))
           then raise(CONSTRAINT-ERROR)
           else (for all fid E dom oldmapdiscrim do
                    (let ov = oldmap(fid),
                         nv = newmap(fid),
                         ed = s-Elem-den(fdens(fid)),
                         rm = oldmap | discrim im
                    check-dyn-elemvalues(nv,ov,ed,rm)env))),
     mk-Array-den( ,tid)                ->
        (let mk-ArrayVal(oldmap, ) = oldval,
             mk-ArrayVal(newmap, ) = newval in
         for all it E dom oldmap do
           check-dyn-values(newmap(it),oldmap(it),env(tid))env),
     T                                  -> I);
  subtype-check(newval,subtpden)env)

type : VAL VAL Subtype-den -> (ENV => )



check-dyn-elemvalues(newval,oldval,elemden,discrvals)env=
  (def mk-(newden,env') : insert-discrimvalues(elemden,discrvals)env;
   check-dyn-values(newval,oldval,newden)env')

type : VAL VAL Elem-den (Field-id m-> VAL) -> (ENV => )



int-Exit(mk-Exit(oplab,cond))env=
  (cond = nil  ->  exit(mk-Ex(oplab)),
   T           ->  (if is-True(eval-Expr(cond)env)
                      then exit(mk-Ex(oplab))
                      else I))

type : Exit -> (ENV => )



int-Return(mk-Return(opexpr))env=
  (if opexpr = nil
     then exit(mk-Ret(nil))
     else (def val : eval-Qualified-expr(opexpr)(env(RESTP))env;
           exit(mk-Ret(val))))

type : Return -> (ENV => )
```

```
int-Procedure-call(mk-Procedure-call(pid,parmexprs))env=
  (let mk-Proc-den(extpdescr,pinit, ,proc) = env(pid) in
   def actid : create-ActId()ₒ
   let env' = env + [ACTID -> actid] in
   always free-locations(actid) in
     (def pla : eval-p-parmassoc(extpdescr,pinit,parmexprs)env';
      let copyenv = extract-copyenv(pla),
          parmassoc = extract-parmassoc(pla) in
      always p-call-epilogue(extpdescr,pla)env' in
        (proc(parmassoc);
         restore-params(parmassoc,copyenv))env')))

type : Procedure-call -> (ENV => )



eval-p-parmassoc(extpdescr,pinit,parmexprs)env=
  (if parmexprs = []
     then eval-default-paramassoc(pinit,extpdescr)env
     else (let parmid E dom parmexprs in
              def mk-(subtpden,varloc,actden) :
                    get-p-varloc(extpdescr(parmid),parmexprs(parmid))env;
              let varden = mk-Var-den(subtpden,varloc),
                  pinit' = pinit{parmid},
                  parmexprs' = parmexprs{parmid} in
              (return([parmid -> mk-(varden,actden)]) U
               eval-p-parmassoc(extpdescr,pinit',parmexprs')env)))

type : (Parm-id m-> (Subtype-den Parmmode (REF ¦ COPY)))
       (Parm-id m-> VAL) (Parm-id m-> Expr) -> (ENV =>
         (Parm-id m-> (Var-den [Var-den])))



get-p-varloc(mk-(subtpden,mode,transf),expr)env=
  cases transf :
    (REF  -> get-p-ref-varloc(subtpden,mode,expr)env,
     COPY -> get-p-copy-varloc(subtpden,mode,expr)env)

type : (Subtype-den Parmmode (REF ¦ COPY)) Expr -> (ENV =>
         (Subtype-den VarLoc [Var-den]))



get-p-ref-varloc(subtpden,mode,expr)env=
  cases mode :
    (IN    -> get-IN-ref-varloc(subtpden,expr)env,
     OUT   -> get-OUT-ref-varloc(subtpden,expr)env,
     INOUT -> get-INOUT-ref-vrloc(subtpden,expr)env)

type : (Subtype-den Parmmode Expr) -> (ENV =>
         (Subtype-den Varloc [Var-den]
```

```
get-IN-ref-varloc(subtpden,expr)env=
  (is-location-expr(expr)  ->
      (def mk-(varloc, , ) : eval-Name(s-Expr'(expr))env;
       def val : value-of(varloc);
       subtype-check(val,subtpden)env;
       let newsubden = get-useable-subden(val,subtpden)env in
       return(mk-(newsubden,varloc,nil))),
   T                                  ->
      (def val : eval-Qualified-expr(expr)(subtpden)env;
       let newsubden = get-useable-subden(val,subtpden)env in
       def varloc : mk-SubLoc(allocate(env(ACTID)),<>,STATIC);
       assign(varloc,val);
       return(mk-(newsubden,varloc,nil))))

type : Subtype-den Expr -> (ENV => (Subtype-den Varloc nil))


get-useable-subden(value,subtpden)env=
  (let mk-Subtype-den(base,constr) = subtpden in
   if constr ≠ nil
      then subtpden
      else (cases env(base) :
                (mk-Array-den( , )                     ->
                   (let indconstr = find-Index-Constraint(s-order(value)) in
                    mk-Subtype-den(base,indconstr)),
                 mk-Record-den(discrim, , , )  ->
                   (if discrim = {}
                       then subtpden
                       else (let mk-RecordVal(vmap) = value,
                                 dmap = vmap | discrim,
                                 dconstr = mk-Discrim-Constraint(dmap) in
                             mk-Subtype-den(base,dconstr))),
                 T                                 ->  subtpden)))

type : VAL Subtype-den -> (ENV -> Subtype-den)


eval-defaultparamassoc(parminit,extpdescr)env=
  (if parminit = []
      then return([])
      else (let parmid E dom parminit in
            def varloc : mk-SubLoc(allocate(env(ACTID)),<>,STATIC);
            assign(varloc,parminit(parmid));
            let subtpden = s-Subtype-den(extpdescr(parmid)),
                parminit' = parminit\{parmid},
                varden = mk-Var-den(subtpden,varloc) in
            (return([parmid -> mk-(varden,nil)]) U
             eval-default-paramassoc(parminit',extpdescr)env)))
type : (Parm-id m-> VAL) (Parm-id m-> (Subtype-den Parmmode (REF|COPY)))

      -> (ENV => (Parm-id m-> (Var-den nil)))
```

```
p-call-epilogue(extpdescr,parmlocassoc)env=
  (for all pid E dom parmlocassoc do
     (let mk-(stden,varloc,actden) = parmlocassoc(pid) in
     if actden = nil
        then I
        else (let mk-Var-den(actstden, ) = actden,
                 mk-( , ,transf) = extpdescr(pid) in
              if transf = COPY
                 then I
                 else subtype-check(value-of(varloc),actstden)env)))

type : (Parm-id m-> (Subtype-den Parmmode (REF | COPY)))
       (Parm-id m-> (Subtype-den VarLoc [Var-den])) -> (ENV => )



restore-params(parmassoc,copyenv)env=
  (for all parmid E dom copyenv do
     (def val : value-of(s-VarLoc(parmassoc(parmid)));
      check-and-assign(copyenv(parmid),val)env))

type : (Parm-id m-> Var-den) (Parm-id m-> Var-den) -> (ENV => )



int-Raise(mk-Raise(opexname))env=
  (opexname = nil
   is-Excp-id(opexname)  ->  (if opexname E dom env
                                 then (let tf = env(opexname) in
                                       raise-failure(s-TV(tf)))
                                 else raise(opexname)),
   T                     ->  (def mk-(varloc, , ) : eval-Name(opexname)env;
                              raise-failure(value-of(varloc))))

type : Raise -> (ENV => )



raise(eid)=
  exit(mk-Excpt(eid))

type : Excp-id =>



int-If(mk-If(condstmtlist,opelse))env=
  (if condstmtlist = <>
     then (if opelse = nil
              then I
              else int-Stmtlist(opelse)env)
     else (let mk-(cond,stmtl) = hd condstmtlist in
           if is-True(eval-Expr(cond)env)
              then int-Stmtlist(stmtl)env
              else int-If(mk-If(tl condstmtlist,opelse))env))

type : If -> (ENV => )
```

```
int-Case(mk-Case(expr,casemap,others))env=
   (def val : eval-Expr(expr)env;
    if val E dom casemap
      then int-Stmtlist(casemap(val))env
      else int-Stmtlist(others)env)

type : Case -> (ENV => )



int-Loop(mk-Loop(oploopid,specloop))env=
   (trap exit (mk-Ex(lid)) with
           (lid = nil or lid = oploopid  ->  I,
            T                            ->  exit(mk-Ex(lid))) in
      (cases specloop :
         (mk-Uncond-loop( )      ->  int-Uncond-loop(specloop)env,
          mk-While-loop( , )     ->  int-While-loop(specloop)env,
          mk-For-loop( , , , )   ->  int-For-loop(specloop)env)))

type : Loop -> (ENV => )



int-Uncond-loop(mk-Uncond-loop(stmtlist))env=
   while true do
      int-Stmtlist(stmtlist)env

type : Uncond-loop -> (ENV => )



int-While-loop(mk-While-loop(expr,stmtlist))env=
   while is-True(eval-Expr(expr)env) do
      int-Stmtlist(stmtlist)env

type : While-loop -> (ENV => )



int-For-loop(mk-For-loop(vid,oprev,discrrange,stmtlist))env=
   (def mk-(tid,rngconstr) : eval-Discrete-range(discrrange)env;
    let forlist = create-forlist(tid,rngconstr,oprev)env in
    if forlist = <>
      then I
      else (let subtpden = mk-Subtype-den(tid,rngconstr) in
            def varloc : mk-SubLoc(allocate(env(ACTID)),<>,STATIC);
            let env' = env + [vid -> mk-Var-den(subtpden,varloc)] in
            for i = 1 to ln forlist do
               (assign(s-VarLoc(env'(vid)),forlist[i]);
                int-Stmtlist(stmtlist)env')))

type : For-loop -> (ENV => )
```

```
create-forlist(tid,mk-Range-Constraint(lb,ub),oprev)env=
  (let list = cases env(tid) :
                (mk-Enum-den(vmap)      ->
                    <vmap⁻¹(i) | vmap(lb) =< i =< vmap(ub)>,
                 mk-Integer-den( , )  ->
                    (let mk-IntegerVal(lv) = lb,
                     let mk-IntegerVal(uv) = ub in
                     <mk-IntegerVal(i) | lv =< i =< uv>)) in
   (oprev = REV  ->  <list[ln list - i] | 0 =< i =< ln list - 1>,
    T            ->  list))

type : Type-id Range-Constraint [REV] -> (ENV -> DiscreteVal*)
```

B.3 Names and Expressions


```
eval-Expr(mk-Expr(tid,expr))env=
  (is-VAL(expr)                  ->  return(expr),
   is-Aggregate(expr)            ->  eval-Aggregate(expr)(tid)env,
   is-Name(expr)                 ->
      (def mk-(locorval, , ) : eval-Name(expr)env;
       (is-VAL(locorval)  ->  return(locorval),
        T                 ->  value-of(locorval))),
   is-Allocator(expr)            ->  eval-Allocator(expr)(tid)env,
   is-Qualified-expr(expr)       ->
      (let mk-Qualified-expr(tid',expr') = expr,
           subtden = (cases env(tid) :
                       (mk-Subtype-den( , )  ->  env(tid'),
                        T                     ->
                          mk-Subtype-den(tid',nil))) in
       eval-Qualified-expr(expr')(subtden)env),
   is-Type-conversion(expr)  ->  eval-Type-conversion(expr)(tid)env,
   is-Prefix(expr)           ->  eval-Prefix(expr)(tid)env,
   is-Infix(expr)            ->  eval-Infix(expr)(tid)env,
   is-Range-test(expr)       ->  eval-Range-test(expr)env,
   is-Subtype-test(expr)     ->  eval-Subtype-test(expr)env)

type : Expr -> (ENV => VAL)



eval-Name(name)env=
  cases name :
    (mk-Simple-name(vid)         ->
       (let mk-Var-den(subtpden,varloc) = env(vid) in
        return(mk-(varloc,subtpden,env))),
     mk-Indexed-component( , ) ->  eval-Indexed-component(name)env,
     mk-Slice( , )             ->  eval-Slice(name)env,
     mk-Field-select( , )      ->  eval-Field-select(name)env,
     mk-Deref( )               ->  eval-Deref(name)env,
     mk-Attribute( , )         ->  eval-Attribute(name)env,
     mk-Fct-call( , )          ->  eval-Fct-call(name)env)

type : Name -> (ENV => ([VarLoc | VAL] Subtype-den ENV))



eval-Indexed-component(mk-Indexed-component(name,exprl))env=
  (def mk-(locorval,subtpden,env') : eval-Name(name)env;
   let mk-Subtype-den(base,constr) = subtpden,
       mk-Array-den(index,elem) = env'(base) in
   def indposlist : eval-indexlist(exprl,index,constr)env';
   let newlocorval = perform-indexing(locorval,indposlist) in
   return(mk-(newlocorval,env'(elem),env')))

type : Indexed-component -> (ENV => ([VarLoc | VAL] Subtype-den ENV))
```

```
eval-indexlist(exprl,index,indconstr)env=
  (let mk-Index-Constraint(bounds,order) = indconstr in
   def indvallist : eval-indices(exprl,index,bounds)env;
   return(order(indvallist)))

type : Expr+ Type-id+ Index-Constraint -> (ENV => N1)



perform-indexing(locorval,indposlist)=
  cases locorval :
    (mk-SubLoc(loc,path,stadyn)                        ->
        mk-SubLoc(loc,path^<indposlist>,stadyn),
     mk-SliceLoc(mk-SubLoc(loc,path,stadyn), , )  ->
        mk-SubLoc(loc,path^<indposlist>,stadyn),   ·
     mk-ArrayVal(vmap, )                               ->
        vmap(indposlist))

type : VarLoc N1+ -> (SubLoc | VAL)



eval-Slice(mk-Slice(name,discrrange))env=
  (def mk-(locorval,subtpden,env') : eval-Name(name)env;
   def mk-(tid,mk-Range-Constraint(lb,ub)) :
              eval-Discrete-range(discrrange)env;
   let mk-Subtype-den(base,constr) = subtpden,
       mk-Array-den(<indextp>,elem) = env'(base),
       mk-Index-Constraint(<mk-(lv,uv)>,order) = constr,
       indbase = get-base(indextp)env' in
   check-ranges(lb,ub,lv,uv,indbase)env';
   let slicelocorval =
         (cases locorval :
            (mk-SliceLoc(subloc, , )  ->
                mk-SliceLoc(subloc,order(lb),order(ub)),
             mk-SubLoc( , , )              ->
                mk-SliceLoc(slicelocorval,order(lb),order(ub)),
             mk-ArrayVal(vmap, )          ->
                slice-value(vmap,order,lb,ub))),
       bounds = <mk-(lb,ub)>,
       neworder = find-order(bounds,<indbase>)env',
       newconstr = mk-Index-Constraint(bounds,neworder),
       newsubtpden = mk-Subtype-den(base,newconstr) in
   return(mk-(slicelocorval,newsubtpden,env')))

type : Slice -> (ENV => ((SliceLoc | VAL) Subtype-den ENV))



slice-value(vmap,order,lb,ub)=
  (let <lov> = order(lb),
       <uov> = order(ub) in
   let neworder = [order⁻¹(<ov>) -> <ov-lov+1> | ov ∈ {lov : uov}],
       newmap = [<ov> -> vmap(<ov+lov-1>) | ov ∈ {1 : uov-lov+1}] in
   mk-ArrayVal(newmap,neworder))

type : N1+ (DiscreteVal+ <-m-> N1+) DiscreteVal+ DiscreteVal+ -> ArrayVal
```

```
eval-indices(exprl,index,bounds)env=
  (if exprl = <>
     then return(<>)
     else (def val : eval-Expr(hd exprl)env;
           let base = get-base(hd index)env,
               mk-(lb,ub) = hd bounds in
           if less-than(val,lb,base)env or less-than(ub,val,base)env
             then raise(CONSTRAINT-ERROR)
             else I;
           def rest : eval-indices(tl exprl,tl index,tl bounds)env;
           return(<val>Rest)))

type : Expr* Type-id* (DiscreteVal DiscreteVal)* -> (ENV => DiscreteVal*)



get-base(tid)env=
  cases env(tid) :
    (mk-Subtype-den(base, )  ->  base,
     T                       ->  tid)

type : Type-id -> (ENV -> Type-id)



eval-Field-select(mk-Field-select(name,fieldid))env=
  (def mk-(locorval,subtpden,env') : eval-Name(name)env;
   cases locorval :
     (mk-SubLoc(loc,path,stadyn)  ->
       (def mk-RecordVal(vmap) : value-of(locorval);
        if fieldid E dom vmap
          then (let newsubloc = mk-SubLoc(loc,path<fieldid>,stadyn),
                    fielddens = s-Field-dens(env'(s-base(subtpden))),
                    elemden = s-Elem-den(fielddens(fieldid)) in
                def mk-(newden,env'') :
                        insert-discrimvalues(elemden,vmap)env';
                return(mk-(newsubloc,newden,env''))
          else raise(CONSTRAINT-ERROR)),
     mk-RecordVal(vmap)           ->
       (if fieldid E dom vmap
          then (let fielddens = s-Field-dens(env'(s-base(subtpden))),
                    elemden = s-Elem-den(fielddens(fieldid)) in
                def mk-(newden,env'') :
                        insert-discrimvalues(elemden,vmap)env';
                return(mk-(vmap(fieldid),newden,env'')))
          else raise(CONSTRAINT-ERROR))))

type : Field-select -> (ENV => ((VarLoc | VAL) Subtype-den ENV))
```

```
eval-Deref(mk-Deref(name))env=
  (def mk-(locorval,subtpden,env') : eval-Name(name)env;
   def val : (cases locorval :
                    (mk-SubLoc( , , ) -> value-of(locorval),
                     T              -> locorval));
   cases val :
     (mk-AccessVal(NULL) -> raise(CONSTRAINT-ERROR),
      mk-AccessVal(loc)  ->
         (let subloc = mk-SubLoc(loc,<>,DYN),
              mk-Subtype-den(base,constr) = subtpden,
              mk-Access-den(objbase, ) = env'(base),
              newsubden = mk-Subtype-den(objbase,constr) in
         return(mk-(subloc,newsubden,env')))))

type : Deref -> (ENV => (SubLoc Subtype-den ENV))


eval-Fct-call(mk-Fct-call(fid,parmexprs))env=
  (let mk-Fct-den(extptps,initmap,restpden,func) = env(fid) in
   def actid : create-ActId()©
   let env' = env + [ACTID -> actid] in
   trap exit(o) with free-locations(actid); exit(o) in
     (def parmassoc : eval-f-parmassoc(extptps,initmap,parmexprs)env';
      def val : func(parmassoc);
      free-locations(actid);
      return(mk-(val,restpden,env))))

type : Fct-call -> (ENV => (VAL Subtype-den ENV))


eval-Allocator(mk-Allocator(objtid,opedi))(accesstid)env=
  (let actid = s-ActId(env(accesstid)) in
   def crid : create-CrId(actid);
   let env' = env + [ACTID -> actid , CRID -> crid] in
       subden = (cases env(objtid) :
                      (mk-Subtype-den( , ) -> env(objtid),
                       T                   -> mk-Subtype-den(objtid,nil))) in
   def val : (is-Expr(opedi) ->
                   (def val' : eval-Expr(opedi)env';
                    subtype-check(val',subden)env';
                    return(val')),
                 opedi = nil ->
                    get-init-VAL(subden)(CREATE)env',
                 T           ->
                    (let subdef = mk-Subtype-def(objtid,opedi) in
                     def subtpden : elab-Subtype-def(subdef)env;
                     get-init-VAL(subtpden)(CREATE)env'));
   def loc : allocate(actid);
   assign(mk-SubLoc(loc,<>,DYN),val);
   activate-tasks(crid);
   return(mk-AccessVal(loc)))

type : Allocator -> (Type-id -> (ENV => AccessVal))
```

```
eval-Qualified-expr(expr)(subden)env=
  (is-Aggregate(expr)   ->   eval-Qualified-Aggr(expr)(subden)env,
   T                    ->   (def val : eval-Expr(expr)env;
                             subtype-check(val,subden)env;
                             return(val))

type : Expr Subtype-den -> (ENV => VAL)



eval-Aggregate(aggregate)(tid)env=
  cases aggregate :
    (mk-Record-Aggregate( )                 ->
        eval-Record-Aggregate(aggregate)(tid)env,
     mk-Named-Array-Aggregate( , )          ->
        eval-Named-Array-Aggregate(aggregate)(tid)env,
     mk-Positional-Array-Agggregate( , )  ->
        eval-Positional-Array-Aggregate(aggregate)(tid)env,
     mk-One-Comp-Aggregate( , )             ->
        eval-One-Comp-Aggregate(aggregate)(tid)env)

type : Aggregate -> (Type-id => VAL)



eval-Record-Aggregate(mk-Record-Aggregate(fieldexprs))(tid)env=
  (def fieldvals : eval-fieldexprs(fieldexprs)env;
   let vmap = [fid -> val | fid E fids and fids E dom fieldvals and
                            val = fieldvals(fids)] in
   check-recordvalue(vmap)(tid)env;
   return(mk-RecordVal(vmap)))

type : Record-Aggregate -> (Type-id -> (ENV => RecordVal))



eval-fieldexprs(fieldexprs)env=
  (if fieldexprs = []
     then return([])
     else (let fids E dom fieldexprs in
           def val : eval-Expr(fieldexprs(fids))env;
           (return([fids -> val] U
            eval-fieldexprs(fieldexprs\{fids})env)))

type : (Field-id-set m-> Expr) -> (ENV => (Field-id-set m-> VAL))



check-recordvalue(vmap)(tid)env=
  (let mk-Recorn-den( ,fdens, , ) = env(tid) in
   for all fid E dom vmap do
      (let elemden = s-Elem-den(fdens(fid)) in
       def mk-(subtpden,env') : insert-discrimvalues(elemden,vmap)env;
       subtype-check(vmap(fid),subtpden)env'))

type : (Field-id m-> VAL) -> (Type-id -> (ENV => ))
```

## B.4 Storage Functions

Functions used by the storage handler, as defined in the tasking model, for manipulating the storage. The basis is the following domains and declarations:

Domains:

```
STG     =   LOC m-> VAL
ACTV    =   ActId m-> LOC-set
LOC     ::  TOKEN
VAL     =   . . . (defined in the section on semantic domains)
ActId   ::  TOKEN
```

Declarations placed in the storage handler:

```
dcl Stg := [] type STG;
dcl Actv := [] type ACTV;
```

Functions:

```
stg-create-ActId()=
  (def actid E ActId s.t. actid ~E dom c Actv ;
   Actv := c Actv U [actid -> {}];
   return(actid))

type : () => ActId


stg-allocate(actid)=
  (def loc E LOC s.t. loc ~E dom c Stg;
   Stg := c Stg U [loc -> UNDEF];
   Actv := c Actv + [actid -> ((cActv)(actid) U {loc})];
   return(loc))

type : ActId => LOC


stg-free-locations(actid)=
  (Stg := c Stg \ (c Actv)(actid);
   Actv := c Actv \ {actid})

type : ActId =>
```

```
stg-value-of(varloc)=
  cases varloc :
    (mk-SubLoc(loc,path, )                      ->
        (def val : (c Stg)(loc);
         def subval : get-subval(val,path);
         return(subval)),
      mk-SliceLoc(mk-SubLoc(loc,path, ),lb,ub)  ->
        (def val : (c Stg)(loc);
         def mk-ArrayVal(vmap,order) : get-subval(val,path);
         get-sliceval(vmap,order,lb,ub)))

type : VarLoc => VAL



get-sliceval(vmap,order,lb,ub)=
  (if ub < lb
     then return(mk-ArrayVal([]),[]))
     else (if {<lb>,<ub>} ⊈ dom vmap
             then raise(CONSTRAINT-ERROR)
             else (let newmap = [<ov> -> vmap(<ov+lb+1>) |
                                        ov E {1 : ub-lb+1}]
                       neworder = [order⁻¹(<ov>) -> <ov-lb+1> |
                                        ov E {lb : ub}] in
                   return(mk-ArrayVal(newmap,neworder)))))

type : (N1+ m-> VAL) (DiscreteVal+ <-m-> N1+) N1 N1 => ArrayVal



get-subval(val,path)=
  (if path = <>
     then return(val)
     else (let first = hd path,
               vmap = (cases val :
                          (mk-ArrayVal(valm, )  ->  valm,
                           mk-RecordVal(valm)   ->  valm)) in
           if first ~E dom vmap
             then raise(CONSTRAINT-ERROR)
             else get-subval(vmap(first),tl path)))

type : VAL (N1+ | Field-id)* => VAL



stg-assign(varloc,val)=
  cases varloc :
    (mk-SubLoc(loc,path, )                      ->
        (def oldval : (c Stg)(loc);
         def newval : update-value(oldval,path,nil,val);
         Stg := c Stg + [loc -> newval]),
      mk-SliceLoc(mk-SubLoc(loc,path, ),lb,ub)  ->
        (def oldval : (c Stg)(log);
         def newval : update-value(oldval,path,mk-(lb,ub),val);
         Stg := c Stg + [loc -> newval]))

type : VarLoc VAL =>
```

```
update-value(oldval,path,opbounds,subval)=
  (if path = <>
     then (if opbounds = nil
             then return(transform-value(subval,oldval))
             else update-slice(oldval,opbounds,subval))
     else (let first = hd path in
             cases oldval :
               (mk-ArrayVal(vmap,order) ->
                  (if first ~E dom vmap
                     then raise(CONSTRAINT-ERROR)
                     else (let v = vmap(first) in
                             def newsubval :
                                   update-value(v,tl path,opbounds,subval);
                             let vmap' = vmap + [first -> newsubval] in
                             return(mk-ArrayVal(vmap',order)))),
                 mk-RecordVal(vmap)      ->
                  (if first ~E dom vmap
                     then raise(CONSTRAINT-ERROR)
                     else (let v = vmap(first) in
                             def newsubval :
                                   update-value(v,tl path,opbounds,subval);
                             let vmap' = vmap + [first -> newsubval] in
                             return(mk-RecordVal(vmap')))))))
```

type : VAL (N1+ | Field-id)* [(N1 N1)] VAL => VAL


```
transform-value(newval,oldval)=
  cases newval :
    (mk-ArrayVal(vmap, )  ->  mk-ArrayVal(vmap,s-order(oldval)),
     T                    ->  newval)
```

type : VAL VAL ->VAL


```
update-slice(oldval,mk-(lb,ub),subval)=
  (let mk-ArrayVal(oldvmap,order) = oldval,
       mk-ArrayVal(newmap, ) = subval in
   if {<lb>,<ub>} $\not\subseteq$ dom oldmap
      then raise(CONSTRAINT-ERROR)
      else (let trnewmap = [<lb+ov-1> -> newmap(<ov>) |
                                          <ov> E dom newmap] in
            return(mk-ArrayVal(oldmap+trnewmap,order))))
```

type : ArrayVal (N1 N1) ArrayVal => ArrayVal

## B.5 Functions used in this Model and defined in the Tasking Model

This is an alphabetic list of functions defined in the tasking model of [Lo 80b] and used in this model.

| Name: | Type: |
|---|---|
| activate-tasks | CrId => |
| allocate | ActId => LOC |
| assign | VarLoc VAL => |
| await-termination | ActId => |
| create-ActId | () => ActId |
| create-Crid | ActId => CrId |
| create-task | Type-id -> (ENV => TV) |
| create-TaskFct | Dcl-part Stmt-list [Excphdl] -> (ENV -> TaskFct) |
| free-locations | ActId => |
| get-new-ActId | () => ActId |
| int-Abort | Abort -> (ENV => ) |
| int-Accept | Accept -> (ENV => ) |
| int-Delay | Delay -> (ENV => ) |
| int-Entry-call | Entry-call -> (ENV => ) |
| int-Select | Select -> (ENV => ) |
| value-of | VarLoc => VAL |
| raise-failure | TV => |

## B.6 Functions used in this Model but not defined

| Name: | Type: |
|---|---|
| elab-Renaming-dcl | Renaming-dcl -> (Dict -> (ENV -> (ENV => ENV))) |
| eval-Attribute | Attribute -> (ENV => . . . ) |
| eval-f-paramassoc | (Parm-id m-> (Subtype-den (<u>REF</u> \| <u>COPY</u>))) (Parm-id m-> VAL) (Parm-id m-> Expr) -> (ENV => (Parm-id m-> Var-den)) |
| eval-Infix | Infix -> (Type-id -> (ENV => VAL)) |
| eval-Named-Array-Aggregate | Named-Array-Aggregate -> (ENV => ArrayVal) |
| eval-One-Comp-Aggregate | One-Comp-Aggregate -> (ENV => ArrayVal) |
| eval-Positional-Array-Aggregate | Positional-Array-Aggregate -> (ENV => ArrayVal |
| eval-Prefix | Prefix -> (Type-id -> (ENV => VAL)) |
| eval-Qualified-aggregate | Qualified-Aggregate -> (Subtype-den -> (ENV => VAL)) |
| eval-Range-test | Range-test -> (Type-id -> (ENV => VAL)) |
| eval-Subtype-test | Subtype-test -> (Type-id -> (ENV => VAL)) |
| eval-Type-conversion | Type-conversion -> (Type-id -> (ENV => VAL)) |
| get-INOUT-ref-varloc | Subtype-den Expr -> (ENV => (Subtype-den VarLoc Var-den)) |
| get-OUT-ref-varloc | Subtype-den Expr -> (ENV => (Subtype-den VarLoc Var-den)) |
| get-p-copy-varloc | Subtype-den Parmmode Expr -> (ENV => (Subtype-den VarLoc <u>nil</u>)) |
| int-Code | Code -> (ENV => ) |
| is-location-expr | Expr -> BOOL    (static function) |
| is-True | EnumVal -> (ENV -> BOOL) |
| less-than | VAL VAL Type-id -> (ENV => BOOL) |

## C. Formula Index

307

# PARALLELISM IN ADA

*Hans Henrik Løvengreen*

Abstract:

This paper tackles, and solves, the (new) problem of modelling all of the Ada tasking semantics as abstractly, i.e. as implementation-unbiased as possible; and of embedding its parallel meta-process model in an otherwise denotational model of sequential Ada.

310

CONTENTS

Each Part has got an individual table of contents

Preface


The present document constitutes (a slightly revised version  of)  a  Master
Thesis for the M.Sc.E.E and C.S at The Technical University of Denmark.  The
project has been carried out at the Department of Computer Science with Professor,  Dr.  D.  Bjorner as responisble supervisor, during the spring and
summer 1980.

The Project has been titled Parallelism in Ada.  The main goals of the  project have been to develop a formal model of concurrency concepts in the programming language Ada, and to examine implementation  principles  for  these
concepts.   This  thesis presents the work that has been done to comply with
these goals.

The thesis has been divided into four rather individual parts;  each one representing a different view on the project.  The reason for this is primarily that a summary paper on the formal model, worked out as part of the  project,  was  accepted  for  the ACM SIGPLAN Symposium, Boston, December 1980.
Therefore, it was natural to let a sketch of the final paper be part of  the
thesis.   As the paper is rather informal, it has been neccessary to compen-
sate with a (rather) technical report on the work.  A system report explains
the  background  and methodology, and finally, the formal definition constitutes a part by itself.

You should start with the first part called "Project Report".   It  presents
the  background  for this and three other companion projects.  The principal
compiler development methodology which is the fundation of the  projects  is
explained,  and  it is shown how this project fits into the method.  It also
describes the project course, and summarizes the results and conclusions  on
the project.

The second part is (a draft of) a paper submitted for the ACM Ada  Symposium
[L¦Bj  80c].   The  paper, called "A Formal Model of the Tasking Concepts in
Ada", is an introduction to the developed formal model.   It  also  explains
the modelling method in an informal way.

Part III:  "Technical Report on Parallism on Ada" is a  complement  to  part
II.   It  describes  the foundations of the formal method, discusses various
modelling strategies, and consider some implementation ideas.

Part IV constitutes a rather bare formal definition of  the  Parallelism  in
Ada.   It  is  referred  to as "The Formal Model".  This part should only be
considered as a reference document or appendix to the introductory part  II,
and  the technical report, part III.  Part II could, however, be read alone,
whereas part III ought to be read together with the model.

Due to the original wish to produce four report which could be  individually
distributed,  it  has  been unavoidable to have overlapping information.   It
should also be noticed that each part has got its own table of contents  and
chapter-numbering.

Finally I would like to thank for the support I have recived during the project.   I would like to thank the Danish Datamatics Centre and its staff for

the use of their fine facilities, and for their sponsoring of my participation in the Ada Europe Implementers Group Meeting in Karlsruhe. I should thank Dines Bjorner for good advices, and other support. Finally I will express my gratefulness for the many interesting hours of discussion and collaboration I have had with my fellow students.

Lyngby, October 1980

Hans Henrik Lovengreen

**Parallelism in Ada**

Part I

PROJECT REPORT

CONTENTS

## 1.0  Introduction

This report describes the background for the M. Sc. Project: "Parallelism in Ada". It will summarize the methodology upon which the project is centred. In chapter 3, the Ada language is characterized, and it is shown how the method is applied and intended to be used in the DDC Ada Compiler Project. The motivation and goals for the tasking sub-project presented here will be given in chapter 4. Then the actual project course is summed up: The working method, and project activities. The report ends with a summary of project results, and a conclusion.

## 2.0  Methodology

The method is based on the idea that compiler development, and other kinds of program development, should start with a formal, mathematically based, description of the language considered. The formal definition will then be used for a systematic derivation of the compiler.

The definition method used here is based on the so-called "Vienna Development Method" [BjJo 78]. The definition principle of this method is primarily that of denotational semantics described in e.g. [St 77], and the meta-language used (META IV) is in principle lambda calculus given another syntax. The meta-language has, however, been extended with some facilities and conventions like the exit mechanism, and the imperative style [BjJo 78].

The realization principle is based on the idea that an implementation can, if not automatically then at least systematically, be derived from the formal definition of the source language and a definition of the target language, through stepwise function-, and object transformation. In the next chapter it will be shown how the derivation principle has been applied to the Ada Compiler.

## 3.0   The Ada Project

In this chapter, the so-called DDC Ada Compiler Project is descrived:   how
it has been organized, and how the methodology is intended to be applied.  A
more comprehensive description of the project can be found in the first  report in this volume [BjOe 80].

## 3.1   What is Ada?

Ada is a high order programming language.  It has been developed by a design
team at CiiHB, France, lead by J. C. Ichbiah, for the Department of Defence, USA.

The language is similar mainly to Pascal, and related languages, but also to
modular languages like Simula, LIS, Modula, Alphard, and CLU.  The complex
type concept of Algol 68 has influenced the design.  Ada represents the
state of the art as it combines many recently presented language concepts
into a single language.  Some primary features are:

1.  Modularity.  Ada consists of units (subprograms and  packages)
    which may be separately compiled.

2.  Visibility.  The usual Algol block structure, combined with
    constructs to restrict visibility. The visibility rules sup-
    port modularity.

3.  Types.  The traditional composite types have  been  parameter-
    ized.  A  subtype  consist  of  a type and a constraint.  All
    type-checking is done at compile time, while check of constra-
    ints may have to be postponed until run-time.

4.  Statements.  A traditional statement repertoire, but  combined
    with an exception concept.

5.  Exceptions.  Possibility to handle error-caused or self-raised
    exceptions at blocklevel.

6.  Tasking.  Tasks are units that may be  executed  in  parallel.
    The  definition of task units is imbedded in the type concept,
    and tasks form a dynamic  hierarchy.   Task  may  synchronize/
    communicate by rendezvous, i.e. passing of parameters between
    the to tasks in connection with  common  execution  of  state-
    ments.

Visibility and static type-checking is described in detail  in  [BuSch 80].
Dynamic type-checking, statements, and handling of exceptions is described
in [StPe 80]. The tasking concept is covered by the present thesis [Lo 80b]
of which this report constitutes part I.

## 3.2  Compiler Components and Development

The following figure shows how the method described in chapter  2  has  been
applied to the Ada Compiler:

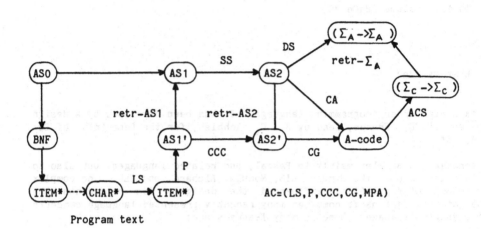

Program text

The formal definition is based on transformation between  abstract  syntaxes
(AS)  which  specify  abstract representations of Ada programs.  An Abstract
Syntax (AS0) which corresponds directly to  the  BNF  description  is  first
stripped  of  all  information  which does not influence neither Static nor Dynamic  semantics.   The  result  is  an  abstract  syntax  AS1.   Now  the
transform-if-wellformed  functions  of  the Static Semantics (SS) are applied
to AS1.  The transformation results in an abstract program AS2, in which all
information  which  does  not influence the Dynamic Semantics is thrown away,
and in which relevant static information has been  inserted.   E.g.  linear
ordering  rudiments  could  often be discharged.  If the program is illegal,
the result of the Static Semantics indicates this.  The Static Semantics  is
extensively  described  in [BuSch 80].  From AS2 we define the Dynamic Semantics (DS) which constists of both sequential and concurrent semantics.   The
result  of the abstract interpretation functions of the Dynamic Semantics is
a "meaning", here represented by a transformation function  on  an  abstract
state      .  The state represents the environment and the store-image of the
program execution.  The sequential semantics of Ada is defined in [StPe 80],
and the concurrent semantics is defined in this thesis [Lo 80b].

Above we showed how the semantics of Ada is formally defined.  Now  we  describe  the  components  of an Ada Compiler (AC), and how they should be derived.  Outside the compiler, the abstract program in the mind  of  the  programmer  (AS0,  AS1, or AS2?) is first given Ada keywords yielding a program
with BNF-structure.  The tree-structured program is  then  linearized  to  a
list  of  ITEM's,  and  finally spelled (non-functional) giving a string of
characters.  This program text is fed into the compiler.   First  a  Lexical
Scanner  (LS) will regroup the characters, and a Parser (P) will recover the
hierarchical structure of the program.  These two compiler components can be
automatically  derived  from  the BNF, and will not be further described.  The
data structure AS1' is a representation of AS1 such that the information  in
AS1  can  be found from AS1' by a retrieve-function.  Now a so-called Context
Condition Checker (CCC) should be applied to the AS1' to check the  legality

of the program. The context condition checker should be derived from the Static Semantics by stepwise operation decomposition. The output of the checker will be an intermediate language AS2' which should again be a representation of AS2. The Lexical Scanner, the Parser, and the Context Condition Checker constitutes a so-called "front end" compiler.

From the intermediate language (AS2'), code can be generated for various target machines. In the following we emphasize on so-called A-Code which is a middle-level language designed for use as target language for Ada compilers. The semantics of A-Code is defined by a so-called virtual A-Code Machine (ACM). The A-code Semantics (ACS) is defined by an A-code interpreter (ACI) and a kernel on an abstract machine-state. The ACM-state ($\Sigma_C$) is a representation of the abstract Ada state $\Sigma_A$. The design and definition of A-Code is described in [Do 80].

When the target language has been defined, we systematically from the Dynamic Semantics derive a Compiling Algorithm (CA) which, for each construct of the (abstract) language AS2, defines the A-Code the construct should be compiled into. The principles of this derivation are given in [Bj 77b] and [Bj 78]. The Compiling Algorithm which goes directly from the abstract program to the target code can be refined once more to give the Code Generator (CG) which inputs the intermediate language (AS2') and outputs A-Code.

It has been shown how the Ada Compiler (AC) which consists of the four components LS, P, CCC, and CG plus a so-called Multi-Pass-Administrator (MPA) can be systematically derived from the formal definition. The idea is that problems should be revealed and solved at the abstract level, such that the implementation will be straightforward.

## 4.0  The tasking Sub-Project

The dynamic semantics of Ada consist of two parts.  Sequential semantics and concurrent  semantics.   The sequential semantics is defined by denotational semantics, and is described in [StPe 80].  Semantics of tasking  is  defined by this thesis [Lo 80b].

The goals of defining tasking semantics formally are the  same  as  for  the rest  of  the  formal definition:  To give a precise semantics definition, to serve as a base for informal and tutorial language descriptions, to  form  a base  for systematic derivation of implementations, and to be used for prov- ing language properties.  For tasking, the formal model can be used for  im- plementation  of  a  a kernel on which to run Ada tasks and for defining the task-kernel communication.

The definition method used for the tasking concepts is operational  compared to  the  more denotational method used for sequential Ada.  The main idea is to imbed a process concept, and a very simple communication/ synchronization concept  into the meta-language, and then use these concepts to model paral- lel execution and complex synchronization.


## 5.0  Project Activities

The work presented here was done in collaboration  with  the  definition  of static semantics by Jorgen Bundgaard and Lennart Schultz, the sequential se- mantics by Jan Storbank Pedersen, and the design and definition of A-Code by Ole Dommergaard.

As Ada was still being revised, many concepts were not consistently defined, and  the team did a great effort to solve vague cases.  This was done by ex- tensive discussions in  the  team,  and  by  various  conferments  with  the language  design  team,  CiiHB  and with the formal definition group, INRIA, France.  The formal definition group develops an (official)  formal  defini- tion  of  sequential  Ada, based upon denotational semantics, but written in Ada syntax.  Unfortunately, during our working period, the state of the for- mal  definition  was  rather inconsistent due to language revisions, so even though we had the definition it was not of much help.  It was a great  help, however,  to  talk  with  Gilles Kahn,  the leader of the formal definition group, when he participated in the IFIP Working Group 2.2 held  in  Copenha- gen,  June 1980.  He gave us a number of information about the intentions of the most inconsistent language constructs and rules.

## 6.0   Summary and conclusion

As part of a full formal definition of Ada including static  semantics,  sequential  semantics;  and concurrent semantics, the concurrent semantics has
been completed.  The model developed is rather operational, but this  partly
due  to implementation influences in Ada.  The model seems to be well suited
for a systematic derivation of a kernel, but is not  ideal  as  a  tool  for
proving properties of concurrent programs.

The coming work on the the compiler derivation  has  to  prove  whether  the
method can bear, but the development of an almost complete dynamic semantics
definition which has already revealed most conceptual and  many  implementa-
tional problems, in about one man-year seems promising.

**Parallelism in Ada**

**Part II**

**A FORMAL MODEL OF THE TASKING CONCEPT IN ADA**

CONTENTS

## 1.0 Introduction

This paper is a draft, comprehensive version of a paper submitted for the ACM SIGPLAN Ada Symposium in Boston, December 1980 [LoBj 80].

The paper is an introduction to the developed model. It describes the ideas of the methods used, the structure of the model, and the behaviour of the model in a very informal way. The full model can be found in the reference part IV. A more technical and analyzing description of the model is given in the Technical Report, part III.

The paper first gives an informal introduction to the concurrent meta-language used for the model. Then the Characteristics of the tasking concepts is given in chapter 3. Chapter 4 is a informal description of the structure and ideas of the model.


## 2.0 Description method


The principal idea of this model is to use a very simple concurrency concept as a primitive to model the more complex tasking concepts of Ada. The simple concept used is based on the idea of "communicating sequential processes" described by Hoare [Ho 78]. The process part of CSP has been extended and the communication part given a new syntax. This concurrency has been imbedded into the meta-language in which the sequential part of Ada has been denotationally defined as described in the introduction. This adaptation of CSP into META-IV has been described and mathematically defined in a paper by Folkjer and Bjorner [FoBj 80].

As the meta-language for convenience is used in an imperative version, the model presented in this paper appears rather operational and mechanical. It is, however, still denotational in the sense that for each language construct the definition assigns a state-to-transition transformation. For concurrency constructs this transition (i.e. next behaviour) becomes so complex that the operational view seems to be more suitable for understanding the task concepts. This may be due to the familiar understanding of parallel and cooperating human activities, which are most often operationally thought of. In the rest of this section the basic principles of the meta-language extensions are informally described.

A simple method for describing concurrency aspects of a programming language is to introduce concurrent activities in the meta-language used for defining the (sequential) semantics of the language. Using this method, the explanation of concurrency is just postponed, and due to this, the method is acceptable only if the concurrency concepts of the meta-language are so simple that they can be given, more ore less formally, an immediately intelligible semantics.

This approach has been taken here. The meta-language, in which the concurrency has been included, is the so-called META-IV of the "Vienna Development Method" [BjJo 78]. This language has been used for the definition of denotational semantics of several large programming languages, e.g. PL/1 [Be 74] and CHILL [HaBj 80]. The imperative version of the language has been extended with the concept of meta-processes. A "running" meta-process corresponds to "sequential elaboration" of meta-statements on a state local to

the process. A process is described in a kind of process type definition
(called processor) containing declarations of local state components, and
the statement list to be "executed" (strictly, applying the
state-transformation denoted by the statement list to the initial state).
Instances of a process description can be created dynamically by
meta-program initialization or by a special start expression. Each process
instance can be parameterized at the point of creation, according to the
process description. A process instance is thus started up by evaluation
and passing of the parameters, then the local state is established as specified in the declaration part, and finally the statement list is elaborated
concurrently with the elaboration of other meta-process instances. Each new
process instance (henceforth just process) is assigned a unique identification by which it can be referenced. A concurrent meta-program thus has the
following form:

```
program( ... )
    pid₁: processor( ... )= (declarations ,statementlist ),
    ...
    pidₙ: processor( ... )= (declarations ,statementlist );
    initialize pidᵢ( ... ), ...,pidⱼ( ... )
end
```

which creates one process instance of each of pidᵢ ,...., pidⱼ . Further
processes can be created by elaborating the start expression:

```
start pidₖ( ... )
```

The unique process indentifications are tokens belonging to a (meta-) domain
called PI (Process Instance). The value of a start expression is the process instance value (piv) of the created process. This value may be assigned to meta-variables of type PI in order to control inter-process references. The start expression may also be used alone as a statement (as a
shorthand for assignment to a dummy variable) in which case the piv is lost.

A process is said to terminate when it reaches the end of the statementlist.
A process can also terminate itself by elaborating the special stop statement.

As no processes share common storage it is necessary to introduce a concept
of inter-process communication and synchronization. The tool chosen is the
high-level, value-passing, handshaking concept of CSP. The concept has been
modified in such a way that it is possible to establish communication chan-
nels dynamically between any active processes. The meta-language has been
extended with several communication constructs of which some are described
below.

OUTPUT:

output vD constraint;

Makes the value vD of type D avaiable for input in any of the processes
specified in the constraint. The process which elaborates the statement is suspended until the value is received. (Handshaking).

**INPUT:**

(<u>input</u> mask  constraint -> clause )

      mask: <u>mk-D</u>( ... )  <u>or</u>  vD

    Accepts certain values specified by the mask from any of the processes
specified by the constraint. The process is suspended until one of
these processes attempts to output a value which fits into the mask;
i.e. values of all domain-types if the mask is an identifier, or only
values of type D if the mask is a tree-constructor for , or metavari-
able of type D. (Further masking is possible.) When the input part (to
the left of the ->) is satisfied, the value is bound to the identifier/
constructor-components/ variable of the mask. (The binding ranges over
the clause.) The process issuing the corresponding output is allowed to
resume, and the input-clause is elaborated.

**Nondeterministic <u>input/output</u>:**

        (i/o-part   -> clause   ,
         i/o-part   -> clause   ,
         ...                 ;
         i/o-part   -> clause   )

  i/o-part:

$$[\underline{if}\ cond] \begin{Bmatrix} \text{input mask} \\ \text{output vD} \end{Bmatrix} \text{constraint}$$

    Guarded nondeterministic input/output. Only unguarded parts or parts
whose condition is true are offered to other processes. The process
elaborating the construct is suspended as long none of the parts can
communicate as described above. When communication is possible, the
value transfer is done, the handshaking partner is allowed to resume,
and the corresponding clause is elaborated. When several parts may
communicate, one of them is chosen in a nondeterministic (but "fair")
way.

**Constraint:**

$$\left[\begin{Bmatrix} \underline{from} \\ \underline{to} \end{Bmatrix} \begin{Bmatrix} \text{one } \underline{in} \text{ pi-set-expr} \\ P \end{Bmatrix}\right] \left[\underline{set}\begin{Bmatrix} \underline{pi} \\ pid \end{Bmatrix}\right]$$

    It is possible to restrict the potential receivers/senders to processes
given in a (dynamic) set-of-piv's expression or to instances of a certain process type P. It is also possible to assign the pi-value of the
contacted process to a meta-variable <u>pi</u> of type PI, or bind it to the
pid ranging over the corresponding clause.

An informal presentation of the meta-extension together with a formal semantics of the constructs is given in [FoBj 80].


## 3.0 Characteristics of tasking in Ada

In this section the tasking concepts of Ada are surveyed for those not familiar with Ada. The description is based on the revised Ada reference manual
[Ada 80].

The aspects of tasking fall into three classes: Task hierarchy, communica-
tion/synchronization, and abnormal situations like abortion and exception
propagation. Each of these groups will be described separately below.


## 3.1 Task Hierarchy

Ada is one of the first languages in which the definitions of the program
units to be executed in parallel (called task in Ada) are imbedded in the
type concept of the language. A task type definition consists of a description of the entries by which other task may communicate with task instances
of the defined type, and a task body consisting of the block to be elaborated by the task. A task type can be used like other types for object declarations and as components of composite types. Task types are, however, implicitly considered as private limited types, implying that objects of task
type cannot be compared with, or assigned to other task objects, see later.


### 3.1.1 Task creation. -

A task type is a template denoting a task executing of which several
co-existing instances may be created. Ada offers two ways to create task
instances, referred to (here) as static and dynamic creation.

Static creation is achieved by means of normal declaration of objects of (or
containing subcomponents of) task type. The elaboration of such a declaration creates an instance of the task type which may be referred to by the
object name.

Dynamic creation is used in connection with access types where the accessed
type is (or contains) a task type. Here the creation of a dynamic object by
means of an allocator automaticcally creates a task instance of the (accessed) task type. This instance may be referred to through the
access-value of the allocated object, and this access-value may, as usual,
be compared and assigned.

## 3.1.2  Task activation. –

A created task (instance) represents just a potential execution of the  task
body.   The task body elaboration is divided into two phases: An activation
phase, during which the declarative part of the task body is elaborated, and
an  execution  phase,  where the statementlist of the task body is executed.
For static tasks declared in the same declarative part (of an package, block
etc.)   the   activation is postponed until the elaboration of the declarative
part has ended.  Then, all the created tasks of that declarative  part  perform  their  activation, and start their independent concurrent execution of
the task body.  The activations are, however, done one at a time.   For dynamic tasks, all tasks created by the same allocator are activated similarly
when the allocator has been completely evaluated.

A task is said to terminate when it reaches the end  of  its  statementlist,
and the task cannot perform further actions.  As described below, a task may
also terminate in other ways.

## 3.1.3  Lifetime and dependence. –

As the task body, and with it instances of the task type , may refer to  the
surroundings of the body according to the usual vivibility rules, it is neccesary to limit the lifetime of the task instances to that of the task  type
definition.   This means that the block (*) containing the task type definition must not be left until all these instances have terminated.  In revised
Ada,  the  lifetime  of  tasks has been even further restricted.  For static
tasks, the lifetime is bound to the block containing the object declaration.
This  is possible only because the referability to such tasks cannot be propagated outside the block because of the illegality of assignment  for  such
objects.    Such propagation of access to tasks is, however, possible for dynamic tasks, but not further out than the scope of the access  type  definition.    In the restrictive style, this scope has been chosen as the lifetime
boundary of dynamic tasks.  This means that a block containing  the  definition of an access type to a task type cannot be left until all of the dynamic tasks created by allocators for the accesstype have terminated.

The above rules introduce a dependence between tasks and blocks.  A task  is
said  to be  dependent on a block (–activation), with the meaning that the
block cannot be left if the task has not terminated.  The dependences form a
dynamic  hierarchy between tasks and blocks which can be illustrated as follows:

---------

(*) In this paper, the term "block" will be used for the three
block–like constructs: Block, procedure body and task body.

Dynamic hierarchy:

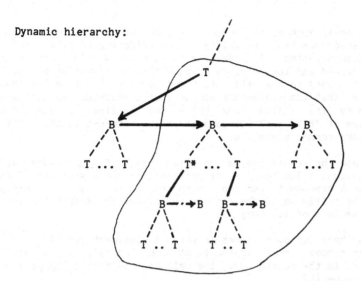

The T's and B's represent task instances and block activations resp.. The T's connected to a B by dashed lines are the tasks dependent on the block. The B's connected to a T are the nested inner blocks currently entered by the task. Thus, the B connected directly to the task is the task body block, the next on the path is the outermost inner block etc. ending with the (dynamically) innermost block activation in which the task is currently executing. The visibility rules of Ada imply that the task marked with an * can, at most, be referred to by the tasks, and from the blocks encircled in the figure.

For use in the following, we define for a task T the tasks dependent on T as all the tasks dependent on any block currently entered by T.


## 3.2 Task communication and synchronization

Tasks normally communicate and synchronize by means of entries. Communication can also be carried out through the use of shared variables together with some synchronizing entry calls, but such communication is not discussed here. An entry is a communication gate which belongs to a task. The entry declarations, which constitutes the declarative part of the task, have the form of procedure heads and specifies the type of the values to be passed during communication. The communication scheme is an extended kind of CSP communication. The so-called rendezvous involves value-passings before and after common execution of statements. The task owning the entry can enable a rendezvous by executing an accept statement whereby the entry is said to be opened. The accept statement includes the statement list to be commonly executed. Other tasks (according to the normal visibility rules) may ask for rendezvous by executing an entry call, which includes the parameters to be passed. If the entry called has not yet been opened by execution of a corresponding accept statement, the calling task is suspended, and the call (including parameter values) is entered into a queue associated with the entry. Likewise, if there are no entry calls waiting in the queue when the owner of an entry executes an accept statement for the entry, the task is suspended until such a call occurs. As the calling task cannot continue until the rendezvous has been fulfilled, no buffering of parameters is involved in the communication. A rendezvous takes place when both an entry call has been issued and the entry is open. Then the values of IN and IN OUT parameters are passed to the called task and bound to the formal parameter names. After that the statements of the accept statement are executed on behalf of both by the called task while the calling is suspended. Finally the values of IN OUT and OUT parameters are returned to the calling task, and both tasks resume execution.

For the calling task the rendezvous is just like a call of a procedure with a dynamic denotation. The body of the procedure is the statements of the corresponding accept statement, and the environment is that of the accept statement. For the called task, the rendezvous is like an execution of some parameterized statements of its body.

The entry call may have two other forms in which a statement-list is executed instead of the rendezvous if, in the first form, the call is not immediately accepted, or, in the second form, the call has not been accepted within a specified time-period.

A special select statement allows for simultaneous acceptance on several entries. It has the form of a set of guarded accept statements. When one or more rendezvous' are possible for the entries, one of them is selected in a non-deterministic way. The selection may be combined with either a time-limit, a possibility to carry on if no rendezvous is immediately possible, or a termination alternative (*). The termination alternative allows for termination of the selecting task if it can be guaranteed that none of its entries can be called after the termination. This will be the case when (but not only when) all of the tasks that may call its entries will have either terminated, can be terminated together with the selecting task, or can leave a block from which the task can be seen. This situation will, as it can be seen from the hierarchy figure above, arise when a task wishes to leave a block, and all task dependent on that block are terminable. A task is called "terminable" either if is has terminated, or if it is waiting at a select statement with termination possibility, and all its dependent tasks are terminable too. When this condition is met, all of the selecting tasks are terminated, and the block can be left. This is a very high level solution to the distributed termination problem and resembles the solution of Francez [Fra 78].

Another kind of synchronization in the language is the possibility for a task to delay itself for a given real time period.

## 3.3 Abortion and exceptions

The language provides two different concepts for external interruption of the sequential execution of a task body: abortion and raise of failure. A

(*) The description of the terminate alternative presented here differs somewhat from the (inconsistent) description in the revised reference manual.

task may impose abortion on, or raise failure in any task it can refer to.

Abortion is a facility to stop the execution of a task and make it terminate. A task can abort any other visible task by means of an abort statement. As mentioned on termination, the aborted task cannot terminate until all of its dependent tasks have terminated. Therefore, to make the abortion "immediate", all tasks in the subtree of the aborted task in the dynamic hierarchy have to be aborted too.

If an aborted task is engaged in a rendezvous, two cases occur:

1. The task is accepting: The task is terminated, and the caller receives a TASKING-ERROR exception at the point of the entry call.

2. The task is calling an entry: The task is terminated, but the called task is unaffected.

Tasks which have called entries of a task being aborted receive the TASKING-ERROR exception. In other cases of task abortion, the implications are a bit vaguely defined in the manual, but the idea seems to be that abortion of a task should affect other tasks as little as possible.

Failure is raised in another task by means of the normal raise statement. When failure is raised in a task, the execution of that task is stopped, and the FAILURE exception is raised at the point of the "current statement". As for abortion, raise of failure in the calling task during a rendezvous does not affect the accepting task. If the accepting task is failed and the exception is not handled within the accept statement, the calling task receives the TASKING-ERROR exception. Raise of failure in an unactivated or activating task is not defined in the manual.

Normal exceptions raised, but not handled, inside the statement list of an accept statement must be propagated to the calling task as well, and raised at the point of the entry call.


## 4.0 Model description


This chapter describes a formal model of Ada tasking. As the full model, including all concurrency aspects has got to a size of about 40 pages of formulas, only parts of it will be presented here. The description will thus be a mixture of model introduction indicating the ideas and structure of the model, and formula extracts to illustrate these.


## 4.1 Meta-Process types and configuration


The semantics of a concurrent Ada program will be modelled by a system of sequential communicating meta-processes. The processes can be grouped into a fixed system, corresponding to the (hard-, and software) environment of the program execution (store, clock, kernel etc.), and a dynamically varying number of processes, each one performing the sequential execution of an Ada task.

The fixed system constists of a fixed number of processes, each one based on its own process type. The process types (and the one and only instance of each of them) are called SYSTEM, STORAGE, MONITOR, TIMER, and CLOCK. The fixed processes exist during the whole program interpretation.

The SYSTEM process is the only process started initially, and it is given the Ada program as a parameter. The only purpose of the process is to initialize the fixed system, wait for the end of program interpretation, and then stop the fixed system.

The STORAGE process, which corresponds to a memory-unit, is used for simulation of shared variables. All variables of the Ada program are held in the local state of the process. The process will accept allocate and access requests from the tasks, and will impose mutual exclusion among these.

As shown above, the three aspects of Ada tasking are connected closely to each other. To handle the tasking facilities, it therefore seems convenient to let one fixed process supervise all TASK processes. Thus, all task creation and interaction is done through this so-called MONITOR process. To simulate real-time tasking the MONITOR uses two auxiliary fixed processes, TIMER and CLOCK.

All dynamic processes are of the TASK type which describes the sequential interpretation of an Ada task.

The figure below shows the interaction paths between the meta-processes, i.e. which processes creates other processes, and which processes communicate with eachother:

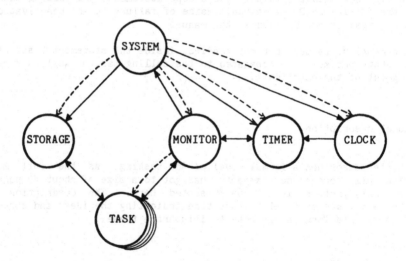

Dashed lines indicate creation. The lines are directed from the creating process (-type) to the created process (-type). Full lines indicate that communication takes place in the shown directions.

The system process only communicate with the fixed processes at the end of program interpretation.

The system is started as follows: The SYSTEM process is started with the

program as a parameter. The SYSTEM process creates one instance of each of
the remaining fixed process types, starts the CLOCK, and passes the program
to the MONITOR which in turn starts up an TASK process. This process starts
interpretation of the outermost task of the program. When the MONITOR can
tell that this task has terminated (and thereby all tasks of the program),
the SYSTEM process is told so, and this process commands all fixed tasks to
terminate. Finally the SYSTEM task terminates itself.

The TASK processes are used for the sequential interpretation of Ada tasks.
For each Ada task instance, a TASK process is created by the monitor. This
task is parameterized with the abstract task body of the task type, and the
environment in which the body should be interpreted. The TASK process then
performs the sequential interpretation of the task body as defined by the
interpretation functions that define the sequential dynamic semantics of Ada
described in [StPe 80].

All manipulation on the storage allocated by the tasks is done through the
STORAGE process. The main purpose of the storage process is to impose mutual exclusion on the storage-accesses. The storage is used at the lowest
level of the interpretation functions of the sequential semantics, where the
state-transformation primitives (like allocate, assign, get-value etc.) simply pass their parameters to the STORAGE and immediately receive their results.

Apart form shared storage, all task interaction is supervised by the monitor. The monitor can be wieved as a slave with respect to the TASK
processes. The principial structure of the monitor must thus be such that
it repeatedly accepts requests from the tasks processes and performs actions
according to these:

```
processor MONITOR( ... )=
  (dcl ...   ;
   cycle{ (input mk-R1( ... ) from TASK set tv -> ... ,
           input mk-R2( ... ) from TASK set tv -> ... ,
           ...                                          ,
           input mk-Rn( ... ) from TASK set tv -> ... ) })
```

The domain-names R1 to Rn are so-called communication domains identifying
the various requests, and their structure (usually in the form of a tree).
The domains can be thought of as channel names where the domain definitions
identifies the information carried by the channel.

The requests to the monitor can be divided into so-called calls and messages
according to the two different communication patterns involved. For calls
the TASK process immediately after the output of the request performs an
"input from monitor" to get a reply. The monitor may then suspend the task
by postponing the output of the reply. Messages simply transfer information
to the monitor about the execution of the task; information which may affect other tasks. A task issuing a message continues immediately by itself.

The semantics of the concurrency constructs in Ada is thus defined by interpretation functions like those for sequential interpretation, but including the communication schemes, or protocols, to be followed to achieve the
concurrency effect. Such functions have a structure similar to:

```
int-Delay(mk-Delay(exp)) env =
    (def period: eval-Expr(exp) env;
    (output mk-DELAY(period) to MONITOR;
    (input mk-CONTINUE()    from MONITOR -> I )))

    type: Delay -> (ENV => )
```

(The double arrow represents the semantic meaning-function of the construct. It could be viewed as a state-transformation on the local state, parameterized by the value of the input function.)

In the following the principal communication schemes of the various constructs are presented in a graphical way which indicates merely the points of input and output during the interpretation of the task, the paths or traces of information and activation flow, and the communication domains used for carrying this flow.

## 4.2  Communication schemes

### 4.2.1  Task creation and termination. –

The execution of each Ada task instance is modelled by an instance of the TASK meta process type.  However, the interpretation must be synchronized to assure correct activation and termination.

As the activation of the task must be postponed until the end of the declarative part in which it has been created, the task first waits for a start-signal from the monitor. The signal starts the activation of the task, i.e. the declarative part is elaborated. Upon completion of the activation, the monitor is informed (so that other tasks of the same declarative part may be activated), and the task continues by execution of its statementlist. When the end of the statement has been reached (or the task ends in other ways), the monitor is told, and the task terminates itself. This communication pattern of the interpretation of the task body of a newly created task is illustrated in the figure below:

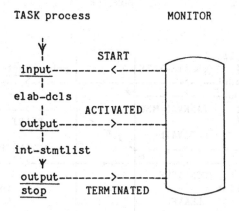

During the elaboration and the statement-interpretation, there may be other communication with the monitor. The figure shows only the communication at task body level, i.e. the communication concerning activation and termination.

Now, we can model the creation of a task. When a task type body is met, the taskfunction, i.e. the tasktype body and the current environment is associated with the tasktype in the environment. When a subsequent object declaration of that type is elaborated, the taskfunction is sent to the monitor, which in turn creates a TASK process with that taskfunction as a parameter and returns an identification of the created task. This identification, called a Task Value (TV), is stored in a location allocated for the task object, and is used for referencing the new task. The monitor must also be told which declarative part the created task belongs to, and which block it depends on.

When a task is about to leave a block, the monitor is called, and the task waits for a continuation signal from the monitor indicating that all tasks dependent on that block have (or have been) terminated.

For a block which declares one task in its declarative part we would thus have the communication patterns shown in the figure below. Notice that the created task (to the right) follows the communication pattern illustrated in the figure above.

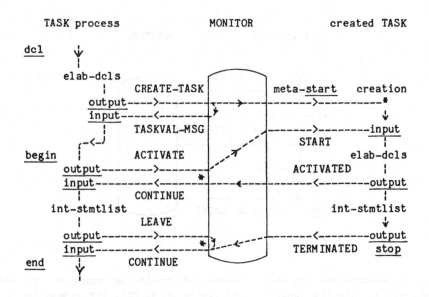

```
      TASK process              MONITOR              created TASK

   dcl      ↓
            ¦
         elab-dcls
            ¦       CREATE-TASK        meta-start    creation
         output---->---------------------->----------*
         input----<---------         ↓                ↓
            ¦       TASKVAL-MSG        ------->--------input
          -<-┘                         START            ¦
   begin    ¦       ACTIVATE                         elab-dcls
         output--------->-----        *              ACTIVATED   ¦
         input---------<------        *     ----<---------output
            ¦       CONTINUE                             ¦
      int-stmtlist                               int-stmtlist
            ¦       LEAVE                                ↓
         output--------->-----             ----<---------output
         input---------<------    *        TERMINATED  stop
   end      ¦       CONTINUE
            ↓
```

The * indicates a potential suspension, i.e. that the MONITOR may not reply
immediately and thereby hold the task waiting for input. The CREATE-TASK
request contains the task body, and the corresponding environment of the
task type of which an instance should be created, plus identification of the
block and the declarative part the task object declaration appears in.  The
ACTIVATE request contains the declarative part of which local tasks should
be activated. The TASKVAL-MSG contains the Task Value assigned to the created task.  LEAVE contains an identification of the block which is being
left.


4.2.2 Delay. -

To illustrate real-time delay, the monitor uses two auxiliary processes.
One of them, the CLOCK, continuously generates pulses. The other process,
the TIMER, uses these pulses to maintain a system clock. The timer receives
delay requests from the monitor, and notifies the monitor when time expires.

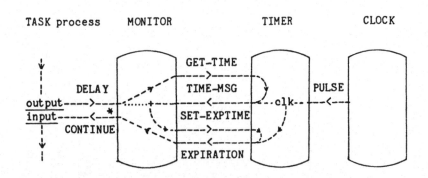

```
      TASK process     MONITOR                TIMER           CLOCK

            ↓                      GET-TIME
            ¦         DELAY        ---->-----         PULSE
         output---->-----         TIME-MSG     clk   ----<---
         input----<--  *          ----<-----
            ¦         CONTINUE     SET-EXPTIME
            ↓                      ---->-----
            ¦                      ----<-----
                                   EXPIRATION
```

The DELAY request contains the delay-time. This time is added to the actual clock value read by a GET-TIME command and a TIME-MSG reply from the TIMER. The calculated expiration-time is sent to the TIMER which will notify the MONITOR when the system-clock reaches this time. The monitor will then allow the task to resume.


4.2.3 Rendezvous. -

The interpretation of an entry call starts by evaluation of the actual parameters. Then these values and an identification of the entry is sent to the monitor as a request for rendezvous. When the rendezvous has ended, the monitor sends the return parameters back, and the task can continue.

If the entry is not open when the entry is called, the calling task is suspended, and entered into the queue of the entry.

The interpretation of an accept statement is slightly more complicated. When the accept statement is met, an indication of this and the entry under consideration is sent to the monitor. If there are no waiting entry calls in the entry queue, the task is suspended in a state indicating, that the entry is open. When a rendezvous is possible, the parameters are sent to the accepting task. The parameters are treated in much the same way as procedure parameters, and the statement list of the accept statement as a procedure body. When the statement list has been interpreted, the called task informs the monitor and continues.

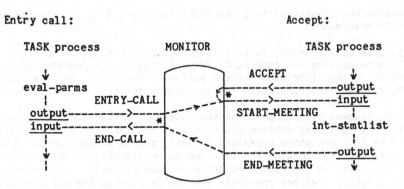

The ENTRY request contains an identification of the called entry, the evaluated parameters, and an indication of whether the call is timed or conditional (these possibilities are not concerned in the figures). The ACCEPT request just identifies the opened entry. The START-MEETING reply carries the parameters from the entry-call.

A select statement is interpreted in a similar but more complex way. First, all the guards and the alternatives are evaluated and each alternative is given an unique label called Alternative Identifier, AltId. Then an association between the open entries of the select statement and their labels is passed to the monitor. Also, the mode of the select statement is given to

the monitor; in the case of a timed select, the mode contains an association between the evaluated delays, and the corresponding alternative labels.
When one of the entries of the entry-association is called, the monitor returns an alternative label for an alternative accepting the entry, and the
statementlist of the corresponding accept statement is interpreted.

4.2.4 Exception and abortion. -

Common for both inter-task exception handling and abortion is the need to
stop a process "immediately" while it is running, i.e. while it is not waiting for response from the monitor. We have chosen to handle this situation by a special function which issues an "interrupt enable" request to the
monitor. The monitor can answer with either a CONTINUE signal, in which
case the function simply continues, or it may send a TERMINATE-, or
FAIL-command, in which case a meta-exit is performed. (The exit mechanism
of the meta-language could be wieved as kind of Ada exception handling where
the exception may be parameterized.) The function is defined by:

enable()=
  (output mk-ENABLE() to MONITOR ;
  (input mk-TERMINATE-CMD() from MONITOR -> exit(mk-TERMINATE()),
   input mk-FAIL-CMD() from MONITOR -> exit(mkExcp(FAILURE)),
   input mk-CONTINUE() from MONITOR -> I ))

type: () =>

(I denotes the identity (state-transfer) function, i.e. it corresponds to
the null statement.)

The purpose of the enable funtion is to abstract the usual hardware interrupt system polling the interrupts request flags. The function has only got
semantical effect inbetween state-transformations, i.e. at the points of
the ";"s in the interpretation and evaluation functions for the program.

However, instead of incorporating the interrupt-enable function at all these
points, it has been decided not to insert the function at all, but instead
let it be implementation dependent at which points a task can be interrupted. One must thus imagine the function to be distributed in the interpretation formulas in an implementation dependent way. However, the
enable-function defines precisely what to be done at the point of interruption.

In certain cases, it must be guaranteed that the interpretation is not interrupted. Therefore, some semicolons in the interpretation functions are
encircled to indicate that they are indivisible, i.e. that the
enable-function cannot be inserted.

As exceptions and abortions may also be imposed on suspended tasks, a task
waiting for monitor response must always be prepared to receive an
TERMINATE-, or FAIL-CMD. To handle this, a special function (monitor-call)
which takes care of such results in the same way as the enable function is
always used for calls to the monitor.

## 4.3  The MONITOR

The purpose of the monitor is to handle all task creation, inter-communication, and synchronization. To be able to do this, the monitor must keep information about the states of all the current tasks. This information is used for handling the various requests properly. In this section, the information maintained by the monitor is first described, and secondly we discuss a few of the functions the monitor will perform as the result of the various requests.

### 4.3.1  Monitor information (Semantic domains). -

The monitor and the tasks should be able to uniquely identify all current (and for tasks, visible, other) tasks. This is done by the Task Value (TV) domain. (Tasks Values as they are stored in task object locations). Each new task is assigned a unique TV at the time of creation. As there is a one to one correspondance between tasks and instances of the TASK process type, the meta-domain PI which identifies the meta-processes could also be used as task values:

   TV  =  PI

As one of its local state-components, the monitor has got a table containing information about all existing tasks:

   TaskTable  =  TV $\xrightarrow{m}$ TaskInfo

Also the dynamic hierarchy must in some way be known to the monitor. To help this, the monitor includes a state-component to keep track of all active blocks, and the task to which they belong. Block-activations (not to be confused with task-activations) are identified by so-called Activation Identifiers (ActId's). These ActId's are maintained by the storage process since they are closely related to the allocation of storage at block entrance. To ease the access to the dynamic hierarchy, it has been decided to record all active blocks together with the tasks they are entered by:

   BlockTable  =  ActId $\xrightarrow{m}$ TV

The block table corresponds directly to the full lines of the hirarchy diagram.

As mentioned, all tasks declared in the same declarative part or in the same allocator should be activated one at a time upon completion of the elaboration or allocation. As declarative parts may be nested in a very unstructured way (due to split packages), it has been neccesary to introduce a special domain called Creation Identifiers (CrId's) to bundle together all tasks of the same declarative part or allocator. The monitor administers all the declarative parts (or allocators) currently being elaborated in the third and final state-component of the monitor:

   CreationTable  =  CrId $\xrightarrow{m}$ (ActId | BEING-ACTIVATED)

(The table also records the block on which all tasks of a declarative part will depend. This is needed in order to clean-up in case the declarative part is never completed due to abortion or exception.)

The information associated with each task is kept in the Task Information. The information has been divided into six rather independent components:

TaskInfo :: Dependence Phase State Queues Partners IntrptReq

The State component contains temporary information, whereas the other components contain information which should be present during the whole lifetime of the task.

The components are described separately below.

4.3.1.1 Dependence -

Dependence = ActId | SYSTEM

This component is fixed during existence of the task. The block Activation Identifier is the ActId of the block the task is dependent of. It thus corresponds to the full lines in the dynamic hierarchy. The main program is considered to belong to a special system activation. All tasks belonging to a block are found by inspection of the Dependence component.

4.3.1.2 Phase -

Phase      = NonActive | ACTIVE
NonActive      :: CrId | SYSTEM

The Phase component indicates whether the task has completed its activation (i.e. the elaboration of the declarative part of the task body) or not. The NonActive Phase is associated with the Creation Identifier of the declarative part in which the task has been created. (The main program is again considered to belong to a special system activation.) All task belonging to the same CrId are found by inspection of the Phase component.

## 4.3.1.3 State –

```
State            =  Initial | Running | Suspended
Suspended        =  Delayed | EntryCalling | Accepting |
                    Selecting | Activating | Leaving |
                    Aborting

Initial          :: ()
Running          :: ()
Delayed          :: Time
EntryCalling     :: TV EV  Status
Status           =  InQueue | ENGAGED
InQueue          :: ParmAssoc [Time]
Accepting        :: EV
Selecting        :: EntryAssoc [ExpirAssoc|TERMINABLE]
EntryAssoc       =  AltId ─m→ EV
ExpirAssoc       :: AltId ─m→ Time
Activating       :: CrId
Leaving          :: ActId
Aborting         :: ()
```

The State component indicates, apart from a classification of the state of a task, the temporary information associated with the state class. When a task is created, it is put in the Initial state. It remains in this until its activation is started. After that, the initial state is not entered again, and it thus characterizes unactivated tasks. The running state indicates that the task is interpreting, and that it may send requests to the monitor. All tasks in suspended states are known to be waiting for a certain response from the monitor, depending on the particular state of a task.

A Delayed task is associated with the time at which is should resume. A task that has issued an entry call is accociated with the called entry identified by the task which owns the entry, and the so-called entry value:

```
EV :: EntryId [DiscrVAL]
```

The entry value consists of the name of the entry and eventually an index value in the case of an entry family. If the entry call has not yet been accepted, the state also contains the parameters to be passed, and eventually an expiration time in the case of a timed entry call.

The accept state has been distinguished from the select state to show its simplicity. In the Accepting state the only information needed is the entry value opened by the accept. For a selecting task, the so-called entry association defines the entries opnened by accept alternatives. The state also indicates whether the select is terminable, unconditional, or timed. If it is timed it contains an association between the open delay alternatives and the corresponding expiration times.

The state-activating of an activating task contains the CrId of which tasks should be activated. It is used to find the activator upon activation of all tasks of the CrId. For a leaving task, the state-component indicates the block activation of the block being left. The Aborting state is an auxiliary state to help proper termination if a task indirectly aborts itself.

#### 4.3.1.4 Queues -

$$\text{Queues} = \text{EV} \xrightarrow{m} \text{TV+}$$

The Queues component indicates the identity of the task waiting for acceptance at the entries of the task, and the order of these. These tasks are
guaranteed to be in an EntryCalling state, and the parameter-information is
placed there. Only non-empty queues are recorded.

#### 4.3.1.5 Partners -

$$\text{Partners} = \text{TV*}$$

The Partner component indicates the tasks with whom the task is presently
having a rendezvous. Due to the proper nesting of accept statements, the
Partner component can be maintained as a stack.

#### 4.3.1.6 Interrupt request. -

$$\text{IntrprReq} = [\underline{\text{FAILREQ|TERMINATED}}]$$

This component of the informantion of a task is used for indicating the wish
to stop the task, until it actually can be stopped, i.e. when it contacts
the monitor. The failrequest is cleared when the exception is actually raised, whereas a task marked as terminated is considered terminated until it
has released its storage (see next section).

#### 4.3.2 Monitor functions. -

The information of the monitor described in the preceeding section is used
by the monitor functions which handle the various requests. In stead of
describing all of these, only a few are described here, and in appendix A an
example is given which shows a trace of calls during a rendezvous.

#### 4.3.2.1 Expiration -

Real-time delay and expiration is simulated with the use of the timer and
clock processes. The monitor can read the actual clock and thereby calcu-
late an expiration-time. This expiration-time is then set in the timer, and
the task is suspended in one of the three expirabel states:

342

```
Delayed          :: Time

EntryCalling     :: TV  EV  Status
Status           =  InQueue | ENGAGED
InQueue          :: ...  [Time]

Selecting        :: ...  [ExpirAssoc|TERMINABLE]
ExpirAssoc       :: AltId --> Time
                            m
```

The timer will notify the monitor each time one of the expiration-times
which have been set by the monitor is reached. The monitor then finds all
expirable tasks which have an expiration-time less than the actual clock,
and makes them resume. No delay queue is maintained. The reason is to
avoid information distribution by separating out the delay information.


## 4.3.2.2  Termination -

Here, the solution to the problem of proper termination is to treat abortion
as a kind of exception which cannot be handled. Thus a process experiences
abortion just as a special exception, and an aborted process will therefore
leave its block in a normal way waiting for local tasks to terminate.
However, as soon as a task is doomed to die it appearently dies as seen from
other tasks. The partners of the task, and tasks waiting on its queues receives the TASKING-ERROR exception, and no task can communicate with it. We
thus have two degrees of termination. Virtual termination where other tasks
cannot reference the task, but where it is still leaving its blokcs
normally; and total termination, where the task has released all of its
storage.

Only total termination affects the hierarchy. When a task terminates totally, it is checked if this termination leads to a block release eventually
combined with termination of selecting task. This is done by sending a termination wave up and down in the hierarchy. This termination wave should be
started when a task terminates (totally), when a block is being left, or
when a task is suspended in a selecting state with the terminate possibility.


## 5.0  Conclusion

It has been shown how the tasking concepts af Ada have been given a semantics definition by means of a formal model. The formal model captures all
aspects of concurrency in Ada, except real-time measurements. It furthermore corresponds directly with a formal model of the sequential parts of
Ada. Apart from being a precise reference document, the model can be used
for a systematic development of an implementation of the concurrency concept. The model is, however, not directly oriented towards proving properties of concurrent Ada programs.

## APPENDIX A

### Example

In this this appendix a trace of a complete rendezvous between an accepting task T1 and an entry-calling task T2 is shown.

We assume that T1 reaches the accept statement before T2 reaches the entry-call. The interpretation function for an accept statement is:

```
int-Accept(mk-Accept(ename,stmtl)) env =
   (def mk-(ev, ) : eval-EntryName(ename) env ;
    let req = mk-ACCEPT(ev) in
    def mk-START-MEETING( ,parmassoc) : monitor-call(req) ;
    int-acceptbody(stmtl,parmassoc)                          )

type: Accept -> (ENV => )


monitor-call(req)=
   (output req to MONITOR ;
    (input rply from MONITOR ->
        cases rply:
        (mk-TERMINATE-CMD()  -> exit(mk-TERMINATE()),
         mk-FAIL-CMD()       -> exit(mk-Excp(FAILURE)),
         mk-RAISE-CMD(eid)   -> exit(mk-Excp(eid)),
         T                   -> return(rply)            )))

type: REQ => REPLY
```

The request sent to the monitor should indicate which entry of the task the accept statement has opened:

```
        ACCEPT  :: EV
```

The request is received by the monitor:

344

```
processor MONITOR(prog)=
   (dcl CT := [] type CreationTable,
        BT := [] type BlockTable,
        TT := [] type TaskTable;
    startup-main(prog);
   (trap exit with (output mk-STOP() to SYSTEM;
                        stop                        ) in
      cycle{ (input req from TASK set tv      ->
                         handle-req(tv,req),
             input mk-EXPIRATION(time) from TIMER ->
                         handle-expiration(tv,time)      )}))

type: Prog =>
```

When the request is received, it is checked whether the calling task  should
be interrupted.  This can be done only for requests where the task waits for
an answer from the monitor, i.e.  only for call-requests.

```
handle-req(tv,req)=
   cases req:
   (mk-LEAVE(actid)  ->
        leave(tv,actid),
    T                 ->
        (is-MSG(req)      ->
               handle-msg(tv,req),
         is-CALL(req)  ->
               cases get-IntrptReq(tv)
               (FAILREQ      -> (resume(tv,mk-FAIL-CMD());
                                 TT.(tv).IntrptReq := nil ),
                TERMINATED -> resume(tv,mk-TERMINATE-CMD()),
                nil          -> handle-call(tv,req)      )))

type: TV  REQ =>
```

The request is passed to the handle-call function which  simply  calls  specialized handle-functions for the various requests.

```
handle-accept(tv,ev)=
   if entry-called(tv,ev)
      then begin-accept(tv,ev,nil)
      else TT.(tv).State := mk-Accepting(ev)

type: TV  EV =>
```

```
entry-called(tv,ev)=
   (def queues : get-Queues(tv);
    return( ev∈ dom queues )   )

type: TV  EV => BOOL
```

We assume that the entry has not yet been called so T1 is suspended  in  the
Accepting state.

Now T2 issues an entry call. The interpretation function is rather complex due to the parameter passing mechanism which is the same as used for procedure calls, and also due to the possibilities of timed and conditional entry calls:

```
int-EntryCall(ec) env=
   (def called : call-entry-with-mode(ec,nil);
    I                                              )

type: EntryCAll -> (ENV => )


call-entry-with-mode(mk-EntryCall(name,ename,parmexprs),cmode) env =
   (def mk-(tv,ev,eden) : eval-entry(name,ename) env ;
    let mk-EntryDen(extpdescr,parminit, , ) = eden in
    def actid : create-ActId() (;)
    always free-locations(actid) in
      (def parmlocassoc :
                  eval-parmassoc(extpdescr,parminit,parmexprs) env ;
       def ecmode : evaluate-cmode(cmode) env;
       let copyenv = extract-copyenv(parmlocassoc),
           parmassoc = extract-parmassoc(parmlocassoc) in
       trap exit(extp) with
                  (p-call-epilouge(extpdescr,parmassoc);
                   exit(extp)             ) in
         (let req = mk-ENTRY-CALL(tv,ev,parmassoc,ecmode) in
          def mk-END-CALL(callresult) : monitor-call(req);
          restore-params(parmassoc,copyenv);
          p-call-epilouge(extpdescr,parmassoc);
          return(callresult)                        )   )

type: EntryCall  CallMode -> (ENV => (CALLED|CLOSED|EXPIRED))
```

During the interpretation, the ENTRY-CALL request is sent to the monitor:

```
ENTRY-CALL       :: TV EV ParmAssoc [COND|Timed]
Timed            :: Duration
```

The taskvalue and the entryvalue uniquely defines the called entry. ParmAssoc is the parameter information. In this model, all parameterlocations are allocated by the caller, so there is no need to pass parameters back. The last component is (here) called the mode of the call, and indicates whether the call is conditional, or timed. We here issue a normal call so the mode is represented by the nil object.

The request passes through the processor, the handle-req, and handle-call as described above. The associated handling function is:

```
handle-entry-call(caller,tv,ev,parmassoc,cmode)=
  (terminated(tv)              ->
                resume(caller,mk-RAISE-CMD(TASKING-ERROR)),
   open(tv,ev)                 ->
                (def altid : find-an-altid(tv,ev);
                 TT.(caller).State:=mk-EntryCalling(tv,ev,ENGAGED);
                 begin-rendezvous(caller,tv,altid,parmassoc)         ),
   cmode = COND                ->
                resume(caller,mk-END-CALL(CLOSED)),
   T                           ->
                (def mcmode : modif-cmode(cmode);
                 let inq = mk-InQueue(parmassoc,mcmode) in
                 TT.(caller).State := mk-EntryCalling(tv,ev,inq);
                 enter-queue(caller,tv,ev)                     )   )

type: TV  TV  EV  ParmAssoc  CallMode =>


open(tv,ev)=
  cases get-State(tv):
  (mk-Accepting(ev)             -> return(true),
   mk-Selecting(eassoc, )       -> return(ev ∈ rng eassoc),
   T                            -> return(false)          )

type: TV  EV => BOOL
```

Here it is checked that the owner of the entry has not terminated.  We assume the entry to be opened by T1, so T2 is suspended in the EntryCalling
state marked engaged, and the rendezvous is started:

```
begin-rendezvous(caller,tv,altid,parmassoc)=
  (TT.(tv).Partners := <caller>^get-Partners(tv);
   resume(tv,mk-START-MEETING(altid,parmassoc))  )

type: TV  TV  [AltId]  ParmAssoc =>


resume(tv,rply)=
  (TT.(tv).State := mk-Running();
   output rply to tv         )

type: TV  REPLY =>
```

The calling task is pushed onto the stack of partners of  the  called  task,
and the called task is resumed with a START-MEETING reply:

```
        START-MEETING    :: [AltId]  ParmAssoc
```

The first component is used only in connection  with  selection  statements,
and  is  nil  in our case.  The parameter information is passed to the accept
statement.  Returning to the accept interpretation function, we see that the
accept body is entered indivisibly with the reciept of the reply:

```
int-acceptbody(stmtl,parmassoc) env =
   (trap exit(mk-Excp(eid) with
            (let eid' = (eid=FAILURE->TASKING-ERROR, T->eid) in
             inform-monitor(mk-ACCEPT-FAIL(eid');
                exit(mk-Excp(eid))                              ) in
    (let env' = env+parmassoc in
    (trap exit(mk-Ret()) with I in
            int-StmtList(stmtl) env'  );
     inform-monitor(mk-END-MEETING())  )                       )
```

type: StmtList  ParmAssoc -> (ENV => )


A trap is set up to catch unhandled exceptions and propagate them to the
monitor.

We assume that the accept statement is completed normally, so the
END-MEETING signal, carrying no information, is sent to the monitor.
(Remember that no returnparameters are needed in this model.) The
END-MEETING request is a message, i.e. the requesting task does not wait
for an answer.  Therefore handle-msg is called:


```
handle-msg(tv,msg)=
   cases msg:
   (mk-ACTIVATED()          -> activation-ended(tv),
    mk-FAILED(excp)          -> activation-failed(tv,excp),
    mk-TERMINATED()          -> handle-termination(tv),
    mk-ENTER-BLOCK(actid) -> BT := c BT U [actid->tv],
    mk-ACCEPT-FAIL(excp)  -> resume-partner(tv,mk-RAISE-CMD(excp)),
    mk-END-MEETING()         -> resume-partner(tv,mk-END-CALL(CALLED)))
```

type: TV  MSG =>


The caller is resumed with an indication that the call was completed normally.

        END-CALL         :: (CALLED¦CLOSED¦EXPIRED)


However, before resumption it should be checked that the caller has not been
terminated  or failed during the rendezvous. (As the caller may pass references to its local storage to the acceptor, the calling task must not be failed  (and  thereby potentially release its storage) until the call has been
completed.  This is an implication of the new  rule  that  the  called  task
should not be aware of failure or termination in the calling task.)

348

```
resume-partner(tv,rply)=
  (def partners : get-Partners(tv);
  let caller = hd partners in
  TT.(tv).Partners := tl partners;
  cases get-IntrptReq(caller):
  (FAILREQ        -> (resume(caller,mk-FAIL-CMD());
                       TT.(caller).IntrptReq := nil   ),
   TERMINATED     -> resume(caller,mk-TERMINATE-CMD()),
   T              -> resume(caller,rply)                ))

type: TV  REPLY =>
```

End of Example

Parallellism in Ada

Part III

TECHNICAL REPORT ON PARALLELISM IN ADA

CONTENTS

## 1.0 Introduction

This report contains technical discussions of the  parallelism  concepts  in
Ada.  The discussion is mainly centred around the formal model given in part
IV.  It is assumed that the reader has got a feeling of the model structure,
acquired from e.g. the model introduction in part II.

First, in chapter 2, the modelling method is  described  and  compared  with
other  methods.   The  extensions  of  the meta-language used in the present
model are also presented.  In chapter 3  various  technical  problems  which
arose during the modelling are discussed, and the chosen solutions are moti-
vated.  Considerations on an implementation of parallel concepts  are  given
in  chapter  4.   It is shown how the monitor directly constitutes a kernel,
and how its data structures may be represented. Also implementation on  existing operating systems is examplified.  The transformation ideas of Habermann-Nassi [HaNa 80] are critisized.  Chapter 5 is a  brief  evaluation  af
Tasking in Ada on the basis of the work on the formal model.

## 2.0 The Method

### 2.1 Why this particular method?

The method used here for defining the semantics of concurrency is based on adaptation of CSP [Ho 78] to the meta-language of the so-called "Vienna Development Method" [BjJo 78]. The main reasons for imbedding CSP-like constructs into the META-IV language are given in the introductory part II together with an informal description of the concurrency construct extensions.

The main reason to choose the META IV concurrency was to make the definition fit together with the companion projects resulting in a semantic definition of sequential Ada written in this notation as described in the introduction part I. Furthermore, the use of concurrent META IV has been used with success in the semantics definition of the programming language CHILL [HaBj 80]. Some of the main features of the method are given below:

1. The CSP constructs fits nicely into the imperative version of the meta-language. All the features of META IV can be used in connection with the concurrency constructs.

2. The interpretation functions for the concurrency constructs of e.g Ada can be imbedded directly into the (denotational) semantics definition of the sequential part of Ada.

3. The interpretation functions for a language shows, although in a rather mechanical way, the behaviour of the concurrency constructs of the language.

4. The formulas of the monitor component leads directly to an implementation of a kernel for the language, and the interpretation functions shows how this kernel should be called.

Thus the practical usefulness of the method compared with other presently known methods to define concurrency semantics (petri-nets, behaviour algebra etc.), and the research in using META IV as a general program specification tool have pointed towards the method. The projects has in a way been used as a test of the capabilities of the method. Indeed, the meta-language did not fit directly with certain problems as described later, but all problems were solved using more or less abstract modelling.

As a student project it has been tried to describe a subset of Ada in behaviour algebra [Mi 80], but the model is still at a trivial stage in relation to the complexity of tasking in Ada.

## 2.2  The foundations of concurrent META IV

The concurrency constructs of META IV have been given a formal semantics model described in [FoBj 80]. Here we summarize the principles of the model, and show how the sequential constructs of the meta-language can be wieved to fit this model.

The main thesis is that a processor (as defined in the introduction part) denotes a so-called transition Tr which describes the external behaviour of a process instance.

```
Tr      =   START | OUT | IN | NDIN | STOP | ...
START   =   ( (PI ≃> Tr)  Pid  Tr)
OUT     =   ( (PI ≃> Tr)  VAL  RCV)
IN      =   ( (PI  VAL ≃> Tr)  SND ... )
NDIN    =   IN-set
STOP    =   (TERMINATED  Result)
```

A transition always (except for STOP) contain the next transition to be used, depending on the interaction with other transtitions. E.g an OUT transition contains a function which yields the next transition to be used depending on which of the Process Instances specified by the ReCieVer component receives the offered VALue. A transition can thus be wieved as an expanded state machine, and the resemblance with e.g. behaviour algebra is obvious [Mi 80].

A concurrent program is defined as the combination of the transitions of the current process instances. Where in behaviour algebra the semantics of such combined transitions is defined algebraically, we use a model to define the combination. The various process instances are identified by a token domain called PI for Process Instance. The "current" transition of each process is held in a so-called kernel-state:

$$\text{KernelState} = \text{PI} \underset{m}{\longrightarrow} ( \text{Tr} | \underline{\text{TERMINATED}})$$

A special kernel function first finds a subset of the possible interactions between the processes and then returns the new kernel state according to "execution" of these interactions. The kernel function is non-determinestic, i.e. strictly a relation on kernel-states. The "result" of running a program is the union of the results delivered by the STOP transactions.

The possible interactions between processes are, as described in the introduction part, very dynamic and powerful.

One of the characteristics of the method is that the transitions are not represented directly, but in a way corresponding to the usual sequential interpretation. A main point is that each process has a local state-component, and that the next transition may depend on the preceding transition in a very complex way due to transformations on this local state.

The transitions are represented by apparently usual state-transforming functions, and concurrency constructs. In [FoBj 80] the interpretation of the concurrency constructs as transitions is formally defined. For this, the idea of continuations is quite useful. Instead of the usual state-to-state continuations, the continuations used here are functions from states to transitions.

$$C = \sum \xrightarrow{\sim} Tr$$

The continuations thus tell the next transition given the current state. The semantics of the meta-constructs ($\theta$) can now be given by an (implicit) interpretation function of the type:

$$\theta \xrightarrow{\sim} (ENV \xrightarrow{\sim} (C \xrightarrow{\sim} C))$$

The ENV is the meta-environment domain which binds the identifiers of the formulas, and the    is the usual meta-state domain:

$$ENV = Id \xrightarrow{m} (VAL \mid LOC \mid \dots )$$
$$\quad = LOC \xrightarrow{m} VAL$$

The usual imperative constructs of META IV which are usually given a state-transformation interpretation can easily be transformed to continuation-transformers, simply by doing the state-transformation and apply the continuation, thereby giving a new continuation. Now the usual state-to-state continuations can be replaced by the state-to-transition continuation. For a processor, this is done for the function defining the processor and this function is applied to an empty state giving the transition of the processor.

We have thus showed how our operational-looking meta-functions and communication constructs can be first transformed or interpreted as continuation-denoting, and then as transition-denoting constructs. A similar work on a combination of Behaviour Algebra and conventional denotational semantics has been done by Brian Mayoh [Ma 80].

## 2.3 Extensions of the concurrent meta-language

For use in the modelling of the Tasking in Ada, it has been convenient to extent the concurrent meta-language with a few straightforward constructs. The most important one, is the introduction of a simultaneous wait for both either input or output:

```
(if ... input   ... from ... -> ...,
 if ... output  ... to   ... -> ...,
        input   ... from ... -> ...,
 ...                                      )
```

To avoid specification of evaluation-order, we demand that the conditions of the guards are pure expressions. The semantics of the construct may easily be incorporated into the existing formal definition of [FoBj 80], involving modifications of about 10 lines! A final extension construct is the parameterization of the metaprogram.

3.0  On the Formal Model


This chapter contains discussions and analyses of the fundamental model
principles, and of the problems which arose during the development of the
formal tasking model. The text is illustrated by extracts from the formal
model. Full details may be found in the reference part IV. A discussion of
the interface between the parallelism model and the sequential semantics  is
found in the paper [StPe 80].


3.1  Configuration

In this section motivations for the chosen system  configuration  consisting
of  the  five process types SYSTEM, STORAGE, MONITOR, TIMER, CLOCK, and TASK
are presented.

The idea of modelling the concurrency as a static number of so-called  fixed
processes,  and  a  dynamic number of process instances corresponding to the
tasks was first used in the formal model of parallelism in CHILL [HaBj  80].
The  idea comes very naturally as the fixed processes corresponds to the environment of the program.  This environment consists of hardware units  like
processors,  storage  units, timers etc., and of software units like kernels
and operating systems.  In CHILL the fixed processes were constituted  by  a
storage,  and  four processes each handling one of the four concurrency concepts of CHILL:  Critical regions, buffers, events, and signals.

It is neccesary to use a process type to interpret the Ada tasks.  In  preliminary  Ada  a  task  could  be initialized several times, and it was then a
question, whether a single TASK process instance should perform all  instantiations,  or a new TASK instance should be created for each initialization.
In revised Ada a task instance may be instantiated only once, and  it  seems
obvious to allocate one TASK instance for each Ada task instance.

Concerning storage, it was considered to keep unshared  locations  in  the
local  state  of the TASK instance owning the locations. However elaboration
of a local task type may make such unshared locations shared  so  that  they
would  have  to be transferred to the common store.  This seemed too hard to
administer, and was rejected.

As shown in the introduction part, all the main concepts of tasking  in  Ada
(hierarchy,  communication, and interruption) are connected closely together
by special rules for the conflicting interferences of the concepts.  (An activating  task  may  receive  a  failure, a selecting task may be terminated
etc).  It was considered to let the meta-process interruption be handled  by
a special process:

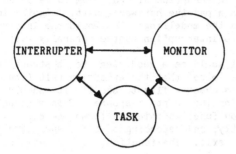

It turned up, however, that the interrupter process had to communicate heavily with the monitor so nothing was gained. In preliminary Ada, the communication concept was the best candidate to be isolated in a special handler, but in revised Ada the termination possibility of the select statement has interferred the concept.

This dependence between the tasking concepts has been the main motivation to use a single process to govern all the tasks. Another reason is that a kernel may be directly derived from the single process, and need not be consistent with several processes. The actual modelling has not indicated that a separation of any concept would have been for any benefit.

The timing processes have been added "for fun", since they have no influence at the semantics. They do, however, illustrate the real time facilities as one might associate certain execution times with the meta-functions. The timer process could have been included in the monitor, but as it did not depend on any other parts of the monitor, and as it corresponds to a hardware unit, it was seperated out.

The system process was introduced to secure proper upstart and termination of the processes.


## 3.2 The Interruption Problem

One of the modelling challenges was to handle the interruption of the "sequential execution" of the meta-processes in conjunction with abortion, and especially when the failure exception is raised in another task. Abortion could be handled by simply ignoring all communication to or from the task in both the storage and the monitor; but this could not handle the need to raise the failure at the point of the "current statement" (whatsoever that is!). As the task processes themselves decide when to communicate, the interruption had to be handled by a trap catching such communication attempts and returning a value indicating that the task should stop the sequential interpretation and terminate or fail. As the tasks communicate heavily with the storage process, it was considered to let the storage do the trap function on demand from the monitor. This solution would have the advantage that the interrupted task could not do any storage-transformations before it would be stopped. However, you could imagine situations in which this model would not work properly. E.g. if a task entered an infinite loop containing nothing but null statements it would not communicate with the storage at all, but it would indeed be nice to stop such a process.

Furthermore, the storage interruption did not seem to be in accordance with the wiev of the storage as a passive hardware unit. Again implementation considerations influenced the modelling: How would the interruption be implemented? By the hardware interruption system naturally (yet, see later).

All this indicated that it would be a good idea to abstract the hardware interruption system, i.e. model that the execution unit (the TASK process) should at "short" intervals check a flag to see if it should continue or stop the execution and do an interrupt- response. This abstraction is given by a special interpretation function which performs the check. The function calls the monitor directly, and depending on the answer, the function continues or performs a meta- exit. The function, called enable, is defined by:

```
enable()=
  (output mk-ENABLE() to MONITOR  ;
  (input mk-TERMINATE-CMD() from MONITOR -> exit(mk-TERMINATE()),
   input mk-FAIL-CMD()       from MONITOR -> exit(mkExcp(FAILURE)),
   input mk-CONTINUE()       from MONITOR -> I                    ))

type: () =>
```

Interruption of the sequential execution has only got effect inbetween state-transformations, i.e. at the points of explicit or implicit meta-semicolons in the interpretation and elaboration functions. It was first considered to insert the function at all these places, but this would have lead to an unreadable definition. Instead the function could be considered inserted at all these points. This would, however, define that a task should always be stopped immediately reaching one of these points. This over-specification could be hard to implement. E.g. for interpreters for A-code, as described in [Do 80], the most convenient interruption points are inbetween A-code instructions. To avoid such over-specification, it was decided not to insert the function at all, but instead let it be considered distributed, or "strayed", out over the interpretation and elaboration functions in an implementation dependent way. The points of interruption were firstly not defined at all, so that a failure exception could be raised "without warning anywhere" in the functions. It was thought that the trap-exit mechanism would take care of all. It was then discovered that in three different situations interruptions during some transformations could not be allowed.

One case is the call (input/output) of the monitor. When the monitor receives a call request it is expected that the calling task immediately performs an input from the monitor to get an answer. If the enable function was inserted after the output, a deadlock situation could occur. (This is mainly a model problem.)

Another case arises when certain actions must always be completed, e.g. freeing of storage upon (normal and abnormal) completion of a block. In the model the storage allocation is centered around so-called Activating Identifiers identifying the "activation records" containing the storage allocated per block. An Activation Identifier (ActId) is allocated from the storage when a block is met, and all variables of the block are marked with this ActId when they are allocated. When block execution has been completed, the storage is asked to remove all locations with the given ActId:

```
int-Block( ... ) env =
  (def actid : create-AcdId;
   always free-locations(actid) in
      ...
                                    )
```

To assure that locations are always released an always trap is set up to catch all exit and normal completion. However, to guarantee this release, a failure exception must not be raised from the point where the create-ActId function receives the actid until the trap is "set up",i.e. until the interpretation of the inner of the trap has started. (This problem is also an implementation problem.)

The third case is very similar to the one above. It concerns the proper exception propagation during rendezvous. To handle this, a special trap must be set up around the interpretation of the statement-list of an accept-statement:

```
( ... ;
  output mk-ACCEPT( ... ) to MONITOR;
  input mk-START-MEETING() from MONITOR;
  trap exit( ... ) with
          output mk-ACCEPT-FAILED( ... ) to MONITOR in
  ...                                                    )
```

Here the task must not be interrupted until the trap has been set up, since the failure would then not be recognized. (The trap cannot just be moved around the input, see later.) (This is really an implementation problem.)

Various solutions to the indivisibility problem were considered. They can be divided into two groups each related to two implementation techniques (again). The first solution class relates to generation of machine code for the Ada which can be interrupted at a very low and unstructured level, and where indivisibility must be implemented by enabling or disabling the EFFECT of the interruption cycle. The corresponding model would in the same way (by calling the monitor) enable and disable the effect of the enable-function, but still let it be distributed in the interpretation functions. The second solution class corresponds to e.g. A-code interpreters which allow for interruption only inbetween the middle-level A-code instructions,i.e. at controlled places. The corresponding model principle is to indicate in the functions the places where the enable function cannot be inserted when spread out.

It was quickly seen that the enabling/disabling solution would be very unstructured and would require insertions in many of the interpretation functions. Various solutions for the second method were considered. It was tried to mark the areas in the interpretation functions where the enable function could not be inserted by special "indivisibility" meta brackets, but this would cut across the block structure of the meta-language, as seen in the examples above, and was rejected. A structure preserving solution would be to mark all areas where the enable function COULD be inserted, but this would be the case in nearly all the interpretation and elaboration functions and would make them more difficult to read.

The solution chosen is of the second class, but it does not use a bracket structure to indicate the points at which the enable function should not be inserted. Instead, it defines which state-transformation compositions could be divided by the enable function and which could not . This is done by use of divisible and indivisible meta-semicolons in the formulas. To assure consistency a few rules had to be added:

1. The enable function may be inserted at all explicit or implicit meta-semicolons, except those encircled. Encircled semicolons guarantee that the preceding elementary state-transformation is composed indivisibily with the following elementary state-transformation both of which could be inside function calls. The elementary state-transformations are the meta-assignment, the input construct, the output construct, and the stop construct.

2. The first statement inside of a trap exit block is also the first state-transformation of the whole block, i.e. the trap is set up indivisibly.

3. An exit is trapped indivisibly.

The following interpretation functions show the use of the indivisible semi-colon in the accept case:

```
int-Accept(mk-Accept(ename,stmtl)) env =
  (def mk-(ev, ) : eval-EntryName(ename) env ;
   let req = mk-ACCEPT(ev) in
   def mk-START-MEETING( ,parmassoc) : monitor-call(req) (;)
   int-acceptbody(stmtl,parmassoc) env                     )

type: Accept -> (ENV => )


int-acceptbody(stmtl,parmassoc) env =
  (trap exit(mk-Excp(eid) with
            (let eid' = (eid=FAILURE->TASKING-ERROR, T->eid) in
             inform-monitor(mk-ACCEPT-FAIL(eid');
                exit(mk-Excp(eid))                          ) in
    (let env' = env+parmassoc in
    (trap exit(mk-Ret()) with I in
       int-StmtList(stmtl) env'  );
     inform-monitor(mk-END-MEETING()) )                     )

type: StmtList  ParmAssoc -> (ENV => )
```

The monitor-call function is a common function used for all calls to the monitor (i.e. monitor request yielding an answer), as a calling process must always be prepared to be interrupted while it waits for an answer. The monitor-call function handles this potential interruption in a way similar to the enable function. It is also indivisible, thereby solving the first of the indivisibility problems:

```
monitor-call(req)=
  (output req to MONITOR ;
  (input rply from MONITOR ->
      cases rply:
      (mk-TERMINATE-CMD() -> exit(mk-TERMINATE()),
       mk-FAIL-CMD()      -> exit(mk-Excp(FAILURE)),
       mk-RAISE-CMD(ied)  -> exit(mk-Excp(eid)),
       T                  -> return(rply)        )))
```

type: REQ => REPLY

The possibility of an exception while a process waits for response from the
monitor explains why the trap could not be moved around the input clause in
the accept example.


3.3  Monitor information domains

It was clear that the monitor should keep information about the state of all
active tasks.  This information may be represented in two different ways.
One is to partition the tasks into state-classes where each class represents
a certain state:

          Running      =  TV-set
          Accepting    =  (TV EV)-set


This representation, which abstracts queue realizations, is well suited for
inquiries like: Find all tasks in a certain state.  It is, however, hard to
administer unless the information which must be associated with each task is
about the same in the different states, such that a common task entity can
be moved simply around between the classes.  This is not the case in Ada, so
another representation was used:

          TaskTable       =  TV $\xrightarrow{m}$ TaskInfo


The information associated with a task is rather different in the various
states.  Some information may be related to only a single state-class while
other information should perhaps be retained and updated during the whole
lifetime of the task.  The information could thus be represented by a hierarchical state-classification where each state-class is associated with the
information common for its members. During the revision of Ada, this hierarchy has varied somewhat, but in the revised version it has turned out that
the type of the information-lifetime belongs to either one of the two ex-
tremes.  Therefore the Task Information has been divided into a State component in which the state-classification and the corresponding temporary information is held, and other components which hold lifetime-bound information groups.  The lifetime-bound information has been divided into five
rather independent components :

  TaskInfo :: Dependence  Phase  State  Queues  Partners  IntrptReq


The components are independent in the sense that they, to some extent, can vary orthogonally. Only the last component binds the five others if an interruption is requested. E.g. only three states are legal in such a case. This indicates that the request could be put in these three states, but since they are not logically connected, no common state-class could be used to hold the information and a lot of information movement between these states would be the result. Therefore, the idea was rejected.

The information components are more carefully described in the introduction part II.

The dependencies between the components can be seen in the well-formedness function for the monitor state given in part IV. Even though the components have been chosen so as to be independent, the well-formedness functions are rather complicated.


## 3.4  Task hierarchy


Somewhere, either in the environments of the tasks, or in the monitor, the dynamic hierarchy must be represented.

Dynamic hierarchy:

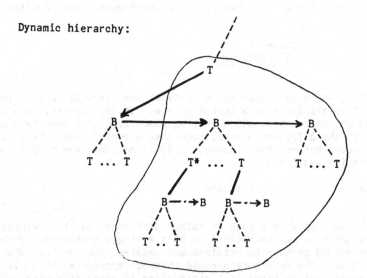

The T's and B's represent task instances and block activations respectively. The T's connected to a B by dashed lines are the tasks dependent on the block. The B's connected to a T are the nested inner blocks currently entered by the task. Thus, the B connected directly to the task is the task body block, the next on the path is the outermost inner block etc. ending with the (dynamically) innermost block activation in which the task is currently executing. The visibility rules of Ada imply that the task marked with an * can, at most, be referred to by the tasks, and from the blocks encircled in the figure.

For use in the following, we define for a task T the tasks dependent on T as all the tasks dependent on any block currently entered by T.

When a block (*) is about to be left, the leaving task must wait for the termination of all tasks dependent on the block. If the dynamic hierarchy is in the environment, the task must search this to find all dependent tasks. This would add rather much new tasking information to the environment, and would be hard to administer. Also handling of abortion and the termination possibility indicates that the dynamic hierarchy should be maintained by the monitor. To help this, the activation identifiers used by the storage to collect locations belonging to the same block activation, are used. When a task is created, the monitor is told which block the task depends on by sending the Activation Identifier to the monitor. When a block is about to be left, the Activation Identifier (ActId) of the block is given to the monitor which then can find all dependent tasks.

To find all dependent tasks of another task, the monitor must be able to find the parent of a task. As the parent is the task that has entered the block on which the task is dependent, the parent may be found by recording the blocks which have been entered by the various tasks. This is the solution used here. This requires that tasks, each time a block is entered, pass the new ActId to the monitor which records it in the BlockTable. Another solution is to associate both the dependent block, and the parent with a task when it is created. This solution is probably better since it is less information demanding. It is,however, a little harder to administer for the tasks.

To sum up: The dynamic hierarchy is maintained by the monitor by means of unique block activation identifications.

## 3.5  Task creation and activation

A great deal of the problems which arose from the new tasking concept in revised Ada are caused by postponed and elaborator-controlled activation. The main problem is that the elaborator of a declarative part must be in contact with the created tasks until the declarative part has been completely elaborated. If the activation rules were connected with the dependence rules, this would probably not be hard to incorporate in the hierarchy. This is unfortunately not the case, mainly because packages introduce more declarative parts than blocks, but also because the dependence rules are more restrictive than neccesary.

To handle the postponed activation of tasks created in the same declarative part or allocator, we could again let either the tasks, or the monitor be the administrator. Again we wish to strip off as much tasking as possible from the sequential semantics. This policy, and interference from other concepts of tasking have made us choose the monitor solution.

The monitor must thus in some way bundle the tasks created in the same declarative part or allocator. If declarative parts were properly nested,

----------
(*) In this paper the term "block" will be used for the three block-like constructs: Block, procedure body, and task body.

i.e. in a parenthesis structure, it would be sufficient for the monitor to have a stack of "bundles":

    CrationStack    =    (TV-set)*

Tasks should inform the monitor each time a declarative part or allocator was entered or left. Upon entry the monitor would push an empty "bundle" on the stack, and insert all subsequent task created by the task in this bundle. Upon end of a declarative part, or allocator, the monitor would pop off a "bundle", and activate all the tasks of this bundle.

Unfortunately, things are not so simple. Due to packages, declarative parts may be split in a very unstructured way as shown in the following example:

    task type TT
    dcl
        A : TT;

        package P1
            B : TT;
        end

        package P2
            C : TT;
        end

        package body P2
            D : TT;
            begin            --- #1
        end

        package body P1

            begin            --- #2
        end

    begin                    --- #3
    end

    Here C and D are activated first at the point of #1. Then B is activated at #2, and finally A at #3.

Thus, the monitor cannot rely on any proper structure, so it must in some other way identify the various bundles, and collect created tasks in these. The block- or package identifier cannot be used to uniquely identify the declarative parts due to recursive procedures. Therefore, the monitor administers a pool of so-called Creation Identifiers (CrId), and associates created tasks with them:

    CreationTable    =    CrId $\xrightarrow{m}$ TV-set

The creation identifiers are allocated from the monitor when the tasks meet a declarative part or allocator, and released upon end of elaboration / evaluation.

All the information needed to create a new task is held in the environment. When a task type body is met, a function which interprets the task body in the given environment is created by the following function:

```
create-TaskFct(mk-DclPart(dict,dcllist),stmtl,excpthdlr) env =
  (trap all exits with (inform-monitor(mk-TERMINATED()) ;
                        stop                              ) in
   await-activation();
   (def actid : get-new-ActId() (;)
   let env' = env+[ACTID->actid]+get-type-dens(dict)(actid) in
   always block-epilouge(actid) in
      (def crid : create-CrId(actid) (;)
      let env'' = env'+[CRID->crid] in
      def env''' : task-extend-env(dict,dcllist) env'' (;)
      (trap exit(mk-Excp(eid)) with
                 handle(mk-Excp(eid),excpthdlr) in
       activate-tasks(crid);
       int-StmtList(stmtl) env'''                    )          )     )

type: DclPart  StmtList  Excpthdlr -> (ENV -> ( ∑ -> ∑ ))
```

The resulting taskfunction is associated with the task type. Instead, only the environment and the task body could be stored, but this would not be in accordance with procedure declarations. The "current" ActId and CrId are always kept in the environment. Thus, when a task object declaration is met, all neccesary information can be found in the environment and this information is sent to the monitor:

```
ENV              = ((Id|QOUT) --m--> DEN) U (ACTID --m--> ActId) U
                   (CRID --m--> CrId) U ...

DEN              = TypeDen | EntryDen | ParmDen | ...
TypeDen          = TaskTypeDen | ...

TaskTypeDen      :: Entries  [TaskFct]

create-task(typeid) env =
  (let mk-TaskTypeDen( ,taskfct) = env(typeid),
       req = mk-CREATE-TASK(taskfct,env(ACTID),env(CRID)) in
   def mk-TASKVAL-MSG(tv) : monitor-call(req);
   return(tv)                                                        )

type: TypeId -> (ENV => TV)
```

The details of handling the environment correctly in relation to tasking is described in detail in [StPe 80].

If a declarative part is not completely elaborated due to exceptions or abortion, the language requires that all tasks created in this declarative part should be (considered) terminated. One plausible solution would be to (indivisibly) put a trap around the declarative part which tells the monitor that the declarative part was not completed. However, for packages this trap should extend over both the head and some of the body, and this cuts across the block structure of the meta-language. Continuations could perhaps be used here, but if so, it would be in a very tricky and unstructured way. Instead it was decided to let the monitor handle this termination "automatically". Each declarative part is associated with the block in which it is elaborated. If the block is left before the completion of all declarative parts or allocators of the block, the monitor knows that still existing CrId's of the block have not been activated, and the corresponding task bundles are terminated.

The abovementioned relationships among CrId's, ActId's and TV's caused a great deal of trouble to model consistently. Various models were tried. The conclusion is that a one-to-many e.g. one A to many B's, should be modelled from B to A i.e. ( B $\xrightarrow{m}$ A ) and not ( A $\xrightarrow{m}$ B-set ).

## 3.6 Communication

Handling of communication has been straightforward, except for interpretation of the select statement. The multi-accept may be executed in one of four here-called modes: Unconditionally, conditionally, timed or terminable. The modes are statically determinable, but instead of letting the mode be an appendix to the statement, it has been imbedded (drowned) in the alternatives, which are a mixture of accept-, delay-, and termination-alternatives.

For pragmatic reasons, the interpretation function for the select statement tries to recover the hidden mode. This has introduced some auxiliary domains and functions, so maybe the intended clarification has instead obscured the description.

The function shows how the labelled entry-values (entry-association) and the mode is extracted from the unstructured set of labelled, evaluated alternatives (alternative-association).

```
int-SelectiveWait(selectwait) env =
  (let kind : find-SelectKind(selectwait) in
   let mk-SelectiveWait(galts,estmtl) = selectwait in
   def altassoc : eval-guarded-alts(galts) env ;
   if none-open(altassoc)  and  estmtl=nil
      then  raise(SELECT-ERROR)
      else (let entryassoc = extract-open-entries(altassoc) in
            let smode = find-smode(kind,altassoc) in
            let req = mk-SELECT(entryassoc,smode)              in
            def rply : monitor-call(req) (;)
            cases rply:
            (mk-START-MEETING(altid),parmassoc)   ->
               (let mk-EAcceptAlt( ,,astmtl,stmtl)=altassoc(altid) in
                int-acceptbody(astmtl,parmassoc) env ;
                int-StmtList(stmtl) env                        ),
            mk-SELECT-EXPIRED(altid)                ->
               (let mk-EDelayAlt( , ,stmtl) = altassoc(altid) in
                int-StmtList(stmtl) env                        ),
            mk-NONE-CALLED()                        ->
               int-StmtList(estmtl) env,                        )))

type: SelectiveWait -> (ENV => )
```

## 3.7  Interruption as seen from the monitor

Early in the planning of the formal definition it was decided to try to  let
abortion  be  modelled  in  the  same  way as failure as both are related to
interruption of the sequential interpretation of tasks.  This has been achieved  by  a  special  kind  of exit, which can trapped only at the outermost
level of a task:

        Terminate      :: ()

It thus behaves as an unhandled exception.  It is of course trapped  by  al-
ways-clauses  which ensures that an aborted task releases all its storage by
itself in a controlled manner.  Thus, under all circumstances  a  task  will
administer  its storage correctly, and the monitor need not communicate with
the storage.

The problem of degrees of termination is analyzed in the next section.  Here
we reconsider indivisibility.

There are certain states of a task in which the task must not be  interrupted.  Of  course a task cannot be interrupted if it is running.  When a task
is about to leave a block, it is known that it will immediately and  indivisibly release the block-storage after the receipt of the continuation signal
from the monitor.  If it is interrupted in this state, the  storage  is  not
released.

```
block-epilogue'(actid)=
  (pass-monitor(mk-LEAVE(actid)) (;)
   free-locations(actid)  )
```

<u>type</u>: ActId =>

An always-trap could be put around the monitor-call, but to avoid release of storage in use, the interruption would then have to be postponed until the block could be left normally. Instead of using this ackward construction, it has been decided not to interrupt a leaving task since it is anyhow doing the same as if interrupted, and since it will be stopped as soon as it tries to do anything else than to leave or terminate.

The third case in which a task cannot be interrupted is when it is calling an entry and is engaged already. Due to the parameter passing mechanism which could be by reference (see [StPe 80]) the calling task may have passed local state references to the called task, and therefore this storage must not be released until the rendezvous has ended.

A task may thus receive an interrupt command in connection with the following events:

1. Call of monitor with any call except LEAVE.

2. Interruption of a suspended task, except for the described entry calling state.

3. When a rendezvous has ended.

This means that the interruption of tasks has been distributed to three places in the monitor functions, but this seems unavoidable. The two functions below contains the three interrupting points.

```
handle-failure(tv,tv')=
  (tv = tv'           ->
       resume(tv,mk-FAIL-CMD()),
   terminated(tv')    ->
       resume(tv,mk-CONTINUE()),
   T                  ->
       (if uninteruptable(tv')
           then mark-failed(tv')
           else cases get-State(tv'):
                (mk-Initial()                              ->
                               terminate(tv'),
                 mk-EntryCalling( ,,mk-InQueue( , ))    ->
                               (queue-remove(tv');
                                resume(tv',mk-FAIL-CMD()) ),
                 T                                         ->
                               resume(tv',mk-FAIL-CMD())    );
        resume(tv,mk-CONTINUE())                                 )

type: TV   TV =>

resume-partner(tv,rply)=
  (def partners : get-Partners(tv);
   let caller = hd partners in
   TT.(tv).Partners := tl partners;
   cases get-IntrptReq(caller):
   (FAILREQ         -> (resume(caller,mk-FAIL-CMD());
                        TT.(caller).IntrptReq := nil   ),
    TERMINATED      -> resume(caller,mk-TERMINATE-CMD()),
    T               -> resume(caller,rply)  ))

type: TV   REPLY =>
```

## 3.8  The termination problem

The termination problem can be simplified to this: When has a  task  terminated?  Look  at  the  following figure which shows the various phases of a
terminating task:

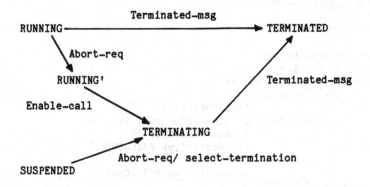

RUNNING and SUSPENDED are the normal state classes. In RUNNING', the task is "doomed to die", i.e. marked that it should termi- nate, but has not been stopped yet. In the TERMINATING phase, the task is "dying", i.e. it has been stopped and commanded to re- lease its storage. In the TERMINATED phase, all storage has been released and the task has stopped itself. The phase transitions are marked with the events that cause the transfer.

Now, we introduce two levels of termination. Virtual termination in which the task seems terminated when seen from other tasks, i.e. they receive the TASKING-ERROR exception if they e.g. try to call its entries. Effective termination means that the termination gets effect on the dynamic hierarchy. Virtual and effective termination of a task can be defined in terms of the (set of) termination phases in which the task is considered to be virtually resp. effectively terminated. As effective termination must also be virtu- al, and as termination cannot be effective in the RUNNING' phase as the task may still refer to its environment, virtual and effective termination can be defined in only five different ways:

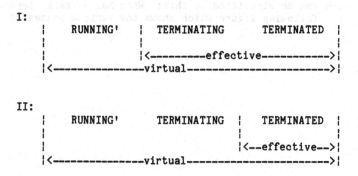

III:
```
        RUNNING'  | TERMINATING     TERMINATED |
                  |                             |
                  |<-----------effective----------->|
                  |<-----------virtual------------->|
```

IV:
```
        RUNNING'  | TERMINATING  | TERMINATED  |
                  |              |             |
                  |              |<--effective-->|
                  |<-----------virtual------------->|
```

V:
```
        RUNNING'    TERMINATING  | TERMINATED  |
                                 |             |
                                 |<--effective-->|
                                 |<---virtual--->|
```

In (I), a task is considered virtually terminated when in one of
the phases: RUNNING', TERMINATING, or TERMINATED, whereas the
termination affects the hierarchy only in the TERMINATING and TER-
MINATED phases. In (II), a task is not considered effectively
terminated until it reaches the TERMINATED phase etc.

Solution (I) and (II) have the advantage that an aborting task need not be
suspended until the virtual termination of the aborted task has been done.
(III) and (V) have the advantage that the two concepts coincide. (IV) corresponds to the termination policy: "Terminate as fast as you can". (V)
corresponds to treatment of abortion exactly like an exception which cannot
be handled.

All these solutions seemed to be equally bad, but a closer study of a
language study note showed that it was desired that an aborting task should
not be suspended. This implied the use of solution (I or (II). From the
phase diagram you can see that solution (I) implies that both internal
events (events caused by the aborted task), and external events (abortion in
a SUSPENDED state) should lead to effective termination, while effective
termination in solution (II) should be done in connection with the one and
same internal event (Termination-msg). For this, and several rather
model-technical reasons, solution (II) was chosen. It corresponds to the
policy that other tasks should feel the abortion as soon as possible, whereas the task itself experiences the termination as an exception which cannot
be handled.

As described in the introduction part, it must, in connection with certain
events, be checked whether selecting terminable tasks can be terminated or a
block can be left. This is done by two functions which call each other recursively while they climb up the dynamic hierarchy tree. We define that a
task is terminable if it is in a terminable selecting state, and all its dependent tasks have terminated, or are terminable to (*).

----------
(*) The treatment of the terminable select-alternative described here is
more general than the (inconsistent) description in [Ada 80].

The try-termination function is called when a task is known to be in a terminable selecting state. It checks whether its dependent tasks are terminable too. If so, there is a chance that the whole tree of terminable tasks can be terminated. Therefore the block on which the task depends is found, and the try-release function is called with this block. (If the Block is the SYSTEM block, the whole program can be terminated.)

The try-release function is called with a block as an argument, when there is a chance that the block could be left. It releases the block if all tasks dependent on the block have effectively terminated. It may also (virtually) terminate the tree of tasks with the block as the root if all these tasks are terminable, or it may propagate the "try" if there is a termination chance. The two functions are given here to show the ideas:

```
try-release(actid)=
  (def parent : (c BT)(actid);
   cases get-State(parent):
  (mk-Leaving(actid)                  ->
      (def bdeps : find-block-dependent(actid);
      (bdeps = {}                     ->
          (BT := (c BT) \ {actid};
           resume(parent,mk-CONTINUE())),
      (∀tv ∈ bdeps) terminable(tv)    ->
          for all tv ∈ bdeps do
              for all tv'∈ find-termination-tree(tv) do
                  terminate(tv')                        ,
      T                               ->
                  I                                     )),
  mk-Selecting( ,TERMINABLE)   ->
      try-termination(parent)                           ))
type: ActId =>
```

```
try-termination(tv)=
  (def tdeps : find-task-dependent(tv);
  if (∀tv'∈ tdeps) terminable(tv')
    then (def actid' : get-Dependence(tv);
          if actid' = SYSTEM
              then for all tv'∈ find-termination-tree(tv) do
                  terminate(tv')
              else try-release(actid')          )
      else I                                            )
type: TV =>
```

Try-release is called when a task terminates totally, or when a task attempts to leave a block. Try-termination is started when a task enters a terminable selecting state.

## 4.0  Implementation Considerations

In this chapter some ideas on how to implement the tasking constructs of Ada will be sketched.

## 4.1  Principle

If we look at the system configuration

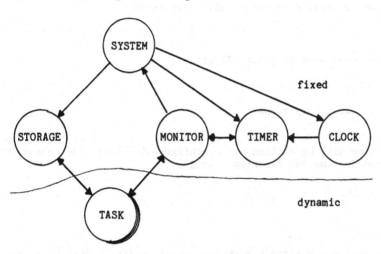

we see that it consists of fixed and dynamic processes as indicated. The main idea is to derive a kernel or specialized Ada operating system from the definition of the fixed processes, mainly the monitor, and to derive a com-piling algorithm for concurrency constructs from the interpretation func-tions of the TASK process. The compiling algorithm will generate calls of the kernel following the schemes given in the interpretation functions. Depending on the target machine, some of the storage functions may be used for the compiling algorithm. For an A-code machine [Do 80] we could thus have the following systematic derivations:

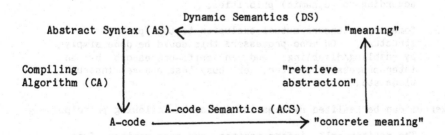

The transformation functions are composite:

$$DS \begin{cases} \text{Interpretation Functions (IF)} \begin{cases} \text{Sequential IF (SIF)} \\ \text{Concurrent IF (CIF)} \end{cases} \\ \\ \text{Monitor and fixed Processes (M)} \end{cases}$$

$$ACS \begin{cases} \text{A-Code Interpreter (ACI)} \\ \\ \text{Kernel (K)} \end{cases}$$

The components can be derived systematically like this:

$$\left. \begin{array}{l} \text{SIF} \\ \text{CIF} \\ \\ \text{ACI} \end{array} \right\} \text{-------------> Compiling Algorithm.}$$

M --------------------> Kernel

The A-code semantics will be defined by an configuration like the abstract configuration used for the Ada semantics [Do 80].

## 4.2  A kernel

We first observe that the MONITOR has the classical monitor structure [Ha 73], i.e. a data structure and some operations (the handle functions) which operate on the data structure in mutual exclusion.

In the following we assume an implementation on a mono- or multi-processor system. The structure and to some extent the deriviation method is very much like the monitor concept presented in [Ha 73], [Ha 77], and [Li 75].

To implement the kernel we principally need:

1. A dispatcher which can create and run a dynamically varying number of processes. The dispatcher should switch
   the avaiable (hardware-) processors among the processes
   according to (dynamic) priorities.

2. Some way to ensure mutual exclusion to the process data
   structure. On mono-processors this could be done simply
   by enabling/disabling, and on multi-processors by an
   inter-processor arbiter, or busy test and set instructions etc.

The kernel can be realized systematically in the following principal way:

1. The monitor-call, inform-monitor, and pass-monitor functions should be transformed to supervisor calls (SVC's)
   where the parameters needed can be derived from the communication domains used.

2. Handling of SVC's will correspond to the handle-functions of the monitor, and will be done by the kernel.

3. The state components of the monitor are represented by a process table data structure accessible also by the dispatcher.

4. Process interruption must be handled either by polling by the processes, or by knowledge of the exception handlers of the processes.

We shall now discuss and illustrate some aspects of this derivation. Process interruption and exception propagation may be handled in two different ways. In the first, which corresponds to the low-level uncontrolled interruption described in chapter 3, the kernel simply asks the dispatcher to stop the process and transfer control to the current exceptionhandler. To do this, the kernel must always know the adress of the code for the current exceptionhandler. An exceptionhandler must naturally always be set up indivisibly corresponding to the discussion in chapter 3.

The other solution, which corresponds to task-controlled interruption, is suitable for interpreters for middle-level instructions like A-code. Here the interpreter polls a flag inbetween the interpretation of the A-code instructions. This can be done without further overhead than caused by the interpretation principle, if a register can be allocated for the purpose! The register acts as the "interrupt flag". It is normally used for the control transfer to restart the interpretation cycle. When the monitor wishes to interrupt the process, it indivisibly (by hardware) changes the register contents :

```
        register R := L1;

        L1:  fetch-instruction
             do-instruction
             goto c R

        L2:  contact-monitor
             do-interrupt-handling(exit)
             R := L1;
             goto L1

        KERNEL:
             Interrupt:  R := L2
```

This solution corresponds to the modelled interruption mechanism. A benefit is that all A-code instructions are performed indivisibly.

Representation of the monitor state is probably the most interesting implementation aspect. We shall here sketch some refinement ideas.

Of course the Task Table can be realized by a conventional list or array structure. The task values would probably be integers in the case of the array implementation, and the kernel would have a list of free task values.

375

Activation identifiers will probably be the adresses of the activation records, and information associated with a block could then be held in this
record.

It is not acceptable that the kernel should search the whole process table
as the find- functions of the formal model do. Instead, the result of the
find- functions should be held and continuously updated in the process descriptions of the processes that use the results.

EXAMPLE:


find-remaining(crid)=
    return({tv | tv∈ c TT and
                ~ terminated(tv) and
                get-Phase(tv)=mk-NonActive(crid) })

type: CrId ==> TV-set


Here we should collect all tasks belonging to the same CrId.

        CreationTable  = CrId ₘ-> (TV-set ... )

This could of course be implemented by a usual list structure. In the same
way, the tasks dependent on a block could be collected. (A collection of
the activation records currently entered by a task, is "built into" the dynamic chain, see [Do 80].)

An interesting problem is to implement the try- functions which searches for
a termination or leave condition. Let us consider them again:


try-release(actid)=
  (def parent : (c BT)(actid);
   cases get-State(parent):
  (mk-Leaving(actid)              ->
      (def bdeps : find-block-dependent(actid);
      (bdeps = {}                 ->
          (BT := (c BT) \ {actid};
           resume(parent,mk-CONTINUE()))),
    (∀tv ∈ bdeps) terminable(tv)   ->
          for all tv∈ bdeps do
              for all tv'∈ find-termination-tree(tv) do
                  terminate(tv')                       ,
      T                          ->
          I                                           )),
  mk-Selecting(~,TERMINABLE)    ->
      try-termination(parent)                         ))

type: ActId =>

```
try-termination(tv)=
  (def tdeps : find-task-dependent(tv);
   if (Ɐtv'∈ tdeps) terminable(tv')
     then (def actid' : get-Dependence(tv);
              if actid' = SYSTEM
                then for all tv'∈ find-termination-tree(tv) do
                              terminate(tv')
                else try-release(actid')              )
     else I                                                    )

type: TV =>
```

We see that the following predicates (based on tree-traversing collector-functions) are used for determining wheter termination or block-exit shall happen:

```
        bdeps = {}
        (Ɐ tv∈ bdeps) terminable(tv)
        (Ɐ tv'∈ tdeps) terminable(tv')
```

These are equivalent to:

```
        card bdeps = 0
        card {tv | tv∈ bdeps and ~terminable(tv)}
        card {tv | tv∈ tdeps and ~terminable(tv)}
```

We could thus save the tree-traversing collector-functions by maintaining two counters for each block and one for each task. One of the counters of the block should count the number of tasks dependent on that block, let us call the counter NO-BDEP. The ouher block-counter NO-BNTERM should count the number of dependent tasks which are not terminable. The counter NO-TNTERM of a task should count the number of nonterminable tasks dependent on the task which are not terminable. We thus have the following rules:

For a block:

```
   NO-DEPS   = "number of tasks dependent on the block"
   NO-BNTERM = "number of nonterminable tasks dependent on the block"

   NO-DEPS   = NO-BNTERM + "number of terminable block-dependent tasks"
```

For a task:

```
   NO-TNTERM = "number of non-terminable tasks dependent on the task"
             = "sum of NO-BNTERM for all blocks currently entered"
```

If these counters are updated correctly, the try-functions need not use the tree-traversing functions for evaluating the predicates. By looking at the colloctor functions find-task-dependent and find-block-dependent and the predicate function terminable, we se that updating of the counters should be triggered by the following events:

```
   1.  Creation of a task:
           The NO-TNTERM is initialized to 0.
           The counters of the parent task, and of the block on
           which the new task is dependent are all incremented.
```

2.  Block entry:
    The counters NO-BNTERM og NO-BDEP of the new block are
    initialized to 0.

3.  Effective termination:
    The counters of the parent and of the block on which the
    task depends are all decremented, and try-release on the
    block is called.

4.  A task enters a terminable selecting state:
    The NO-TNTERM of the parent and NO-BNTERM of the depen-
    dence block are decremented, and try-termination of the
    task is called.

5.  A task leaves a terminable selecting state:
    This can happen in three ways:
    (a) A redezvous is possible.
    (b) Failure is raised in the selecting task.
    (c) The selecting task is aborted.
    In all cases, the NO-TNTERM of the parent and NO-BNTERM
    of the dependence block are incremented.

We see from this informal description of the implementation, that the predicates used by the try-functions now have to be maintained at many different
points. Points which were good candidates for errors if not based on derivation from the formal model. In Appendix A we exemplify how the formulas
may be modified to handle the counters according to these rules.

The described implementation means that the "try" just moves up in the hierarchy, and only as long as there is a chance to terminate or leave. The
overhead is negligible!!

We have thus arrived at a representation which looks like this:

```
CreationTable    = CrId --> (ActId    TV-set ... )
Storage          = ActId --> (no-deps:N   no-nterm:N   TV .. )
TaskTable        = TV --> TaskInfo'
TaskInfo'        :: no-tnterm:N   Dependence  Phase ...
```

Notice that the data structures could easily be implemented in Ada.


4.3  Implementation on existing operating systems


To implement a kernel on an existing operating system, we must require the
following features of that operating system:

1.  Creation of dynamic number of processes run with priori-
    ties.

2.  Synchronization primitives to ensure mutual exclusion.

3.  Synchronization primitives to suspend a process.

Semaphores could be used for 2 and 3.  The kernel function could  (should?)

be run by the processes themselves by elimination of the kernel with Habermann-Nassi transformations.


## 4.4 Criticism of Habermann-Nassi transformations


This section is related to the acticle by Habermann and Nassi [HaNa 80] on implementation of Ada tasking constructs. The discussion will be on three points.

H-N starts with the postulate that if the task calling an entry executes the accept body instead of the acceptor, a scheduling point will be saved in both the case of the caller being first, and the case of the acceptor being first. This appears to be wrong. As long as always the caller or always the acceptor executes the body, no scheduling points are saved. Only if the task that comes most late for the rendezvous executes the body, scheduling can be saved.

Their elimination of a monitor structured task works (almost) right for uninterrupted tasks, but it will be difficult, and certainly not effective, to administer e.g. the raise of FAILURE in a eliminated task.

Finally they describe code motion to make a task have the pure monitor structure. This code motion should be done with extreme care as e.g. movement of concurrency constructs or exception handlers could change the semantics.

The conclusion is: Do not use Habermann-Nassi to implement the concurrency directly. Instead use it for implementing a kernel.

## 5.0 Evaluation of the Tasking Concepts in Ada

This evaluation is based on the work on the formal model. Of course the modelling revealed a number of undefined special cases. In this chapter the language will be evaluated at a conceptual level.

The imbedding of tasking into the type concept has given a very dynamic and flexible task creation concept. The dependence principle which ensures that environments in use cannot disappear is really consistent and nice. The distinction between dynamic and static creation and the corresponding lifetime rules, which are unneccesary restrictive, seem a bit artificial and complicate creation.

The postponed activation under control of the activator (unnecesarily) introduced with the task type concept gave rise to a number of creation problems. Especially the interaction with failure and abortion is inconsistent. Instead all tasks should be immediately activated after creation, and automatic abortion should take place if a declarative part was left abnormally.

The rendezvous concept is nice, but the select statement should be given a pragmatically better syntax, which in a more explicit way as described in 3.6. This could be done e.g. by separating out the terminate/ delay/ conditional alternatives and colloct them at the end of the statement.

Abortion and raise of failure are principally good, but the implications of raising failure should be more presicely described.

The terminate possibility as it has been described here (and which is not quite the same as the manual reads) is a nice solution to the problem of distributed termination [Fra 78], as it is powerful, logical, fits the dynamic hierarchy, and can be efficiently implemented. We have shown that the restriction in the manual (that tasks may only be dependent on the outermost block of a task) seems unnecesary.

Thus, the tasking concept seems nice although non-trivial, but the activation problem could be solved in a more satisfactory way, and the termination possibility in a more general way.

6.0   Conclusion


As described, there have been a number of  problems  in  making  the  formal
model  consistent.    This  has been partly due to conflicts between language
concepts, partly due to lack of concept generality, and partly due to an in-
adequate  description tool.However, all problems have been solved, but often
in a non-abstract, mechanical, and implementation directed way.

One cause of the problem is the lack of structure of the  syntactic  domains
(the communication domains), and semantic domains of the monitor.   Thus, the
monitor functions do not have the same syntax  directed  structure  as  e.g.
interpretation  or is-wf functions.  Instead, the monitor has become a great
(50 functions) unstructured program.

Another reason for the mechanical structure, is that  tasking,  as  well  as
other concepts in Ada are very implementation oriented.  However, concurrency is so complicated that many implementation problems seem unelaborated.

A probable  solution  to  both  the  design  and  modelling  problem  is  to
(re-)search  for  more  general  concurrency concepts.  CSP, and the derived
rendezvous concept, as well as the termination possibility are steps in this
direction, but I hope and believe that many more will follow.

## Appendix A

### Implementation of termination-wave

We exemplify how to the modufy the formulas of the formal tasking definition to realize the termination wave problem according to the principles outlined in chapter 4.

The semantic domains are modified to hold the counters described in the sketch. The selector corresponding to the counters NO-BDEP, NO-BNTERM, and NO-TNTERM are called ndep, nnt, and ntnt respectively:

```
BlockTable      = ActId --> (ndep:N   nnt:N  TV)
TaskTable       = TV --> TaskInfo
TaksInfo        :: ntnt:N   Dependence ...
```

If the fields are correctly updated, they can be used directly by the two try-functions as shown:

```
try-release(actid)=
  (def parent : (c BT)(actid);
   cases get-State(parent):
  (mk-Leaving(actid)                    ->
       (s-ndep(c(BT.(actid))=0           ->
               (BT := (c BT) \ {actid};
                resume(parent,mk-CONTINUE())),
        s-nnt(c(BT.(actid))=0           ->
             for all tv ∈ find-block-dependent(actid) do
                 for all tv' ∈ find-termination-tree(tv) do
                     terminate(tv')                          ,
        T                               ->
                I                                             )),
   mk-Selecting( ,TERMINABLE)   ->
       try-termination(parent)                                ))

type: ActId =>



try-termination(tv)=
  if s-ntnt(c(TT.(tv))
     then (def actid' : get-Dependence(tv);
           if actid' = SYSTEM
               then for all tv' ∈ find-termination-tree(tv) do
                       terminate(tv')
               else try-release(actid')               )
     else I                                              )

type: TV =>
```

We see, that the tree-traversing need only be called when termination is known to be possible.

When a block is entered, or a task is created, the counters should of course be initialized to 0.

Upon effective termination, the counters should be decremented. The handle-termination function then becomes:

```
handle-termination(tv)=
  (def actid : get-Dependence(tv);
   if ~ terminated(tv) then clear-queues(tv) else I;
   TT := (c TT) \ {tv};
   if actid = SYSTEM
       then exit
       else (BT.(actid).ndep:= c(BT.(actid).ndep)-1;
             BT.(actid).nnt := c(BT.(actid).nnt)-1;
             (def parent : s-TV(c(BT.(actid))));
             TT.(parent).ntnt:= c(TT.(parent).ntnt)-1;
             try-release(actid)                        )))

type: TV =>
```

Likewise in handle-select, the non-terminable counters of the parent and the block should be decremented:

```
        ...
        if cmode'=TERMINABLE
            then (def actid : c(TT.(tv).Dependence);
                  def parent : C(BT.(actid).TV);
                  BT.(actid).nnt:=c(BT.(actid).nnt)-1;
                  TT.(parent).ntnt:=c(TT.(parent).ntnt)-1;
                  try-termination(tv)                      )
```

The other way from the terminable state is more distributed as mentioned in chapter 4.

End of examples

# Parallelism in Ada

## Part IV

## THE FORMAL MODEL

CONTENTS

387

# CONTENTS (contd.)

## 1.0 Introduction

This report contains a complete (*) formal model of the concurrency concepts in the programming language Ada [Ada 80]. The report should not be read as a self-contained paper, but rather as a reference document for the introduction part and the technical report, parts II and III.

As described in the project report, this model is part of a total formal definition of the Ada language. This means that the present model should be understood in connection with the Dynamic Semantics in this volume [StPe 80]. Also, the syntactic constructs of the language described by the abstract syntax should satisfy the static context conditions as described in the thesis on static semantics of Ada included in this volume [BuSch80]. However, most of the model presented here could be understood without further knowledge of the dynamic semantics than given in the introduction part.

The meta-language used for the formal model is the so-called META-IV of the "Vienna Development Method" , described in e.g. [BjJo 78]. The meta-language is in principle applicative, and the formal model denotational. Various sequential features of the language (e.g. the imperative style, and the exit mechanism) are described in [StPe 80]. The meta-language has also been extended with concurrency (CSP-,behavior algebra-like) constructs. This aspect is described in the introductory part II, and is further discussed in the technical report. A formal definition of the extension has been given in [FoBj 80].

As there are still a few vague cases which are not defined properly in the manual, it has been necessary to make some assumptions and decisions during the modelling work. In chapter 3, these assumptions and decisions are summarized.

---

(*) The only concept not covered is priorities, esecially the (rather trivial) handling of these during rendezvous has been left out.

## 2.0 Formulas

The following formulas are given in META-IV in the usual mathemathics-like style. However, a few modifications are described together with some general remarks below:

Due to printer limitations the following syntactical changes have been made:

The logical operators are denoted by: ˜ and or

The concatenation operator is denoted by: ^

All functions (->) are implicit partial (≈>), except for is-wf- functions.

The => symbol is a shorthand for -> ( Σ -> Σ ).
i.e. A =>    means A -> ( Σ -> Σ )  and
    A => B means A -> ( Σ -> Σ B ). (*)

In the functions for the monitor process it has turned out to be convenient to let almost all functions be impure (i.e. state-transforming). However, some of the functions merely reads the state and do not modify it. To indicate these functions, their names have been prefixed with find-, or get-, or (in the case of predicates on the state) have been given questioning forms. In the same style, the potential state-changing functions have been given imperative names. This differentiation is for pragmatic reasons only.

---

(*) The ( Σ --> Σ ) should, as described in the technical report, strictly be (C --> C) where the continuation is ( Σ --> Tr). However, for correspondence with the sequential semantics, the state-transformation is retained.

## 2.1  Semantic Domains


### 2.1.1  Communication Domains –

The communication domains describe the structure of the messages  which  are
communicated  among  the  meta-processes.  The domains have been grouped according to the communication path they are used in.  P <--> Q1,Q2,...Qn  indicates the communication between P on one side, and Q1,Q2,..Qn on the other
side.  The communication domains used  between  the  MONITOR  and  the  TASK
processes have been subdivided according to the concurrency concept they are
related to.


### 2.1.1.1  SYSTEM <--> MONITOR, STORAGE, TIMER, and CLOCK-GENERATOR –

STOP             :: ()


### 2.1.1.2  TIMER <--> MONITOR, and CLOCK-GENERATOR –

```
GET-CLOCK        :: ()
TIME-MSG         :: Time
SET-EXPTIME      :: Time
EXPIRATION       :: Time
PULSE            :: ()
```


### 2.1.1.3  MONITOR <--> TASK –


### 2.1.1.3.1  Classes –

```
REQ              = CALL | MSG

CALL             = LEAVE | CREATE-CRID | CREATE-TASK | ACTIVATE |
                   DELAY | ENTRY-CALL | ACCEPT | SELECT |
                   RAISE-FAILURE | ABORT | ENABLE | TERMINATED-REQ |
                   CLOCK-REQ | COUNT-REQ

MSG              = ACTIVATED | FAILED | TERMINATED | ENTER-BLOCK |
                   ACCEPT-FAIL | END-MEETING

REPLY            = START | TASKVAL-MSG | CRID-MSG | END-CALL |
                   START-MEETING | SELECT-EXPIRED | NONE-CALLED |
                   TERMINATE-CMD | FAIL-CMD | RAISE-CMD |
                   CONTINUE | TERMINATED-MSG | CLOCK-MSG |
                   COUNT-MSG
```

## 2.1.1.3.2  Task creation/termination. -

```
START           :: ()
ACTIVATED       :: ()
FAILED          :: (ExcpId|ABORTED)
TERMINATED      :: ()
```

## 2.1.1.3.3  Block entry/leave. -

```
ENTER-BLOCK     :: ActId
LEAVE           :: ActId
```

## 2.1.1.3.4  Task activation. -

```
CREATE-CRID     :: ActId
CRID-MSG        :: CrId
CREATE-TASK     :: TaskFct  ActId   CrId
TASKVAL-MSG     :: TV
ACTIVATE        :: CrId
```

## 2.1.1.3.5  Delay -

```
DELAY           :: Duration
```

## 2.1.1.3.6  Task communication -

```
ENTRY-CALL      :: TV  EV  ParmAssoc  [COND|Timed]
END-CALL        :: CALLED | CLOSED | EXPIRED

ACCEPT          :: EV
SELECT          :: EntryAssoc  [DelayAssoc|COND|TERMINABLE]
START-MEETING   :: [AltId]  ParmAssoc
SELECT-EXPIRED  :: AltId
NONE-CALLED     :: ()
ACCEPT-FAIL     :: ExcpId
END-MEETING     :: ()
```

2.1.1.3.7  Failure, exception and abortion. -

```
RAISE-FAILURE    :: TV
ABORT            :: TV-set
ENABLE           :: ()
TERMINATE-CMD    :: ()
FAIL-CMD         :: ()
RAISE-CMD        :: ExcpId
```

2.1.1.3.8  Auxiliary -

```
CONTINUE         :: ()
TERMINATED-REQ   :: TV
TERMINATED-MSG   :: BOOL
CLOCK-REQ        :: ()
CLOCK-MSG        :: Time
COUNT-REQ        :: EV
COUNT-MSG        :: N
```

2.1.1.4  TASK <--> STORAGE -

```
STGREQ           = CREATE-ACTID | ALLOCATE | FREE-LOCS | ASSIGN |
                   GET-VALUE

CREATE-ACTID     :: ()
ACTID-MSG        :: ActId
ALLOCATE         :: ActId
LOC-MSG          :: LOC
FREE-LOCS        :: ActId
ASSIGN           :: Varloc  VAL
ASSIGNED         :: ()
GET-VALUE        :: VarLoc
VALUE-MSG        :: VAL
```

## 2.1.2 Monitor Domains –

```
CreationTable    =  CrId  --->  (ActId|BEING-TERMINATED)
                         m

BlockTable       =  ActId  --->  TV
                          m

TaskTable        =  TV  --->  TaskInfo
                        m
TaskInfo         :: Dependence  Phase  State  Queues  Partners
                    IntrptReq

Dependence       =  ActId
Phase            =  NonActive | ACTIVE
NonActive        :: CrId
State            =  Initial | Running | Suspended
Queues           =  EV  --->  TV+
                        m
Partners         =  TV*
IntrptReq        =  [FAILREQ|TERMINATED]

Suspended        =  Delayed | EntryCalling | Accepting | Selecting |
                    Activating | Leaving | Aborting
Initial          :: ()
Running          :: ()
Delayed          :: Time
EntryCalling     :: TV  EV  Status
Status           =  InQueue | ENGAGED
InQueue          :: ParmAssoc  [Time]
Accepting        :: EV
Selecting        :: EntryAssoc  [ExpirAssoc|TERMINABLE]
Activating       :: CrId
Leaving          :: ActId
Aborting         :: ()

TV               =  PI
EV               :: EntryId [DiscrVal]
```

2.1.3  Wellformedness of Monitor Domains. -

These functions show the dependencies among the monitor domains. These dependencies are invariants of the monitor, i.e. they must always be satisfied inbetween handling of request.

NOTE

The functions given in this version are incomplete in the sense that they show only the
most fundamental relationships.


is-wf-monitorstate(tt,bt,ct)=
  ((rng ct\{BEING-ACTIVATED} $\subseteq$ dom bt) and
   (rng bt $\subseteq$ dom tt)  and
   ($\forall$ tv $\in$ dom tt) (is-wf-TaskInfo(tv,tt,bt,ct))  )

type: TaskTable  BlockTable  CreationTable -> BOOL

```
is-wf-TaskInfo(tv,tt,bt,ct)=
  (let mk-TaskInfo(actid,ph,state,queues,partners,ireq) = tt(tv) in
  (actid ∈ (dom bt U {SYSTEM}))
  and
    cases ph:
    (mk-NonActive(crid)    -> ((crid ∈ (dom ct U {SYSTEM})) and
                                 ~is-Accepting(state)        and
                                 ~is-Selecting(state)        and
                                 partners = <>                  ),
    ACTIVE                 -> ~is-Initial(state)               )
  and
    cases state:
    (mk-EntryCalling(tv',ev,mk-InQueue( , ))      ->
                ( (tv'∈ dom tt) and
                  (ev ∈ dom(s-Queue(tt(tv'))) and
                   tv∈ elems(s-Queue(tt(tv'))(ev)) ) ),
    mk-EntryCalling(tv', ,ENGAGED)              ->
                ( (tv'∈ dom tt)and(tv∈ elems(s-Partners(tt(tv'))))),
    mk-Accepting(ev)                            ->
                ( ev ~ ∈ dom queues),
    mk-Selecting(eassoc, )                      ->
                ( rng eassoc ∩ dom queues ={}),
    mk-Activating(crid)                         ->
                ( (crid ∈ dom ct) and
                  (∀ tv'∈ dom tt\{tv})
                       s-State(tt(tv'))≠mk-Activating(crid)),
    mk-Leaving(actid)                           ->
                ( (actid ∈ dom bt) and (bt(actid) = tv)) and ... ),
    T                                           ->
                true                                            )
  and
    (∀ ev ∈ dom queues)
       (∀ tv'∈ rng queues(ev))
          s-State(tt(tv'))=mk-EntryCalling(tv,ev,mk-InQueue( , ))
  and
    (∀ tv'∈ elems partners)
       (s-State(tt(tv')) = mk-EntryCalling(tv, ,ENGAGED)
  and
    cases ireq:
    (nil        -> true,
    T           -> ( is-Running(state) or
                     is-Leaving(state) or
                    (is-EntryCalling(state) and
                          s-Status(state) = ENGAGED ) ) )  )

type: TV TaskTable  BlockTable  CreationTable -> BOOL
```

## 2.1.4  Auxiliary Semantic Domains -

```
SelectKind       = COND ¦ TIMED ¦ TERMINABLE ¦ UNCOND

AltAssoc         = AltId ⇉> EvaluatedAlt
EvaluatedAlt     = EAcceptAlt ¦ EDelayAlt ¦ ETermAlt
EAcceptAlt       :: BOOL  EV  StmtList  StmtList
EDelayAlt        :: BOOL  Duration  StmtList
ETermAlt         :: BOOL

EntryAssoc       = AltId ⇉> EV

SelectMode       = [DelayAssoc¦ExpirAssoc¦COND¦TERMINABLE]
DelayAssoc       :: AltId ⇉> Duration
ExpirAssoc       :: AltId ⇉> Time

CallMode         = [Timed¦COND]
Timed            :: Duration

AltId            = TOKEN

Time             = ...
Duration         = ...
```

Note: The relational metaoperators (+,<,.. ) are overloaded to
      handle Time and Duration in a way corresponding to the
      predefined ADA functions.


## 2.1.5  Extracts from the Semantic Domains of the Sequential Semantics. -

```
ENV          = ((Id¦QOUT) ⇉> DEN) U (ACTID ⇉> ActId) U
               (CRID ⇉> CrId) U ...

DEN          = TypeDen ¦ EntryDen ¦ ParmDen ¦ ...
TypeDen      = TaskTypeDen ¦ ...

EntryDen     :: ExtdTypeDescr  init:(ParmId ⇉> VAL)
                order:(ParmId ⇉> N )  fam:[SubtypeDen]
PackageDen   :: CrId
TaskTypeDen  :: Entries [TaskFct]
Entries      = EntryId ⇉> EntryDen
TaskFct      = ( Σ ≈> Σ )
```

## 2.2  Syntactic Domains (for concurrency constructs)

| | | |
|---|---|---|
| Block | :: | DclPart  StmtList  [Excpthdlr] |
| | | |
| TaskTypeDcl | :: | TypeId  Dict  EntryDcl* |
| EntryDcl | :: | EntryId  [DiscrRange]  FormalPart |
| | | |
| TaskTypeBody | :: | TypeId  DclPart  [StmtList]  [Excpthdlr] |
| | | |
| EntryCall | :: | Name  EntryName  (ParmId --> Expr) |
| EntryName | :: | EntryId  [Expr] |
| | | |
| Accept | :: | EntryName  StmtList |
| | | |
| Delay | :: | Expr |
| | | |
| Select | = | SelectiveWait \| |
| | | CondEntryCall \| |
| | | TimedEntryCall |
| | | |
| SelectiveWait | :: | ([Expr]  SelectAlt)-set  [StmtList] |
| | | |
| SelectAlt | = | AcceptAlt \| DelayAlt \| TerminateAlt |
| AcceptAlt | :: | Accept  StmtList |
| DelayAlt. | :: | Delay  StmtList |
| TerminateAlt | :: | () |
| | | |
| CondEntryCall | :: | EntryCall  StmtList  StmtList |
| | | |
| TimedEntryCall | :: | EntryCall  StmtList  DelayAlt |
| | | |
| Abort | :: | Name+ |

We here consider a program to consist of a block:

| | | |
|---|---|---|
| Prog | = | Block |

2.3   The meta-program

```
program (prog,starttime,unit)=
    SYSTEM : processor,
    CLOCK : processor,
    TIMER :    processor,
    MONITOR : processor,
    STORAGE : processor,
    TASK : processor;
    initialize SYSTEM(prog,starttime,unit)
end
```

Note: The various processors are defined in the sections below.


2.4   The SYSTEM process

```
processor SYSTEM(prog,starttime,unit)=
   (start STORAGE();
    start TIMER(starttime,unit);
    start CLOCK();
    start MONITOR(prog);
   (input mk-STOP() from MONITOR  ->
                 (output mk-STOP() to STORAGE ;
                  output mk-STOP() to TIMER ;
                  output mk-STOP() to CLOCK )))
```

type: Prog  Time  Duration =>

## 2.5  The TIMER and CLOCK processes

```
processor TIMER(starttime,unit)=
  (dcl clock:=starttime type Time,
       times:={}          type Time-set;
  (trap exit with stop in
   cycle{(def acttimes : c times;
          def actclock : c clock;
          let expird={t|t ∈ acttimes  and  t<=actclock} in
          (if expird ≠ {}
          output mk-EXPIRATION(actclock) to MONITOR        ->
                          times := acttimes \ expird,
          input mk-PULSE() from CLOCK              ->
                          clock := actclock+unit,
          input mk-SET-EXPTIME(time) from MONITOR        ->
                          times := acttimes U {time},
          input mk-GET-CLOCK() from MONITOR            ->
                          output mk-TIME-MSG(actclock) to MONITOR,
          input mk-STOP() from SYSTEM              ->
                          exit                                   ))}))

type: Time  Duration =>



processor CLOCK()=
  (trap exit with stop in
   cycle{(output mk-PULSE() to TIMER    -> I,
          input mk-STOP() from SYSTEM  -> exit)})

type: () =>
```

## 2.6  The MONITOR process

### 2.6.1  Processor and main handle-functions. –

```
processor MONITOR(prog)=
  (dcl CT := [] type CreationTable,
       BT := [] type BlockTable,
       TT := [] type TaskTable;
   startup-main(prog);
   (trap exit with (output mk-STOP() to SYSTEM;
                    stop                          ) in
    cycle{ (input req from TASK set tv              ->
                         handle-req(tv,req),
            input mk-EXPIRATION(time) from TIMER  ->
                         handle-expiration(tv,time)      )}))

type: Prog =>


startup-main(prog)=
  (let mk-Block(dclpart,stmtl,excpthdlr) = prog in
   let taskfct = create-TaskFct(dcllist,stmtl,excpthdlr)([]) in
   def tv : start TASK(taskfct );
   TT := [tv ->initial-taskinfo(SYSTEM,SYSTEM)];
   activate-next(SYSTEM)                            )

type: Prog =>


handle-req(tv,req)=
  cases req:
  (mk-LEAVE(actid)  ->
       leave(tv,actid),
   T                ->
       (is-MSG(req)      ->
                  handle-msg(tv,req),
        is-CALL(req)    ->
                  cases get-IntrptReq(tv)
                  (FAILREQ      -> (resume(tv,mk-FAIL-CMD());
                                    TT.(tv).IntrptReq := nil ),
                   TERMINATED -> resume(tv,mk-TERMINATE-CMD()),
                   nil          -> handle-call(tv,req)          )))

type: TV  REQ =>
```

```
handle-msg(tv,msg)=
   cases msg:
   (mk-ACTIVATED()          -> activation-ended(tv),
    mk-FAILED(excp)         -> activation-failed(tv,excp),
    mk-TERMINATED()         -> handle-termination(tv),
    mk-ENTER-BLOCK(actid)   -> BT := c BT U [actid->tv],
    mk-ACCEPT-FAIL(excp)    -> resume-partner(tv,mk-RAISE-CMD(excp)),
    mk-END-MEETING()        -> resume-partner(tv,mk-END-CALL(CALLED)))

type: TV  MSG =>



handle-call(tv,call)=
   cases call:
   (mk-CREATE-CRID(actid)                  ->
                (def crid s.t. crid ~ e dom c CT;
                 CT := (c CT) + [crid->actid];
                 resume(tv,mk-CRID-MSG(crid))            ),
    mk-CREATE-TASK(taskfct,actid,crid)   ->
                handle-creation(tv,taskfct,actid,crid),
    mk-ACTIVATE(crid)                  ->
                (TT.(tv).State := mk-Activating(crid);
                 CT := (c CT) + [crid->BEING-ACTIVATED];
                 activate-next(crid)                 ),
    mk-DELAY(dur)                     ->
                handle-delay(tv,dur),
    mk-ENTRY-CALL(tv',ev,parmassoc,cmode) ->
                handle-entry-call(tv,tv',ev,parmassoc,cmode),
    mk-ACCEPT(ev)                     ->
                handle-accept(tv,ev),
    mk-SELECT(eassoc,smode)              ->
                handle-select(tv,eassoc,smode),
    mk-RAISE-FAILURE(tv')                 ->
                handle-failure(tv,tv'),
    mk-ABORT(tvs)                       ->
                handle-abort(tv,tvs),
    mk-ENABLE()                        ->
                resume(tv,mk-CONTINUE()),
    mk-TERMINATED(tv')                  ->
                (def term : terminated(tv');
                 resume(tv,mk-TERMINATED-MSG(term)),
    mk-CLOCK-REQ()                      ->
                (def time : read-clock();
                 resume(tv,mk-CLOCK-MSG(time)),
    mk-COUNT-REQ(ev)                   ->
                (def n : find-count(tv,ev);
                 resume(tv,mk-COUNT-MSG(n) )                  )

type: TV  CALL =>
```

2.6.2  Task creation and activation. –
(See chapter 3: cases 1, 2, and 3.)

```
handle-creation(tv,taskfct,actid,crid)=
  (def newtv : start TASK(taskfct);
   TT := (c TT) U [newtv->initial-taskinfo(actid,crid)];
   resume(tv,mk-TASKVAL-MSG(newtv))                    )

type: TV  TaskFct  ActId  CrId =>
```

```
initial-taskinfo(actid,crid)=
  (let ph = mk-NonActive(crid) in
   mk-TaskInfo(actid,ph,mk-Initial(),[],<>,nil)  )

type: ActId  CrId -> TaskInfo
```

```
activation-ended(tv)=
  (def mk-NonActive(crid) : get-Phase(tv);
   TT.(tv).Phase := ACTIVE;
   activate-next(crid)                        )

type: TV =>
```

```
activate-next(crid)=
  (def tvs : find-remaining(crid);
   if tvs = {}
      then (CT := (c CT) \ {crid};
            resume-activator(crid,mk-CONTINUE()) )
      else (let tv є tvs in
            resume(tv,mk-START())          )     )

type: (CrId|SYSTEM) =>
```

```
find-remaining(crid)=
  return({tv | tv є c TT  and
               ~ terminated(tv)  and
               get-Phase(tv)=mk-NonActive(crid) })

type: CrId => TV-set
```

```
activation-failed(tv,excp)=
  (def mk-NonActive(crid) : get-Phase(tv);
   if excp = ABORTED
      then activate-next(crid)
      else (mark-terminated(tv);
            terminate-remaining(crid);
            resume-activator(crid,mk-RAISE-CMD(excp)) )

type: TV  (ExcpId¦ABORTED) =>



resume-activator(crid,rply)=
  (crid = SYSTEM                          ->
                  I,
   (∃ tv ∈ dom c TT) activating(tv,crid)  ->
                  (def tv ∈ dom c TT s.t. activating(tv,crid);
                   resume(tv,rply)                          ),
   T                                      ->
                  I                                              )

type: (CrId¦SYSTEM)  REPLY =>



activating(tv,crid)=
   return( ~terminated(tv) and get-State(tv)=mk-Activating(crid))

type: TV  CrId => BOOL
```

2.6.3 Task termination and block exit -
(See chapter 3: case 4.)

```
handle-termination(tv)=
  (def actid : get-Dependence(tv);
   if ~ terminated(tv) then clear-queues(tv) else I;
   TT := (c TT) \ {tv};
   if actid = SYSTEM
      then exit
      else try-release(actid)   ))

type: TV =>
```

```
try-release(actid)=
  (def parent : (c BT)(actid);
   cases get-State(parent):
   (mk-Leaving(actid)              ->
        (def bdeps : find-block-dependent(actid);
        (bdeps = {}                     ->
               (BT := (c BT) \ {actid};
                resume(parent,mk-CONTINUE())),
          (∀tv ∈ bdeps) terminable(tv)      ->
               for all tv ∈ bdeps do
                   for all tv' ∈ find-termination-tree(tv) do
                       terminate(tv')
        T                               ->
                I                                      )),
    mk-Selecting( ,TERMINABLE)     ->
        try-termination(parent)                        ))

type: ActId =>
```

```
try-termination(tv)=
  (def tdeps : find-task-dependent(tv);
   if (∀tv' ∈ tdeps) terminable(tv')
      then (def actid' : get-Dependence(tv);
            if actid' = SYSTEM
               then for all tv' ∈ find-termination-tree(tv) do
                       terminate(tv')
               else try-release(actid')             )
      else I                                         )

type: TV =>
```

```
terminable(tv)=
  return( get-State(tv) = mk-Selecting( ,TERMINABLE)
          (∀tv' ∈ find-task-dependent(tv)) terminable(tv')  )

type: TV => BOOL
```

```
find-termination-tree(tv)=
  (def deps : find-task-dependent(tv);
   def ts : {find-termination-tree(tv') | tv'∈ deps};
   return( {tv} U union ts )                              )

type: TV => TV-set
pre:  terminable(tv)



leave(tv,actid)=
  (clear-unactivated-crids(actid);
   TT.(tv).State := Leaving(actid);
   try-release(actid)        )

type: TV  ActId =>



clear-unactivated-crids(actid)=
  (def uacrids : {crid|crid∈ dom(c CT) and (c CT)(crid)=actid};
   for all crid∈ uacrids do
        terminate-remaining(crid)                              )

type: ActId =>



find-block-dependent(actid)=
   return({tv | tv∈ dom c TT  get-Dependence(tv)=actid})

type: ActId => TV-set



find-task-dependent(tv)=
   return({tv | ( ∃actid  dom (c BT))
                    ((c BT)(actid) = tv  and
                     tv'∈ find-block-dependent(actid) })

type: TV => TV-set
```

2.6.4 Delays and expiration. –
(See chapter 3: case 5.)


```
handle-delay(tv,dur)=
  (def time : read-clock();
  (let time'= time+dur in
   TT.(tv).State := mk-Delayed(time');
   setup-expiration-time(time')           ))

type: TV  Duration =>


read-clock()=
  (output mk-GET-CLOCK() to TIMER;
   input mk-CLOCK-MSG(time) form TIMER  -> return(time))

type: () => Time


setup-expiration-time(time)=
  (output mk-SET-EXPTIME(time) to TIMER)

type: Time =>


handle-expiration(time)=
  (def exprd : find-expired(time);
   for all tv ∈ exprd do
     cases get-State(tv):
     (mk-Delayed()                         ->
               resume(tv,mk-CONTINUE()),
      mk-EntryCalling( ,, )                ->
               (queue-remove(tv);
                resume(tv,mk-END-CALL(EXPIRED))),
      mk-Selecting( ,mk-ExpirAssoc(expm)) ->
               (def altid ∈ dom expm s.t. expm(altid)<=time;
                resume(tv,mk-SELECT-EXPIRED(altid))             ))

type: Time =>
```

```
find-expired(time)=
  return({tv | tv ∈ dom(c TT)    and
                ~terminated(tv)    and
                cases get-State(tv):
                (mk-Delay(time')                         ->
                        time' <= time,
                 mk-EntryCalling( ,,mk-InQueue( ,time)   ->
                        time'≠nil and time' <= time,
                 mk-Selecting( ,mk-ExpirAssoc(expm))      ->
                        (∃ altid ∈ dom expm) (expm(altid)<=time),
                 T                                        ->
                        false                                   )})

type: Time => TV-set
```

2.6.5  Task communication. -


2.6.5.1  Entry call. -


```
handle-entry-call(caller,tv,ev,parmassoc,cmode)=
  (terminated(tv)            ->
               resume(caller,mk-RAISE-CMD(TASKING-ERROR)),
   open(tv,ev)               ->
               (def altid : find-an-altid(tv,ev);
                TT.(caller).State:=mk-EntryCalling(tv,ev,ENGAGED);
                begin-rendezvous(caller,tv,altid,parmassoc)    ),
   cmode = COND              ->
               resume(caller,mk-END-CALL(CLOSED)),
   T.                        ->
               (def mcmode : modif-cmode(cmode);
                let inq = mk-InQueue(parmassoc,mcmode) in
                TT.(caller).State := mk-EntryCalling(tv,ev,inq);
                enter-queue(caller,tv,ev)                )   )

type: TV  TV  EV  ParmAssoc  CallMode =>
```


```
modif-cmode(cmode)=
  cases cmode:
  (mk-Timed(dur)          -> (def time : read-clock();
                              let time'= time+dur in
                              setup-expiration-time(time');
                              return(time')              ),
   nil                    -> return(nil)                  )

type: [Timed] => [Time]
```


```
enter-queue(caller,tv,ev)=
  (def oldqueqes : get-Queues(tv);
   let newqueues = if ev ∈ dom oldqueues
                   then (let queue = oldqueues(ev) in
                         let queue'= queue^<caller> in
                         oldqueues + [ev->queue']    )
                   else oldqueues U [ev-><caller>]        in
   TT.(tv).Queues := newqueqes                            )

type: TV  TV  EV =>
```

```
find-an-altid(tv,ev)=
   cases get-State(tv):
   (mk-Accepting( )          ->
                 return(nil),
    mk-Selecting(eassoc, ) ->
                 (let altid ∈ dom eassoc be s.t. eassoc(altid)=ev in
                  return(altid)                              ) )

type: TV  EV => [AltId]
pre: open(tv,ev)



open(tv,ev)=
   cases get-State(tv):
   (mk-Accepting(ev)                    -> return(true),
    mk-Selecting(eassoc, )              -> return(ev  rng eassoc),
    T                                   -> return(false)                )

type: TV  EV => BOOL
```

## 2.6.5.2  Accept and Select. -

```
handle-accept(tv,ev)=
   if entry-called(tv,ev)
      then begin-accept(tv,ev,nil)
      else TT.(tv).State := mk-Accepting(ev)

type: TV  EV =>



handle-select(tv,eassoc,smode)=
   ((∃ ev ∈ rng eassoc) entry-called(tv,ev)          ->
                 (def ev ∈ rng eassoc s.t. entry-called(tv,ev);
                  let altid ∈ dom eassoc be s.t. eassoc(altid)=ev;
                  begin-accept(tv,ev,altid)                          ),
    smode = COND                                      ->
                 resume(tv,mk-NONE-WAITING()),
    T                                                 ->
                 (def smode' : modif-smode(smode);
                  TT.(tv).State := mk-Selecting(eassoc,smode');
                  if cmode' = TERMINABLE
                     then try-termination(tv)
                     else I                                           )

type: TV  EntryAssoc  SelectMode =>
```

```
entry-called(tv,ev)=
  (def queues : get-Queues(tv);
   return( ev ∈ dom queues )    )

type: TV  EV => BOOL


begin-accept(tv,ev,altid)=
  (def caller : remove-first(tv,ev);
   def mk-InQueue(parmassoc, ) : c(TT.(caller).State.Status);
   TT.(caller).State.Status := ENGAGED;
   begin-rendezvous(caller,tv,altid,parmassoc)          )

type: TV  EV  [AltId] =>


remove-first(tv,ev)=
  (def first : hd(get-Queues(tv)(ev));
   queue-remove(first);
   return(first)                )

type: TV  EV => TV
pre: entry-called(tv,ev)


queue-remove(caller)=
  (def mk-EntryCalling(tv,ev,mk-InQueue( , )) : get-State(caller);
   def queues : get-Queues(tv);
   let queue = queues(ev) in
   let i be s.t. queues[i]=caller in
   let queue' = <queue[j]|1<=j<=i-1>^<queue[j]|i+1<=j<=ln queue> in
   let newqueues = (queue'=<>  -> queues \ {ev},
                    T          -> queues + [ev->queue']) in
   TT.(tv).Queues := newqueues                           )

type: TV  EV =>
pre: is-EntryCalling(get-State(tv))


modif-smode(smode)=
   cases smode:
  (mk-DelayAssoc(delm)   ->
       (def time : read-clock();
        let expm=[altid->(time+delm(altid )|altid∈dom delm] in
        for all time' rng expm do
             setup-expiration-time(time');
        return(mk-ExpirAssoc(expm )                         ),
   T                     ->
       return(smode)                                        )

type: SelectMode => SelectMode
```

2.6.5.3  Common rendezvous functions. -

```
begin-rendezvous(caller,tv,altid,parmassoc)=
  (TT.(tv).Partners := <caller>^get-Partners(tv);
   resume(tv,mk-START-MEETING(altid,parmassoc)   )

type: TV   TV  [ActId]  ParmAssoc =>


resume-partner(tv,rply)=
  (def partners : get-Partners(tv);
   let caller = hd partners in
   TT.(tv).Partners := tl partners;
   cases get-IntrptReq(caller):
   (FAILREQ        -> (resume(caller,mk-FAIL-CMD());
                         TT.(caller).IntrptReq := nil    ),
    TERMINATED     -> resume(caller,mk-TERMINATE-CMD()),
    T              -> resume(caller,rply)                 ))

type: TV   REPLY =>


find-count(tv,ev)=
  return( (~entry-called(tv,ev)    -> 0,
                T                   -> ln (get-Queues(tv)(ev)) ))

type: TV   EV => N
```

2.6.6 Failure, abortion and virtual termination. -
(See chapter 3: case 1, 2, and 3.)


```
handle-failure(tv,tv')=
  (tv = tv'              ->
        resume(tv,mk-FAIL-CMD()),
   terminated(tv')  ->
        resume(tv,mk-CONTINUE()),
   T                  ->
        (if uninteruptable(tv')
            then mark-failed(tv')
            else  cases get-State(tv'):
                  (mk-Initial()                              ->
                                     terminate(tv'),
                   mk-EntryCalling( ,,mk-InQueue( , ))    ->
                                     (queue-remove(tv');
                                      resume(tv',mk-FAIL-CMD()) ),
                        T                                   ->
                                     resume(tv',mk-FAIL-CMD())    );
         resume(tv,mk-CONTINUE())                                )

type: TV  TV =>
```


```
mark-failed(tv)=
   TT.(tv).IntrptReq := FAILREQ

type: TV =>
```


```
handle-abort(tv,tvs)=
  (def closure : union{find-abortion-tree(tv')|tv'∈ tvs};
   TT.(tv).State := mk-Aborting();
   for all tv'  closure do terminate(tv');
   if terminated(tv)
      then I
      else resume(tv,mk-CONTINUE())                   ))

type: TV  TV-set =>
```


```
find-abortion-tree(tv)=
   if terminated(tv)
      then return({})
      else (def deps : find-task-dependent(tv);
            def ts : {find-abortion-tree(tv') | tv'∈ deps};
            return( {tv} U union(ts) )                     )

type: TV => TV-set
```

```
terminate(tv)=
  (mark-terminated(tv);
   if uninterruptable(tv)
      then I
      else cases get-State(tv):
            (mk-EntryCalling( ,,mk-InQueue( , )) ->
                              (queue-remove(tv);
                               resume(tv,mk-TERMINATE-CMD(()) ),
                      T                        ->
                               resume(tv,mk-TERMINATE-CMD(())  ) ;
   clear-queues(tv);
   clear-partners(tv)                                              )

type: TV =>



mark-terminated(tv)=
   TT.(tv).IntrptReq := TERMINATED

type: TV =>



terminated(tv)=
   return( tv ~∈ dom(c TT) or get-IntrptReq(tv) = TERMINATED )

type: TV => BOOL



uninteruptable(tv)=
   cases get-State(tv):
   (mk-Running()                      -> return(true),
    mk-Leaving( )                     -> return(true),
    mk-EntryCalling( ,,ENGAGED)       -> return(true),
    T                                 -> return(false)   )

type: TV => BOOL



clear-queues(tv)=
  (def tvs : union{elems q | q∈ rng(get-Queues(tv))};
   for all tv'∈ tvs do
        (queue-remove(tv');
         resume(tv',mk-RAISE-CMD(TASKING-ERROR)) )          )

type: TV =>



clear-partners(tv)=
   while get-Partners(tv) ≠ <> do
              resume-partner(tv,mk-RAISE-CMD(TASKING-ERROR))

type: TV =>
```

```
terminate-remaining(crid)=
  (for all tv ∈ find-remaining(crid) do
          terminate(tv)                          ;
    CT : ⊆ CT \ {crid}                           )

type: CiId =>
```

2.6.7  Auxiliary monitor functions. -


```
resume(tv,rply)=
  (TT.(tv).State := mk-Running();
   output rply to tv               )
```

type: TV  REPLY =>


SCHEMA:

```
get-X(tv)=
   return(c(TT.(tv).X))
```

type: TV => X

X one of Dependence, Phase, State, Queues, Partners and IntrptReq.

2.7  The STORAGE process

```
processor STORAGE()=
  (dcl stg := [] type STG,
       actv := [] type ACTV;
  (trap exit with stop in
   cycle{ (input  req from TASK set tv  -> handle-stgreq(tv,req),
           input mk-STOP() from SYSTEM -> exit                  )})

type: () =>


handle-stgreq(tv,req)=
  (trap exit(mk-Excp(eid)) with
                (output mk-EXCP-MSG() to tv) in
   cases req:
  (mk-CREATE-ACTID()        ->
                (def actid : stg-create-ActId();
                 output mk-ACTID-MSG(actid) to tv),
    mk-ALLOCATE(actid)     ->
                (def loc : stg-allocate(actid);
                 output mk-LOC-MSG(loc) to tv ),
    mk-FREE-LOCS(actid)    ->
                stg-free-locations(actid),
    mk-ASSIGN(varloc,val) ->
                (stg-assign(varloc,val);
                 output mk-ASSIGNED() to tv ),
    mk-GET-VALUE(varloc)   ->
                (def val : stg-value-of(varloc);
                 output mk-VALUE-MSG(val) to tv )    ))

type: TV  STGREQ =>
```

2.8  The TASK process

```
processor TASK(taskfct)=
    taskfct()

type: TaskFct =>
```

2.9  Interpretation functions for concurrency constructs

The formulas should be understood in connection with the interpretation formulas of the sequential semantics [StPe80]. The syntactic domains must be
wellformed according to the static semantics given in [BuSch80].

The enable function may be inserted in the interpretation functions at the
points of explicit and implicit meta-";"s. The insertion is implementation
defined. The function must not, however, not be inserted at the points of
encircled ";"s. The details are discussed in part III of this thesis [Lo
80b] and in [StPe 80] (in this volume).

2.9.1  Task creation, activation and termination in blocks. -

```
int-Block(mk-Block(mk-DclPart(dict,dcllist),stmtl,excpthdlr)) env =
  (def actid : get-new-ActId() (;)
    let env'=env+[ACTID->actid]+get-type-dens(dict)(actid) in
    always block-epilogue(actid) in
      (def crid : create-CrId(actid);
      let env''=env'+[CRID->crid] in
      def env''' : extend-env(dect,dcllist)(env'') env''' ;
      trap exit(mk-Excp(eid)) with
                    handle(mk-Excp(eid),excpthdlr) env'''  in
        (activate-tasks(crid);
          int-StmtList(stmtl) env''')                      )   )

type: Block -> (ENV -> (   ->   ))
```

```
get-new-ActId()=
  (def : create-ActId() (;)
    inform-monitor(mk-BLOCK-ENTER(actid) (;)
    return(actid)                         )

type: () -> ActId
```

```
block-epilouge(actid)=
  (await-termination(actid) (;)
   free-locations(actid)        )

type: ActId =>



activate-tasks(crid)=
   pass-monitor(mk-ACTIVATE(crid))

type: CrId =>



await-termination(actid)=
   pass-monitor(mk-LEAVE(actid))

type: Actid =>



elab-TaskTypeBody(mk-TaskTypeBody(tid,dclpart,stmtl,excpthdlr)) env =
   (let mk-TaskTypeDen(entries,nil) = env(tid) in
    let env' = env+entries in
    let taskfct = create-TaskFct(dclpart,statl,excpthdlr) env' in
    return(env+[tid->mk-TaskTypeDen(entries,taskfct) ]            )

type: TaskTypeBody -> (ENV => ENV)



create-TaskFct(mk-DclPart(dict,dcllist),stmtl,excpthdlr) env =
   (trap all exits with (inform-monitor(mk-TERMINATED()) (;)
                          stop                           ) in
    await-activation();
   (def actid : get-new-ActId() (;)
    let env' = env+[ACTID->actid]+get-type-dens(dict)(actid) in
    always block-epilouge(actid) in
       (def crid : create-CrId(actid) (;)
        let env'' = env'+[CRID->crid] in
        def env''' = task-extend-env(dict,dcllist) env''  (;)
        (trap exit(mk-Excp(eid)) with
               handle(mk-Excp(eid),excpthdlr) in
         activate-tasks(crid);
         int-StmtList(stmtl) env'''                )        )        )

type: DclPart  StmtList  Excpthdlr -> (ENV -> ( Σ -> Σ ))
```

```
task-extend-env(dict,dcllist) env =
  (trap exit(extp) with
       (cases extp:
       (mk-Excp(eid)      -> inform-monitor(mk-FAILED(eid)),
        mk-Terminate()   -> inform-monitor(mk-FAILED(ABORTED)));
        exit(extp)                                                ) in
    (def env' : extend-env(dict,dcllist) (env) env' ;
     inform-monitor(mk-ACTIVATED()) (;)
     return(env')                                        )            )


type: Dict  DclList -> (ENV => ENV)



create-task(typeid) env =
  (let mk-TaskTypeDen( ,taskfct) = env(typeid),
       req = mk-CREATE-TASK(taskfct,env(ACTID),env(CRID)) in
    def mk-TASKVAL-MSG(tv) : monitor-call(req);
    return(tv)                                                 )

type: TypeId -> (ENV => TV)
```

2.9.2  Task creation, and activation in allocators -

```
eval-Allocator(mk-Allocator(objtid,opedi))(accesstid) env =
  (let actid = s-ActId(env(accesstid)) in
   def crid : create-CrId(actid);
   let env' = env+[ACTID->actid]+[CRID->crid],
       subden = cases env(objtid):
                  (mk-SubtypeDen( , )  -> env(objtid),
                   T                   -> mk-SubtypeDen(tid,nil)) in
   def val : (is-Expr(opedi)    ->
                        (def val' : eval-Expr(opedi) env' ;
                         check-subtype(val',subden) env';
                         return(val')                        ),
              opedi=nil          ->
                        get-init-VAL(subden)(CREATE) env',
              T                  ->
                        (let subdef = mk-SubtypeDef(objtid,opedi) in
                         def subtpden:elab-SubtypeDef(subdef) env';
                         get-init-VAL(subtpden)(CREATE) env'   ));
   def loc : allocate(actid);
   assign(mk-Subloc(loc,<>,DYN),val);
   activate-tasks(crid);
   return(mk-AccessVal(loc))                                       )

type: Allocator -> (TypeId -> (ENV => AccessVal))
```

2.9.3  Entry calls -

```
int-EntryCall(ec) env=
  (def called : call-entry-with-mode(ec,nil);
   I                                           )

type: EntryCAll -> (ENV => )
```

```
int-CondEntryCall(mk-CondEntryCall(ec,stmtl,estmtl)) env =
  (def callresult : call-entry-with-mode(ec,COND) env ;
   cases callresult:
   (CALLED        -> int-StmtList(stmtl) env,
    CLOSED        -> int-StmtList(estmtl) env )            )

type: CondEntryCall -> (ENV => )
```

```
int-TimedEntryCall(mk-TimedEntryCall(ec,stmtl,delayalt)) env =
   (let mk-DelayAlt(delay,dstmtl) = delayalt in
    def callresult : call-entry-with-mode(ec,delay) env ;
    cases callresult:
    (CALLED     -> int-StmtList(stmtl) env,
     EXPIRED    -> int-StmtList(dstmtl) env )               )

type: TimedEntryCall -> (ENV => )



call-entry-with-mode(mk-EntryCall(name,ename,parmexprs),cmode) env =
   (def mk-(tv,ev,eden) : eval-entry(name,ename) env ;
    let mk-EntryDen(extpdescr,parminit, , ) = eden in
    def actid : create-ActId() (;)
    always free-locations(actid) in
      (def parmlocassoc :
                  eval-parmassoc(extpdescr,parminit,parmexprs) env ;
       def ecmode : evaluate-cmode(cmode) env;
       let copyenv = extract-copyenv(parmlocassoc),
           parmassoc = extract-parmassoc(parmlocassoc) in
       trap exit(extp) with
                  (p-call-epilouge(extpdescr,parmassoc);
                   exit(extp)                     ) in
         (let req = mk-ENTRY-CALL(tv,ev,parmassoc,ecmode) in
          def mk-END-CALL(callresult) : monitor-call(req);
          restore-params(parmassoc,copyenv);
          p-call-epilouge(extpdescr,parmassoc);
          return(callresult)                         )    )

type: EntryCall  CallMode -> (ENV == (CALLED|CLOSED|EXPIRED))



eval-entry(name,ename) env =
   (def mk-(varloc,mk-SubtypeDen(tpid, ), ) : eval-Name(name) env ;
    let mk-TaskTypeDen(entries, ) = env(tpid) in
    def tv : value-of(varloc);
    def mk-(ev,eden) : eval-EntryName(ename)(env+entries);
    return(mk-(tv,ev,eden))                          )

type: Name  EntryName -> (ENV => (TV  EV  EntryDen))



eval-EntryName(mk-EntryName(eid,expr)) env =
   (let eden = env(eid) in
    let mk-EntryDen( , , ,subtypeden) = eden in
    if subtypeden = nil
       then  return(mk-(mk-EV(eid,nil),eden))
       else (def discrval : eval-Expr(expr) env ;
             check-subtype(discrval,subtypeden) env ;
             return(mk-(mk-EV(eid,discrval),eden))   )  )

type: EntryName -> (ENV => (EV  EntryDen))
```

```
eval-callmode(cmode) env =
  cases cmode:
  (mk-Delay(expr)           -> (def dur : eval-Expr(expr) env ;
                                 return(mk-Timed(dur))          ),
   T                        ->  return(cmode)                          )

type: CallMode -> (ENV => CallMode)


call-entry(tv,ev,parmassoc)=
  (let req = mk-ENTRY-CALL(tv,ev,parmassoc,nil) in
   def mk-END-CALL(called) : monitor-call(req);
   I                                               )

type: TV  EV  ParmAssoc =>
```

2.9.4  Accept and Select statements -


```
int-Accept(mk-Accept(ename,stmtl)) env =
  (def mk-(ev, ) : eval-EntryName(ename) env ;
   let req = mk-ACCEPT(ev) in
   def mk-START-MEETING( ,parmassoc) : monitor-call(req) ⊙
   int-acceptbody(stmtl,parmassoc) env                      )

type: Accept -> (ENV => )
```


```
int-acceptbody(stmtl,parmassoc) env =
  (trap exit(mk-Excp(eid) with
        (let eid' = (eid=FAILURE->TASKING-ERROR, T->eid) in
         inform-monitor(mk-ACCEPT-FAIL(eid'));
           exit(mk-Excp(eid))                              ) in
   (let env' = env+parmassoc in
   (trap exit(mk-Ret()) with I in
      int-StmtList(stmtl) env'  );
    inform-monitor(mk-END-MEETING())  )                       )

type: StmtList  ParmAssoc -> (ENV => )
```


```
int-Select(select) env =
   cases select:
   (mk-SelectiveWait( , )        -> int-SelectiveWait(select) env ,
    mk-CondEntryCall( , , )       -> int-CondEntryCall(select) env ,
    mk-TimedEntryCall( , )        -> int-TimedEntryCAll(select) env )

type: Select -> (ENV => )
```

```
int-SelectiveWait(selectwait) env =
  (let kind : find-SelectKind(selectwait) in
   let mk-SelectiveWait(galts,estmtl) = selectwait in
   def altassoc : eval-guarded-alts(galts) env ;
   if none-open(altassoc)  and  estmtl=nil
      then  raise(SELECT-ERROR)
      else (let entryassoc = extract-open-entries(altassoc) in
            let smode = find-smode(kind,altassoc) in
            let req = mk-SELECT(entryassoc,smode)            in
            def rply : monitor-call(req) (;)
            cases rply:
            (mk-START-MEETING(altid),parmassoc)   ->
                (let mk-EAcceptAlt( ,,astmtl,stmtl)=altassoc(altid) in
                 int-acceptbody(astmtl,parmassoc) env ;
                 int-StmtList(stmtl) env                       ),
            mk-SELECT-EXPIRED(altid)              ->
                (let mk-EDelayAlt( , ,stmtl) = altassoc(altid) in
                 int-StmtList(stmtl) env                        ),
            mk-NONE-CALLED()                     ->
                int-StmtList(estmtl) env,                   )))

type: SelectiveWait -> (ENV => )
```

2.9.4.1  Auxiliary functions used for the selective wait. -

```
find-SelectKind(mk-SelectiveWait(galts,estmtl))=
  (estmtl ≠ nil                                  -> COND,
   (∃ mk-( ,alt)∈ galts) is-DelayAlt(alt)        -> TIMED,
   (∃ mk-( ,alt)∈ galts) is-TerminateAlt(alt)    -> TERMINABLE,
   T                                             -> UNCOND   )

type: SelectiveWait -> SelectKind
```

```
eval-guarded-alts(galts) env =
  if galts={}
     then return([])
     else (let galt ∈ galts in
           def ealt : eval-guarded-alt(galt) env ;
           def altassoc' : eval-guarded-altlist(galts\{galt}) env ;
           let altid∈ AltId be s.t. altid ~∈dom altassoc' in
           return(altassoc'+[altid->ealt])            )

type: (Expr SelectAlt)-set -> (ENV => AltAssoc)
```

```
eval-guarded-alt(galt) env =
  (def cond : (expr=nil  -> true,
                T        -> is-true(eval-Expr(expr) env ) );
   cases alt:
  (mk-AcceptAlt(mk-Accept(ename,astmtl),stmtl)  ->
       (def mk-(ev, ) : eval-EntryName(ename) env ;
        return(mk-EAcceptAlt(cond,ev,astmtl,stmtl)) ),
   mk-DelayAlt(expr,stmtl)                        ->
       (def dur : eval-Expr(expr) env ;
        return(mk-EDelayAlt(cond,dur,stmtl)),
   mk-TerminateAlt()                              ->
       return(mk-ETermAlt(cond)                        )   )

type: ([Expr] SelectAlt) -> (ENV => EvaluatedAlt)



none-open(altassoc)=
  (∀ ealtεrng altassoc) (~s-BOOL(ealt))

type: AltAssoc -> BOOL



extract-open-entries(altassoc)=
  [altid->s-EV(altassoc(altid))|altid ε dom altassoc    and
                               (let ealt = altassoc(altid) in
                                is-EAcceptAlt(ealt)    and
                                s-BOOL(ealt))                  ]

type: AltAssoc -> EntryAssoc



find-smode(kind,altassoc)=
  cases king:
  (COND        -> COND,
   TIMED       -> mk-DelayAssoc(extract-open-delays(altassoc)),
   TERMINABLE  -> if terminate-open(altassoc)
                     then TERMINABLE
                     else nil,
   UNCOND      -> nil                                     )

type: SelectKind  AltAssoc -> SelectMode



extract-open-delays(altassoc)=
  [altid->s-Duration(altassoc(altid))|altid ε dom altassoc  and
                               (let ealt=altassoc(altid)in
                                is-EDelayAlt(ealt)   and
                                s-BOOL(ealt)               )]

type: AltAssoc -> (AltId -> Duration)
```

2.9.5  Delay -

```
int-Delay(mk-Delay(expr)) env =
  (def dur : eval-Expr(expr) env ;
   if dur <= 0
      then I
      else pass-monitor(mk-DELAY(dur))  )

type: Delay -> (ENV => )
```

2.9.6  Failure and abortion -
(See chapter 3: case 6.)

```
int-Abort(mk-Abort(namel)) env =
  (def tvs : eval-abortlist(namel) env ;
   pass-monitor(mk-ABORT(tvs))            )

type: Abort -> (ENV => )
```

```
eval-abortlist(namel) env =
   if namel = <>
      then return({})
      else (let name = hd namel in
               def tv : eval-Expr(name) env ;
               return( {tv} U eval-abortlist(tl namel) env ) )

type: Name* -> (ENV => TV-set)
```

2.9.7  Functions for communication with the storage. -


```
create-ActId()=
  (def mk-ACTID-MSG(actid) : call-stg(mk-CREATE-ACTID())  ;
   return(actid)                                          )

type: () => ActId


allocate(actid)=
  (def mk-LOC-MSG(loc) : call-stg(mk-ALLOCATE(actid));
   return(loc)                                        )

type: ActId => LOC


free-locations(actid)=
  (output mk-FREE-LOCS(actid) to STORAGE )

type: ActId =>


assign(varloc,val)=
  (def assigned : call-stg(mk-ASSIGN(varloc,val));
   I                                              )

type: VarLoc  VAL =>


value-of(varloc)=
  (def mk-VALUE-MSG(val) : call-stg(mk-GET-VALUE(varloc));
   return(val)                                           )

type: VarLoc => VAL


call-stg(stgreq)=
  (output stgreq to STORAGE ;
  (input result from STORAGE  ->
        cases result:
        (mk-EXCP-MSG(eid)  -> exit(mk-Excp(eid)),
         T                 -> return(result)     ) ))

type: STGREQ => (ACTID-MSG | LOC-MSG | ASSIGNED | VALUE-MSG)
```

2.9.8  Functions for communication with the monitor. -

```
monitor-call(req)=
  (output req to MONITOR (;)
  (input rply from MONITOR  ->
        cases rply:
        (mk-TERMINATE-CMD()  -> exit(mk-TERMINATE()),
         mk-FAIL-CMD()       -> exit(mk-Excp(FAILURE)),
         mk-RAISE-CMD(eid)   -> exit(mk-Excp(eid)),
         T                   -> return(rply)            )))

type: REQ => REPLY


enable()=
  (output mk-ENABLE() to MONITOR (;)
  (input mk-TERMINATE-CMD() from MONITOR  -> exit(mk-TERMINATE()),
   input mk-FAIL-CMD()      from MONITOR  -> exit(mk-Excp(FAILURE)),
   input mk-CONTINUE()      from MONITOR  -> I                     ))

type: () =>


pass-monitor(req)=
  (def continue : monitor-call(req);
   I                                  )

type: REQ =>


inform-monitor(msg)=
  (output msg to MONITOR)

type: MSG =>


await-activation()=
  (input mk-START() from MONITOR )

type: () =>
```

## 3.0  Summary of assumpsions and decisions

The main cases of concern are:

1.  The manual does not explicitly specify that tasks do not start their activation until the declarative part in which they have been declared has been elaborated, and that the activations are done one at a time. This is though indicated in the examples, and has thus been assumed here.

2.  The language description does not specify the effect of raising failure in a task which has not completed its activation. In the case where it has not even started its activation, it has been decided to make the task terminate without any effect on other tasks of the same declarative part. In case it has already started its activation, the failure is simply raised and handled as a normal exception. If a task is aborted during its activation, it is assumed that the other tasks of the same declarative part are still subject to be activated, i.e. activation continues as if the aborted task had been properly activated.

3.  If a parent task, which is suspended after elaboration of a declarative part waiting for the local tasks to become active, is aborted, or suffers a failure, it has been decided to do the interruption of the parent task immediately, and let it have no effect on the local tasks. When all local tasks have become active, this does not, as usual, affect the parent.

4.  The select-to-terminate concept applied in the whole of this thesis is more general than the one described in the manuals, as in the manuals it is required that task that can terminate in this way are bound to be dependent to the outermost block of a task, i.e. the task body.

5.  The language manual does not specify the effect of a negative duration in connection with timed entry calls and select statements. The solution adopted here is that negative delays do not take priority over immediately possible rendesvous', and that negative durations are incomparable with eachother, i.e. that any negative duration may be selected if a rendezvous is not immediately possible.

6.  It is assumed that the identification of the tasks to be aborted of an abort statement are found from left to right.

## 4.0  Formula index

# THE DESIGN OF A VIRTUAL MACHINE FOR ADA

*Ole Dommergaard*

Abstract:

This document formally defines a virtual machine. The design of the instruction set and state components of the machine is based on a semantic analysis of the basic concepts of Ada. The result is a high-level machine especially suited to run Ada programs.

## Acknowledgements

This document constitutes the thesis presented to attain the degree of master of science in engineering. The work was carried out in collaboration with Jørgen Bundgaard, Hans Henrik Løvengreen, Lennart Schultz and Jan Storbank Pedersen. Regular discussions with these people gave me a thorough understanding of the ideas behind Ada, as well as they revealed the deepest implications of the language changes that came up during the project period.

I owe my deepest thanks to Jørgen Bundgaard, Hans Henrik Løvengreen, Lennart Schultz and Jan Storbank Pedersen for their never-ending interest in my work. I would also like to thank my instructor Ole Oest for many valuable comments. Finally a very special thanks goes to my teacher professor Dines Bjørner for making the last years of my study most instructive and pleasant.

## Notation

This document is produced by a primitive text-processing system, lacking a number of features. The following special symbols will be used:

$\qquad$ E $\qquad$ : The membership operator.

$\qquad$ ∀,A : The universal quantifier.

$\qquad$ E : The existential quantifier.

$\qquad$ S : The State Domain.

.. $\xrightarrow{m}$ .. : Denotes a mapping from .. to ..

.. -> .. : Denotes a function from .. to ..

X.Y : Denotes a derived reference in X.

The appendix META-IV-CSP reference manual further defines the notation.

Document Structure

The document describes the design of a virtual machine. The machine is designed to run compiled Ada programs, so-called A-code.

The machine is described using the Vienna development method [BjJo78], that
is as a Meta-IV program decribing the meaning of running an A-code program
on the machine.

Chapter one contains a brief discussion on Ada, A-code, what A-code is and
why A-code is selected instead of code for a real machine. The design criteria for the machine will also be given in this chapter.

Chapter two discusses systematic compiler and interpreter construction.

Chapter three describes the design of the machine. The state-components,
structure and the instruction-set of the machine are derived from a semantic
analysis of the relevant Ada constructs.

Chapter four will describe a method to derive a concrete A-code interpreter
from the more abstract model of the A-code-machine.

Finally chapter five will comment on the design of the machine and the development project.

Appendix A contains the complete formal model of the virtual machine.

Appendix B contains a rudimentary compiling algorithm from a subset of Ada
into A-code.

Table of contents

## 1.0 Introduction

### 1.1 What is Ada ?

Ada is a modern high-level language. The features of Ada are carefully selected to give an easy-to-learn yet powerful language. The language is intended to be used when programming embedded systems as well as for general
purpose programming. Only a brief discussion will be given here, the complete language definition [Ada80] should be consulted for further details.

Ada mainly consists of features known from other high-level languages. This
includes a rather ordinary set of statement types like if-statements,
case-statements, loop-statements, assignment-statements, procedure-calls and
so on.

The predefined data types includes the types integer, boolean, character and
floating point. Fixed precision, fractional numbers can be expressed
through the type fixed. Pointers are represented by access types. Only two
structured types are included: array-types and record-types.

The type mechanism of Ada allows the programmer to define his own types.
Dynamically evaluated constraints can be applied to types by means of subtypes.

Variables and types can be protected from unintended use by means of packages. A package can be used to define a datatype principally through the
legal operations applicable to objects of the type. The private-type concept can be used to disallow any other operations on objects of a protected
type.

The concept of generic program units provides a macro-like way of generating
parameterised versions of a single package or subprogram definition.

Names of procedures and functions can be overloaded, that is: one name can
be used for several procedures. The meaning of such a name is determined
from its context.

An exception-mechanism allows the programmer to specify the handling of
unexpected events occurring during program execution.

Concurrently executing processes can be generated by means of tasks. Tasks
are synchronised by means of entry-calls, that is calls of procedure-like
entities defined in other tasks. Entry-calls are synchronised through a
handshaking mechanism.

## 1.2 Why A-code ?

Several reasons can be given for generating virtual code instead of code for a real machine. The two most important will be given here.

 To obtain a highly portable compiler.

 To be able to control a distributed system of different processors by means of compiled Ada programs.

The first reason is well-known. The method of using virtual code in the bootstrapping of a compiler, has succesfully been applied to languages like Pascal [No76] and BCPL [Ri71]. The second reason is not so wellknown: it is not common to control a computer network by means of programs written in high-level languages.

## 1.3 What is A-code ?

A-code is code for a virtual (hypothetical) machine. The machine is designed to run compiled Ada-programs.

The machine is a high-level machine with a structured storage and a powerful set of specialised instructions. The instructions-set features instructions to deal with Ada-specialities like task-communication and exception-handling. The instruction-set is designed to allow a simple code-generation from all Ada-statements.

Two sorts of virtual code exists.

 One used as an intermediate language that can be interpreted, however the interpretation is very slow.

 Another type is used as a final language and is designed to be interpreted efficiently.

The first sort is used during the bootstrap operation of a compiler that later shall generate real code for the machine on which it is to run. The slow interpretation is not important because the interpreter is only used until a codegenerator for the new target machine is running. The second sort is used both during the bootstrap-operation and in the final compiler. For this purpose it is important to be able to interpret the virtual code efficiently.

The instruction types of the two types of virtual code are rather different.

The first type usually contains a small set of very general instructions. The second one contains a large set of more or less specialised instructions.

A good example of the first type of virtual code is the INTCODE used during the bootstrap of a BCPL compiler [Ri72]. The second type is represented by the virtual code generated by the Pascal-compilers of the SOLO-operating system [Ha77].

The effort necessary to obtain a reasonable fast compiler is much bigger when using the former method than when using the latter. The final compiler, however will be faster if the first method is used. The difference in implementation effort arise from the fact that a new code-generator must be written when the first method is used. The task of writing a code-generator is considered to be much larger than the task of writing an efficient interpreter. The interpreter needed by the first method can be written in an high-level language and may therefore be provided as part of an implementation-kit.

As portability is considered more important than efficiency, the second type of virtual code is chosen. This choice is supported by the fact that the first method is of little use in a distributed network of different processors. In a network it is desirable to be able to delay the choice of processor a program shall run on, until the program is to be started. The first method uses real machine-code and the choice of processor would therefore have to be performed before the program is compiled.

The design of the A-code machine is carried out along the following guidelines.

It must be possible to translate every Ada-construct into an equivalent sequence of A-code instructions, and it should be possible to argue this equivalence.

It must be easy to implement A-code interpreters on various computers.

The A-code interpreters must be reasonable efficient.

A-code need not be a good starting point for the generation of real machine code.

Optimisations of the instruction set are not performed during the design phase. Due to the unusual structure of the machine it is deemed that such optimisations should be based on a statistical analysis of data collected during the use of the machine described. This implies that instructions which can only be generated when certain relations exist between the subcomponents of a program construct, will not be presented.

2.0  Systematic Compiler and Interpreter Construction

This section describes a systematic method for compiler and interpreter construction and implementation. A more elaborate description can be found in [Bjørner & Oest, this volume].

Before starting to implement a compiler for Ada, a precise description of the language must be available. The description is in this case derived from the language reference manual. The result is a three part document.

Part one is the definition of the static semantics. This document describes the conditions an Ada program must satisfy to be statically correct. These conditions state all rules that can be checked without running the program. The description takes the form of an is-well-formed-function that maps an abstract representation of an Ada program into truth if the program is statically well-formed, falsehood otherwise. Such a definition of Ada can be found in [Bundgaard & Schultz, this volume].

Part two of the document is the definition of the dynamic semantics. The dynamic semantics colloquially speaking defines the meaning of running a statically well-formed program. The meaning is described through a set of evaluation- and interpretation functions, each describing the meaning of some construct in the language. A definition of the dynamic semantics of Ada can be found in [Storbank Pedersen, this volume].

Part three is the definition of Ada-tasking.
The document describes the task-related aspects of Ada. A mechanical model of task-creation and communication is given. This definition will use the functions of the dynamic semantics definition to ascribe meaning to non-task related features. Likewise the functions of the tasking model will be used by the dynamic semantics definition. A tasking model can be found in [Loevengreen, this volume].

When the formal definition of the language has been completed the first implementation step can be started. For this purpose another document is needed.

A formal definition of the target machine semantics.
This paper gives the meaning of running a machine-code program on the target machine.

A first implementation step is hence the derivation of a compiling algorithm.

The compiling algorithm is a function that maps an Ada program into an equivalent sequence of machine code instructions. To realistically be able to argue this equivalence, the structure of the compiling algorithm should correspond closely to the structure of the dynamic semantics definition from which the compiling algorithm will be derived and against which its correctness will be argued. The correctness arguments will use the machine semantics definition mentioned above.

The next implementation step is a series of program transformations.

From the definition of the static semantics the corresponding parts of the compiler is derived. These parts are called the context condition checker and constitutes the declaration- and name-analysis parts of the compiler.

The codegenerator part of the compiler is derived from the compiling algorithm.

Finally the kernel or runtime system is derived from the definition of tasking.

If the target machine is to be a virtual machine and this machine is not yet designed, the first implementation step should be altered slightly. Instead of just deriving the compiling algorithm from the dynamic semantics definition, both the compiling algorithm and the virtual machine should be derived in parallel. This method will ease the correctness arguments of the compiling algorithm considerably as the instructions can be designed to suit the compiling algorithm. At the same time the design of the virtual machine will be almost automatic as the semantics of the instructions will arise directly from the compiling algorithm. The instructions should be designed so powerful that only short sequences of instructions are needed to handle the "basic" operations of Ada. The basic operations are those that are described without the use of functioncalls and implicit constructions in the functions of the dynamic semantics definition.

A similar method can be used to derive the interface to the tasking kernel.

When the model of the virtual machine has been completed, it must be implemented on the real machine. Chapter four is aimed at this point.

Unfortunately this method could not be used during this project. The definition of the dynamic semantics and the tasking model were not available until the first project period was nearly over. In spite of that, instructions for handling most of Ada has been designed. This has only been possible through a careful study of Ada and as a result of long discussions with Jan Storbank Pedersen who wrote the dynamic semantics definition and Hans Henrik Lovengreen who created the tasking model.

3.0  The Model of the A-Code Machine

This chapter describes the derivation of the state components, structure and instruction set of the virtual machine. The main criterion of the design is to facilitate a simple codegeneration. The goal is to be able to generate all code in a single left to right pass of the program (parsetree).

First the structure of the model will be described, then the following chapters will show how different Ada concepts influenced the design of the machine.
The following concepts will be treated.

        Blocks, variables and addressing,
        Procedures,
        Tasks,
        Exceptions and handlers,
        Types, subtypes and variables,
        Expressions,
        Declarations and
        Statements.

Some concepts have been left out for the moment.

The problems around discriminants seem extremely complex, the implications on the A-Code machine can therefore hardly be seen before the definition of the dynamic semantics of Ada have been completed. The omission of discriminants implies the omission of variant records.

A similar situation is present in the case of exceptions occurring during task creation. Here the semantics has not yet been decided, and it can therefore not be described.

Aggregates and initialisation values in record-type definitions have been left out for the same reasons.

Other features has been left out because they are considered less important and uncomplicated, this is the case with attributes of types and objects.

Files and file-operations have been left out because treatment of files would imply the treatment of a file-system, which was considered beyond the limits of this project.

The model is described in the VDM style [BjJo78], that is as a Meta-IV program. For the purpose of modelling concurrently executing processes Meta-IV is extended with a CSP-like process mechanism [FoBj79].

The model inherits the structure of the definition of the dynamic semantics, that is as a set of communicating META-IV processors.

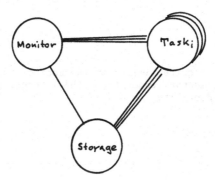

The Monitor-processor handles the intricate parts of task-creation, deletion and communication.

The Storage-processor provides indivisible access to the storage and schedules storage-operation-requests among the Task-processors.

Each Task-processor executes the program of an Ada-task.

## 3.1 The Monitor Processor

The Monitor processor takes as argument the program to be executed. When
started it will start the storage processor. Then it will start a task processor to execute the main program. After the main program has been started
the monitor processor is ready to handle requests from task processors.

The main structure of the monitor is:

```
monitor processor(code)=
  ( def store : start stg();
    def main  : start task(code,1, );
    dcl pi type processor(task);

    trap exit with I in

      cycle

        {
            .
            .

            input mk-?request( ... )  from task set pi
              -> output handle-?request( ... ) to c pi,

            .
            .

        }

  )
```

As the monitor should be quite similar to the monitor in the definition of
Ada-tasking, only rudimentary comments on the internal parts of the monitor
will be given in this document.

## 3.2 The Storage Processor

The storage-processor protects the storage state-component by defining and executing the legal operations applicable to it. Such operations are performed indivisibly in response to requests from the task processors.

The structure of the Stg-processor:

```
stg processor()=
  ( dcl stg := [] type Stg;
    dcl pi         type processor(task);

    trap exit with I in

      cycle

        {
           .
           .

           input mk-?request( ... ) from task set pi
             -> output handle-?request( ... ) to c pi,

           .
           .

           input mk-command?( ... ) from task
             -> handle-command?( ... ),

           .
           .
        }
  )
```

The structure of the storage-variable, stg, as well as the operations defined to manipulate it will be derived from various Ada-concepts in the later parts of this document.

## 3.3 The Task Processors

A task processor executes the program of an Ada-task. The arguments to the task processor is an A-Code program and the index of the initial instruction. When started the task processor will interpret instructions one by one.

The program is a sequence of instructions. Indexes in the program are called labels. The instructions will be carefully designed to handle the "elementary operations" of Ada.

The task processor structure:

```
task processor(code,entry, )=
  ( dcl ins-cnt := entry type Label;

    trap exit with I in

      cycle

        {
          ( def ins : code[c ins-cnt];
            ins-cnt := c ins-cnt + 1;
            int-ins(ins)
          )
        }
  )


  int-ins(ins)=
    ( cases ins:
        (

              .
              .

            mk-?( ... )        ->  int-?(ins),

              .
              .

        )
    )
```

To use the storage the task processors must communicate with the storage processor. This is done by a set of interface functions, one for each entry in the storage processor. The interface functions are all very simple. Two schemes are used:

```
stg-op( ,,, )=
  ( output mk-Stg-op( ,,, ) to stg;
    input answ               from stg
```

```
        -> return answ
  )


stg-op( ,,, )=
( output mk-Stg-op( ,,, ) to stg
)
```

The first is used when calling value returning entries in the  storage  processor.   After the message is sent the answer is awaited and returned.  The second is used when calling non-value returning entries in the storage  processor.

For readability reasons the names and the number and types of the  arguments to  the  interfacefunctions  will  be the same as those of the corresponding functions in the storage processor.

The storage interface functions will not be discussed further.

A set of interface functions to the monitor will also be defined.   In  this case  the names of the communication domains will be overlaid with the names of the corresponding A-code instructions.

## 3.4  Blocks, Variables and Addressing

From the A-code point of view the most important feature of Ada is the concept of nested blocks. A block is a collection of declarations and a statementlist. Procedures and tasks is seen as a sort of blocks, that can be invoked at several points in the program. Invocation of such blocks might cause several instances of a single block to become active at the same time. Although procedures and tasks are not treated explicitly in this section, the problems of several active occurrences of the same block will be taken into account.

In this section the problems of addressing variables declared in nested blocks will be discussed.

At a given point in the program only a limited subset of the variables of the program can be used. The visible variables are those declared in the current block or in blocks surrounding the current one in the program text. Only visible variables can be addressed directly. The same identifier may be used in several blocks. At a given point in the program a visible variable name is uniquely identified by its name in connection with the nesting level number of the block in which it is declared. Such a unique identifier can be computed at compile time. The unique identifier of a variable is henceforth called an static address, the term 'Addr' will be used as well. As several instances of the same block may be active at a time several instances of a variable can be active too. Thus it is not sufficient to identify the name of a variable, it must be possible to address one of several instances of it. Such an address can only be evaluated at run time, it will henceforth be called a dynamic address or a 'Loc'. During program execution it must at any program point be possible to compute the dynamic address of every visible variable from its static address. The storage is structured as a collection of named, dynamically created instances of blocks. Usually a dynamically created instance of a block is called an "activation record". This term will also be used in this document. The dynamic names of activation records will be called activation pointers. An activation record is created when a block is entered and deleted when the block is left. This scheme allows storage of a task to be structured in a stack-like way. Each activation record contains the information of an instance of a block. This information, in addition to the variables of the block, also includes bookkeeping information to be used for storage management, addressing and so on.

The first, simplified model of the storage is now presented.

$$\text{Stg} \qquad = \text{Actvptr} \underset{m}{\to} \text{Actv}$$

$$\text{Actvptr} \qquad = \text{TOKEN}$$

$$\text{Actv} \qquad :: \text{lastactv: Actvptr}$$
$$\qquad\qquad\quad \text{vars: Id} \underset{m}{\to} \text{Val}$$
$$\qquad\qquad\quad \cdot$$
$$\qquad\qquad\quad \cdot$$

$$\text{Val} \qquad = \dots$$

The field 'lastactv' contains a pointer to the activation record of the block that caused this activation record to be created. In the simple case of blocks this will always be the activation record of the block surrounding the current one in the program text. To be able to handle procedures and tasks however the field is necessary.

The basic operations used to manipulate activation records and addressing variables are as follows:

Create-activation:          Create a new activation-record.

Delete-activation:          Delete the youngest activation record.

Get-link:                   Find the activationpointer of the activation record corresponding to some static nesting level.

In addition operations for allocating and using variables will be necessary.

Extend-stg:                 Extend the local storage of an activation-record with a number of variables.

Read:                       Read the contents of some location.

Write:                      Store a new value in some location.

Several techniques can be used to handle the access to variables. Three of these will be described briefly.

The following program will be used in examples of the storage structure used by the three methods.

```
declare  X : integer := 1;    -- Block 1
begin

        declare  Y : integer  := 2;    -- Block 2
        begin

                declare  X : integer  := 3;    -- Block 3
                begin

                        end;
                end;
        end;
```

3.4.1  The Simple Display Mechanism. -

A stack of pointers to the activation records (the display) are maintained. The pointer to the activation record corresponding to static nesting level 'n' is kept in the 'n'th position (counting from the bottom) of the stack. When an activation record is created a pointer to it is pushed on the stack.

Likewise when an activation record is deleted, the pointer to it is removed from the stack. The simple display mechanism has several limitations. The problems appear when procedurecalls and task—creation is to be handled. However a slightly modified version of the display mechanism is able to handle the problems.

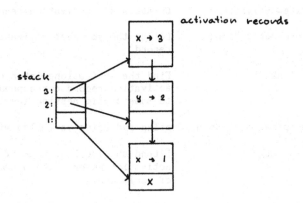

### 3.4.2 The Modified Display Mechanism. –

In the modified display mechanism the display is stored in the activation records. Only the display contained in the youngest activation record is used at any time. To be able to find the youngest activation record a pointer to it must be maintained. When an activation record is created the display of the statically surrounding block is extended with a pointer to the new activation record to get the display of the new activation record. When an activation record is deleted the display of the statically surrounding block automatically becomes active. Except from the deletion of the activation record only the pointer to the current activation record need be updated at block—exit.

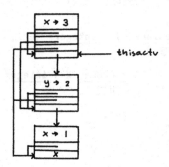

### 3.4.3 The Chaining Mechanism. –

Activation records are identified by activation pointers. In each activation record a pointer to the activation record corresponding to the statically surrounding block is stored. In addition a pointer to the youngest

activation record is maintained.
A pointer to the activation record corresponding to some static nesting
level 'n' is obtained by starting in the activation corresponding to the
most recent block 'm' to follow the chain of activation pointers 'm-n'
times.

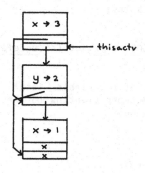

As mentioned the simple display mechanism has several disadvantages and it
will therefore not be given much attention in the following. The two other
mechanisms are quite similar and the model is not influenced much by the
choice. Although the modified display-model is selected for the model, the
differences to the chaining model will be described at appropriate points.


3.4.3.1 A partial Model of the Storage. -

The design of the storage is influenced by many other Ada concepts, therefore only a partial model can be given at this stage.


The semantic domains of the storage:


        Stg     = (Actvptr $\underset{m}{\rightarrow}$ Actv) U (ROOT $\underset{m}{\rightarrow}$ Actv)

        Actvptr = TOKEN

        Actv    :: display:    Display
                   lastactv:   Actvptr
                     ·
                     ·
                   loc-stg:    (Id $\underset{m}{\rightarrow}$ Val)
                     ·
                     ·

        Display = Actvptr#

        Id      = TOKEN

        Val     = ...

```
Addr    :: level: N1  Id

Loc     :: actv: Actvptr  Id
```

To get started the storage must be initialised to a dummy activation record
containing an empty display:

```
dcl stg := [ROOT -> mk-Actv(<>,undefined,undefined)];
```

Assuming the existence of a variable 'stg' of type Stg and a variable
'thisactv' of type Actvptr pointing to the youngest activation record, the
basic operations would be:

```
create-actv(actv)=
  ( def newactvp E Actvptr s.t. newactvp ~E dom c stg;
    def newdisp : c(stg.(actv).disp)) ^ <newactvp>;
    def newactv : mk-Actv(newdisp,actv,[]);
    stg := c stg U [newactvp -> newactv];
    return newactvp
  )

type:   Actvptr   ->  S  ->  S Actvptr



delete-actv(actv)=
  ( def old-actv : c(stg.(actv).lastactv);
    stg := stg \ {actv};
    return old-actv
  )

type:   Actvptr   ->  S  ->  S Actvptr



get-link(actv,level)=
  c(stg.(actv).disp.[level])

type:   Actvptr Level   ->  S  ->  S Actvptr



extend-stg(actv,xstg)=
  stg.(actv).loc-stg := c(stg.(actv).loc-stg) U  xstg

type:   Actvptr Id -> Val   ->  S  ->  S



read(mk-Loc(actv,id)=
  c(stg.(actv).loc-stg.(id))
```

<u>type</u>:   Loc   -> <u>S</u> -> <u>S</u> Val

```
write(mk-Loc(actv,id),val)=
  stg.(actv).loc-stg.(id) := val
```

<u>type</u>:   Loc Val   -> <u>S</u> -> <u>S</u>

Only minor changes are needed to convert the model to use the chaining technique:

```
Actv     :: surr-actv:   Actvptr
            last-actv:   Actvptr
            .
            .
            loc-stg:     Id ⇒ Val
            .
            .

Addr:    :: level-diff: NO  Id
```

Note the change in 'Addr', as mentioned in the chaining model variables are addressed through the difference of the nesting level of the current block and the nesting level of the block containing the declaration of the variable.

```
create-actv(actv)=
  ( def newactvp E Actvptr s.t. newactvp ~E dom c stg;
    def newactv : mk-Actv(actv,actv,[]);
    stg := c stg  U  [newactvp -> newactv];
    return newactvp
  )
```

<u>type</u>:   Actvptr   -> <u>S</u> -> <u>S</u> Actvptr

```
get-link(actv,leveldiff)=
  ( dcl a := actv type Actvptr;
    for i=1 to leveldiff do
      a := c(stg.(c a).surr-actv);
    return c a
  )
```

<u>type</u>:   Actvptr NO   -> <u>S</u> -> <u>S</u> Actvptr

3.4.4  Block Entry and Exit. -

Two A-Code instructions are used in connection with blocks:

> Enter-block:     Create an activation record for a new
> block. Then allocate storage for the
> local variables of the block.
>
> Exit-block:      Delete the activation record
> corresponding to the most
> recent block.

3.4.4.1  Enter-block and Exit-block. -

```
Enter-block    :: vars: Id-set
Exit-block     :: ()
```

```
int-Enter-block(mk-Enter-block(vars))=
  ( def newactv : create-actv(c thisactv);
    let newstg = [id -> undefined | id E vars] in
  extend-stg(newactv,newstg);
    thisactv := newactv
  )
```

type:   Enter-block  -> $\underline{S}$ -> $\underline{S}$

```
int-Exit-block(mk-Exit-block())=
  thisactv := delete-actv(c thisactv)
```

type:   Exit-block  -> $\underline{S}$ -> $\underline{S}$

3.5  Procedures, Parameters and Procedurecalls

Procedures are viewed as named and parameterised blocks, which can be invoked (called) at several points in the program. Procedures can be defined
(declared) inside blocks or inside other procedures. When a procedure is
invoked an activation record for it must be created. This activation record
must correspond to the static level of the procedure definition, not to the
level of the point of invocation. The addressing mechanism must be able to
handle this.

The parameters can be of any type of the language. Each parameter has an associated mode. The mode describes whether the parameter is used to transfer values from the point of invocation to the procedure body (IN), from the procedure to the invocation point (OUT) or both (INOUT). The type check necessary in connection with parameterpassing influence the choice of parameterpassing mechanism.


3.5.1 Parameter-passing and Parameter-addressing. -

Parameterpassing gives rise to two problems:

    Where are parameters to be stored and
    When are copying and type-checking to be performed.


The definition of Ada states the semantics of parameterpassing as:

    "The formal parameters of a subprogram are considered
    local to the subprograms. A parameter has one of the
    following tree modes:

    IN:    The parameter acts as a local constant whose
           value is provided by the corresponding actual
           parameter.

    OUT:   The parameter acts as a local variable whose
           value is assigned to the corresponding actual
           parameter as a result of the execution of the
           subprogram.

    INOUT: The parameter acts as a local variable and
           permits access and assignment to the
           corresponding actual parameter.               "

This semantics together with the semantics of assignment implies typecheck-ing after evaluation of actual IN or INOUT parameters and typechecking be-fore the assignment of formal OUT or INOUT parameters to the corresponding actual parameters. This means that at the point of return the actual value of the local variable corresponding to OUT and INOUT parameters must lie within the type of the actual parameter. Such a check cannot be performed within the procedure body as the type of the actual parameter is not known at that point.


The solution to the parameterpassing problem is quite simple but somewhat unconventional.

In the procedure body the parameters of the procedure is seen as variables declared in a virtual block enclosing the procedure body. At the calling point the parameterlist is seen as a block containing declarations of the formal parameters. After entering this block the actual parameters are eva-luated, checked and assigned to the corresponding formal parameter-variable. Then the addressing mechanism of the parameter-block is changed to reflect the change of environment of the virtual block, and the procedure body is entered. When the execution of the procedure body is completed the address-ing mechanism is restored to its initial state, and execution is resumed at the point following the call. At this point typechecking of OUT and INOUT parameters are performed and assignment of the formal-parameter variables to the actual ones are done. Finally the parameter-block is left.

This parameter-passing mechanism offers several advantages:

> Parameters are addressed in the same
> way as ordinary variables,
>
> Parameterpassing is performed by ordinary
> assignments and
>
> Type-checking of parameters are done by
> the usual type-checking during assignment.

To be able to use this method it must be possible to change the addressing mechanism when the change of environment of the parameters is to take place. This change is not difficult and can be done in all three mechanisms. More serious is the problem of restoring the addressing mechanism when a procedure is left. This requires the old status of the mechanism to be stored somewhere. If this is to be added to the simple display mechanism it will be cumbersome to use. The two other mechanisms already contain copies of the old status and the restore operation is thus no problem.

The concept of procedures adds a field containing the return address to the activation record:

```
        Actv    :: .
                   .
                   ret-addr:    [Label]
                   .
```

Four new basic storage operations are added:

>     proc-context:    Change the addressing mechanism to
>                      reflect the fact that the most recent
>                      activation record is the formal
>                      parameterlist of a procedure that
>                      is now to be entered.
>
>     parm-context:    Change back the addressing mechanism.
>                      The block is now seen as a block defined
>                      at the calling point (the actual
>                      parameter list).
>
>     set-ret-addr:    Save a label as return-address in some
>                      activation record.
>
>     get-ret-addr:    Fetch the return-address of some
>                      activation record.

Two A-code instructions are defined to handle the call/return aspects of procedure management.

Call:   Save the instruction-counter as the return
        address of the current (parameter) activation
        record. Change the environment of the
        youngest activation record (the
        parameterlist) and continue the execution
        at the entrypoint of the procedure.

Return: Restore the context of the youngest activation
        record to that of the calling point, and restore
        the instruction-counter from the return-address
        field of that activation record.

Note that the return instruction is only intended to be used as the last instruction of the compiled procedure body, it is not able to return from a
point inside a block.

3.5.1.1 Proc-context, Parm-context, Set-ret-addr & Get-ret-addr. –

The storage operations are simple to define in both the display-model and
the chaining model.

The display-model:

```
proc-context(parmactv,defactv)=
  stg.(parmactv).disp := c(stg.(defactv).disp) ^ <parmactv>

type:   Actvptr Actvptr  -> S -> S


parm-context(actv)=
  ( def lastactv : c(stg.(actv).lastactv);
    stg.(actv).disp := c(stg.(lastactv).disp) ^ <lastactv>
  )

type:   Actvptr   -> S -> S


set-ret-addr(actv,addr)=
  stg.(actv).ret-addr := addr

type:   Actvptr Label  -> S -> S


get-ret-addr(actv)=
  c(stg.(actv).ret-addr)

type:   Actvptr   -> S -> S [Label]
```

The chaining model (only changed functions):

```
proc-context(parmactv,defactv)=
  stg.(parmactv).surractv := defactv

type:   Actvptr Actvptr  -> S -> S



parm-context(actv)=
  stg.(actv).surractv := c(stg.(actv).lastactv)

type:   Actvptr   -> S -> S
```

## 3.5.1.2 Call and Return. -

```
Call     :: deflevel: Level   entry: Label
Return   :: ()

int-Call(mk-Call(deflevel,entry))=
  ( def defactv : get-link(c thisactv,deflevel);
    set-ret-addr(c thisactv, c ins-cnt);
    proc-context(c thisactv, defactv);
    ins-cnt := entry
  )

type:   Call  -> S -> S


int-Return(mk-Return())=
  ( parm-context(c thisactv);
    ins-cnt := get-ret-addr(c thisactv)
  )

type:   Return  -> S -> S
```

## 3.6 Tasks

Ada provides a way to run processes concurrently. A process is created by
the declaration or allocation of an object of a task type. Task types are
defined in a way similar to that of procedures. This means that taskdefini-
tions can be nested in blocks, procedures or other task type definitions.
The consequence is that tasks can share storage as well as procedures.
Therefore:

> The addressing mechanism must be able to handle
> the sharing of parts of the storage between a
> number of tasks.
>
> Procedures and functions must be reentrant.

Ada states that a task cannot leave a block while another task is dependent
on the block. A task is dependent on a block if the type of the task is defined in the block. This implies monitor-communication when a block is to
be left.

Special problems arise from the fact that one task can stop the execution of
another task at arbitrary points in time. This requires the task-processors
regularly to check if some (other) task is requesting it to be aborted.
When a task is aborted all its subtasks, that is all tasks whose type is declared inside the aborting task will be aborted too.

The monitor must be able to handle continuation-requests as well as it must
be able to convert an abort-request into several terminate-commands to a
family of tasks.

To be able to identify all tasks in the system, they must be uniquely named.
The monitor is responsible for creating such names.


The tasking facility also influence the choice of addressing mechanism. In
the two display models the display of a newly created task must be the display corresponding to the block containing the definition of the task type.
In the simple display model this display might be stored away and would then
not be directly accessible. The simple display model is therefore not suited to handle the addressing involved in tasking.

Both the modified display model and the chaining model are able to handle
the sharing of storage between tasks.

In the modified display model the right display is obtained by letting the
current activation pointer of a new task be the pointer to the activation
record corresponding to the block containing the declaration of the type of
the new task.

The chaining model only requires the pointer to the current activation record of a newly created task to be the same as the pointer to the activation
record corresponding to the block in which the task type is defined.

The storage of the machine when running a program with several tasks will be
a tree-structure of stacks (a cactus-stack) [Or73] and [HaDe]. Each task
owns a branch of the tree. Note that a 'Loc' is still sufficient to address
any variable in the storage. This is needed, in order to be able to pass
addresses (pointers) among the different tasks.

463

As an example consider the following program:

```
task t1;
task body t1 is

            i : integer;

                task type t;
                task body t is
                        j : integer;
                begin
                    declare k : integer;
                    begin  -- P1
                    end;
                end;

                t2,t3 : t;

        begin
            declare l : integer;
            begin  -- P2
            end;
    end;
```

Imagine that t1 has reached the point P2 and, at the same  time  t2  and  t3
have both reached P1, then the 'cactus stack' would look like this:

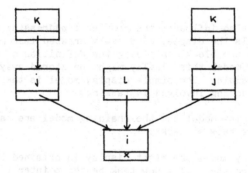

The model for procedure-calls ensures that procedures and functions are reentrant.

The storage does not need extensions to handle tasking; other than it already be a separate meta-process.

Changes in the task-processor is required to take into account the problems of blockexits and the abort facility. For this purpose the monitor must have two entries, one to be called when a block is to be left, another to be called at not further specified intervals to check if the task is to be aborted.

When a task is going to terminate it must leave all its active blocks. If task types are defined in such a block, the block-exit will be delayed until all occurrences of tasks of such types have terminated.

A number of auxiliary functions are defined in the task-processor to handle the problems of monitor-communication, block-exits and task-termination.

| | |
|---|---|
| monitor-fct-call: | Pass a message to the monitor and wait for an answer. If the answer is a 'terminate'-command the execution of the task is terminated, otherwise the answer is returned. |
| monitor-call: | Pass a message to the monitor and await an answer. If the answer is a 'terminate'-command the execution of the task is terminated, otherwise the answer is ignored. |
| exitlevel: | Ask for permission to delete a block. When permission is granted, the youngest activation-record is deleted. |
| unwind: | Delete the activation records corresponding to a number of blocks. |
| terminate: | Leave all active blocks, then stop the execution of this task. |

Only a few extra A-code instructions are needed to handle the basic concepts of tasking.

| | |
|---|---|
| Create-task: | Create a new task-processor to execute a program of a task defined in some block. The operation must provide a unique name for the new task. |
| Initiate: | Release a series of newly created tasks. The semantics of this instruction can not be given at this stage as the |

465

                                    the semantics of Ada has not yet been
                                    defined for this area.

    Terminate:        Stop the execution of this task.

    Abort:            Stop the execution of a set of named
                      tasks.


## 3.6.1 Monitor Function Create-task. -


```
create-task(defactv,depactv,entry)=
  ( def newtask : start task(code,entry,defactv);
    return mk-Task-descr(newtask)
  )
```

type:    Actvptr Actvptr Label   -> $\underline{S}$ -> $\underline{S}$ Task-val


## 3.6.2 Task Processor. -


```
task  processor(code,entry,defactv)=

  ( dcl thisactv := defactv type Actvptr,
        ins-cnt  := entry   type Label;

    trap exit with I in

      cycle

        { monitor-call(mk-Continue?());
          ( def ins : code[c ins-cnt];
            ins-cnt := c ins-cnt + 1;
            int-Ins(ins)
          )
        };

    output mk-Terminated() to monitor

  )
```

466

```
monitor-fct-call(msg)=
  ( output msg to monitor;
    input answ from monitor
     -> cases answ:
          ( mk-Terminate()    -> terminate(),
            T                  -> return answ
          )
  )

type:  Actvptr Message  -> S -> S Answer


monitor-call(msg)=
  def dummy : monitor-fct-call(msg)

type:  Actvptr  -> S -> S


exitlevel()=
  ( monitor-call(mk-Exit-block(c thisactv));
    thisactv := delete-actv(c thisactv)
  )

type:  ()  -> S -> S


unwind(levels)=
  for i=1 to levels do
    exitlevel()

type:  NO  -> S -> S


terminate()=
  ( while c thisactv ≠ defactv do
      exitlevel();
    exit
  )

type:  ()  -> S -> S
```

3.6.2.1  Create-task, Initiate, Terminate and Abort. -


    Create-task    :: deflevel: Level   deplevel: Level
                      entry-addr: Label

```
Initiate        :: ()
Terminate       :: ()
Abort           :: N1


int-Create-task(mk-Create-task(deflevel,deplevel,entry))=
  ( def defactv : get-link(c thisactv, deflevel),
        depactv : get-link(c thisactv, deplevel),
        loc     : pop(c thisactv);
    let msg     = mk-Create-task(defactv,depactv,entry)in
    def newtask : monitor-fct-call(msg);
    write(loc, newtask)
  )

type:   Create-task  ->  S  ->  S



int-Initiate(mk-Initiate())=
  monitor-call(mk-Initiate(c thisactv))

type:   Initiate  ->  S  ->  S



int-Terminate(mk-Terminate())=
  terminate()

type:   Terminate  ->  S  ->  S



int-Abort(mk-Abort(n))=
  ( dcl tasks := {} type processor(task)-set;
    for i = 1 to n do
      tasks := c tasks U pop(c thisactv);
    monitor-call(mk-Abort(c tasks))
  )

type:   Abort  ->  S  ->  S
```

## 3.7  Exceptions and Handlers

Exceptions are unexpected events that can arise during program execution. Ada offers a mechanism to handle exceptions, so called exception-handlers. An exception-handler is a piece of program designed to handle a class of exceptions. Exception-handlers are attached to blocks.

When an exception occurs (is raised) the execution of the task is is switched to a search for a handler. The search starts in the current block and continues in dynamically surrounding blocks, deleting blocks lacking an appropriate handler. If an appropriate handler is found the execution is resumed at the entry point of that handler, otherwise the task is terminated. Before blocks are deleted the termination of all tasks whose task-type are defined in the block must be awaited. A set of auxiliary functions are provided to handle these aspects.

Exceptions can be raised explicitly by a 'raise-statement' or implicitly if something happens during computation e.g. overflow.

A special feature is the ability to reraise the exception that caused the transfer to some handler. Since new exceptions can be raised and handled (in nested blocks) during the treatment of one exception, the machine must be able to treat more than one exception at a time.

Another feature is the 'failure-exception'. One task can raise the failure exception in another task. When this happens the execution of the task in which the exception is raised is switched to the search for a handler for the exception. Similarly to the abort-statement this requires the task-processors at further unspecified program points to check if some other tasks have raised the failure exception in the task itself. The monitor-fct-call function of the task processor is used to check for the terminate-command at such intervals and it is now extended to handle exception-messages as well.

Exception-handlers are attached to blocks. Information on entry addresses to handlers and current exception names are therefore stored in the activation records. Several operations are needed to manipulate these fields.

    Set-excph-addr: Set the exception-handler address
                    field of some activation record.

    Get-excph-addr: Fetch the contents of the exception
                    handler address field of some
                    activation record.

    Set-curr-excp:  Declare some exception to be the
                    current of some handler (block).

    Get-curr-excp:  Get the current exception of the
                    handler connected to some block.

Several A-code instructions are needed to deal with exceptions:

    Set-handler:    Declare an address to be the entry
                    address of the first handler of

the current block.

Handle:          Check whether the current exception is in
some class of exceptions, if not then
jump to some other handler.

Raise:           Raise an exception.

Reraise:        Reraise the current exception of
this block

Raise-failure:  Raise the failure exception in a
named task.


3.7.1  Set-excph-addr, Get-excph-addr, Set-curr-excp & Get-curr-excp. -


```
Actv      :: .
                .
          excph:      [Label]
          curr-excp:  [QUOT]
                .
                .
```

```
set-excph-addr(actv,addr)=
  stg.(actv).excph := addr
```

type:   Actvptr [Label]   -> $\underline{S}$ -> $\underline{S}$


```
get-excph-addr(actv)=
  c(stg.(actv).excph)
```

type:   Actvptr   -> $\underline{S}$ -> $\underline{S}$ [Label]


```
set-curr-excp(actv,excp)=
  stg.(actv).curr-excp := excp
```

type:   Actvptr QUOT  -> $\underline{S}$ -> $\underline{S}$


```
get-curr-excp(actv)=
  c(stg.(actv).curr-excp)
```

type:   Actvptr   -> $\underline{S}$ -> $\underline{S}$ [QUOT]

### 3.7.2   Auxiliary Functions Raise, Reraise and Findhandler. –

```
raise(exception)=
  find-handler(exception)

type:   QUOT   ->  S  ->  S



reraise()=
  ( def exception : get-curr-excp(c thisactv);
    find-handler(exception)
  )

type:   ()   ->  S  ->  S



find-handler(exception)=
  ( ins-cnt := get-excph-addr(c thisactv);
    while c ins-cnt = nil do
      if c thisactv = defactv
      then exit
      else ( exitlevel();
             ins-cnt := get-excph-addr(c thisactv)
           );
    set-curr-excp(c thisactv, exception)
  )

type:   QUOT   ->  S  ->  S
```

### 3.7.3   Extended Monitor-fct-call. –

```
monitor-fct-call(msg)=
  ( output msg to monitor;
    input  answ from monitor
      -> cases answ:
           ( mk-Terminate()     -> terminate(),
             mk-Exception(excp) -> raise(excp),
             T                  -> return answ
           )
  )

type:   Message   ->  S  ->  S
```

3.7.4  Set-handler, Handle, Raise, Reraise and raise-failure. -

```
Sethandler      :: Label
Handle          :: excps: QUOT-set  afterhandler: Label
Raise           :: QUOT
Reraise         :: ()
Raise-failure   :: ()
```

```
int-Sethandler(mk-Sethandler(handleraddr))=
  set-excph-addr(c thisactv,handleraddr)
```

<u>type</u>:   Sethandler  ->  <u>S</u>  ->  <u>S</u>

```
int-Handle(mk-Handle(excps,nxth))=
  ( def exception : get-curr-excp(c thisactv);
    if exception ~E excps
    then ins-cnt := nxth
    else I
  )
```

<u>type</u>:   Handle  ->  <u>S</u>  ->  <u>S</u>

```
int-Raise(mk-Raise(excp))=
  raise(excp)
```

<u>type</u>:   Raise  ->  <u>S</u>  ->  <u>S</u>

```
int-Reraise(mk-Reraise())=
  reraise()
```

<u>type</u>:   Reraise  ->  <u>S</u>  ->  <u>S</u>

```
int-Raise-failure(mk-Raise-failure())=
  ( def task : pop(c thisactv);
    output mk-Raise-failure(task) to monitor
  )
```

<u>type</u>:   Raise-failure  ->  <u>S</u>  ->  <u>S</u>

## 3.8  Types, Subtypes and Variables

Ada provides a number of predefined types. From these the user can define
his own types and subtypes. No sharp distinction between types and subtypes
is carried out in this document. The term 'type' will sometimes be used in
both cases.

The predefined types of the language are:

> Integer,
> Float,
> Fixed,
> Character,
> Boolean and
> Access.

User-defineable types are:

> Enumeration-types,
> Array-types,
> Record-types and
> Task-types.

In addition it is possible to generate derived types, that is types equivalent to, but not compatible with, existing types. This is a purely "static"
feature and will therefore not influence the design of the A-Code machine.

The machine must be able to store values of all the mentioned types. This
implies the ability to express the sharing of storage between compound locations and their sub-locations. Partly evaluated addresses can be stored for
later use (renaming) and it is therefore essential to have a powerful addressing mechanism.

Declared objects belong to some subtype. A subtype is a constrained (parameterised) type. Some sorts of constraints can be general expressions, and
can therefore not be evaluated at compiletime. This means that it must be
possible to evaluate and store constraints at run time, as well as it must
be possible to check whether or not some value obey a certain dynamically
evaluated constraint.

The existing 'loc-stg' field of the activation records are not able to handle the overlay of compound locations with their sublocations. Therefore the storage component must be redesigned.

The new model uses a two-part storage-component:

```
Actv            :: .
                   .
                   dstg: Descr-stg
                   vstg: Val-stg
                   .
                   .


Descr-stg       =  Id ⇒ₘ Descr

Val-stg         =  Id ⇒ₘ Simple-val

Descr           =  Comp-descr    | Simple-descr

Simple-descr    :: Id

Comp-descr      =  A-descr        | R-descr

A-descr         :: INTG+ ⇒ₘ Loc

R-descr         :: Id ⇒ₘ Loc

Loc             :: Actvptr Id


Val-stg         =  Id ⇒ₘ Simple-val

Simple-val      =  .....
```

The idea is to describe all overlaying in the descriptor-storage, while keeping only simple values, that is values whose sub-components cannot be accessed separately, in the value-storage.

A 'Simple-descriptor' gives the name (displacement) of a simple value in the value storage. A 'Composite-descriptor' describes the mapping from the composite location to its sublocations.

To use the new storage stucture the storage-operations 'read' and 'write' must be redesigned.


Only a few datatypes are needed in the A-Code-machine. The basic types of the machine are:

```
Integer,
Floating-point,
Boolean,
Task-val,
Location (pointer),
Array-types and
```

Record-types.

Values of these types are represented as values of the domains:

| | | |
|---|---|---|
| Int-val | :: | INTG |
| Float-val | :: | NUM |
| Bool-val | :: | BOOL |
| Task-val | :: | processor(task) |
| Loc | :: | actv: Actvptr  Id |
| A-val | :: | INTG+ $\underset{m}{\Rightarrow}$ Val |
| R-val | :: | Id $\underset{m}{\Rightarrow}$ Val |

Where the first five types are considered "simple".

The absence of the types fixed, character and enumeration-types are due to the fact that these types can (and should) easily be mapped into the type integer. The mappings are simple:

A fixed value is represented by the integer
value that if multiplied by the delta of the
fixed type would give the fixed value.

A character value is represented by the
integer being the ascii representation
of the character value.

Enumeration values are represented by their
positional number in the definition of the
enumeration type.

The location type covers the class of access-types as well as other dynamic addresses computed during the execution. As mentioned array and record values are not stored as such, but rather as a collection of simple values.

Array indices are always integers. The only type of Ada that can be used as an indextype and that is not mapped into the the machinetype integer, is the type boolean. When a boolean value is to be used as index in an array it must therefore be converted to an integer. An instruction is provided for this purpose.

The problems around constraints will be dealt with in a later section.

3.8.1 Read and Write. −

```
read(mk-Loc(defactv,id))=
   ( def d : c(stg.(defactv).dstg.(id));
```

```
      cases d:
        ( mk-Simple-descr(id')
            -> c(stg.(defactv).vstg.(id')),
          mk-A-descr(ds)
            -> mk-A-Val([it->read(ds(it)) |
                                      it E dom ds]),
          mk-R-descr(ds)
            -> mk-R-val([id->read(ds(id)) |
                                      id E dom ds])
        )
      )

type:   Loc   ->  S  ->  S Val


write(mk-Loc(defactv,id),val)=
  ( def d : c(stg.(defactv).dstg.(id));
    cases d:
      ( mk-Simple-descr(id')
          -> stg.(defactv).vstg.(id') := val,
        mk-A-descr(ds)
          -> for all it E dom ds do
                write(ds(it),val(it)),
        mk-R-descr(ds)
          -> for all id E dom ds do
                write(ds(id),val(id))
      )
    )

type:   Loc Val   ->  S  ->  S
```

## 3.9 Expressions

The language offers several types of expressions; that is: several ways of generating values or addresses. Expressions can be divided into the following classes:

> Constants,
> Aggregates,
> Names,
> Allocators,
> Prefix-expressions,
> Infix-expressions,
> Range-tests,
> Subtype-tests and
> Type-conversions.

The class of Names covers the following sub-classes:

> Variables,
> Indexed-components,
> Slices,
> Selected-components,
> Attributes and
> Function-calls.

all of which can generate either values or addresses, depending on the context. The term 'expression' will henceforth cover both addresses and values. During the evaluation of expressions a need for temporary storage arises. A stack of temporary results (the evaluation stack) is used for this purpose. Evaluation using a stack as temporary storage forces expressions to be converted into reverse polish notation. This is however the easiest way to compile expressions and the method therefore appears to be reasonable. To deal with the different types of expressions a set of instructions are defined. Most of them operate on the top of the evaluation stack, some of them also use the storage.

## 3.9.1 The Evaluation Stack. -

As different tasks can evaluate expressions concurrently, each task must have its own stack. The design of the evaluation stack is also influenced by the exception concept. Exceptions can be both raised and handled during the evaluation of a single expression. That is an exception raised inside a function can be handled by a handler attached to the function itself. Such an exception will not be seen at the point of the function-call. When such an exception is raised and handled the evaluation stack must be cleaned up. The clean-up operation must remove the part of the evaluation stack used inside the function body. The clean up action is connected to the handlers and thus to the blocks. The simplest solution is to distribute the evaluation stack in the activation records. The part of the evaluation stack residing in an activation record is the part used by the corresponding block. When an unhandled exception causes the deletion of an activation record the invalid part of the stack will be removed automatically.

Now we are able to give the final version of the activation record:

```
Actv               :: disp:         Display
                      lastactv:     Actvptr
                      ret-addr:     [Label]
                      excph:        [Label]
                      curr-excp:    [Id]
                      dstg:         Descr-stg
                      vstg:         Val-stg
                      stack:        Stack

Stack              = Stackelm*

Stackelm           = Val            | ...

Val                = Simple-val     | A-val        |
                     R-val

Simple-val         = Scalar-val     | Task-val     |
                     Loc            | nil          |
                     Type-descr

Scalar-val         = Int-val        | Float-val    |
                     Bool-val

Type-descr         = Range-descr    | A-tp-descr   |
                     R-tp-descr
```

A set of storage-operations applicable to the evaluation stack is added:

> push:      push a value on the evaluation
> stack in some activation record.

> pop:       pop off and return the top element
> of the evaluation stack in some
> activation record.

> top:       read the value of the top element.

> unstack:   remove the top element of the stack.

No operations for using non-top-elements of the stack are given.


3.9.1.1  Push, Pop, Top and Unstack. -


```
push(actv,val)=
    stg.(actv).stack := <val> ^ c(stg.(actv).stack)

type:  Actvptr Val  -> S -> S


pop(actv)=
    ( def val : hd c(stg.(actv).stack);
```

```
      stg.(actv).stack := tl c(stg.(actv).stack);
      return val
   )
```

type:   Actvptr   -> S -> S Val


```
top(actv)=
   hd c(stg.(actv).stack)
```

type:   Actvptr   -> S -> S Val


```
unstack(actv)=
    stg.(actv).stack := tl c(stg.(actv).stack)
```

type:   Actvptr   -> S -> S


## 3.9.2  Expression Evaluation. -

A powerful set of instructions is needed to handle the various kinds of expressions.  The different kinds of expressions are studied in order to define such an instruction set.


## 3.9.2.1  Constants. -

Whenever a constant is met it must be pushed onto the stack.  A  single  instruction is sufficient for this purpose.

        Load-imm:        Push some constant onto the
                         evaluation stack.


## 3.9.2.1.1  Load-imm. -

        Load-imm      :: Val


```
int-Load-imm(mk-Load-imm(Val))=
   push(c thisactv,val)
```

type:   Load-imm   -> S -> S

## 3.9.2.2 Aggregates. -

Aggregates will not be treated in this document.

## 3.9.2.3 Names. -

The class of names covers a large class of expressions. A name can, depending on its context denote either a value or a location.

The simplest form of a name is a variable. Two operations are needed to handle names of simple variables, one to load the contents of a variable on the stack, another to load the address of the variable on the stack.

> Load-var:      Push the contents of a variable onto
> the evaluation stack.

> Load-addr:      Push the address of a variable onto
> the stack.

Three classes of names are used for the selection of sublocations or subvalues of composite locations respectively values. Compound locations are described by descriptors in the descriptor storage. To compute a sublocation of a composite location it must be possible to fetch the descriptor of a such a location. In addition instructions for reading values from and storing values in locations described by descriptors must be added to the storage . It should be noted that only sublocations of arraylocations are needed, record sublocations will never be described by a descriptor.

Three storage-operations are provided to handle descriptors.

> Read-descr:      Fetch the descriptor of a composite
> location.

> Read-array:      Fetch the array-value stored in the
> composite location described by a
> descriptor.

> Write-array:      Store an array-value using a
> descriptor of a composite location.
> The store operation include a
> transformation of the index tuples
> of the array-value to the index
> tuples of the descriptor.

Two A-code instructions to load the descriptor of a compound location are available.

> Load-var-descr: Push the descriptor of some
> compound variable onto the stack.

> Load-descr:      Pop the address of some compound
> location off the stack. Push the

descriptor for the compound location
at this address onto the stack.

Three instructions are designed to compute sublocations or descriptors from
a descriptor.

Loc-index:      First pop a number of index-values
from the stack, then pop an array-
descriptor. Finally apply the index
values to the descriptor to get a
location and push this location onto
the stack.

Loc-slice:      Pop the upper and lower bounds of
the slice from the stack, then pop
an array descriptor. Now construct
a new descriptor describing the
slice and push it onto the stack.

Loc-field:      Pop a record descriptor from the
stack. Apply a field name to the
descriptor to get the sublocation
of the field and push this location
onto the stack.

The corresponding instructions operating on values are:

Val-index:      Pop a set of index values and
an array value from the stack.
Apply the index values to the
array value to get an element
value and push this value onto
the stack.

Val-slice:      Pop the slice bounds and an
arrayvalue from the stack.
From these compute the array
slice value and push it onto
the stack.

Val-field:      Pop a record value from the stack.
Apply a field name to it to get
out the field value and push
this value onto the stack.

The store instruction is used when a value is to be stored in a location
computed on the stack.

Store:      Pop the value to be stored from the
evaluation stack, then pop the
address of the location in which the
value is to be stored from the stack.
Finally store the value in the storage
cell denoted by the location.

To load and store array values using descriptors two instructions are needed.

Read-array:    Pop an array-descriptor from the stack.
               then fetch the array stored in the
               compound location described by the
               descriptor and push it onto the stack.

Write-array:   Pop an array value and an array
               descriptor from the stack. If the
               length of the array value is the
               same as the "length" of the location
               described by the descriptor, then
               store the value in the location,
               otherwise raise the CONSTRAINT-ERROR
               exception.

In order to convert a final address to the value addressed by it another instructions are needed.

Load:          Pop a location off the stack, then
               push the value of the location.

Certain attributes are connected to objects and types. Some attributes
(like SIZE,FIRST and TERMINATED) can only be computed at run-time and a set
of instructions to do that is therefore needed. The instructions will all
be simple and will not be described in this document.

The last class of names is function-calls. A function call is treated much
like a procedure call, the only difference being that the function call delivers a result. The result must be passed from the point of the
return-statement inside the function body to the top of the evaluation-stack
in the calling environment. The mechanism provided is a special
'exit-block'-instruction called 'result'. To use this instruction the result-value must be stored in a variable in the activation record containing
the parameters.

Result:        Fetch the result-value from a variable
               in the current activation-record, then
               delete the current activation-record
               and push the result-value on the stack
               in the new current activation record.

3.9.2.3.1  Read-descr, Read-array & Write-array Storage Operations. -

read-descr(mk-Loc(defactv,id))=
  c(stg.(defactv).dstg.(id))

type:   Loc  -> S  -> S (A-descr | R-descr)

```
read-array(mk-A-descr(ds))=
  mk-A-val([it -> read(ds(it)) | it E dom ds])

type:   A-descr   -> S -> S A-val



write-array(mk-A-descr(ds),mk-A-val(av))=
  ( for all it E dom ds do
      ( let it' = transform-index-tuple(it,ds,av) in
        write(ds(it),av(it'))
      )
  )

type:   A-descr A-val   -> S -> S



transform-index-tuple(it,ds,av)=
  ( let dds = dom ds,
        dav = dom av in
    <it[i] - min{it'[i] | it' E dds}
          + min{it'[i] | it' E dav} | 1<=i<=len it>
  )

type:   INTG* A-descr A-val   -> INTG*
```

3.9.2.3.2  "Name-handling" A-code-instructions. -

```
        Load-var        :: Addr
        Load-var-descr  :: Addr
        Load-descr      :: ()
        Loc-Index       :: N1
        Loc-Slice       :: ()
        Loc-Field       :: Id
        Val-Index       :: N1
        Val-Slice       :: ()
        Val-Field       :: Id
        Store           :: ()
        Read-array      :: ()
        Write-array     :: ()



int-Load-var(mk-Load-var(mk-Addr(deflevel,id)))=
  ( def defactv : get-link(c thisactv,deflevel);
    def val     : read(mk-Loc(c defactv,id));
    push(c thisactv,val)
  )

type:   Load-var   -> S -> S
```

```
int-Load-addr(mk-Load-addr(mk-Addr(deflevel,id)))=
  ( def defactv : get-link(c thisactv,deflevel);
    push(c thisactv,mk-Loc(defactv,id))
  )
```

type:   Load-addr   ->  S  ->  S


```
int-Load-var-descr(mk-Load-var-descr(addr))=
  ( let mk-Addr(deflevel,id) = addr in
    def defactv : get-link(c thisactv, deflevel);
    def descr   : read-descr(mk-Loc(defactv,id));
    push(c thisactv, descr)
  )
```

type:   Load-var-descr   ->  S  ->  S


```
int-Load-descr(mk-Load-descr())=
  ( def loc   : pop(c thisactv);
    def descr : read-descr(loc);
    push(c thisactv, descr)
  )
```

type:   Load-descr   ->  S  ->  S


```
int-Load(mk-Load())=
  ( def loc : pop(c thisactv);
    def val : read(loc);
    push(c thisactv,val)
  )
```

type:   Load   ->  S  ->  S


```
int-Loc-Index(mk-Loc-Index(dim))=
  ( dcl it := <> type INTG*;
    for i = 1 to dim do
      ( def mk-Int-val(indx) : pop(c thisactv);
        it := <indx> ^ c it
      );
    ( def mk-A-descr(d): pop(c thisactv);
      if c it ~E dom d
      then raise(OBJECT-ERROR)
      else push(c thisactv, d(c it))
    )
  )
```

type:   Loc-index   ->  S  ->  S


```
int-Loc-Slice(mk-Loc-Slice())=
```

```
( def mk-Int-val(ub) : pop(c thisactv);
  def mk-Int-val(lb) : pop(c thisactv);
  def mk-A-descr(d)  : pop(c thisactv);
  ( lb > ub and lb E dom d
      -> push(c thisactv, mk-A-descr([])),
    lb ~E dom d or ub ~E dom d
      -> raise(OBJECT-ERROR),
    T
      -> ( let nd = [<i>->d(<i>) | <i> E dom d and
                                   lb <= i <= ub ]in
           push(c thisactv, mk-A-descr(nd))
         )
  )
)

type:  Loc-slice   -> S -> S


int-Loc-Field(mk-Loc-Field(fid))=
  ( def mk-R-descr(descr) : pop(c thisactv);
    push(c thisactv, descr(fid))
  )

type:  Loc-field   -> S -> S


int-Val-Index(mk-Val-Index(dim))=
  ( dcl it := <> type INTG*;
    for i = 1 to dim do
      ( def mk-Int-val(indx) : pop(c thisactv);
        it := <indx> ^ c it
      );
    ( def mk-A-Val(a) : pop(c thisactv);
      if c it ~E dom a
      then raise(OBJECT-ERROR)
      else push(c thisactv, a(c it))
    )
  )

type:  Val-index   -> S -> S


int-Val-Slice(mk-Val-Slice())=
  ( def mk-Int-val(ub) : pop(c thisactv);
    def mk-Int-val(lb) : pop(c thisactv);
    def mk-A-Val(a)    : pop(c thisactv);
    ( lb > ub and lb E dom a
        -> push(c thisactv, mk-A-Val([]),
      lb ~E dom a or ub ~E dom a
        -> raise(OBJECT-ERROR),
      T
        -> ( let na = [<i>->a(<i>) | <i> E dom a and
                                    lb <= i <= ub ] in
             push(c thisactv, mk-A-val(na))
           )
```

```
    )
  )

type:   Val-slice   -> S -> S



int-Val-Field(mk-Val-Field(fid))=
  ( def mk-R-val(r) : pop(c thisactv);
    push(c thisactv, f(fid))
  )

type:   Val-field   -> S -> S



int-Store(mk-Store())=
  ( def val : pop(c thisactv);
    def loc : pop(c thisactv);
    write(loc,val)
  )

type:   Store   -> S -> S



int-Read-array(mk-Read-array())=
  ( def ds : pop(c thisactv);
    push(c thisactv, read-array(ds))
  )

type:   Read-array   -> S -> S



int-Write-array(mk-Write-array())=
  ( def val : pop(c thisactv);
    def ds  : pop(c thisactv);
    if card dom val ≠ card dom ds
    then raise(CONSTRAINT-ERROR)
    else write-array(ds,val)
  )

type:   Write-array   -> S -> S
```

### 3.9.2.4 Allocators. -

An allocator causes the dynamic allocation of a piece of storage. Normally the storage is allocated in a global heap and cannot be explicitly released thereafter. Garbage-collection may be implemented; however techniques for that are well-known and the problem will not be included here.

A special feature in Ada allows the programmer to assign a fixed amount of storage to an access type. When objects are allocated to pointers of this type the storage will be taken from a fixed pool connected to the type. As

486

the  size  of the pool is fixed and since the type rules of Ada ensures that
objects in the pool cannot be referenced from outside the block in which the
type  is  defined,  the  storage of the pool can safely be released when the
block containing the definition of the accesstype is left.

The mechanism necessary to handle this technique is much simpler  (and  faster) than a general garbage-collection mechanism.

Only a few extensions are needed to handle allocation  of  storage  in  such
local heaps.

A heap is allocated in the activation record of the block containing the definition  of the corresponding access type.  In this way the deletion of the
heap will be automatic.  A heap is described by a heap descriptor stored  in
the  value-storage component of the activation record.  A heap-descriptor is
just a set of reserved entries in the descriptor storage  component  of  the
same activation record.


        Heap-descr        :: free-ids: Id-set


A special storage operation to handle the allocation of an object in a local
heap is given.


        heap-allocate(mk-Loc(actv,id),val)=
          ( def mk-Heap-descr(ids) : c(stg.(actv).vstg.(id));
            if ids = {}
            then mk-Exception(STORAGE-OVERFLOW)
            else ( def i E Id s.t. i E ids;
                   def newheap : mk-Heap-descr(ids \ {i});
                   stg.(actv).vstg.(id) := newheap;
                   allocate(mk-Loc(actv,i),val);
                   return mk-Loc(actv,i)
                 )
          )

        type:  Loc Val   ->  S  ->  S Loc



The allocator expression is compiled into an Heap-alloc instruction.

        Heap-alloc:      Pop a value from the stack and
                         store it in a location in the
                         head addressed by an address
                         provided in the instruction.
                         Push a pointer to the new object
                         on the stack.

### 3.9.2.4.1 Heap-alloc. -

```
Heap-alloc        :: heap: Addr


int-Heap-alloc(mk-Heap-alloc(mk-Addr(deflevel,id)))=
  ( def defactv : get-link(c thisactv,deflevel);
    def val     : pop(c thisactv);
    def res     : heap-allocate(mk-Loc(defactv,id),val);
    cases res:
      ( mk-Exception(STORAGE-OVERFLOW)
            -> raise(STORAGE-OVERFLOW),

        mk-Loc( , )
            -> push(c thisactv,res)
      )
  )

type:   Heap-alloc  -> S -> S
```

### 3.9.2.5  Prefix Expressions. -

Ada provides a small set of unary operators.  Unary operators are treated by instructions operating on the top of the evaluation stack.  Only one example will be given.  The rest is found in appendix A.

```
Not:              Pop a boolean value off the stack and
                  push its logical complement.
```

### 3.9.2.5.1 Not. -

```
Not               :: ()


int-Not(mk-Not())=
  ( def mk-Bool-val(v) : pop(c thisactv);
    push(c thisactv, mk-Bool-val(~v))
  )

type:   Not  -> S -> S
```

### 3.9.2.6  Infix Expressions. –

An elaborated set of dyadic operators exist. Most of them are handled by instructions operating on the two topmost values of the stack. Only a few examples will be given. The rest is given in appendix A.

      Add-int:          Add the two integer-values on the
                           the top of the stack. The result is
                           pushed on the stack.

      Cat:               Catenate the two array-values on the
                           top of the stack.

      And-then:          Inspect the boolean value on the top
                           of the stack, if the value is true
                           then remove the value from the stack,
                           otherwise jump to some label.

### 3.9.2.6.1  Add-int, Cat and And-then. –

```
Add-int     :: ()
Cat         :: index-type: Addr
And-then    :: Label


int-Add-int(mk-Add-int())=
  ( def mk-Int-val(rv) : pop(c thisactv);
    def mk-Int-val(lv) : pop(c thisactv);
    push(c thisactv, mk-Int-val(lv + rv))
  )

type:  Add-int  -> S -> S


int-Cat(mk-Cat(mk-Addr(deflevel,id)))=
  ( def defactv : get-link(c thisactv,deflevel);
    def mk-A-tp-descr(<(lb, )>, ) : read(mk-Loc(defactv,id));
    def mk-A-val(rv)                : pop(c thisactv);
    def mk-A-val(lv)                : pop(c thisactv);
    let lvlgth = card dom lv,
        lvlb   = min{i | <i> E dom lv},
        rvlb   = min{i | <i> E dom rv}  in
    let la = [<i-lvlb+lb>->lv(<i>)        | <i> E dom lv],
        ra = [<i-rvlb+lb+lvlgth>->rv(<i>) | <i> E dom rv] in
    push(c thisactv, mk-A-val( la U ra ))
  )

type:  Cat  -> S -> S
```

```
int-And-then(mk-And-then(addr))=
  ( def mk-Bool-val(cond) : top(c thisactv);
    if cond
    then unstack(c thisactv)
    else ins-cnt:= addr
  )
```

type:   And-then  -> S -> S

### 3.9.2.7  Range Tests. -

The membership operators of Ada test whether a value lie within a given range. A similar set of instructions are designed in the A-code-machine. As an example:

> In-range-int:    Pop the upper and lower bounds and
>                  the value from the stack. If the
>                  value lies within the range the
>                  boolean value true is pushed
>                  otherwise the value false is pushed.

### 3.9.2.7.1  In-range-int. -

In-range-int   :: ()

```
int-In-range-int(mk-In-range-int())=
  ( def mk-Int-val(ub) : pop(c thisactv);
    def mk-Int-val(lb) : pop(c thisactv);
    def mk-Int-val(v)  : pop(c thisactv);
    push(c thisactv, mk-Bool-val(lb <= v <= ub))
  )
```

type:   In-range  -> S -> S

### 3.9.2.8  Subtype Test. -

Ada provides an operator to check if a value is in a certain subtype. To handle this operator a set of instructions must be added. The instructions use a stored type descriptor in the check. Scalar values can be tested by the 'In-range' instructions if a possibility to load the range of a range-descriptor is given. The 'load-range-descr' instruction is designed to do this.

Load-range-descr:       Load the range of the range
descriptor stored in some
address.

## 3.9.2.8.1 Load-range-descr. -

Load-range-descr :: Addr

```
int-Load-range-descr(mk-Load-range-descr(mk-Addr(l,id)))=
  ( def actv : get-link(c thisactv, l);
    def mk-Range-descr(lb,ub) : read(mk-Loc(actv,id));
    push(c thisactv, mk-Int-val(lb));
    push(c thisactv, mk-Int-val(ub))
  )
```

type:   Load-range-descr  -> S -> S

## 3.9.2.9 Type Conversions. -

To facilitate conversions between the predefined types of Ada a set of type conversion instructions are provided. All type conversion instructions operate on the top stack element. Only two examples will be given. One is the instruction used to convert a floating point value to the integer value representing a fixed point value. For this purpose the delta of the fixed type must be provided. As the delta of a fixed type is a "static" attribute, it can be given as part of the conversion instruction. The other instruction is the conversion instruction used to convert a boolean value to an integer value. The conversion is necessary when boolean expressions are used as indices in arrays or as selectors in case statements. The conversion operation must preserve the ordering given by the boolean type, but the specific values are not important.

Conv-float-fixed:     Convert a floating-point value
to the integer value representing
a fixed value given the delta of
the fixed type.

Conv-bool-int:       Convert a boolean value to an
integer value.

### 3.9.2.9.1 Conv-float-fixed. –

```
Conv-float-fixed :: delta: NUM
Conv-bool-int   :: ()


int-Conv-float-fixed(mk-Conv-float-fixed(delta))=
  ( def mk-Float-val(v) : pop(c thisactv);
    push(c thisactv, mk-Int-val(round(v / delta)))
  )

type:   Conv-float-fixed   -> S -> S


int-Conv-bool-int(mk-Conv-bool-int())=
  ( def mk-Bool-val(v) : pop(c thisactv);
    push(c thisactv, mk-Int-val((v -> 1, T -> 0)))
  )

type:   Conv-bool-int   -> S -> S
```

## 3.10  Declarations

The declarative part of an Ada program describes the types, objects, procedures, functions and tasks to be used in the program. At run-time some actions must take place at the point where declarations occurred. These are:

Type-definitions could induce the evaluation and storing of constraints.

Object declarations may imply the evaluation and storing of initial values.

Procedures and functions can have default values for parameters, these must be evaluated and stored at the place of the procedure definition.

Ada provides the ability to apply constraints on types. Some constraints may contain general expressions and can therefore only be evaluated at run-time. To be able to handle such constraints some extra care must be taken. Several types of constraints exist:

        Range-constraints,
        Accuracy-constraints,
        Index-constraints and
        Discriminant-constraints.

Accuracy-constraints are of purely static nature and will not influence the design of the machine.

Information on the other types of constraints is stored in the storage as type-descriptors.

Corresponding to the constraint types are the descriptor-types:

        Range-descriptors,
        Array-type-descriptors and
        Discriminant-descriptors.

A range-descriptor describes the lower- and upper- bounds of a subtype of integer, float, fixed, boolean or enumeration type.

        Range-descr     :: lb: Val   ub: Val

An array-type-descriptor defines the index bounds and the element type of an array-type.

        A-tp-descr:: (lb: INTG  ub: INTG)+  etp: Loc

Finally a record-type-descriptor describes a record-type (as discriminants is not taken into account the internal structure of a record type descriptor cannot be given yet).

        R-tp-descr :: ...

To allocate space for a composite location a special entry in the storage processor is necessary. The operation is called 'stack-allocate' to indicate the difference to the 'heap-allocate' operation. The operation will just allocate the space necessary to hold the composite value provided and update the descriptor storage correspondingly. The value provided will then be stored in the new location. A similar A-code instruction is provided. Both operations are quite simple and will not be discussed further here.

A set of A-code-instructions for handling constraints is provided. Some examples will be given.

Range-constr:  The two top elements of the stack
               is stored as lower and upper bounds
               in a range-descriptor in the
               current activation record.

Range-check:   Check if the stack-top element obeys
               a stored range constraint. If not
               then raise the CONSTRAINT-ERROR
               exception.

Null-check:    Check if the stack-top element is the
               null access value. If that is the case
               the CONSTRAINT-ERROR is raised.

An initialisation expression can be connected to the declaration of a list of variables. In that case the initialisation expression must be evaluated once and the value yielded must be assigned to the variables in the list. The usual 'store' instruction will remove the value to be stored from the stack, it is therefore not suited for initialisations. A similar problem is present in the case of default values of parameters. Two instructions are provided to handle the storing of initial values of variables or default parameters.

Save:          Inspect the stack-top element
               and store its value in a variable
               in the current activation record.

Unstack:       Remove the stack-top element
               from the stack.

## 3.10.1  Range-constr, Range-check and Null-check. -

```
Range-constr   :: Id
Range-check    :: Addr
Null-check     :: ()
```

```
int-Range-constr(mk-Range-constr(id))=
  ( def mk-Int-val(ub) : pop(c thisactv);
    def mk-Int-val(lb) : pop(c thisactv);
    write(mk-Loc(c thisactv,id),mk-Range-descr(lb,ub))
  )
type:  Range-constr  -> S -> S
```

```
int-Range-check(mk-Rangecheck(mk-Addr(deflevel,id)))=
  ( def defactv : get-link(c thisactv,deflevel);
    def mk-Range-descr(lb,ub) : read(mk-Loc(defactv,id));
    def mk-Int-val(val) : top(c thisactv);
    if ~(lb <= val <= ub)
    then raise(OBJECT-ERROR)
    else I
  )
```

type:   Range-check  -> S -> S


```
int-Null-check(mk-Null-check())=
  ( def v : top(c thisactv);
    if v = nil
    then raise(CONSTRAINT-ERROR)
    else I
  )
```

type:   Null-check  -> S -> S


## 3.10.2  Save and Unstack. -

```
Save    :: Id
Unstack :: ()
```


```
int-Save(mk-Save(id))=
  ( def val = top(c thisactv);
    write(mk-Loc(c thisactv,id),val)
  )
```

type:   Save  -> S -> S


```
int-Unstack(mk-Unstack())=
  unstack(c thisactv)
```

type:   Unstack  -> S -> S

## 3.11 Statements

Ada offers several classes of statements:

> Null-statements,
> Assignment-statements,
> If-statements,
> Case-statements,
> Blocks,
> Loop-statements,
> Goto-statements,
> Exit-statements,
> Procedure-call-statements,
> Return-statements,
> Entry-call-statements,
> Accept-statements,
> Delay-statements,
> Abort-statements and
> Select-statements.

The A-Code-machine must provide an instruction set powerful enough to allow an easy and adequate compilation from these statement types into A-code. To ensure this every statement-type is considered and special purpose instructions are designed to handle the different statement types.

### 3.11.1 The Null Statement. -

Execution of the null statement has no effect. This can be obtained by generating no code, the null statement will therefore not influence the design of the instruction set.

### 3.11.2 The Assignment Statement. -

An assignment statement consists of two parts: the left-hand-side and the right-hand side. Execution of an assignment statement implies the evaluation of both the left-hand and the right-hand sides. The evaluation of the left-handside leads to a location, the right-hand side evaluates to a value. After evaluation the value of the right-hand side is type checked. If the value of the right-hand side is not within the type of the left-hand side the 'CONSTRAINT-ERROR' exception is raised, otherwise the value is stored in the location denoted by the left-hand side.

The instructions needed to perform the actions of an assignment statement, namely instructions to evaluate locations and expressions, to check constraints and to store a value in a location, have already been shown. No extra instructions are needed.

### 3.11.3 The If Statement. -

To execute an if statement the condition of the if statement must first be evaluated, then if the condition evaluates to true the statementlist of the then part is executed otherwise the statementlist of the else part is executed. This scheme calls for some way of conditional jumping. As the code-generation is to be performed in a single left to right scan of the parse-tree, the instruction needed is a jump on the condition false. In addition an unconditional jump instruction will be needed.

      False-jump:      Pop a boolean value from the stack.
                        If the value is FALSE then jump to
                        some label.

      Jump:           Perform an unconditional jump to
                        some label.

## 3.11.3.1 Falsejump and Jump. -

```
Falsejump      :: Label
Jump           :: Label


int-Falsejump(mk-Falsejump(addr))=
   ( def mk-Bool-val(cond) : pop(c thisactv);
     if ~ cond
     then ins-cnt := addr
     else I
   )
```

type:    False-jump  -> S -> S

```
int-Jump(mk-Jump(addr))=
   ins-cnt := addr
```

type:    Jump  -> S -> S

## 3.11.4 The Case Statement. -

Execution of a case statement causes the evaluation of the selector value. When the value is obtained a search for a statementlist labeled with the value is performed. If such a list is found it is executed, otherwise the statementlist labeled by 'others' are executed. Note that an 'others'-part is always present if the search can possibly fail. The search can always be implemented by a sequence of if statements. This solution is sometimes both inefficient and cumbersome and a special instruction is therefore provided. The instruction performs an indexed jump via a jumptable. This is the usual way to implement a case statement.

      Casejump:      Pop the selector value from the stack.

If the value lie in the domain of the
the jumptable of the instruction, then
fetch the continuation address from the
table, otherwise use the others-label
as continuation address.


3.11.4.1  Casejump. -


Casejump :: jumptable: (INTG $\xrightarrow{m}$ Label)  others: Label


```
int-Casejump(mk-Casejump(table,others))=
  ( def mk-Int-val(sel) : pop(c thisactv);
    if sel E dom table
    then ins-cnt := table(sel)
    else ins-cnt := others
  )
```

type:   Casejump  -> S -> S


3.11.5  The Block Statement. -

Blocks have already been treated in a previous chapter.  The  only  instructions  needed for block-statements are the enter/exit-block instructions and
the instructions for handling declarations.


3.11.6  Loop Statements. -

Three kinds of loop statements exist:

        the unconditional loop statement,
        the while loop statement and
        the for loop statement.

The unconditional loop statement causes an  unconditional  repetition  of  a
statementlist.   This is obtained by generating at the end of the statementlist a jump instruction which designate a jump to the start of the code corresponding to the statementlist.

The while loop statement causes a conditional repetition of a statementlist.
The repetition stops when a control expression evaluates to false.  The test
is performed at the top of the loop and the  'false-jump'  instruction  is
therefore able to do the job.

The for loop statement repeats the execution of a statementlist while count-

ing a variable through a range. The direction of the scan is determined at
compile-time and the control structure necessary to control the loop is thus
not complicated and can therefore be built from existing instructions.


As can be seen from the previous the loop statements need not extend the instruction repertoire.


### 3.11.7 The Goto Statement. -

Execution of a goto statement causes an unconditional jump to some other
point in the program.
It is possible to leave a block through a goto statement. The execution of
a goto statement may therefore lead to deletion of activation records. The
usual jump instruction is not able to handle this, therefore a new instruction is needed.

> Goto:        Leave a number of blocks, then
>              jump to some label.


### 3.11.7.1 Goto. -


> Goto            :: levels: NO   addr: Label


```
int-Goto(mk-Goto(levels,addr))=
  ( unwind(levels);
    ins-cnt := addr
  )
```

type:   Goto   ->   S   ->   S




### 3.11.8 The Exit Statement. -

Execution of an exit-statement causes the termination of one or more enclosing loop statements.
An exit statement is equivalent to a goto statement leading to a point just
after the end of the corresponding loop. The exit statement can therefore
be handled by the same mechanism as the goto statement.

3.11.9  The Procedure-call Statement. -

The procedure call statement have already been treated in chapter 3.5.


3.11.10  The Return Statement. -

Execution of a return statement stops the execution of a procedure or function. If a function is left, a return value is passed to the calling point.

As mentioned (in 3.5.1) the return instruction will restore the environment to that of the calling point and jump to the stored return address.

The return instruction can not return from a point nested in a block local to the procedure body. Such a return statement is treated as a goto statement leading to a point just after the last statement of the procedure body. The return instruction expanded at the end of the procedure body will then restore the environment to that of the calling point.

Return statements leading out of functions are treated slightly different. First the return value is evaluated and stored in a variable in the parameter activation. Then, if necessary a jump to the end of the function body is made. Finally the usual exit block instruction of the function body is replaced with a result instruction. The result instruction is used to delete the current activation record and then push the function result onto the stack.

> Result:            Read the result value from a variable
>                    in the current activation record. Then
>                    delete the current activation record.
>                    Finally push the result value onto the
>                    evaluation stack.


3.11.11  The Entry-call Statement. -

Ada tasks can only be synchronised by means of entry-calls. An entry-call is a call of a procedure owned by another task. An entry-call can only take place if the task owning the entry are performing an 'accept' statement on the same entry. Only one task can use an entry at any time. Entry-calls are queued up by the monitor until the task owning the entry performs an accept statement on the entry. When this happens the entry body is executed by the task owning the entry on behalf of, and using parameters received from, the task in the head of the queue corresponding to the entry. At the same time the calling task is removed from the queue. Only the Entry-call instruction will be mentioned here. A simple instruction to create an entry-name is left uncommented.

> Entry-call:        Pass the latest activation record
>                    as a parameterlist to the entry

call to the monitor, then await
termination of the call.


## 3.11.11.1 Entry-call. -


Entry-call        :: task: Addr   entry-name: Addr


```
int-Entry-call(mk-Entry-call(taskaddr,entryaddr))=
  ( let mk-Addr(tle,tid) = taskaddr,
        mk-Addr(ile,iid) = entryaddr in
    def ta        : get-link(c thisactv, tle),
        ia        : get-link(c thisactv, ile);
    def task      : read(mk-Loc(ta,tid)),
        entry-name : read(mk-Loc(ia,iid));
    let msg=mk-Entry-call(task,entry-name,c thisactv) in
    monitor-call(msg)
  )
```

type:   Entry-call   -> S -> S


## 3.11.12  The Accept Statement. -

When an accept statement is executed a parameterlist is received from the
task  in  the head of the queue corresponding to the entry. If the queue is
empty the task executing the accept statement is delayed until another  task
performs  an  entry-call on the entry. After reception of the parameterlist
the entrybody is executed by the task owning the entry on behalf of the task
calling  the  entry.  Finally the updated parameterlist is passed back to the
calling task which can then write back the out-parameters of the call.

Special attention is needed concerning exceptions raised during  the  execution of the entry body. If such an exception is not handled inside the body
special  actions  must  be  taken.   If  the  exception  is  not  the
'FAILURE'-exception  it must be propagated in both the task owning the entry
and  in  the  task calling the  entry.     If  the  exception  is  the
'FAILURE'-exception, the exception 'TASKING-ERROR' must be propagated in the
task calling the entry while the 'FAILURE' exception is  propagated  in  the
task  executing the accept-statement. Similarly if the task owning an entry
is aborted while executing the entry-body the 'TASKING-ERROR' is  passed  to
the  task  calling the entry. To handle such exceptions a special exception
handler is used. The address of this handler must be available AS  SOON  AS
the  execution  of the entry body is started. The setting up of the handler
is thus critical and must be performed indivisibly with  the  acceptance  of
the  entry-call. Likewise the handler must be removed BEFORE the parameter-
activation is passed back to the calling task.

Three instructions are needed to take care of the details of the accept statement.

Accept:             Receive a parameterlist for the entry
                    call from the monitor. Then set up an
                    exceptionhandler to handle exceptions
                    raised inside the accept body.

End-accept:         Take down the exception handler.
                    Return the parameters to the calling
                    task and tell the monitor that the
                    entry-call has ended.

Handle-excp-in-accept:
                    Handle an exception raised but not
                    handled inside the body of an
                    accept statement.


3.11.12.1  Accept, End-accept and Handle-excp-in-accept. -


Accept                 :: pseudoh: Label
End-accept             :: surr-level: Level
Handle-excp-in-accept  :: surr-level: Level



```
int-Accept(mk-Accept(hdlr))=
  ( def entry-name : pop(c thisactv);
    def call-actv :
              monitor-fct-call(mk-Accept(entry-name));
    proc-context(call-actv, c thisactv);
    thisactv := call-actv;
    set-excp-addr(c thisactv,hdlr)
  )
```

type:    Accept   -> S -> S


```
int-End-accept(mk-End-accept(surr-level))=
  ( def old-this : get-link(c thisactv, surr-level);
    set-excp-addr(c thisactv, nil);
    parm-context(c thisactv);
    monitor-call(mk-End-accept());
    thisactv := old-this
  )
```

type:    End-accept   -> S -> S

```
int-Handle-excp-in-accept(ins)=
  ( let mk-Handle-excp-in-accept(surrlevel) = ins in
    def excp : get-curr-excp(c thisactv);
```

```
      def old-this : get-link(c thisactv, surrlevel);
      set-excph-addr(c thisactv, nil);
      parm-context(c thisactv);
      monitor-call(mk-Excp-in-accept(excp));
      thisactv := oldthis;
      raise(excp)
   )
```

type:  Handle-excp-in-accept  -> S -> S


## 3.11.13  The Delay Statement. -

Execution of a delay statement causes the task executing it to be delayed
for the specified time. A single instruction is sufficient to handle this
statement-type.

    Delay:          Pop the delay period length from
                    the stack, then call the monitor
                    to get delayed for this period.


## 3.11.13.1  Delay. -

    Delay           :: ()


```
int-Delay(mk-Delay())=
  ( def time : pop(c thisactv);
    monitor-call(mk-Delay(time))
  )
```

type:  Delay -> S -> S


## 3.11.14  The Abort Statement. -

Execution of an abort-statement causes the execution of a number of named
tasks to be terminated. The abort instruction is made for this purpose.

    Abort:          Pop a number of task-names from
                    the stack, then tell the monitor
                    to terminate these tasks.

3.11.14.1  Abort. –


    Abort           :: N1


```
int-Abort(mk-Abort(n))=
  ( dcl tasks := {} type processor(task)-set;
    for i = 1 to n do
      tasks := c tasks U pop(c thisactv);
    output mk-Abort(c tasks) to monitor
  )
```

    type:    Abort   -> S -> S


3.11.15  The Select Statement. –

There are three types of select statements:

     Selective-wait,
     Conditional-entry-call and
     Timed-entry-call.

A selective wait is a nondeterministic selection between a number of select-alternatives.  Three types of alternatives exist:

     Accept-alternative,
     Delay-alternative and
     Terminate-alternative.

Finally an 'else'-part can be present, if so and if no alternative can be immediately selected, the statementlist of the else-part is executed.  A delay or terminate alternative can only be selected if no accept alternative can be selected.  A terminate alternative can only be present if there are no delay alternatives or else part.  Each alternative can be protected by a guard.  A guard is a boolean expression.  If the boolean expression evaluates to false the alternative cannot be selected for execution, the alternative is said to be 'closed'.
The accept and delay alternatives are similar to respectively the accept and delay statements.  They can both be followed by a statement list which will be executed as the last part of the alternative.
Execution of a terminate alternative causes the termination of the task executing the select statement.  A terminate alternative will not be selected as long as it is possible for other tasks to call entries in the select statement.

A conditional entry call issues an entry call if it does not cause a delay, otherwise the statementlist of the else part is executed.

A timed entry call issues an entry-call if it can be started within a certain time, otherwise an alternative statement list is executed.

Three instruction are designed to handle the three types of select statements.

Select:

For each alternative all information concerning the alternative must be stacked.
That is for each alternative its type, continuation address and guard must be stacked.
Additional information is needed in the case
of accept or delay alternatives. If the select statement contains an else part information about this must also be stacked. The
select instruction pops all the information
from the stack and collects information on
'open' alternatives. This information is
sent to the monitor which decides which alternative to select. Information on this
alternative is then (sooner or later) passed
back to the task.

If the selected alternative is an accept alternative the activation- pointer to the activation record containing the parameters
will be included in the information passed
back. This activation record is then established as the current one and execution is
resumed at the continuation address of the
alternative.

If a delay alternative is selected the
answer will first arrive when the delay has
taken place. In this case execution is resumed at the statement list following the
delay alternative.

If a terminate alternative is selected execution is resumed at a point corresponding
to this sort of alternative. A terminate
instruction must be generated at this point.

Finally if an else part is selected execution resumes at the statementlist of the
else part.

Conditional-entry-call:

Issues a conditional entry call. If the
call cannot be performed immediately, the
parameter activation is removed and execution is resumed at the instruction list corresponding to the else part of the select
statement.

Timed-entry-call:

Issues a timed entry call. If the call cannot be initiated within the specified time,
the parameter activation is removed and execution is resumed at the instruction list

corresponding to the alternative of the de-
laystatement.


3.11.15.1  Select, Conditional-entry-call and Timed-entry-call. -


```
    Select          :: N1  pseudoh: Label
    Cond-entry-call :: task: Addr  entry-name: Addr
                       not-called: Label
    Timed-entry-call:: task: Addr  entry-name: Addr
                       not-called: Label


    int-Select(mk-Select(n,hdlr))=
      ( dcl msg := {} type Select-alt-set;
        for i=1 to n do
          ( def tp    : pop(c thisactv),
                entry : pop(c thisactv);
            cases tp:
              ( ACCEPT
                  -> ( def entry-name: pop(c thisactv);
                       def mk-Bool-val(guard) :
                                     pop(c thisactv);
                       let alt =
                           mk-Accept-alt(entry-name,entry) in
                       if guard
                       then msg := c msg U {alt}
                       else I
                     ),
                DELAY
                  -> ( def time  : pop(c thisactv);
                       def mk-Bool-val(guard) :
                                     pop(c thisactv);
                       let alt = mk-Delay-alt(time,entry) in
                       if guard
                       then msg := c msg U {alt}
                       else I
                     ),
                TERMINATE
                  -> ( def mk-Bool-val(guard) :
                                     pop(c thisactv);
                       let alt = mk-Terminate-alt(entry) in
                       if guard
                       then msg := c msg U {alt}
                       else I
                     ),
                ELSE
                  ->  msg := c msg U {mk-Else-alt(entry)}
          );

        if c msg = {}
        then raise(SELECT-ERROR)
```

506

```
        else ( def mk-Select-answ(callactv,lab) :
                  monitor-fct-call(mk-Select(c msg));
               ins-cnt := lab;
               if callactv = nil
               then I
               else ( proc-context(callactv, c thisactv);
                      thisactv:= callactv;
                      set-excp-addr(c thisactv, hdlr)
                    )
             )
      )

type:   Select  -> S -> S



int-Cond-entry-call(ins)=
   ( let mk-Cond-entry-call(taskvar,entryvar,nc) = ins in
     let mk-Addr(tle,tid) = taskvar,
         mk-Addr(ele,eid) = entryvar in
     def ta : get-link(c thisactv,tle),
         ea : get-link(c thisactv,ele);
     def task : read(mk-Loc(ta,tid)),
         entry-name : read(mk-Loc(ea,eid));
     let msg = mk-Cond-entry-call(task,entry-name,c thisactv)in
     def answ : monitor-fct-call(msg);
     if answ = ELSE
     then ( ins-cnt := nc;
              exitlevel()
          )
     else I
   )

type:   Cond-entry-call  -> S -> S



int-Timed-entry-call(ins)=
   ( let mk-Timed-entry-call(taskvar,entryvar,nc) = ins in
     def time : pop(c thisactv);
     let mk-Addr(tle,tid) = taskvar,
         mk-Addr(ele,eid) = entryvar in
     def ta : get-link(c thisactv,tle),
         ea : get-link(c thisactv,ele);
     def task : read(mk-Loc(ta,tid)),
         entry-name : read(mk-Loc(ea,eid));
     let msg = mk-Timed-entry-call(task,entry-name,c thisactv)in
     def answ : monitor-fct-call(msg);
     if answ = DELAYED
     then ( ins-cnt := nc;
            exitlevel()
          )
     else I
   )

type:   Timed-entry-call  -> S -> S
```

4.0 Deriving A-code-interpreters

The derivation of an A-code interpreter from the definition of the A-code machine is intended to take place in three steps.

In step one the model is refined to mirror the structure of the target system. Three kinds of systems can be imagined.

>    Monoprocessors,
>    Multiprocessors with shared storage and
>    Distributed systems without shared storage.

The main differences between the obtained model and the original one, will be found in the processor structure and the processor communication. Most of the instruction interpretation functions will be unchanged. Likewise the main part of the storage-access functions will be unchanged.

Step two of the derivation will take into account the datatypes of the target system, that is machine attributes will be added as well as several lengths (short,long) of integers and reals might be implemented. This step will add machine dependent exceptions (like overflow) to the repertoire. In addition several copies of the arithmetic instructions will be created.

The third and final step will map the still abstract domains and instruction of the model on the concrete storage and instructions of the targetmachine. Representation of instructions and data must be chosen, the choice must be based on a study of the targetsystem. The representation of instructions and operands can either be chosen to save space or to save execution-time. This choice will therefore depend on the size and use of the target system [Ne79]. The choice must in addition to space-requirements and efficiency also take into account possible idiosyncrasies arround word-boundary problems and so on. It must be emphasized that this choice of representation need not harm the portability of the compiler. The representation of instructions and data can easily be parameters to the code-generator part of the compiler.

## 5.0  Comments and Conclusion

### 5.1  Ada versus A-code

One of the design goals for the development of the  A-code  machine  was  to
allow  a simple code generation from Ada into A-code.  I think this goal has
been reached.  The preliminary compiling algorithm shows that  almost  every
Ada-statement can be compiled into a simple sequence of A-code instructions.
Only the most complicated statements for  task  communication  are  compiled
into  less  simple  sequences,  but  as these statements are by far the most
powerful in Ada, it should not be surprising that the corresponding code  is
not trivial.

### 5.2  CHILL versus A-code

CHILL is a high-level language designed the CCITT to be used for programming
automatic telephone- exchange equipment [CH80],[HaBj80].

One of the sub-goals of this project was to find out whether it was possible
to  construct  a common virtual machine that can run both Ada and CHILL programs.
At a first glance it seems that Ada and CHILL share a large set of features.
Clearly  the  more  special  parts of the languages would have to be treated
separately.

As will be shown in the following the subset of common instructions would be
so small and trivial that it is not advisable to design a common virtual machine.

In the search for a common  instruction-set,  the  common  features  of  the
languages  must  be  identified.  Uncommon features cause extra instructions
that can only be used by programs  compiled  from  one  of  the  languages.
Common  features  with a different degree of generality in the two languages
will lead to general instructions able to handle the most general  language.
When  such instructions are used for the more specialised language they will
lead to unnecessary overhead.  Such an overhead cannot be accepted when  the
interpretation  technique  is to be used in a production environment.  If the
overhead should be avoided, two sets of instructions would be  necessary  to
handle  such concepts, one for the general case, another for the more specialised.

The mechanisms for task definition, creation and task communication  are  so
different in the two cases that common features can hardly be seen.

Ada features approximate numbers of the types float and  fixed,  such  types
are not present in CHILL.

CHILL contains special types like rows and mode-free pointers.  Of more normal  CHILL  features, not supported in Ada, powerset-types and procedure values can be mentioned.

Of common features with different degree of generality the following will be mentioned.

The case statement of CHILL allows a decision-table like selection with several selector expressions. The case statement of Ada certainly does not call for this kind of generality.

The for-loop of CHILL is much more complex than the for-loop of Ada. The CHILL-loop would need a set of special instructions to handle the for-loop, this is not necessary in Ada.

CHILL allows multiple assignment statements, these cannot be handled by the mechanisms necessary to handle Ada-assignments.

Ada allows run-time evaluated constraints on ranges and array index-types. The mechanisms necessary to handle these concepts would be unhandy and slow in the CHILL case, where such constraints are evaluated at compile-time and could as well be expanded into the instructions.

In Ada exceptionhandlers can only be connected to blocks, CHILL allows exceptionhandlers on all types of statements.

When all such differences have been taken into account, only a small, trivial instruction set would be common to the two languages. The common set would only contain trivial instructions to handle the simplest features of the languages like integer-arithmetics, simple assignment statements and if statements.

The price of a common machine would be an instruction-set much larger than necessary to handle a single of the languages. The interpreters would be larger and slower than necessary.

As only a small amount of work is saved this price is too high, and not worth paying.


5.3 P-code versus A-code

The P-code used in this comparison is the one generated by the Sequential Pascal compiler used in the SOLO operating system [Ha77].

The P-code is much simpler than the A-code. The only exception being the instructions for handling powersets in the P-code machine, such instructions are not present in the A-code machine.

The difference in complexity arises from the simple fact that Sequential Pascal is much simpler than Ada. Sequential Pascal does not feature tasks, exception handling, dynamic arrays, dynamic constraints and nested procedure definitions. These differences are so big that any further comparison would be meaningless.

## 5.4  Conclusion

A formal model of a special-purpose, high-level machine has been given.  The machine is designed for the sole purpose of running Ada programs.  The resulting machine is therefore very attractive as a target machine when an Ada compiler is to be implemented.  As it should be a manageable job to implement a software interpreter for the A-code-machine, it is deemed that this is the way to go.
The size and complexity of the model are about the same as those of a similar model of a modern minicomputer [Do78].  This means that a special-purpose high-level machine constructed in modern hardware technology need not be more complex than an ordinary minicomputer.  Therefore it is quite possible that such Ada machines will be introduced in the future.

**Appendix A**

**A formal model of the A-Code-Machine**

# Table of contents

Semantic Domains


Stg      = (Actvptr $\xrightarrow{m}$ Actv) $\underline{U}$ (ROOT $\xrightarrow{m}$ Actv)

Actvptr    :: TOKEN

Actv     :: disp:   Display
        lastactv:  Actvptr
        ret-addr: [Label]
        excph:   [Label]
        curr-excp: [QUOT]
        dstg:   Descr-stg
        vstg:   Val-stg
        stack:   Stack

Display    :: Actvptr+

Level     = N1

Id      = TOKEN

Label     = N1


Descr-stg   = Id $\xrightarrow{m}$ Descr

Descr     = Comp-descr ¦ Simple-descr

Simple-descr  :: Id

Comp-descr  = A-descr  ¦ R-descr

A-descr    :: INTG+ $\xrightarrow{m}$ Loc

R-descr    :: Id $\xrightarrow{m}$ Loc

Loc     :: Actvptr Id


Val-stg    = Id $\xrightarrow{m}$ Simple-val

Simple-val  = Scalar-val ¦ Type-descr ¦ Heap-descr ¦
        Loc     ¦ nil    ¦ Task-val   ¦
        Entry-name

Scalar-val  = Int-val   ¦ Float-val  ¦ Bool-val

```
Stack          =  Stackelm*

Stackelm       =  Val          | A-descr        | R-descr

Val            =  Simple-val   | A-val          | R-val

A-val          :: INTG+ --> Val
                        m

R-val          :: Id --> Val
                     m

Heap-descr     :: free-ids: Id-set

Int-val        :: INTG

Float-val      :: NUM

Bool-val       :: BOOL

Task-val       :: processor(task)

Entry-name     :: entry-id: Id  index: [INTG]

Type-descr     =  Range-descr  | A-tp-descr     | R-tp-descr

Range-descr    :: lb: Val  ub: Val

A-tp-descr     :: (lb: INTG  ub: INTG)+  etp: Loc

R-tp-descr     :: ...
```

**Syntactic Domains**


Program = Ins*


| Ins | = Call | Return | |
| | Result | | |
| | | | |
| | Enterblock | Exitblock | |
| | | | |
| | Sethandler | Handle | |
| | Raise | Reraise | |
| | | | |
| | Jump | Falsejump | |
| | Goto | Casejump | |
| | | | |
| | Load-addr | Load | |
| | Load-imm | Load-var | |
| | Store | Store-var | |
| | Save | Unstack | |
| | | | |
| | Load-var-descr | Load-descr | |
| | Loc-Index | Loc-Slice | |
| | Loc-Field | | |
| | Val-Index | Val-Slice | |
| | Val-Field | | |
| | Read-array | Write-array | |
| | | | |
| | Add-int | Sub-int | |
| | Mul-int | Div-int | |
| | Mod-int | Rem-int | |
| | Exp-int | | |
| | | | |
| | Add-float | Sub-float | |
| | Mul-float | Div-float | |
| | Exp-float | | |
| | | | |
| | Cat | | |
| | | | |
| | Eq-int | Neq-int | |
| | Gt-int | Lt-int | |
| | Ge-int | Le-int | |
| | | | |
| | Eq-float | Neq-float | |
| | Gt-float | Lt-float | |
| | Ge-float | Le-float | |
| | | | |
| | Eq-bool | Ne-bool | |
| | Gt-bool | Lt-bool | |
| | Ge-bool | Le-bool | |
| | | | |
| | And | Or | |
| | Xor | | |
| | And-then | Or-else | |

| | |
|---|---|
| Neg-int | Neg-float |
| Not | |
| | |
| Conv-int-float | Conv-int-fixed |
| Conv-float-int | Conv-float-fixed |
| Conv-fixed-int | Conv-fixed-float |
| Conv-fixed-fixed | |
| Conv-bool-int | |
| | |
| In-range-int | Not-in-range-int |
| In-range-float | Not-in-range-float |
| In-range-bool | Not-in-range-bool |
| | |
| Range-constr | |
| Load-range-descr | |
| Index-constr | |
| Range-check | |
| Null-check | |
| | |
| Heap-alloc | Alloc-comp |
| | |
| Create-task | Initiate |
| Terminate | |
| Abort | |
| Raise-failure | |
| Entry-call | Create-entry-name |
| Accept | End-Accept |
| Handle-excp-in-accept | |
| Delay | |
| Select | |
| Cond-entry-call | |
| Timed-entry-call | |

```
Call              :: def-level: Level   entry-addr: Label
Return            :: ()
Result            :: res-var: Id

Enterblock        :: init-stg: Id ‒ₘ> Val   vars: (Id,Type)-set
Exitblock         :: ()

Sethandler        :: Label
Handle            :: excps: QUOT-set   afterhandler: Label
Raise             :: QUOT
Reraise           :: ()

Jump              :: Label
Falsejump         :: Label
Goto              :: levels: NO   addr: Label
Casejump          :: jumptable: INTG ‒ₘ> Label   others: label


Load-addr         :: Addr
Load              :: ()
Load-imm          :: Val
Load-var          :: Addr
Store             :: ()
Store-var         :: Addr
Save              :: Id
Unstack           :: ()

Load-var-descr    :: Addr
Load-descr        :: ()
Loc-Index         :: N1
Loc-Slice         :: ()
Loc-Field         :: Id
Val-Index         :: N1
Val-Slice         :: ()
Val-Field         :: Id
Read-array        :: ()
Write-array       :: ()

Add-int           :: ()
Sub-int           :: ()
Mul-int           :: ()
Div-int           :: ()
Mod-int           :: ()
Rem-int           :: ()
Exp-int           :: ()
Add-float         :: ()
Sub-float         :: ()
Mul-float         :: ()
Div-float         :: ()
Exp-float         :: ()

Cat               :: index-type: Addr
```

```
Eq-int          :: ()
Neq-int         :: ()
Gt-int          :: ()
Lt-int          :: ()
Ge-int          :: ()
Le-int          :: ()
Eq-float        :: ()
Neq-float       :: ()
Gt-float        :: ()
Lt-float        :: ()
Ge-float        :: ()
Le-float        :: ()
Eq-bool         :: ()
Neq-bool        :: ()
Gt-bool         :: ()
Lt-bool         :: ()
Ge-bool         :: ()
Le-bool         :: ()

And             :: ()
Or              :: ()
Xor             :: ()

And-then        :: Label
Or-else         :: Label

Neg-int         :: ()
Neg-float       :: ()
Not             :: ()

Conv-int-float  :: ()
Conv-int-fixed  :: delta: NUM
Conv-float-int  :: ()
Conv-float-fixed:: delta: NUM
Conv-fixed-int  :: delta: NUM
Conv-fixed-float:: delta: NUM
Conv-fixed-fixed:: delta1: NUM  delta2: NUM
Conv-bool-int   :: ()

In-range-int            :: ()
Not-in-range-int        :: ()
In-range-float          :: ()
Not-in-range-float      :: ()
In-range-bool           :: ()
Not-in-range-bool       :: ()
```

```
Range-constr      :: Id
Load-range-descr :: Addr
Index-constr      :: Id   dim: N1   etp: Addr
Range-check       :: Addr
Null-check        :: ()

Alloc-comp        :: comp: Id
Heap-alloc        :: heap: Addr

Create-task       :: deflevel: Level   deplevel: Level
                     entry-addr: Label
Initiate          :: ()
Abort             :: N1
Raise-failure     :: ()
Entry-call        :: task: Addr   entry-name: Addr
Create-entry-name :: entry-id: Id
Accept            :: pseudoh: Label
End-accept        :: surr-level: Level
Handle-excp-in-accept :: surr-level: Level
Delay             :: ()
Terminate         :: ()
Select            :: N1   pseudoh: Label
Cond-entry-call :: task: Addr   entry-name: Addr   nocall: Label
Timed-entry-call:: task: Addr   entry-name: Addr   delayed: Label


Addr              :: Level   Id
```

Communication Domains


Stg / Task, communication-domains

|              |                                          |
|--------------|------------------------------------------|
| Push         | :: Actvptr Stackelm                      |
| Pop          | :: Actvptr                               |
| Top          | :: Actvptr                               |
| Unstack      | :: Actvptr                               |
| Read         | :: Loc                                   |
| Read-descr   | :: Loc                                   |
| Read-array   | :: A-descr                               |
| Write-array  | :: A-descr  A-val                        |
| Write        | :: Loc     Stgelm                        |
| Create-actv  | :: Actvptr                               |
| Delete-actv  | :: Actvptr                               |
| Proc-context | :: call-actv: Actvptr  defactv: Actvptr  |
| Parm-context | :: Actvptr                               |
| Get-link     | :: Actvptr Level                         |
| Extend-stg   | :: Actvptr  Id $\underset{m}{\Rightarrow}$ Val |
| Stack-allocate | :: Id  Val                             |
| Heap-allocate | :: Loc  Val                             |
| Set-ret-addr | :: Actvptr Label                         |
| Get-ret-addr | :: Actvptr                               |
| Set-excph-addr | :: Actvptr Label                       |
| Get-excph-addr | :: Actvptr                             |
| Set-curr-excp | :: Actvptr QUOT                         |
| Get-curr-excp | :: Actvptr                              |

**Task / Monitor, communication-domains**

| | | |
|---|---|---|
| Continue? | :: | () |
| Continue | :: | () |
| Exception | :: | QUOT |
| Abort | :: | () |
| Terminated | :: | () |
| Create-task | :: | defactv: Actvptr  depactv: Actvptr  entry: Label |
| Initiate | :: | Actvptr |
| Abort | :: | processor(task)-set |
| Raise-failure | :: | processor(task) |
| Entry-call | :: | Task-val  Entry-name  Actvptr |
| Accept | :: | Entry-name |
| Accept-answ | :: | Actvptr |
| Excp-in-accept | :: | QUOT |
| End-accept | :: | () |
| Delay | :: | Time |
| Terminate | :: | () |
| Select | :: | Select-alt-set |
| Select-alt | = | Accept-alt  \| Delay-alt  \|  Terminate-alt\| Else-alt |
| Accept-alt | :: | Entry-name  Label |
| Delay-alt | :: | Time  Label |
| Terminate-alt | :: | Label |
| Else-alt | :: | Label |
| Select-answ | :: | [Actvptr]  Label |
| Cond-entry-call | :: | Task-val  Entry-name  Actvptr |
| Timed-entry-call | :: | Task-val  Entry-name  Actvptr  Time |
| Entry-name | :: | Id  [NO] |

**Monitor / Stg, communication-domain**

    **Terminate**        :: ()

Monitor-processor

```
monitor  processor(code)=

  ( def store : start stg();
    def main  : start task(code,1,ROOT);
    dcl tbl   := {main} type processor(task) =ₘ> Actvptr;
        pi             type processor(task);

    trap exit with I in

      cycle

        {
            input mk-Continue?()              from task set pi
               -> output continue(c pi)                to c pi,

            input mk-Terminated()             from task set pi
               -> output stop-task(c pi)               to c pi,

            input mk-Create-task(defactv,entry,createactv)
                                         from task set pi
              -> output create-task(defactv,depactv,entry)
                                                   to c pi,

            input mk-Initiate(create-actv) from task set pi
               -> output initiate(c pi, create-actv) to c pi

            input mk-Abort(tasks)             from task set pi
               -> output abort(tasks)                  to c pi

            input mk-Raise-failure(task) from task set pi
               -> output raise-failure(task)       to c pi,

               ...
               ...
        };

    output mk-Terminate() to stg

  )
```

Monitor-processor:  Local functions

```
create-task(defactv,depactv,entry)=
  ( def newtask : start task(code,entry,defactv);
    tbl:= c tbl  U  [newtask -> depactv];
    return mk-Task-val(newtask)
  )
```

type:   Actvptr Actvptr Label  ->  S  ->  S


```
initate(create-actv)=
  ( ....
    return mk-Continue()
  )
```

type:   Actvptr  ->  S  ->  S


```
abort(tasks)=
  ( ....
    return mk-Continue()
  )
```

type:   Task-val-set  ->  S  ->  S

```
raise-failure(task)=
  ( ...
    return mk-Continue()
  )

type:  .Task-val -> S -> S


stop-task(pi)=
  ( ...
    tbl := c tbl \ {pi};
    if c tbl = {}
    then exit
    else return mk-Continue()
  )

type:  Task-val  -> S -> S


continue(pi)=
  ( ...  -> mk-Abort(),
    ...  -> mk-Exception( ... ),
    ...  -> mk-Continue()
  )

type:  Task-val  -> S -> S (Abort | Exception | Continue)
```

Storage-processor

```
stg  processor()=

( def ra : mk-Actv(<>,undefined,nil,nil,nil,[],[],<>);
  dcl stg := [ROOT -> ra] type Stg;
      pi                    type processor(task);

  trap exit with I in

    cycle

      {
          input mk-Push(actv,val)
             -> push(actv,val),

          input mk-Pop(actv)                      set pi
             -> output pop(actv)                  to c pi,

          input mk-Top(actv)                      set pi
             -> output top(actv)                  to c pi,

          input mk-Unstack(actv)
             -> unstack(actv),

          input mk-Read(loc)                      set pi
             -> output read(loc)                  to c pi,

          input mk-Write(loc,val)
             -> write(loc,val),

          input mk-Read-descr(loc)                set pi
             -> output read-descr(loc)            to c pi,

          input mk-Read-array(descr)              set pi
             -> output read-array(descr)          to c pi,

          input mk-Write-array(descr,val)
             -> write-array(descr,val),

          input mk-Create-Actv(actv)              set pi
             -> output create-actv(actv)          to c pi,

          input mk-Delete-Actv(actv)              set pi
             -> output delete-actv(actv)          to c pi,

          input mk-Proc-context(callactv,defactv)
             -> proc-context(callactv,defactv),

          input mk-Parm-context(actv)
             -> parm-context(actv),
```

527

```
          input mk-Get-link(actv,level)          set pi
             -> output get-link(actv,level)      to c pi,

          input mk-Extend-stg(actv,xstg)
             -> extend-stg(actv,xstg),

          input mk-Stack-allocate(loc,val)
             -> stack-allocate(loc,val),

          input mk-Heap-allocate(loc,val)         set pi
             -> output heap-allocate(loc,val)     to c pi,

          input mk-Set-ret-addr(actv,addr)
             -> set-ret-addr(actv,addr),

          input mk-Get-ret-addr(actv)             set pi
             -> output get-ret-addr(actv)         to c pi,

          input mk-Set-excph-addr(actv,addr)
             -> set-excph-addr(actv,addr),

          input mk-Get-excph-addr(actv)           set pi
             -> output get-excph-addr(actv)       to c pi,

          input mk-Set-curr-excp(actv,excp)
             -> set-curr-excp(actv,excp),

          input mk-Get-curr-excp(actv)            set pi
             -> output get-curr-excp(actv)        to c pi,



          input mk-Terminate()                    from monitor
             -> exit

      };

   assert  dom c stg = ROOT

)
```

Storage-processor:  Local functions


```
push(actv,val)=
  stg.(actv).stack := <val> ^ c(stg.(actv).stack)
```

type:    Actvptr Val  ->  S  ->  S


```
pop(actv)=
  ( def val : hd c(stg.(actv).stack);
    stg.(actv).stack := tl c(stg.(actv).stack);
    return val
  )
```

type:    Actvptr  ->  S  ->  S Val


```
top(actv)=
  hd c(stg.(actv).stack)
```

type:    Actvptr  ->  S  ->  S Val


```
unstack(actv)=
  stg.(actv).stack := tl c(stg.(actv).stack)
```

type:    Actvptr  ->  S  ->  S

```
read(mk-Loc(defactv,id))=
  ( def d : c(stg.(defactv).dstg.(id));
    cases d:
      ( mk-Simple-descr(id')
          -> c(stg.(defactv).vstg.(id')),
        mk-A-descr(ds)
          -> mk-A-Val([it->read(ds(it)) | it E dom ds]),
        mk-R-descr(ds)
          -> mk-R-val([id->read(ds(id)) | id E dom ds])
      )
  )

type:  Loc -> S -> S Val



write(mk-Loc(defactv,id),val)=
  ( def d : c(stg.(defactv).dstg.(id));
    cases d:
      ( mk-Simple-descr(id')
          -> stg.(defactv).vstg.(id') := val,
        mk-A-descr(ds)
          -> for all it E dom ds do
                write(ds(it),val(it)),
        mk-R-descr(ds)
          -> for all id E dom ds do
                write(ds(id),val(id))
      )
  )

type:  Loc Val -> S -> S



read-descr(mk-Loc(defactv,id))=
  c(stg.(defactv).dstg.(id))

type:  Loc -> S -> S A-descr



read-array(mk-A-descr(ds))=
  mk-A-val([it -> read(ds(it)) | it E dom ds])

type:  A-descr -> S -> S A-val



write-array(mk-A-descr(ds),mkA-val(av))=
  for all it E dom ds do
    ( let it' = transform-index-tuple(it,ds,av) in
      write(ds(it),av(it'))
    )

type:  A-descr A-val -> S -> S
```

```
transform-index-tuple(it,ds,av)=
  ( let dds = dom ds,
        dav = dom av in
    <it[i] - min{it'[i] | it' E dds}
           + min{it'[i] | it' E dav} | 1<=i<=len it>
  )

type:   INTG* A-descr A-val  ->  INTG*



allocate(mk-Loc(actv,id),val)=
  ( let vst = stg.(actv).vstg,
        dst = stg.(actv).dstg  in
    cases val:
      ( mk-A-val(av)
          -> ( dst := c dst U [id -> mk-A-descr([])];
               for all it E dom av do
                 ( def id' E Id s.t. id' ~E dom c dst;
                   dst.(id) := c(dst.(id)) U [it -> id'];
                   allocate(mk-Loc(actv,id'),av(it))
                 )
             ),
        mk-R-val(rv)
          -> ( dst := c(dst) U [id -> mk-R-descr([])];
               for all fid E dom rv do
                 ( def id' E Id s.t. id' ~E dom c dst;
                   dst.(id) := c(dst) U [fid -> id'];
                   allocate(mk-Loc(actv,id'),rv(id))
                 )
             ),
        T
          -> ( def id' E Id s.t. id' ~E dom c vst;
               vst := c vst U [id' -> val];
               dst := c dst U [id -> mk-Scalar-descr(id')]
             )
      )
  )

type:   Loc Val ->  S  ->  S



stack-allocate(loc,val)=
  allocate(loc,val)

type:   Loc Val ->  S  ->  S
```

```
create-actv(actvp)=
  ( def newactvp E Actvptr s.t. newactvp ~E dom c stg;
    def newdisp = c(stg.(actvp).disp) ^ <newactvp>;
    def actv : mk-Actv(newdisp,actvp,nil,nil,nil,[],[],<>);
    stg := c stg U [newactvp -> actv];
    return newactvp
  )

type:   Actvptr  ->  S  ->  S Actvptr



delete-actv(actv)=
  ( def lastactv : c(stg.(actv).lastactv);
    stg := c stg \ { actv };
    return lastactv
  )

type:   Actvptr  ->  S  ->  S Actvptr



proc-context(callactv,defactv)=
  stg.(callactv).disp := c(stg.(defactv).disp) ^ <callactv>

type:   Actvptr Actvptr  ->  S  ->  S



parm-context(actv)=
  ( def lastactv : c(stg.(actv).lastactv);
    stg.(actv).disp := c(stg.(lastactv).disp) ^ <actv>
  )

type:   Actvptr  ->  S  ->  S



get-link(actv,deflevel)=
  c(stg.(actv).disp.[deflevel])

type:   Actvptr Level  ->  S  ->  S Actvptr



extend-stg(actv,newstg)=
  for all id E dom newstg do
    allocate(mk-Loc(actv,id),newstg(id))

type:   Actvptr Id -> Val  ->  S  ->  S
```

```
heap-allocate(mk-Loc(actv,id),val)=
  ( def mk-Heap-descr(ids) : c(stg.(actv).vstg.(id));
    if ids = {}
    then return mk-Exception(STORAGE-OVERFLOW)
    else ( def i E Id s.t. i E ids;
           def newheap : mk-Heap-descr(ids \ {i});
           stg.(actv).vstg.(id) := newheap;
           allocate(mk-Loc(actv,i),val);
           return mk-Loc(actv,i)
         )
  )

type:   Loc Val  ->  S  ->  S Loc
```

```
set-ret-addr(actv,addr)=
  stg.(actv).ret-addr := addr
```

type:    Actvptr Label  ->  <u>S</u>  ->  <u>S</u>

```
get-ret-addr(actv)=
  c(stg.(actv).ret-addr)
```

type:    Actvptr  ->  <u>S</u>  ->  <u>S</u> [Label]

```
set-excph-addr(actv,addr)=
  stg.(actv).excph := addr
```

type:    Actvptr [Label]  ->  <u>S</u>  ->  <u>S</u>

```
get-excph-addr(actv)=
  c(stg.(actv).excph)
```

type:    Actvptr  ->  <u>S</u>  ->  <u>S</u> [Label]

```
set-curr-excp(actv,excp)=
  stg.(actv).curr-excp := excp
```

type:    Actvptr QUOT  ->  <u>S</u>  ->  <u>S</u>

```
get-curr-excp(actv)=
  c(stg.(actv).curr-excp)
```

type:    Actvptr  ->  <u>S</u>  ->  <u>S</u> [QUOT]

534

Task-processor

```
task  processor(code,entry,defactv)=

( dcl thisactv := defactv type Actvptr,
      ins-cnt  := entry   type Label;

  trap exit with I in

    cycle

    {  monitor-call(mk-Continue?());
       ( def ins : code[c ins-cnt];
         ins-cnt := c ins-cnt + 1;
         int-Ins(ins)
       )
    };

    output mk-Terminated() to monitor

)
```

**Task-processor:**  Communication functions

```
push(actv,val)=
  output mk-Push(actv,val)                to   stg

type:   Actvptr Val  ->  S  ->  S


pop(actv)=
( output mk-Pop(actv)                     to   stg;
  input  val                              from stg
    ->  return val
)

type:   Actvptr  ->  S  ->  S Val


top(actv)=
( output mk-Top(actv)                     to   stg;
  input  val                              from stg
    ->  return val
)

type:   Actvptr  ->  S  ->  S Val


unstack(actv)=
  output mk-Unstack(actv)                 to   stg

type:   Actvptr  ->  S  ->  S
```

```
read(loc)=
  ( output mk-Read(loc)                    to   stg;
    input val                              from stg
      -> return val
  )

type:   Loc -> S -> S Val



write(loc,val)=
  output mk-Write(loc,val)                 to   stg

type:   Loc Val -> S -> S



read-descr(loc)=
  ( output mk-Read-descr(loc)              to   stg;
    input descr                            from stg
      -> return descr
  )

type:   Loc -> S -> S (A-descr ¦ R-descr)



read-array(ds)=
  ( output mk-read-array(ds)               to   stg;
    input val                              from stg
      -> return val
  )

type:   A-descr -> S -> S A-val



write-array(ds,av)=
  output mk-write-array(ds,av) to   stg

type:   A-descr A-val -> S -> S
```

537

```
create-actv(actv)=
  ( output mk-Create-actv(actv)          to   stg;
    input  newactv                       from stg
     -> return newactv
  )

type:   Actvptr -> S -> S Actvptr


delete-actv(actv)=
  ( output mk-Delete-actv(actv)          to   stg;
    input  oldactv                       from stg
     -> return oldactv
  )

type:   Actvptr -> S -> S Actvptr


proc-context(callactv,defactv)=
  output mk-Proc-context(callactv,defactv) to stg

type:   Actvptr Actvptr -> S -> S


parm-context(actv)=
  output mk-Parm-context(actv)  to stg

type:   Actvptr -> S -> S


get-link(actv,level)=
  ( output mk-Get-link(actv,level)       to   stg;
    input  defactv                       from stg
     -> return defactv
  )

type:   Actvptr Level -> S -> S Actvptr


extend-stg(actv,xstg)=
  output mk-Extend-stg(actv,xstg)        to   stg

type:   Actvptr Id -> Val -> S -> S
```

```
stack-allocate(loc,val)=
  output mk-Stack-allocate(loc,val)      to stg

type:   Loc Val  ->  S  ->  S


heap-allocate(loc,val)=
  ( output mk-Heap-allocate(loc,val)     to   stg;
    input  res                           from stg
     -> return res
  )

type:   Loc Val  ->  S  ->  S Loc
```

```
set-ret-addr(actv,addr)=
  output mk-Set-ret-addr(actv,addr)        to    stg

type:   Actvptr Label -> S -> S



get-ret-addr(actv)=
  ( output mk-Get-ret-addr(actv)           to    stg;
    input  addr                            from stg
     -> return addr
  )

type:   Actvptr -> S -> S [Label]



set-excph-addr(actv,addr)=
  output mk-Set-excph-addr(actv,addr) to    stg

type:   Actvptr [Label] -> S -> S



get-excph-addr(actv)=
  ( output mk-Get-excph-addr(actv)         to    stg;
    input  addr                            from stg
     -> return addr
  )

type:   Actvptr -> S -> S [Label]



set-curr-excp(actv,excp)=
  output mk-Set-curr-excp(actv,excp)       to    stg

type:   Actvptr QUOT -> S -> S



get-curr-excp(actv)=
  ( output mk-Get-curr-excp(actv)          to    stg;
    input  excp                            from stg
     -> return excp
  )

type:   Actvptr -> S -> S [QUOT]
```

Task-processor:  Auxiliary functions


```
unwind(levels)=
  for i=1 to levels do
    exitlevel()

type:   NO -> S -> S


terminate()=
  ( while c thisactv ≠ defactv do
      exitlevel();
    exit
  )

type:   () -> S -> S


exitlevel()=
  ( monitor-call(mk-Exit-block(c thisactv));
    thisactv := delete-actv(c thisactv)
  )

type:   () -> S -> S
```

```
raise(excption)=
  find-handler(exception)

type:   QUOT -> S -> S



reraise()=
  ( def exception : get-curr-excp(c thisactv);
    find-handler(exception)
  )

type:   () -> S -> S



find-handler(exception)=
  ( ins-cnt := get-excph-addr(c thisactv);
    while c ins-cnt = nil do
      if c thisactv = defactv
      then exit
      else ( exitlevel();
             ins-cnt := get-excph-addr(c thisactv)
           );
    set-curr-excp(c thisactv, exception)
  )

type:   QUOT -> S -> S
```

```
monitor-fct-call(msg)=
  ( output msg to monitor;
    input  answ from monitor
      -> cases answ:
           ( mk-Terminate()     -> return terminate(),
             mk-Exception(excp) -> return raise(excp),
             T                  -> return return  answ
           )
  )
```

type:   Message  ->  S  ->  S Answer


```
monitor-call(msg)=
  def dummy : monitor-fct-call(msg)
```

type:   Message  ->  S  ->  S

Task-processor:   Interpretation functions


```
    int-Ins(ins)=

      ( cases ins:

            ( mk-Call( )                -> int-Call(ins),
              mk-Return( )              -> int-Return(ins),
              mk-Result( )              -> int-Result(ins),

              mk-Enterblock( , )        -> int-Enterblock(ins),
              mk-Exitblock( )           -> int-Exitblock(ins),,

              mk-Sethandler( )          -> int-Sethandler(ins),
              mk-Handle( ,, )           -> int-Handle(ins),
              mk-Raise( )               -> int-Raise(ins),
              mk-Reraise( )             -> int-Reraise(ins),

              mk-Jump( )                -> int-Jump(ins),
              mk-Falsejump( )           -> int-Falsejump(ins),
              mk-Goto( , )              -> int-Goto(ins),
              mk-Casejump( , )          -> int-Casejump(ins),

              mk-Load-addr( )           -> int-Load-addr(ins),
              mk-Load( )                -> int-Load(ins),
              mk-Load-imm( )            -> int-Load-imm(ins),
              mk-Load-var( )            -> int-Load-var(ins),
              mk-Store( )               -> int-Store(ins),
              mk-Save( )                -> int-Save(ins),
              mk-Unstack( )             -> int-Unstack(ins),

              mk-Load-var-descr( )      -> int-Load-var-descr(ins),
              mk-Load-descr()           -> int-Load-descr(ins),
              mk-Loc-Index( )           -> int-Loc-Index(ins),
              mk-Loc-Slice( )           -> int-Loc-Slice(ins),
              mk-Loc-Field( )           -> int-Loc-Field(ins),
              mk-Val-Index( )           -> int-Val-Index(ins),
              mk-Val-Slice( )           -> int-Val-Slice(ins),
              mk-Val-Field( )           -> int-Val-Field(ins),
              mk-Read-array( )          -> int-Read-array(ins),
              mk-Write-array( )         -> int-Write-array(ins),


              mk-Add-int( )             -> int-Add-int(ins),
              mk-Sub-int( )             -> int-Sub-int(ins),
              mk-Mul-int( )             -> int-Mul-int(ins),
              mk-Div-int( )             -> int-Div-int(ins),
              mk-Mod-int( )             -> int-Mod-int(ins),
              mk-Rem-int( )             -> int-Rem-int(ins),
              mk-Exp-int( )             -> int-Exp-int(ins),
              mk-Add-float( )           -> int-Add-float(ins),
              mk-Sub-float( )           -> int-Sub-float(ins),
              mk-Mul-float( )           -> int-Mul-float(ins),
              mk-Div-float( )           -> int-Div-float(ins),
              mk-Exp-float( )           -> int-Exp-float(ins),
```

```
mk-Cat( )                  -> int-Cat(ins),

mk-Eq-int( )               -> int-Eq-int(ins),
mk-Neq-int( )              -> int-Neq-int(ins),
mk-Gt-int( )               -> int-Gt-int(ins),
mk-Lt-int( )               -> int-Lt-int(ins),
mk-Ge-int( )               -> int-Ge-int(ins),
mk-Le-int( )               -> int-Le-int(ins),
mk-Eq-float( )             -> int-Eq-float(ins),
mk-Neq-float( )            -> int-Neq-float(ins),
mk-Gt-float( )             -> int-Gt-float(ins),
mk-Lt-float( )             -> int-Lt-float(ins),
mk-Ge-float( )             -> int-Ge-float(ins),
mk-Le-float( )             -> int-Le-float(ins),
mk-Eq-bool( )              -> int-Eq-bool(ins),
mk-Neq-bool( )             -> int-Neq-bool(ins),
mk-Gt-bool( )              -> int-Gt-bool(ins),
mk-Lt-bool( )              -> int-Lt-bool(ins),
mk-Ge-bool( )              -> int-Ge-bool(ins),
mk-Le-bool( )              -> int-Le-bool(ins),

mk-And( )                  -> int-And(ins),
mk-Or( )                   -> int-Or(ins),
mk-Xor( )                  -> int-Xor(ins),

mk-And-then( )             -> int-And-then(ins),
mk-Or-else( )              -> int-Or-else(ins),

mk-Neg-int( )              -> int-Neg-int(ins),
mk-Neg-float( )            -> int-Neg-float(ins),
mk-Not( )                  -> int-Not(ins),

mk-Conv-int-float( )       -> int-Conv-int-float(ins),
mk-Conv-int-fixed( )       -> int-Conv-int-fixed(ins),
mk-Conv-float-int( )       -> int-Conv-float-int(ins),
mk-Conv-float-fixed( )     -> int-Conv-float-fixed(ins),
mk-Conv-fixed-int( )       -> int-Conv-fixed-int(ins),
mk-Conv-fixed-float( )     -> int-Conv-fixed-float(ins),
mk-Conv-fixed-fixed( )     -> int-Conv-fixed-fixed(ins),
mk-Conv-bool-int( )        -> int-Conv-bool-int(ins),

mk-In-range-int( )         -> int-In-range-int(ins),
mk-Not-in-range-int( )     -> int-Not-in-range-int(ins),
mk-In-range-float( )       -> int-In-range-float(ins),
mk-Not-in-range-float( )-> int-Not-in-range-float(ins),
mk-In-range-bool( )        -> int-In-range-bool(ins),
mk-Not-in-range-bool( )    -> int-Not-in-range-bool(ins),

mk-Range-constr( )         -> int-Range-constr(ins),
mk-Load-range-descr()      -> int-Load-range-descr(ins),
mk-Index-constr( ,, )      -> int-Index-constr(ins),
mk-Range-check( )          -> int-Range-check(ins),
mk-Null-check( )           -> int-Null-check(ins),

mk-Alloc-comp( )           -> int-Alloc-comp(ins),
mk-Heap-alloc( )           -> int-Heap-alloc(ins),

mk-Create-task( ,,, )      -> int-Create-task(ins),
```

```
        mk-Initiate( )          -> int-Initiate(ins),
        mk-Abort( )             -> int-Abort(ins),
        mk-Raise-failure( )     -> int-Raise-failure(ins),
        mk-Entry-call( , )      -> int-Entry-call(ins),
        mk-Create-entry-name( ) -> int-Create-entry-name(ins),
        mk-Accept( , )          -> int-Accept(ins),
        mk-End-accept( )        -> int-End-accept(ins),
        mk-Handle-excp-in-accept( )->
                        int-Handle-excp-in-accept(ins),
        mk-Delay( )             -> int-Delay(ins),
        mk-Terminate( )         -> int-Terminate(ins),
        mk-Select( ,, )         -> int-Select(ins),
        mk-Cond-entry-call( ,, )-> int-Cond-entry-call(ins),
        mk-Timed-entry-call( ,, )->int-Timed-entry-call(ins)
    )
  )

type:  Ins -> S -> S
```

```
int-Call(mk-Call(deflevel,entry))=
  ( def defactv : get-link(c thisactv,deflevel);
    set-ret-addr(c thisactv, c ins-cnt);
    proc-context(c thisactv,defactv);
    ins-cnt := entry
  )

type:   Call  ->  S  ->  S


int-Return(mk-Return())=
  ( parm-context(c thisactv);
    ins-cnt := get-ret-addr(c thisactv)
  )

type:   Return  ->  S  ->  S


int-Result(mk-Result(res))=
  ( def ret-val : read(mk-Loc(c thisactv, res));
    exitlevel();
    push(c thisactv, ret-val)
  )

type:   Result  ->  S  ->  S
```

```
int-Enterblock(mk-Enterblock(init-stg,vars))=
  ( def newactv : create-actv(c thisactv);
    let xstg = [id -> undef-val(tp) | (id,tp) Ε vars] in
    let newstg = init-stg U xstg in
    extend-stg(newactv, newstg);
    thisactv := newactv
  )

type:   Enterblock  ->  S  ->  S



int-Exitblock(mk-Exitblock())=
  exitlevel()

type:   Exitblock  ->  S  ->  S



int-Sethandler(mk-Sethandler(handleraddr))=
  set-excph-addr(c thisactv, handleraddr)

type:   Sethandler  ->  S  ->  S



int-Handle(mk-Handle(excps,nxth))=
  ( def exception : get-curr-excp(c thisactv);
    if exception ~Ε excps
    then ins-cnt := nxth
    else I
  )

type:   Handle  ->  S  ->  S



int-Raise(mk-Raise(excp))=
  raise(excp)

type:   Raise  ->  S  ->  S



int-Reraise(mk-Reraise())=
  reraise()

type:   Reraise  ->  S  ->  S
```

```
int-Jump(mk-Jump(addr))=
   ins-cnt := addr

type:   Jump -> S -> S



int-Falsejump(mk-Falsejump(addr))=
   ( def mk-Bool-val(cond) : pop(c thisactv);
     if ~ cond
     then ins-cnt := addr
     else I
   )

type:   Falsejump -> S -> S



int-Goto(mk-Goto(levels,addr))=
   ( unwind(levels);
     ins-cnt := addr
   )

type:   Goto -> S -> S



int-Casejump(mk-Casejump(table,others))=
   ( def mk-Int-val(sel) : pop(c thisactv);
     if sel E dom table
     then ins-cnt := table(sel)
     else ins-cnt := others
   )

type:   Casejump -> S -> S
```

```
int-Load-addr(mk-Load-addr(mk-Addr(deflevel,id)))=
  ( def defactv : get-link(c thisactv,deflevel);
    push(c thisactv,mk-Loc(defactv,id))
  )

type:   Load-addr  ->  S  ->  S



int-Load(mk-Load())=
  ( def loc : pop(c thisactv);
    def val : read(loc);
    push(c thisactv,val)
  )

type:   Load  ->  S  ->  S



int-Load-imm(mk-Load-imm(Val))=
  push(c thisactv,val)

type:   Load-imm  ->  S  ->  S



int-Load-var(mk-Load-var(mk-Addr(deflevel,id)))=
  ( def defactv : get-link(c thisactv,deflevel);
    def val     : read(mk-Loc(c defactv,id));
    push(c thisactv,val)
  )

type:   Load-var  ->  S  ->  S
```

```
int-Store(mk-Store())=
  ( def val : pop(c thisactv);
    def loc : pop(c thisactv);
    write(loc,val)
  )

type:   Store -> S -> S


int-Store-var(mk-Store-var(mk-Addr(deflevel,id)))=
  ( def val     : pop(c thisaactv);
    def defactv : get-link(c thisactv, deflevel);
    write(mk-Loc(defactv,id),val)
  )

type:   Store-var -> S -> S


int-Save(mk-Save(id))=
  ( def val = top(c thisactv);
    write(mk-Loc(c thisactv,id),val)
  )

type:   Save -> S -> S


int-Unstack(mk-Unstack())=
  unstack(c thisactv)

type:   Unstack -> S -> S
```

```
int-Load-var-descr(mk-Load-var-descr(mk-Addr(deflevel,id)))=
  ( def defactv : get-link(c thisactv, deflevel);
    def descr   : read-descr(mk-Loc(defactv,id));
    push(c thisactv, descr)
  )
```

**type:**  Load-var-descr  ->  <u>S</u>  ->  <u>S</u>

```
int-Load-descr(mk-Load-descr())=
  ( def loc   : pop(c thisactv);
    def descr : read-descr(loc);
    push(c thisactv, descr)
  )
```

**type:**  Load-descr  ->  <u>S</u>  ->  <u>S</u>

```
int-Loc-Index(mk-Loc-Index(dim))=
  ( dcl it := <> type INTG*;
    for i = 1 to dim do
      ( def mk-Int-val(indx) : pop(c thisactv);
        it := <indx> ^ c it
      );
    ( def mk-A-descr(descr): pop(c thisactv);
      if c it ~E dom descr
      then raise(OBJECT-ERROR)
      else push(c thisactv,descr(c it))
    )
  )

type:   Loc-index  ->  S  ->  S




int-Loc-Slice(mk-Loc-Slice())=
  ( def mk-Int-val(ub)    : pop(c thisactv);
    def mk-Int-val(lb)    : pop(c thisactv);
    def mk-A-descr(descr): pop(c thisactv);
    ( lb > ub and lb E dom descr
        -> push(c thisactv, mk-A-descr([])),
      lb ~E dom descr or ub ~E dom descr
        -> raise(OBJECT-ERROR),
      T
        -> ( let nd = [<i>->descr(<i>) | <i> E dom descr and
                                         lb <= i <= ub   ] in
             push(c thisactv, mk-A-descr(nd))
           )
    )
  )

type:   Loc-slice  ->  S  ->  S




int-Loc-Field(mk-Loc-Field(fid))=
  ( def mk-R-descr(descr) : pop(c thisactv);
    push(c thisactv, descr(fid))
  )

type:   Loc-Field  ->  S  ->  S
```

```
int-Val-Index(mk-Val-Index(dim))=
  ( dcl it := <> type INTG*;
    for i = 1 to dim do
      ( def mk-Int-val(indx) : pop(c thisactv);
        it := <indx> ^ c it
      );
    ( def mk-A-Val(a) : pop(c thisactv);
      if c it ~E dom a
      then raise(OBJECT-ERROR)
      else push(c thisactv, a(c it))
    )
  )

type:   Val-index -> S -> S



int-Val-Slice(mk-Val-Slice())=
  ( def mk-Int-val(ub) : pop(c thisactv);
    def mk-Int-val(lb) : pop(c thisactv);
    def mk-A-Val(a)    : pop(c thisactv);
    ( lb > ub and lb E dom a
        -> push(c thisactv, mk-A-Val([]),
      lb ~E dom a or ub ~E dom a
        -> raise(OBJECT-ERROR),
      T
        -> ( let na = [<i>->a(<i>) | <i> E dom a and
                                      lb<=i<= ub    ] in
             push(c thisactv, mk-A-val(na))
           )
    )
  )

type:   Val-slice -> S -> S



int-Val-Field(mk-Val-Field(fid))=
  ( def mk-R-val(r) : pop(c thisactv);
    push(c thisactv, f(fid))
  )

type:   Val-field -> S -> S
```

```
int-Read-array(mk-Read-array())=
  ( def ds : pop(c thisactv);
    push(c thisactv, read-array(ds))
  )
```

type:    Read-array  ->  S  ->  S


```
int-Write-array(mk-Write-array())=
  ( def val : pop(c thisactv);
    def ds  : pop(c thisactv);
    if card dom val ≠ card dom ds
    then raise(CONSTRAINT-ERROR)
    else write-array(ds,val)
  )
```

type:    Write-array  ->  S  ->  S

```
int-Add-int(mk-Add-int())=
  ( def mk-Int-val(rv) : pop(c thisactv);
    def mk-Int-val(lv) : pop(c thisactv);
    push(c thisactv, mk-Int-val(lv + rv))
  )

type:   Add-int  ->  S  ->  S



int-Sub-int(mk-Sub-int())=
  ( def mk-Int-val(rv) : pop(c thisactv);
    def mk-Int-val(lv) : pop(c thisactv);
    push(c thisactv, mk-Int-val(lv - rv))
  )

type:   Sub-int  ->  S  ->  S



int-Mul-int(mk-Mul-int())=
  ( def mk-Int-val(rv) : pop(c thisactv);
    def mk-Int-val(lv) : pop(c thisactv);
    push(c thisactv, mk-Int-val(lv * rv))
  )

type:   Mul-int  ->  S  ->  S



int-Div-int(mk-Div-int())=
  ( def mk-Int-val(rv) : pop(c thisactv);
    def mk-Int-val(lv) : pop(c thisactv);
    if rv = 0
    then raise(NUMERIC-ERROR)
    else push(c thisactv, mk-Int-val(lv div rv))
  )

type:   Div-int  ->  S  ->  S
```

```
int-Mod-int(mk-Mod-int())=
  ( def mk-Int-val(rv) : pop(c thisactv);
    def mk-Int-val(lv) : pop(c thisactv);
    if rv = 0
    then raise(NUMERIC-ERROR)
    else push(c thisactv, mk-Int-val(lv mod rv))
  )

type:   Mod-int -> S -> S


int-Rem-int(mk-Rem-int())=
  ( def mk-Int-val(rv) : pop(c thisactv);
    def mk-Int-val(lv) : pop(c thisactv);
    if rv = 0
    then raise(NUMERIC-ERROR)
    else push(c thisactv, mk-Int-val(lv rem rv))
  )

type:   Rem-int -> S -> S


int-Exp-int(mk-Exp-int())=
  ( def mk-Int-val(rv) : pop(c thisactv);
    def mk-Int-val(lv) : pop(c thisactv);
    if rv = 0
    then raise(NUMERIC-ERROR)
    else push(c thisactv, mk-Int-val(lv ** rv))
  )

type:   Exp-int -> S -> S
```

```
int-Add-float(mk-Add-float())=
  ( def mk-Float-val(rv) : pop(c thisactv);
    def mk-Float-val(lv) : pop(c thisactv);
    push(c thisactv, mk-Float-val(lv + rv))
  )

type:   Add-float -> S -> S



int-Sub-float(mk-Sub-float())=
  ( def mk-Float-val(rv) : pop(c thisactv);
    def mk-Float-val(lv) : pop(c thisactv);
    push(c thisactv, mk-Float-val(lv - rv))
  )

type:   Sub-float -> S -> S



int-Mul-float(mk-Mul-float())=
  ( def mk-Float-val(rv) : pop(c thisactv);
    def mk-Float-val(lv) : pop(c thisactv);
    push(c thisactv, mk-Float-val(lv * rv))
  )

type:   Mul-float -> S -> S



int-Div-float(mk-Div-float())=
  ( def mk-Float-val(rv) : pop(c thisactv);
    def mk-Float-val(lv) : pop(c thisactv);
    if rv = 0
    then raise(NUMERIC-ERROR)
    else push(c thisactv, mk-Float-val(lv / rv))
  )

type:   Div-float -> S -> S



int-Exp-float(mk-Exp-float())=
  ( def mk-Float-val(rv) : pop(c thisactv);
    def mk-Float-val(lv) : pop(c thisactv);
    push(c thisactv, mk-Float-val(lv ** rv))
  )

type:   Exp-float -> S -> S
```

```
int-Cat(mk-Cat(mk-Addr(deflevel,id)))=
  ( def defactv                      : get-link(c thisactv,deflevel);
    def mk-A-tp-descr(<(lb, )>, ) : read(mk-Loc(defactv,id));
    def mk-A-val(rv)                 : pop(c thisactv);
    def mk-A-val(lv)                 : pop(c thisactv);
    let lvlgth = card dom lv                                in
    let la = [<i-lvlb+lb>->lv(<i>) | <i>€ dom lv  and
                                     lvlb=min{i|<i>€dom lv}],
        ra = [<i-rvlb+lb+lvlgth>->rv(<i>) | <i>€ dom rv  and
                                     rvlb=min{i|<i>€ dom rv}] in
    push(c thisactv, mk-A-val( la U ra ))
  )

type:  Cat -> S -> S
```

```
int-Eq-int(mk-Eq-int())=
( def mk-Int-val(rv) : pop(c thisactv);
  def mk-Int-val(lv) : pop(c thisactv);
  push(c thisactv, mk-Bool-val(lv = rv))
)

type:   Eq-int -> S -> S


int-Neq-int(mk-Neq-int())=
( def mk-Int-val(rv) : pop(c thisactv);
  def mk-Int-val(lv) : pop(c thisactv);
  push(c thisactv, mk-Bool-val(lv ≠ rv))
)

type:   Neq-int -> S -> S



int-Gt-int(mk-Gt-int())=
( def mk-Int-val(rv) : pop(c thisactv);
  def mk-Int-val(lv) : pop(c thisactv);
  push(c thisactv, mk-Bool-val(lv > rv))
)

type:   Gt-int -> S -> S



int-Lt-int(mk-Lt-int())=
( def mk-Int-val(rv) : pop(c thisactv);
  def mk-Int-val(lv) : pop(c thisactv);
  push(c thisactv, mk-Bool-val(lv < rv))
)

type:   Lt-int -> S -> S



int-Ge-int(mk-Ge-int())=
( def mk-Int-val(rv) : pop(c thisactv);
  def mk-Int-val(lv) : pop(c thisactv);
  push(c thisactv, mk-Bool-val(lv >= rv))
)

type:   Ge-int -> S -> S



int-Le-int(mk-Le-int())=
( def mk-Int-val(rv) : pop(c thisactv);
  def mk-Int-val(lv) : pop(c thisactv);
  push(c thisactv, mk-Bool-val(lv <= rv))
)

type:   Le-int -> S -> S
```

```
int-Eq-float(mk-Eq-float())=
  ( def mk-Float-val(rv) : pop(c thisactv);
    def mk-Float-val(lv) : pop(c thisactv);
    push(c thisactv, mk-Bool-val(lv = rv))
  )
```

type:    Eq-float  ->  S  ->  S

```
int-Neq-float(mk-Neq-float())=
  ( def mk-Float-val(rv) : pop(c thisactv);
    def mk-Float-val(lv) : pop(c thisactv);
    push(c thisactv, mk-Bool-val(lv ≠ rv))
  )
```

type:    Neq-float  ->  S  ->  S

```
int-Gt-float(mk-Gt-float())=
  ( def mk-Float-val(rv) : pop(c thisactv);
    def mk-Float-val(lv) : pop(c thisactv);
    push(c thisactv, mk-Bool-val(lv > rv))
  )
```

type:    Gt-float  ->  S  ->  S

```
int-Lt-float(mk-Lt-float())=
  ( def mk-Float-val(rv) : pop(c thisactv);
    def mk-Float-val(lv) : pop(c thisactv);
    push(c thisactv, mk-Bool-val(lv < rv))
  )
```

type:    Lt-float  ->  S  ->  S

```
int-Ge-float(mk-Ge-float())=
  ( def mk-Float-val(rv) : pop(c thisactv);
    def mk-Float-val(lv) : pop(c thisactv);
    push(c thisactv, mk-Bool-val(lv >= rv))
  )
```

type:    Ge-float  ->  S  ->  S

```
int-Le-float(mk-Le-float())=
  ( def mk-Float-val(rv) : pop(c thisactv);
    def mk-Float-val(lv) : pop(c thisactv);
    push(c thisactv, mk-Bool-val(lv <= rv))
  )
```

type:    Le-float  ->  S  ->  S

```
int-Eq-bool(mk-Eq-bool())=
  ( def mk-Bool-val(rv) : pop(c thisactv);
    def mk-Bool-val(lv) : pop(c thisactv);
    push(c thisactv, mk-Bool-val(lv = rv))
  )

type:   Eq-bool  ->  S  ->  S


int-Neq-bool(mk-Neq-bool())=
  ( def mk-Bool-val(rv) : pop(c thisactv);
    def mk-Bool-val(lv) : pop(c thisactv);
    push(c thisactv, mk-Bool-val(lv ≠ rv))
  )

type:   Neq-bool  ->  S  ->  S


int-Gt-bool(mk-Gt-bool())=
  ( def mk-Bool-val(rv) : pop(c thisactv);
    def mk-Bool-val(lv) : pop(c thisactv);
    push(c thisactv, mk-Bool-val(lv and ~rv))
  )

type:   Gt-bool  ->  S  ->  S


int-Lt-bool(mk-Lt-bool())=
  ( def mk-Bool-val(rv) : pop(c thisactv);
    def mk-Bool-val(lv) : pop(c thisactv);
    push(c thisactv, mk-Bool-val(~lv and rv))
  )

type:   Lt-bool  ->  S  ->  S


int-Ge-bool(mk-Ge-bool())=
  ( def mk-Bool-val(rv) : pop(c thisactv);
    def mk-Bool-val(lv) : pop(c thisactv);
    push(c thisactv, mk-Bool-val(lv))
  )

type:   Ge-bool  ->  S  ->  S


int-Le-bool(mk-Le-bool())=
  ( def mk-Bool-val(rv) : pop(c thisactv);
    def mk-Bool-val(lv) : pop(c thisactv);
    push(c thisactv, mk-Bool-val(rv))
  )

type:   Le-bool  ->  S  ->  S
```

```
int-And(mk-And())=
  ( def mk-Bool-val(rv) : pop(c thisactv);
    def mk-Bool-val(lv) : pop(c thisactv);
    push(c thisactv, mk-Bool-val(lv and rv))
  )

type:   And  ->  S  ->  S


int-Or(mk-Or())=
  ( def mk-Bool-val(rv) : pop(c thisactv);
    def mk-Bool-val(lv) : pop(c thisactv);
    push(c thisactv, mk-Bool-val(lv or rv))
  )

type:   Or  ->  S  ->  S


int-Xor(mk-Xor())=
  ( def mk-Bool-val(rv) : pop(c thisactv);
    def mk-Bool-val(lv) : pop(c thisactv);
    push(c thisactv, mk-Bool-val(lv xor rv))
  )

type:   Xor  ->  S  ->  S


int-And-then(mk-And-then(addr))=
  ( def mk-Bool-val(cond) : top(c thisactv);
    if cond
    then unstack(c thisactv)
    else ins-cnt:= addr
  )

type:   And-then  ->  S  ->  S


int-Or-else(mk-Or-else(addr))=
  ( def mk-Bool-val(cond) : top(c thisactv);
    if ~ cond
    then unstack(c thisactv)
    else ins-cnt:= addr
  )

type:   Or-else  ->  S  ->  S
```

```
int-Neg-int(mk-Neg-int())=
  ( def mk-Int-val(v) : pop(c thisactv);
    push(c thisactv, mk-Int-val(- v))
  )

type:   Neg-int -> S -> S



int-Neg-float(mk-Neg-float())=
  ( def mk-Float-val(v) : pop(c thisactv);
    push(c thisactv, mk-Float-val(- v))
  )

type:   Neg-float -> S -> S



int-Not(mk-Not())=
  ( def mk-Bool-val(v) : pop(c thisactv);
    push(c thisactv, mk-Bool-val(~ v))
  )

type:   Not -> S -> S
```

```
int-In-range-int(mk-In-range-int())=
  ( def mk-Int-val(ub) : pop(c thisactv);
    def mk-Int-val(lb) : pop(c thisactv);
    def mk-Int-val(v)  : pop(c thisactv);
    push(c thisactv, mk-Bool-val(lb <= v <= ub))
  )
```

type:   In-range-int -> S -> S


```
int-Not-in-range-int(mk-Not-in-range-int())=
  ( def mk-Int-val(ub) : pop(c thisactv);
    def mk-Int-val(lb) : pop(c thisactv);
    def mk-Int-val(v)  : pop(c thisactv);
    push(c thisactv, mk-Bool-val(~(lb <= v <= ub)))
  )
```

type:   Not-int-range-int -> S -> S


```
int-In-range-float(mk-In-range-float())=
  ( def mk-Float-val(ub) : pop(c thisactv);
    def mk-Float-val(lb) : pop(c thisactv);
    def mk-Float-val(v)  : pop(c thisactv);
    push(c thisactv, mk-Bool-val(lb <= v <= ub))
  )
```

type:   In-range-float -> S -> S


```
int-Not-in-range-float(mk-Not-in-range-float())=
  ( def mk-Float-val(ub) : pop(c thisactv);
    def mk-Float-val(lb) : pop(c thisactv);
    def mk-Float-val(v)  : pop(c thisactv);
    push(c thisactv, mk-Bool-val(~(lb <= v <= ub)))
  )
```

type:   Not-in-range-float -> S -> S

```
int-In-range-bool(mk-In-range-bool())=
  ( def mk-Bool-val(ub) : pop(c thisactv);
    def mk-Bool-val(lb) : pop(c thisactv);
    def mk-Bool-val(v)  : pop(c thisactv);
    let res = (~v and ~lb) or (v and ub) in
    push(c thisactv, mk-Bool-val(res))
  )

type:  In-range-bool -> S -> S


int-Not-in-range-bool(mk-Not-in-range-bool())=
  ( def mk-Bool-val(ub) : pop(c thisactv);
    def mk-Bool-val(lb) : pop(c thisactv);
    def mk-Bool-val(v)  : pop(c thisactv);
    let res = (~v and lb) or (v and ~ub) in
    push(c thisactv, mk-Bool-val(res))
  )

type:  Not-in-range-bool -> S -> S
```

```
int-Conv-int-float(mk-Conv-int-float())=
  ( def mk-Int-val(v) : pop(c thisactv);
    push(c thisactv, mk-Float-val(v))
  )

type:   Conv-int-float  ->  S  ->  S


int-Conv-int-fixed(mk-Conv-int-fixed(delta))=
  ( def mk-Int-val(v) : pop(c thisactv);
    push(c thisactv, mk-Int-val(round(v / delta)))
  )

type:   Conv-int-fixed  ->  S  ->  S


int-Conv-float-int(mk-Conv-float-int())=
  ( def mk-Float-val(v) : pop(c thisactv);
    push(c thisactv, mk-Int-val(round(v)))
  )

type:   Conv-float-int


int-Conv-float-fixed(mk-Conv-float-fixed(delta))=
  ( def mk-Float-val(v) : pop(c thisactv);
    push(c thisactv, mk-Int-val(round(v / delta)))
  )

type:   Conv-float-fixed  ->  S  ->  S
```

```
int-Conv-fixed-int(mk-Conv-fixed-int(delta))=
  ( def mk-Int-val(v) : pop(c thisactv);
    push(c thisactv, mk-Int-val(round(v * delta)))
  )

type:   Conv-fixed-int  ->  S  ->  S


int-Conv-fixed-float(mk-Conv-fixed-float(delta))=
  ( def mk-Int-val(v) : pop(c thisactv);
    push(c thisactv,mk-Float-val(v * delta))
  )

type:   Conv-fixed-float  ->  S  ->  S


int-Conv-fixed-fixed(mk-Conv-fixed-fixed(delta1,delta2))=
  ( def mk-Int-val(v) : pop(c thisactv);
    push(c thisactv, mk-Int-val(round(v*delta1/delta2)))
  )

type:   Conv-fixed-fixed  ->  S  ->  S


int-Conv-bool-int(mk-Conv-bool-int())=
  ( def mk-Bool-val(v) : pop(c thisactv);
    push(c thisactv, mk-Int-val((v -> 1, T -> 0)))
  )

type:   Conv-bool-int  ->  S  ->  S
```

```
int-Range-constr(mk-Range-constr(id))=
  ( def mk-Int-val(ub) : pop(c thisactv);
    def mk-Int-val(lb) : pop(c thisactv);
    write(mk-Loc(c thisactv,id),mk-Range-descr(lb,ub))
  )

type:   Range-constr  ->  S  ->  S



int-Load-range-descr(mk-Load-range-descr(mk-Addr(1,id)))=
  ( def actv : get-link(c thisactv, 1);
    def mk-Range-descr(lb,ub) : read(mk-Loc(actv,id));
    push(c thisactv, mk-Int-val(lb));
    push(c thisactv, mk-Int-val(ub))
  )

type:   Load-range-descr  ->  S  ->  S



int-Index-constr(mk-Index-constr(id,dim,etpa))=
  ( let mk-Addr(deflevel,id') = etpa in
    def defactv : get-link(c thisactv, deflevel);
    let etpl    = mk-Loc(defactv,id') in
    dcl it := <> type INTG*;
    for i = 1 to dim do
      ( def mk-Int-val(ub) : pop(c thisactv);
        def mk-Int-val(lb) : pop(c thisactv);
        it := <(lb,ub)> ^ c it
      );
    write(mk-Loc(c thisactv,id), mk-A-tp-descr(it,etpl))
  )

type:   Index-constr  ->  S  ->  S



int-Range-check(mk-Rangecheck(mk-Addr(deflevel,id)))=
  ( def defactv : get-link(c thisactv,deflevel);
    def mk-Range-descr(lb,ub) : read(mk-Loc(defactv,id));
    def mk-Int-val(val) : top(c thisactv);
    if ~(lb <= val <= ub)
    then raise(OBJECT-ERROR)
    else I
  )

type:   Range-check  ->  S  ->  S
```

```
int-Null-check(mk-Null-check())=
  ( def v : top(c thisactv);
    if v = nil
    then raise(CONSTRAINT-ERROR)
    else I
  )

type:   Null-check  ->  S  ->  S



int-Alloc-comp(mk-Alloc-comp(id))=
  ( def val : pop(c thisactv);
    stack-allocate(mk-Loc(c thisactv,id),val)
  )

type:   Alloc-comp  ->  S  ->  S



int-Heap-alloc(mk-Heap-alloc(mk-Addr(deflevel,id)))=
  ( def defactv : get-link(c thisactv,deflevel);
    def val     : pop(c thisactv);
    def res     : heap-allocate(mk-Loc(defactv,id),val);
    cases res:
      ( mk-Exception(STORAGE-OVERFLOW)
            -> raise(STORAGE-OVERFLOW),

        mk-Loc( , )
            -> push(c thisactv,res)
      )
  )

type:   Heap-alloc  ->  S  ->  S
```

```
int-Create-task(mk-Create-task(deflevel,deplevel,entry))=
  ( def defactv : get-link(c thisactv, deflevel),
        depactv : get-link(c thisactv, deplevel),
        loc     : pop(c thisactv);
    let msg     = mk-Create-task(defactv,depactv,entry) in
    def taskval : monitor-fct-call(msg);
    write(loc, taskval)
  )
```

type:   Create-task -> $\underline{S}$ -> $\underline{S}$

```
int-Initiate(mk-Initiate())=
  monitor-call(mk-Initiate(c thisactv))
```

type:   Initiate -> $\underline{S}$ -> $\underline{S}$

```
int-Terminate(mk-Terminate())=
  terminate()
```

type:   Terminate -> $\underline{S}$ -> $\underline{S}$

```
int-Abort(mk-Abort(n))=
  ( dcl tasks := {} type processor(task)-set;
    for i = 1 to n do
      tasks := c tasks U pop(c thisactv);
    output mk-Abort(c tasks) to monitor
  )
```

type:   Abort -> $\underline{S}$ -> $\underline{S}$

```
int-Raise-failure(mk-Raise-failure())=
  ( def task : pop(c thisactv);
    output mk-Raise-failure(task) to monitor
  )
```

type:   Raise-failure -> $\underline{S}$ -> $\underline{S}$

```
int-Entry-call(mk-Entry-call(mk-Addr(tle,tid),mk-Addr(il,iid)))=
  ( def ta : get-link(c thisactv, tle),
        ia : get-link(c thisactv, il);
    def task : read(mk-Loc(ta,tid)),
        entry-name : read(mk-Loc(ia,iid));
    monitor-call(mk-Entry-call(task,entry-name,c thisactv))
  )

type:   Entry-call  ->  S  ->  S



int-Create-entry-name(mk-Create-entry-name(eid))=
  ( def indx : pop(c thisactv);
    if   indx = nil
    then push(c thisactv, mk-Entry-name(eid,nil))
    else ( let mk-Int-val(v) = indx in
           push(c thisactv, mk-Entry-name(eid,v))
         )
  )

type:   Create-entry-name  ->  S  ->  S
```

```
int-Accept(mk-Accept(hdlr))=
  ( def entry-name : pop(c thisactv);
    def call-actv  : monitor-fct-call(mk-Accept(entry-name));
    proc-context(call-actv, c thisactv);
    thisactv := call-actv;
    set-excp-addr(c thisactv,hdlr)
  )

type:   Accept -> S -> S


int-End-accept(mk-End-accept(surr-level))=
  ( def old-this : get-link(c thisactv, surr-level);
    set-excp-addr(c thisactv, nil);
    parm-context(c thisactv);
    monitor-call(mk-End-accept());
    thisactv := old-this
  )

type:   End-accept -> S -> S


int-Handle-excp-in-accept(mk-Handle-excp-in-accept(surrlevel))=
  ( def excp : get-curr-excp(c thisactv);
    def old-this : get-link(c thisactv, surrlevel);
    set-excph-addr(c thisactv, nil);
    parm-context(c thisactv);
    monitor-call(mk-Excp-in-accept(excp));
    thisactv := oldthis;
    raise(excp)
  )

type:   Handle-excp-in-accept -> S -> S


int-Delay(mk-Delay())=
  ( def time : pop(c thisactv);
    monitor-call(mk-Delay(time))
  )

type:   Delay -> S -> S
```

```
int-Select(mk-Select(n,hdlr))=
  ( dcl msg := {} type Select-alt-set;

    for i=1 to n do
      ( def tp    : pop(c thisactv),
            entry : pop(c thisactv);
        cases tp:
          ( ACCEPT
              -> ( def entry-name: pop(c thisactv);
                   def mk-Bool-val(guard) : pop(c thisactv);
                   let alt = mk-Accept-alt(entry-name,entry) in
                   if guard
                   then msg := c msg U {alt}
                   else I
                 ),
            DELAY
              -> ( def time  : pop(c thisactv);
                   def mk-Bool-val(guard) : pop(c thisactv);
                   let alt = mk-Delay-alt(time,entry) in
                   if guard
                   then msg := c msg U {alt}
                   else I
                 ),
            TERMINATE
              -> ( def mk-Bool-val(guard) : pop(c thisactv);
                   let alt = mk-Terminate-alt(entry) in
                   if guard
                   then msg := c msg U {alt}
                   else I
                 ),
            ELSE
              -> msg := c msg U {mk-Else-alt(entry)}
          );

    if c msg = {}
    then raise(SELECT-ERROR)
    else ( def mk-Select-answ(callactv,lab) :
                 monitor-fct-call(mk-Select(c msg));
           ins-cnt := lab;
           if callactv = nil
           then I
           else ( proc-context(callactv, c thisactv);
                  thisactv:= callactv;
                  set-excp-addr(c thisactv, hdlr)
                )
         )
  )

type:  Select -> S -> S
```

```
int-Cond-entry-call(mk-Cond-entry-call(taskvar,entryvar,nc))=
  ( let mk-Addr(tle,tid) = taskvar,
        mk-Addr(ele,eid) = entryvar in
    def ta : get-link(c thisactv,tle),
        ea : get-link(c thisactv,ele);
    def task : read(mk-Loc(ta,tid)),
        entry-name : read(mk-Loc(ea,eid));
    let msg = mk-Cond-entry-call(task,entry-name,c thisactv)in
    def answ : monitor-fct-call(msg);
    if answ = ELSE
    then ins-cnt := nc
    else I
  )

type:  Cond-entry-call  ->  S  ->  S


int-Timed-entry-call(mk-Timed-entry-call(taskvar,entryvar,nc))=
  ( def time : pop(c thisactv);
    let mk-Addr(tle,tid) = taskvar,
        mk-Addr(ele,eid) = entryvar in
    def ta : get-link(c thisactv,tle),
        ea : get-link(c thisactv,ele);
    def task : read(mk-Loc(ta,tid)),
        entry-name : read(mk-Loc(ea,eid));
    let msg = mk-Timed-entry-call(task,entry-name,c thisactv)in
    def answ : monitor-fct-call(msg);
    if answ = DELAYED
    then ins-cnt :=nc
    else I
  )

type:  Timed-entry-call  ->  S  ->  S
```

# Function index

577

581

Appendix B


A Rudimentary Compiling Algorithm

from an Ada-subset into A-code

This appendix, B, contains a compiling algorithm from an Ada-subset into A-code. The compiling algorithm is sketchy and its sole purpose is to show how simple sequences of A-code instructions most Ada statements lead to.

The language subset compiled is described by an abstract syntax. This syntax is an extract of the syntax used in the dynamic semantics definition. The subset contains all statementtypes (except the code statement) and the most interesting type of declarations, namely procedure declarations.

Optimisations are not even considered and most bookkeeping is left inconsistent. In spite of that the main ideas remain valid.

Only a few comments on the compiling algorithm will be given.

The compiling algorithm is a set of functions which traverse the program tree. The result of every function is the code generated for the sub-tree the function handles. To compile a composite construct implies the compilation of its subconstructs. The result of such a compilation is the joint sequences of instructions generated from the subtrees, possibly with extra instructions expanded before, after and in-between the tuples of the subconstructs. The only serious bookkeeping done in the compiling algorithm is the account of block-level numbers. Every function has the current block-level number as a parameter ('l'). The level is increased when block-bodies and parameterlists are compiled. All other bookkeeping information is kept in the 'dict' parameters. This dictionary is not the same as the 'dict'-components found in the abstract parsetree.

For readability reasons the generated code is not described in Meta-IV, instead an informal, assembler-like notation is used, e.g.

```
"lab:  Load-var      (l,id)          "  ^
"      Store-var     (l',id')        "
```

means:

```
        define 'lab' to denote the symbolic label (index) of
        the instruction 'mk-Load-var( ... )' in


        <       mk-Load-Var     mk-Addr(l,id)    >  ^
        <       mk-Store-var    mk-Addr(l',id')  >
```

A special function 'gen-label' is used to generate unique, symbolic labels.

**Abstract syntax of the Ada subset.**

5.1

```
Stmt-list      = Stmt*

Stmt           :: [Label-id]  Unlab-stmt

Unlab-stmt     = Null               |
                 Assign             |
                 Exit               |
                 Return             |
                 Goto               |
                 Procedure-call     |
                 Entry-call         |
                 Delay              |
                 Abort              |
                 Raise              |
                 Code               |
                 If                 |
                 Case               |
                 Loop               |
                 Block              |
                 Accept             |
                 Select

Null           :: ()
```

5.2

```
Assign         :: Name  Expr
```

5.3

```
If             :: (Expr  Stmt-list)+  [Stmt-list]
```

5.4

```
Case           :: Expr  (DiscreteVal ─m→ Stmt-list)
                                        [Stmt-list]
```

5.5

```
Loop           :: [Loop-id] ( Uncond-loop  |
                              While-loop   |
                              For-loop         )

Uncond-loop    ::                                     Stmt-list

While-loop     :: Expr                                Stmt-list

For-loop       :: Var-id  [REV]  Discrete-range  Stmt-list
```

5.6

```
Block          :: Dcl-part  Stmt-list  [Excphdl]
```

5.7

```
Exit           :: [Loop-id]  [Expr]
```

5.8

     Return              :: [Expr]

5.9

     Goto               :: Label-id


6.1

     Proc-dcl        :: Proc-id  Formal-part

     Fct-dcl         :: Fct-id   Formal-part  Subtype-def

     Formal-part     = Parm-id-<u>set</u> $_{\overline{m}}$> ( Subtype-def [Expr])

6.3

     Subprog-body  :: (Proc-id | Fct-id)  Block

6.4

     Procedure-call :: Proc-id  (Parm-id $_{\overline{m}}$> Expr)

     Fct-call       :: Fct-id   (Parm-id $_{\overline{m}}$> Expr)


7.1

     Package-dcl   :: Package-id  Dcl-part

     Package-body  :: Package-id  Dcl-part  Stmt-list  [Excphdl]


9.1

     Task-type-dcl :: Type-id  Dict  Entry-dcl*

     Task-type-body :: Type-id  Dcl-part
                       Stmt-list  [Excphdl]

9.5

     Entry-dcl      :: Entry-id  [Discrete-range]  Formal-part

     Entry-call    :: Name  Entry-name  (Parm-id $_{\overline{m}}$> Expr)

     Entry-name    :: Entry-id  [Expr]

     Accept        :: Entry-id  [Expr]  Stmt-list

9.6

     Delay         :: Expr

9.7

     Select        = Selective-wait                 |

```
                         Conditional-entry-call        |
                         Timed-entry-call
```

9.7.1

```
     Selective-wait   :: ([Expr] Select-alt)* [Stmt-list]

     Select-alt      =  Accept-alt                     |
                        Delay-alt                      |
                        Terminate-alt

     Accept-alt      :: Accept  Stmt-list

     Delay-alt       :: Delay   Stmt-list

     Terminate-alt   :: ()
```

9.7.2

```
     Conditional-entry-call
                     :: Entry-call  Stmt-list  Stmt-list
```

9.7.3

```
     Timed-entry-call
                     :: Entry-call  Stmt-list  Delay-alt
```

9.10

```
     Abort           :: Name+
```

11.2

```
     Excphdl         :: (Excp-id ⇒ Stmt-list)  oth: [Stmt-list]
                                  m
```

11.3

```
     Raise           :: [Excp-id | Name]
```

Compiling algorithm.

5.1

```
C-Stmt-list(sl)(dict,l)=
  ( {  C-Stmt(sl[i])(dict,l)  | 1<=i<=len sl  }
  )

type:  Stmt-list -> (Dict Level) -> Ins*


C-Stmt(mk-Stmt(lbl,stmt))(dict,l)=
  ( if lbl = nil
    then C-Unlab-stmt(stmt)(dict,l)
    else ( let mk-Label-inf(lab,lev) = dict(lbl) in
           "lab:                        " ^
            C-Unlab-stmt(stmt)(dict,l)
         )
  )

type:  Stmt -> (Dict Level) -> Ins*


C-Unlab-stmt(stmt)(dict,l)=
  ( cases stmt:
      ( mk-Null( )                 -> "",
        mk-Assign( , )             -> C-Assign(stmt)(dict,l),
        mk-Exit( , )               -> C-Exit(stmt)(dict,l),
        mk-Return( )               -> C-Return(stmt)(dict,l),
        mk-Goto( )                 -> C-Goto(stmt)(dict,l),
        mk-Procedure-call( , )     -> C-Procedure-call(stmt)(dict,l),
        mk-Entry-call( ,,, )       -> C-Entry-call(stmt)(dict,l),
        mk-Delay( )                -> C-Delay(stmt)(dict,l),
        mk-Abort( )                -> C-Abort(stmt)(dict,l),
        mk-Raise( )                -> C-Raise(stmt)(dict,l),
        mk-Code( )                 -> C-Code(stmt)(dict,l),
        mk-If( , )                 -> C-If(stmt)(dict,l),
        mk-Case( ,, )              -> C-Case(stmt)(dict,l),
        mk-Loop( , )               -> C-Loop(stmt)(dict,l),
        mk-Block( ,, )             -> C-Block(stmt)(dict,l),
        mk-Accept( ,,, )           -> C-Accept(stmt)(dict,l),
        mk-Select( )               -> C-Select(stmt)(dict,l)
      )
  )

type:  Unlab-stmt -> (Dict Level) -> Ins*
```

5.2

```
C-Assign(mk-Assign(le,e))(dict,l)=
(    C-Loc-expr(le)(dict,l)   ^
     C-Expr(e)(dict,l)        ^

   if is-array-expr(e)
   then "  Write-array   "
   else "  Store         "
)
```

type:   Assign  ->  (Dict Level)  ->  Ins*


5.3

```
C-If(mk-If(esl,es))(dict,l)=
  ( def out : gen-label();

    { ( def pass : gen-label();
        let (e,sl) = esl[i] in

           C-Expr(e)(dict,l)        ^

        " Falsejump    pass  "      ^

           C-Stmt-list(sl)(dict,l)  ^

        " Jump         out   "      ^
        "pass:               "   ¦ 1<=i<=len esl   } ^

     if es ≠ nil
     then C-Stmt-list(es)(dict,l)
     else ""                        ^

     "out:                   "
  )
```

type:   If  ->  (Dict Level)  ->  Ins*

5.4

```
C-Case(mk-Case(e,cl,oth))(dict,l)=
  ( def ent  : gen-label();
    def out  : gen-label();
    def em   : [stmt -> gen-label() | stmt E rng cl];
    def eoth : gen-label();
    let jtbl = [val -> em(cl(val)) | val E dom cl] in

        C-Expr(e)(dict,l)                    ^

      "  Jump    ent    "                    ^

    { "em(stmt):              "              ^

          C-Stmt-list(stmt)(dict,l)  ^

        "  jump   out      "    | stmt E rng cl }  ^

    if oth ≠ nil
    then ( "eoth:              "                  ^

               C-Stmt-list(oth)(dict,l)  ^

          "  Jump   out  "
        )
    else ""                          ^

    "ent:                "  ^
    "  Casejump   jtbl,eoth  "  ^
    "out:                "
  )

type:  Case  ->  (Dict Level)  ->  Ins*
```

5.5

```
    C-Loop(mk-Loop(exitlbl,loop))(dict,l)=
    ( def out   : gen-label();
      let ex    = mk-Label-inf(out,l) in
      let dict' = dict + [EXIT -> ex]
                       + [exitlbl=nil -> [],
                          T -> [exitlbl -> ex] in
         cases loop:
           ( mk-Uncond-loop( )         -> C-Uncond-loop(loop)(dict,l),
             mk-While-loop( , )        -> C-While-loop(loop)(dict,l),
             mk-For-loop( ,,, )        -> C-For-loop(loop)(dict,l),
           )         ^

        "out:                         "
    )

    type:  Loop  ->  (Dict Level)  ->  Ins*



    C-Uncond-loop(mk-Uncond-loop(sl))(dict,l)=
      ( def up : gen-label();

        "up:                  "          ^

            C-Stmt-list(sl)(dict,l)  ^

        "  Jump    up          "
      )

    type:  Uncond-loop  ->  (Dict Level)  ->  Ins*



    C-While-loop(mk-While-loop(e,sl))(dict,l)=
      ( def up  : gen-label();
        def out : gen-label();

        "up:                   "      ^

            C-Expr(e)(dict,l)            ^

        "   Falsejump    out      "     ^

            C-Stmt-list(sl)(dict,l)  ^

        "   Jump        up        "     ^
        "out:                     "
      )

    type:  While-loop  ->  (Dict Level)  ->  Ins*
```

```
C-For-loop(mk-For-loop(id,rev,drng,sl))(dict,l)=
  ( def test : gen-label();
    def out  : gen-lebel();
    def lim  : alloc-temp-var();

        C-Discrete-range(drng)(dict,l)  ^

    if rev = REV
    then ( "    Store-var    (l,id)   "  ^
           "    Store-var    (l,lim)  "  ^
           "test:                     "  ^
           "    Load-var     (l,id)   "  ^
           "    Load-var     (l,lim)  "  ^
           "    Ge-int                "  ^
           "    Falsejump    out      "  ^

                C-Stmt-list(sl)(dict,l)  ^

           "    Load-var     (l,id)   "  ^
           "    Load-imm     1        "  ^
           "    Sub-int               "  ^
           "    Store-var    (l,id)   "  ^
           "    Jump         test     "
         )
    else ( "    Store-var    (l,lim)  "  ^
           "    Store-var    (l,id)   "  ^
           "test:                     "  ^
           "    Load-var     (l,id)   "  ^
           "    Load-var     (l,lim)  "  ^
           "    Le-int                "  ^
           "    Falsejump    out      "  ^

                C-Stmt-list(sl)(dict,l)  ^

           "    Load-var     (l,id)   "  ^
           "    Load-imm     1        "  ^
           "    Add-int               "  ^
           "    Store-var    (l,id)   "  ^
           "    Jump         test     "
         )                              ^

    "out:                   "
  )

type:  For-loop -> (Dict Level) -> Ins*
```

```
5.6
        C-Block(mk-Block(dclp,sl,excph))(dict,l)=
          ( def init-stg : extr-init-stg(dclp),
                vars     : extr-vars(dclp,sl,excph),
                dict'    : dict + extr-block-dict(dclp,sl,excph);

            "    Enterblock    init-stg,vars    "          ^

                C-Dcl-part(dclp)(dict',l+1)                ^

            if excph = nil
            then C-Stmt-list(sl)dict',l+1
            else ( def pass   : gen-label();
                   def excpha : gen-label();

                   "    Sethandler    excpha        "      ^

                       C-Stmtlist(sl)(dict',l+1)           ^

                   "    Jump          pass          "   ^
                   "excpha:                         "   ^

                       C-Excphdl(excph)(dict',l+1)        ^

                   "pass:                           "
                   )                                      ^

            "    Exitblock                          "
            )

        type:  Block  ->  (Dict Level)  ->  Ins*
```

5.7

```
C-Exit(mk-Exit(cond,lid))(dict,l)=
  ( let mk-Label-inf(lab,lev) =
                  (lid=nil -> dict(EXIT), T -> dict(lid)) in
    let levels = l-lev                                      in
    if cond = nil
    then "  Goto    levels,lab  "
    else ( def pass : gen-label();

              C-Expr(cond)(dict,l)                    ^

           "  Falsejump   pass        "   ^
           "  Goto        levels,lab   "   ^
           "pass:                       "
         )
  )

type:  Exit -> (Dict Level) -> Ins*
```

5.8

```
C-Return(mk-Return(e))(dict,l)=
  ( let mk-Proc-inf( ,lev,ret-val-var,... ) = dict(PROC),
        mk-Label-int(lev,lab) = dict(RETURN)              in

    if e ≠ nil
    then (   C-Expr(e)(dict,l)                   ^
          "  Storevar   (lev+1,ret-val-var)  "
         )
    else ""    ^

    "  Goto   (l-lev),lab  "
  )

type:  Return -> (Dict Level) -> Ins*
```

5.9

```
C-Goto(mk-Goto(lid))(dict,l)=
  ( let mk-Label-inf(lab,lev) = dict(lid) in

    "  Goto   (l-lev),lab  "
  )

type:  Goto -> (Dict Level) -> Ins*
```

6.1
```
C-Proc-dcl(mk-Proc-dcl(pid,fmlprt))(dict,l)=
( C-Formal-part(pid,fmlprt)(dict,l)
)
```

type:   Proc-dcl -> (Dict Level) -> Ins*


```
C-Fct-dcl(mk-Fct-dcl(fid,fmlprt,subtype-def))(dict,l)=
( C-Formal-part(fid,fmlprt)(dict,l)       ^
    C-Subtype-def(subtype-def)(dict,l)
)
```

type:   Fct-dcl -> (Dict Level) -> Ins*


```
C-Formal-part(pid,fmlprt)(dict,l)=
( let mk-Subprog-inf(lab,lev,defparmlocs,... ) = dict(pid) in

  {    C-Expr(fmlprt(ids))(dict,l)    ^

      { "  Save    defparmlocs(id)    " | id E ids }  ^
        "  Unstack   1               " | ids E dom fmlprt }
)
```

type:   Id Formal-part -> (Dict Level) -> Ins*


6.3
```
C-Subprog-body(mk-Subprog-body(id,block))(dict,l)=
( let pinf = dict(id) in

    C-Block(block)(dict+[PROC -> pinf],l+1)  ^

  "   Return    "
)
```

type:   Subprog-body -> (Dict Level) -> Ins*

6.4

```
C-Procedure-call(mk-Procedure-call(pid,parms))(dict,l)=
  ( let mk-Subprog-inf(lev,entry,... ) = dict(pid) in

    C-Call-prologue(pid,parms)(dict,l)        ^

    "   Call    level,entry          "   ^

    C-Call-epilogue(pid,parms)(dict,l)
  )

type:   Procedure-call  ->  (Dict Level)  ->  Ins*
```

```
C-Call-prologue(id,parms)(dict,l)=
  ( def vars : extract-parm-ids(id)dict;
    def mk-Subprog-inf( ,,parminf,defparms) = dict(id);

    "   Enterblock  [],vars   "  ^

    ( let inparms    = {id | parminf(id) =
                              mk-Parmlocinf(IN,, )},
        inoutparms = {id | parminf(id) =
                              mk-Parmlocinf(INOUT,, )},
        outparms   = {id | parminf(id) =
                              mk-Parmlocinf(OUT,, )}  in

      { ( let mk-Parmlocinf( ,,vid) = parminf(id) in
          if id E parms
          then (      C-Expr(parms(id))(dict,l)     ^
                  "   Store-var  (l+1,vid)       "
               )
          else (  "   Load-var   defparms(id)    "  ^
                  "   Store-var  (l+1,vid)       "
               ) )              | id E inparms       } ^

      { ( let mk-Parmlocinf( ,lid,vid) = parminf(id) in

          C-Loc-expr(parms(id))(dict,l)     ^

          "   Save    lid               "   ^
          "   Load                      "   ^
          "   Store-var (l+1,vid)       " )
                                | id E inoutparms } ^

      { ( let mk-Parmlocinf( ,lid, ) = parminf(id) in

          C-Locexpr(parms(id))(dict,l)   ^

          "   Store-var   (l+1,lid)  " )| id E outparms }
      )
  )

type:   Id  Id -> Expr  ->  (Dict Level)  ->  Ins*



C-Call-epilogue(id,parms)(dict,l)=
  ( let mk-Subprog-inf( ,,parminf) = dict(id) in
    let updateparms = {id | s-mode(parminf(id)) ≠ "IN"} in

    { ( let mk-Parminf( ,lid,vid) = parminf(id) in
        "   Load-var   (l+1,lid)  "  ^
        "   Load-var   (l+1,vid)  "  ^
        "   Store               "
                              ) | id E updateparms } ^
    "   Exitblock            "
  )

type:   Id  Id -> Expr  ->  (Dict Level)  ->  Ins*
```

7.1

```
C-Package-dcl(mk-Package-dcl(id,dclp))(dict,l)=
  ( C-Dcl-part(dclp)(dict,l)
  )

type:   Package-dcl  ->  (Dict Level)  ->  Ins*



C-Package-body(mk-Package-body(id,dclp,sl,excph))(dict,l)=
  ( C-Dcl-part(dclp)(dict,l)   ^

    if excph = nil
    then C-Stmt-list(sl)(dict,l)
    else ( def pass : gen-label();
           def excpha : gen-label();

           "    Enterblock   [],{}       "    ^
           "    Sethandler   excpha      "    ^

               C-Stmt-list(sl)(dict,l)        ^

           "    Jump    pass             "    ^
           "excpha:                      "    ^

               C-Excphdl(excph)(dict,l)       ^

           "pass:                        "    ^
           "    Exitblock                "
         )
  )

type:   Package-body  ->  (Dict Level)  ->  Ins*
```

```
9.1
        C-Task-type-dcl(mk-Task-type-dcl( ,,edcll))(dict,l)=
          ( {   C-Entry-dcl(edcll[i])(dict,l) | 1<=i<=len edcll }
          )

        type:   Task-type-dcl -> (Dict Level) -> Ins*



        C-Task-type-body(tbody)(dict,l)=
          ( let mk-Task-type-body(taskid,dclp,sl,excph) = tbody,
                mk-Task-inf(ent,... ) = dict(taskid)              in
            def init-stg : extr-init-stg(dclp),
                vars     : extr-vars(dclp,sl,excph),
                dict'    : dict + extr-block-dict(dclp,sl,excph);

            "ent:                            "  ^
            "   Enterblock   init-stg,vars   "  ^

                C-Dcl-part(dclp)(dict',l+1)        ^

            if excph = nil
            then C-Stmt-list(sl)dict',l+1
            else ( def pass   : gen-label();
                   def excpha : gen-label();

                   "   Sethandler   excpha   "  ^

                       C-Stmtlist(sl)(dict',l+1)    ^

                   "   Jump          pass    "  ^
                   "excpha:                  "  ^

                       C-Excphdl(excph)(dict',l+1) ^

                   "pass:                    "
                 )                              ^

            "   Exitblock                 "  ^
            "   Terminate                 "
          )

        type:   Task-type-body -> (Dict Level) -> Ins*
```

9.5

```
C-Entry-dcl(mk-Entry-dcl(eid,dr,fmlp))(dict,l)=
  ( if dr ≠ nil
    then C-Discrete-range(dr)(dict,l)
    else ""              ^

    C-Formal-part(fmlp)(dict,l)
  )

type:   Entry-dcl -> (Dict Level) -> Ins*
```

9.5

```
C-Entry-call(mk-Entry-call(task,eid,indx,parms))(dict,l)=
  ( def taskvar  : alloc-temp-var(),
        entryvar : alloc-temp-var();

        C-Expr(task)(dict,l)                          ^

     "  Store-var    (l,taskvar)            "  ^

        C-Entry-name(eid,indx)(dict,l)               ^

     "  Store-var    (l,entryvar)           "  ^

        C-Call-prologue(eid,parms)(dict,l)   ^

     "  Entry-call  taskvar,entryvar        "  ^

        C-Call-epilogue(eid,parms)(dict,l)   ^

  )

type:   Entry-call -> (Dict Level) -> Ins*
```

```
C-Entry-name(eid,indx)(dict,l)=
  ( if indx = nil
    then "  Load-imm   nil    "
    else ( let mk-Subpgminf( ,,,,mk-Entryinf(indxtp)) =
                                                  dict(eid) in
              C-Expr(indx)(dict,l)              ^
              C-Range-check(indxtp)(dict,l)
         )      ^

     "  Create-entry-name   eid  "
  )

type:   Id  Expr -> (Dict Level) -> Ins*
```

9.5

```
C-Accept(mk-Accept(eid,indx,sl))(dict,l)=
  ( def pseudoh : gen-label();
    def pass    : gen-label();

        C-Entry-name(eid,index)            ^

     "    Accept    eid,pseudoh      "  ^

        C-Stmt-list(sl)(dict,l)            ^

     "    End-accept l            "  ^
     "    Jump        pass        "  ^
     "pseudoh:                    "  ^
     "    Handle-excp-in-accept   "  ^
     "pass:                       "
  )
```

<u>type</u>:   Accept  ->  (Dict Level)  ->  Ins*

9.6

```
C-Delay(mk-Delay(time))(dict,l)=
  (    C-Expr(time)(dict,l)       ^
    "  Delay              "
  )
```

<u>type</u>:   Delay  ->  (Dict Level)  ->  Ins*

9.7

```
C-Select(select)(dict,l)=
  ( cases select:
      ( mk-Selective-wait( , )
                  -> C-Selective-wait(select)(dict,l),
        mk-Conditional-entry-call( ,, )
                  -> C-Conditional-entry-call(select)(dict,l),
        mk-Timed-entry-call( ,, )
                  -> C-Timed-entry-call(select)(dict,l)
      )
  )

type:   Select -> (Dict Level) -> Ins*
```

9.7.1

```
C-Selective-wait(mk-Selective-wait(al,alt))(dict,l)=
  ( def out     : gen-label();
    def pseudoh : gen-label();

    { ( let (e,a) = al[i] in
        if e = nil
        then "   Load-imm    true    "
        else C-Expr(e)(dict,l)                      ^

        C-Select-alt(a)(out)(dict,l) | 1<=i<=len al }  ^

    if else ≠ nil
    then ( def l    : gen-label();
           def pass : gen-label();
           "    Load-imm    1         "  ^
           "    Load-imm    ELSE      "  ^
           "    Jump        pass      "  ^
           "l:                        "  ^
               C-Stmt-list(alt)(dict,l) ^
           "    Jump        out       "  ^
           "pass:                     "
         )
    else ""                         ^

    ( let n = len al + (alt=nil -> 0, T -> 1) in
      "    Select   n,pseudoh "                   )  ^

    "pseudoh:                 "  ^
    "    Handle-excp-in-accept"  ^
    "out:                     "
  )

type:   Selective-wait -> (Dict Level) -> Ins*
```

9.7.1

```
        C-Select-alt(alt)(out)(dict,l)=
          ( cases alt:
              ( mk-Accept-alt( , )
                          -> C-Accept-Alt(alt)(out)(dict,l),
                mk-Delay-alt( , )
                          -> C-Delay-alt(alt)(out)(dict,l),
                mk-Terminate-alt( , )
                          -> C-Terminate-alt(alt)(out)(dict,l)
              )
          )

        type:   Select-alt  ->  Label  ->  (Dict Level)  ->  Ins*
```

9.7.1

```
        C-Accept-alt(mk-Accept-alt(accept,sl2))(out)(dict,l)=
          ( let mk-Accept(eid,indx,sl1) = accept in
            def pass : gen-label();
            def ent  : gen-label();

                C-Entry-name(eid,indx)(dict,l)  ^

            "    Load-imm    ent              "  ^
            "    Load-imm    ACCEPT           "  ^
            "    Jump        pass             "  ^
            "ent:                             "  ^
                C-Stmt-list(sl1)(dict,l+1)       ^

            "    End-accept  l                "  ^

                C-Stmt-list(sl2)(dict,l)         ^

            "    Jump        out              "  ^
            "pass:                            "
          )

        type:   Accept-alt  ->  Label  ->  (Dict Level)  ->  Ins*
```

9.7.1

```
C-Delay-alt(mk-Delay-alt(mk-Delay(time),sl))(out)(dict,l)=
  ( def pass : gen-label();
    def ent  : gen-label();

        C-Expr(time)(dict,l)          ^

    "    Load-imm     ent        "  ^
    "    Load-imm     DELAY      "  ^
    "    Jump         pass       "  ^
    "ent:                        "  ^

        C-Stmt-list(sl)(dict,l)       ^

    "    Jump         out        "  ^
    "pass:                       "
  )
```

type:   Delay-alt  ->  Label  ->  (Dict Level)  ->  Ins*

```
C-Terminate-alt(mk-Terminate-alt())(out)(dict,l)=
  ( def pass : gen-label();
    def ent  : gen-label();

    "    Load-imm     ent        "  ^
    "    Load-imm     TERMINATE  "  ^
    "    Jump         pass       "  ^
    "ent:                        "  ^
    "    Terminate               "  ^
    "pass:                       "
  )
```

type:   Terminate-alt  ->  Label  ->  (Dict Level)  ->  Ins*

9.7.2

```
C-Cond-entry-call(cond-entry-call)(dict,l)=
( let mk-Cond-entry-call(entry-call,cons,alt) =
                                   cond-entry-call in
  let mk-Entry-call(task,eid,indx,parms) = entry-call in
  let mk-Subprog-inf(lev,ent,   ) = dict(eid)          in
  def out : gen-label();
  def lelse : gen-label();
  def task-var : alloc-temp-var();
  def entry-var : alloc-temp-var();

      C-Expr(task)(dict,l)                               ^

   "  Store-var     task-var                          "  ^

      C-Entry-name(eid,indx)(dict,l)                     ^

   "  Store-var     entry-var                         "  ^

      C-Call-prologue(eid,parms)(dict,l)                 ^

   "  Cond-entry-call    taskvar,entryvar,lelse      "  ^

      C-Call-epilogue(eid,parms)(dict,l)                 ^
      C-Stmt-list(cons)(dict,l)                          ^

   "  Jump    out                                     "  ^
   "lelse:                                            "  ^

      C-Stmt-list(alt)(dict,l)                           ^

   "out:                                              "  ^
  )

type:   Conditional-entry-call  ->  (Dict Level)  ->  Ins*
```

9.7.3

```
C-Timed-entry-call(timed-entry-call)(dict,l)=
( let mk-Timed-entry-call(entry-call,cons,delay) =
                                       timed-entry-call in
  let mkEntry-call(task,eid,indx,parms) = entry-call    in
  let mk-Delay-alt(mk-Delay(time),alt)  = delay          in
  let mk-Subprog-inf(lev,ent,  )= dict(eid)              in
  def out : gen-label();
  def del : gen-label();
  def task-var : alloc-temp-var();
  def entry-var : alloc-tem-var();

      C-Expr(task)(dict,l)                             ^

  "   Store-var    task-var                         "  ^

      C-Entry-name(eid,indx)(dict,l)                   ^

  "   Store-var    entry-var                        "  ^

      C-Call-prologue(eid,parms)                       ^
      C-Expr(time)(dict,l)                             ^

  "   Timed-entry-call    task-var,entry-var,del    "  ^

      C-Call-epilogue(eid,parms)(dict,l)               ^
      C-Stmt-list(cons)(dict,l)                        ^

  "   Jump     out                                  "  ^
  "del:                                             "  ^
      C-Stmt-list(alt)(dict,l)                         ^
  "out:                                             "
)

type:   Timed-entry-call -> (Dict Level) -> Ins*
```

9.10
```
C-Abort(mk-Abort(nt))(dict,l)=
( let n = len nt in
{   C-Expr(nt[i])(dict,l)   | 1<=i<=n }  ^
  "   Abort   n              "
)
```

type:   Abort  ->  (Dict Level)  ->  Ins*


11.2
```
C-Excphdl(mk-Excphdl(el,oth))(dict,l)=
( def out : gen-label();

   "    Sethandler    nil   "  ^

   { ( let ids = {id | id E dom el and el(id) = sl} in
       def pass : gen-label();

       "   Handle ids,pass      "  ^

           C-Stmt-list(sl)(dict,l)  ^

       "   Jump    out           "  ^
       "pass:                     "  | sl E rnl el  }  ^

   if oth ≠ nil
   then (    C-Stmt-list(oth)(dict,l)  ^
        "   Jump    out             "
        )
   else ""     ^

   "   Reraise       "  ^
   "out:             "
)
```

type:   Excphdlr  ->  (Dict Level)  ->  Ins*


11.3
```
C-Raise(mk-Raise(excp))(dict,l)=
( excp = nil          ->  "    Reraise        ",
  is-Excp-id(excp)    ->  "    Raise    excp  ",
  is-Name(excp)       ->  (    C-Expr(excp)(dict,l)  ^
                          "   Raise-failure       "
                          )
)
```

type:   Raise  ->  (Dict Level)  ->  Ins*

# REFERENCE MANUAL FOR THE META-LANGUAGE

*Dines Bjørner*

# CONTENTS

# 1. DATA TYPES

The language constructs for expressing Domains of objects, for constructing and representing objects, and for operating upon objects are defined. Each subsection is accordingly presented in three parts. For operations we state their type, i.e. types of ordered input argument(s) and result value.

## 1.1. Elementary Data Types

### 1.1.1. The Boolean Data Type

**Domain Expression :   BOOL**

BOOL denotes the Domain of truth values, i.e. the set : {true,false}.

**Object Representation :    true, false**

**Object Operations :**

| Symbol | Name | Type | | |
|--------|------|------|---|---|
| ` | negation | BOOL | $\rightarrow$ | BOOL |
| $\wedge$ | and | BOOL BOOL | $\rightarrow$ | BOOL |
| $\vee$ | or | BOOL BOOL | $\rightarrow$ | BOOL |
| $\supset$ | implies | BOOL BOOL | $\rightarrow$ | BOOL |
| $\equiv$ | equivalent | BOOL BOOL | $\rightarrow$ | BOOL |

Operators $\vee$ and $\wedge$ are not commutative. Thus :

$$a \vee b \;\triangleq\; \text{if } a \text{ then true else } b$$
$$a \wedge b \;\triangleq\; \text{if } a \text{ then } b \text{ else false}$$
$$a \supset b \;\triangleq\; \text{if } a \text{ then } b \text{ else true}$$
$$a \equiv b \;\triangleq\; \text{if } a \text{ then } b \text{ else (if } b \text{ then false else true)}$$

### 1.1.2. The Integer Data Type

**Domain Expressions :   INTG, $N_0$, $N_1$**

INTG denotes the Domain of integer values, i.e. the infinite set : $\{...,-2,-1,0,1,2,...\}$. $N_i$ denotes the Domain of positive integers larger than or equal to $i$.

**Object Representation :    ...,-2,-1,0,1,2,...**

**Object Operations :**

| Symbol | Name | Type | |
|--------|------|------|---|
| - | minus | **INTG** | → **INTG** |
| **abs** | numerical | **INTG** | → **N₀** |
| - | subtract | **INTG INTG** | → **INTG** |
| + | add | **INTG INTG** | → **INTG** |
| ★ | multiply | **INTG INTG** | → **INTG** |
| / | integer division | **INTG INTG** | → **INTG** |
| **mod** | modulus | **N₀ N₁** | → **N₀** |
| = | equal | **INTG INTG** | → **BOOL** |
| ≠ | different | **INTG INTG** | → **BOOL** |
| < | less than | **INTG INTG** | → **BOOL** |
| ≤ | < or equal | **INTG INTG** | → **BOOL** |
| > | larger than | **INTG INTG** | → **BOOL** |
| ≥ | > or equal | **INTG INTG** | → **BOOL** |

Integer division leads to the largest integer smaller than or equal to the real quotient. Modulus (of $i,j$) gives the largest natural number, $r$, less than $j$ such that there exist a natural number multiplier $m$ such that : $i = j \star m + r$.

### 1.1.3. The Quotation Data Type

**Domain Expression :  QUOT**

QUOT denotes the Domain of quotations; these are represented as any bold-face sequence of uppercase letters or digits.

**Object Representation :    A, B, ... , Z, 0, 1, ... , AA, AB, ... , A9, AAA, ...**

**Object Operations :**

| Symbol | Name | Type | |
|--------|------|------|---|
| = | equal | **QUOT QUOT** | → **BOOL** |
| ≠ | different | **QUOT QUOT** | → **BOOL** |

(Two quotations are equal if they form exactly the same "sequence" (or "pattern") of characters.)

### 1.1.4. The Token Data Type

**Domain Expression :    TOKEN**

TOKEN denotes the Domain of tokens. This Domain can be considered as consisting of a potentially infinite set of otherwise distinct, elementary, i.e. further unanalysed objects for which no representations (designators) are required.

**Object Representation :    -- not applicable  (N/A)**

**Object Operations :**

| Symbol | Name | Type | |
|--------|------|------|---|
| = | equal | **TOKEN TOKEN** | → **BOOL** |
| ≠ | different | **TOKEN TOKEN** | → **BOOL** |

### 1.2. Composite Data Types

Composite objects are such which are composed from other objects. A composite data type (or Domain) has objects, all of which are composite. Whereas fixed names where prescribed for the elementary data type Domains, viz. : **BOOL**, **INTG**, **TOKEN**, and **QUOT**, the definer, if required, must use abstract syntax definition facilities to ascribe names to composite Domains. In all of the subsections below suitable decorated $A$'s and $B$'s denote arbitrary Domains. Suitable decorated $a$'s and $b$'s represent objects of corresponding Domains.

### 1.2.1. The Set Data Type

**Domain Expression :**  $A$-set

-set is a suffix operator. As an operation, it applies to Domains, $A$, and yields the possibly infinite Domain of objects all of which are finite, possibly empty, subsets of $A$, i.e. unordered collections of distinct $A$ objects.

**Object Construction :**

Explicit enumeration :  $\{a_1, a_2, \ldots, a_s\}$
Implicit enumeration :  $\{a \mid P(a)\}$ , $\{a \; \varepsilon \; aset \mid P(a)\}$

Usually $s = 0$ or $1$, i.e. $\{\ \}$, which denotes the empty set of no $(A)$ objects, respectively $\{a\}$, which denotes the singleton set of exactly one object. $\{a \; \varepsilon \; aset \mid P(a)\}$ is a short-hand for writing $\{a \mid a \; \varepsilon \; aset \wedge P(a)\}$. The ellipsis (...) is meta linguistic. The explicit enumeration lists all members of the set. The implicit enumeration constructs the (finite) set of all those objects which satisfy the predicate (see sect. 1.5.2) $P(a)$.

**Object Operations :**

| Symbol | Name | Type | |
|--------|------|------|--|
| $\varepsilon$ | membership | $A \quad SET$ | $\rightarrow$ BOOL |
| $\cup$ | union | $SET \quad SET$ | $\rightarrow$ SET |
| $\cap$ | intersection | $SET \quad SET$ | $\rightarrow$ SET |
| $\setminus$ , - | complement, difference | $SET \quad SET$ | $\rightarrow$ SET |
| $\subset$ | proper inclusion, subset | $SET \quad SET$ | $\rightarrow$ BOOL |
| $\check{c}$ | inclusion | $SET \quad SET$ | $\rightarrow$ BOOL |
| $=$ | equal | $SET \quad SET$ | $\rightarrow$ BOOL |
| $\neq$ | distinct | $SET \quad SET$ | $\rightarrow$ BOOL |
| **card** | cardinality | $SET$ | $\rightarrow N_0$ |
| **union** | distributed union | $SET$-set | $\rightarrow$ SET |

If $a$ is in the set $aset$ then $a \; \varepsilon \; aset$ holds. If the set $aset$ is empty then for no $a$ does $a \; \varepsilon \; aset$ hold. If $aset$ is not empty then it is possible to extract an arbitrary member of $aset$ : (let $a \; \varepsilon \; aset$ in ... ).

$$as_1 \cup as_2 \quad \triangleq \{a \mid a \; \varepsilon \; as_1 \; \vee \; a \; \varepsilon \; as_2\}$$
$$as_1 \cap as_2 \quad \triangleq \{a \mid a \; \varepsilon \; as_1 \; \wedge \; a \; \varepsilon \; as_2\}$$
$$as_1 - as_2 \quad \triangleq \{a \mid a \; \varepsilon \; as_1 \; \wedge \; a \; '\varepsilon \; as_2\}$$
$$as_1 \subset as_2 \quad \triangleq (A \; a \; \varepsilon \; as_1)(a \; \varepsilon \; as_2) \wedge (E \; a \; \varepsilon \; as_2)(a \; '\varepsilon \; as_1)$$
$$as_1 \; \check{c} \; as_2 \quad \triangleq (A \; a \; \varepsilon \; as_1)(a \; \varepsilon \; as_2)$$
$$as_1 = as_2 \quad \triangleq (A \; a \; \varepsilon \; as_1)(a \; \varepsilon \; as_2) \wedge (A \; a \; \varepsilon \; as_2)(a \; \varepsilon \; as_1)$$
$$as_1 \neq as_2 \quad \triangleq \; '(as_1 = as_2)$$
$$\textbf{card } as \quad = (as = \{\ \} \rightarrow 0, \; T \rightarrow (\text{let } a \; \varepsilon \; as \text{ in } 1 + \textbf{card} (as - \{a\})))$$
$$\textbf{union } sas \quad = \{a \mid as \; \varepsilon \; sas \; \wedge \; a \; \varepsilon \; as\}$$
$$\{m:n\} \quad = \{i \mid m \leq i \leq n\}$$

### 1.2.2. The Tuple Data Type

**Domain Expressions :**  $A^*, A^+$

$*$ and $+$ denote (suffix) Domain operations which yield Domains of objects all of which are finite, possibly zero-, respectively non-zero-, length, ordered sequences (lists, tuples) of not necessarily distinct $A$ objects.

**Object Constructions :**

Explicit enumeration :  $\langle a_1, a_2, \ldots, a_t \rangle$
Implicit enumeration :  $\langle F(i) \mid m \leq i \leq n \wedge P(i) \rangle$,
$\langle G(i) \mid i \; \varepsilon \; \{m:n\} \wedge P(i) \rangle$

Usually $t = 0$ or $1$, which denotes the empty tuple of no $(A)$ objects and zero length, respectively $\langle a \rangle$, which denotes the unit-length tuple of exactly the $a$ object. The head, or first, $[1]$, element or object of the explicitly enumerated tuple is $a_1$; the second, $[2]$, is $a_2$, ... , with the $t$'th, $[t]$, being $a_t$. $F$ and $G$ are arbitrary functions defined over the domains for which $P$ holds. The first object of the implicitly defined, $F$ produced tuple is $F(j)$ where $j$ is the smallest integer, in the range $\{m:n\}$, for which $P(j)$ holds. The next object is the $F(k)$ where $k$ is the next-smallest, etc.. The last element is the $F(l)$ where $l$ is the largest integer, in the range $\{m:n\}$, for which $P(l)$ holds. In the $G$

produced tuple no ordering of $G(i)$ elements is prescribed; thus any permutation of $<G(i) \mid m \leq i \leq n \land P(i)>$ is denoted.

**Object Operations :**

| Symbol | Name | Type | |
|--------|------|------|---|
| hd | head,first | $A^+$ | $\rightarrow A$ |
| tl | tail | $A^+$ | $\rightarrow A^\star$ |
| [.] | index | $A^+ \ N_1$ | $\rightarrow A$ |
| len | length | $A^\star$ | $\rightarrow N_0$ |
| elems | elements | $A^\star$ | $\rightarrow A$-set |
| ind | indices | $A^\star$ | $\rightarrow N_1$-set |
| ^ | concatenation | $A^\star \ A^\star$ | $\rightarrow A^\star$ |
| conc | distributed concatenation | $A^{\star\star}$ | $\rightarrow A^\star$ |
| = | equal | $A^\star \ A^\star$ | $\rightarrow$ BOOL |
| $\neq$ | distinct | $A^\star \ A^\star$ | $\rightarrow$ BOOL |

The head of a non-empty tuple is its first element, the tail the tuple of remaining elements. Selecting the $i$th *tuple* element, for $1 \leq i \leq$ len *tuple*, yields that element :

$$tuple[i] \quad \triangleq \ ((1 \leq i \leq \text{len } tuple) \rightarrow ((i=1) \rightarrow \text{hd } tuple, \ T \rightarrow (\text{tl } tuple)[i-1]), \quad T \rightarrow \text{undefined}),$$
$$\text{elems } tuple \triangleq \{tuple[i] \mid i \, \varepsilon \text{ ind } tuple\},$$
$$\text{ind } tuple \quad \triangleq \{i \mid 1 \leq i \leq \text{len } tuple\}.$$

Concatenation, $t_1 \,\hat{}\, t_2$, of two tuples, yields a tuple, $t$, whose $i$th element for $1 \leq i \leq$ len $t_1$ is the $i$th element of $t_1$, and for $i = j + $ len $t_1$, where $1 \leq j \leq$ len $t_2$, is the $j$th element of $t_2$.

$$\text{conc } tt \quad \triangleq \text{ if } tt = <> \text{ then} <> \text{ else hd } tt \,\hat{}\, \text{conc tl } tt.$$
$$t_1 = t_2 \qquad \triangleq (t_1 = <> \equiv t_2 = <>) \lor ((\text{len } t_1 = \text{len } t_2) \land (\text{hd } t_1 = \text{hd } t_2) \land (\text{tl } t_1 = \text{tl } t_2))$$

Where equality with empty tuples is assumed a primitive.

### 1.2.3. The Map Data Type

**Domain Expression :** $A \ _m\!\rightarrow B$

$_m\!\rightarrow$ is an infix Domain operator. As an operation it yields the Domain of all finite, possibly empty domain, partial maps, i.e. finitely constructable functions, from objects in a subset of $A$ into $B$. Partiality because not all of A need be the domains of denoted maps.

(**Observe :** 'Domain', spelled with capital 'D', is the name used for the concept of a possibly infinite set of objects defined by some Domain expression; whereas 'domain', spelled whith 'd', is the name used for the concept of the set of objects for which a function is defined, i.e. to which it applies & yields well-defined values.)

**Object Construction :**

      Explicit enumeration :   $[a_1 \rightarrow b_1, a_2 \rightarrow b_2, ..., a_m \rightarrow b_m]$
      Implicit enumeration :   $[F(o) \rightarrow G(o) \mid P(o)]$

Usually $m = 0$ or $1$, i.e. [ ], which denotes the empty map, i.e. the totally undefined function, which functionally associates no $A$ objects with any $B$ object, respectively $[a \rightarrow b]$, which denotes the one domain element function which maps $a$ into $b$. Assume $F$, $G$ and $P$ to denote $A$-, $B$- respectively BOOL object producing functions where $F$ and $G$ apply to all those $O$ objects, $o$, for which at least $P(o)$ holds. Then the implicit map enumeration expression denotes a map which functionally associates, or "pairs", exactly those $F(o)$ objects with $G(o)$ objects for which $P(o)$ holds.

**Object Operations :**

| Symbol | Name | Type |
|--------|------|------|
| (.) | apply | $(A \xrightarrow{m} B)\ A \quad \xrightarrow{\sim} B$ |
| U | merge | $(A \xrightarrow{m} B)\ (A \xrightarrow{m} B) \xrightarrow{\sim} (A \xrightarrow{m} B)$ |
| + | override extend | $(A \xrightarrow{m} B)\ (A \xrightarrow{m} B) \xrightarrow{\sim} (A \xrightarrow{m} B)$ |
| \ | complement restrict (with) | $(A \xrightarrow{m} B)\ A\text{-set} \quad \to (A \xrightarrow{m} B)$ |
| \| | restrict (to) | $(A \xrightarrow{m} B)\ A\text{-set} \quad \to (A \xrightarrow{m} B)$ |
| dom | domain | $(A \xrightarrow{m} B) \qquad\qquad \to A\text{-set}$ |
| rng | range | $(A \xrightarrow{m} B) \qquad\qquad \to B\text{-set}$ |
| = | equal | $(A \xrightarrow{m} B)\ (A \xrightarrow{m} B) \to \textbf{BOOL}$ |
| $\neq$ | distinct | $(A \xrightarrow{m} B)\ (A \xrightarrow{m} B) \to \textbf{BOOL}$ |
| merge | distributed merge | $(A \xrightarrow{m} B)\text{-set} \quad \to (A \xrightarrow{m} B)$ |

Let $m, m_1, m_2 \in (A \xrightarrow{m} B)$. If $a$ is in the domain of $m$, i.e. if $a \in \textbf{dom}\ m$ holds, then $m(a)$ yields the $b$ to which $a$ is functionally associated, i.e. with which $a$ is "paired".

If domains of $m_1$ and $m_2$ do not share $A$ objects, then :

$$m_1 \cup m_2 \triangleq [a \to b \mid (a \in \textbf{dom}\ m_1 \wedge m_1(a) = b) \vee (a \in \textbf{dom}\ m_2 \wedge m_2(a) = b)]$$

If domains of $m_1$ and $m_2$ (potentially) overlap, then :

$$m_1 + m_2 \triangleq [a \to b \mid (a \in \textbf{dom}\ m_2 \wedge m_2(a) = b) \vee (a \in \textbf{dom}\ m_1 \setminus \textbf{dom}\ m_2 \wedge m_1(a) = b]$$
$$m \setminus aset \triangleq [a \to b \mid a \in \textbf{dom}\ m \setminus aset \wedge m(a) = b]$$
$$m \mid aset \triangleq [a \to b \mid a \in aset \cap \textbf{dom}\ m \wedge m(a) = b]$$
$$m_1 = m_2 \triangleq (\textbf{dom}\ m_1 = \textbf{dom}\ m_2) \wedge (\textbf{A}\ a \in \textbf{dom}\ m_1)(m_1(a) = m_2(a))$$

Let $mab \in (A \xrightarrow{m} B)$ and $mbc \in (B \xrightarrow{m} C)$, then

$$mab \circ mbc \triangleq [a \to c \mid a \in \textbf{dom}\ mab \wedge mab(a) \in \textbf{dom}\ mbe \wedge mbc(mab(a)) = c]$$
$$\textbf{merge}\ sms \equiv ((sms = \{\}) \to [], \quad \textbf{T} \to (\textbf{let}\ m \in sms\ \textbf{in}\ m \cup \textbf{merge}(sms \setminus \{m\})))$$

provided $(\textbf{A}\ m_1, m_2 \in sms)((m_1 \neq m_2) \supset (\textbf{dom}\ m_1 \cap \textbf{dom}\ m_2 = \{\}))$, i.e. that any two distinct maps, of the set of maps **merged**, have disjoint domains.

**Bijections :** $\quad A \xleftarrow{m} B \qquad$ **(Domain Expression)**

A map is a bijection iff to each distinct range object there corresponds a distinct domain object. Let $m \in (A \xleftarrow{m} B)$, then for defined $a$, $(m(a) = b) \triangleq (m^{-1}(b) = a)$.

**1.2.4. The Function Data Type**

**Domain Expressions :** $\quad A \to B \qquad (A \xrightarrow{\sim} B)$

$A \to B$ $(A \xrightarrow{\sim} B)$ denote the Domain of all total (partial) functions from $A$ ((i.e. subsets of $A$)) into $B$.

**Object Construction :**

1. $\lambda a.C(a)$,
2. $(\textbf{let}\ f(a) = C(a)\ \textbf{in} ...),$
3. $(\textbf{let}\ f = \lambda a.C(a)\ \textbf{in} ...),$
4. $(\textbf{def}\ f(a) : C(a); ...),\ \text{etc.}$

Forms 1.-3. basically define the same function, namely : "that function of $a$ which $C(a)$ is". Forms 2.-3. gives the name, $f$, to the defined function (with this name appearing free in the bodies ... of the block). Forms 2.-3. therefore permits the recursive definition of $f$; i.e. $f$ to appear free in $C(a)$. Thus $(\textbf{let}\ f = \lambda a.C(a)\ \textbf{in} ...)$ is equal to $(\textbf{let}\ f = Yf.\lambda a.C(a)\ \textbf{in} ...)$ where the latter **let** is not recursive, but where Y is the least-fix-point finding function(al). Forms 1.-3. define applicative functions which rely on no state (see sect 1.3). Form 4. defines an imperative function since it is assumed that evaluation of $C(a)$ relies on the state. The $f$ of forms 1.-3. returns a value, whereas the $f$ of form 4. may return a value - potentially changing the state - , or may potentially change the state, not returning any value. In the former case $f$ is a value-returning ("applicative") function, in the latter case $f$ is a state-changing ("imperative") function. In the former case references, $f(arg)$, may occur anywhere an expression occurs; in the latter case anywhere a statement occurs. $C(a)$ is·any clause, which for forms 1.-3. is an expression; for form 4. an expression, respectively a statement.

Form 1., when encountered during elaboration of a meta-program, and the right-hand-sides of the **let** and **def** specifications of forms 2.-4., are not elaborated. A function is (instead) defined which, if (and when) applied, to some argument, say *arg*, yields the same effect as would elaboration of *C(arg)* (i.e. where all free *a* in *C(a)* have been replaced by *arg*), in the defining environment, i.e. in the bindings present at the point of elaboration of the function definition.

**Object Operation :**

| Symbol | Name | Type | |
|--------|------|------|---|
| (.) | apply | $(A \to B)\ A$ | $\to B$ |

is the only operation defined on lambda ($\lambda$) defined functions. (Thus function objects cannot be tested for equality/distinction - and any such operation on other composite objects which involve functional ones is hence not defined.)

### 1.2.5. The Tree Data Type

**Domain Expressions :**

$$0.: \qquad (B_1\ B_2\ ...\ B_n)$$

**Domain Definitions :**

$$1.: \qquad A_1 = (B_1\ B_2\ ...\ B_n) \qquad \text{(Abstract Syntax Rule)}$$
$$2.: \qquad A_2 :: B_1\ B_2\ ...\ B_n \qquad \text{(Abstract Syntax Rule)}$$

Forms 0.-1. defines a Domain of anonymous, i.e. root-non-labelled trees, whereas form 2. defines $A_2$-root-labelled, i.e. non-anonymous, trees. The defined trees all have exactly $n$, non-ordered, sub-components, of Domains $B_1, B_2, ... , B_n$.

**Object Constructions :**

$$0.-1.: \qquad (b_1,b_2,...,b_n) \qquad \text{where } b_i \,\epsilon\, B_i$$
$$2.: \qquad \text{mk-}A_2(b_1,b_2,...,b_n) \qquad \text{where } b_i \,\epsilon\, B_i$$

forms 0.-1. are interchangeably written as :  $\text{mk}(b_1,b_2,...,b_n)$.

**Axiom :**     **if :**

$$A_1 :: B_1\ B_2\ ...\ B_m,$$
$$A_2 :: C_1\ C_2\ ...\ C_n, \quad \text{and}$$
$$\text{mk-}A_1(b_1,b_2,...,b_m) = \text{mk-}A_2(c_1,c_2,...,c_n),$$

     **then**

$$A_1 \equiv A_2,$$
$$m = n,$$
$$B_i \equiv C_i \quad \text{for all } 1 \leq i \leq m, \quad \text{and}$$
$$b_i = c_i \quad \text{for all } 1 \leq i \leq m.$$

This axiom secures disjointness of Domains of root-labelled trees labelled with distinct roots ($A_1$, respectively $A_2$).

**Object Operations**

| Symbol | Name | Type | |
|--------|------|------|---|
| s-$B_i$ | select | $A$ | $\to B_i$ |
| = | equal | $A\ A$ | $\to$ **BOOL** |
| $\equiv$ | distinct | $A\ A$ | $\to$ **BOOL** |

where $A$ is either $A_1$ or $A_2$, or some such tree Domain.
    Let

$$t_1 = (b_1,b_2,...,b_n)$$
$$t_2 = \text{mk-}A_2(b_1,b_2,...,b_n)$$

and $B_i$ be an identifier distinct from other identifiers $B_j$ $(1 \leq j \neq i \leq n)$, then

$$s\text{-}B_i(t_1) = b_i = s\text{-}B_i(t_2)$$

Equality of trees holds only for trees of the same Domain, $(B_1\ B_2\ ...\ B_n)$, $A_1$ or $A_2$, i.e. let :

$$t' = mk\text{-}A_2(b_1',b_2',...,b_n')$$
$$t'' = mk\text{-}A_2(b_1'',b_2'',...,b_n'')$$

$t' = t''$ holds iff $b_i' = b_i''$ for all $1 \le i \le n$. Etcetera.


## 1.3. The Access Data Type and The State

**Domain Expressions :**    ref $A$

The Domain **ref** $A$ is the Domain of all references, i.e. meta-locations, of variables declared of type $A$.

**Object Constructions :**    (dcl ra [:= expr] type A; ...)

ra is the name of an assignable, i.e. updateable, meta-variable. [its content may be initialized, to the value of *expr*.] Values of the location must always be of type $A$.

**The State :**    $\Sigma$        **(Domain Name)**

If the following declarations :

> dcl   $v_1$ ...  type $A_1$
>
> ...
>
> dcl   $v_2$ ...  type $A_2$
>
> ...
>
> ...
>
> dcl   $v_n$ ...  type $A_n$

are in effect at a given point in the elaboration of a meta-program, then the state Domain is defined as :

$$(v_{1\ m} \to A_1)\ \cup\ (v_{2\ m} \to A_2)\ \cup\ ...\ \cup\ (v_{n\ m} \to A_n)$$

(see sect. 2.1 for $\cup$). If e.g. $v_i$ is recursively declared, i.e. there is a (potentially) indefinite number of $v_i$ locations, all of type **ref** $A_i$, then the term :

$$(v_{i\ m} \to A_i)$$

instead becomes :

$$(\text{ref } A_{i\ m} \to A_i).$$

etcetera.

**Object Operations :**

| Symbol | Name | Type | |
|--------|------|------|---|
| c | contents | ref $A$ | $\to (\Sigma \to (\Sigma A))$ |
| := | assignment | ref $A$   $A$ | $\to (\Sigma \to \Sigma)$ |

Let $\sigma$ be the (hidden) state, then :

> c v      $\equiv$ if v $\varepsilon$ dom $\sigma$ then $(\sigma, \sigma(v))$ else **undefined**
>
> v := *val*    $\equiv$ if v $\varepsilon$ dom $\sigma$ then $\sigma + [v \to val]$ else **undefined**

## 1.4. The Process Instance Data Type

**Domain Expression** :.  $\Pi$ ,  $\Pi(pid)$

$\Pi$ denotes a possibly infinite Domain of process instance values, possibly identifying instances of the processor definition *pid*. See sect. 5.1.

**Object Construction** :   not applicable, see however sect. 5.2.1

**Object Operations** :

| Symbol | Name | Type | |
|--------|---------|-------|---------|
| = | equal | $\Pi$ $\Pi$ | → **BOOL** |
| ≠ | distinct | $\Pi$ $\Pi$ | → **BOOL** |

For special uses of $\Pi$-objects see sects. 5.2.2-3.

## 1.5. Descriptor and Quantified Expressions

Although not defining new data types we here introduce some auxiliary expression forms.

### 1.5.1. Descriptor Expressions

**Schema** :   $(\triangle obj \; \varepsilon \; Set)(P(obj))$

-- denotes the unique object in the *Set* for which the *P*redicate holds. If the predicate holds for several, or no, objects of *Set*, then the expression, as a whole is undefined.

### 1.5.2. Quantified Expressions

**Schemas** :   1.:   $(A \; obj)(P(obj)), \; (A \; obj \; \varepsilon \; Set)(P(obj))$
2.:   $(E \; obj)(P(obj)), \; (E \; obj \; \varepsilon \; Set)(P(obj))$
3.:   $(E! \; obj)(P(obj)), \; (E! \; obj \; \varepsilon \; Set)(P(obj))$

The right-hand column specifies bound quantification. The schemas reads : 1.: for all objects, *obj*, [in the *Set*] it is the case that *P(obj)* holds; 2.: there exist at least one object [in the *Set*] for which the precicate holds; and 3.: there exists a unique object [in the *Set*] for which the predicate holds. The expressions all yield truth values, i.e. denote objects in **BOOL**. [The *Set* may be infinite.] For finite sets, *Set*, the schemas can be explained :

Let   $Set = \{o_1, o_2, ..., o_n\}$

1.:   $P(o_1) \wedge P(o_2) \wedge ... \wedge P(o_n)$
2.:   $P(o_1) \vee P(o_2) \vee ... \vee P(o_n)$

and :

3.:   if $(E \; o_i \; \varepsilon \; Set)(P(o_i))$
then $(let \; o_i \; \varepsilon \; Set \; be \; s.t. \; P(o_i)$ in
$(A \; o \; \varepsilon \; Set \setminus \{o_i\})(\cap P(o)))$
else false

In the clause :   if   $(E \; obj)(P(obj))$
then   ...
else   ...

the free occurrences of *obj* in ... are considered bound by the quantified expression, so that e.g. 3. above reads:
if $(E \; o_i \; \varepsilon \; Set)(P(o_i))$
then $(A \; o \; \varepsilon \; Set \setminus \{o_i\})(\cap P(o))$
else false

Observe :   $(A \; o)(P(o)) \equiv {}'(E \; o)(\cap P(o)),$
$'(E \; o)(P(o)) \equiv (A \; o)(\cap P(o))$

# 2. ABSTRACT SYNTAX

## 2.1. Domain Expressions

**Domain Operators**

| Symbol | Name | Sect-Reference |
|--------|------|----------------|
| -set | power-Domain | 1.2.1 |
| * | tuple-Domain | 1.2.2 |
| + | tuple-Domain | 1.2.2 |
| $_m\rightarrow$ | map-Domain | 1.2.3 |
| $\rightarrow$ | total-function-Domain | 1.2.4 |
| $\rightarrow$ | partial-function-Domain | 1.2.4 |
| (...) | anonymous-tree-Domain | 1.2.5 |
| ref | access-Domain | 1.3 |
| \| | arbitrary, non-discriminated-union Domain | |
| [...] | Domain optionality | |
| U | non-discriminated-map-merge Domain | |

*Explanations :* $A \mid B \equiv \{ab \mid ab \, \varepsilon \, A \ \lor \ ab \, \varepsilon \, B\}$. $[A] \equiv A \mid \{nil\}$, where nil is just an arbitrarily chosen symbol denoting itself! $(A_1 \, _m\rightarrow B_1) \ \cup \ (A_2 \, _m\rightarrow B_2)$ etcetera denotes the Domain of maps whose $A_i$ domain objects (for $i$ either 1 or 2) map into $B_i$ objects (for pairwise $i$'s either both = 1, or both = 2, etcetera). The $\rightarrow$ operators associate to the right, i.e. $(A_1 \rightarrow A_2 \rightarrow ... \rightarrow A_{n-1} \rightarrow A_n) \equiv (A_1 \rightarrow (A_2 \rightarrow (... \rightarrow (A_{n-1} \rightarrow A_n)...)))$ commute. Note that sometimes, as in above expressions, parentheses are used for breaking or indicating precedence (grouping), rather than for tree Domain construction; context shows which.

## 2.2. Rule Definitions

**Schemas :**

| | | |
|---|---|---|
| 0.: | $A = B_1 \mid B_2 \mid ... \mid B_n$ | |
| 1.: | $B_1 :: C_{11} \, C_{12} ... C_{1 \, m1}$ | See sect. 1.2.5 |
| 2.: | $B_2 :: C_{21} \, C_{22} ... C_{2 \, m2}$ | - " - |
| ... | ... | |
| n.: | $B_n :: C_{n1} \, C_{n2} ... C_{n \, mn}$ | - " - |

Rule 0. defines $A$ to denote the same Domain as its right-hand side expression, giving a "handy" way of naming it. Rules $i$ (for $1 \leq i \leq n$) denotes distinct tree Domains (insofar as '$(B_j \equiv B_k)$' for j ≠ k, etcetera).

**Domain Function :**  is-$A$,  is-$B_i$     (for $1 \leq i \leq n$)

Any rule defines a predicate function of the form is- composed with the left-hand side rule identifier :

$$is\text{-}A(obj) \equiv (obj \ \varepsilon \ A)$$
$$is\text{-}B_i(obj) \equiv (obj \ \varepsilon \ B_i)$$

# 3. FUNCTION DEFINITIONS

**Schema :**

$$fid(p_1,p_2,...,p_m)(s_1)(s_2) ... (s_n) =$$
$$Clause(...)$$
$$\text{type:} \quad P_1 \ P_2 \ ... \ P_M \rightarrow (S_1 \rightarrow (S_2 \rightarrow ... \rightarrow (S_N \rightarrow D)...))$$

Commas in the formal parameter lie, as in ALGOL 60, be replaced by back-to-back parentheses : ")(". The **type** clause specifies the function type : parameters $p_i$ are of type $P_i$, $s_j$ of $S_j$, and applying the function to arguments of corresponding types $(P_1 - P_m, S_1 - S_n)$ yields an object of type $D$. Elaboration of the function, named *fid*, proceeds by elaborating its body, *Clause(...)*, in which all free occurrences of formal parameters have been replaced by corresponding actual arguments. If that elaboration accesses, but does not change, the state, and returns a value of type $E$, then the type clause part "$\rightarrow D$" reads : "$\rightarrow (\Sigma E)$", for short "$=> E$". If the elaboration, in addition, changes the state "$\rightarrow D$" reads : "$\rightarrow (\Sigma \rightarrow (\Sigma E))$", for short "$=> E$". Thus we shall consider "$\rightarrow (\Sigma \rightarrow E)$" only as an abbreviation for "$\rightarrow (\Sigma \rightarrow (\Sigma E))$", permitted whereever there is no (chance of) state change. If elaboration alone potentially changes the state the part : "$\rightarrow D$" reach "$\rightarrow (\Sigma \rightarrow \Sigma)$", for short "$=>$". The *Clause* can be any expression or statement, inclusive blocks.

The function definition header *fid(mk-D(a,...,w))(...) = Clause(...)* is an abbreviation for : *fid(p)(...) = (let mk-D(a,...,w) = p in Clause(...))*.

## 3.1. Blocks

**Schemas :**

| | |
|---|---|
| 0.: | *(let id = expr in Clause)* |
| 1.: | *(def id : expr; Clause)* |
| 2.: | *(dcl v [:= expr] type A; Clause)* |

Form 0. applicatively defines all free occurrences of *id* in *Clause* to denote what expr denotes; as such form 0. is a short-hand for *Clause'* where all free occurrences of *id* in *Clause* have been syntactically replaced by *'expr'*. Form 1. imperatively defines all free occurences of *id* in *Clause* to denote the value of *'expr'*, elaborated before elaboration of *Clause*; hence semicolon in form 1. means: "first evaluate *expr*, then bind *id* to that value, then elaborate *Clause* in the context of that binding". Form 1. is used wherever evaluation of *expr* requires access to a potentially changing state. Form 2. imperatively declares a variable, named v, possibly initializes it to the value of *expr*, fixes the type of variable values to $A$, and then elaborates *Clause*.

### 3.1.1. Let Clause Variants

Variants to the let clause of form 0. above and its use are often found useful:

**Schemas :**

| | |
|---|---|
| 1.: | *(let id $\varepsilon$ Set [be s.t. P(id)] in ...),* |
| 2.: | *(let mk-B(b_1,b_2,...,b_n) = tree in ...),* |
| 3.: | *(let $id_1 = e_1$,* |
| | $\quad id_2 = e_2$, |
| | $\quad ...$ |
| | $\quad id_n = e_n$ in ...), and |
| 4.: | *(let f(a) = e in ...)* |
| 5.: | *(let $id_1 = e_1$ in* |
| | let $id_2 = e_2$ in |
| | $\quad ...$ |
| | let $id_n = e_n$ in ...) |

Form 1. reads: let *id* be (the name of) an object in *Set* [for which the *Predicate* holds]. Form 2. assumes $B :: B_1 \ B_2 \ ... \ B_n$ and corresponds to form 3. where $id_i \equiv b_i$ and $e_i \equiv s\text{-}B_i(tree)$. Form 3. simultaneously defines n quantities. Forms 0., 1., 3. and 4. permit recursive definitions of *id*, *id*, $id_i$'s, respectively f. If there are no mutually recursive definitions of any $id_i$ in 3., then form 3. corresponds to form 5. which is an abbreviation of:

| | |
|---|---|
| 5.: | *(let $id_1 = e_1$ in* |
| | *(let $id_2 = e2$ in* |
| | $\quad ...$ |
| | *(let $id_n = e_n$ in ...)...))* |

Form 4. was explained in sect. 1.2.4.


## 3.2. Statement Composition


### 3.2.1. Sequential Statement Composition

**Schema** :     $(s_1; s_2; ...; s_n)$

$s_i$, for all $i$, are statements. These are to be interpreted in the order listed. (See however sect. 4.)


### 3.2.2. [Quasi-] Parallel Statement Composition

**Schema** :     $//(s_1, s_2, ..., s_n)$

$s_i$, for all $i$, are statements. These are to be interpreted in parallel. [In order not to confuse this "parallelism" with the notion of meta-processes, see sect. 5, you may choose to constrain the above to "quasi-parallel"; that is: operations of all $s_i$ are serially performed, in any order, while preserving operator precedences.]


## 3.3. The Assignment Statement

**Schema** :     v := expr

The value of *expr* replaces the current value of v, see sect. 1.3.


## 3.4. Function References

**Schema** :     $fid(arg_1, arg_2, ..., arg_n)(d_1)(d_2)...(d_n)$

If the **type** of the *fid* function definition, see begin sect. 3., has "→ $D$" containing no mention of the state Domain $\Sigma$, then *fid* is an applicative function, and the above form is an expression. If "→ $D$" is of the form: "=> $E$" then *fid* is an "applicative" function accessing (and possibly changing) the state, and the form is an "imperative" expression. If "→ $D$" is of the form "=>", i.e. "→ $(\Sigma \to \Sigma)$", then fid is an imperative function, and the form is a statement. For further details see beginning of section 3.


## 3.5. The error Clause

**Schema:**     error

Indicates a semantically erroneous construct. As used in this definition it indicates an error which must be detected.


## 3.6. The undefined Clause

**Schema:**     undefined

Indicates a construct to which no semantics is (can be) given. As used in this definition it indicates an error situation which should not necessarily be detected.


## 3.7. Structured Clauses


### 3.7.1. Conditional Clauses

### 3.7.1.1. If-then-else

**Schema :**        if  $e$  then  $c_c$  [else  $c_a$]

$e$ is any expression evaluating to **true** or **false**. If to **true** then the consequent clause, $c_c$, is elaborated; otherwise the alternative clause, $c_a$. If $c_c$ is an expression, then the else part is mandatory and $c_a$ and the entire construct are expressions. If $c_c$ is a statement and if $c_a$ is present, it too is a statement; the entire construct is a statement.

### 3.7.1.2. McCarthy Conditional

**Schema :**        $(e_1 \rightarrow c_1, e_2 \rightarrow c_2, ..., e_n \rightarrow c_n)$,      $n \geq 2$

is semantically explained by translation into: (if $e_1$ then $c_1$ else (if $e_2$ then $c_2$ else (if ... then ( ... else (if $e_n$ then $c_n$ else not-defined)...)...))). If the $e_n$ is T then the innermost phrase above reads: else $c_n$.

### 3.7.1.3. Cases

**Schema :**        cases $e_0$ : $(e_1 \rightarrow c_1, e_2 \rightarrow c_2, ..., e_n \rightarrow c_n)$

Is explained by translation into: (let $v = e_0$ in $((e_1 = v) \rightarrow c_1, (e_2 = v) \rightarrow c_2, ..., (e_n = v) \rightarrow c_n)$, respectively (det $v$ : $e_0$; $((e_1 = v) \rightarrow ...$ etc.), depending on whether evaluation of $e_0$ does not or do require access to the state.
    A case construct of the form: cases $e_0$ : (mk-$D(a,...,w) \rightarrow c_1$, etc.) is explained as follows: (let $v = e_0$ in (is-$D(v) \rightarrow$ (let mk-$D(a,...,w) = v_0$ in $c_1$, etc.)).

### 3.7.2. Iterative Statements

### 3.7.2.1. Indexed Iteration

**Schema :**        for  $i = m$  to  $n$  do  $S(i)$

$S(i)$ is any statement; $m$ and $n$ are integer, usually natural number, valued, expressions (where $m$ usually is 1 and $n$ of the form len *tuple*). The expression evaluation usually is 'static', i.e. does not require access to the state. Let $j$ and $k$ be the values of $m$, respectively $n$, then the semantic is explained by translation into: $(S(j); S(j + 1); ...; S(k - 1); S(k))$, where for $j > k$ the whole thing collapses to I.

### 3.7.2.2. Un-ordered Iteration

**Schema :**        for all  $id \ \varepsilon \ Set$  do  $S(id)$

$S(id)$ is any statement, $id$ an identifier free in the context, and $Set$ a set-valued, usually 'static', expression. Let the value of $Set$ be $\{o_1, o_2, ..., o_n\}$ , in any order, then the semantics can be explained by translation into: $(S(o_1); S(o_2); ...; S(o_n))$. [The definer should be ready to assert that any ordering of $Set$ leaves the effect invariant.]

### 3.7.2.3. Conditional Iteration

**Schema :**        while  $e$  do S

$e$ is a boolean valued expression usually dependent upon the state for its evaluation; S is any statement. The semantics can be explained by repeated "translation": (if $e$ then (S; while $e$ do S) else I).

# 4. EXIT MECHANISM

There are two parts to the exit story: the generation of exits, and their handling. There are basically three ways of taking care of exits: always trapping them, trapping them recursively in a tixe clause (exit spelled backwards), and trapping them non-recursively.

## 4.1. The exit Clause

Schemas :         exit, exit(expr)

In an imperative context the clauses are ("return-like") statements; whereas in a pure applicative context they are ("return-like") expressions. Their execution leads to a termination of further elaboration of whatever meta-language construct they occur in. Control is transferred back to the dynamically, most recently, embracing handler capable of "fielding" the exit. expr is evaluated in the exiting scope and the value carried back to the fielding handler.

(exits are phrase-structured "gotos". Instead of statically designating a clause label, exits transfer control "down" the activation "stack" of most recently elaborated meta-blocks and meta-function bodies.)

## 4.2. The exit Handlers

### 4.2.1. The always Clause

Schema :         (always $Clause_e$ in $Clause_b$)

$Clause_e$ is always elaborated after elaboration of $Clause_b$, whether this latter was terminated "normally" or by an exit. The schema can be explained, using the trap construct of sect. 4.2.2, by:

$$(trap \; [ALWAYS \quad\quad \rightarrow Clause_e ,$$
$$T \quad\quad\quad\quad\quad \rightarrow (Clause_e; \; exit/] \quad in$$
$$(Clause_b; \; exit(ALWAYS))) ,$$

that is, if $Clause_b$ is terminated by an exit, $Clause_e$ is elaborated, and if this in itself does not terminate by an exit, the exit of $Clause_b$ is passed on to an embracing handler; otherwise the exit generated by $Clause_e$ is passed on. If $Clause_b$ terminates normally, $Clause_e$ is elaborated, and the entire construct terminates.

### 4.2.2. The trap Clause

Schemas :     1.:         (trap exit with $Clause_e$ in $Clause_b$)
           2.:         (trap exit(id) with $Clause_e$ in $Clause_b$) , (trap [id → $Clause_e$] in $Clause_b$)

exits of $Clause_b$ (not handled in $Clause_b$) are trapped by the trap ... $Clause_e$ handler and cause elaboration of $Clause_e$. exits of $Clause_e$ (not handled in $Clause_e$) are passed on to embracing handlers. Form 2. bind, in $Clause_e$, the free identifier, id, to the object, v, carried with an exiting exit(v).

### 4.2.3. The tixe Clause

Schema :         (tixe [F(i) → Clause(i) | P(i)] in $Clause_b$)

exits of $Clause_b$ (not handled in $Clause_b$), and exiting with a value v which equals some F(j), for which the predicate P(j) holds, is (recursively) trapped in the tixe [...] handler, and leads to elaboration of the corresponding Clause(j) construct. The same holds for exits of any Clause(k) for which P(k) holds and for which Clause(k) does not specify a handler. (Hence "recursively".) exits of $Clause_b$ or clauses Clause(k), of the form exit -- or exit(v), for which v does not equal any F(i), etc. -- are passed on to embracing handlers.

(Note: thus (trap exit(id) with if id = val then $Clause_e$ else exit(id) in $Clause_b$) is not equivalent to (tixe [val → $Clause_e$] in $Clause_b$), since an exit(val) of $Clause_e$ in the former is passed on to embracing handlers while it is recursively handled by the same $Clause_e$ of the latter.)

# 5. META PROCESSES

The meta process concept is a non-denotational extension to the otherwise denotational meta notation described in this summary. It is based on the principles of Hoare's "Communicating Sequential Processes" otherwise described.

## 5.1. Processor Definition

**Schema:**     *pid* processor*(...)* = *(declarations; clause-list)*

A processor definition consists of three parts: a formal parameter list, a set of declarations, and a list of clauses. For each start of a process the usual mechanism of actual argument/formal parameter passing is applied. Then the internal state (local storage) of that process is established in the usual manner as specified in the declarations. Finally all clauses are obeyed in the order listed. No two processors share storage.

## 5.2. Process Clauses

The following clauses are those explicitly dealing with/relating to meta peocesses. They may (anywhere) occur freely mixed with other (sequential) clauses.

### 5.2.1. The Start Expression

**Schema:**     start *pid(expression-list)*

The start expression specifies that a new (meta) process instance, based on the *pid* processor definition is to be started up. This process instance is passed an appropriately evaluated argument list, and it will run in parallel with the process instance in which the start expression occurs. The start expression creates a new, unique instance object identifying the started process instance. This instance object is the value of (returned by) the start expression.

### 5.2.2. The Output Statement

**Schema :**                     output mk-*A(expression-list)* to *pid*
                              output mk-*A(expression-list)* to $\pi$

The output statement specifies first the evaluation of the (possibly empty) expression-list. An *A* object (tree) is constructed of the yielded values, and this named, composite object is then communicated to one other process instance. If *pid* is specified, the receiving process instance may be any process instance based on the *pid* processor definition. If $\Pi$ (which is an instance value denoting let-type identifier) is specified, only the denoted process instance may receive the output object. The output statements terminates only when some receiving process actually inputs, i.e. consumes, the communicated object. Reference objects may not by communicated.

### 5.2.3. The Input Statement

**Schema :**     .1.:                 {input mk-$A_1$(id-list) from *pid* => Clause$_1$,
                              input mk-$A_2$(id-list) from $\pi$   => Clause$_2$,
                              ...
                              input mk-$A_n$(id-list) from *pid* => Clause$_n$}
                 2.:         input mk-*A(id-list)* from $\pi$ [ => Clause]

Form 1. is a non-deterministic input statement, consisting of a set of pairs (input => *Clause*). The input statement specifies that one of its clauses should be elaborated. The elaboration of a clause requires its corresponding input to be satisfied, i.e. another process instance must be in a situation where it attempts to output an object of the named type ($A_i$). If several inputs are simultaneousty satisfied, then an arbitrary one of these is selected. The outputting (sending) process instance is either an arbitrary process based on the *pid* processor definition, or an arbitrary process to whose identifying instance value the identifier $\pi$ is bound throughout the corresponding *Clause* (i.e. this latter has the effect of: *(let $\pi$ =* "the identifying instance object of the sending

623

process" in *Clause*)). Upon receival of the output object, it is decomposed into its constituent values, the identifiers of id-list are bound to those (i.e. corresponding to: *(let mk-A$_i$(id$_1$, ... ,id$_n$) = "received object tree" in Clause)*), and the *Clause* is elaborated. The input statement terminates when elaboration of one of its clauses terminates. Form 2. requires a specific input object. Omission of the *Clause* implies pure synchronisation, i.e. a transmitted value is not used.

Hence, the input and output statements specifies complete synchronisation (rendez-vous) of some sending and some receiving process instance.

### 5.2.4. The Cycle Clause

**Schema :**          cycle *Clause*

Specifies eternal repetition (**while true do**) of *Clause*.

REFERENCES AND BIBLIOGRAPHY

References and Bibliography


Ada 79a        Preliminary Ada Reference Manual. ACM Sigplan Notices, vol. 14,
               no. 6, June 1979 (Part A).

Ada 79b        Rationale for the design of the Ada programming language. ACM
               Sigplan Notices, vol. 14, no. 6, June 1979 (Part B).

Ada 80         Reference Manual for the Ada Programming Language. Proposed
               Standard Document. Cii Honeywell Bull, 1980.

Ba 72          F.T. Baker: "Chief Programmer Team Management of Production
               Programming". IBM systems journal vol. 11, no. 1, 1972.

BeWa 71        H. Bekic, K. Walk: "Formalization of Storage Properties", in:
               'Formal Semantics of Algorithmic Languages' (ed. E. Engeler),
               Springer Verlag Lecture Notes in Mathematics, vol. 188, 1971.

Be 74          H. Bekic, D. Bjørner, W. Henhapl, C.B. Jones & P. Lucas: "A
               Formal definition of a PL/I Subset", Parts I & II, Technical
               Report TR25.139, IBM Vienna Laboratory, Dec. 1974.

Bj 77a         D. Bjørner: "Programming Languages: Linguistics & Semantics",
               in: 'European ACM "International Computing Symposium 1977"',
               (eds E. Morlet & Ribbens) North-Holland Publ., 1977.

Bj 77b         D. Bjørner: "Programming Languages: Formal Development of
               Interpreters & Compilers". Techn. Report ID 673, Department of
               Computer Science, Technical University of Denmark, 1977 - and in
               same as above.

Bj 78          D. Bjørner: "The Systematic Development of a Compiling
               Algorithm". Department of Computer Science, Technical University
               of Denmark, 1978., & in: 'State of the Art of Compilation' (eds.
               Amirchachy & Neel), IRIA Publ.

Bj 80          D. Bjørner (ed.): "Abstract Software Specifications", Springer
               Verlag Lecture Notes in Computer Science, vol. 86, 1980.

BjJo 78        D. Bjørner, C.B.Jones (eds.): "The Vienna Development Method:
               The Meta-Language", Springer Verlag Lecture Notes in Computer
               Science, vol. 61, 1978.

BjOe 80        D. Bjørner, O. Oest: "The DDC Ada Compiler Development Project",
               in: 'Towards a Formal Definition of Ada', Springer Verlag
               Lecture Notes in Computer Science, vol. 98, 1980 (these lecture
               notes).

BuSch 80       J. Bundgaard, L. Schultz: "A (Denotational) Semantics Method for
               Defining Ada Context Conditions", in: 'Towards a Formal
               Definition of Ada', Springer Verlag Lecture Notes in Computer
               Science, vol. 98, 1980 (these lecture notes).

CH 80          CHILL Language Definition, C.C.I.T.T. Period 1977-1980, Study
               Group XI, May 1980.

DDC 80/14      O. Oest, J. Storbank Pedersen: "Systematic Derivation of an A-
               Code Compiling Algorithm from a Denotational Semantics
               Definition of Ada". DDC 80/14, Danish Datamatics Centre, 1980
               (draft paper).

Do 78   O. Dommergaard: "IBM/Series 1: En formel model". Technical Report ID 777 (in Danish). Dept. of Computer Science, Technical University of Denmark, May 1978.

Do 80   O. Dommergaard: "The Design of a Virtual Machine for Ada", in: 'Towards a Formal Definition of Ada', Springer Verlag Lecture Notes in Computer Science, vol. 98, 1980 (these lecture notes).

DoBo 80   O. Dommergaard, S. Bodilsen: "A Formal Definition of P-Code". Dept. of Computer Science, Technical University of Denmark, 1980.

ErKr 75   S.H. Eriksen, B.B. Kristensen, O. Lehrmann Madsen, B.B. Jensen: "An Implementation of P-Code on RIKKE-MATHILDA". DAIMI (Computer Science Department), Aarhus University, Denmark, 1975.

FoBj 79   P. Folkjaer, D. Bjørner: "A Formal Model of a Generalized CSP-like Language. ID 879, Department of Computer Science, Technical University of Denmark, 1979 - also in IFIP 8th World Computer Conference Proceedings, North-Holland Publ. Co., Amsterdam 1980.

Fr 78   N. Francez: "On Achieving Distributed Termination", Dept. of Computer Science, Technion -- Israel Institute of Technology, Haifa, Israel, 1978.

Ha 73   P. Brinch Hansen: "Operating System Principles", Prentice Hall Series in Automatic Computation, 1973.

Ha 77   P. Brinch Hansen: "The Architecture of Concurrent Programs". Prentice-Hall, 1977.

HaBj 80   P. Haff, D. Bjørner (eds.): "A Formal Definition of CHILL. A Supplement to the CCITT recommendation Z.200". Danish Datamatics Centre, 1980.

HaDe   E.A. Hauck and B.A. Dent: "Burroughs B6500/B7500 Stack Mechanism". Burroughs Corporation, California.

HeJo 78   W. Henhapl, C.B. Jones: "A Formal Definition of ALGOL 60 as described in the 1975 Modified Report". In [BjJo 78].

Ho 78   C.A.R. Hoare: "Communicating Sequential Processes". Comm. ACM vol. 21, no. 8, Aug 1978.

Jo 74   C.B. Jones: "On Formal Definition in Program Development", In: 'Programming Methodology', Springer Verlag Lecture Notes in Computer Science, vol. 23, 1974.

Jo 76   C.B. Jones: "Formal Definition in Compiler Development", IBM Vienna Techn. Rept. TR25.145, Febr. 1976.

Jo 78   C.B. Jones: "The Vienna Development Method: Examples of Compiler Development", in: 'State of the Art of Compilation' (eds. Amirchachy & Neel), IRIA Publ.

Jo 79   C.B. Jones: "Models of Programming Language Concepts", in: 'Abstract Software Specifications' (ed. D. Bjørner), Springer Verlag Lecture Notes in Computer Science, vol. 86, 1980.

Jo 80        C.B.  Jones:  "Program  Development  -  A  Rigorous  Approach",
             Prentice-Hall International (International  Series  in  Computer
             Science, ed. C.A.R.Hoare), 1980.

JoLu 71      C.B.  Jones,  P.  Lucas:  "Proving Correctness of Implementation
             Techniques", in same as [BeWa 71].

Kn 79        D.E. Knuth: "TEX and METAFONT, New Directions in Typesetting".
             Digital Press & Amer. Math. Society 1979.

KoKrMa       P.  Kornerup,  B.B.  Kristensen,  O.  Lehrmann  Madsen:
             "Interpretation  and  Code  Generation  Based  on  Intermediate
             Languages".  DAIMI  (Computer  Science  Department),  Aarhus
             University, Denmark.

KrMaJe 74    B.B.  Kristensen,  O.  Lehrmann  Madsen,  B.B.  Jensen:"A Pascal
             Environment  Machine  (P-Code)".  DAIMI  (Computer  Science
             Department) PB-28, Aarhus University, Denmark, 1974.

LaBu 69      P.  Landin,  R.M.  Burstall:  "Programs  and  their  Proofs:  An
             Algebraic Approach", in: 'Machine Intelligence' (ed. D. Michie),
             Edinburg Univ. Press, vol. 4, 1972.

Li 75        A.M.  Lister:  "Fundamentals  of  Operating  Systems", MacMillan
             Comp. Science Series, 1975.

Lø 80a       H.H.  Løvengreen:  "Formal  Definition of Ada: A Storage Model",
             Technical Report ID 904, Dept. of  Computer  Science,  Technical
             University of Denmark, 1980.

Lø 80b       H.H.  Løvengreen:  "Parallelism  in  Ada", in: 'Towards a Formal
             Definition of Ada', Springer Verlag Lecture  Notes  in  Computer
             Science, vol. 98, 1980 (these lecture notes).

LøBj 80      H.H.  Løvengreen,  D. Bjørner: "On a Formal Model of the Tasking
             Concepts in Ada", Proc. ACM SIGPLAN Ada Symp., Boston 1980.

Ma 79        Brian  Mayoh:  "Parallelism  in Ada: Program Design and Meaning",
             PB-103, DAIMI (Computer Science Department), Aarhus  University,
             Denmark, 1979.

McCaPa 67    J.  McCarthy,  J.  Painter:  "The  Correctness of a compiler for
             Arithmetic Expressions", in: Amer.  Math.  Soc.  Proc.:  'Math.
             Aspects of Computer Science', Proc. Symp. Appl. Math., vol. 19,
             1967.

Mi 80        R. Milner: "Behaviour Algebras", in 'A Calculus of Communication
             Systems',  Springer  Verlag  Lecture  Notes  in  Computer Science,
             vol. 92, 1980.

MiSt 77      R.  Milne  &  C.  Strachey:  "A  Theory  of Programming Language
             Semantics", Chapman and Hall, London, Halsted Press/John  Wiley,
             New York, 1976.

Mo 73        F. Lockwood Morris: "Advice on Structuring Compilers and Proving
             them  Correct",  Conf.Rec.of  ACM  Symp.  on:  'Principles  of
             Programming Languages', Boston, 1973.

Na 63    P. Naur: "The design of the GIER Algol Compiler". BIT 3, 2 (1963).

Ne 77    M.C. Newey: "Proving Properties of Assembly Language Programs", IFIP Information processing 77 (ed. B. Gilchrist), North-Holland Publ. Company, 1977.

Ne 79    P.A. Nelson: "A Comparison of Pascal Intermediate Languages". Proceedings of the SIGPLAN Symposium on Compiler Construction, Denver, Colorado, August 6-10, 1979.

No 76    K.V. Nori et al.: "The Pascal <P> Compiler Implementation Notes". Eidgenossische Technische Hochschule, Zurich 1976.

Or 73    E.I. Organick: "Computer System Organization, the B5700/B6700 Series". Academic Press 1973.

PeWi 79  G. Persch, G. Winterstein, M. Dausman, S. Drossopoulou: "Overloading in Ada". University of Karlsruhe, Inst. f. Informatik II, 1979.

Re 72    J.C. Reynolds: "Definitional Interpreters for Higher-Order Programming Languages", ACM Proc. 25th Nat Conf., Boston, vol.2, 1972.

Ri 71    M. Richards: "The Portability of the BCPL Compiler". Software Practice and Experience, Vol. 1, 135-146 (1971).

Ri 72    M. Richards: "INTCODE An Interpretive Machine Code for BCPL." The Computer Laboratory, Corn Exchange Street, Cambridge, December 1972.

Sc 72    D. Scott: "Mathematical Concepts in Programming Language Semantics", in: Proc.Spring Joint Comp.Conf., AFIPS Press, vol. 40, 1972.

ScSt 71  D. Scott & C. Strachey: "Towards a Mathematical Semantics for Computer Languages", in: 'Computers & Automata', (ed. J. Fox), Polytechnic Institute of Brooklyn Press, Microwave Research Institute Series, vol. XXI, 1971.

Stoneman  Requirements for Ada Programming Support Environments, "STONEMAN". US Department of Defense, Research and Engineering, Feb. 1980.

St 77    J.E. Stoy: "Denotational Semantics", MIT Press, Cambridge, Mass., 1977.

St 79    J.E. Stoy: "Foundations of Mathematical Semantics", in same as (Jo 79).

StPe 80  J. Storbank Pedersen: "A Formal Semantics Definition of Sequential Ada", in: 'Towards a Formal Definition of Ada', Springer Verlag Lecture Notes in Computer Science, vol. 98, 1980 (these lecture notes).

Sø 75    O. Sørensen: "The Emulated O-Code Machine for the Support of BCPL". DAIMI (Computer Science Department) PB-45, Aarhus University, Denmark, 1975.

Te 76        R.D. Tennent: "The Denotational Semantics of Programming Languages". Comm. ACM vol. 19, no. 8, August 1976.

Wa 72        K. Walk: "Modelling of Storage Properties of High-Level Languages", Intel Journal of Computer & Information Sciences, vol. 2, no. 1, 1973.

WeHe 75      F. Weissenbock, W. Henhapl: "A Formal Mapping Description", IBM Vienna Lab. Techn. Note, TN25.3.105, Feb. 1975.

WeMi 72      R.W. Weyrauch, R. Milner: "Program Correctness in a Mechanized Logic", Proc. 1st USA-Japan Comp.Conf., 1972.

Wo 80       "Semantics-Directed Compiler Generation". Proceedings of a Workshop. Springer Verlag Lecture Notes in Computer Science, vol. 94. Workshop held at Computer Science Dept., Aarhus University, Denmark, January 14-18, 1980. Selected papers:

            H. Ganzinger: "Transforming Denotational Semantics into Practical Attribute Grammars", pp. 1-69.

            M-C. Gaudel: "Specification of Compilers as Abstract Data Type Representations", pp. 140-164.

            M. Raskovsky, P. Collier: "From Standard to Implementation Denotational Semantics", pp. 94-139.

            J.W. Thatcher, E.G. Wagner, J.B. Wright: "More on Advice on Structuring Compilers and Proving them Correct", pp. 165-188.

        Relevant Hand-outs at the workshop were:

            M. Raskovsky: "Compiler Generation and Denotational Semantics".

            R. Sethi: "Transformations between Semantic Descriptions".